seventh edition

Personal Finance
for Canadians

Kathleen H. Brown
Thomas F. Chambers

Elliott J. Currie
University of Guelph

Prentice
Hall

Toronto

Canadian Cataloguing in Publication Data

Brown, Kathleen H. (Kathleen Helen), 1926-
    Personal finance for Canadians

Irregular.
[1st ed. (1981)]-
Sixth edition by Kathleen H. Brown, Thomas F. Chambers, Elliott J. Currie.
Includes bibliographical references.
ISSN 1202-9386
ISBN 0-13-029068-8 (7th ed.)

I. Finance, Personal — Canada. 2. Consumer credit — Canada. 3. Financial security. I. Title.

0-13-029068-8

Vice President, Editorial Director: Michael Young
Executive Editor: Dave Ward
Marketing Manager: Deborah Merry
Developmental Editor: Laurie Goebel
Production Editor: Gillian Scobie
Copy Editor: Nancy Carroll
Production Coordinator: Patricia Ciardullo
Page Layout: Jack Steiner
Permissions/Photo Research: Susan Wallace-Cox
Art Director: Julia Hall
Cover and Interior Design: Carole Knox
Cover Image: Stock Illustration Source

2 3 4 5   06 05 04 03 02

Printed and bound in Canada.

To my wife Ann. — E.C.
To my wife Heather. — T.C.

Brief Table of Contents

Table of Contents

Preface

It is essential for most people in our increasingly complex society to understand and control their financial affairs. Financial planning tools permit an individual or family to set realistic economic and financial goals, establish a viable plan, monitor progress, and take appropriate action when the need arises. Without these tools, financial matters can become a morass of mistakes and confusion, leading to frustration and despair. The best way to master the skills necessary for achieving financial success is to start by studying the basic principles, building on that knowledge, and using the tools. It is then possible to assess the many pieces of financial and economic information available and to apply them constructively.

There is a caveat about personal finance: a cloud of uncertainty surrounds the subject. No matter how experienced an investor or financial manager is, no one knows for certain what tomorrow's financial news will bring. Evidence of this was obvious to everyone, early in January 2001 when Alan Greenspan, the U.S. Federal Reserve Chairman, unexpectedly lowered the federal funds rate (the equivalent of Canada's bank rate) by half a percentage point. Events of this nature can, and do, happen frequently and usually without warning. They can wreak havoc on investment portfolios and mutual funds. They can cost new home owners who took out mortgages at an inopportune time considerably more money over the terms of their mortgages. They can also benefit people with sound financial plans. Such people should be able to sleep peacefully. We hope that you, the readers of this book, will be members of this elect group.

The earlier editions, as well as this edition, consider the memorization of many details to be of limited value in the ever-changing environment of financial planning. Therefore, we undertake in this book to explore the basic principles, concepts, and vocabulary. There are many sources of information and many perspectives for each individual to consider. This book is designed to help you understand, evaluate, and apply financial information in an effective way.

Content and Organization

The depth of coverage of the topics in this text varies, due partly to the availability of other excellent sources of information. Some topics, such as taxes and wills, are covered very well in other publications. Our goal, then, is to ensure that the reader understands when to see a professional or to seek further information. Topics not covered in great depth in other sources are explored here in more depth. The authors have not presented the more complex forms of investments, such as derivatives, but have provided a solid overview of the whole investment environment. For further information, the reader is directed to the references at the end of each chapter.

Some topics in this book, such as tax law, have not been covered in depth, due to their ever-changing nature. To deal with the rapidly changing environment of financial planning, we have delivered a textbook current as of the date of writing to allow the reader to become familiar with the variety of information available and the use of other sources of current information such as the Internet. At the same time, we encourage our readers to keep up-to-date and to use the most current information available when applying the information learned in this book to their situation.

The book is organized in three sections; the first section (Chapters 1-3) deals with the planning process and those two inevitabilities—death and taxes. The second section (Chapters 4 through 11) addresses security aspects such as the risks faced by each of us and the means of mitigating these risks, and their fallout, usually through insurance or building one's own personal net worth. After introducing the concepts of interest, the second section moves on to examine the fundamental methods of saving and investing everything from debt instruments to stocks and mutual funds. The third section (Chapters 12 through 14) starts with consumer credit, progresses to mortgages, and finally discusses the worst-case scenario, bankruptcy. Keep in mind that the laws governing many of these topics vary by province. Every effort has been made to identify the variations across the country.

New to this Edition

We have thoroughly updated the information in this latest edition to reflect changes in the financial, legal, and economic environment. And to better suit the users of the book, we have made the following changes:

- Recent changes to the income Tax Law have been incorporated in Chapter 2.
- We have expanded on topics such as Joint Tenancy/Tenancy in Common in Chapter 3, Segregated Funds in Chapter 7, and Stock Analysis in Chapter 11.
- New "hot" topics have been added, including Day Trading in Chapter 11 and Telephone/Internet Banking in Chapter 9.
- About half of the Personal Finance in Action boxes have been replaced.
- About 25 percent of the existing end-of-chapter problems are new.
- An Internet exercise has been added to each chapter.
- The list of references and Weblinks at the end of each chapter has been thoroughly revised and updated.

Features

We have enhanced the features for this edition to facilitate learning and highlight applications:

A set of **Learning Objectives** is provided at the beginning of each chapter.

Key Terms are boldfaced where they are defined in the text. They are also listed alphabetically, with page references, near the end of each chapter. The index at the back of the book also clearly indicates where to find the definitions.

Personal Finance In Action Boxes throughout the book present a wide variety of practical scenarios.

A **Summary** is provided for each chapter.

A set of **Problems** near the end of each chapter offers the opportunity to apply the material to a variety of situations. An Internet problem is included in each chapter to keep the questions current and as applied as possible.

References near the end of each chapter will help guide users to further readings.

The section entitled **Personal Finance On The Web** at the end of each chapter lists useful Internet sites that provide further information and current material.

Downloadable Excel Files

The special Excel files available for download from our Web site (www.pearsoned.ca/brown) contain the following 12 financial worksheets to help students personalize basic financial planning concepts:

Table 1.1 Net Worth Statement	Table 1.4 Estimated Annual Expenses
Table 1.2 Analysis of Net Worth	Table 1.5 The Budget
Table 1.3 Estimated Annual Income	Table 2.1 Estimate Your Income Tax Bill

Table 6.1 Current Life Insurance Needs Future Value of Investments

Mortgage Payments Annual Income Required for Retirement

Loan Payments Retirement Savings

Supplements

The following supplements have been carefully prepared to accompany this new edition:

An **Instructor's Resource Manual** includes an overview, answers to all the text problems, and suggested supplementary activities for each chapter of the text. It also provides a printout of the Financial Planning Worksheets downloadable from the book's Web site, along with Transparency Masters of all the Figures and Tables in the text.

A **Test Item File** provides multiple-choice questions, true-false questions, and problems for each chapter. The number of questions has been increased for this edition. Each question has been classified by level of difficulty (i.e., easy, moderate, or challenging) and a page reference to the text has been added.

Test Manager consists of a special computerized version of the Test Item File that allows instructors to create and distribute tests and analyze the results electronically.

Our **Companion Website** contains self-test material for the students (multiple choice, true-false, and short essay questions), links to other Web sites where students will find information relevant to personal finance, and Excel files containing financial worksheets for download. PowerPoint presentations containing the figures and tables from the text are also available for download on the site. Visit the site often at **www.pearsoned.ca/brown**.

Acknowledgments

Without the help of many individuals and their organizations, this book could not have been written. We would like to thank the following for their assistance:

Brenda Bunting, Credit Manager, McCain International, Florenceville, New Brunswick; Mark Bardsley, Fiona Winter, LeeAnn Acton, and Doug Newlands, Nesbitt Burns, Private Client Division, Toronto; Dan Bouley, Fontaine and Associates, Trustee in Bankruptcy, North Bay; John Charlton, London Life, North Bay; Professor Bernie McGaughey, North Bay; Lloyd Burke and Craig Harvey KPMG, Chartered Accountants, North Bay; Herb Kast, Wood Gundy, Private Client Investments, North Bay; Professor Ken Deck, Coordinator Math Department, Canadore College, North Bay; Randy Harris, London Life, London; Cornelia Breen, Economical Insurance, Waterloo; Joyce Luxton, Guelph; Wellington Credit Union, Guelph,; Jim Golem, Clarica Insurance, Waterloo; Professor Rick Bates, Erin; and Donald Muck, Great-West Life, Waterloo.

We are also grateful to the following instructors for providing formal reviews of the manuscript:

Sid Dolgoy, George Brown College John Cavaliere, Sault College

Rosemary Vanderhoeven, University of Guelph John Churchill, Acadia University

Sherry Finney, University College of Cape Breton Vincent Durant, St. Lawrence College

Michael Bozzo, Mohawk College Bob McCrae, Sheridan College

Finally, we would like to thank Laurie Goebel, Developmental Editor, Pearson Education Canada for her suggestions and help with this edition.

Kathleen Brown *Tom Chambers* *Elliott Currie*

The Pearson Education Canada

companion Website...

Your Internet companion to the most exciting, state-of-the-art educational tools on the Web!

The Pearson Education Canada Companion Website is easy to navigate and is organized to correspond to the chapters in this textbook. The Companion Website comprises these distinct, functional features:

Customized Online Resources

Online Interactive Tests

Web links

Communication

Learning Objectives

Explore these areas in this Companion Website. Students and distance learners will discover resources for indepth study, research, and communication, empowering them in their quest for greater knowledge and maximizing their potential for success in the course.

A NEW WAY TO DELIVER EDUCATIONAL CONTENT

Course Management

Our Companion Websites provide instructors and students with the ability to access, exchange, and interact with material specially created for our individual textbooks.

- **Syllabus Manager** provides instructors with the option of creating online classes and constructing an online syllabus linked to specific modules in the Companion Website.

- **Grader** allows the student to take a test that is automatically marked by the program. The results of the test can be e-mailed to the instructor and then added to the student's record.

- **Help** includes an evaluation of the user's system and a tune-up area that makes updating browsers and plug-ins easier. This new feature will facilitate the use of our Companion Websites.

Instructor Resources

This section features modules with additional teaching material organized by chapter for instructors. Downloadable PowerPoint Presentations, Electronic Transparencies, and an Instructor's Manual are just some of the materials that may be available in this section. Where appropriate, this section will be password protected. To get a password, simply contact your Pearson Education Canada representative or call Faculty Sales and Services at 1-800-850-5813.

General Resources

This section contains information that is related to the entire book and that will be of interest to all users of the site. A Table of Contents and a Glossary are just two examples of the kind of information you may find in this section.

The General Resources section may also feature *Communication facilities* that provide a key element for distributed learning environments:

- **Message Board** – This module takes advantage of browser technology to provide the users of each Companion Website with a national newsgroup to post and reply to relevant course topics.

- **Chat Room** – This module enables instructors to lead group activities in real time. Using our chat client, instructors can display website content while students participate in the discussion.

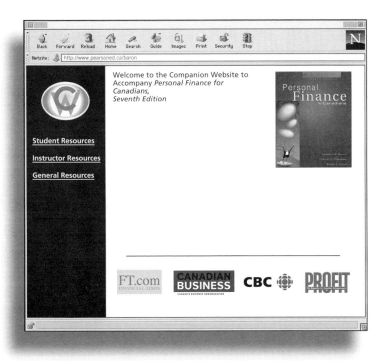
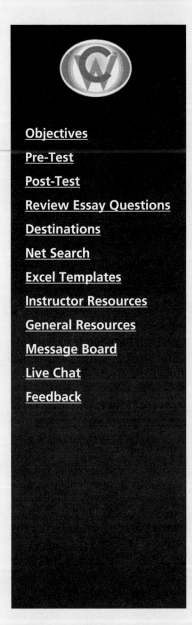

PART ONE

Financial Planning

Current interest in financial planning has generated increasing numbers of books and articles on the subject and a developing profession dedicated to helping people solve their financial problems. But what is financial planning? It can be whatever you want it to be: a tax plan, an investment strategy, a life insurance needs assessment, or a comprehensive financial appraisal. Analyzing or forecasting almost any personal financial activity may be labelled financial planning; consequently, the results can range in scope from a very specific tax plan to a complete strategy covering all personal financial affairs.

In Chapter 1 the general process of making financial plans is explained, including why future cash flow projections should be based on identification of future goals and knowledge of present resources. Most financial planning involves some understanding of basic tax concepts, which are outlined in Chapter 2. After this introduction to the topic, income tax will come up again in later chapters dealing with retirement income, savings, and investments.

Financial planning is important not only in directing the management of resources during our lives but also in preparing for the disposition of our estate after death. Therefore, this section includes a chapter on wills and planning for the distribution of estates. A wise man once said, "the only inevitables in life are death and taxes." Let's start our discussions here.

Chapter 1

Financial Planning

objectives

1. Explain how the use of economic resources can be improved by financial planning.

2. Examine ten reasons for taking a lifetime perspective in personal financial planning.

3. Demonstrate how a financial plan can influence decisions about spending, income tax, insurance, and investments.

4. Explain the basic principles of financial planning.

5. Identify the functions of net worth statements, expenditure records, and budgets in the financial planning process.

6. Evaluate a net worth statement.

7. Distinguish between income and wealth.

8. Evaluate four methods of controlling expenditures, and identify six obstacles to successful control.

9. Identify behaviours with a psychological or social origin that may interfere with successful implementation of a financial plan.

10. Examine the costs and benefits of various models for handling finances in a two-income family.

11. Identify reasons why women face greater economic risks than men do.

12. Examine the status of the financial planning industry.

Introduction

We live in a very materialistic world. Money and the quantity of possessions one can acquire with it are important to many people. Even those for whom money is not an obsession are forced to pay attention to it. We depend on it to acquire the goods and services we need. We need it to maintain our standard of living. Our place in the world is based on our monetary resources, our ability to earn money, and our attitude toward money.

How we think about money and how we use it are determined by our cultural and family values and by our personalities. The wants and desires of many Canadians exceed their financial resources. This gap has led to an enormous amount of consumer debt and financial insolvency, as well as to serious social problems.

This text is written from an economic and financial perspective. It realizes, however, that subjective influences also determine how people manage their affairs. People may fully comprehend the importance of budgeting and financial planning, but they may be unable to implement their ideas because of personal or family problems. A list of books dealing with the psychology of money is included at the end of this chapter to help readers understand their own financial behaviour.

Even though a financial plan makes sense, few people have one. One reason for not having such a document is the complexity of the financial industry and the many choices available. Often, people just don't know where to start. Another reason may be that financial planning requires discipline and a commitment many people lack. The result is a failure to begin and a serious shortfall of financial resources when one is older. This chapter discusses how to start a financial plan and some of the psychological concerns involved.

Financial decisions may be made with long-term goals in mind, or they may be made with no plan at all. Without a plan of some sort, it is difficult for most of us to achieve the financial security advertised on television and in the press. With a plan in mind to guide us and the discipline to carry out the plan, we can improve our quality of life. As famed baseball player and coach Yogi Berra is reputed to have said, "If you don't know where you're going, you'll probably end up somewhere else." Financial security is within the grasp of everyone, no matter how limited his or her resources.

Need for Financial Plans

What Is a Financial Plan?

A **financial plan,** like any other kind of plan, begins with goals that indicate what is to be achieved. After available resources are identified and assessed, they are allocated to the desired objectives. Finally, a strategy is developed to ensure that goals are reached. Although the procedure for making a plan is straightforward, implementing it is quite another matter, especially if some change in behaviour is required.

Financial plans come in many degrees of completeness and complexity. A small plan might be devised to control spending on entertainment and recreation; such a plan would include specific goals, a set limit for this category, and some ways to ensure that you do not overspend. At the other extreme, a very comprehensive financial plan can include all aspects of a person's financial affairs, starting with financial objectives and including current spending and saving projections, investment strategies, income tax plans, estate plans, and schemes for financing such specific goals as retirement. In most cases, people make financial plans that fall somewhere between these two extremes of complexity. Several examples of financial plans are included later in this chapter.

Why Plan Financial Affairs?

Planning makes it possible for you to live within your income, save money for short-term and long-term goals, and reduce financial worries and stresses in the household. Do you hope to purchase expensive goods, take a big trip, buy a house, send your children to university, or just make ends meet? Do you want to achieve financial independence and have a comfortable retirement? Do you wish to leave your dependents well provided for if something should happen to you? A financial plan will help you to take control of your finances and attain these goals.

There are both non-economic and economic reasons for making financial plans. Taking control of your finances can reduce anxiety, raise self-confidence, and increase satisfaction. In addition to helping you feel much better about yourself and your finances, planning can help you accomplish a number of economic goals:

(a) balancing cash flows,

(b) accumulating funds for special goals,

(c) adjusting lifetime earnings to expenses and saving for retirement,

(d) meeting the needs of dependents in case of death or disability,

(e) minimizing income taxes,

(f) maximizing investment returns.

BALANCE CASH FLOWS Everyone faces the necessity of ensuring that current income is adequate to cover expenses, a task otherwise known as making ends meet. Those with financial plans are in a better position to balance receipts and expenditures because of their overall view of the situation. Some non-planners go through cycles of feast and famine, spending money when they have it and doing without when it is gone. Others have a sufficient margin between income and expenses so that such problems do not arise. Taking control of current cash flows leads to peace of mind and greater success in achieving financial goals.

SPECIAL GOALS We all dream of things we would like to do or buy but know the cost is too much to handle on our current income. We have a choice: to wait until we have saved enough or to do it now and pay later. Each option has costs and benefits. Is it better to submit to the discipline of waiting and saving or to pay the extra costs of using credit? (See Personal Finance in Action Box 1.1, "The Credit Trap," for an example of a family facing this challenge.) If the expenditure can be postponed, there is much to be said for selecting a savings target and gradually accumulating the needed funds. This way, you earn interest while waiting instead of paying it to someone else as a credit charge. Good money managers try to receive interest, not pay it. It is usually worthwhile to save before buying a house, because a large down payment substantially reduces interest costs. The key point is that your goals will be more easily reached if you have a plan for achieving them.

LIFETIME PERSPECTIVE A planner has a long time horizon, looking ahead to future years and not just this month or year. For instance, most people can expect the relation between their income and expenses to vary over their life span: generally, living expenses will be more stable than employment earnings. Living costs tend to rise somewhat as our expectations increase—and they definitely expand when children join the family. Earnings, on the other hand, may be very small or nonexistent for a student, take a jump with labour force involvement, increase gradually with experience, be interrupted by unemployment or a return to school, and reach a peak just before terminating at retirement.

The Credit Trap

Sean and Melanie married shortly after graduating from college. Student life had been good, and their government-sponsored student loans enabled them to attend college. Sean and Melanie like having a car, so despite their tight budget, they purchased one with a graduation package offered by an automobile manufacturer.

Shopping for their new apartment became a virtual hobby for them; in fact, shopping on-line with their new computer has become one of their favourite pastimes. Sean is now working for a large foreign-owned manufacturing firm, and Melanie works in the hospitality industry.

Their finances are always tight, especially now that they are making payments on their student loans. Even with the maximum time allowed to repay the loans, the payments for the car, rent, and insurance make money very tight. Unable to pay off their credit card balance every month, they are only paying the minimum. Consequently, they have a large amount owing and are paying a very high rate of interest. Fortunately, the car is less than a year old, but with no money in the bank for emergencies, they are beginning to worry: there are rumours that the foreign company that Sean works for is going to rationalize its worldwide operations and Sean's department may be closed.

In the early stages of family formation, it is not unusual to find expenses exceeding income, with a consequent dependence on consumer credit. In middle age, as the children leave home and earnings are reaching a peak, opportunities to save may be particularly good. At retirement, there may be income from deferred earnings in the form of pensions, but often this is inadequate to support your accustomed lifestyle. At this stage, investment income can make life much more comfortable. In summary, an important planning task is to develop a way of distributing resources to support a fairly stable consumption level throughout the life span. A lifetime perspective on income and expenses is suggested in the diagram in Figure 1.1.

NEEDS OF DEPENDENTS If you have dependents, you will want to consider the economic consequences of your untimely death. Should you die tomorrow or become seriously ill, would there be enough money to support your dependents for as long as needed? Young families, who usually lack enough wealth to cope with such situations, buy life insurance and disability insurance to fill the gap. Another aspect of planning is to make a will to ensure that funds will be distributed as you intend after your death.

MINIMIZE INCOME TAX The income tax system has become very complex. While there are ways to minimize your tax bill, the responsibility is yours to know and take advantage of all the possibilities. By tax filing time in April, it is usually too late to implement most tax-saving strategies. Plans must be made well in advance.

MAXIMIZE INVESTMENT INCOME Some people who are good savers have no idea how to go about investing. They find the subject of investments so overwhelming that they leave too much money in low-yielding securities. If increasing wealth is one of your goals, you must not only save but also invest prudently.

When to Start Planning

Planning is best not postponed on the assumption that there will be more money in the future. Start right now to make the best use of what you have. You can achieve financial independence

FIGURE 1.1 INCOME AND LIVING COSTS: AVERAGE LIFETIME PROFILE

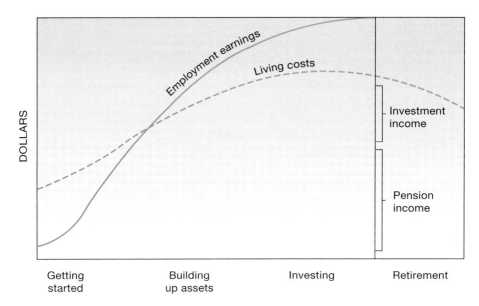

STAGES IN THE FINANCIAL LIFE CYCLE

if you are determined to do so. It will mean taking deliberate control of your own financial affairs, rather than delaying decisions, letting things drift, and becoming a victim of circumstances. Many opportunities have been missed by those who considered financial matters beyond their control. Numerous people have retired with insufficient funds for a comfortable life because they did not save and invest during their working years.

Reaching Financial Independence

The way to financial independence is to spend less than you earn and to invest the savings. As your wealth gradually grows, you will be able to achieve more of your financial goals and perhaps even retire earlier. The key is to increase your wealth steadily so that eventually investment income can replace or augment your employment income. Naturally, it helps to have a high income, but many highly paid people spend their money as quickly as they get it. The sooner you begin to plan, save, and invest, the more time the money will have to grow. It is not how much you make, but how much you save and invest.

Life Cycle Differences

Although there are individual differences, most of us will go through a series of phases in our lifetimes. Sociologists call these "**life cycle stages.**" In terms of financial management, they could be designated as follows:

(a) getting started (to mid-thirties),

(b) building up assets (mid-thirties to fifties),

(c) investing (fifties to retirement),

(d) retirement.

Financial planning is dynamic. Expect your plans to change as you move through the life cycle.

GETTING STARTED Students are naturally concerned with educational and living costs and with obtaining a job in a chosen field. It is wise to invest money saved from summer employment in secure short-term deposits (savings account, term deposit, Canada Savings Bonds) that will generate as much interest as possible. Careful spending plans can be helpful in ensuring that funds last until the end of term. Perhaps you have noticed that for some students, the money ends before the term does. Others manage to put themselves through college or university and still have a nest egg at the end of it all. Why the difference? Could it be planning?

After graduation, high priority will be given to career advancement, saving for an emergency fund, paying off student debt, perhaps buying a house, and starting a modest investment portfolio. If you are raising a family, life insurance may be needed to cover the risk that you might die while supporting dependents. The funds available to do all these things will usually come from earnings, since you have not yet had time to build up wealth that will generate investment income.

BUILDING UP ASSETS The middle years are the time to concentrate on paying off the mortgage on the house, increasing savings and investments, and giving some thought to retirement planning. (See Personal Finance in Action Box 1.2, "When to Start Saving for Retirement.")

INVESTING In middle age, most people have the best opportunity to save and to acquire a variety of assets. Obligations to children usually diminish, the house becomes mortgage-free, and income is at or near its peak. This is the time to give a high priority to increasing assets in a way that will provide an adequate retirement income.

RETIREMENT After retirement, your opportunities to increase wealth will be much diminished. Your attention will be focused on sound management of previously acquired assets and on changing the mix of assets to emphasize income rather than growth.

This review of changes in financial management as one moves through the life cycle demonstrates that long-term planning is essential. A small investment that is left to grow for many years will take advantage of the time effects of compounding, but those who wait until age 55 to start saving for retirement will have to save more to compensate for the shorter time for growth. To achieve financial independence, we must be willing to pay the price in time, effort, and self-discipline.

Personal Finance in Action 1.2

When to Start Saving for Retirement

Yolanda and Dan were debating when they should start saving for their retirement. Yolanda thought that if they put away $2 000 each year for the next 30 years, they would have a useful sum when they turned 65. Dan, however, argued that with a young family it would be too hard for them to do without $2 000 now. He said that if he started at age 55 and saved $6 000 a year, he would be just as far ahead as Yolanda. Either way they would be saving the same amount—$60 000. To support her position, Yolanda decided to look up some compound interest tables. Assuming an average return of 5% compounded annually, she found that in 30 years her savings would have grown to $139 522. With ten years of investment, Dan's $60 000 would become only $79 241. The results are shown in Figure 1.2.

FIGURE 1.2   VALUE OF ANNUAL DEPOSITS OF $2 000 FROM AGE 35–64 AND $6 000 FROM AGE 55–64 AT 5%

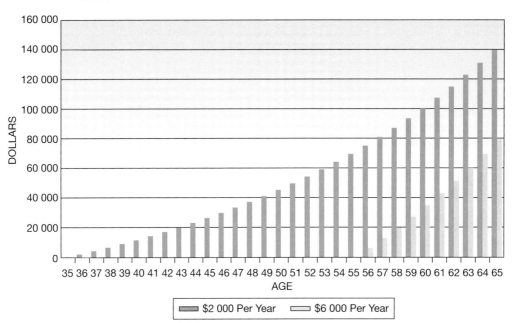

The Financial Planning Process

Financial planning is the currently popular name for an age-old process, usually known as "budgeting." However, financial planning sometimes means a more comprehensive plan than the traditional budget. A word here about terminology: the word "budget," which has a strict technical meaning, is often misused. A **budget** is a plan for using financial resources, a projection for the future. It is not a record of what was spent last year. Very often "budget" is used to imply thrift, scrimping, or lower quality. This book adheres to the technical definition of a budget.

The basic principles of management apply just as much to handling financial affairs as to any other kind of activity. In this section, a general overview of the financial planning process will be followed by more detailed discussion of each component. The time span used for financial planning is entirely personal, but for simplicity we will assume that the planning period is one year. During that time, most kinds of expenses and income will have occurred at least once.

The first principle of financial management—as with any other type of management—is that goals must be identified before they can be achieved. Because it is usual to have more objectives than financial resources, priorities must be attached to goals to reflect their relative importance. The second principle is that an analysis of present financial resources is basic to future planning. Assemble all records of income and expenses for the past year, as well as a list of your assets and debts.

The third principle is that successful planning requires balanced cash flows. Refer to past spending records as a basis for estimating the cost of accomplishing your objectives. Draw up a plan or forecast for a specific period, perhaps a year, which includes a statement of your anticipated financial resources and their allocation; this plan is called a budget.

Fourth, strategies for the implementation and control of the plan are essential. Plans are intended to direct some action and to manage changes as they occur. The fifth and final principle

FIGURE 1.3 STEPS IN THE FINANCIAL PLANNING PROCESS

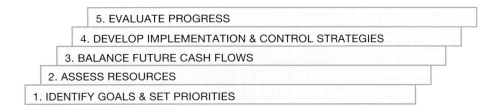

is that effective financial management requires the ongoing evaluation of plans and implementation strategies to keep the plan relevant and effective. A summary of the process is shown in Figure 1.3.

Identify Values, Goals, and Priorities

All people have personal goals, whether they are aware of them or not. To some, a major goal may be to have a comfortable life; for others, it may be to travel or to own a Maserati. Perhaps the goals may be to raise a family, to have a vacation property, and to retire comfortably. Every person's goals are different and incorporate different time frames. A financial goal is usually the quantitative portion and concrete measurement that coincides with the personal goal. If the desire is to have a comfortable lifestyle, then the household must determine the level of comfort. The Maserati has a price tag and can easily be measured. It is, therefore, also a financial goal; it merely lacks another aspect of financial planning—timing. When does the individual want the car, the house, or the vacation? When does the family want children, and how much will it cost to send each child to college or university? Now the goals have financial aspects, which are the major focus of this book.

It is imperative to set goals for the household to ensure that it is attaining what it desires. Knowing where we want to go, when we want to get there, and how much it will cost are the fundamental building blocks of financial planning and goal setting. Starting the whole planning process with where you want to end up will help with the actual planning by providing a measuring stick for determining progress as well as a regular re-evaluation of the goals. The financial elements of goals are easier to quantify and discuss and are the primary focus of this book.

Three major areas in which many people have goals with financial elements are (i) level of living, (ii) financial security, and (iii) estate planning. In allocating financial resources, each individual creates his or her own balance among desires for comforts and amenities in the present, the need to develop a reserve of funds to be used in emergencies and on retirement, and the wish to amass an estate that can be bequeathed to others.

Establishing financial goals is a very personal matter. A counsellor or advisor can ask questions to help you identify goals and the priorities you place on them, but cannot and should not attempt to decide what your goals are. Once the goals and their attached priorities are made explicit, a financial advisor can help you learn the management process necessary to reach the goals.

Conflicts in Goals and Values

Unfortunately, it is a common family problem that people who share economic resources do not always share financial goals. For example, one partner may want to save as much as possible for a down payment on a house, while the other has a strong need to pursue an expensive hobby or other recreation. With limited resources, such a couple will have difficulty in reaching both goals. Furthermore, they will likely have problems in their relationship until they settle their differences. Recognizing that a difference in values is at the root of their problem is an essential first step in resolving these difficulties. In this era of dual-income households, the tasks of goal setting and following through on the plan become even more complex.

Financial management may sound easy, but it can be difficult to accomplish because conflicts in attitudes, beliefs, and values continually intrude. As you would expect, the greater the number of individuals involved in the financial management of a common set of resources, the greater the potential for conflict. One might think, though, that a person who lives alone and who does not have to share resources or cooperate with others in determining goals would have no problems. Not so. Single individuals often experience financial difficulties because of a lack of clarity in goals, unresolved conflicts in priorities, lack of self-discipline, and poor methods of control. You may wish to do further reading about clarifying values and handling interpersonal conflicts; here it is emphasized that attitudes, values, and motivation are probably the most important components in the financial management process. Books, courses, and financial advisors can tell you how to manage your money, but only you can decide whether to act.

Assess Resources

Once you are clear about goals and priorities, the next step is to take an inventory of the resources you either have or can expect to receive that may be used to achieve these goals. There are two components to this resource assessment: (i) an inventory of assets, called a net worth statement, and (ii) an income statement. The distinction between income and wealth is important. A net worth statement shows the stock of assets and the amount of liabilities at a specific time—that is, your net **wealth. Income,** which is not a stock but a flow of resources over a period of time, is usually expressed as an amount per week, per month, or per year. An analogy may help to clarify this point. Think of income as the rate at which water flows into a pond, and net worth as the amount of water in the pond. Those people who do not let some water stay in their ponds will find that their net worth fails to grow.

Net Worth

An essential requirement for financial planning is knowledge of exactly what you own and what you owe. Begin by making a list of all your assets and liabilities, or a net worth statement. Subtract the liabilities from the assets to find your actual **net worth,** or wealth. Those who make a wealth inventory are usually surprised by what they find. They may have more assets than they thought, or more debts than they imagined, or they may find that their assets are not sufficiently diversified.

MEASURE OF ECONOMIC PROGRESS If your goal is to increase wealth for financial security and independence, you must have some way to measure your progress. A series of annual net worth statements will reveal the rate at which your wealth is growing and will indicate whether you should make changes in your saving or investing practices. Think of a net worth statement as a snapshot of wealth on a given day; since it may be larger or smaller at another time, it should always be dated.

NET WORTH STATEMENT When making a net worth statement, list all your assets at their current value and the total amounts currently outstanding on all existing liabilities, as shown in Table 1.1. Assets that are not fully paid for, such as a house or car, are listed at their present market value in the asset column, and the amount owing is listed under liabilities.

Total each column, and find the difference between the two. If your assets exceed your liabilities, you have a positive net worth. Many people start their working lives with a negative net worth, but expect a growing positive net worth as middle age nears. In summary:

$$\text{Net worth} = \text{total assets} - \text{total liabilities}$$

Use the sample net worth statement in Table 1.1 or download the worksheet at our Web site, www.pearsoned.ca/brown, as a guide in preparing your own. A couple is advised to make individual net worth statements as well as a joint one. Since Canadians prepare individual tax returns, it is helpful for tax planning to be able to analyze the assets of each partner separately. For instance, a family might decide that the spouse with the lower income will own those assets that generate the most income. For later analysis, calculate what proportion of the total is represented by each asset.

WHAT TO INCLUDE   What to include in a net worth statement will depend on how you intend to use it. Be consistent in your choice of items in annual net worth statements used to measure economic progress, so that you can compare your results from year to year. You may decide that household furnishings and clothing are fairly constant and can be excluded. On the other hand, if you need to monitor the growth in your personal household capital goods, you may decide to include specific items. When an estate is being settled, a very detailed net worth statement may be required that includes all the personal possessions of the deceased. For loan applications, the credit manager might ask enough questions to estimate the borrower's net worth, with emphasis mainly on liquid assets and real property. When preparing a net worth statement for retirement planning, the attention will be on assets that have income-producing potential.

VALUING ASSETS AND LIABILITIES   Setting a value on the assets you own can be a very complicated process, especially when considering personal property. Certified individuals can appraise your collectibles, such as artwork or jewellery; this may help establish the required levels of insurance coverage, but is frequently beyond what is needed for a net worth statement. Financial assets can be easily valued from recent statements, but when it comes to real estate it is advisable to use a recent selling price for a similar house in your neighbourhood. For vehicles, check newspaper ads for the selling prices of similar vehicles. As stated above, your personal property may be excluded, but should it be of significant value, include it either at what you consider a reasonable value or at its appraised value. Debts can be easily valued from your most recent statements or by calling your financial institution for a current amount.

USES FOR NET WORTH STATEMENTS   What uses are there for net worth statements, other than to measure economic progress, obtain a loan, or settle an estate? An analysis of assets and debts can help determine whether the asset mix is appropriate and whether the debt/asset ratio is satisfactory. When making plans for retirement, you will want to know what wealth you have available to generate future investment income. Should you need to draw on net worth in a time of crisis, it will help if you have a clear idea of what your resources are. If you are trying to decide whether you need life insurance, the net worth statement can be examined to see whether there is a gap between the resources your dependents would need and what the family already has.

ANALYZE NET WORTH   Once made, a net worth statement should be analyzed, not just filed. Use Table 1.2 and the following questions as a guide for evaluating net worth.

TABLE 1.1   NET WORTH STATEMENT

ASSETS	SELF OR JOINT		SPOUSE	
	Amount	% of Total	Amount	% of Total
Liquid Assets				
Cash, bank accounts (savings & chequing)	$ 500	0.13%	$ 950	0.42%
Canada Savings Bonds	$ 5 000	1.27%	$ 500	0.22%
Term deposits	$ 8 000	2.04%	$ 5 000	2.20%
Life insurance cash surrender value	$ 1 750	0.45%	$ —	0.00%
(A) TOTAL LIQUID ASSETS	$ 15 250	3.89%	$ 6 450	2.84%
Other Financial Assets				
Stocks and equity mutual funds	$ 10 000	2.55%	$ 10 000	4.40%
Bonds and bond mutual funds	$ 5 000	1.27%	$ 15 000	6.59%
Loans to others	$ 5 000	1.27%	$ —	0.00%
GICs	$ 2500	0.64%	$ 5 000	2.20%
RRSPs	$ 17 500	4.46%	$ 2 500	1.10%
Pension plan credits	$ 5 000	1.27%	$ 25 000	10.99%
(B) TOTAL OTHER FINANCIAL ASSETS	$ 45 000	11.47%	$ 57 500	25.28%
Real Estate				
Home (market value)	$ 175 000	44.61%	$ —	0.00%
Other real estate	$ —	0.00%	$ 45 000	19.78%
(C) TOTAL REAL ESTATE	$ 175 000	44.61%	$ 45 000	19.78%
Personal Property				
Vehicles	$ 32 500	8.29%	$ 25 000	10.99%
Artwork, collectibles, jewellery, etc.	$ 4 500	1.15%	$ 3 500	1.54%
Furnishings, stereos, etc.	$ 45 000	11.47%	$ 15 000	6.59%
(D) TOTAL PERSONAL PROPERTY	$ 82 000	20.91%	$ 43 500	19.13%
(E) BUSINESS EQUITY	$ 75 000	19.12%	$ 75 000	32.97%
(F) TOTAL ASSETS (A+B+C+D+E)	$ 392 250	100.00%	$ 227 450	100.00%

LIABILITIES				
Short-Term Debt				
Loans, instalment contracts, leases	$ 25 000		$ 12 500	
Credit card debts	$ 4 500		$ 2 500	
Life insurance loans	$ —		$ —	
Long-Term Debt				
Mortgages	$ 125 000		$ 35 000	
Other debts: tuition, business, etc.	$ 25 000		$ 25 000	
(G) TOTAL LIABILITIES	$ 179 500		$ 75 000	
TOTAL ASSETS (F)	$ 392 250		$ 227 450	
ASSETS (F) − LIABILITIES (G) = NET WORTH	$ 212 750		$ 152 450	
COMBINED NET WORTH OF SELF AND SPOUSE	$ 365 200			

DATE: May 21, 2001

TABLE 1.2 ANALYSIS OF NET WORTH

1. ANNUAL GROWTH IN NET WORTH

Present net worth	$ 365 200
Previous net worth	$ 305 250
Change in net worth	$ 59 950
Percentage change in net worth	19.6%
Inflation rate for same period	6.5%
Net change after inflation (real rate of growth)	13.1%

2. LIQUIDITY

Total liquid assets	$ 21 700
Total Assets	$ 619 700
Liquid assets/total assets ratio	3.5

3. DEBT RATIOS

Total short-term debt	$ 44 500
Liquid assets	$ 21 700
Short-term debt/liquid asset ratio	2.05
Total assets in property and other investments	$ 598 000
Total debts for property and other investments	$ 210 000
Investment asset/debt ratio	2.85
Total short-term debt	$ 44 500
Total long-term debt	$ 210 000
Short-term/long-term debt ratio	0.21

4. DIVERSITY

Deposits and other debt securities	$ 26 000
Total liquid assets	$ 21 700
Total RRSPs	$ 20 000
Bonds and bond mutual funds	$ 20 000
Other loans (you are the lender)	$ 5 000
Total debt securities	$ 92 700
Total stocks and equity mutual funds	$ 20 000
Total equity in property	$ 60 000
Total business equity	$ 100 000
Total equity securities	$ 180 000
Debt securities/equity securities ratio	0.52

DATE: May 21, 2001

(a) **Has your net worth grown faster than inflation in the past year?**

If not, assets have been losing purchasing power. Look for a minimum long-term growth of about 3 percent after inflation. For instance, if net worth increased 8 percent in a year when inflation was 5 percent, there would be a net change of 3 percent after inflation, also known as the **real rate of return.** Next, check to see whether all the growth has been in the value of your home. If so, this increase may be overshadowing a lack of growth in other assets.

(b) **What is the ratio of liquid assets to total assets?**

In order to answer this question, you need to know that **liquid assets** are those that can readily be converted to cash without loss of principal, such as bank deposits or Canada Savings Bonds. Too much or too little liquidity can be unwise, as will be discussed in the chapter on investments. Some liquid assets, perhaps the equivalent of three months' wages, may be reserved for emergencies. However, since liquid assets tend to earn less than other investments, an overemphasis would mean a loss of potential income. Many people have too large a proportion of their assets in liquid form.

(c) What is the ratio of short-term debt to liquid assets?

A high ratio indicates a precarious position if anything should happen to income. Is the ratio appropriate for your stage in the life cycle? Normally, the debt/income ratio will decrease with age.

(d) What is the ratio of investment assets to investment debt?

Just after you purchase a house with a large mortgage, this ratio may be low, but with time, it should increase.

(e) What is the ratio of short-term to long-term liabilities?

Short-term debt should not be greater than long-term debt. Are you using most of the long-term debt to acquire assets? Is your short-term debt for living expenses? Borrowing to buy assets such as property makes sense, but too much dependence on credit for day-to-day living costs is a drain on resources and impedes the growth of wealth.

(f) How diversified are the assets?

Add up all the assets that are deposits, bonds, or investment certificates, also referred to as debt securities. These assets are usually low risk, and pay interest income.

Compare this total with the total of the assets that you own, such as property, mutual funds, or stocks. These are called equity securities. What is the ratio of debt securities to equity securities? Are the various kinds of risks balanced? What might happen to the assets' purchasing power if we were to have a period of high inflation? Generally, debt securities lose purchasing power in periods of inflation, and equity securities are more likely to appreciate. How much is exposed to market risk, as in a business or the stock market? Different types of risks are explained in Chapter 9.

Income

The second task in assessing financial resources is to predict your income for the planning period by examining past income records. Use either Table 1.3 or download the spreadsheet at our Web site, www.pearsoned.ca/brown, to record your income for the last calendar year. Income tax records can be helpful for this task. Enter your gross income before any deductions, not your take-home pay. All deductions, including income tax, will be shown in the expenditure record.

OTHER RESOURCES Include in the income statement any other resources you used last year to cover living expenses, such as savings, credit, or gifts, if you expect to use those resources again in the next planning period.

Expenditures

ESTIMATE LIVING COSTS Before making plans for next year, it is best to have the most complete information possible about current living costs. Those who have been keeping records

TABLE 1.3 ESTIMATED ANNUAL INCOME

SOURCE	SELF	SPOUSE
Employment		
Gross income from employment	$ 45 000	$ 75 000
Other (bonuses, etc)	2 500	2 500
(A) TOTAL EMPLOYMENT INCOME	$ 47 500	$ 77 500
Government Payments		
Employment Insurance	$ 1 350	—
Workers' Compensation	—	—
Pensions (Veterans', CPP, OAS, Other)	3 600	—
Welfare, family benefits	250	750
(B) TOTAL GOVERNMENT PAYMENTS	$ 5 200	$ 750
Investment		
Interest	$ 152	$ 257
Dividends	350	1 125
Rent (net income)	—	—
Capital gains	365	2 587
Profit	—	—
Annuities	—	—
Other	—	—
(C) TOTAL INVESTMENT INCOME	$ 867	$ 3 969
Other Income		
Self-employment	$ 2 540	—
Other	—	250
(D) TOTAL OTHER INCOME	$ 2 540	$ 250
Total Annual Income (A+B+C+D)	$ 56 107	$ 82 469
Total Family Income	$ 138 576	
Other Resources Used		
Savings spent	$ 5 000	—
Money borrowed	25 000	—
Gifts received	125	125
Total Other Resources	$ 30 125	$ 125

DATE: January 31, 2001

will have a great advantage here. Otherwise, make the best and most detailed estimates possible of your costs for the past year by using Table 1.4 or the spreadsheet on our Web site as a guide. Try to reconstruct the outward cash flow, using cheque stubs, receipts, and any records available. Anyone who feels overwhelmed by the detail required in Table 1.4 can skip to the end and use the summary part only. For those using the spreadsheet, the summary will be automatically calculated based on your input. This approach may be quicker, but you will recognize that these estimates may not be as accurate.

TABLE 1.4   ESTIMATED ANNUAL EXPENSES

EXPENSE ITEM	Per Week	Biweekly	Per Month	Per Year	Check Fixed Expenses
Deductions from Pay					
Income tax (include with security and taxes at the end)					
Canada Pension Plan (max $1329.90 each)	$ —	$ 107.88	$ —	$ 2 659.80	✓
Employment Insurance (max $936.00 each)	—	98.08	—	1 872.00	✓
Parking	—	—	15.04	180.48	✓
Company pension	—	181.56	—	4 720.56	✓
Association/union dues	—	—	35.00	420.00	✓
Health insurance	—	25.46	—	661.96	✓
Group life insurance	—	7.50	—	195.00	✓
Long-term disability insurance	—	25.60	—	665.60	✓
Dental plan	—	4.85	—	126.10	✓
Extended health insurance	—	2.85	—	74.10	✓
Other	—	—	—	—	
TOTAL DEDUCTIONS	$ —	$ 453.78	$ 50.04	$ 11 575.60	
Food					
Groceries	$ —	$ 250.00	—	$ 6 500.00	
Dining out	$ 25.00	—	—	1 300.00	
TOTAL FOOD	$ 25.00	$ 250.00	—	$ 7 800.00	
Housing					
Rent or mortgage	$ —	$ 550.00	—	$ 14 300.00	✓
Real estate taxes	—	—	185.00	2 220.00	✓
Hydro, water	—	—	65.00	780.00	✓
Heat	—	—	48.00	576.00	✓
Telephone	—	—	75.00	900.00	✓
Cable TV	—	—	35.00	420.00	✓
Household operation and help	—	—	200.00	2 400.00	
Home maintenance	—	60.00	100.00	2 760.00	
Purchase of furniture and appliances	—	—	250.00	3 000.00	
Home insurance	—	—	34.25	411.00	✓
TOTAL HOUSING	$ —	$ 610.00	$ 992.25	$ 27 767.00	

continued

TABLE 1.4   ESTIMATED ANNUAL EXPENSES (CONTINUED)

EXPENSE ITEM	Per Week	Biweekly	Per Month	Per Year	Check Fixed Expenses
Medical					
Insurance premiums	$ —	$ —	$ 8.50	$ 102.00	✓
Dental	—	—	12.50	150.00	✓
Drugs	—	—	—	—	
Optical (annual coverage)	—	—	—	—	
Other	—	—	—	—	
TOTAL MEDICAL	$ —	$ —	$ 21.00	$ 252.00	
Transportation					
Vehicle payments	$ —	$ —	$ 375.00	$ 4 500.00	✓
Vehicle purchase	—	—	—	30 000.00	
Vehicle insurance	—	—	112.00	1 344.00	✓
Operation (gas, oil, licence, and parking)	—	—	200.00	2 400.00	✓
Vehicle maintenance	—	—	100.00	1 200.00	✓
Travel and public transportation	—	50.00	—	1 300.00	✓
TOTAL TRANSPORTATION	$ —	50.00	$ 787.00	$ 40 744.00	
Personal Needs					
Pocket money	$ —	$ 200.00	—	$ 5 200.00	
Personal care	—	—	95.00	1 140.00	
TOTAL PERSONAL NEEDS	$ —	$ 200.00	$ 95.00	$ 6 340.00	
Gifts and Donations					
Gifts	$ —	$ —	$ 150.00	$ 1 800.00	
Charitable donations	—	—	50.00	600.00	
Religious contributions	10.00	—	—	520.00	
TOTAL GIFTS AND DONATIONS	$ 10.00	$ —	$ 200.00	$ 2 920.00	
Clothing					
Spouse	$ —	$ —	$ 150.00	$ 1 800.00	
Spouse	—	—	150.00	1 800.00	
Other family members	—	—	150.00	1 800.00	
Laundry and cleaning	10.00	—	—	520.00	
TOTAL CLOTHING	$ 10.00	$ —	$ 450.00	$ 5 920.00	

continued

TABLE 1.4   ESTIMATED ANNUAL EXPENSES (CONTINUED)

EXPENSE ITEM	Per Week	Biweekly	Per Month	Per Year	Fixed Expenses
Recreation and Entertainment					
Hobbies	$ —	$ —	15.00	$ 180.00	
Liquor and tobacco	—	—	50.00	600.00	
Books and subscriptions	—	—	25.00	300.00	
CDs, tapes etc.	—	—	50.00	600.00	
Other (i.e., travel)	—	—	250.00	3 000.00	
TOTAL RECREATION	$ —	$ —	390.00	$ 4 680.00	
Security and Taxes					
Life insurance	$ —	$ —	$ 95.00	$ 1 140.00	✓
Annuities, RRSPs	—	—	450.00	5 400.00	
Regular savings	—	—	250.00	3 000.00	
Income tax (from deductions)	—	815.00	—	21 190.00	✓
TOTAL SECURITY AND TAXES	$ —	$ 815.00	$ 795.00	$ 30 730.00	
Other Expenses	$ —	—	—	—	
TOTAL OTHER EXPENSES	$ —	—	$ —	$ —	
Debt Repayment (excluding mortgage)	$ —	$ —	$ 375.00	$ 4 500.00	
TOTAL DEBT REPAYMENT	$ —	$ —	$ 375.00	$ 4 500.00	

Summary of Expenses

Expense Item	Per Year
1. Deductions	$ 11 575.60
2. Food	7 800.00
3. Housing	27 767.00
4. Medical	252.00
5. Transportation	36 244.00
6. Personal needs	6 340.00
7. Gifts and donations	2 920.00
8. Clothing	5 920.00
9. Recreation and entertainment	4 680.00
10. Security and taxes	30 730.00
11. Debt repayment	4 500.00
12. Other	—
TOTAL EXPENSES	$ 138 728.60
TOTAL FIXED EXPENSES	$ 64 508.60
TOTAL SAVINGS	$ −152.60 −0.1% of Income

Note that in Table 1.4 a check mark is to be placed beside all expenses that are considered fixed. It is helpful in planning to distinguish between **flexible expenses** (which can be altered if needed) and **fixed expenses** (which are difficult to change in the short term). In the long run, of course, all expenses can be altered. Whenever quick adjustments are required, changes will probably have to be made in the flexible expenses. Enter expenses by week or month as convenient, and then convert them all to annual amounts.

ANALYZE EXPENSE RECORD   Review the expense record to discover whether there is consistency between the way money has been spent and the statement of goals and priorities. Quite often we say one thing but do another. Identify spending categories that may need better methods of control. Is debt repayment too large a proportion of expenses? Will next year's expenses be about the same as those for last year, or are changes expected?

SAVING   What proportion of income was saved last year? Is this satisfactory, or could it be increased? A discussion of savings strategies may be found in Chapter 9.

Balance Future Cash Flows

Income

Based on the data you have assembled, estimate your income for next year. If you are at all unsure whether you will receive some income, do not include it. There will be fewer unpleasant surprises if you are conservative in predicting income, but generous in estimating expenses. Enter the amounts in Table 1.4. You can download it from our Web site at www.pearsoned.ca/brown.

IRREGULAR INCOME   When income is irregular or seasonal, it is harder to make a forecast unless there are adequate records from past years. Make the best estimate possible of next year's income, but be restrained. Since expenses are likely to be more regular than income, divide total expenses by 12 and allocate this amount for monthly living expenses and savings.

Other Resources

If you expect that your income will not be high enough to cover your expenses, list the other resources that you will use, such as savings, borrowed funds, and gifts from others. Such resources may be needed by students, the unemployed, or the retired if they have insufficient income to support their living costs. At other times in the life cycle, it should be possible to add to savings rather than use them. It has been observed, however, that those who have been good savers all their lives are often reluctant to use these assets to support their lifestyle when they are old. They have saved for a rainy day, and they are concerned that things may be worse in the future. Sometimes it is difficult to decide whether you have arrived at a rainy day!

Savings

Plan your savings for the year first; don't just hope that some money will be left over. How much must be saved to meet various long-term and short-term objectives? For instance, if you are planning a large purchase in four years, determine how much you must save each year. Is there enough in the emergency fund? What part of the savings is going toward a retirement fund? Keeping in mind goals and annual resources, decide how much would be realistic to save for the year. This subject is explored in more detail in Chapter 9.

Living Expenses

How much does it cost to run a household, to clothe and feed family members, to take an annual holiday? How much will be needed for those desired expensive items or for the down payment on a house? Past records of expenditures will be helpful in predicting regular costs.

If you lack adequate records, or expect that next year will be very different from the last, it may be difficult to make realistic projections. Allow for flexibility in your plan. Estimate your total expenses for the year to come using a table similar to the summary part of Table 1.4, and enter total predicted expenses in Table 1.5. If you use the spreadsheet available on our Web site at www.pearsoned.ca/brown, these numbers, excluding savings, will be automatically calculated from your earlier input.

PERSONAL ALLOWANCES Designate a sum of money for each individual in the family to use without having to account for its use to others. This will simplify record-keeping and also enhance family harmony. Obviously, you will need to reach some agreement about what sorts of expenditures will be covered by these personal allowances.

Balance Income and Expenses

Use Table 1.5 as a guide for comparing total budget figures. Will the financial resources you expect to have available during the budget period cover predicted saving and spending? It is not unusual at this stage to find that there is not enough money for everything and that adjustments are therefore needed. To balance the budget, you have the choice of increasing resources, reducing wants, or doing some of both. This balancing step is a critical one in financial management, because goals, priorities, and the total expected financial situation for a year (or other period) are being taken into consideration. A calm look at the overall plans will lead to a more careful and rational allocation of resources than will hasty *ad hoc* decisions made while shopping.

TABLE 1.5 THE BUDGET

Planning period from January 1st, 2001 to December 31st, 2001

Available Resources

Income	$ 138 576.00
Savings	5 000.00
Borrowing	25 000.00
TOTAL RESOURCES AVAILABLE	$ 168 576.00

Allocation of Resources

Savings

Emergency funds	3 000.00	
Short-term goals	2 500.00	
Long-term goals	5 000.00	
TOTAL SAVINGS		$ 10 500.00

Expenses

TOTAL EXPENSES	$ 138 728.60	
TOTAL SAVINGS AND EXPENSES		149 228.60
Difference between total resources and total savings and expenses		$19 347.40

When trying to make a budget balance, review estimates to ensure that they are as accurate as possible. Has uncertain income been included? Are the expenditure estimates inflated? What has been included that is not essential or important? Could better use be made of the money?

Develop Implementation and Control Strategies

A critical part of the planning process is controlling the plan. Many splendid budgets have been prepared and filed away by their creators, who thought the task was finished. In fact, a plan for any type of activity is ineffective until it is put into action. Once the saving and spending estimates have been balanced with expected resources, consider how you can make the plan work.

The following generalizations summarize key points about controlling financial plans:

(a) All those handling the money share a commitment to the plan.

(b) The control system is compatible with an individual's personality and habits.

(c) Controlling a plan requires that someone know where the money is going.

(d) The funds for major groups of expenditures are segregated in some way to prevent overspending.

Shared Commitment

All those who are sharing income and expenses and have a common budget must not only be informed about the budget but also be committed to it. Any plan not supported by all those concerned is doomed from the outset. For instance, a family argument may result in one person using money to punish the other by running up large bills on a spending spree. Such a family relations problem must be dealt with before any budget can be effective. Ideally, all those in the spending unit will work together in preparing the financial plan, taking time to resolve conflicts in values as they arise.

A System to Suit Your Personality

It is impossible to prescribe a system of control for another person's financial affairs; we can only suggest possible alternatives. People differ too widely in their styles of handling money and in their willingness to maintain written records. Consider your own habits and personality, and develop ways to ensure that your money will be spent or saved as planned. If money burns holes in your pockets, you will need to do something to curb your impulsiveness.

Know Where the Money Is Going

In order to keep track of expenses, you will need to do some kind of record-keeping, but make the system simple enough that it does not become onerous and thus neglected. (See Personal Finance in Action Box 1.3, "Simple Record-Keeping and Control.") Decide how much detail is needed or wanted, and proceed accordingly. Often the very act of recording expenditures serves as a control on spending, because having to write down what you spend tends to encourage reflection on your financial habits. There are numerous reasonably priced software packages to help in this area. Quicken from Intuit is the most popular. Money from Microsoft is second in popularity.

Control the Allocations

There are several ways to control allocations. The simplest method is to operate strictly on a cash basis, putting the allocated amounts in envelopes, purses, or sugar bowls. During a specific period, restrict spending to the sum in each container. This system is not practical for many people, both because of the danger of theft and loss and because of the inconvenience of handling complex affairs this way. However, this concrete approach is useful for people who have difficulty with abstract thinking. At the opposite extreme is the completely abstract method of control by double-entry bookkeeping, which can be very effective if you are committed to the system.

A possible compromise is to establish several levels of control by opening a number of savings and chequing accounts. For example, you could have one account for long-term savings, one for short-term goals, one for irregular expenditures, and one for regular living expenses. These accounts serve the same function as the envelopes or sugar bowls mentioned above. Decide which expenditures can be handled by the same account, and deposit the planned amount each time a paycheque is received. To make certain that this system will work, cheques or debits must be taken from the appropriate account and records kept up-to-date. If you have a joint account, each user must inform the other of deposits and withdrawals.

Actions or Events that Jeopardize Plans

UNEXPECTED EXPENSES As many will attest, unexpected expenses occur just about every month, so you may as well plan for them. Add such a category to the budget to prevent frustration when the unforeseen occurs. It is virtually impossible to plan spending exactly to the last dollar, but with experience it becomes easier to approximate how much to allow for the unexpected.

USE OF CREDIT How does the use of credit cards affect the control system? If purchases are charged as a convenience and you pay off the total bill monthly, they can be treated in the same way as other bills. However, if you are susceptible to the impulse buying that credit cards encourage, you will need to develop restrictions on having or carrying credit cards. If charge account balances are growing because you pay only a portion of the total each month, consider how much you are spending on costly credit charges and also whether you have a tendency to overspend.

IRREGULAR EXPENSES Everyone has irregular large bills that cannot be paid from the monthly allocation without planning for them. Using last year's records as a guide, find the annual total of expenses such as insurance, taxes, auto licence and maintenance, and income tax. Divide the total by the number of paydays, and deposit the appropriate amount in the account earmarked for these bills.

UNREALISTIC PLAN If your plans never seem to materialize, it could be because they are unrealistic. The first time you make a budget, lack of experience and inaccurate records may result in poor plans. Do not give up, but do expect to make adjustments to your plans. Remember that you can change the plan at any time, and that as time goes on, your plans will become more realistic.

A budget may be most needed just when predictions are most difficult to make. For instance, when there is a change in living arrangements or in household composition, or a drop in income, it is evident that things are going to be different but it is hard to know how different. A couple establishing a new household will have no past records to refer to. They will have to make the best estimates they can for a few months, and then review those estimates and make a better plan. Likewise, the arrival of a child will add to costs, but new parents lack sufficient data to make accurate forecasts.

Personal Finance in Action 1.3

Simple Record-Keeping and Control

Ann works for a large financial institution as an analyst/manager and is also working towards an accounting designation. As part of her training, she has become aware that she needs to manage the household funds through budgeting and a system of controls. Ann and her husband, Francis, believe they can achieve financial freedom through financial management. The problem is, after Ann's two-hour commute and studying for the accounting program, she feels too exhausted to set up a system for managing their money.

Francis now manages their money, while running his commercial artist service from their home. They have two bank accounts: one joint and one for Francis' business. All bills are paid from the joint account. Francis keeps track of their expenses and inflows on his computer. The expenses are broken down into categories such as household expenses; utilities; telephone; savings; education; business; emergencies; food; pocket money; and gifts. He records all paycheques on these tables as well as the receipts from his business.

He records each expense and allocates the inflows to the different accounts, with a proportional share from the business for tax reasons and to ensure that the business pays for its particular expenses. Francis pays all of their bills at night on his computer; this saves money on postage and frees his time during the day for his business.

INFLEXIBLE PLANS Do not consider plans to be unchangeable. A plan is a device to help achieve goals, not a straitjacket. If it becomes inappropriate for some reason, it can be revised. Consider plans to be your servants, not your masters.

TOO MUCH PRECISION EXPECTED Decide how precise financial plans and records must be to achieve the desired goals, and proceed accordingly. Do not make the mistake of embarking on a first financial plan with unrealistic notions of how much record-keeping will be done and how precisely the actual expenses must match the budgeted amount.

USING A FINANCIAL PLAN TO REFORM BEHAVIOUR If you are feeling guilty about the way you are now spending money, you might want to make a plan on the assumption that certain vices will be cut out. How successful will that plan be? Reforming yourself may be a good idea, but it would be best to separate that goal from financial planning. We need to accept the fact that changing behaviour, even our own, is difficult. Anyone who intends to change his or her spending habits, record-keeping practices, or savings goal must plan for a series of small changes, not a large one. Success with each small change achieved will provide the motivation for undertaking another modification. Attempts to make too big a change usually result in failure.

Evaluate Progress

Since the purpose of making a budget is to have a blueprint that will guide financial decisions, there must be a mechanism for measuring progress. Periodically, compare the plan with what is actually happening. Are goals being met? If what is happening does not correspond very well with the plan, ask why. Was the plan unrealistic, perhaps because it was based on wrong assumptions or on incomplete data? Is the problem with the methods of control? Do not expect too perfect a match between the actual and the budgeted amounts for each category of spending.

Rather, look for a balance in overall cash flow, and check whether any particular category is out of line.

Develop some system for simplifying comparisons between the amounts budgeted and actual cash flow, and check on this often enough to prevent things from getting out of control. An annual review of changes in net worth should be adequate, but allocations for savings and living expenses need a closer watch—perhaps monthly, or at least quarterly. Successful monitoring and review of budgets requires a system of records.

Financial Records

CASH FLOW CONTROL WORKSHEET   There are three steps in this record-keeping task:

(a) collecting the data,

(b) summarizing or finding monthly and annual totals,

(c) analyzing the results.

Some may get stuck at the first step, because they have no system for recording what they have spent. It may help to begin by concentrating on regular, fixed expenses, which are usually well known or are recorded in chequebooks. Once all the information on the fixed expenses has been obtained, the flexible expenses can be added.

Develop a method that suits you and that provides enough information for your purposes. Do not attempt a scheme that is too ambitious; such a system may be neglected because it is too time-consuming. Some people use a ledger book, or ruled loose-leaf pages, with columns for all the expense categories. Enter each expense, as it occurs, under the appropriate column. Others carry a small notebook to record expenditures as they occur, and later transfer the information to a ledger.

Analyze the results by comparing the actual monthly totals with the budgeted amounts. This can be done on another summary sheet that has space for 12 months.

A computer can be helpful for record-keeping. A number of commercial software programs have been developed for this purpose. Although they do not eliminate the task of collecting the data, such programs do other tasks well, making it much easier for you to categorize entries, create totals, and calculate percentages so that you can summarize and analyze the data and do some basic planning and projections. If you find working with a computer more fun than working with pencil and paper, use it for your record-keeping and analysis. Some programs will even interact with your bank to pay bills and balance accounts. Take a look at Quicken or Money.

Strategies for Two-Income Households

Changing Family Patterns

Among the many dramatic changes in family structure we have witnessed in recent decades, the increasing number of women in the labour force is one that has had an impact on many households' finances. In the late 1960s, women with young children or with high-earning husbands tended not to take paid employment, but that is no longer true. It is clear that nowadays dual-earner families have become the most common type, even when the husband receives a high income.

By 1994, the number of two-earner households had increased to 3.3 million versus 1.9 million single-earner households. This trend has almost exactly reversed the situation of 20 years earlier. The presence of children—even preschoolers—in the home has almost no impact on the incidence of two-earner households. This significant shift has had major implications for the way household finances are managed. A strategy that may have been reasonable for a one-earner family, such as pooling all resources, may be less appropriate when there are two earners. Some models used by dual-income families to organize their finances are outlined below.

(a) *Pooled funds.* All income is combined, and expenses are paid from this pool. This approach requires frequent discussion to achieve shared values and goals.

(b) *Equal split.* Each partner puts the same amount into a common pool to cover specified joint expenses. They also have separate personal and savings accounts. This system works best if both partners earn about the same amount.

(c) *Proportionate contributions.* When one partner earns more than the other, their contributions to the common pool are based on agreed proportions of their incomes to make it more equitable.

(d) *Dividing the bills.* Instead of pooling funds, each person agrees to handle certain expenses.

When deciding what model to try, couples should take stock of their personalities and values. (See Personal Finance in Action Box 1.4, "A Plan That Works for Them.") Some systems require more discussion and agreement than others do. The pooled fund system works best if both people share values and attitudes toward money. When one partner is a spendthrift and the other a tightwad, it might work better to have each individual handle more of his or her money on a personal basis.

Personal Finance in Action 1.4

A Plan That Works for Them

Ilona and Pierre belong to the ranks of people who don't like to keep a regular record of their expenses and who prefer to plan their budget in their heads. However, now that their children have reached university age, they find that they need to maintain a reserve fund to cover some of the children's expenses. Also, they want to be able to finance the family's hobbies of cycling and skiing, both of which are becoming more expensive with each new high-technology development. To find the least demanding and least tiresome method of financial planning, they attended a one-day workshop that also included information about planning for retirement.

After deliberating briefly, they decided that the best method for them was to create a budget based on their current spending habits. To start, they needed to estimate their expenses for the coming year. This involved figuring out how much they would spend on

three major categories: (i) the house (e.g., mortgage, utilities, taxes, insurance, telephone, landscaping, repairs, and maintenance); (ii) personal/discretionary (e.g., groceries, drugstore, cosmetics, clothes, medical, non-essentials for the house, gifts, books, ski and bicycle accessories, race fees, and boots), and (iii) savings and investment (e.g., RRSPs, mutual funds, savings account).

Their paycheques, with combined earnings of $83 000 per year, are deposited into their personal chequing account. Automatic monthly transfers of funds have been arranged for RRSPs, investments, life insurance, mortgage payments, and savings. To avoid recording detailed grocery expenditures, they set aside $850 per month ($180 a week) for this purpose.

Once a month, Ilona and Pierre spend a few hours recording the previous month's cash flows. They use a transaction log to record deposits, automatic transfers,

continued

cheques, cash withdrawals (from automatic tellers), and any other transactions. From credit card statements and chequebook records, they are able to categorize all expenses according to their two major categories: personal/discretionary and house. Next, the amounts for each category are totalled and entered on the monthly budget page and also on a year-to-date statement.

Like everyone else, they find that there are times when they have overspent in one or more categories. They are then able to bring the budget in line over the next several months either by spending less in each category or by skipping a category (for example, buying no new cycling outfits, or renting videos instead of going to the movies).

By choosing a budget method that suits their personalities, Ilona and Pierre have been able to gain control over their expenses without drastically changing their lifestyle and without feeling bound by too stringent a system. In their case, flexibility and ease of administration were the key factors that made their financial planning successful.

In summary,

(a)   Inflow/Outflow

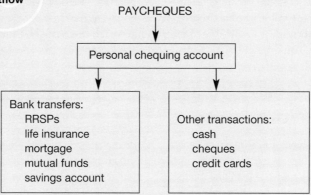

(b)   Monthly Budget Control Sequence and Records

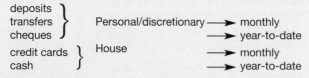

(c)   Categories and Items

HOUSE	PERSONAL/ DISCRETIONARY		SAVINGS/ INVESTMENT
mortgage	groceries	race fees	RRSPs
utilities	clothes	books	mutual funds
taxes	car	magazines	Canada Savings Bonds
insurance	cosmetics	medical	savings account
telephone	gifts	entertainment	
landscaping	ski & bicycle accessories	donations	
repairs	travel	miscellaneous	
maintenance			
furnishings			

Reasons for *Not* Making Plans

Although almost anyone will tell you that it is a good idea to make a financial plan, fewer people actually do much planning. Why the discrepancy? Making and using a financial plan requires motivation, knowledge, time, effort, and finally, discipline and persistence. Planning is easily postponed in favour of more interesting or more pressing activities. This chapter, like other sections of this book, is intended to increase your motivation for taking control of your personal financial affairs and to show you how to do it, but only you can provide the other necessary components.

Those who think they ought to do some financial planning, but don't, should ask themselves what obstacles are preventing them from taking greater control of their finances. Is it lack of motivation or lack of a reason for getting involved? Is it not knowing how to get started? Is it a perceived lack of time? Or is it a general distaste for financial matters? Once the reason for not doing more planning has been identified, steps can be taken to improve matters. You may choose to learn how, to delegate planning to someone else in the family, or to hire assistance.

People have a variety of reasons for not making financial plans. Some people say that their income and expenses are too unpredictable to plan anything; others feel that plans are much too confining or that planning takes all the fun out of spending. Discouragement with a plan that did not work effectively may be the result either of unrealistic estimates or of inadequate methods of controlling the plan. It would be better to try again than to abandon all plans.

Women and Financial Independence

For several reasons, women often face higher economic risks than men do. Although the situation has improved in the past few decades, women's economic well-being often still depends on their relationships with men; any time such a relationship breaks down, a woman may find her finances in jeopardy. Because of family responsibilities to children and older relatives, women tend to have less regular labour force attachment than men do; they usually earn less than men do; and they generally live longer than men do. As a result, they have less opportunity to acquire personal financial assets or to accumulate pension credits either with the Canada Pension Plan or with employer-sponsored pension plans. When families break up, women are often left with dependent children and uncertain child support.

Many women, who will probably spend years living on their own, will encounter economic uncertainty in their senior years because they do not have enough personal assets or pension credits. What steps can younger women take to ensure their future financial security? Perhaps the most important thing is to have a long planning horizon, so that current decisions are taken with reference to future implications. Women who have a marketable skill and who keep it up-to-date will have more economic independence than those who do not. Those who establish a savings or investment account in their own name and keep adding to it will have a nest egg. Anyone who has personal assets before marriage may do well to get advice about a marriage contract. Family laws differ in various provinces with regard to dividing matrimonial property after a separation, and it is wise to know your rights.

Planning for economic self-sufficiency is not always easy. It may seem disloyal to be thinking about independence while in a happy marriage. Nevertheless, women who are informed about financial affairs, have some personal assets, avoid co-signing loans with spouses, have a marriage contract, and maintain a paper trail of any personal gifts and inheritances will have an advantage if the unthinkable happens.

Professional Financial Advisors

Professional advice on personal financial affairs has long been available to certain segments of society. The wealthy pay investment counsellors for advice on investments and tax planning. The overindebted go to publicly and privately supported credit counsellors, who suggest ways of coping with too much debt. Where do the rest of us go for advice? There is no shortage of people who *want* to advise us—to invest in term deposits, guaranteed investment certificates, Canada Savings Bonds, mortgages, real estate, stocks, bonds, mutual funds, or limited partnerships, or to buy insurance. Each advisor has a special interest in promoting ways to invest our spare cash, and each is knowledgeable in a special area. Since many of these salespeople depend on sales commissions, their advice may not be unbiased.

The various kinds of financial advisors may be categorized as follows:

(a) investment counsellors,

(b) credit counsellors,

(c) officers and sales representatives of financial institutions (e.g., bankers, trust company officers, life insurance agents, brokers, mutual fund agents),

(d) financial planners,
    — fee-only
    — commissions-only (may be the same as (c) above)
    — mixture of commission and fees.

Investment Counsellors

For years, professional **investment counsellors** have advised the wealthy on how to handle their finances, with special attention to minimizing income tax and maximizing investment return. Many investment counsellors will invest funds and handle all the day-to-day decisions for their clients, although some are not interested in clients with less than $200 000 or even $500 000. For ongoing investment services, the management fee is usually based on a percentage of assets. Clearly the assistance of an investment counsellor is beyond the reach of most families. Some, however, will work with groups of people with assets totalling in the millions.

Credit Counsellors

At the other end of the financial spectrum are the overindebted—people who often, although not always, have low incomes. When facing a debt crisis, they may turn to **credit counsellors** for help in reducing the pressure from creditors and debt collectors. Such counsellors make every effort to find ways to help families and individuals cope with such a crisis. People who are not yet overindebted may also come to a credit counsellor for information and assistance in financial management. These services, now available in most major communities, may or may not be free to clients. There is more about credit counselling in Chapter 14.

Financial Advice for the Majority

The majority of citizens, who are neither very wealthy nor overindebted, generally lack independent financial counsellors to turn to for help. If they want to know more about financial management, they must read books, take courses, or consult those who sell various financial products. The high cost of providing advice, and people's reluctance to pay for this kind of service, means that independent financial advisors have not been widely available to the middle class.

In the 1980s, both the availability of microcomputers and greater family affluence (partly the result of an increase in the number of two-earner households) caused some changes. As the sums of money being handled by families increased and the services and products offered by financial institutions became ever more complex, the demand for information about and help with financial management grew. This need was recognized by publishers, who rapidly expanded the number of books, magazines, and newsletters about personal finance, and by companies selling such products as mutual funds, stocks, life insurance, annuities, and RRSPs. The offer of some financial planning became a new marketing tool for a variety of companies. Large financial institutions, such as banks and trust companies, began to offer financial planning without charge, to entice customers. Computers made the planning process quicker and cheaper.

Financial Planners

Financial planners may be categorized in three groups, based on the source of their remuneration. Many people who call themselves financial planners actually sell financial products, such as mutual funds, guaranteed investment certificates, life insurance, bonds, and stocks; they gain their incomes from sales commissions. A much smaller number are fee-only planners, whose incomes depend solely on client fees and who sell no financial products. The third group consists of planners who combine characteristics of the other two: they charge fees for financial planning and also receive commissions on any products they sell.

A big issue is the potential conflict of interest that arises when a financial advisor does not charge for advice but gains his or her income from product commissions. It would be natural for such a planner to find that a client's solutions included some of the products he or she is particularly well informed about and is licensed to sell.

Financial planning, a rapidly growing business in the United States and Canada, may soon become an accepted profession. In the meantime, though, efforts are being made to reduce the confusion resulting from its rapid expansion. It has been a largely unregulated activity to date, but is under review by securities branches in several provinces, where discussions are going on about establishing standards for education, liability insurance coverage, and ethics. In 1989, Quebec became the first province to pass legislation linking the use of the term "financial planner" with specific educational criteria and mandatory registration. Other provinces are studying the matter; some are expected to take similar action soon. Until then, anyone can call him- or herself a financial planner, financial consultant, or financial advisor.

The Canadian Association of Financial Planners, founded in 1983, is eager to solve the problems of educational requirements and certification. People with two years' experience who complete six correspondence courses become "Chartered Financial Planners."

The Financial Planners' Standards Council has established standards with input from accountants, the insurance industry, the credit unions, and international organizations.

COMPUTER PROGRAMS FOR FINANCIAL PLANNERS Since it may take a financial planner up to 40 hours to create a comprehensive financial plan for a family, and cost as much as $3 000 or $4 000, a way was needed to deliver financial planning to clients more cheaply. The solution was found in computers. Software programs have been developed that will use the data provided by a client to generate a financial plan fairly inexpensively. The programs vary widely in the extent to which they make adjustments for personal habits and preferences, as well as in the assumptions they use. The expansion of financial planning coincided with the availability of microcomputers and suitable programs, and most financial planners now depend heavily on computers.

Choosing a Financial Advisor

It is wise to make some inquiries before entrusting your financial affairs to an unknown advisor.

(a) Find out how the financial planner is paid. Is his or her income based only on fees, on fees and commissions, or only on commissions?

(b) Ask about the planner's qualifications. What educational background, experience, and licences does the person have? Does he or she have any recognized certificates?

(c) Does this planner have certain areas of specialization?

(d) What sort of planning is he or she offering? Will you receive a very detailed, comprehensive plan or the solution to a specific problem? Will there be a written report with recommendations? Does the planner have a sample plan to show you?

(e) Will the planner provide an analysis of the costs and benefits of the various alternatives suggested?

(f) What will the plan cost?

(g) Has the planner ever been sued by a client?

(h) How does the planner keep up-to-date on financial and legal matters?

(i) What institutes is the planner affiliated with?

Summary

We have examined the reasons why individuals should take control of their own financial affairs, rather than letting them drift. People who take such control will increase their chances of reaching their financial goals and improving their quality of life. Although money is not everything, it is the means of achieving many desires. The process of planning and managing finances begins with specifying definite goals and assessing what resources are available to reach them. With this information, a plan can be made for the next year or other time period. To ensure that the plan becomes reality, means must be designed to implement the plan and to control spending behaviour. Periodic review of the process will reveal whether progress is satisfactory.

Financial planning requires some record-keeping. In this chapter, we presented sample forms for assessing and analyzing net worth, assessing income, summarizing expenditures, and creating a one-year budget. We used several examples to illustrate less complex ways of planning and controlling expenditures.

Women often have special economic problems, either because of social attitudes or because of interrupted labour force involvement, and should give thought to ways of ensuring their personal economic security.

Financial planning is a growing and evolving profession. Financial planners offer advice on personal financial affairs, sometimes for a fee. Those who do not charge fees for their advice depend on commissions from the sale of financial products, such as mutual funds, life insurance, stocks, bonds, annuities, and RRSPs.

Key Terms

budget (p. 8)

credit counsellor (p. 28)

financial plan (p. 3)

financial planner (p. 29)

fixed expenses (p. 19)

flexible expenses (p. 19)

income (p. 10)

investment counsellor (p. 28)

life cycle stage (p. 6)

liquid assets (p. 13)

net worth (p. 10)

real rate of return (p. 13)

wealth (p. 10)

Problems

1. Where Does All the Money Go?

    Jan and Dave, a couple in their early thirties, have recently purchased a new house in
    Vegreville, Alberta. The purchase price of $145 000 was a little more than they had
    anticipated, but they love the life in this small town. Dave is able to commute to his of-
    fice in Edmonton, where he works as a sales manager for a scientific supply company.
    Jan, an elementary school teacher, is just getting back into the work force now that
    eight-year-old Brent and six-year-old Karen are both attending school. Since she is
    working as a substitute teacher until a full-time position becomes available, her income
    is quite uncertain and irregular.

    With a down payment of $49 000 from the sale of their old home, a mortgage of
    $96 000, to be paid off in 25 years, costs them $748.80 a month. In the excitement of
    buying the new house, however, they forgot to allow for legal bills, moving costs, and
    the need for new draperies, so they had to get a $3 000 personal loan with a two-year
    term. Recently, they purchased a new car for Jan, costing $12 500, financed with a
    $10 000 loan on which the monthly payments are $308.32.

    They have $1 500 in Canada Savings Bonds (a gift from Jan's grandmother), $355
    in Jan's savings account, and about $456 in their joint chequing account. Last year they
    received about $82.50 in interest from Canada Savings Bonds. Except for a pension
    plan refund put into an RRSP a few years ago (when Dave transferred from another
    company), which is now worth about $3 755, their only major asset is their home.

    When they married, Jan and Dave each bought a $100 000 life insurance policy. If
    they were to cash in these policies, each would have a cash surrender value of $2 000.

    They rely on a line of credit from the bank for emergencies, but apart from this
    would have very little flexibility if Dave should be off work for any length of time. He
    does have insurance coverage at work that would pay about half his usual wages if he
    should become disabled for longer than three months. During the three-month waiting
    period, there would be a small Employment Insurance benefit and a few days' sick leave
    with pay.

    Dave's benefits at work include the use of a leased car and an expense account for
    lunches and the occasional dinner. He also has comprehensive dental, drug, and vision
    care plans, along with some group life insurance coverage.

Fortunately, their new house seems to need little maintenance work, but Jan and Dave would like to start fixing up the basement. They are hoping that Jan will get full-time work soon, so that they will be able to clear some debts and be able to start on the basement.

Dave feels that with his relatively high income of $55 000 a year, including commissions, they should not have the money worries they are currently experiencing and should be in a better position to invest some funds in RRSPs to save for the future and take advantage of the tax saving, but at the moment he does not see how they can afford to do so.

Jan confesses that before the children came along they were used to spending quite freely, since both were earning good wages. Now, with no established management pattern, the money just seems to disappear.

Following is the list Jan and Dave made of their monthly income and expenses. They do not keep records, so these are their best estimates. The income figures are net of deductions at the source, such as income tax, Canada Pension Plan and Employment Insurance premiums, and registered pension plan contributions.

Income	Per month
Dave's take-home pay	$2 909.00
Jan's average salary	600.00
TOTAL	$3 509.00
Short-term debt repayment	
Bank loan for car	$308.33
Bank loan	134.00
TOTAL	$ 442.33
Expenses	
Mortgage	$ 748.00
Heating	90.00
Electricity and water	115.00
Telephone	35.00
Home insurance	25.00
Property taxes	120.00
Food	650.00
Entertainment	120.00
Clothes	200.00
Babysitter	40.00
Books, magazines, CDs	35.00
Gifts	100.00
Life insurance	110.00
Transportation (Jan's car)	200.00
Miscellaneous	300.00
TOTAL	$2 888.00

(a) Make a net worth statement for this couple.

Analyze their net worth position and make a list of issues you would raise in a discussion with them if you were their financial counsellor.

(b) Make a summary cash flow statement for Jan and Dave, noting which expenditures are fixed and which are flexible.

Analyze their cash flow situation. Do any expense categories seem to be missing?

(c) Evaluate this couple's financial security. How well prepared are they for a financial emergency?

(d) Do you think this couple ought to be saving more? What do you suggest? What future difficulties do you foresee for them if they continue as at present?

(e) Evaluate this couple's financial management strategies in terms of the basic steps of financial planning. If they were really motivated to make a change, where might they begin?

2. Decide whether you AGREE or DISAGREE with each of the following statements:

(a) Making and sticking to a financial plan is easier if some rewards are built into the system.

(b) A budget takes all the fun out of spending.

(c) Financial planning makes more sense for people with a good income; for people who are poor, planning is impossible.

(d) If you and your spouse cannot agree on some financial goals, perhaps the solution is to handle your money separately instead of pooling it.

(e) If your financial affairs have been stable for some years and you have reached a comfortable agreement with your spouse about who pays for what and how much to spend on various things, your need for detailed budget analysis may be less than that of a recently married couple.

(f) Students can't really make spending plans, because they have no regular income.

(g) If your income is very irregular, your spending must necessarily be adjusted to the fluctuations of your income.

(h) It is impossible to make a budget work because of all the unexpected expenses that occur.

(i) The reason there is more belief in the value of budgets than in actually making them is the amount of paperwork involved.

3. Explain the difference between the following pairs of terms:

(a) budget and expenditure record.

(b) assets and liabilities.

(c) net worth (wealth) and income.

(d) credit counsellor and financial planner.

(e) investment counsellor and financial planner.

(f) cash flow control worksheet and net worth analysis.

(g) budget and methods of control.

4. Julie was taught that responsible financial management requires that a record be kept of every penny she spends. She has kept such records throughout her life. She keeps them

in a running diary, without any expenditure categories, and never totals the figures or does any analysis. What value does this record-keeping probably have for Julie? What is your opinion of its usefulness?

5. How important is it to have an emergency fund when you do not know whether you will ever need it and you feel that you could always borrow in a pinch?

6. a) List some internal factors that may cause people to become financially distraught.

   b) What external factors may cause people to become financially distraught?

7. Refer to Personal Finance in Action Box 1.1, "The Credit Trap." Why do you think this couple got caught in this trap? Is this a problem mostly for low-income families?

8. What methods will you use to assist your children, if you have any, to manage their money while attending college or university?

9. How did your parents help you learn about money? What will you do differently for your children when they are growing up?

10. Refer to Figure 1.2. Why did Yolanda's $30 000 grow to a larger sum than Dan's?

11. For Darryl and Ilana, life was progressing well, but not the way they wanted it to progress. Darryl's career challenges and opportunities were limited in his current position. Consequently, they were exploring the possibility of Darryl returning to school to complete an MBA. This would require both Darryl and Ilana to quit their jobs and move to a larger city. Ilana would then have to find another job, thus putting her career on hold for Darryl's two-year MBA. After his graduation, they would likely have to move again to whatever job he might get.

    Both agreed to this arrangement, but once they'd moved, Ilana could not find a job. Darryl felt he was too busy to work as a teaching assistant. Meanwhile, the bills continued to roll in. The savings they had set aside for Darryl's MBA only proved adequate for tuition and books; living expenses became the sole responsibility of Ilana. Employment insurance proved inadequate as only Ilana could collect it. The situation was extremely stressful for the two of them, so they went to the graduate student counsellor for advice.

    As their advisor, what advice would you give this couple?

12. Lucy called a financial advisor, saying that she did not know how to cope with her financial affairs. She had never had to give money much thought before her recent divorce from a well-to-do businessman. When she decided to look for work, she found herself at a disadvantage without previous work experience. However, she did land a job in a women's clothing store, where she enjoyed selling clothes and getting things for herself at a discount. She loves clothes and always dresses well. Her two children are grown and independent, and she owns a spacious condominium apartment in a good part of town.

    Lucy had initially tried to maintain her accustomed level of living, but she had lately begun to dip into her divorce settlement funds to make ends meet. Also, she was having trouble with a trust company over the way her money was being handled and was quite confused about what kinds of accounts she had. Now in her late forties, Lucy has been too absorbed in recent family crises to think about her own future. She does not feel very enthusiastic about the advisor's suggestion that they make a long-term financial plan for her. She had wanted an immediate solution and freedom from financial stress.

(a) If you were in Lucy's shoes, what would you do now?

(b) Identify the factors that have created Lucy's current problems.

(c) What sources of income will Lucy probably have when she turns 65?

13. On the Web at www.cfp-ca.org, determine the steps a financial planner is expected to proceed through compared to the five steps outlined in Figure 1.3. What are the differences and what are the similarities between the two? Which entails the most work, and is the planner's work and time worth the $3 000 to $4 000 mentioned in this textbook?

References

BOOKS AND ARTICLES

BAMBER, LORI M., *The Complete Idiot's Guide to Personal Finance for Canadians*. Scarborough: Pearson Education Canada, 2001. Part of the popular "Complete Idiot's Guide" series, which presents clear, understandable information about difficult topics (the kind that make many intelligent adults feel like complete idiots—hence the series' title). Numerous complementary titles also available.

BOOK, JANICE, SANDY CIMORONI, and SUSAN SWAYZE. *Women in the Know: How to Build a Strategy to Achieve Financial Success*. Toronto: Key Porter, 1996. A book written by women for women.

CHAKRAPANI, CHUCK. *Financial Freedom on Five Dollars a Day*. Sixth edition. Vancouver: Self Counsel Press, 1994. A frugal perspective on financial independence.

CHARETTE, DAN. "Hours of Working Couples." *Perspectives on Labour and Income*, Summer 1995, Vol. 7, No. 2. Ottawa: Statistics Canada (Catalogue 75-001E). A government overview of the changing nature of the working family in Canada.

CHUN, ANNE, and PATRICIA JERMEY. *Planning Your Financial Future: A Guide for Canadians*. Toronto: ITP Nelson, 1997. A how-to book on the topic of planning.

COHEN, BRUCE, and ALYSSA DIAMOND. *The Money Adviser: The Canadian Guide to Successful Financial Planning*. Toronto: Stoddart, 1996. Part of a financial series for Canadians, with a focus on planning.

DELOITTE and TOUCHE. *Canadian Guide to Personal Financial Management 2000*. Scarborough: Prentice Hall Canada, annual. A team of accountants provides guidance on a broad range of topics, including planning finances, estimating insurance needs, managing risk, and determining investment needs. Instructions and the necessary forms for making plans are also included.

DOUGLAS, ANN. *Family Finance: The Essential Guide for Canadian Parents*. Scarborough: Pearson Education Canada, 2000. An excellent methodology for managing finances for your family.

JACKS, EVELYN. *Jacks on Personal Finance: Money Management for Utterly Confused Canadians*. Toronto: McGraw-Hill Ryerson, 1994. A good overview from an author with a strong background in income tax.

KINGSTON, ANNE. "Can a Planner Help You Get a Grip on Your Finances?" Toronto: *The Globe and Mail*, March 20, 1993, p. B22. An article about whether or not to have a planner help you.

McKINNON, ALLAN JAMES. *Success in the Nineties Through Personal Financial Planning: A Practical Guide for Personal Financial Planning*. Calgary: McKinnon, 1992. Practical advice for professionals such as medical practitioners.

PAPE, GORDON. *The Best of Pape's Notes: 15 Years of Sound Financial Advice*. Toronto: ITP Nelson, 1998. A review of Pape's past writings.

Personal Finance on the Web

Each of the following Web sites provides high-quality links to many other Internet resources.

Canada WealthNet

www.nucleus.com/wealthnet An index of Canadian financial and investment news and a list of advisors accessible via the Net. Extensive investment information.

Canadian Financial Network

www.canadianfinance.com Provides solid information about finance for Canadians, along with extensive links to other relevant sites and a window on Canada for global investors.

Quicken Financial Network

209.146.210.203/ A Canadian site provided by the developers of the popular software programs Quicken and QuickTax that encompasses a financial fitness test, expert advice, and analysis, investment tracking, and other financial help.

RetireWeb

www.retireweb.com A site that emphasizes planning for retirement, no matter what your life cycle stage. Includes valuable calculators.

Financial Planners Standards Council

www.cfp-ca.org An excellent source of information for consumers and professionals in the industry. A number of links to other professional organizations.

Chapter 2

Introduction to Personal Income Tax

Introduction

The intent of this chapter is to provide an overview of the personal income tax system, rather than an in-depth treatment of what is a very large and complex topic. The explanations of basic terminology offered here, along with a simplified framework that shows the relationships among a few key concepts, should make it easier for you to understand the many articles and books available on personal income tax. In addition to the discussion in this chapter, you will find income tax mentioned elsewhere in the book in relation to other topics, especially retirement income and investments.

In the late 1980s, Canada's federal government made major revisions to the income tax system, reducing the kinds of allowable deductions, increasing tax credits, changing tax rates, and shifting some taxation from income to expenditures. To keep up-to-date with the details of our ever-changing tax rules, it is necessary to follow the financial press or read some of the regularly revised tax guides. These are especially important with all the recent tax cuts.

Such matters become even more important for those who are self-employed or who own their own business. The tax laws vary considerably depending on whether you are an employee or are responsible for calculating and remitting your own taxes. People in the ranks of the self-employed can avail themselves of tax deductions that are not available to those who work for others. Some of these details will be discussed both in this chapter and in later chapters.

The Tax Burden

Personal income tax has become an increasing burden. In 1999, Canadians paid $134 billion in income taxes to federal and provincial governments: that works out to about $4 400 for each man, woman, and child in the country. Since 1950, Canadians' income tax burden has been steadily increasing, as shown by the per capita data in Figure 2.1. These data have been adjusted for the effects of inflation by converting all values to 1986 dollars using the Consumer Price Index. Thus, it is possible to see the trend in the income tax burden while holding population and inflation constant. The percentage of income paid in income taxes to both federal and provincial governments has also grown over this period, as shown in Figure 2.2. The rate has increased from over 4 percent of income in 1950 to just under 18 percent of the average annual income in Canada of over $25 000 in 1999. More recently, the tax cuts have eased the burden, but it will take some time to see a major impact from these changes.

Income tax was introduced in 1917 as a temporary measure to help pay the costs of World War I. It has been continued ever since to meet governments' ever-increasing need for funds. Canadians have become accustomed to a wide variety of government-provided and government-funded services and comprehensive income security programs supported by large amounts of public funds. So it is not surprising to find that we are paying increasing amounts of income tax to fund these programs.

The Personal Income Tax System

Who Pays Income Tax?

All Canadian residents with incomes above a certain level are taxed on their Canadian income as well as on any income received from outside the country. Each of us must file an individual income tax return; spouses must file individually, not jointly, as they do in the United States. Contrary to popular belief, members of the First Nations do pay income tax. Should

FIGURE 2.1 PERCENTAGE INCOME PAID IN INCOME TAXES (1986 $), 1950–1999

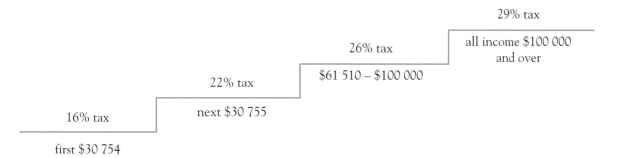

YEAR

⎯⎯ Percentage paid in taxes

SOURCE: Statistics Canada, *Canadian Economic Observer*, Historical Supplement, 1999/00, Catalogue No 11-210-XPB, Table 2 p.10.

they live off the reserve, they pay tax like any other Canadian resident. Even those living on the reserves pay income tax on earnings from off the reserve if the earnings exceed 10 percent of their income. The rules are complex and worth investigating for First Nations' people.

Federal Income Tax Rates

In Canada, we use a **progressive tax rate** system, which means that as taxable income increases, the tax rate increases. Taxable income is calculated by subtracting certain deductions from gross income (more about this later). The diagram below illustrates the progressive nature of federal income tax (using taxable income and 2001 tax rates).

29% tax

all income $100 000
and over

26% tax

$61 510 – $100 000

22% tax

next $30 755

16% tax

first $30 754

FIGURE 2.2   AVERAGE INCOME AND INCOME TAXES PER CAPITA (1986 $), 1950–1999

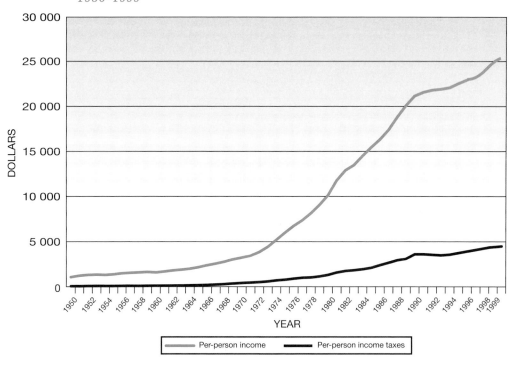

SOURCE: Statistics Canada, *Canadian Economic Observer*, Historical Supplement, 1999/00, Catalogue No 11-210-XPB, Table 2 p. 10.

Under this system, a taxable income of $30 754 or less is taxed at 16 percent. If your taxable income is higher than that, the next $30 755 is taxed at 22 percent; income over $61 510 but less than $100 000 is taxed at 26 percent; anything beyond $100 000 is taxed at 29 percent.

The highest rate that you personally pay on taxable income is referred to as your **marginal tax rate.** Understanding this concept is basic to understanding the significance of tax shelters and to choosing investment alternatives. For example, if you are now paying 22 percent as your highest federal tax rate, that would be your federal marginal rate: each extra dollar of taxable income you receive will be taxed at this rate. Obviously, if your taxable income increases enough, you will move to the next step: your marginal tax rate will become 26 percent. In other words, your marginal tax rate is the rate of taxes that you pay on the last dollar earned.

Your **average tax rate** is the percentage of your gross income that is paid in income tax. Generally, this concept is less useful in tax planning than the marginal tax rate, although occasionally there may be a need to know what proportion of your income was paid in taxes.

Provincial Income Tax Rates

Although all Canadian provinces and territories levy income taxes in addition to those imposed by the federal government, all except Quebec have arranged for Canada Customs Revenue Agency to collect this tax for them. This approach makes life simpler for most of Canada's taxpayers, who must complete only one combined tax return. (Quebec residents file separate provincial returns.) The above provincial rates are for planning purposes only and do not reflect the actual tax one would have to pay. Most provinces actually charge a percentage of the taxable income, same as the Federal government, but the rates vary for each province and change regularly with each new government and provincial budget. Check with your provincial finance ministry for the rates charged in your province. For approximate percentages for 2000 provincial rates, see Table 2.1.

   After calculating the amount of your federal tax, you must add on the appropriate provincial tax. For example, if you lived in New Brunswick and your federal taxes were $2 000, you would add 2 000 × 0.468 = $936, making your combined tax a total of $2 936.

   Quebec tax rates including the federal tax are included in the spreadsheet for reference only and are not all-inclusive of all situations such as an individual with dependents. The Quebec tax system is provincially administered and exceeds 25 percent of taxable income over $52 000.

Combined Marginal Tax Rate

To find your **combined marginal tax rate,** multiply your federal marginal tax rate by the provincial rate, and then add the result of that calculation to the federal rate. Assume, for example, that you have a federal marginal tax rate of 22 percent and that your provincial rate is 45 percent of your federal tax. Your combined marginal tax rate would be 22 + (0.45 × 22) = 31.9 percent.

How Much Tax to Pay

Stripped of detail, the process of calculating how much federal income tax you need to pay annually can be summarized in three steps:

(a) Total relevant income   −   Deductions   =   Taxable income

(b) Taxable income   ×   Tax rate   =   Total tax

(c) Total tax   −   Tax credits   =   Tax payable

   If you analyze the articles on income tax in the financial press, you will find that much of their content has to do with these three issues:

(a) What is counted as relevant income for tax purposes?

(b) Which deductions can be used to reduce taxable income?

(c) How can a person make the most effective use of tax credits?

   The following sections will examine each of these topics in turn.

What Is Income?

Gross and Net Income

Gross income is all the income you received before anything was subtracted. Wage rates are usually quoted as gross income. **Net income** is harder to define: it simply refers to your income after something has been subtracted. Any use of this term should therefore be accompanied by information about what the income is "net *of*." For instance, it may be "net of deductions by the employer" or "net of income tax" or "net of expenses related to generating self-employed earnings."

Legislative Concept of Income

Income can be quite difficult to define. In economic terms, **income** is a flow of economic resources over a specified time period, usually expressed as a rate per hour, per day, per week, per month, or per year (for example, you might say that your new job pays "$35 000 a year"). The Income Tax Act uses a legislative concept of income for the purposes of taxation, and thus does not necessarily define income in the way economists do. Therefore, we find that as a result, some types of income are currently subject to income tax, and some are not. Here is an abbreviated list of some forms of income that are taxable and some that are not:

Income Subject to Tax	**Income Exempt from Tax**
Income from employment	
• wages, salaries, commissions, bonuses	
• net income from self-employment (after expenses)	
• value of employment benefits	
Pensions and social security	*Income support payments*
• Canada/Quebec Pension Plan	• Guaranteed Income Supplement
• Old Age Security	• Spouse's Allowance
• Employment Insurance	• Workers' Compensation
• employment-related retirement pensions	• welfare
• income from an annuity bought with RRSP funds	
Investment income	
• interest	
• dividends	
• rent	
• net profit	
• withdrawals from RRSPs	

EMPLOYMENT BENEFITS   In addition to income, employees may receive taxable benefits: the value of these benefits must be added to your income for tax purposes. Some examples are employee loans, personal use of a company car, medical care plans, and travel benefits. Some benefits—such as employers' contributions to employee pension plans or group insurance—are exempt from taxation until you have actually received them.

Capital Gains

In addition to taxing income, governments may tax changes in wealth. In the past, Canada's governments have taxed estates, inheritances, and gifts, but these taxes have all been discontinued. Currently, however, Canadians do pay taxes on capital gains. A **capital gain** is not income; it is a change in wealth—that is, the windfall accruing to an owner because property or possessions have increased in value. In simple terms, a capital gain is the difference between an asset's original cost and its selling price. The income tax literature makes a distinction between capital gains and **taxable capital gains,** because only a portion of any capital gain (currently 50 percent) is taxable.

Deductions from Income

Once income and the changes in wealth that are subject to tax have been identified and listed, the next step is to examine what deductions may be used to reduce taxable income. (Although technically there is a difference between an exemption and a deduction, both serve to reduce taxable income, and the terms are often used interchangeably.) The exact nature and amounts of deductions allowed may change whenever the federal government amends the Income Tax Act. Deductions from income may be classified in the following three categories, with the specific examples changing from time to time. In many cases, there are limits on the amounts that may be deducted.

(a) Contributions to retirement pension plans
   • registered pension plans (RPPs)
   • registered retirement savings plans (RRSPs)

(b) Specified expenditures associated with any of the following activities:
   • earning a living, such as self-employed earnings or commissioned sales income
      — union and professional dues
      — moving expenses
      — child care
      — travel expenses
   • investing (excluding RRSPs)
      — interest on money borrowed to invest
      — rent for safety deposit box
      — accounting fees
      — investment counsel fees
   • paying child support under an arrangement dated before May 1, 1997
   • paying alimony and spousal support

(c) Capital gains exemption for small businesses and farm property
   • net capital gains

Contributions to Retirement Plans

Since the 1950s, encouraging Canadians to save for retirement has been a matter of public policy implemented through the income tax system. Contributions to employer-sponsored registered pension plans (RPPs) and to registered retirement saving plans (RRSPs) have been exempt from tax, within limits. Since money goes into these plans tax-free, while any return generated within the plan is also not taxed, such plans are known as **tax-sheltered funds**. Only when the money is withdrawn or turned into a retirement pension does it come

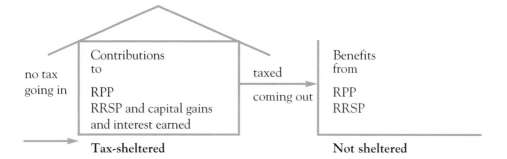

out of the shelter; at that point, it becomes fully taxable. A major reason for putting money in a tax shelter is to defer taxes until a time (such as retirement) when you expect to have a lower marginal tax rate.

Specified Expenditures

Within limits, a few types of expenditures are deductible for tax purposes, including some associated with earning a living, investing, and family support. Some examples are listed above, in the introduction to this section.

Capital Gains Exemption

The opportunity to make a capital gain is always associated with the possibility of having a capital loss. For tax purposes, capital losses are therefore subtracted from capital gains, to get **net taxable capital gains.** These terms and relationships are summarized in the following calculations.

Sale price	−	Purchase price	=	Capital gain (or loss)
Capital gain	−	Capital loss	=	Net capital gain
Net capital gain	×	0.50	=	Net taxable capital gain

PRIMARY RESIDENCE Any capital gain realized on the sale of your home is not subject to tax, but there are limits on this exemption: you (and your spouse) can have only one primary residence at any given time. This means that any capital gains on the family cottage would be taxable, but the family's primary home would not generate taxable capital gains. This matter can be of significant concern to some families and will therefore be discussed in more detail in later chapters. (Income properties—properties that are owned by you but rented or leased to others—are considered investment properties; capital gains on such properties are automatically taxed.)

LIFETIME EXEMPTION For a while (from 1985 until the February 1994 federal budget), all Canadian taxpayers were allowed up to $100 000 in tax-exempt capital gains during their lifetime. This general personal exemption has now been eliminated, but the federal government has left two exemptions still available: the small business corporation shares exemption and the exemption for family farms. Under the first of these categories, individuals who own shares in a corporation that conducts (or conducted) the majority of its business in Canada can deduct up to $500 000 of any capital gain from the sale of those shares. In the second instance, the owners of family farms or farm quotas are entitled to a tax exemption up to the same $500 000 limit.

NON-TAXABLE CHANGES IN WEALTH If you receive an inheritance, win a lottery, or make a gain from another form of gambling, these increases in your wealth are not subject to income tax. In the case of an inheritance, any taxes owing on the estate of the deceased will have been paid before the estate was distributed. Life insurance is not taxed and is paid directly to the beneficiary unless there is foul play. Insurance is paid for with after-tax dollars, and hence has already been taxed.

Tax Credits

After calculating your total federal income tax, determine your eligibility for certain tax reductions, called tax credits. A **tax credit** is subtracted after total tax has been determined. Because, as we'll see shortly, deductions tend to be of the greatest benefit to those with higher incomes, many income deductions were replaced with tax credits in the 1988 tax reforms. To see how tax credits make the tax burden more equitable, consider this example: under the previous rules, a person with a combined marginal tax rate of 48 percent and a $1 000 deduction would have saved $480 in taxes, while someone with a marginal rate of 30 percent and the same deduction would have saved only $300. If both persons were instead eligible for the same tax credit, each would receive the same benefit, regardless of his or her income.

Most tax credits are not refundable, which means that they are useful only if you have some taxable income. Suppose, for example, you calculate that your federal tax will be $5 000 and your tax credits will be $1 000; the tax credits reduce your federal tax to $4 000. But if your taxable income is so low that you owe no tax, that non-refundable tax credit does you no good: your tax is still zero. (If, on the other hand, the tax credit were refundable, you'd get a $1 000 "tax refund" from the government, even though you paid no taxes into the system. See the next section for more details.)

Some tax credits—for example, the basic personal amount that every taxpayer is allowed to claim, and the married amount—are indexed: that is, they are adjusted to reflect the annual change in the Consumer Price Index. If the price index rose 3 percent in the previous year, these credits would be increased by the same 3 percent. For instance, an annual inflation rate of 5.5 percent would mean an increase of 5.5 percent in certain tax credits. (For another example of indexations, see Personal Finance in Action Box 2.1, "Indexation of Pensions.")

REFUNDABLE TAX CREDITS Sometimes the federal income tax system also includes **refundable tax credits.** If you are eligible for such a tax credit, how you receive it will depend on whether or not you have taxable income. If you have no taxable income, you can claim the tax credit anyway; the government will issue it to you by cheque. If you have a taxable income, you can use a refundable tax credit to reduce the taxes you owe. One example of a refundable tax credit is the GST tax credit. Designed to provide benefits for low-income

---

Personal Finance in Action 2.1

Indexation of Pensions

Marina's CPP retirement pension, which was $540 a month last year, will be revised in January to take account of the inflation rate. Since prices rose an average of 4 percent the previous year, her pension will be increased by 4 percent: $540 + (540 × 0.04) = $561.60. This is an example of **full indexation.**

Unfortunately for her, the pension from her previous employment is only partially indexed, with adjustments made for inflation greater than 3 percent. Under **partial indexation,** a pension of $750 a month would be adjusted as follows: $750 + (750 × [0.04 − 0.03]) = $757.50.

individuals, it is negatively related to taxable income. This means that the more you earn, the smaller the credit you receive, and vice versa.

NON-REFUNDABLE TAX CREDITS Most tax credits fall into this category. Here is a partial list of the types of **non-refundable tax credits** available to qualified taxpayers in 2000:

Basic personal amount	Age amount
Married amount	Dependent children
Pension income	Disability
Tuition fees	Medical expenses
Charitable donations	Donations to political parties
Dividend	Employment Insurance contributions
Canada or Quebec Pension contributions	

Because the specifics of each of these tax credits (how much, who is eligible, and so on) can and do change, we will not discuss them in further detail here: to learn more about the credits currently available, consult a recent income tax guide. The dividend tax credit, because of its significance for investment planning, will be explained in detail in Chapter 11. Some of these credits, such as tuition and charitable donations, can be transferred from one family member to another; again, refer to current tax books for specific details.

Table 2.1 presents a simple form for calculating your income tax, with a particular view to planning for the current year or the upcoming year. The spreadsheet, which you can download from our Web site at www.pearsoned.ca/brown, is almost identical to Table 2.1, with basic information on exemptions and tax deductions included in tables at the bottom of the file.

TABLE 2.1 ESTIMATE YOUR INCOME TAX BILL

Year 2001

Income

Employment income	$56 000.00	
Pension income	—	
Employment Insurance benefits	—	
Dividends (125% of amount received)	1 250.00	
Other investment income	—	
Rental income (or loss)	—	
Business or self-employed income (or loss)	—	
1/2 of capital gains	666.67	
Other income	—	
Total Income		$57 916.67

Less Deductions

RRSP or RPP contributions	$ 3 750.00
Union or professional dues	450.00
Eligible child- and attendant-care expenses	3 500.00
Allowable business investment losses	—
Moving expenses	—
Alimony and maintenance expenses	—
Other deductions	375.00
Clawback of OAS	—

TABLE 2.1   ESTIMATE YOUR INCOME TAX BILL (CONTINUED)

Non-capital losses from previous years	—	
Net capital losses from previous years (only against capital gains)	125.00	
Capital gains deductions	—	
Other deductions (E.I., CPP, etc.)	2 265.90	
Total Deductions		$ 10 465.90
Total Taxable Income		$ 47 450.77

Income Tax

Federal Tax:

16% of first $30 754 taxable income (maximum income tax of $4 921)	$ 4 921.00	
22% of next $30 774 taxable income (maximum income tax of $7 201)	3 673.29	
26% of next $38 491 taxable income (maximum income tax of $10 007)	—	
29% of taxable income $100 000 and over	—	
Total Federal Tax		$ 8 594.29

Less Tax Credits

Personal tax credits *	1 229.00	
Dividend tax credit: 13.33% of grossed-up dividends		
(in Quebec use 8.897%)	166.63	
Total Tax Credits		$ 1 395.63
Basic Federal Tax (Total Tax less Tax Credits)		$ 7 198.66

Plus

CPP or QPP Contributions (maximum $1 329.90 or $2 659.80		
if self-employed)	$1 329.90	
Employment Insurance contributions (maximum $936;		
zero if self-employed)	936.00	
Total		$ 2 265.90
Net Federal Income Tax		9 464.56
Provincial Tax		
45% x Basic Federal Tax		3 239.40
Total Income Tax Payable		$ 12 703.96

Provincial Income Tax Rates for 2000

British Columbia	48.7%	Nova Scotia	47.3%
Alberta	39.5%	Prince Edward Island	47.4%
Saskatchewan	45.0%	Newfoundland	48.6%
Manitoba	46.5%	Yukon	49.0%
Ontario	46.4%	Northwest Territories	45.0%
New Brunswick	46.8%	Non-resident	48.0%

Quebec tax rates require a separate calculation that exceeds the capability of this form. Tax credits in Quebec are also more diverse than this form is capable of calculating.

Quebec, which collects its own income tax, uses the following rates:

Taxable Income	Tax Rate
$ 0 to $26 000	18.0%
$26 000 to $52 000	$4 680 plus 22.5% of excess over $26 000
$52 000 and over	$10 530 plus 25% of excess over $52 000

Note: These rates apply only to a single filer with no dependents.

continued

TABLE 2.1   ESTIMATE YOUR INCOME TAX BILL (CONTINUED)

* Personal Tax Credits	
Individual credit	$1 229.00
Spousal credit: if spouse's income is less than $614, claim	$1 044.00
Spousal credit: if spouse's income is more than $615 and is less than $7 231, reduce claim from	$1 044.00
Equivalent to married (supporting a child)	$1 044.00
Child tax credits are included under child-care expenses and claimed by spouse with lower income	

Tax Planning

The aim of personal tax planning is to pay no more taxes than necessary at present and, whenever possible, to defer tax to a future time when your marginal rate may be lower. Tax planning cannot be done effectively if you leave it until April, when you are completing your tax return; instead, it should be an ongoing process. Most tax planning possibilities may be classified as either (i) tax avoidance, or (ii) tax deferment. A few examples to be discussed here include avoiding tax by income splitting and by transferring deductions or credits, and deferring tax with registered retirement savings plans or registered educational savings plans.

Tax Avoidance

Arranging one's affairs to minimize income tax is considered perfectly acceptable and is called **tax avoidance.** Many Canadians pay more tax than necessary through ignorance of the tax rules and failing to report deductions or tax credits for which they are eligible. Such errors are quite understandable, given the increasing complexity of our income tax system. The solution is either to become knowledgeable yourself by following the financial press, or to obtain advice from a tax accountant.

Deliberate **tax evasion,** on the other hand, is a violation of the law. Our system depends on voluntary compliance, which is encouraged by unannounced audits of a sample of taxpayers each year. During an audit, CCRA examines records, receipts, cancelled cheques, bank statements, and other background documents. It is in your own interest to keep your records in good order. Less complex than a tax audit is a tax *reassessment*. Revenue Canada may conduct a reassessment of your taxes for any year within the past three; this process typically involves a request for more information to support your claims.

INCOME SPLITTING   A family unit, which pools income and expenses, may have one or more members who earn a great deal more than the other family member(s); nevertheless, each person in the family must file an individual tax return. Tax planning aims to shift some of the income from high earners to low earners, who have lower marginal tax rates, thus reducing the family's total income tax. Income splitting is a complicated matter, and is best attempted only after seeking professional advice.

A basic principle to be considered when contemplating intrafamilial transfers of funds is that of **attribution of income** (see Personal Finance in Action Box 2.2, "Attribution of Income"). Under income tax legislation, all reported income must be identified with a specific earner. In most cases, the person who earned the income also received it. However, if Person A earns revenue but arranges for that revenue to be received by Person B, that income is generally

Personal Finance in Action 2.2

Attribution of Income

Matt and Stephanie wanted to provide all the best for their son Peter—especially the opportunity to go to university, something they didn't get a chance to do. So to help Peter pay for his education, they saved money for him, putting $1 000 a year, every year, into Canada Savings Bonds. When Peter was 16, Matt and Stephanie gave him the money which now totaled $20 000. The plan was that Peter would now receive the interest in his name and hence reduce the taxes owed on the annual interest earned on the CSBs.

Unfortunately, Matt and Stephanie did not understand the laws regarding the transfer of wealth to family members. Although this money was gifted, the laws of attribution apply, and Matt and Stephanie must still pay taxes on the interest earned on the CSBs. However, any earnings that Peter keeps and reinvests will then be his, and the earnings on his new investments will be taxable in his hands. It is best if Matt and Stephanie keep the earnings on the CSBs in a separate account. This will more easily allow them to keep track of the earnings and Peter's taxable income.

"attributed" to the person who earned it (A), who is liable for the tax on it. Attribution rules are designed to discourage income splitting.

With professional advice, some income splitting can be achieved. For instance, attribution rules do not generally apply to business income earned by a spouse or child from funds lent or transferred to them. Funds may be contributed to a spouse's RRSP, which will be discussed further in Chapter 7. As a gift, the higher-income spouse may pay the income tax of the lower-income spouse as a way of transferring funds. Or, if one spouse has more income than the other, the higher-income earner can pay as many of the family expenses as possible, leaving the other to invest his or her personal income. For example, if Joan has a higher income than John does, she could pay more than her share of expenses. John would then invest much of his income. The family's investment income would thus be reported by the lower-income spouse, thereby attracting less tax. A common practice is for a spouse or child to be paid an income for work performed in the family's business or for a self-employed parent or spouse.

TRANSFER OF TAX CREDITS If your spouse cannot use all the tax credits for which he or she is eligible, those credits can be transferred to you. For instance, if one spouse is eligible for but cannot use tax credits, such as the age amount, the pension income amount, or the allowance for charitable donations, they may be transferred to the other spouse.

Tax Deferment

With careful planning, you may be able to defer income tax by arranging for some income not to come into your hands until a later time, such as retirement, when you expect to have a lower marginal tax rate.

REGISTERED RETIREMENT SAVINGS PLANS **RRSPs** are good examples of vehicles used for tax deferment. While you are earning wages, you can shift some funds into an RRSP or into another type of tax shelter without paying any tax. The money you have invested in such a plan will grow, sheltered from tax (that is, you will not be required to pay tax on any income generated within the plan—such as interest income or dividend income), until you "deregister"

Personal Finance in Action 2.3

Should She Use a Tax Shelter?

Maya has $1 000 (before tax) to invest and is wondering whether to put the money in a 5-year guaranteed investment certificate inside her RRSP or in a GIC outside her RRSP.

Maya's combined marginal tax rate is 39%. She can obtain 7% on a certificate. A comparison of the two alternatives is shown below.

Year 1	Alternative 1, RRSP	Alternative 2, No Shelter
Investment	$1 000.00	$1 000.00
Income tax	0.00	390.00
Net investment	1 000.00	610.00
Interest earned @ 7%	70.00	42.70
Income tax @ 39%	0.00	16.65
Balance	$1 070.00	$ 636.05
Year 2		
Interest	$ 74.90	$ 44.52
Income tax @ 39%	0.00	17.36
Balance	$1 144.90	$ 663.21
Year 3		
Interest	$ 80.14	$ 46.42
Income tax @ 39%	0.00	18.11
Balance	$1 225.04	$ 691.52
Year 4		
Interest	$85.75	$ 48.41
Income tax @ 39%	0.00	18.88
Balance	$1 310.79	$ 721.05
Year 5		
Interest	91.76	$ 50.47
Income tax @ 39%	0.00	19.68
Balance	1 402.55	751.84
Income tax @ 39%	546.99	0.00
Balance	$ 855.56	$ 751.84
Total interest earned	$ 402.55	$ 232.52
Total income tax paid	$ 546.99	$ 480.68
After-tax value year 5	**$ 855.56**	**$ 751.84**

It is apparent that deferring the payment of taxes represents a "win" for the investor, the investment community, and the government, based on the amount of taxes paid and on the amount of money invested in the Canadian economy. In this example, if the individual retired and was then taxed at the lower combined marginal tax rate of 25.5 percent, then she would pay only $357.65 in taxes and would be able to keep $1 044.90.

Another valuable perspective regarding before- and after-tax dollars can be acquired by calculating the actual values of the two kinds of money. If a person needs $1 000 to purchase a new stereo, this money is considered after-tax dollars. But how many before-tax dollars does this person need to earn, and pay tax on, in order to be left with $1 000? Using the same tax rates as above, $1 000 after tax equals X before tax times (1 minus the marginal tax rate); to put this another way, X before tax equals $1 000 after tax divided by (1 minus 39 percent). Maya would therefore have to earn $1 639.34 in before-tax dollars in order to have the equivalent of $1 000 in after-tax dollars.

the plan. Of course, when you take funds out of an RRSP, you must pay income tax on those funds, but if you choose to withdraw the funds during a year when you have a lower-than-usual income, the funds will be taxed at a lower rate. Even if your marginal tax rate is not expected to be lower in the future, funds held in a tax shelter will grow faster than unsheltered funds. (This point is illustrated in Personal Finance in Action Box 2.3, "Should She Use a Tax Shelter?")

Whenever you have income that you do not currently need—for example, when you receive a pension plan refund after changing jobs, or when you receive an allowance for taking early retirement—give some thought to ways of deferring the payment of tax on that income. You may be able to transfer these types of funds directly from your employer into your RRSP.

REGISTERED EDUCATION SAVINGS PLANS To create a fund to support a child's post-secondary education or your own and to defer tax on investment income, you might enroll in an **RESP.** The money put into an RESP is not tax deductible, but the money earned while it is in the plan is tax-sheltered. If the beneficiary pursues a post-secondary education, the money will be paid to the student and taxed in his or her hands, presumably at a lower marginal rate. For parents, there may be a disadvantage in such a plan, in that if the child does not continue past the secondary level of education, and no other children in the family continue either, the money earned in the fund may be forfeited; only the invested capital would be refunded to the parents. However, some plans permit the funds to be paid to almost any designate attending a post-secondary educational program.

The two main types of RESPs are individual plans or group plans. Group plans operate similar to a pension, investing on behalf of the contributors. Individual RESPs, like RRSPs, can be invested in mutual funds. However, they are not limited to foreign content.

Before-Tax and After-Tax Dollars

Articles on tax planning or investing often mention the terms before-tax and after-tax dollars. It is important to make a distinction between money on which income tax has already been paid, or **after-tax dollars,** and money that has been received but on which no tax has yet been paid, or **before-tax dollars.** Personal Finance in Action Box 2.3 ("Should She Use a Tax Shelter?") illustrates the difference.

Summary

This chapter presented a simplified framework for understanding personal income tax, setting the stage for further study of the subject. Knowing how key concepts are related is basic to understanding the current information on tax planning that is available in the financial press.

Canadian income tax rates are progressive—that is, they increase as taxable income rises. Taxable income is gross income minus deductions. Once you have determined your taxable income, you can determine your total tax by multiplying that number by the tax rate. Tax credits are deducted directly from total tax owed, thereby reducing your actual tax payable. In addition to income, some increases in wealth or capital gains are also subject to taxation.

To be effective, tax planning must be a year-round activity. It is important to pay attention to your marginal tax rate (the rate that applies to your last dollar of income) and to distinguish between before-tax and after-tax dollars. Much tax planning involves either avoiding income tax or deferring tax until a time when your marginal tax rate may be lower. While couples may wish to avoid taxes by income splitting (shifting some of the income of the higher-earning spouse so that it will be taxed in the hands of the lower-earning spouse), attribution rules must be considered.

Key Terms

after-tax dollars (p. 51)	net taxable capital gain (p. 44)
attribution of income (p. 48)	non-refundable tax credit (p. 46)
average tax rate (p. 40)	partial indexation (p. 45)
before-tax dollars (p. 51)	progressive tax rate (p. 39)
capital gain (p. 42)	refundable tax credit (p. 45)
combined marginal tax rate (p. 41)	RESP (p. 51)
	RRSP (p. 49)
full indexation (p. 45)	taxable capital gain (p. 43)
gross income (p. 41)	tax avoidance (p. 48)
income (p. 42)	tax credit (p. 45)
marginal tax rate (p. 40)	tax evasion (p. 48)
net income (p. 41)	tax-sheltered funds (p. 43)

Problems

1. If you received any of the following, should they be reported as income on your tax return?

    (a) an inheritance from your grandfather's estate

    (b) a lottery winning

    (c) the Old Age Security pension

    (d) a capital gain from selling your primary residence

    (e) Employment Insurance benefits

2. If you have dependent children, can you claim a deduction for them, a tax credit, or both? Explain.

3. Decide whether you AGREE or DISAGREE with each of the following statements:

    (a) The money put into a tax shelter would be classified as after-tax dollars.

    (b) The proportion of taxable income on which tax is paid is called the marginal tax rate.

    (c) To find your taxable income, you would deduct from gross income any applicable tax credits.

    (d) Capital gain is a change in wealth rather than a kind of income.

    (e) Persons over the age of 65 are allowed special tax credits.

    (f) On a per capita basis, the federal income tax burden has not changed significantly over the past 25 years.

    (g) Spouses have a choice regarding whether to file individual or joint income tax returns.

    (h) Interest income is deductible from gross income.

    (i) Capital loss is deducted from capital gain before determining net taxable capital gain.

(j) RRSPs are tax shelters because the funds put into these plans are not taxed, even though the income gained while in the shelter is taxed.

4. Jean, who lives in Manitoba, has determined that she owes $8 997 in federal income tax. How much provincial tax does she owe? Find the current tax rate for Manitoba, or use the rates given in this chapter.

5. Assume that you have a mortgage at 8 percent and also have $6 000 that can be used either to reduce the mortgage or to invest at 7 percent. Should you (i) reduce your mortgage by $6 000 and borrow money to invest, or (ii) simply invest the money?

   Assumptions: the mortgage company will not charge a penalty if you decide to reduce your mortgage; your combined federal and provincial marginal tax rate is 39 percent; if you borrow money to invest, the interest will be a tax deduction, but the interest paid on your mortgage is not deductible.

6. Obtain a current income tax form and complete it for Karen, aged 40, who lives in Vancouver, is employed full-time, and has one dependent. She has never before reported any capital gains. The information she provides is as follows:

Employment income	$38 750
Interest income	950
Net capital gain from selling property (not her home)	8 500
Contributions to	
Employment Insurance	936
Canada Pension Plan	1 329
RRSP	2 500
registered pension plan	3 000
professional dues	500
Charitable donations	750
Rent on safety deposit box	25
Accountant's fee	200
Donation to the Alliance party	250

(a) Find Karen's
   — taxable income
   — federal tax
   — provincial tax

(b) What is her federal marginal tax rate?

(c) Does Karen have any tax credits? If so, which ones?

(d) How much income tax does she owe or will she receive back?

7. Suggest some ways of reducing a family's income tax. For each approach, indicate whether it would be considered tax avoidance or tax evasion.

8. Proceed to the Canada Customs Revenue Agency Web site or an accountant's Web

site such as the one listed at the end of the chapter. Then determine the income tax for your province and a province next to it to be paid by a single parent who is earning $40 000 and supporting two children.

References

BOOKS AND ARTICLES

BEACH, WAYNE, and LYLE R. HEPBURN. *Are You Paying Too Much Tax?* Toronto: McGraw-Hill Ryerson, annual. A tax planning guide for the general reader that discusses capital gains, RRSPs, and investment income.

CESTNICK, TIM. *Winning the Tax Game 2001*, Toronto, Prentice Hall Canada, 2000, annual. A non-technical book to assist those interested in keeping more of the money they earn. Helps in building a solid tax plan no matter what stage in life you're in.

DELOITTE and TOUCHE. *Canadian Guide to Personal Financial Management*. Scarborough: Prentice Hall Canada, annual. A team of accountants provides guidance on a broad range of topics, including planning finances, estimating insurance needs, managing risk, and determining investment needs. Instructions and the necessary forms for making plans are also included.

DELOITTE and TOUCHE. *How to Reduce the Tax You Pay*. Toronto: Key Porter Books, annual. A non-technical guide, prepared by tax accountants, that explains the basics of personal income tax.

DENHAMER, JANET. *Taxation in Canada*. Fourth Edition. Toronto: McGraw-Hill Ryerson, 1997. A technical textbook for students of tax and accounting.

HOGG, R.D. *Preparing Your Income Tax Returns*. Toronto: CCH Canadian, annual. A complete and technical guide to income tax preparation.

JACKS, EVELYN. *Jacks on Tax Savings*. Toronto: McGraw-Hill Ryerson, annual. Explains the current tax rules and demonstrates how to prepare a tax return.

KPMG. *Tax Planning for You and Your Family 2001*. Scarborough: Carswell Thomson Professional Publishing, annual. Accountants provide a general perspective to help families reduce their overall income tax. Explains the general rules and offers advice on some of the opportunities to reduce income tax.

PERIODICALS

DRACHE, ARTHUR B.C., editor. *The Canadian Taxpayer*. Toronto: Richard De Boo Publishers, bi-monthly. A newsletter with up-to-date income tax information. Includes articles on tax cases, relevant political events, recent changes to regulations, and other topics of interest related to tax planning.

———, editor. *Canada Tax Planning Service*. Toronto: Richard De Boo Publishers, subscription service (four-volume looseleaf set). A detailed professional reference that is kept up-to-date through regular mailings of replacement pages.

The National Post. Daily. 300–1450 Don Mills Rd, Toronto, ON M3B 3R5. Up-to-date information on business, economics, income tax, and investments.

Report on Business. Daily. A section of *The Globe and Mail*. Important source of information on the financial markets.

Personal Finance on the Web

Each of the following Web sites provides high-quality links to many other Internet resources.

Canadian Taxpayers Federation
> **www.taxpayer.com** A taxpayers' advocacy group with extensive commentary on the tax system in Canada. Numerous links to political parties and right-wing money groups.

Ernst & Young
> **www.eycan.com** Another of Canada's large accounting firms; provides information on taxes and other accounting concerns. Significant current information available. Sponsor of Canada's Entrepreneur of the Year Award.

KPMG
> **www.kpmg.ca/tax** One of Canada's largest accounting firms; keeps up-to-date with the tax laws and can provide significant information for those interested in assistance. Still, you may need to see an accountant and pay for professional advice.

Canada Customs and Revenue Agency
> **www.ccra-adrc.gc.ca** You might as well go to the horse's mouth for information. This site contains information, brochures, and forms; you can even get some questions answered here. Recent changes are posted for up-to-date information as well.

The Waterstreet Group
> **www.waterstreet.ca** A Web site maintained by the tax education and consulting firm out of Toronto. The president, Tim Cestnick, writes extensively on tax and appears in *The Globe and Mail*'s, "Report on Business" and CBC's "Newsworld." The site updates current tax rates and other tax topics of interest.

Chapter 3

Wills: Planning for the Distribution of Assets

objectives

1. Explain how wills fit into comprehensive financial planning.

2. Differentiate among the responsibilities involved in drawing a will, witnessing a will, and acting as executor of an estate.

3. Compare the effects of the existence of a valid will and no will (intestacy) on the settling of an estate.

4. Identify two situations in which assets are not distributed by a will.

5. Explain the purpose of probate.

6. Explain the distribution of an estate in the case of intestacy.

7. Evaluate the legal position of dependents who are not provided for in the will.

8. Distinguish between the following pairs of terms: testator and testatrix; executor and administrator; bequest (or legacy) and beneficiary (or legatee); codicil and holograph will; joint tenancy and tenancy in common.

9. Explain the following terms: letters of administration, letters probate, preferential share, testamentary trust, and power of attorney.

10. Differentiate among the various types of powers of attorney.

11. Explain how the transfer of ownership of assets underlies most of the formalities associated with wills and with the settling of estates.

Introduction

The general discussion of financial planning in Chapter 1 focused on the maximization of resources during one's lifetime. Persons with assets also need to make provision for the distribution of their estate after death, but estate planning is often postponed because there is no sense of urgency. Unfortunately, those who die leaving no legal statement covering how they wish to dispose of their possessions and assets often create difficulties for the surviving family members. In such cases, as we shall see, provincial laws direct how the estate is distributed.

A will provides an orderly procedure for changing the ownership of assets after a death, indicating which assets should be transferred to which people. When a person dies without a will, that person's assets are distributed according to the law of the province, which may or may not coincide with the desires of the deceased. A comprehensive financial plan thus includes a will that will ensure the orderly transfer of assets at death.

Some of the general procedures and terminology associated with wills and estates are introduced in this chapter. Although they may seem confusing at first, there is a logic in the process that, once identified, makes it quite understandable.

After death, the person named to act in your place—your executor—gets the power to do so from the will. Often the will is submitted to a special court to verify that it is valid. Then the executor makes a list of the assets of the deceased, pays the bills, and distributes the estate according to the will. Much of the legal formality associated with wills is concerned with transferring the ownership of assets from the deceased to other people.

There has been an increasing concern about the management of an individual's assets while that individual is still alive and about the appropriate use of powers of attorney. These powerful documents enable one person to manage the affairs of another person. As well, Ontario's new Power of Attorney for Personal Care or "living will" is discussed, along with the likely future of the laws governing the control of an individual's estate while the person is still living but possibly incapable of making financial or personal-care decisions for him- or herself.

Need for a Will

What Is a Will?

A **will** is a legal document that gives someone the power to act as your financial representative after your death and directs how your assets should be distributed. The person named in the will to act as your agent is called an **executor** if a man, and an **executrix** if a woman. A will has no effect or power during your lifetime; while you are alive, you can change your will as often as you wish, give away the possessions listed in your will, or write new wills. A will takes effect when the person who signs the will (the **testator** if a man and the **testatrix** if a woman) dies.

Who Needs a Will?

Most adults should have a will for two reasons: it ensures that their estate is distributed according to their wishes after their death; and because the will names an executor, it simplifies the handling of the estate. Most people have a larger estate than they realize, because they tend to forget about those assets that do not form part of their estate until they die, such as the proceeds from privately purchased life insurance, the lump-sum death benefit from the Canada Pension Plan, group life insurance plans in connection with their employment, registered retirement savings plans, and credits in company pension plans. All of these assets become part of your estate at death, even though some may not be accessible during your lifetime.

Legal Capacity to Make a Will

To make a valid will, the testator must meet the following criteria:

(a) He or she must have reached the age of majority (17 in Newfoundland; 18 in Alberta, Manitoba, Ontario, Quebec, Prince Edward Island, and Saskatchewan; 19 in New Brunswick, the Northwest Territories, Nova Scotia, British Columbia, and the Yukon). A person is permitted to make a legal will before reaching the age of majority only if he or she is married or is a member of the military.

(b) He or she must be of sound mind—i.e., he or she must understand what is being done. People who are mentally unfit may not meet this requirement. This is a particular concern with those who may have some degree of senility, or with regard to anyone who is undergoing psychiatric treatment. If the will is contested (disputed before a court) after such a person's death, and it can be shown that the person was not of sound mind when signing it, the will may be considered invalid.

(c) He or she must be free of undue influence by another person. If a will is signed under conditions of coercion or persuasion, there may be a basis for contesting it.

Drawing up a Will

How to Begin

First, take stock of possessions, assets, and any other moneys that would form part of your estate. Next, decide how you want to allocate this estate. If you take this list to a lawyer, along with the name of your executor, a will can be drafted for you. The lawyer's role is to translate your wishes into legal language and to suggest ways of allowing for various contingencies that you may not have considered, such as naming an alternate executor, including a common-disaster clause in case husband and wife are killed in the same accident, and allowing for children who have not yet been born.

It is not essential that a will be drawn up by a lawyer. The law does not require any special format, or legal words, or even typing. You can write a will in your own words or use a standard form bought at a stationery store. However, if you are not experienced in writing wills, your choice of words may not make your intentions perfectly clear, and you may forget important clauses. Lawyers charge nominal fees for drawing up a will, and it is worthwhile to have the assistance of such a professional.

What to Include in a Will

A will usually includes the following information:

(a) the domicile (or home) of the testator.

(b) a statement that previous wills made by the testator are revoked.

(c) a direction to pay funeral expenses, debts, and taxes before distributing the estate.

(d) possible specific bequests (or legacies) of certain possessions or moneys to named persons.

(e) a clause that covers how to dispose of the residue of the estate (e.g., naming one or more persons as **residual legatees** to receive any balance remaining after debts, taxes, and specific bequests).

(f) the appointment of an executor and possibly an alternate executor.

(g) the naming of a guardian if the testator has any minor children.

(h) possibly, a common-disaster clause to cover such situations as the death of a couple as a result of one event.

A person who benefits from a will is called a **beneficiary,** and an asset or possession left to this person is called a **bequest** (or **legacy**); if it is real property, it is called a **devise.**

Guardians for Children

A guardian for children is often designated in a will, but the testator does not have the final word on this decision. After the death of their parents, the court appoints a guardian for the children; in many cases, of course, the guardian named in the will is appointed by the court if that person is agreeable and able to act. You cannot bequeath a human being; only possessions and property may form part of an estate and be distributed according to the wishes you express in your will. Not being bound by the terms of a will, the court has the flexibility to make the most appropriate decision about the guardianship of children after the death of their parents.

Can the Family Be Disinherited?

Contrary to the hopes of some children, there is no legal requirement that a person must leave his or her estate to family members. However, if a spouse or children who were financially dependent on the deceased at the time of the latter's death are disinherited, these survivors may have a basis for contesting the will under provincial legislation. If they can show that they have financial needs, and that the deceased did financially care for them, the court may award them a share of the estate. The relevant acts are as follows:

Alberta, Newfoundland	*Family Relief Act*
British Columbia	*Wills Act and The Wills Variation Act*
Manitoba	*The Dependents Relief Act and The Marital Property Act*
New Brunswick	*Wills Act and The Provision for Dependents Act*
Nova Scotia	*Family Maintenance Act*
Ontario	*Succession Law Reform Act*
Quebec	*Civil Code*
Prince Edward Island	*Dependents of a Deceased Person Relief Act*
Saskatchewan and the Territories	*Dependents' Relief Act*

Provisions in family law acts regarding the division of family property (after family breakup or the death of one of the spouses) can affect the spouse's share of an estate. For instance, under the *Ontario Family Law Act* of 1986, a spouse may choose either (i) the provisions accorded to him or her under the will or (ii) a half-share of the net family property calculated according to this legislation. Certain property of the deceased, such as a prior inheritance, may be excluded from net family property. This legislation has implications for wills written before 1986. For instance, a will that leaves an estate in trust for a spouse during that person's lifetime, with the balance going to a third party after the spouse's death, may be put aside if the spouse elects to take half the net family property. If there is no will, the family will have to take the share outlined later in this chapter.

Signing and Witnessing a Will

A will must be signed at its end almost simultaneously by the testator and by two witnesses; all three signers must be present together. By their signatures, the witnesses attest that they watched the testator sign this will, but they need not read the will or know the contents. It is advisable that neither a spouse nor a person who is to benefit from a will serve as a witness to that will. Ignoring this suggestion could mean that any gift to that person would be declared void. Check provincial legislation on this point.

A person named in a will as executor may also be, and often is, a beneficiary. For instance, if a man names his wife as executrix and leaves his estate to her, this choice should present no difficulty.

How to Choose an Executor

When selecting an executor, consider the person's age, willingness to handle your business, and capability of doing so. It is wise to appoint an executor who may be expected to survive you. Often close relatives are appointed executors, but in cases involving large and complex estates, a trust company may be appointed either sole executor or joint executor with a family member. If, for instance, the testator believes that managing the estate may be a burden for the survivor, the spouse may be appointed a **co-executor** with a trust company. Such arrangements allow the spouse to be involved in settling the estate and aware of what is being done without taking the sole responsibility. However, few trust companies are very interested in small estates, because of the limited revenue generated compared to the amount of work required to settle the estate.

An executor named in a will is not bound to accept this appointment and may refuse if unable or disinclined; therefore, it is wise to determine your nominee's preference in advance. The executor need not see the will, but he or she would no doubt appreciate knowing where the document is kept. More than one executor can be named to act as co-executors, although for small estates this can be an unnecessary complication. Requiring the signatures of several people to implement each action when settling an estate can cause inconvenience. However, it is wise to name an alternate executor—someone who would act if the person originally selected is unwilling or unable to act, or has died.

Where to Keep a Will

A will should be kept in a spot that is safe, but easy for the survivors to find. The main alternatives are to leave it with a trust company or a lawyer (to be kept in the company's or the lawyer's vault) or to put it in a safety-deposit box. There is only one signed copy of a will, but an unsigned duplicate could be kept at home with other personal papers.

Disposing of Small Personal Possessions

People often change their minds about which relative should receive the grandfather clock or the antique rocker, but it may be inconvenient and expensive to have a new will drawn to accommodate each change. One solution is to attach a memorandum to the will listing such possessions and who should receive each. The list can easily be changed because it is not part of the will; as long as there is harmony in the family about the distribution of possessions, the executor is likely to follow these instructions. However, remember that such a memorandum carries no legal weight; thus, if the will were contested, this list might not be followed. Although it has no legal weight, it is wise to refer to the memorandum within the will.

Instructions About Funeral Arrangements

Funeral or memorial instructions need not be included in a will, because after an individual's death, that person's body belongs to his or her next of kin, who will decide on its disposition.

Mike and Tara Had Wills

Shortly after Mike and Tara married, they prudently went to Mike's parents' lawyer and had their wills drawn up. They ensured that each would be the sole beneficiary of the other's estate as well as the executor of the estate. No arrangements were discussed regarding their funerals or future children. The lawyer advised them that since they had no children as yet, there was no need to accommodate them in the will until they were born. Mike and Tara planned to postpone starting a family until they were more secure in their careers.

Later, after moving to a new city and acquiring their first house, Mike and Tara had their dream family—a boy and a girl. Life was busy and their wills remained in their hometown with their lawyer, a matter to be dealt with when they had more time.

Tragedy struck when an automobile accident took the lives of Mike and Tara. Because they had both died, there was no executor to manage their estate. And because their wills had not been updated, there were no legal guardians for their children (age one and three). With the two sets of grandparents disagreeing over who should raise the children, the responsibility for the children had to be brought before a judge.

In most cases, though, relatives try to follow the wishes of the deceased. Such instructions can therefore be filed with the will if desired, but it is important to ensure that others know about the instructions; otherwise, they may not be found until it is too late to act on them. This matter is of particular interest when a prepaid funeral has been arranged or when the deceased has died far from home.

Marriage and Wills

Usually a will made before marriage is rendered void by the event of marriage, unless the spouse elects in writing to uphold it after the testator's death. To avoid having to make a will on your wedding day, you may write a "will in contemplation of marriage," which takes effect after the marriage. Such a document states that it was written in contemplation of marriage and names the expected spouse.

Revoking or Altering a Will

While you are alive, you can alter your will or make a new one as often as you wish, because the document has no power until after your death. A will may be cancelled or **revoked** by (i) destroying it, (ii) writing a new will that expressly states that previous wills are revoked, or (iii) getting married. You can change your will after it has been drafted but not yet signed, as long as each alteration is signed and witnessed. To alter an existing will without writing a new one, you must add a codicil. Although it is really a separate document, a **codicil** is merely a postscript to a will. It must contain a reference to the will to which it is appended and must be dated, signed, and witnessed.

Some lawyers believe that it is better to rewrite a will than to add a codicil. However, if there could be any doubt about the testator's mental capacity at the time the new will is being made, it might be better to add a codicil. Better that the codicil alone should fail than that the entire will should be declared invalid.

FIGURE 3.1   MRS. HASTINGS'S HOLOGRAPH WILL

For Winston

In case I should be taken before Cedric R.M. Hastings

July 30, 1933

If my brother, Winston, should outlive me, there are a few things that I wish he would attend to, viz:-

If my Husband, Cedric Hastings, outlives me and there is any of my property left, please see that he is provided for.

I should like to see my personal property, such as the family silver, bedding, and my trinkets, brooches, etc., divided among my nieces Camille, Mabel, and Beatrice. Likewise, the furniture that was mine at the time of our marriage. I should like Cedric to have the gold (Howard) watch that Dad gave me. The books and pictures are left for Winston to dispose of as he sees fit. If there are any items that Cedric particularly wished to keep, please see that he has them.

Rebecca Maud Hastings

The Holograph Will

A will entirely in the handwriting of the testator, dated and signed, but not witnessed, is called a **holograph will.** Such documents are valid in some provinces (e.g., in Ontario, if the will was written after 1978; in Quebec; New Brunswick and in Saskatchewan). Note that a will prepared using a stationery-store form on which the testator fills in the blanks is not a holograph will; this type of will must therefore be properly witnessed. Holograph wills are not valid in British Columbia, Nova Scotia, or Prince Edward Island, all of which require that the testator's signature be witnessed. An example of a holograph will is shown in Figure 3.1.

Settling an Estate with a Will

Finding the Will

After a death, the first and perhaps most obvious step in settling the estate involves finding the most recent will. A thorough search of the deceased's home, safety-deposit boxes, and appropriate lawyers' offices must be conducted before concluding that there is no will.

Duties of the Executor

A will usually names one or more persons to act as executors—that is, as the personal financial representatives of the deceased. The executor is charged with a variety of duties, which may be categorized as follows:

(a) proving the validity of the will,

(b) assembling and administering the assets of the estate in trust,

(c) distributing the estate to the heirs.

In situations where (i) no executor was named (ii) the named executor either is deceased or is unable or unwilling to act, or (iii) the deceased has died without a will, someone with a financial interest in the estate must apply to the appropriate Surrogate Court for **Letters of Administration,** which appoint an administrator to act for the deceased. The **Surrogate Court** is the provincial court that arbitrates matters relating to wills and to the settling of estates. Once appointed, an **administrator** has the same duties and responsibilities as an executor. The only difference between an executor, who is named by a will, and an administrator, who is given authority by the Surrogate Court, is in the manner of their appointment and in the possible requirement that the administrator be bonded. A bond, equivalent to the value of the estate, can be posted by paying a fee to a bonding company to ensure that the administrator is trustworthy in carrying out his or her duties. Bonding, of course, represents an additional cost to the estate. Clearly, having an administrator appointed means additional steps before the settling of the estate can begin. In Quebec, should there be no executor named or should the named person prove unwilling or unable to act, the settling of the estate falls to the heirs and legatees.

Proving the Will

A will is submitted to the Surrogate Court for **probate,** a process whereby the Court verifies the authenticity of the will and the appointment of the executor. The confirming document is called **Letters Probate.** In the subsequent steps of assembling the assets and paying the taxes, the Letters Probate are used to support the authority of the executor to conduct these transactions.

Some wills are not probated, especially when the estate is small and uncomplicated. The legal transfer of the ownership of assets from the name of the deceased to the name(s) of the heir(s), the crucial task in settling an estate, is sometimes accomplished without probate. However, the financial institutions involved require adequate documentation if there are no Letters Probate.

Administering the Estate in Trust

After the testator's death, the property included in the will comes under the authority and control of the executor, whose duty it is to implement the provisions of the will. An executor usually engages a lawyer, delegating to this person certain tasks involved in fulfilling the legal formalities connected with the estate. Final responsibility, however, rests with the executor. The extent of the executor's task depends on the complexity of the deceased's estate and on whether or not the estate was left in good order.

ASSEMBLING THE ASSETS Once the executor's or administrator's authority to proceed has been established, the next task is to compile an inventory of the deceased's assets and liabilities. In the process of doing so, the executor informs all financial institutions holding these assets that the testator has died. The executor opens a trust account, into which funds belonging to the deceased may be deposited temporarily. This account is needed in order to handle the estate's business, including the payment of bills and the final distribution of the estate to the beneficiaries.

PAYING THE DEBTS Once the financial institutions that hold accounts in the name of the deceased are given proof that the person has died and that the executor is empowered by the will to act, funds are usually released. While the estate is being settled, the assets may be generating income in the form of interest, dividends, rent, or profit, or any combination thereof. For income tax purposes, the executor must keep a record of the income received by the estate during the time it was held in trust.

FIGURE 3.2   INCOME TAX RETURNS FOR DECEASED PERSONS

Return I	Return II
INCOME RECEIVED WHILE THE PERSON WAS ALIVE	INCOME RECEIVED BY THE ESTATE WHILE IT WAS HELD IN TRUST
January 1 until date of death	Date of death until the estate is distributed

Before the estate can be distributed, all debts must be paid, with taxes and funeral expenses taking first priority. There are no longer any succession duties or estate taxes in Canada, but there are probate taxes, which vary by province. Should the debts of the deceased exceed the assets, the executor must devise a way to distribute what there is among the creditors, perhaps on a pro rata basis.

The executor has to pay any income tax that is due on (i) any income the deceased received from January 1 of the year in which the person died until the date of his or her death, and (ii) any income generated by the estate between the date of death and the date of distribution. An executor should contact the local office of CCRA Taxation for instructions about income tax for deceased persons and their estates. Essentially, the first task is to complete an income tax return for the portion of the year during which the deceased was alive. The executor must pay whatever income tax is owing from the estate funds that are being held in trust. Just before distributing the estate, another income tax return must be completed; this return reports any estate income and must be accompanied by payment of the appropriate tax. This process is summarized in Figure 3.2.

RECORDING THE ACCOUNTS The executor is responsible for maintaining a record of accounts showing all receipts and disbursements, but this task may be delegated to a lawyer. Beneficiaries with questions may wish to see the accounts, and if there is concern about the misuse of funds, the court may require that the accounts be submitted for inspection, a process known as **passing the accounts.**

Distributing the Estate

When the executor has paid the deceased's debts, filed an income tax return, and paid the legal fees, the estate may be distributed to the beneficiaries according to the will. In some instances, it may be necessary to sell certain assets in order to pay the debts and make the distribution; other assets may be transferred to new owners. Whether all assets must be converted into cash or whether some may be transferred in their present form depends both on the instructions in the will and on the wishes of the beneficiaries.

In some cases, the executor may have to sell property in order to divide the estate among several people. For instance, if the estate's chief asset is a house and there are three beneficiaries, the house could be sold and the proceeds divided, or one of the heirs could buy the house by paying the other beneficiaries their shares. In cases where dividing the asset is not necessary, the executor may simply transfer ownership of the property.

The demands on the executor at this stage depend on the estate's complexity. A lawyer can help with the legal formalities of transferring various forms of property.

FEES FOR SETTLING AN ESTATE Settling an estate involves two sets of fees: one for the services of a lawyer, and one for those of the executor. Lawyers prepare applications for probate, and there is usually a Surrogate Court tariff setting the fee (not including disbursements) that a lawyer may charge for handling an estate of average complexity— for example, $5 per $1 000 of value for the first $50 000 and $15 per $1 000 of value over $50 000.

Because executors are responsible for all the other work involved in settling the estate, they are entitled to a fee based on the estate's complexity and on the time and effort they have expended. This fee is usually around 4 to 5 percent of the estate's value. The actual amount or rate of pay can be stated in the will. If the executrix wants the lawyer to do her work, the lawyer charges the executrix, who pays the lawyer from the moneys due to her as executrix. If more than one executor is involved, the fee is divided between them. Frequently, family members act as executors without taking any fees from the estate.

Legal fees depend on the amount of work the lawyer has to do for the estate. Such fees may be based either on the time the lawyer spends or on a percentage of the assets. The executor should discuss the fee schedule with the lawyer before work on the estate begins. Legal fees can be reduced if the executor decides to do some tasks, such as assembling the assets and paying debts. These fees are paid from the estate funds that are being held in trust before the distribution of the estate.

Settling an Estate without a Will

It is not uncommon to discover that a deceased person has left no will; many people—even those who are fond of talking about their wills and about their plans for disposing of their possessions—have never made a will at all. We tend to postpone this task, thinking that it is not an urgent matter. Also, we are reluctant to contemplate our mortality. However, before concluding that no will was left, a thorough search must be made.

If the deceased's relatives believe that a will existed at some time, but it cannot be found, the will is presumed to have been revoked unless evidence can be discovered to the contrary. Should a will be found subsequent to the distribution of the estate, altering the distribution may prove very difficult or even impossible.

Naming the Administrator

If you die without a will, or **intestate,** someone with a financial interest in your estate must apply to the court to be appointed administrator of your estate. If family members do not do so, a creditor (for example, the funeral director) may press for action. This application includes an inventory of the estate's assets and debts, a list of close relatives, and an affidavit stating that the deceased left no will. As previously mentioned, the applicant may also be asked to post a **bond of indemnity** with the court so that the estate is protected should the administrator prove to be dishonest. If the administrator absconds with the assets or dissipates the estate and fails to render a true accounting to the court, beneficiaries can call on the bond of indemnity to protect their financial interests. A fee also must be paid to the Surrogate Court. After the applicant receives the Letters of Administration, he or she can begin to settle the estate.

WILL BUT NO EXECUTOR   If a will is found, but no executor is prepared to act, someone must apply to the court for Letters of Administration and the appointment of an administrator. Such a situation is referred to as an **administration with will annexed.**

The Administration

The administrator carries out the same duties as an executor does, but may be required to withhold distribution of the assets of the estate until one year after the deceased's death, unless there has been an advertisement for creditors. This requirement does not apply to an executor, but it is often done anyway, for convenience and for the protection of the executor: an executor can be held personally liable if the estate is distributed to beneficiaries without prior repayment of debts. The one-year waiting period is one way to ensure that all creditors are informed of the death and have an opportunity to submit any outstanding bills.

Distributing the Intestacy

When there is no will (an *intestacy*), the estate is distributed according to the provisions of the appropriate provincial law. An outline of some rules regarding intestacy is shown in Table 3.1. For greater accuracy and completeness you should consult the appropriate provincial statute. You may note a reference to **preferential shares** in this table, which means that the spouse gets a specified share before any other beneficiary. For example, if the spouse's preferential share is $50 000, this must be paid to the spouse before anyone else gets anything. If the estate is less than $50 000, then the spouse gets it all. (For an example, see Personal Finance in Action Box 3.2, "Brent Left No Will.")

TABLE 3.1   PROVINCIAL LEGISLATION REGARDING INTESTATE SUCCESSION

Although legislation governing intestate succession varies from province to province, there are a number of aspects that are the same in all 10 jurisdictions. Similarities will be outlined first, with differences listed below.

(I)   GENERAL RULES FOR INTESTATE SUCCESSION

If the deceased left	the estate goes
spouse, no children	all to the spouse
spouse and 1 child*	preferential share to spouse; excess split 50/50 between spouse and child
spouse and 2 or more children*	preferential share to spouse; excess split 1/3 to spouse and 2/3 shared equally among children
no spouse, but children	all to children, shared equally
no spouse	all to parents or children
no spouse, children, or parents	all to brothers and sisters
no relatives	all to the government

(II)   INTESTATE SUCCESSION AND VARIATIONS FROM GENERAL RULES

Province	Relevant Legislation	Variations from General Rules
Alberta	Intestate Succession Act	• spouse's preferential share is $40 000
British Columbia	Estate Administration Act (Pt. 10)	• spouse's preferential share is $65 000
Manitoba	Intestate Succession Act	• spouse's preferential share is $50 000 • spouse gets 1/2 excess regardless of number of children
New Brunswick	Devolution of Estates Act	• spouse receives all joint (matrimonial property) and shares all other assets equally with children
Newfoundland	Intestate Succession Act	• no preferential share to spouse, see above rules
Nova Scotia	Intestate Succession Act	• spouse's preferential share is $50 000, plus 1/2 to spouse if one child or 1/3 to spouse and balance equally to children

Province	Relevant Legislation	Variations from General Rules
Ontario	Succession Law Reform Act	• spouse's preferential share is $200 000, set by order of Lieutenant Governor in Council
Prince Edward Island	Probate Act	• spouse shares equally with any children
Quebec	Civil Code of Quebec	• no preferential share to spouse • spouse gets 1/3 of estate; children get 2/3
Saskatchewan	Intestate Succession Act	• spouse's preferential share is $100 000

*Predeceased children are "represented" by their surviving children.

CONSANGUINITY   There is a method of classifying relatives according to the nearness of their relationship to the deceased. To illustrate how the system works, an abbreviated table of **consanguinity** (blood relationships) is shown in Table 3.2. Relatives beyond the nuclear family are grouped in classes. Should the deceased die intestate leaving no spouse or children, the estate may be divided equally among the next-of-kin in the class closest in blood relation. If there are no relatives in Class I, the estate is divided equally among all those in Class II. When there is even one relative in a class, that person gets the whole estate, and the distribution does not continue to the next class. If the deceased leaves grandchildren, but no living children, the estate goes to the grandchildren through a process called **representation,** because they receive their parents' share.

COMMON-LAW SPOUSES   The status of common-law spouses is changing gradually, but at this time there is no generally accepted treatment of such spouses under all conditions. While the Canada Pension Plan, as well as some other pension plans (such as RRSPs and RRIFs), may provide benefits to a common-law spouse, some provincial statutes have considered them to be legal spouses in cases of intestacy. Therefore, it is difficult to generalize about their rights. At the time of writing, common-law spouses do not automatically receive a share of an intestacy, but may go to the court to argue for a portion because of financial dependency. Of course, if there is a will, a common-law spouse can be named a beneficiary.

STEPCHILDREN   With the increasing number of blended families due to divorce and remarriage, the legal status of stepchildren is a growing concern. In the case of marriage, all

TABLE 3.2   ABBREVIATED TABLE OF CONSANGUINITY

Beyond children, all blood relatives are ranked in numbered classes as follows:

Class I	father, mother, brother, sister
Class II	grandmother, grandfather
Class III	great-grandmother, great-grandfather, nephew, niece, uncle, aunt
Class IV	great-great-grandfather, great-great-grandmother, great-nephew, great-niece, first cousin, great-uncle, great-aunt
Class V	great-great-uncle, great-great-aunt, first cousin once removed, etc.

Brent Left No Will

Brent, like most people aged 26, had never thought he would need a will. After his accidental death, his widow, Alanna, who was appointed administrator, discovered that his estate totalled about $105 000. According to Saskatchewan law where they lived, the estate was to be divided as follows:

To Alanna, the preferential share of

$100 000, plus one-half of the balance, making a total of $102 500.

To Brent's two year-old son Simon, one-half of the balance, $2 500.

Now Alanna was faced with the question of how to manage the money for Simon for the next 16 years.

spouses have the same legal rights before the law, whether or not either spouse has been previously married. This is not so for stepchildren. The difficulty is that stepchildren are not considered "children" of the stepparent, especially if the biological parent of the same gender is still alive. Only if the stepparent names the stepchildren in his or her will, will they inherit; otherwise they will likely be excluded as beneficiaries. Conversely, if one partner of the new couple dies and leaves his or her estate to the surviving spouse with no other beneficiaries, then the surviving spouse will inherit. When the surviving spouse dies, his or her estate will passs to his or her children, which may totally exclude the children of the previously deceased spouse. This is why widowed seniors particularly require a will. When the will is drawn up, the desired beneficiaries are named, thus ensuring that the deceased's wishes are followed and the beneficiaries do inherit.

Transferring the Ownership of Assets

The main purpose of settling an estate is to transfer the ownership of assets from the deceased to designated beneficiaries, and the various formalities are necessary in order to ensure that this transfer is done correctly. The diagram in Figure 3.3 summarizes the transfer of the ownership from the deceased to the executor (administrator) in trust, and finally to the beneficiaries.

FIGURE 3.3   TRANSFER OF THE DECEASED'S ASSETS

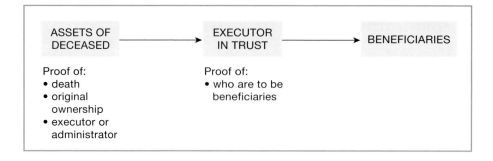

Estate Assets Not Distributed by the Will

There are two situations in which the deceased's assets go directly to a beneficiary, independently of the will, *by contract* and *at law*. Certain financial assets—such as life insurance, annuities, and registered retirement savings plans—may have a designated beneficiary who was named in the contract by the deceased during his or her lifetime. On proof of death, the financial institution that holds these assets automatically transfers ownership to the beneficiary; the will is not involved. If the named beneficiary has predeceased the testator, the assets are generally paid into the estate unless an alternate beneficiary was named.

Other assets that are not distributed by the will are those held in **joint tenancy,** a situation that confers the right of survivorship. For instance, if a couple has a joint bank account, the wife, through right of survivorship, becomes the sole owner of the account when her husband dies. Real property such as a house held in joint tenancy is handled similarly. Note that joint tenancy is not the same as **tenancy in common.** In the latter instance, each owns an undivided share of the asset. If a couple owns the family house as tenants in common, and one partner dies, only half the value of the house forms part of the deceased's estate; the other half continues to belong to the survivor. However, if the house was held in joint tenancy, ownership of the house passes to the survivor.

Frequently with elderly relatives, bank accounts are jointly held to enable the children to manage their parents' money. This also reduces the costs of probate. Tenancy in Common is more likely to be used in remarriage situations to ensure that each set of children inherits.

Testamentary Trusts

A will may state that particular assets or property are to be held in trust for some person or persons. Such an arrangement is called a **testamentary trust,** because the trust is established by a will; in contrast, a **living trust** becomes operative during the lifetime of the person who established it. A testamentary trust must be managed by an appointed trustee. Usually the trustee (and perhaps an alternate) is named in the will. Trust companies specialize in this service, and have trust departments that offer advice in planning the trust. The company acts as trustee when the trust becomes operative. When trust companies are involved in planning an estate, with or without a trust, they usually insist that the company be named executor or co-executor of the will. If there is to be a trust, the company may be named the trustee. Trust companies, of course, charge a fee for managing assets on someone's behalf. In fact all trustees, whether they are corporations or individuals, are entitled to charge a fee, subject to review by the court. In some situations, the executor may also be the trustee, and he or she may decide to appoint someone to carry out the management of the trust property. In such a case, the executor retains ultimate responsibility.

It is wise to select a trustee who does not have a conflict of interest. As an example, suppose that Jane has been named the trustee of funds for her disabled brother, John. The will states that the income from the estate is to be used for John, and that after his death the balance of the estate goes to Jane. There can be a conflict of interest in such a situation; by restricting the money available for her brother, Jane may inherit a larger estate. A trustee, however, is obliged to be even-handed in dealing with the interests of beneficiaries. Consideration must be given to the life interest of one beneficiary as well as to the ultimate interest of the other.

Power of Attorney

Another aspect of financial planning involves providing for the possibility that you may become incapacitated through accident or illness. As has been explained in this chapter, there is a process for handling the affairs of a deceased person. An incompetent person presents different problems. Unless the client has a legally appointed representative, the officers of financial institutions have no choice but to follow the client's instructions, regardless of his or her competency level. Family members are helpless to intervene unless a power of attorney has previously been signed or unless they initiate the slow, painful court process of having the person ruled mentally incompetent and naming a legal representative. In some situations, a joint bank account for depositing income and paying expenses may be a practical and informal alternative, at least for a time.

A **power of attorney** is a legal document that names someone to handle your finances under certain conditions. It is a wise precaution to assign power of attorney to a trusted person who can handle your financial affairs if necessary. It is also advisable to name an alternate, in case your first choice is unable to act. There are various ways to make a power of attorney restrictive enough so that you do not lose control of your affairs prematurely. For instance, the family lawyer can keep the document and can be instructed to release it only when two doctors have stated in writing that the person can no longer handle his or her own affairs. Such an arrangement should of course be discussed clearly with your lawyer and your physician.

It is easier, cheaper, and less cumbersome for the family if a power of attorney is signed when the individual is capable. Several additional safeguards are built into the more complex court process of determining incompetence. The person named by the court to manage assets must submit regular detailed reports to the court for approval. Should the individual who has been declared incompetent die, the power of attorney dies as well, and the will comes into force.

In 1996, Ontario enacted the *Substitute Decisions Act of 1992* and the *Health Care Consent Act*, both of which addressed the area of "living wills." Residents of Ontario can now legally specify the level of medical care they wish to receive in the event that a serious injury or illness leaves them incapacitated. This may be done by issuing specific instructions to their medical caregivers or, more frequently, by assigning a trusted family member or friend to make what he or she considers to be appropriate decisions regarding their personal care. Known as the **power of attorney for personal care,** this document is similar to the power of attorney for financial matters described earlier, but is limited to making decisions about the level and costs of the physical care that will be given to an incapacitated person.

A point that is of major concern to all parties involves knowing when this power of attorney comes into force: when does a person cease to have the ability to make his or her own decisions about the desirable level of physical care? The legislation has established limits on the professions that can decide an individual's ability, but this matter remains one of some contention among health care practitioners and medical ethicists. While Ontario residents must be 18 in order to decide financial matters for themselves, the law enables anyone older than 16 to decide on his or her own health care. This area of law is rapidly evolving and will probably take many years to establish firm standards, so anyone considering a power of attorney for personal care would be wise to discuss the matter with both his or her lawyer (who will draw up the document) and the attorney whom he or she plans to appoint with the document.

Summary

Most adults should have a will, and most should obtain help from a lawyer in drawing one up. A trusted, capable, and willing person should be named executor or executrix, with a second person as a designated alternate. It is wise to review and revise your will periodically to ensure that it reflects any changes in your financial resources or family composition. A will is not operative until death, when it becomes the plan for disposing of the estate. The executor has responsibility for carrying out the provisions of the will. The estates of those who die intestate are disposed of according to provincial law. The status of common-law spouses is changing in Canada, but in most jurisdictions they are not given spouse status in cases of intestacy. With the increase in blended families, the legal status of stepchildren is also a growing concern.

There are sound arguments for giving power of attorney to someone to act as your representative if you should become incompetent to handle your own financial affairs. Residents of Ontario may also wish to prepare a power of attorney for personal care, specifying who may make medical decisions on their behalf if they become incapacitated.

Key Terms

administration with will
    annexed (p. 65)

administrator (p. 63)

beneficiary (p. 59)

bequest (p. 59)

bond of indemnity (p. 65)

codicil (p. 61)

co-executor (p. 60)

consanguinity (p. 67)

devise (p. 59)

executor (p. 57)

executrix (p. 57)

holograph will (p. 62)

intestate (p. 65)

joint tenancy (p. 69)

legacy (p. 59)

Letters of Administration (p. 63)

Letters Probate (p. 63)

living trust (p. 69)

passing the accounts (p. 64)

power of attorney (p. 70)

power of attorney for personal
    care (p. 70)

preferential shares (p. 66)

probate (p. 63)

representation (p. 67)

residual legatee (p. 58)

revoke (p. 61)

Surrogate Court (p. 63)

tenancy in common (p. 69)

testamentary trust (p. 69)

testator (p. 57)

testatrix (p. 57)

will (p. 57)

Problems

1. A Case of Intestacy

When he died, Eugene Markotic was living with his common-law wife, Mrs. Anna Pavlicek, and her children, and was operating a successful pig-raising business with the help of Anna's son, Larry. Because Mr. Markotic left no will, there was much uncertainty about who should look after his affairs, including the growing pigs. Mr. Markotic was divorced and had no children of his own, and his parents were deceased; by the rules of intestacy, the collateral relatives (in this case, his three brothers) would be the heirs. It was agreed that one brother, Tom, would apply to be the administrator of the estate.

Initially, Mr. Markotic's affairs appeared quite straightforward. He left two rented barns full of pigs, a truck, some supplies and equipment, personal belongings, and a bank account. But a search of his apartment revealed seven burlap bags of personal papers dating from the late 1940s. Tom found that his brother had held two mortgages, several bank accounts, stocks, bonds, and two life insurance policies with named beneficiaries—in one case his deceased mother and in the other his divorced wife.

Mr. Markotic had lived with Mrs. Pavlicek for a number of years, treating her family as his own. However, Mr. Markotic's brothers did not approve of this situation and had kept their distance. Gradually it was revealed that Mr. Markotic had had plans for the disposition of his estate, but had not put those plans in writing. He had often mentioned making Larry a partner in the business, and he had always meant to change his life insurance policies to name Anna as beneficiary, and also to cancel the mortgage he had held for her daughter and son-in-law. His lawyer had known about his intention to make a will that would name one brother as executor and recipient of 60 percent of the estate, and that would divide the remaining 40 percent so that half would go to Anna and the other half would be split between the other two brothers. Unfortunately, he died before making a will; as a result, his plans could not be implemented.

(a) Would probate be involved in settling Mr. Markotic's estate?

(b) Since Mr. Markotic did not leave a will, what steps would be necessary to have Tom appointed to handle his estate?

(c) Would there be any additional costs or delays incurred because Mr. Markotic did not name an executor?

(d) Who would receive the benefits of the two life insurance policies?

(e) In your province, what is the name of the law that specifies how Mr. Markotic's estate would be distributed?

(f) Assume that this situation had occurred in your province; estimate the share that Anna Pavlicek would receive under the intestacy law.

(g) Make a list of things that would probably have turned out better if Mr. Markotic had written a will.

(h) Do you think the common-law wife should investigate the possibility of making a claim as a dependent? What law would be involved?

(i) Does Larry Pavlicek have a basis for contesting the distribution of this estate?

2.   Wills of All Sorts

When Mrs. Hastings died in 1972 at the age of 94, her family began to search for her will. Someone remembered that there had been a letter in her brother's desk for years, with instructions to open it after her death. That turned out to be the holograph will reproduced in Figure 3.1. The search did not end there, however, because someone thought that Mrs. Hastings had once said something about keeping her will at a certain bank. A search of several banks revealed some Canada Savings Bonds, a life insurance policy belonging to her husband, and his will.

After the funeral, a careful search of her room uncovered a second will, which had been drawn by a lawyer in 1939 (Figure 3.4). Mrs. Hastings had made some revisions to this will nine years later, cutting out certain sections and pasting in changes. Finally, the matron of the nursing home where Mrs. Hastings had been living just before her death produced yet another will, which was on a stationery store form (Figure 3.5). This last will was the most recent, and it was submitted for probate.

FIGURE 3.4   MRS. HASTINGS'S SECOND WILL

ON THIS twenty-first day of the month in February, in the year one thousand nine hundred and thirty-nine, at the Village of Rockport, County of Crompton, District of St. Francis, and Province of Quebec:

Before the undersigned Witnesses, Catherine Ross, Advocate, and Mary Goodman, Accountant, both of the Village of Rockport, said County, District, and Province,

CAME AND APPEARED

REBECCA M. HASTINGS (née Cassells), of the Township of Smithton, said District and Province, who, being of sound mind, memory, and understanding, has declared the following to be her Last Will and Testament:

1. I commend my soul to Almighty God.

2. Hereby revoking any and all former Wills, I hereby will, devise and bequeath any and all property, real and personal, which I now own, or may own or possess at the time of my death, in the following manner:

November 25, 1948

If my good and faithful husband, Cedric Hastings, outlives me, I wish what property is left to be used for his benefit as my dear brother Winston Cassells sees fit. Also that the Sun Life Insurance money be used for Cedric's benefit.

I should like a double tombstone erected for both of us, whenever seems most suitable, the cost thereof to come out of our estate. I wish Cedric to have my large trunk and the best black suitcase. Also Dad's gold "Howard" watch. Will Winston and Camille please be my executors?

3. I desire my niece Camille H. Cassells to have the Blue and White bedspread woven by her grandmother. And my niece Mabel Cassells to have the White bedspread with "Theresa A. Green" woven thereon. And to my niece Beatrice Cassells the silk quilt.

4. I desire my furniture, books, pictures, silverware, and household effects generally, to be divided among my three nieces, Camille, Mabel, and Beatrice Cassells abovementioned, as my Executrix may see fit.

After due reading of this Will by the Testatrix, she has signed the same in the presence of the Witnesses, who have also signed in her presence and in the presence of each other.

<u>WITNESSES</u>   *Rebecca M. Hastings*
                                                                  ‾‾‾‾‾‾‾‾‾‾‾‾‾‾‾‾‾‾‾‾

Catherine Ross
‾‾‾‾‾‾‾‾‾‾‾‾‾‾‾‾

FIGURE 3.5   MRS. HASTINGS'S LAST WILL

THIS IS THE LAST WILL AND TESTAMENT OF ME, Rebecca Maud Cassells Hastings, at present residing at Eliza Gregson Home, in the Township of Smithton, in the District of St. Francis, retired.

I hereby revoke all former wills and testamentary dispositions heretofore made by me.

I NOMINATE AND APPOINT my brother, Winston Charles Cassells, farmer, residing on Rural Route 4, Crompton, Quebec, and my nieces, Camille Cassells, teacher, residing in Perth, Ontario, and Mabel Cassells, nurse, residing in Toronto, Ontario, and the survivor of them, to be the Executors and Trustees of this, my Will.

I GIVE, DEVISE, AND BEQUEATH all the Real and Personal estate of which I shall die possessed or entitled to unto my said Executors and Trustees hereinbefore named, in Trust for the purposes following:

Firstly, to pay my just debts. Secondly, to pay the expenses of my burial, which I wish to have undertaken by L.O. Cass and Son, Ltd., funeral directors, of Crompton, Que. Thirdly, to provide for the erection of a modest headstone over the grave of my husband and myself, and to cover all testamentary expenses. Fourthly, to pay to Eliza Gregson Home in the Township of Smithton, Que., whatever may be required for the maintenance of my husband, Mr. Cedric Hastings, during his lifetime. Fifthly, to divide among my nieces, Camille Cassells and Mabel Cassells (aforementioned) and Beatrice (Mrs. B.M. Thomas), my pictures, trinkets, and personal things. All the rest and residue of my estate, both Real and Personal, I GIVE, DEVISE AND BEQUEATH unto Eliza Gregson Home in the Township of Smithton in the Province of Quebec absolutely.

With full power and authority to my Executors and Trustees to sell and dispose of all or any part of my Real or Personal estate, where necessary, for the carrying out of the purpose of this my will, and to execute any and all documents that may be necessary for so doing.

IN WITNESS WHEREOF I have subscribed these presents at Eliza Gregson Home in the Township of Smithton, this 14th day of September, Nineteen hundred and sixty-five.

SIGNED published and declared by the above-named
testatrix as and for her last Will and Testament in
the presence of us both present at the same time,
who at her request and in her presence have
hereunto subscribed our names as witnesses.   Rebecca M. Hastings

(Witnesses)

Name	*Terry Petrie*	Name	*Miss Betty McDonald*
Address	*290 Oba St. Sherbrooke*	Address	*Eliza Gregson Home*

(a) When Mrs. Hastings died, her holograph will, written in 1933, would have been valid in Quebec if she had not written later wills. Would it be acceptable now in British Columbia or Ontario?

(b) What is your opinion of the way Mrs. Hastings revised her second will? Do you think the entire will would be valid, or only a part of it? If your will needed revision, how would you do it?

(c) Changes occurred during Mrs. Hastings's long life, and some personal possessions listed in her various wills were disposed of before she died. In your opinion, how might this matter of designating the distribution of personal possessions be handled?

(d) How many executors did Mrs. Hastings name in her third will? Were they to act as co-executors, or were some of them alternates in case the others were unable or unwilling to act? How many executors and alternates would you suggest that she needed for a very small estate?

3. John Vander Kamp died leaving an estate estimated at approximately $235 000. There was no will, but he did have a wife and three children under age 15 plus his parents. John's share of the farm that he jointly owned with his father was $125 000, the value of his estate.

   a) How would his estate be distributed if he died in your province?

   b) There was also a mortgage life insurance policy on the farm mortgage. What happens to this money and the farm ownership?

   c) The $150 000 life insurance John owned had also stated his wife as the beneficiary. What happens to this money?

   d) If John and his father owned the farm as tenants in common, what would happen to his ownership of the farm?

4. Marie, who lived common-law for 15 years, tells the following story:

Intestacy and Common-law Spouses

My common-law husband was a wonderful man, but although I tried and tried to get him to make a will, he said that he considered wills to be meaningless pieces of paper. As the years went by, I worried less about this and concentrated on planning our future together. I never gave up my well-paying job, because we needed the money. We pooled our finances to pay current expenses as we raised his three daughters, bought a house, and established a retirement fund.

Suddenly, my husband died, leaving me not only grief-stricken but also penniless. Now I am living alone in a nearly empty apartment with very few of the lovely things we had over the years. Our house is for sale, and the antique furniture that I collected as a hobby has been distributed among my husband's grasping family, who never approved of our relationship. I never thought my stepchildren would show such disloyalty to their father by doing things he never would have wanted.

(a) What can a common-law wife like Marie do to protect her financial security?

(b) Do you think she has a strong case for contesting the distribution of this estate?

(c) If a person dies without a will in your province, does that person's common-law spouse automatically get a preferential share? Does the length of time the couple lived common-law make any difference?

5. Mrs. DeMelo has a dependent daughter who is severely handicapped and has a limited capacity to handle financial affairs. Mrs. DeMelo's will leaves her estate in equal shares to her daughter and to her son, but she is wondering whether she should revise her will to establish a testamentary trust for the daughter. Because her son is financially independent and her daughter is not, Mrs. DeMelo proposes leaving her total estate in trust for her daughter, with the residue to go to her son after her daughter's death.

   (a) List some factors that should be considered in deciding whether to leave the estate in trust for the daughter.

   (b) Do you think a testamentary trust would be a wise approach in this case?

   (c) Do you see a potential conflict of interest for the son if he is made a trustee?

6. Mr. Schwartz left a will stating that his estate was to be divided equally among three of his four children. His youngest son, Leon, now 32, with whom he had been on bad terms for some years, was left out of the will. Does the fact that Leon was the only child excluded from the will form a good basis for him to contest the will?

7. (a) Why does an executor need a trust account?

   (b) The main task of an executor is to assemble the assets of the deceased and distribute them to the designated beneficiaries. Why is there so much formality associated with transferring the assets?

   (c) If the beneficiaries of a will suspect that an executor is not acting in their best interests, what can they do to check on this?

8. When Mrs. Mears died, her will appointed her two daughters, both now in their 70s as co-executors. One daughter was suffering from Alzheimer's disease, and the other lived a couple of days travel away. Given that one of the executors may not be capable to administer the estate and the other daughter may decline the task due to the significant travelling required, how will the estate be settled? Do both daughters have to act to fulfill the will's requirements?

9. Maisie had often talked about how she would leave her estate, but after her death no will could be found. As a result, her estate had to be treated as an intestacy and was administered by her cousin John. Maisie's estate included the following assets:

   - Cash and deposits of $26 000
   - A house, valued at $185 000, which she had owned as a tenant in common with her estranged husband
   - Canada Savings Bonds, worth $5 000
   - A car, valued at $8 000
   - A life insurance policy with a face value of $38 000, which named her husband as beneficiary
   - A $3 600 RRSP
   - A pension plan credit of $6 849

In addition to her estranged, but never legally divorced, husband, Maisie left a mentally disabled daughter and an elderly mother.

(a) Make a list of the assets that would form part of Maisie's estate.

(b) Using the rules for intestacy for your province, show how this estate would be divided.

(c) Might there be a reason for applying to the Surrogate Court for a change in this division to favour the mentally disabled daughter? What information about the family would you need to know in order to determine whether such a case could be made?

(d) If the husband wanted the house, would it have to be sold or could it go directly to him?

10. Arrange for a debate on the following resolution:

"Resolved that a young couple without children does not need a will."

11. Proceed to the Living Will Registry Web site at www.livingwills.com and find the four tests to assess competency. Who is the most likely person(s) to determine competency? What do you think is his or her legal responsibility and to whom?

References

BOOKS AND ARTICLES

CESTNICK, TIM. *Winning the Estate Planning Game, Estate Planning Strategies for Canadians*. Toronto: Pearson Education Canada Inc., 2001. A regular *Globe and Mail* contributor in tax and financial planning provides insight into wills, trusts, succession planning, and life insurance matters.

DELOITTE and TOUCHE. *Canadian Guide to Personal Financial Management*. Toronto: Prentice Hall Canada, annual. A team of accountants provides guidance on a broad range of topics, including planning finances, estimating insurance needs, managing risk, and determining investment needs. Instructions and the necessary forms for making plans are also included.

DRACHE, ARTHUR B.C., and SUSAN WEIDMAN SCHNEIDER. *Head and Heart: Financial Strategies for Smart Women*. Toronto: Macmillan, 1987. Recognizing the needs and perspectives of women, a tax lawyer and a journalist collaborate to present basic financial information that takes into account women's concerns at different stages in their lives.

FISH, BARRY M., and LESLIE S. KITZER. *Speaking of Wills*. Thornhill, ON: Continental Atlantic Publications, 1992. A lawyer's perspective on developing a will, dispersing an estate and other issues to think about before having a will prepared.

FORMAN, NORM. *Mind over Money: Curing Your Financial Headaches with Moneysanity*. Toronto: Doubleday Canada, 1987. A psychologist examines the effects money has on behaviour, looking at the origins of money problems and suggesting therapies that can help us better understand our relationship with money.

FOSTER, SANDRA E. *You Can't Take It with You*. Second Edition. Toronto: John Wiley & Sons Inc., 1998. A current Canadian perspective on death and the transactions surrounding estate disbursements.

GOTTSELIG, CHERYL. *Wills for Alberta*. Eighth Edition. Vancouver: International Self-Counsel Press, 1992. A lawyer explains the hows and whys of writing a will and offers some pointers on estate planning.

HULL, RODNEY, Q.C., and IAN M. HULL. *Macdonnell, Sheard and Hull on Probate Practice*. Fourth Edition. Toronto: Thomson Canada, 1996. Legal textbook with focus on Ontario laws pertaining to wills and on legal practices involving wills and estates.

KRUZENISKI, RONALD, and JANE E. GORDON. *Will/Probate Procedure for Manitoba and Saskatchewan*. Fourth Edition. Vancouver: International Self-Counsel Press, 1990. A basic explanation of the terminology and procedures involved in drawing or probating a will.

LIFE UNDERWRITERS ASSOCIATION OF CANADA. *Elements of Estate Planning, 1994 Edition*. Toronto: Life Underwriters Association of Canada, 1994. An academic book used in the life insurance industry to help agents deal with clients who require estate-planning services.

OLKOVICH, EDWARD. *The Complete Idiot's Guide to Estate Planning in Six Simple Steps for Canadians*. Toronto: Pearson Education Canada Inc., 2001. Another in the popular line of how-to books that is practical for individuals who wish to take control of their own estate and protect their beneficiaries.

SPENCELEY, ROBERT. *Estate Administration in Ontario*. Toronto: CCH Canada Limited, 1996. A professional reference for estate administrators.

WONG, STEVEN G. *Wills for British Columbia*. Fifteenth Edition. Vancouver: International Self-Counsel Press, 1991. Gives the general reader an explanation of the basic processes involved with wills.

WYATT, ELAINE. *The Money Companion: How to Manage Your Money and Achieve Financial Freedom*. Toronto: Penguin, 1997. A guide to personal financial management that focuses on planning, investment strategy, and retirement needs.

WYLIE, BETTY JANE, and LYNNE MACFARLANE. *Everywoman's Money Book*. Fourth Edition. Toronto: Key Porter, 1989. A journalist and a stockbroker collaborated on this wide-ranging treatment of a variety of personal finance topics, including women and credit; the budget; insurance; retirement; children; and money.

Personal Finance on the Web

Living Wills Registry (Canada)
www.livingwills.com This site discusses and registers information regarding powers of attorney and related matters.

Wills and Estate Planning
www.preplannet.com This site provides information regarding the prearrangement of funerals and basic information regarding wills and estates. There are some links to legal firms and other government authorities regarding tax, especially for Quebec.

PART TWO

Financial Security

The processes of making financial plans to maximize the use of resources during one's lifetime and afterward were the focus of Part I. An integral part of financial planning involves ensuring financial security for oneself and one's dependents. The objective of Part II is to examine in some depth a variety of ways to protect financial security, such as buying insurance or increasing net worth.

Before becoming too involved with specific information about insurance, pensions, annuities, bonds, and stocks, it is essential to reflect on the necessity for any of them. Part II therefore begins with an introductory chapter, which explains financial security and identifies economic risks. The rest of the chapters in this section are concerned with ways of enhancing financial security by reducing risk. Two chapters explain the risks that can be handled by general and life insurance. Next, retirement income, an important aspect of financial security, is explored: both social security programs and private savings—including annuities and registered retirement savings plans—are discussed. The section's three final chapters are concerned with the offensive portions of finance, saving, and investing—indispensable ways of increasing financial security.

Economic Risks and Financial Security

objectives

1. Define what is meant by financial security.

2. Explain how the need for financial security affects decisions about the use of economic resources—e.g., saving for the future or selecting insurance.

3. Identify three events that pose economic risks for individuals or families.

4. Differentiate between assuming risk and sharing risk.

5. Distinguish between the steps an individual can take to enhance financial security and the means provided by society to do so.

6. Identify the threats to financial security that are posed by a serious disability, and two ways to alleviate the consequences of disability.

7. Analyze the meaning of disability as defined by various insurers.

8. Identify important features in disability insurance coverage.

Introduction

Maintaining a feeling of financial security, or assurance that we can cope with whatever may happen, is of prime concern to everyone. This feeling of security can be enhanced if we know what our economic risks are and if we can take steps to reduce their consequences. Life is full of economic risk, but sometimes we fail to recognize the particular risks that most threaten our economic well-being. Perhaps that explains why some people buy life insurance regardless of whether or not they need it, and why some others who really need such protection fail to buy it. This chapter first helps to identify the economic risks that pose the greatest threats to personal welfare and then suggests ways to minimize those risks. Certain risks, such as the untimely death of a person with dependents, or theft of or damage to personal property, may be shared through the purchase of insurance. Canada has social programs (e.g., Old Age Security, the Canada/Quebec Pension Plan, Employment Insurance, welfare) to minimize the effects of some events, such as loss of income. The serious risk of becoming disabled and unable to earn a living is too often ignored.

The chapters that follow this one consider in some detail several important ways to reduce economic risk, such as insuring your possessions or your life, planning for retirement income, and saving and investing to build up your net worth.

Financial Security

What do we mean by financial security? You will experience a feeling of **financial security** if you are confident that you will have the economic means to meet your needs in the present and in the future. Just as there are many conceptions regarding what is needed for a satisfactory level of living, so there are many notions of what constitutes financial security. Your feelings about risk, as well as your economic situation, will have much to do with the nature of your concerns about financial security. For instance, a family living on welfare may well consider that having enough money to pay the current bills for food, shelter, and clothing represents financial security for them, while a family living in affluent circumstances may have much more expansive ideas about what is required to maintain their financial security. The latter may feel economically threatened if they have to give up a vacation home, regular holidays, or restaurant meals.

If you feel financially secure, it may be assumed that you feel confident that you will be able to handle the following needs: (i) maintaining your accustomed level of living, (ii) coping with financial emergencies or unusual expenses, and (iii) making provisions for replacing income lost because of illness, unemployment, retirement, aging, or disability. When you know that you are protected from financial threats, you can feel reasonably secure about the future. But is such peace of mind possible for many of us? Who among us can be certain of what our future needs will be or of what resources we will have as we move through the various stages in our life cycle?

As individuals and as a society, we have taken an increasing interest in ensuring financial security. For one thing, we have become used to a complex level of living with more to protect. For another, our society has changed within a few generations to feature less economic self-sufficiency and more economic interdependence. In an agrarian society, many families can supply more of their needs outside the market than is possible in a society like ours. We rely, for the most part, on money income rather than on household production to support our desired lifestyle; anything that interrupts or halts the flow of income is therefore a serious threat. In response to social changes, government-sponsored programs have been instituted to provide partial financial security for the young, the old, the disabled, the unemployed, and the poor. Since most of us want more than partial financial security, we must take further steps to protect ourselves against a variety of economic risks.

Economic Risks

Before we can make any plans to enhance our financial security, we must first identify what events pose economic risks for us. The list of risks will not be identical for everyone, nor will it be the same at all stages of our lives. If you do not own a house, you do not face the risk of having it burn down; if you do not have dependent children, you need not worry about the risk of being unable to support them; if you do not own a car, damage to it is not one of your risks. It is essential to remember that economic risks and our ideas about financial security will change constantly as our lives change. Most of our economic risks can be categorized as follows:

(a) loss of income

—destruction of earning capacity

—loss of market for your services

(b) unexpected large expenses

—destruction or loss of property

—illness and death

—personal liability

(c) loss in value of capital

—drop in market value

—inflation

Loss of Income

Anything that causes the income stream to stop poses a very serious threat to economic security. As long as your income continues, there is some possibility of coping with unexpected expenses or with a loss of capital; but without a regular income, it is difficult to obtain enough resources. The reason for termination of income is usually either the destruction of your earning capacity or the disappearance of the market for your services.

DESTRUCTION OF EARNING CAPACITY   The ability to earn income may be lost temporarily (through illness) or permanently (through disability, aging, or death). Of these possibilities, permanent disability presents a particularly serious risk. Not only would you be unable to work, you would have to be supported and might also need expensive care. Social mechanisms for coping with this financial burden have not developed as fully as those for coping with aging or death, perhaps because we all expect to get older and eventually to die, but few people expect to be disabled. See Personal Finance in Action 4.1, "Things Were Going So Well."

LOSS OF MARKET FOR YOUR SERVICES   People who are self-employed must consider the possibility that the market for their goods or services may disappear, leaving them without income. Under such circumstances, they will need to change what they produce if possible. People who are employees may find that their services are no longer needed because the demand for particular skills has fallen, because economic conditions have reduced economic activity, because a change in technology has made their skills obsolete, or because of many other reasons. So employees, like the self-employed, may have to acquire new skills to fit into the labour market again.

Personal Finance in Action 4.1

Things Were Going So Well

Victor and Benita met in college, where she had returned to improve her employment opportunities by completing her business administration diploma in retail management. Finances were tight, as Benita had to support her daughter from her first marriage with student loans, part-time work, and infrequent support payments from her first husband.

Victor graduated from an engineering program and obtained a promising position with a Japanese auto maker in a nearby town. The salary and overtime pay was far in excess of their hopes and dreams for this entry-level position. The two decided to marry in six months, after Benita graduated and her divorce was final. Victor, in the meantime, would continue to live with his parents and save as much money as possible towards a down payment on a house.

During an evening snowfall Victor lost control of his car while returning from working overtime at the factory. Thanks to the prompt action of the snowplow operator and the emergency crews, Victor was saved, but never again would he be able to work the way he used to. After the accident, he was in the hospital for four months before he was able to return to his parents' home. They had to purchase a new van so his wheelchair could be accommodated.

With no income and only a disability pension from work, Victor became dependent on his parents as well as on the occupational therapists who helped him manage his new life. Benita once again had to support herself and her daughter on her own.

Unexpected Large Expenses

Many kinds of unexpected large expenses may threaten financial security, but only three will be discussed here:

(a) destruction or loss of personal property,

(b) illness and death,

(c) personal liability.

DESTRUCTION OF PROPERTY   The more we own, the greater the risk in the event that our possessions are lost or destroyed. Loss can be the result of many factors, including theft, fire, or severe weather. Should a family lose their house and all the contents through fire, they would probably be unable to replace everything by using only their own resources (e.g., savings); for this reason, they buy home insurance.

ILLNESS AND DEATH   Here in Canada, many, but not all, of the large expenses associated with illness and death have for decades been shared through our health insurance program. But caring at home for a person who is ill for a long time can be very expensive, and some or all of this expense may have to be borne by the family. Therefore, some personal resources may be needed in addition to health insurance and other social programs. In this age of AIDS and other long-term illnesses, some insurance companies have started to introduce **critical illness insurance** to cover just such instances. These policies generally pay a lump sum of money if you survive over 30 days.

PERSONAL LIABILITY Any one of us could face a very large unexpected expense if we were to be found liable for damage or injury because of negligence. We are probably most aware of this possibility in relation to our cars, because of the potential for destruction and death from a moment's inattention while driving. This concept will be more fully developed in the chapter on general insurance.

Loss in Value of Capital

Things that you own can lose value because of a reduction in the demand for them. If a highway is built close to your house, if interest in a certain artist wanes, or if no one wants your mining stocks, your capital—in the form of a house, a painting, or shares, respectively—diminishes through no action of yours.

Inflation affects various assets differently: some lose value, while others gain it. The value of money saved in deposits tends to suffer substantial loss during inflationary times. For instance, a dollar earned in 1980 and saved under your mattress until 1999 would buy only 43 percent of what it would have purchased 19 years earlier. That is why it should have been invested to earn a return equal to or greater than the rate of inflation. To do so, your annual return would have to be over 5 percent after taxes to maintain your buying power over the 19 years. Real estate, on the other hand, appreciated significantly during the same period.

What Are Your Economic Risks?

Make a list of economic risks that could threaten your financial security this year. Which events might cause a loss of income, even temporarily? What are some unexpected large expenses that would create hardship? How much of your net worth is at risk from price changes? Next, assign priorities to your list so that you can make plans to handle these risks.

Second, make a list of future economic risks—issues that are not concerns currently but may become important at another time—such as insufficient retirement income and inability to support children or other relatives.

Need for Savings

Even if you are fortunate enough to go through life without experiencing a disability, a major illness, or unemployment, you will probably retire sometime. When you do, your employment income will stop, and you will become dependent on pensions and investment earnings. Unless you spend your entire working life with the same employer, you may find that your work pension will not support you in the style you would wish. Public pensions will help, but many people find retirement much more comfortable if they also have private investment income. However, before you get any investment income, you must first save some money and then invest it.

Handling Risks

Having identified your economic risks, the next step is to decide what to do about them. Essentially, there are three possibilities:

(a) try to prevent the event from happening,

(b) assume the risk yourself,

(c) share the risk with others.

The task of thinking of ways to reduce or prevent risks is left to you. Some possibilities for assuming and sharing risk are outlined here, but the concept will be more fully developed in subsequent chapters on general insurance, life insurance, and annuities.

Assuming Risk

If you have enough financial resources, you can assume your own risks: that is, you can handle unfortunate events without jeopardizing your level of living. You can expect to have the funds to cope with unemployment, an unexpected large expense, illness, or retirement. Accumulating net worth is clearly one way of preparing to handle whatever risks come your way. That is why all sound advice on financial planning stresses the importance of saving three months of take-home pay for unforeseen needs, emergencies, and retirement.

Another way a family can assume risk is to expect individuals to help each other. When one earner is unable to work, someone else in the family may be able to support the household. Two-income families have spread the risk of having something happen to the income stream. Still, most of us are unable to assume all potential risks; usually, we must depend on some risk-sharing.

Sharing Risk

When a risk is too much for individuals or families to bear alone, it can be shared, either through private insurance or through social income-security programs. Collecting small contributions from many people allows for the creation of a fund that will be sufficient to compensate those few people who experience an unfortunate event. For example, all car owners contribute to car insurance, but only those who have accidents draw on the fund. The participating in a risk-sharing program enhances financial security by providing the knowledge that compensation would be available if the insured people required it.

PRIVATE EFFORTS General insurance allows us to share the risks that our personal property may be lost or damaged, as well as the risk that we may be held personally liable for injury to another person or damage to another person's property. Life insurance is designed to protect against the financial risk of the premature death of a person with dependents. Annuities, by turning capital into an income stream guaranteed for life, protect against the risk of living so long that there are no savings left.

PUBLIC PROGRAMS Canada's public income-security programs are based on risk-sharing, one way or another. The Canada and Quebec Pension Plans, along with Employment Insurance, are social insurance programs to which employed people make contributions; your eligibility for benefits under these programs depends on your having been a contributor. Such programs offer protection against the risks of becoming unemployed or disabled, of aging, and of dying. Canadians fund several other programs, such as Old Age Security and social welfare, through taxes rather than by direct contributions. In this way, those in the labour force provide support for those who are old or are unable to work.

In addition to these income-security programs, society takes other steps to help us plan for our own financial security. Canada's income tax system encourages retirement planning by offering tax deductions for people who invest in RRSPs or contribute to employment-related pension plans.

Disability: A Serious Risk

In this chapter, brief mention will be made of personal disability, a very significant economic risk that people too often ignore. A common hazard is the potential loss of one's ability to earn a living because of temporary or permanent disability due to an accident or an illness. The case study in Personal Finance in Action Box 4.2, "His Life Was Changed by a Fall"—which is based on a real situation—illustrates the disastrous effect that permanent disability can have on a family's financial security.

People under the age of 65 have a greater probability of suffering a disability than of dying. Yet people of any age are more likely to have life insurance than to have disability insurance. The gender differences in the probability of being disabled for more than six months between the ages of 25 and 55 are illustrated in Figure 4.1. Females in this age group face a significantly greater risk of being disabled than of dying, but have a lower mortality rate than males of the same age. Experience has shown that anyone who is disabled for more than three months will probably still be disabled five years later. The risk of becoming disabled is one that few of us are financially able to assume alone. How many people have enough savings to support themselves for a year or more?

To protect ourselves against the risk of becoming disabled, we can purchase **disability insurance** (sometimes called income replacement insurance). Without such protection, we would have to depend on others—our families or the social welfare system—to support us.

Disability Insurance

Disability insurance may be purchased either privately (the more expensive of the two options) or through a group policy (which is a less expensive approach). When an insurance company insures a group of people in one policy, each person's coverage is less costly than if he or she had bought it separately. Many people have some group disability insurance through their place of work. It is critical, however, to find out exactly what coverage you have. Policies

---

Personal Finance in Action 4.2

His Life Was Changed by a Fall

Simon, a self-employed mason, fell 15 metres from a scaffold, injuring himself so badly that despite having spent months in the hospital, he still lives in constant pain and walks with difficulty. He can't lift or carry anything. Fortunately, he was covered by Workers' Compensation, which provides him with a small pension, but he was inexplicably classified as only 25 percent disabled. Two years after the accident, Simon is still negotiating with Canada Pension about the extent of his disability. His first application was rejected because of the possibility that he might be able to return to work. He has now applied again.

At 40, Simon is unable to work to support his wife and three teenage children. He has given up his business and sold the family's home; they lived on their savings as long as they lasted. The monthly Workers' Compensation cheque is just large enough to pay the rent on a subsidized apartment. The small additional amount that Simon gets from welfare is insufficient to buy the family's food. Applying for disability benefits involves considerable red tape and waiting, as Simon has discovered. Simon's fall drastically changed life for him and for his family.

FIGURE 4.1   PROBABILITY OF DEATH OR LONG-TERM DISABILITY (OVER SIX MONTHS) OCCURRING WITHIN A YEAR, BY GENDER

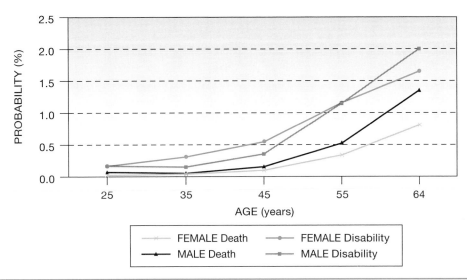

SOURCE: Clarica's group insurance data. Reproduced with the permission of Clarica of Canada.

vary in many ways: the waiting period before benefits start may be shorter or longer, the definition of disability may be broader or narrower, the amount of benefits may be higher or lower, the benefit period may be shorter or longer, and other options may also differ. The cost of the coverage typically depends on what features are included; better benefits cost more. Cost may also vary due to the rate of claims, especially for group plans.

WAITING PERIOD When assessing your coverage, it is important to know how long you would need to be considered unable to work before disability payments would begin. If you have sick-leave coverage at your place of work, that might or might not be enough to cover you until the income replacement benefits begin. Either way, you could have to wait several months before receiving any payments. Policies can have waiting periods as short as one week or as long as four months. Consider how long you could survive without any income; then, to keep the cost of your premiums down, choose the longest waiting period you could manage.

DEFINITION OF DISABILITY How disabled must you be in order to become eligible for benefits? It is essential that you read this part of a policy very carefully; many disabled people have been surprised to find that, although they have insurance, the policy's definition of disability excludes them. A distinction is usually made between partial and total disability; as well, benefits may be withheld if the insurance company deems you capable of working part-time or working at an occupation other than your usual one. By paying more, you can get a policy that provides benefits until you are able to return to your usual occupation. For instance, consider a teacher who has suffered some voice impairment. He might be unable to continue teaching, but able to do a clerical job. Since he would not be considered totally disabled, some disability policies would not provide support for him, because he appears able to handle certain types of work—just not the career he has chosen and trained for. Personal Finance in Action Box 4.3, "Collecting Disability Benefits Can Be Difficult," illustrates a similar scenario.

AMOUNT OF BENEFITS Even if you obtain the most coverage you can afford, at best the benefits will probably amount to only 60 or 70 percent of your usual income. Depending on the

Personal Finance in Action 4.3

Collecting Disability Benefits Can Be Difficult

A decade ago, Ken was happily employed as a nursing assistant in a Nova Scotia hospital. Then disaster struck: while he was lifting a heavy patient, he had a heart attack that left him with a poorly functioning heart. Various medications and treatments added to his miseries and disability. After a 27-year career, Ken was no longer able to work as a nursing assistant.

He applied for benefits under his group income replacement insurance. To his surprise, the insurance company refused his claim, on the grounds that he did not qualify as totally and permanently disabled, since he would be able to work at some occupation, though not necessarily nursing. He took his case to court and eventually received a settlement.

policy's payment process, this amount may or may not be tax free. If it is tax free (and most are) it may prove adequate. No insurance company will offer a policy that would make it profitable for anyone to become disabled. For an additional premium, it is sometimes possible to have a policy that would index benefits to inflation.

BENEFIT PERIOD What limits are there on the benefit period? Policies may restrict benefits to a few weeks, one year, five years, or until you reach age 65. Again, you will want the longest benefit period you can afford.

RENEWABILITY Is there a clause in the policy that guarantees that it is non-cancellable or renewable? You would not want to find, as you get older, that the company will not renew your policy.

Social Support for the Disabled

Are there social programs for which you might be eligible if you became disabled? Eligibility requirements could include your having contributed to the program previously or your having a disability as a result of an injury sustained either on the job or during military service. Here is a list of the major social supports for disabled people in Canada:

(a) **Employment Insurance**—a federal program that provides short-term benefits to contributors.

(b) **The Canada and Quebec Pension Plans**—a disability pension for contributors with a severe or prolonged disability, and for their dependents and survivors.

(c) **Workers' Compensation**—provincial plans that offer medical, financial, and rehabilitative assistance to workers who become disabled by accidents or illness related to their jobs.

(d) **Short-term or Long-term Welfare**—municipal and provincial programs for those with few other resources.

Summary

Financial security is something we take for granted when things are going well, actively endeavour to protect if it is threatened, and vigorously try to regain if we lose it. It involves feeling assured that we have the capacity to maintain our desired level of living in the face of any life crisis. Prudent people take steps to protect their financial security as much as possible from the kinds of economic risks that can result in loss of income or can require unexpected large expenditures. This can be done by trying to reduce some risks, by assuming others, and by sharing the largest risks with a group. The latter principle underlies all forms of insurance. A serious but frequently neglected risk is the possibility of becoming disabled.

This chapter may have alerted you to economic risks that could threaten your financial security at some time in your life, but has not specified exactly what you can do to protect yourself. Following chapters will discuss the protection offered by general and life insurance, by private and public pensions, and annuities. Building your net worth, which is, of course, helpful in any financial crisis, is achieved by regular saving and wise investing.

Key Terms

critical illness insurance (p. 83)   financial security (p. 81)
disability insurance (p. 86)

Problems

1. When Disaster Struck

   Six years ago, Luke and Vera never imagined that they would find themselves in such dire financial straits that they would have to apply for welfare. He was a self-employed, skilled construction worker who was making a good income when suddenly he developed a heart condition that required open-heart surgery. Complications ensued; after an extended hospitalization, Luke went home, but was not well enough to work. His doctor advised him that any physical activity could cause a coronary.

   The stress of Luke's illness, the financial problems, and having to look after the home and children on her own caused a gastric condition that made Vera miserable and not well enough to go out to work. And even if she had been able to do so, who would have looked after the children (a five-year-old, a four-year-old, and a ten-month-old)?

   When Luke stopped working, the couple had $5 000 in the bank and had built up equity amounting to about $30 000 in the semi-detached home they were buying. They did not apply for welfare immediately, because they were afraid they would have to sell their house and car; instead, they lived on their savings as long as they could. Because he was self-employed, Luke was not covered by Employment Insurance, but he had been paying into the Canada Pension Plan. He had once thought about disability insurance but had decided against purchasing it because of the high premiums. Besides their regular living expenses, costly drugs were needed for Luke, along with a special formula for the baby, who was allergic to milk.

   Finally this family became so desperate that they called Social Services. They were immediately granted short-term welfare, which included a waiver of their health insurance premium, free prescription drugs and dental care, and an allowance for the baby's special diet. They were advised to see their bank about the mortgage payment (which was one month in arrears) to ask that it be deferred and that the mortgage be extended a month. They discovered to their surprise that welfare recipients are allowed to have a car and a few assets, and that if they had applied sooner, they could have kept their savings in the bank.

(a) Can you think of anything this family could have done to be better prepared for such an economic disaster?

(b) Should they be applying for disability benefits from the Canada Pension Plan?

(c) Do you have any other suggestions for ways they could obtain more resources?

2. Interview people you know, and compare two families who have quite different ideas of what financial security means to them.

3. At what stage in the life cycle do you think economic risks are most threatening?

4. Make a list of the five major economic risks you will face after you graduate. What major risks are you likely to face 15 years from now?

5. What features would you like to see in a disability insurance policy? What other major health risks are not covered by disability insurance or life insurance for which it would be advisable to be covered? Hint: Go to Statscan.ca.

6. What major factors cause people to ignore the need for a) life insurance and b) disability insurance?

7. In this chapter, we have mentioned a variety of economic risks and suggested various ways to minimize the effects of encountering each. As an aid in summarizing this information, complete the following chart. In addition to the material in this chapter, you should be able to draw on your general knowledge. The first and last lines have been filled in as examples.

Economic risks	Ways to Handle Economic Risks		
	As an individual or family member	As an employee	As a citizen
A. LOSS OF INCOME 1. Earning capacity destroyed (a) temporarily (e.g., illness)	*Use savings. Income of another family member.*	*Sick leave with pay*	*Health insurance*
(b) permanently —disability			
—aging			
—death			
2. Market for earner's services destroyed (a) unemployment			
(b) fall in profits for self-employed			

continued

Economic risks	Ways to Handle Economic Risks		
	As an individual or family member	As an employee	As a citizen
B. UNEXPECTED LARGE EXPENSES			
1. Destruction or loss of personal property			
2. Illness, death			
3. Personal liability			
C. LOSS OF VALUE OF CAPITAL			
1. Drop in market value (e.g., house, stock)	*Diversify assets*	*n/a*	*n/a*
2. Price changes (e.g., inflation)	*Diversify assets*	*n/a*	*n/a*

8. Evaluate the following long-term disability plan, which covers one group of employees. How effective do you think it will be in meeting the needs of employees who become disabled?

   Benefits: $66\frac{2}{3}$ percent of basic monthly earnings, to a maximum of $3500. This will be reduced by any amount to which you are entitled from Workers' Compensation or Canada Pension (benefits for dependents are excluded). The employer will supplement this at $13\frac{1}{3}$ percent of the basic salary for a period of four months, to a maximum of 80 percent of your basic earnings.

   Waiting Period: Benefits begin on the 91st consecutive day of total disability.

   Benefit Period: Until age 65 for total disability; two years for a temporary disability that prevents you from performing the duties of your occupation. Benefits are payable beyond two years if you are disabled to such an extent that you cannot engage in any occupation for which you are or could reasonably become qualified as determined by your doctor.

9. Decide whether you AGREE or DISAGREE with each of the following statements.

   (a) What you already possess affects your concept of financial security.

   (b) Employment Insurance protects against the risk of personal liability.

   (c) You have to contribute to the Canada/Quebec Pension Plan or to Employment Insurance in order to become eligible for disability benefits under these programs.

   (d) Employment Insurance will assist a family when the breadwinner dies suddenly.

   (e) For those aged 30, the probability of becoming disabled (for more than three months) is greater than the probability of dying.

   (f) Social programs tend to provide income support for people who are unable to work, but such programs leave individuals to arrange their own protection for risks to property or capital.

10. Try to find out the cost of buying disability insurance privately for employed 25-year-old males and females. If possible, compare this amount to the cost of group protection.

11. Explore the Web site of Statistics Canada at www.statcan.ca, proceed to the People, and then the Health area. Determine your personal expectations of illness or disability. Now do the same for your other family members. How significant are these risks?

12. Find any one of the major life and health insurance Web sites and examine their offerings for disability and critical illness insurance. How do they define these terms and what do they offer? Is this individual or group coverage? Suggested companies: Manulife, Clarica, Sun Life, and Great West Life.

References

BOOKS AND ARTICLES

MATTHEWS, BETSY, and RICHARD BIRCH. *Taking Care of Tomorrow: The Canadian Money Book for Prime Time Women*. Toronto: McGraw-Hill Ryerson, 1992. A practical guide that deals with the financial needs and realities of women in various social and financial circumstances.

WYATT, ELAINE. *The Money Companion: How to Manage Your Money and Achieve Financial Freedom*. Toronto: Penguin, 1997. A guide to personal financial management that focuses on planning, investment strategy, and retirement needs.

Personal Finance on the Web

Statistics Canada
www.statcan.ca/English[or French]/Pgdb/People/health.htm Contains some illuminating data that can help you determine how much risk you face depending on your gender, age, profession, or place of residence.

Useful Resource from the Insurance Industry
www.iicc.ca An industry Web site with significant reference material on property and casualty insurance information.

Canadian Life and Health Insurance Association Inc.
www.clhia.ca An industry body representing the 100 life and health insurance companies in Canada. An overview of the industry and the role it plays as well as the self-established rules of the industry.

Insurance Canada
www.insurance-canada.ca A consumer-focused site with information regarding the needs and intricacies of the industry. It is co-sponsored by the Consumers Council of Canada and the Consumers Association of Canada.

Chapter 5

General Insurance

objectives

1. Identify two major financial risks associated with owning a house and its contents, personal possessions, or an automobile, and also, the appropriate type of insurance coverage for each risk.

2. Understand and demonstrate applications of the following basic insurance principles: sharing risk, indemnification, subrogation, and co-insurance.

3. Distinguish between the following terms: pure cost of insurance and loading charge; premium and policy; insurable interest and insurable risk; insured and insurer; actual cash value and replacement value; deductible and policy limits; scheduled property rider and clause covering possessions taken from home; and, named-peril and all-risks coverage.

4. Explain the different functions of the following: an actuary, an insurance agent, an insurance broker, an adjuster, and a claims department.

5. Determine, from an insurance policy, the risks that the policy covers, and excludes.

6. Identify at least two factors that insurers consider when settling claims.

7. Explain how the concept of negligence affects insurance claims.

8. Explain the following terms: depreciation, rider or endorsement, short rate, and accident benefits.

Introduction

The analysis of financial security in Chapter 4 led to the conclusion that some risks can be minimized by purchasing insurance. This chapter identifies economic risks that are of concern to anyone who owns real property or personal possessions, explains the basic concepts and principles of general insurance, and examines in detail three types of general insurance: property insurance, personal liability insurance, and automobile insurance. Life insurance, which is not considered a type of general insurance, is discussed in the next chapter.

The Economic Risks of Ownership

Two types of risk are associated with ownership: (i) the property itself may be damaged, destroyed, or lost, and (ii) people may be held responsible for injury to others or for damage to their possessions because of what they do or own. Fire and theft are examples of the first type of risk. The second type of risk is known as a personal liability risk, and is perhaps less easily understood than the former. A person may have a financial responsibility (or liability) if his or her car, dog, or broken steps causes damage or injury, although it is usually necessary for those making the claim to prove that there was negligence involved. Moreover, liability risks need not be related to ownership; careless behaviour can also create liability.

Damage to or Loss of Property

Both tenants and home owners must consider the risk that their furnishings and other possessions could be damaged by fire or stolen; owners must also consider the possibility that their house could burn. Damage to or loss of a car is another risk to consider, but a less serious one than being responsible for injury to other people. At the very worst one would be left without a car, but burdened with a monstrous debt for many years.

Liability for Damages

Being found responsible, because of negligence, for damage to the lives or property of others is one of the risks that anyone may be exposed to. Here we are speaking not about damage to you or your possessions, but about claims against you by others for their losses. A tenant may be held responsible for damage to rented premises. If, for instance, the tenant's careless smoking or forgetfulness in using a cooking or heating appliance were to cause an apartment fire, the landlord's insurer would reimburse the landlord for the damage to the building, but would probably bill the tenant for the cost of the repairs. The extent of the tenant's liability would depend on the circumstances.

A home owner faces the risk that his or her walks, yards, trees, and so on could cause injury. A tree could fall on the neighbour's car, or someone could fall on the home owner's broken steps. An automobile owner faces the serious risk of being held liable for a death or an injury, with potentially enormous financial consequences. Recent Canadian settlements for personal injury in automobile accidents have been as high as several million dollars. Cars can also damage other people's cars or property, but claims involving such incidents are usually lower than those related to personal injury.

Most of us consider the risks outlined above to be too great to accept entirely on our own, so we buy insurance in order to share the risks with others. In fact, society considers the liability risks associated with car ownership so serious that liability insurance coverage is mandatory in most jurisdictions. Before we examine the various types of insurance, it is necessary to review and understand a few basic insurance concepts and principles.

Basic Concepts and Principles

The Insurance Principle

Since a major fire or auto accident can financially cripple an individual or a family, methods have been devised that allow people to spread the risk of these events. If a large number of people who face a common risk decide to pool their money, the result will be a fund that is sufficient to compensate the few who actually experience the disaster in question. This sharing or **pooling risk** is the basic principle on which all types of insurance are based. But because this approach depends on the law of large numbers, it will not work for a small group. The insurance companies that collect, manage, and disperse the pooled funds employ specialized mathematicians called **actuaries** to predict the probability that a particular event will occur among a group of 1 000 people in a 12-month period. Such predictions can be fairly accurate when large numbers of people or events are involved, but actuaries cannot, of course, identify which persons will be affected in a particular year. The amount that each person must contribute to the insurance pool or fund depends on several factors:

(a) the probability (according to actuarial estimates) that the event will occur,

(b) the amount that compensation can be expected to cost,

(c) the number sharing the risk.

The simplified example in Personal Finance in Action Box 5.1, "Sharing the Risk," illustrates this principle.

To summarize, the principle of sharing risk works when a large number of people are willing to pay a regular fee that is certain in exchange for protection against a hazard that is uncertain. Those who experience a loss will be compensated from the pooled funds, and those who are fortunate enough not to have had a loss will not need to claim anything from the insurance fund. Nevertheless, all participants will have enhanced their financial security by having insurance.

Personal Finance in Action 5.1

Sharing the Risk

In the town of Bayfield there are 1 000 houses, all wooden and of approximately equal value. Past records reveal that, on average, one house burns down each year, and that the cost of rebuilding a house is approximately $100 000. (It is not necessary to take into account the value of the land on which the house stands, because fire does not destroy the lot.)

The loss of a house is such a serious disaster that the community does not expect the affected family to cope alone. In nineteenth-century North America, it was customary for neighbours to come to the rescue, providing temporary shelter for the homeless family while they felled logs and sawed boards to construct a new house. Now the scarcity of trees and the complexity of house construction has caused the house-building "bee" to be abandoned in favour of property insurance.

How large a fund will be needed in Bayfield to cover the potential fire losses to houses?

Number of home owners
sharing the risk: 1 000

Probability of fire: . . . . 1 per 1 000/year

Cost of compensation: $100 000/house

If each owner contributes $100 per year, there will be a fund of $100 000. At the end of a typical year, with one claim for $100 000, the fund will be exhausted.

Factors Affecting Cost

The cost of property insurance, as we have said, depends on the probability that a particular peril will occur, the cost of compensation, and the number of people sharing the risk. In practice, actuaries take into consideration many more complex factors than those in the above example. The probability of fire and the extent of damage are affected by the availability of fire-fighting facilities, the proximity of hazards such as paint factories or oil storage tanks, and the flammability of the house. The cost of compensation depends on the value of the property that would need to be repaired or replaced, which can, of course, vary considerably in the case of houses.

Once the probability that the event will occur has been established and the cost of compensation estimated, an actuary can determine the cost of covering this risk, which is called the **pure cost of insurance**. To this amount will be added a **loading charge,** which covers the costs that the insurance company incurs in collecting and managing the insurance funds, settling the claims, and returning profits to the company's shareholders. Not surprisingly, the estimates of all these costs vary from company to company. The cost of insuring a property, called a **premium**, is paid at regular intervals to keep the insurance in force and is reviewed at least annually by the insurance company.

Risk Management

INSURABLE INTEREST It is impossible to buy insurance against a risk unless it can be shown that the buyer has an **insurable interest** in the risk in question. In other words, would the buyer suffer a financial loss if the event occurred? A property owner has an insurable interest in the possibility of it being stolen or destroyed, but a relative or friend who has no legal relation to the property cannot insure it. This principle applies to all types of insurance, including life insurance.

INSURABLE RISKS Insurance is concerned with **insurable risks** only; such risks result from chance events and are not caused by deliberate action on the part of the person insured. If a fire starts because of lightning, it is a chance risk, but if a fire is started by the property owner, it is not. Insurance companies must be certain about the cause of the damage before settling the claim.

HANDLING RISK As noted earlier, there are three possible ways of dealing with insurable risks:

(a) taking steps to eliminate or reduce the risk,

(b) preparing to handle the loss oneself,

(c) sharing the risk with others.

An example of reducing the risk of injury or damage from fire would be to install smoke detectors or a sprinkler system in one's home. The risk of theft could be reduced by improving the locks on the doors and windows. Some people decide to handle some risks themselves when the risk is not too high and their financial resources are adequate. A person who decides not to buy collision coverage (which, unlike liability coverage, is a matter of choice rather than a legal requirement for car owners) on an old car is accepting the risk that the car could be destroyed instead of sharing that risk by buying insurance. Sharing risks through insurance is prudent whenever the possible loss would be too heavy to handle alone. In planning for financial security, it may be wise to use a combination of these three options. Most people probably need some insurance, but they may be able to reduce the cost of that insurance by taking steps to minimize the risk and by assuming some portion of the risk themselves.

The Insurance Contract

A person who decides to buy insurance may contact an **agent** (someone who represents a single insurance company) or a **broker** (someone who represents several companies). The broker can do comparison shopping for the client among the several companies that he or she represents to find the most economical and most appropriate coverage.

A buyer applying for insurance completes an application form and receives an explanation of the policy from the agent. Generally, purchasers are more likely to be given a complete copy of a home insurance policy than an automobile policy. Perhaps that is because, in some provinces, there is a standard car insurance policy for the whole province, irrespective of insurance company.

The legal contract or agreement between the person buying insurance (called the **insured**) and the insurance company (called the **insurer**) is known as a **policy.** Traditionally, policies have been written in legal language that is difficult to understand, but some insurers are now writing their policies in a more simplified form. Refer to your home insurance policy, or to the sample policy in Appendix 5A, for practice reading. A policy will seem less daunting if you begin by identifying the following main components:

(a) the preamble or declaration sheet,

(b) the insuring agreement,

(c) the statutory and policy conditions,

(d) any endorsements or riders.

DECLARATION SHEET The preamble, or declaration sheet, is a separate page that is filled in for each insurance buyer, giving the names of the insurer and the insured, the dates the insurance will be in effect, the amounts paid, and the risks to be covered in the agreement. Without this sheet, it is impossible to know what coverage the insured has bought. This page can be easily identified, because the spaces in it have been filled in by writing or typing.

The rest of the policy consists of several printed pages that the company routinely uses for all similar risks. For instance, the company may have a standard fire insurance policy that can be adjusted to fit individual requirements by the selections made on the declaration sheet. If the space beside a risk on the declaration sheet is not filled in, that risk is not covered in that particular agreement. When reading a policy, first determine what coverage is in force by examining the declaration sheet, and then locate the relevant sections of the policy's printed portion.

INSURING AGREEMENT The printed part of the policy will contain an insuring agreement

Insurance Terminology

Insured—the person whose risks are covered by the insurance, usually the purchaser

Insurer—the insurance company

Policy—the contract between the insured and the insurer that specifies the terms of the agreement

Premium—the regular payment made by the insured for insurance coverage

Peril—a risk of some damage or injury

Endorsement or **rider**—a statement appended to an insurance policy that may specify additional coverage and a change in ownership or in risk

that sets out which kinds of property are covered, which perils are insured against, the exclusions (situations not covered by the policy), and the circumstances under which insurance settlements will be made.

POLICY CONDITIONS Statutory and policy conditions include statements about the responsibilities of the insurer and the insured, including the duty to avoid misrepresentation, why and how the policy may be terminated, the actions required after a loss, and the consequences of fraud.

ENDORSEMENTS Insurance policies may be modified by the use of an **endorsement** or **rider,** which is a statement that is appended to the contract. Some examples of possible riders include a change in the ownership of the property, a change in the risk situation of the property owner, or additional coverage.

CANCELLATION The insured may cancel a policy at any time, but if this occurs, the insurer may choose to retain a portion of the premium calculated at the **short rate.** This means that the insurer keeps more than the just the prorated share of the premium. For instance, if a one-year policy is cancelled after six months, the refund will be less than half of the premium paid.

Insurance Settlements

CLAIMS PROCESS After a loss has occurred, it is the insured's responsibility to provide proof of the loss. Specialists called **adjusters,** who may either be on the regular staff of the insurance company or be working independently for a number of companies, immediately go to the scene of the misfortune to begin estimating the extent of the damage. They report their results to the insurance company's claims department, which negotiates a settlement. Agents and brokers have little, if any, part in the claims procedure. Police, on the other hand, have to be called if the loss is as a result of any criminal act or contravention of some other law. The police report may be used in the insurance investigation or any lawsuit that may arise later.

There are two approaches to determining the amount of an insurance settlement: (i) actual cash value (indemnification), or (ii) replacement value. Traditionally, most claims were settled using the principle of cash value or indemnification; but in recent years, insurers have offered replacement value coverage. Actual cash value coverage will be considered first.

ACTUAL CASH VALUE Property insurance, unlike life insurance, is based on the principle of indemnifying the insured for a loss. **Indemnification** is defined as compensating the insured at such a level that the insured will be returned to approximately the same financial position enjoyed before the loss (since it is not intended that anyone should profit from an insurance settlement). The concept of indemnification may sound simple. But in practice it may not

How to Read a Policy

Examine the sample home insurance policy in Appendix 5A to find the answers to the following questions.

1. *What* property is covered?

2. *What* are the financial limits of the coverage?
3. *What* is the total premium?

Your instructor may have other questions about the rest of the policy.

be easy to determine exactly what the previous financial position of the insured was with regard to the lost or damaged property.

Some property insurance policies promise to indemnify on the basis of the **actual cash value** of the property at the date of the loss—that is, the cost of replacing it less the use already received from it. Therefore, it is the cash value when the loss occurred that is significant, not the value of the property either when it was bought or when it was insured.

There are various methods of arriving at the actual cash value, but a common one is to determine the **replacement value** of the loss and then deduct any accumulated depreciation. The replacement value of a house is the cost of rebuilding it, not the amount it might have sold for. The replacement value of a household possession is the cost of buying a similar new one. **Depreciation** is the monetary value that has been used up since the item was new. Different objects wear out at different rates because of the object's characteristics or the way it is used or cared for. Insurance companies have tables of standard rates of depreciation for many household goods. Adjusters may adapt these rates somewhat to allow either for especially good care or for very hard usage. The well-established depreciation rates for cars are found in tables possessed by most automobile dealers. The way to calculate actual cash value is shown in the Personal Finance in Action Box 5.2, "Actual Cash Value."

The insurer has the option of offering the following:

(a) a cash settlement,

(b) a similar article as a replacement for the damaged one,

(c) the repair of the damaged article.

If the repair results in an improvement of the property, the value of the betterment is charged to the insured. In addition to the factors mentioned, the condition of the property and the standard of maintenance also affect the estimated cash value. In the case of a building that has been destroyed or damaged, the insurer usually settles by paying for the repair or rebuilding, but does not take possession of the property.

Personal Finance in Action 5.2

Actual Cash Value

A fire in Nathan's kitchen damaged his appliances beyond repair as well as the cabinetry and some of the contents. The insurance company adjuster adequately accounted for the repairs to the house, but Nathan was quite upset about the amount of money he was to receive for the appliances he purchased three years earlier for $3 000. The adjuster advised that since Nathan had purchased the least expensive policy, he was only covered for the cash value of the appliances, which equals the replacement cost less depreciation. The settlement was calculated as follows with depreciation being estimated at 10 percent per year, or 30 percent in total for the three years:

$$\begin{aligned} \text{Actual Cash Value} &= \text{Replacement Cost} - \\ &\quad \text{Depreciation} \\ &= \$3\ 500 - (0.30 \times \$3\ 500) \\ &= \$3\ 500 - \$1\ 050 \\ &= \$2\ 450 \end{aligned}$$

Nathan was very upset, as this money would barely cover the loan to the furniture store that sold the appliances on their delayed payment program. Now Nathan would have to go out and buy new appliances all over again. From now on, Nathan would review his policy and purchase full replacement coverage, not just indemnification for a loss.

In cases of partial loss, the insured might be reimbursed for a total loss, but any **salvage value** of the damaged property subsequently belongs to the insurance company. For instance, if a heavily damaged car is replaced by the insurer, the owner has no claim on the remnants of the smashed car; the wreck would belong to the insurance company as salvage. To retain the salvage value, the owner must pay the insurer for it.

REPLACEMENT VALUE INSURANCE   In recent years insurers have begun offering replacement value insurance—that is, they may now agree to replace used possessions with similar new ones. This practice increases the cost of compensation and consequently raises the premium that must be charged. Replacement value insurance does not follow the classic principle of indemnification of losses, because replacing used furniture with new may leave the insured in a better position than before the loss. Replacement value insurance is now very popular, and some companies report that it predominates over actual cash value coverage. Claimants, pleased to receive settlements that enable them to replace lost articles without considering depreciation, have proved willing to pay the higher premiums.

INSURER'S LIABILITY   The insured is entitled to compensation for personal loss, but this amount can never be greater than the **policy limits** purchased. An $80 000 fire insurance policy limits the insurer's liability on this contract to $80 000. For any claim, the insurer will pay the lesser of the policy limits, the actual cash value of the loss, or the cost of repairs. If a replacement value policy has been purchased, the insurer will pay the lesser of the policy limits or the replacement value. A person who has had a loss valued at $7 000 but has a policy limit of $5 000 will receive only $5 000. In the case of automobiles, the insurer's liability is the lesser of the actual cash value or the cost of repairs.

Since small claims are expensive for an insurance company to handle, it is customary to offer the insured the opportunity to pay a lower premium and carry a certain amount of the risk personally. If the insured agrees to assume responsibility for the first $200 of damages, the contract is said to have a **deductible clause** of $200. The higher the deductible, the lower the premium.

SUBROGATION   When an insurer indemnifies a claimant for a loss, the insurer is entitled to attempt to recover damages from any other persons who may have been responsible for the loss—a procedure called **subrogation.** For instance, if a tenant is responsible for fire damage in an apartment, the building's insurer may indemnify the landlord and then, by subrogation, attempt to collect from the tenant who caused the damage.

Property Insurance

In the interests of clarity, this discussion of property insurance will be limited to coverage on personal possessions, houses, and liability, and will look at each type separately. However, in practice, coverage for several risks is often combined in one policy—as, for example, is common in the case of home owners' or tenants' policies.

The Risks

The many perils that may befall a house (or apartment) or its contents can be categorized as either (i) accidental or (ii) the result of criminal actions. Such perils as fire, smoke, water, windstorms, and falling objects represent accidental damage; vandalism and stealing are examples of criminal actions. Defining perils and specifying exclusions (situations not covered in the contract) can be quite complex. For instance, stealing is subdivided into theft, burglary, or robbery. Theft means the loss of property by stealing without either violence against persons or forced entry. Burglary involves theft accompanied by forcible entry that leaves visible marks on the premises. Robbery is theft accompanied by violence or the threat of violence to a person.

Coverage

Most insurance companies sell two types of home owner coverage: (i) **named-peril coverage,** which provides protection for losses from a list of perils named in the contract, or (ii) **all-risks coverage,** which covers all risks except for any that may be specifically excluded. The more comprehensive coverage may be limited to the house, while the contents are covered for named perils only. All-risks insurance is also more expensive than the more basic named-peril policies.

It is possible to insure only certain possessions against all risks by having an endorsement or rider added to the policy. Such added coverage includes all the kinds of risks associated with direct physical loss or damage, limited only by any exclusions that may be listed. It is usually specified that the extra coverage applies only to accidental damage and not to damage that is due to the nature of the property itself (for example, rust or age). When all-risks coverage is bought for such items as cameras, furs, jewellery, and collections, these items are listed as scheduled property. It is prudent to update your list from time to time, especially after a wedding or a major birthday.

A **scheduled property rider,** also called a **valued contract endorsement,** lists the items covered, along with their value, and also includes identifying information such as descriptions and serial numbers. To confirm the value, the insurer will require either a bill of sale (if the item was recently acquired) or an official appraisal (if the item was previously purchased). In the event of loss or damage, the insurer's maximum liability is the value placed on the property when it was insured. Such contracts are generally used to insure items whose true value is difficult to determine after a loss, such as jewellery, works of historic value, antiques, and stamp and coin collections. Unfortunately, in periods of rapid inflation the maximum liability established when the insurance was bought can become outdated quickly. Unless the insurance company offers automatic adjustment for inflation, the owner should have new appraisals done periodically. (See Personal Finance in Action Box 5.3, "Scheduled Property Rider.")

Personal Finance in Action 5.3

Scheduled Property Rider

Emil and Anne had built up quite an art collection over the years, primarily from the artists that they had gone to school with. Paintings hung all over their apartment and were constantly changing as they rearranged and framed their artworks. Carvings and crafts were everywhere. In many ways, the art proved to be a good investment; a few of the pieces were purchased from artists who later became quite famous. Some of their creations were worth over $10 000 each. To protect their investment, Emil and Anne had an artist friend appraise their collection for insurance purposes.

Five years later, their apartment was burglarized and three of the artworks were stolen. The insurance company offered them $7 500 for the three works based on the appraisal their friend had done five years earlier. This amount was not even a quarter of the value of one of the paintings alone. If Emil and Anne had wanted to be fully insured, they should have had the artwork appraised more frequently and by an expert, at least whenever the coverage limits of their policy changed.

PERSONAL PROPERTY TAKEN AWAY FROM HOME Policies often contain a personal property clause that covers personal items when they are taken away from home temporarily. The key word here is *temporarily*: possessions taken on a trip, to a summer cottage for a few weeks, or by a student to a college residence would be considered temporarily away. The amount of coverage for possessions under such circumstances varies with the policy. For instance, if the policy states that possessions taken away from home are covered for 10 percent of the total coverage on all personal possessions, and if the household contents are insured for $30 000, there would be coverage of $3 000. Read the policy to find out the extent of the coverage.

Co-Insurance

Actuaries base the premium structure for property insurance on the assumption that property owners will carry sufficient insurance to cover a total loss of the building. In fact, however, very few buildings burn completely; thus, most claims involve damage costing only a few thousand dollars. Knowing this, the insured might decide to buy a policy with very low limits. If many insured people were to take this approach, the pooled insurance funds would be insufficient to provide compensation for all claims. To prevent such under-insurance, many companies include a co-insurance clause in each policy; such clauses apply to the building, but not to its contents.

A **co-insurance** clause states that the insured must carry policy limits to a level considered adequate by the company. An adequate level might be defined, for example, as 80 percent or 100 percent of the building's replacement value. If the owner fails to carry sufficient insurance, any claims made for damage to the building will be prorated. For instance, if the policy's limits are only half of what is considered adequate, the claim for damages from a small fire will be reduced by half. Personal Finance in Action Box 5.4, "Under-Insured," illustrates how a claim is prorated if the insured has not been carrying sufficient insurance. The purpose of the co-insurance clause is to encourage the purchase of adequate limits. Those who choose not to do so must share the risk with the insurance company—hence the term co-insurance. In the event that the house has a mortgage on it, the lender usually requires full insurance coverage and a certificate to that effect.

Personal Finance in Action 5.4

Under-Insured

The Wongs bought a policy on their house with limits of $80 000. A few years later they had a bad fire, which resulted in damage calculated at $40 000. At that time, their house was estimated to have a replacement value of $140 000. Their policy had a co-insurance clause requiring that they have coverage for 80 percent of the replacement value.

Policy limits . . . . = $80 000
Replacement value. . . . . = $140 000
Adequate coverage . . . . = 80% of replacement value

. . . . = 0.80 x $140 000
. . . . = $112 000
Claim . . . . = $40 000

The insurance settlement was calculated as follows:

$$\frac{\text{Policy limits they had}}{\text{Policy limits they should have had}} \times \text{Claim} = \text{Settlement}$$

$$\frac{\$80\ 000}{\$112\ 000} \times \$40\ 000 = \$28\ 571$$

Although their loss was estimated at $40 000, they received a settlement of only $28 571, because they were under-insured.

Property Insurance and Mortgages

Property insurance may include a mortgage clause; such a clause recognizes that there is a mortgage on the property and specifies the rights and obligations of both the lender and the insurer. The effect of this clause is to express an agreement between the mortgage lender and the insurer that is independent of the agreement between the insured and the insurer, even though this clause is attached to the insured's policy.

The lender has the right to share in any insurance settlement on the property as long as the insured still has an outstanding balance owing. Once the mortgage is completely repaid, the mortgage lender no longer has a claim. The mortgage clause entitles the lender to receive a loss payment regardless of any act or neglect of the home owner or borrower. For example, the insured could breach a condition of the contract with the insurance company, making the insured's claim for damages void; even so, the lender would still be entitled to compensation. Thus, an insured who commits arson cannot collect insurance on the burned property, but the lender can.

The mortgage lender is obliged to inform the insurer of any factors that may change the risk situation. If the risk should increase, and the insured does not pay the additional amount required, the lender is responsible for this amount. The lender's rights in an insurance settlement would take into account the amount still owing on the property at that time. Conversely, if the insured/borrower fails to make a premium payment, the insurer notifies the lender, who in turn ensures that the premium is paid.

The Inventory

When a loss is experienced, it is necessary to produce proof of what was lost. In some instances, enough evidence may remain for the adjusters to see what sorts of possessions the insured had; at other times, though, very little if anything may be left. It is therefore best to be prepared by keeping an up-to-date inventory of possessions in a secure place away from the house—for example, in a safety-deposit box. An inventory will not be of much help if it burns up along with the possessions it lists.

For those who feel that creating a written inventory is too tedious, a camera, video camera, tape recorder, or some combination of these devices can be used. With a video camera or a tape recorder, someone can go through the house describing all that is seen, including the contents of cupboards. These records should be supplemented with sales receipts, lists of serial numbers, and any other relevant information, especially for major items.

Preparing a detailed inventory and attaching current values to each item will also help you determine how much insurance coverage you require. Consideration should be given to the need for additional coverage for such items as jewellery, special collections, or antiques. Preparing this inventory will not be a one-time event; your list of possessions will change, and some of what is listed may increase in value over time. Regular valuation of possessions is therefore recommended. Generally, though, insurance companies estimate the value of a house's contents to equal 30 percent of the value of the house, excluding land.

Inflation

If the insurance company does not automatically adjust policy limits in relation to changes in general price levels, the policyholder may have to review his or her coverage regularly. Replacement costs tend to increase during periods of inflation, leaving policy limits too low to cover a total loss. For this reason, many home owners' policies now contain an automatic inflation clause, particularly for the coverage that applies to the building.

Personal Liability Insurance

The Risks

Anyone's financial security may be jeopardized if he or she should be found responsible either for damage to someone else's property or for an injury to another person. However, in order to succeed with such a liability claim, the person seeking damages must prove that the loss or damage was caused by negligence. Negligence is defined as either (i) failing to do what a reasonable and prudent person would do in a similar situation, or (ii) doing what a prudent person would not do in a similar situation. Everyone lives under the legal requirement not to cause harm to others or to their property and to take reasonable steps to preserve the safety of others. Besides being held liable for their own negligent acts, people with employees are also legally responsible for the employees' work-related actions. Each of us is responsible for any losses that may be caused by our animals and, to some extent, for our children's carelessness and, in some provinces, criminal acts. The examples in Personal Finance in Action Box 5.5, "Personal Liability Insurance Claims," illustrate some types of personal liability claims that have been successfully made.

Personal Finance in Action 5.5

Personal Liability Insurance Claims

1. Ten-year-old Rosa, whose broken leg was in a cast, was sitting in an ice cream parlour with her friends when an elderly woman who was walking down the aisle tripped and fell over Rosa's cast. The woman broke her leg and claimed $10 000 for damages. Rosa's father's insurance company investigated the circumstances; finding that the woman's companion, who had preceded her down the aisle, had maneuvered safely around the cast, the insurer decided that there was not a strong case for finding Rosa negligent. Rather than go through the expense of defending itself against a suit, however, the company paid the woman $2 000 *ex gratia*, without admitting any liability. The settlement was made under Rosa's father's personal liability insurance.

2. Larry's children broke the windshield of the car next door while playing baseball. Larry's insurance company paid to replace the windshield.

3. A child who was visiting the Duval family was attacked by their dog and required stitches and plastic surgery. The Duvals' insurer paid the extra medical bills.

4. At a campground, a young woman broke her neck by diving into water that was only 1.2 metres deep. She eventually recovered with only a 20 percent disability. Because she had earned various Red Cross swimming certificates, it was established that she was 25 percent at fault for not having investigated the water's depth before diving; the campground owner was held to be 75 percent at fault. His insurer paid the woman $50 000.

5. Mr. Nielsen, a self-employed handyperson, was called to a commercial building to check the plumbing. He proceeded to thaw frozen pipes with a blowtorch and succeeded in igniting the whole building, resulting in a total claim that exceeded $2 000 000. His liability coverage was only $1 000 000, leaving him responsible for the difference.

Coverage

Liability insurance (sometimes called legal liability) covers the risk of being found responsible for damage caused by your own negligence or by the negligence of your family members, employees, animals, and so on. Such policies are known as third-party insurance, because they involve not only the insured and the insurer, but also some third party who is seeking compensation for a loss. The need to establish who was at fault makes liability insurance claims more involved with legal matters than other kinds of insurance are.

Under liability insurance coverage, the insurer agrees to pay for damages attributed to the policyholder, including the costs of a court defence, interest, and reimbursement for some immediate expenses. Because the insurance company defends the insured in a liability suit, it is important that there be no admission of liability or offer to make payments, because such actions or statements could prejudice the defence. In some situations, there must be a court case to prove negligence; in others, an out-of-court settlement may be reached. Before the insurance company will settle a liability claim, however, it must be satisfied (i) that the insured was indeed legally liable in this instance and (ii) that the policy covers this particular liability.

Liability insurance may be bought separately or, more commonly, as a part of another policy, such as home or auto insurance. A home owners' or tenants' policy that includes comprehensive personal liability may cover damage to property or injury to people as a result of the use or maintenance of the insured property, the personal acts of the insured, the ownership of animals, the ownership of boats, and children's carelessness. It may cover the insured's legal liability for fire, explosion, and smoke in rented premises. In addition, some policies include a small amount of coverage for damage caused by the insured without reference to negligence. Subject to a list of exclusions, personal liability coverage applies wherever the insured is engaged in normal activities as a private individual; business pursuits are commonly excluded from personal liability policies. Personal liability insurance is an inexpensive way to protect yourself against risks that may have a low probability of occurring but can be extraordinarily costly if they do happen.

People who operate home-based businesses must be sure to examine any household policy that is in force to determine whether it covers "business use of the home." If, as may very well be the case, the policy does not cover the business, then additional liability coverage should be acquired to apply to any visitors to the home and any assets that are at the home and used in the business. Similar consideration should be given to the family automobile: if the car is used for business, you need to have business insurance for it. In most instances, the increase in coverage for a home-based business will have only a minimal impact on your premiums for both the home and auto insurance.

Automobile Insurance

This section is intended to provide an understanding of basic principles and concepts associated with auto insurance, not to supply the details of coverage available in each province or territory. There is too much variation to go into all the possible features here. The social and financial risks associated with automobiles—risks that are widely considered too significant to be left to people's personal discretion—are protected against, to some degree, by minimum insurance laws in each jurisdiction. Three major categories of risks will be identified, and the relevant types of insurance protection associated with each will be explained. With this basic knowledge, you will be prepared to investigate the specific arrangements for auto insurance that apply where you live.

Two important distinguishing features of the various provincial arrangements for automobile insurance relate to (i) who supplies the insurance coverage (a public body, private companies, or a combination of public and private resources), and (ii) how fault is handled. We will discuss fault after identifying the risks associated with car ownership and explaining the basic types of insurance protection.

Insurance Providers

In British Columbia, Manitoba, and Saskatchewan, basic automobile insurance coverage is provided by the provincial government, with extra insurance available from private insurers. Quebec splits auto insurance coverage between government and private companies, and the other provinces and territories leave the provision of auto insurance to private companies. Wherever auto insurance is publicly provided, there is just one price for coverage and one place to get it; where insurance is offered by private enterprise, there may be many competing suppliers, and prices may vary.

The Risks

As noted earlier, car ownership poses such a significant threat to society as well as to the financial security of individuals that governments have made carrying a minimum amount of public liability and accident benefits coverage mandatory. Three major categories of financial risks that a car owner assumes, along with the basic types of protection against those risks, are outlined below:

Risk	Insurance Coverage
1. Liability to others for injury, death, or property damage	Public liability (third-party)
2. Injury to or death of self or passengers	Accident benefits
3. Damage to insured's vehicle	Physical damage (e.g., collision, comprehensive)

Liability to Others

Anyone who owns or drives a car faces the risk that, because of negligence, he or she could be held financially responsible for injuries caused to others or for damage to their property. When assessing your own liability risk, reflect on the high probability of being involved in a car accident at some time, simply because of the large number of vehicles on our roads. Despite our best intentions, a little mistake can cause a serious accident. The consequences of severely injuring one or more persons could be financially disastrous; courts have been awarding increasingly large settlements—sometimes as high as several million dollars—in successful negligence suits. The rising costs of car repair, medical care, and income replacement for killed or injured persons have increased settlements to the point where some insurers are now advising their customers to have at least $1 000 000 in liability coverage. The legal requirement for liability insurance is $50 000 in Quebec and $200 000 elsewhere in Canada.

POLICY LIMITS As with most types of insurance, the liability policy limits determine the maximum that the insurer will pay on a claim. However, a court can order that an accident victim be awarded a settlement that exceeds the policy limits. The insured is then responsible for paying the difference, unless the policy includes specific coverage for such situations.

NEGLIGENCE Public liability insurance does not apply either to damage to your car or to injury to you; instead, it is limited to situations where others suffer loss due to your negligence. Because liability claims depend on proving negligence, it is important to give some thought to the legal concept of negligence. Sometimes distinctions are made between ordinary negligence and gross negligence. Ordinary negligence involves either failing to do what a reasonable person would do or doing what a reasonable person would not do. Gross negligence, on the other hand, constitutes reckless, wanton, and willful misconduct in which someone fails by a wide margin to exercise due care, thereby reflecting an indifference to the probable consequences of his or her actions.

A basic rule in our society is that each of us has the duty to take proper care no matter what we are doing, and to take responsibility for any injury caused by our carelessness. Motorists can be held negligent for not keeping a proper lookout or for failing to have their vehicles under complete control at all times. Icy roads or storms are not an excuse; drivers are expected to adjust their driving to suit the conditions. In some jurisdictions, a car owner is also held responsible for the consequences of any negligence on the part of anyone who is driving his or her car with consent. When a friend borrows a car and has an accident with it, liability or collision claims may be handled by the owner's insurance. It is wise, therefore, to know the terms of the policy when lending or borrowing a car. If the owner is liable, the claim will be submitted to his or her insurer, who in turn might raise future premiums if the friend is found to be at fault.

HIGHWAY TRAFFIC ACT Where a highway accident involves an infraction of a traffic regulation, the insurer may use that information when determining negligence. However, being found not guilty of a traffic offence does not necessarily mean absolution of negligence as far as the insurance company is concerned or in a civil court.

PROVING FAULT A serious problem for insurance companies is the difficulty of proving negligence in auto accidents, where events happen very fast and there may be no witnesses. If there is uncertainty about who was at fault, the issue can be decided in court; alternatively, the two insurers may reach an out-of-court agreement in which the responsibility for the accident is divided between them. For instance, a 60/40 split would mean that 60 percent of all the damages resulting from the accident would be assessed to one driver and 40 percent to the other; both would in turn refer these claims to their respective insurance companies as third-party liability claims. High legal costs, prolonged court processes, and the difficulty of determining fault have created so many problems that some measures have been devised to expedite certain types of claims by not requiring that fault be established. In a later section we will examine so-called no-fault auto insurance, but first we will consider the two other categories of risks faced by motorists.

Questions to Ask About Your Liability Coverage

1. **Who is covered by this part of the policy and in which situations?**

   There should be protection for you (the car owner), and for anyone who drives the vehicle with your consent, if the driver's negligence causes injury, death, or property damage to others. Find out whether you are covered when driving cars that you do not own or use regularly, such as temporary substitute cars or uninsured cars. Whose insurance would cover you if you

   continued

were found negligent in an accident while driving a friend's car? Also, does your liability coverage protect you if family or passengers sue you for negligence?

2. **How much liability coverage do you need?**

Inquire about the size of recent liability settlements to get an idea of the amount of coverage you need.

3. **What is not covered by your liability insurance?**

Liability insurance does not cover injuries sustained by you, and it does not cover your death. Additionally, it won't cover damage to your own car or to property that is being carried in or on it.

4. **What other things does your insurer agree to do?**

Besides paying claims that result from your negligence, the insurer may cover the costs of investigating the accident, negotiating a settlement, settling a claim, and defending you in court. Also, the insurer may reimburse you for out-of-pocket costs for immediate expenses associated with the accident, and pay court costs and interest on the insured portion of settlements charged to you. Such costs are paid even where they exceed your policy's liability limit.

5. **Does the insurer cover business use of your car?**

Even if you are an employee who is reimbursed for mileage, this condition should be explained to the insurance company to ensure that you are covered when travelling for work.

Personal Injury or Death

The second major risk is that the car's driver or passengers will be injured. Medical insurance or accident benefits coverage is designed to provide benefits in case of bodily injury to the occupants of a vehicle or to anyone struck by the vehicle. Note that the term **accident benefits** refers to insurance coverage for personal injury or death. Payment of claims for accident benefits occurs without reference to fault, and claims are made to the policyholder's insurance company. All provinces except Newfoundland require compulsory accident benefits coverage as part of auto insurance. There is some variation by province, but essentially, accident benefits cover (to defined limits), such things as medical and rehabilitation costs in excess of provincial health plan coverage, disability income, death payments, and funeral expenses. Find out what the accident benefits are where you live.

Damage to Your Vehicle

The least serious risk faced by car owners is that their vehicle may be stolen or damaged. Insurance coverage is generally not mandatory for this risk (with the exception of Saskatchewan and Manitoba). Physical damage coverage does not have a dollar limit, but is based on the car's actual cash value at the time of the loss. Because of the rapid rate at which cars depreciate, it is best to review physical damage insurance from time to time; the coverage may then be dropped when the premium becomes too high in relation to the size of the risk being covered. For instance, if an old car has an actual cash value of only a few hundred dollars, that would be the maximum settlement in the event of a total loss of the car. How much is it worth in annual premiums to protect this small amount of capital in the car?

Coverage for physical damage to a car is often subject to some deductible amount. The deductible is the amount of each claim that the insured pays; for instance, if you purchase collision coverage with a $500 deductible, you will take responsibility for paying the first $500 in damages. By sharing the risk with the company, you lower your insurance costs.

Most insurance companies will offer a choice of physical damage coverage, such as (i) all-perils, (ii) specified-perils, (iii) collision, and (iv) comprehensive. All-perils coverage is the broadest, encompassing everything that is included in the other three categories and possibly more. Such a policy should be examined to find out what is excluded, because everything else will be covered. By contrast, specified-perils coverage includes only named risks. The two other types of coverage, collision and comprehensive, are widely used.

COLLISION   Collision coverage applies when a car collides with another object. Usually a collision involves the car's striking or being struck by another car, but it also includes one-vehicle accidents (those in which the car strikes a tree, a guard rail, another object, or the surface of the ground).

If a collision is caused by the negligence of another person, the car owner's insurer will pay the damage claim if it is greater than the deductible; then, by the right of subrogation, will endeavour to collect from the person responsible for the accident. The insurer has agreed to indemnify the owner under the collision coverage whether or not the driver was at fault. If the insurer is successful in collecting from the third party, the policyholder will be reimbursed for the deductible amount.

COMPREHENSIVE   To be protected against perils other than collision that may happen to a car, you need comprehensive coverage. The distinction between collision and comprehensive coverage can seem confusing. If a loss is specifically excluded under your collision coverage, it may be included under your comprehensive coverage. Some of the perils included in comprehensive coverage are theft, vandalism, fire, lightning, windstorm, hail, and falling or flying objects. Such coverage is usually subject to a deductible amount, but the deductible may not apply in certain situations—for example, when the entire auto is stolen.

Mandatory Provincial Coverage

A summary of how auto insurance is provided and what coverage is mandated in various provinces and territories is presented in Table 5.1.

Factors Affecting Insurance Rates

Usually we pay more to insure our cars than we do to insure our houses—even though a house is much more valuable—because cars pose a greater risk to financial security. The number of accidents and the rising cost of settlements have caused car insurance premiums to escalate. Auto insurance premiums reflect not only the coverage requested, but often a number of other factors as well. These factors can be grouped according to (i) the personal characteristics of the insured, (ii) the type of car, (iii) the use that is made of the car, and (iv) the region where the insured lives.

PERSONAL CHARACTERISTICS   Traditionally, statistics linking accident frequency to car drivers' personal characteristics (for example, age, gender, and marital status) have been used in determining auto insurance premium rates. Although there has been discussion of eliminating these criteria, not all provinces have yet done so. Modifications to the risk-according-to-age method may be made in the case of young people who have had driver training, since they are expected to present less risk to the insurer. Likewise, a driver who has had no accidents for sev-

TABLE 5.1   AUTOMOBILE INSURANCE PROVIDERS AND MANDATED COVERAGE BY PROVINCE, CANADA, 2000

Province/ Territory	Public liability minimum	Mandatory accident benefits	Mandatory collision coverage
Public Insurer			
B.C.	$200 000	X	
Sask.	$200 000	X	X
Man.	$200 000	X	X
Public & Private Insurers			
Que.	$50 000*	X	
Private Insurers			
Alta.	$200 000	X	
Ont.	$200 000	X	
N.B.	$200 000	X	
N.S.	$200 000	X	
P.E.I.	$200 000	X	
Nfld.	$200 000		
Yukon	$200 000	X	
N.W.T.	$200 000	X	

* Quebec residents are compensated for injury without regard to fault. Liability limits are $50 000 for property damage claims within Quebec, and for personal injury and property damage claims outside the province.

SOURCE: Data from Web sites of provincial legislatures, Oct. and Nov., 2000.

eral years is considered a much better risk than one with a record of accidents or traffic violations. After an accident, insurers reassess the insured's risk classification and usually increase the premium if the insured is deemed to have been at fault.

TYPE OF CAR The type of car will have an obvious effect on the cost of collision and comprehensive coverage because of the variations in repair costs. In addition, insurers often increase liability and accident benefits premiums for powerful cars because of their potential for causing substantial damage.

USE OF CAR The number of kilometres driven in a year and the number of people who normally drive a particular car also affect the risk situation. The more a car is driven, the more it is exposed to risk. Whether or not the car is used for driving to work is also a consideration, as is the distance driven to work. A vehicle that is to be used for business purposes, as mentioned earlier, will also require a revised risk assessment. (For the insurance options that are typically available to people who rent a car, see Personal Finance in Action Box 5.6, "Damage to Rental Cars.")

REGION More accidents occur in certain regions of the country, usually either because of population density or because of adverse driving conditions due to weather.

PROVINCIAL DIFFERENCES Provinces differ in the factors used for determining premium rates. Quebec, for instance, has a set premium for a given class of vehicle, regardless of the risk presented by the individual. In Manitoba, rates are based on the make and model of the vehicle, its use, geographical location, and the insured's driving record, with no dis-

Damage to Rental Cars

Denise and her friend plan to rent a car for two weeks while they are on holiday. A friend has pointed out to them that they will be expected to sign a rental agreement stating they are responsible for returning the car in the same condition as it was when they took it, meaning that they bear the risk of any damage. When Denise made inquiries about supplementary insurance for rented cars, she found three alternatives. The first option was to buy the extra coverage offered by whichever rental company they choose. One firm offers a damage waiver for about $10 a day that protects customers against damage to the vehicle from just about any cause, including collision, vandalism, falling trees, etc., with no deductible. Another company offers a waiver that covers damage only if it is caused by a collision. Clearly, it is important to read a car rental contract before signing it.

Next, Denise checked her own car insurance policy to see whether it had a clause regarding rental cars. She found that she can buy additional coverage for the duration of her holiday for a small fee ($15 to $20), but that her own deductible amounts would apply if she submits a claim. Furthermore, if she decides to have her own insurance company protect her against damage to a rented car, she will be required by the rental company to provide written documentation of that coverage.

Denise's third option is to use her premium credit card to pay for the car rental. The card, which costs her over $100 a year for a variety of services, provides the same protection as that sold by the first rental company—broad damage coverage with no deductible.

Since circumstances vary with the individual, each person must make his or her own decision in such situations.

crimination based on age, sex, or marital status. British Columbia drivers pay premiums determined by the value of the vehicle, its use, geography, and their claims experience.

Insurance for High-Risk Drivers

There are some drivers whose accident records or other characteristics make them very high risks and thus unacceptable to insurers. However, if they are able to get a driver's licence, and if car insurance is mandatory where they live, there must be some way to insure them in order to protect society as well as to protect them. The insurance industry has solved this problem by creating an arrangement whereby insurers pool the high risks, which makes it possible to cover all

Comparison Shopping for Insurance

If you want to find the best rates for car or home insurance, you have several choices. You can get prices from a number of agents, an approach that can be time-consuming. Or you can consult an insurance broker, who, by definition, represents a number of companies.

However, a broker who subscribes to a computerized rating service will give you access to the broadest rate comparison. Both insurance brokers and insurance agents (who represent only one insurance company) are listed in your telephone book.

licensed drivers and registered owners. The high-risk driver applies for auto insurance the same way that anyone else does, but the policy is then transferred to the insurance pool—which in turn assigns these high-risk cases to companies in proportion to their share of auto insurance in each province. Thus, no single company receives more than its fair share of bad risks, and all those who want insurance can obtain it. Naturally, the premiums paid by high-risk drivers are very high. Claims made on these policies, however, are handled in the usual way by the insurer concerned.

Responsibility of the Insured

The agreement with the insurer requires the policyholder to give the company written notice containing details of an accident as soon as possible after the event occurs. At the scene of an accident, information about the other driver (including his or her name and address, the name and address of his or her insurance company, and the licence-plate number of his or her car) should be collected. Names and addresses of passengers and other witnesses may also prove useful later. At the time of the accident, the driver should not say anything to suggest assuming any obligation or accepting any responsibility for the accident, nor should the driver offer or make any payments to the victim or victims.

After the accident, the car owner must cooperate with the insurer by providing information as needed; forwarding all summonses, notices of suit, and other correspondence received; and appearing in court if required. The victim's claims are being made against the car owner, not against the insurer. If a victim named Smith brings a driver case to court concerning an accident involving a car that Jones was driving, the court case will be labelled *Smith v. Jones*, not *Smith v. Jones's Insurer*. The insurer is responsible only for helping to resolve the problem, not for taking it over entirely.

No-Fault Automobile Insurance

The Fault System

Under the law of torts, which has descended to us from the English common-law system, each person has a basic duty to take care not to harm other people or damage other people's property, either intentionally or unintentionally. When applied to car accidents, this system often creates problems, because in many instances it is difficult to clearly establish fault. Besides driving errors, accidents may be caused by adverse road or weather conditions, or by cars or pedestrians who are not involved in the crash. Naturally, the more extensive the injuries and damage, the greater the need to establish fault in order to receive compensation, but such cases often take years to settle because of long delays in getting court hearings. Some accident victims are never compensated, because no one can be shown to have been negligent. Still, fault is frequently assigned by the police through the assessment of moving violations and is used to reassess insurance premiums.

No-Fault Insurance

Claims under accident benefits and claims for physical damage to one's own car have usually been paid without regard to fault. Much of the controversy that has occasionally surrounded the introduction of no-fault insurance has been in relation to third-party liability claims. In a pure no-fault system, proof of fault would not be required in order to settle claims for injuries and damages resulting from car accidents. Instead, each person would claim damages from his or her own insurer, thus saving litigation costs and considerable time, while also ensuring that all claims are paid. However, this simple idea raises some important questions. Should the insurance premium be raised because the policyholder was paid a large settlement for damages caused by another? Should a consistently bad driver continue driving without penalty? Should those who have been seriously injured be deprived of the right to sue for damages?

Many modifications of the basic no-fault approach have been tried in a number of provinces and states, with the result that we have now reached a state of terminological confusion. The term no-fault has been applied to so many versions of the basic idea that it is no longer meaningful. For example, a partial no-fault scheme may pay claims without regard to fault up to some maximum amount, but permit claimants to sue for further damages in court.

Examples of No-Fault Insurance

Quebec and Manitoba have no-fault insurance programs that have eliminated claims entirely, substituting tribunals and legal rights to compensation by the injured party. In Ontario, a partial no-fault insurance system permits injured parties to sue in situations involving serious injury or death. By instituting such plans, all three provinces are attempting to speed the payment of claims for minor injuries and to prevent all but the most serious cases from involving the time and expense of a court case. These programs are constantly evolving and operate differently in each province as they are revised by the different governments. It is vital for residents of any province that permits lawsuits to ensure that they carry adequate liability insurance, preferably above the prescribed minimum coverage.

Summary

This chapter introduced the insurance principle, and explained its application to the risks associated with owning property. The importance of identifying risk exposure before selecting insurance coverage has been emphasized. The concepts of indemnity, depreciation, subrogation, and co-insurance were illustrated in relation to property insurance. Car owners face a number of risks, the most significant of which involves their liability to others. It cannot be emphasized too strongly that adequate liability coverage is most essential for car owners. The car's age and condition has little to do with the risk of causing damage or injury. Physical damage to a car presents a smaller risk; by accepting some of this risk personally (through arranging for a larger deductible amount), an insured person can reduce the cost of his or her insurance.

Although Canadian legislators and policymakers have often discussed the merits of a truly no-fault auto insurance system, problems have prevented the implementation of such a scheme. However, modified versions of no-fault plans are now used in several provinces. Modest coverage for personal injuries, where proof of fault is not required for compensation, remains mandatory in most provinces.

Key Terms

accident benefits (p. 108)

actual cash value (p. 99)

actuary (p. 95)

adjuster (p. 98)

agent (p. 97)

all-risks coverage (p. 101)

broker (p. 97)

co-insurance (p. 102)

deductible clause (p. 100)

depreciation (p. 99)

endorsement (rider) (p. 98)

indemnification (p. 98)

insurable interest (p. 96)   pooling risk (p. 95)
insurable risk (p. 96)   premium (p. 96)
insured (p. 97)   pure cost of insurance (p. 96)
insurer (p. 97)   replacement value (p. 99)
liability insurance (third-party   salvage value (p. 100)
    insurance) (p. 105)   scheduled property rider
loading charge (p. 96)   (valued contract endorse-
named-peril coverage (p. 101)   ment) (p. 101)
policy (p. 97)   short rate (p. 98)
policy limits (p. 100)   subrogation (p. 100)

Problems

1. To answer this question, you need to refer to Appendix 5A.

   (a) Look for the answers to the questions posed in the box "How to Read a Policy."

   (b) Is there any automatic inflation adjustment of the policy limits? If so, does it apply to both the house and the contents?

   (c) How much coverage is there for personal property taken away from home?

   (d) Does the policy include coverage for personal liability? If so, what is the liability limit?

   (e) If the owner of this policy were to lose all of his or her personal possessions in a fire, would the maximum settlement represent the actual cash value of the loss or the policy limits?

   (f) Would this policy cover a theft that occurred while the family was away?

   (g) Are there any riders or endorsements attached to the policy?

   (h) Is this an all-risks policy or a named-perils policy?

   (i) Is there a co-insurance clause? If so, what is the policyholder's responsibility?

   (j) Is there coverage for property away from home?

2. The Bates returned home to find their townhouse under the fire department's careful watch for a fire recently extinguished. A candle left burning while they went for a walk had probably started the fire. The townhouse was seriously damaged with the walls and ceilings smoke damaged and extensive water damage throughout. The land manage-ment company was claiming damages to the property as well as the neighbours on either side. The contents portion of their insurance policy provides for replacement coverage with $500 000 personal liability coverage.

   (a) Who pays for what in this case?

   (b) Would the Bates' receive a settlement large enough to replace their damaged furniture? How would the insurance company account for the depreciation of the furniture and the inflation in the costs of the furniture and appliances?

   (c) Would the insurance company pay for the lost computer and its contents for the home business?

3. The MacDonalds have bought their first house for $160 000. The building itself is estimated to have a replacement cost of $120 000.

    (a) How much insurance do they require?

    (b) Who else will likely be listed on the policy?

    (c) The co-insurance clause of their insurance policy requires that they cover 80 percent of the replacement value of the property. During a windstorm they lost their roof, a number of pieces of outdoor furniture, and the garden shed. They had insured for $100 000, as that was the amount of their mortgage. Calculate the amount of the settlement, if the damages totalled $12 000 in value.

4. (a) What are the pros and cons of buying a replacement value insurance policy on your household effects?

    (b) How does replacement value insurance alter the basic principle of indemnification?

    (c) What should you do on a regular basis to maintain adequate coverage?

5. Obtain an automobile insurance policy, and examine it to find answers to the following questions:

    (a) If you or your passengers should be injured in an accident and as a result become unable to work, would there be any income replacement payments? How much? For how long?

    (b) If one of your passengers were to be killed, would there be any compensation for funeral costs?

    (c) If your injuries included some that were not covered by the provincial health insurance, would the accident benefits portion of your car insurance policy provide some help? Is there any limit on the amount?

    (d) Do you have collision coverage? What is the deductible amount?

    (e) Is there a deductible amount on the comprehensive coverage?

    (f) Are there any exclusions to the coverage for damage to the insured's automobile?

    (g) Is there a no fault rider?

    (h) If so, what can you still sue for?

6. When Dave Hill's father was buying a new car, he found that his old one was valued at only $1 900 as a trade-in. He offered it to 19-year-old Dave, on the condition that Dave would handle all the operating costs and insure it. Dave was delighted—he would have his own car at last. The insurance agent was happy to help him arrange suitable coverage for the car, but Dave was dismayed to find that the premium would be higher than the value of the car. To economize, he decided that he could cut down on some parts of the insurance. He told the agent that he would take collision coverage but drop the third-party liability, because the car was getting old; however, he definitely wanted coverage for theft and fire.

    Consider each of the following statements in relation to Dave's case, and decide whether you AGREE or DISAGREE.

    (a) If Dave doesn't buy public liability coverage, he will not be able to register his car.

    (b) If Dave buys an automobile insurance policy, he is required to have at least $100 000 in public liability coverage.

(c) In Dave's case, it is probably a good idea for him to skip the public liability coverage, because it wouldn't be a great disaster if the old car were wrecked.

(d) If Dave takes out a policy with collision coverage that has a $500 deductible and then later runs into a bridge, completely demolishing his car, he will have to pay the first $500 of damages, but his insurance company will pay him $1400 to buy another car.

(e) Dave is wise to insist on coverage for fire and theft even if he must do without some other coverage in order to afford it.

(f) Because of the province's mandatory no-fault accident benefits insurance coverage, Dave would not be held accountable if he injured another person in an auto accident.

7. Analyze the following complaints from car owners regarding insurance claims, and note how you would explain the situation to each.

(a) Sam writes, "under conditions of icy roads and high winds, our car was blown off the road. When I presented a claim for damage to my car, I was told that my policy did not include collision coverage. On reading the policy, I find that we are covered for windstorm damage. The company still insists that it has no responsibility for paying my car repairs."

(b) The summer before last, Bob was in a head-on collision with a car that suddenly appeared on his side of the road. Because he had no collision coverage, he was advised to settle on a 50/50 basis, since it would cost too much to prove that he was in the right. His lawyer will not take the case: she says that it will cost more to fight the case than the car is worth. Bob wonders what to do.

(c) Until recently, Sophie considered her car insurance quite adequate: she has collision, comprehensive, and public liability coverage. Then an unknown driver damaged her car when it was parked legally on the street. She assumed that such damage would be covered under the comprehensive clause (which had only a $50 deductible), because she believed that collision would, by definition, mean that her car had collided with another vehicle or with some object. The insurer, however, says that since her car was hit by another car, rather than by, for example, a stone, the accident is indeed classified as a collision. To Sophie, this seems impossible: she was not even in the car, and the car was not moving. She thinks that collision coverage should pay for damage caused by her own carelessness, not someone else's. She says that comprehensive ought to cover this event, since it covers vandalism. But the insurer wants her to pay for the damage in full, because it amounted to less than the deductible amount that applies to her collision coverage. Is this right?

8. What is the extent of no-fault auto insurance coverage where you live? To what extent may a victim or his or her family sue for loss or damages?

9. One Man Dead, Another Paralyzed in Two-Car Crash

The foggy wet weather and poor driving conditions on Saturday evening accounted for a head-on collision involving cars driven by Richard Chaney and Russell Talcott. Police reports indicate that Chaney's car went out of control in the northbound lane and crossed the slippery pavement into the southbound lane, where it collided with the vehicle driven by Talcott. On arrival at the General Hospital, Russell Talcott was pronounced dead. He is survived by his wife, Mary, and their young son, Jason. At present Richard Chaney is reported to be in critical condition as a result of a serious spinal injury. No charges were laid in this case.

Assume the following information about the insurance and other security plans of these men:

	Chaney	Talcott
Health insurance	covered	covered
Canada Pension	contributor	contributor
Group life insurance	$70 000	$35 000
Personal life insurance	$75 000	$150 000
Disability insurance	none	pays 1/2 salary
Auto insurance:		
Collision insurance	none	$250 deductible
Comprehensive	none	$50 deductible
Accident benefits	yes	yes
Public liability	$500 000	$1 000 000

(a) In the chart below, identify by check marks the areas of probable financial need for each man's family as a result of this accident.

	Chaney	Talcott
Personal injury		
Funeral expenses		
Property damage		
Liability to others		
Loss of income		
Other		

(b) Using the chart below, note the resources that these families could call on and what each resource would cover.

	Chaney	Talcott
Health insurance		
Canada/Quebec Pension		
Group insurance		
Personal life insurance		
Disability insurance		
Auto insurance:		
Collision		
Comprehensive		
Public liability		

Note: When answering the following questions, assume that the accident happened in your province.

(c) Will Chaney's insurer immediately authorize repairs to his car, and look after the bill? Would you expect Talcott's company to do this? Explain.

(d) Both of these drivers had third-party liability. Explain how claims against this portion of their coverage would proceed. Would the case necessarily have to go to court? What would the claims be for?

(e) If the case does go to court and if Chaney is declared to be more than 50 percent responsible for the accident, will Chaney receive any compensation for his disability from Talcott's insurer?

(f) From the information provided, which of the two families seems to be in the worst financial position as a result of this accident? Why?

(g) Does the fact that the police did not press charges under the province's *Highway Traffic Act* mean that the insurer will not make any settlement under the liability coverage?

10. Explore the Insurance Bureau of Canada Web site at **www.ibc.ca** and determine the process recommended for an accident claim and report.

(a) How should you act when asked questions at the scene of an accident?

(b) What rights do pedestrians have if struck by a car?

(c) Under whose policy are the accident benefits paid if the pedestrian also is an insured driver?

References

BOOKS AND ARTICLES

DELOITTE and TOUCHE. *Canadian Guide to Personal Financial Management*. Toronto: Prentice Hall Canada, annual. A team of accountants provides guidance on a broad range of topics, including planning finances, estimating insurance needs, managing risk, and determining investment needs. Instructions and the necessary forms for making plans are also included.

FLEMING, JAMES. *Merchants of Fear, An Investigation of Canada's Insurance Industry*. Toronto: Penguin, 1986. An investigative report on the life insurance and general insurance industries.

HUEBNER, S.S., KENNETH BLACK JR., and BERNARD WEBB. *Property and Liability Insurance*. Scarborough: Prentice Hall Canada, 1996. An appropriate reference for students of the industry and of the changes facing consumers.

INSURANCE BUREAU OF CANADA. *Facts*. Toronto: Insurance Bureau of Canada, annual. An annual summary of industry statistics.

PRASKEY, SALLY, and HELENA MONCRIEFF. *The Insurance Book: What Canadians Really Need to Know Before Buying Insurance*: Toronto: Pearson Education Canada Inc., 2000. A straightforward book with information and answers to various questions for Canadians at all stages of their lives. The focus is on making informed decisions on insurance.

TIERNEY, FRANCIS, and PAUL BRAITHWAITE. *A Guide to Effective Insurance*. Toronto: Butterworths, 1992. A Canadian reference to help readers in the selection of insurance and to help them understand the complexity of the industry and language. Helps readers focus on what it is they want and need and how they can make an informed purchase.

Personal Finance on the Web

Insurance Bureau of Canada

www.ibc.ca An overview of the industry with extensive coverage of the legal aspects of property and casualty insurance. Many links are provided to the member companies. Available in both English and French but does not cover life and health insurance.

Insurance Canada

www.insurance-canada.ca A consumer-focused site with information regarding the needs and intricacies of the industry. Co-sponsored by The Consumers Council of Canada and the Consumers Association of Canada.

Appendix 5A

Excerpt from a Home Insurance Policy

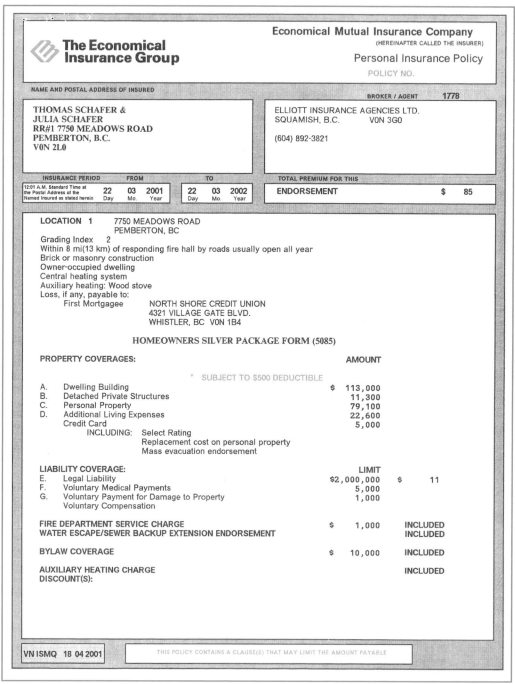

continued

5085 (05/2001) BC

PRINCIPAL AND SEASONAL RESIDENCE

HOMEOWNERS
SILVER PACKAGE FORM

AGREEMENT

We provide the insurance described in this policy in return for payment of the premium as stated on the Policy Declaration Page and subject to the terms and conditions set out. This form consists of two sections.

SECTION I describes the insurance for your property.

SECTION II describes the insurance for your legal liability to others because of bodily injury and property damage, and provides for certain voluntary payments.

SECTION I -- PROPERTY COVERAGES
DEFINITIONS (Applicable to Section I)

"You" or **"Your"** refers to the Insured.

"Insured" means the person(s) named as Insured on the Coverage Summary page and, while living in the same household:

> his or her spouse
>
> the relatives of either, and
>
> any person under 21 in their care

Spouse includes either of two persons who are living together in a conjugal relationship outside marriage and have so lived together continuously for a period of 3 years or, if they are the natural or adoptive parents of a child, for a period of 1 year.

In addition, a student who is enrolled in and actually attends a school, college or university and who is dependent on the Named Insured or his or her spouse for support and maintenance is also insured even if temporarily residing away from the principal residence stated on the Coverage Summary page.

Only the person(s) named on the Coverage Summary page may take legal action against us.

"We" or **"Us"** means the Company or Insurer providing this insurance.

"Dwelling" means the building described on the Coverage Summary page, wholly or partially occupied by you as a private residence.

"Premises" -- means the land contained within the lot lines on which the dwelling is situated.

"Residence Employee" means a person employed by you to perform duties in connection with the maintenance or use of the insured premises. This includes persons who perform household or domestic services or duties of a similar nature for you. This does not include persons while performing duties in connection with your business.

"Occupancy" means the presence of the Insured or a representative in the described seasonal dwelling. A seasonal dwelling will be considered occupied if an interior and exterior inspection is carried out by a competent adult at least once every 60 days.

"Unoccupied" means the dwelling is uninhabited.

Seasonal Dwelling only - "unoccupied" means the absence of the Insured or a representative in the described furnished seasonal dwelling. A seasonal dwelling will not be considered unoccupied if an interior and exterior inspection is carried out by a competent adult at least once every 60 days.

"Vacant" refers to the circumstance where, regardless of the presence of furnishings: all occupants have moved out with no intention of returning and no new occupant has taken up residence; or in the case of a newly constructed house, no occupant has yet taken up residence.

"Ground water" means water in the soil beneath the surface of the ground including but not limited to water in wells and in underground streams, and in percolating waters.

"Surface waters" means, but it is not limited to, water on the surface of the ground where water does not usually accumulate in ordinary watercourses, lakes or ponds.

"Domestic appliance" means a device or apparatus for personal use on the premises for containing, heating, chilling or dispensing water.

Coverages

The amounts of insurance are shown on the Policy Declaration Page. These include the cost of removing debris of the insured property, or the debris that damaged the property, as a result of an Insured Peril.

If you must remove insured property from your premises to protect it from loss or damage, it is insured by this form for 30 days or until your policy term ends - whichever occurs first. The amount of insurance will be divided in the proportions that the value of the property removed bears to the value of all property at the time of loss.

COVERAGE A -- Dwelling Building

We insure:

1. The dwelling and attached structures.
2. Permanently installed outdoor equipment on the premises.
3. Outdoor swimming pool and attached equipment on the premises.
4. Materials and supplies located on or adjacent to the premises intended for use in construction, alteration or repair of your dwelling or private structures on the premises. The peril of theft applies only when dwelling is occupied or completed and ready to be occupied.

continued

5085 (05/2001) BC

Tear Out

If any walls, ceilings or other parts of insured buildings or structures must be torn apart before water damage from a plumbing, heating, air conditioning or sprinkler system or domestic appliance can be repaired we will pay the cost of such repairs. The cost of tearing out and replacing property to repair damage related to outdoor swimming pools or public watermains is not insured.

Building Fixtures and Fittings

You may apply up to 10% of the amount of insurance on your dwelling to insure building fixtures and fittings temporarily removed from the premises for repair or seasonal storage.

Outdoor Trees, Lawns, Shrubs and Plants

You may apply up to 5% in all of the amount of insurance on your dwelling to trees, lawns, plants and shrubs on your premises. We will not pay more than $500 for any one tree, plant or shrub including debris removal expenses. We will also reimburse you for up to $500 in total for removal of trees due to a peril not covered.

We insure these items against loss caused by fire, lightning, explosion, theft, impact by aircraft or land vehicle, riot, vandalism and malicious acts, as described under Insured Perils.

We do not insure lawns or items grown for commercial purposes.

COVERAGE B -- Detached Private Structures

We insure structures or buildings separated from the dwelling by a clear space, on your premises but not insured under Coveage A. If they are connected to the dwelling by a fence, utility line or similar connection only, they are considered to be detached structures.

COVERAGE C -- Personal Property

1. We insure the contents of your dwelling and other personal property you own, wear or use, while on your premises, which is usual to the ownership or maintenance of a dwelling.

    If you wish, we will include uninsured personal property of others while it is on that portion of your premises which you occupy but we do not insure property of roomers or boarders who are not related to you.

    We do not insure loss or damage to motorized vehicles, trailers and aircraft or their equipment (except watercraft, wheelchairs, lawn mowers, gardening equipment or snow blowers). Equipment includes audio, visual, recording or transmitting equipment powered by the electical system of a motor vehicle or aircraft.

2. We insure your personal property while it is temporarily removed from your premises anywhere in the world. We also insure newly acquired personal property in situations where there has not been an opportunity to take such property to your premises. If you wish, we will include personal property belonging to others while it is in your possession or belonging to a residence employee travelling for you.

    The coverage is extended to cover personal property normally kept in a land recreation vehicle you own.

    This coverage is extended to insure the personal property of students insured by this policy while temporarily residing away from home and in full time attendance at school.

    Personal property kept at any other location you own, rent, lease or occupy, except while you are temporarily living there, is not insured. Personal property stored in a warehouse is only insured for 30 days unless loss or damage is caused by theft. To extend cover in storage for a further period we must be notified in writing and endorse your policy as required.

3. We insure your personal property damaged by change of temperature resulting from physical damage to your dwelling or equipment by an Insured Peril. This only applies to personal property kept in the dwelling.

4. If the insurance is governed by the law of Quebec, the words "Personal Property" shall, subject to the coverages, exclusions and conditions of this insurance, mean corporeal, moveable property other than the right to property.

5. We insure your personal property that is being moved to another location within Canada which is to be occupied by you as your principal dwelling, the limit insurance for personal property will be divided between the premises, in transit, and at the new location on the basis of the percentage of the total value of the property at your premises, in transit and at the new location. This coverage applies only for a period of 30 days from the date you commenced removal.

6. We insure your personal property up to $500 in all, normally kept at your place of business.

7. We agree to insure the personal property of a named insured or a parent who is dependent on the named insured or his or her spouse for support and maintenance if residing in a nursing home for up to a total of $10,000.

Special Limits of Insurance

We insure:

(1) Books, tools and instruments pertaining to a business, profession or occupation for an amount up to $2,000 in all, but only while on your premises. Other business property, including samples and goods held for sale, is not insured;
(2) Securities up to $2,000 in all;
(3) Money, bank notes, bullion, gold other than goldware, silver other than silverware, platinum, coins, medals and medallions up to $300 in all;
(4) Watercraft, their furnishings, equipment, accessories and motors up to $1,000 in all;
(5) Computer software up to $1,000 in all. We do not insure the cost of gathering or assembling information or data;
(6) Garden type tractors including attachments and accessories up to $5,000 in all.

The following special limits of insurance apply if the items described below are stolen:

(7) Jewellery, watches, gems, fur garments and garments trimmed with fur up to $3,000 in all;
(8) Numismatic property (coin collections) up to $300 in all;
(9) Manuscripts, stamps and philatelic property (such as stamp collections) up to $1,000 in all;
(10) Silverware, silver-plated ware, goldware, gold- plated ware and pewterware up to $10,000 in all;

continued

5085 (05/2001) BC

We will pay for the cost of supplying or renewing artificial limbs or braces, made necessary by the accident, for up to 52 weeks after the accident, subject to a maximum of $5,000.

We do not insure you for costs recoverable from other insurance plans.

All other items and conditions of the policy to which this rider applies remain unchanged.

SPECIAL LIMITATIONS

Watercraft -- Watercraft You Own: You are insured against claims arising out of your ownership, use or operation of watercraft equipped with an outboard motor or motors of not more than 18kW (24 HP) in total when used with or on a single watercraft. You are also insured if your watercraft has an inboard or an inboard-outboard motor of not more than 38kW (50 HP) or for any other type of watercraft not more than 8 metres (26 feet) in length. We do not insure damage to the watercraft itself.

If you own any motors or watercraft larger than those stated above, you are insured only if they are shown on the Policy. If they are acquired after the effective date of the policy, you will be insured automatically for a period of thirty days only from the date of their acquisition.

Watercraft You Do Not Own. You are insured against claims arising out of of your use or operation of watercraft which you do not own, provided:

1. the watercraft is being used or operated with the owner's consent;
2. the watercraft is not owned by anyone included in the definition of "you" or "your" in Section II of this form.

You are not insured for damage to the watercraft itself.

Vehicles You Own. You are insured against claims arising out of your ownership, use or operation of the following including their trailers or attachments:

1. self-propelled lawn mowers, snow blowers, garden-type tractors, of not more than 19kW (25 H.P.), used or operated mainly on your property, provided they are not used for compensation or hire;
2. motorized golf carts while in use on a golf course;
3. motorized wheelchairs, including motorized scooters having more than two wheels and specifically designed for the carriage of a person who has a physical disability.

Vehicles You Do Not Own. You are insured against claims arising out of your use or operation of any self-propelled land vehicle, amphibious vehicle or air cushion vehicle including their trailers, which you do not own, provided that:

1. the vehicle is not licensed and is designed primarily for use off public roads;
2. you are not using it for business or organized racing;
3. the vehicle is being used or operated with the owner's consent;
4. the vehicle is not owned by anyone included in the definition of "you" or "your" in Section II of this form.

You are not insured for damage to the vehicle itself

Trailers: You are insured against claims arising out of your ownership, use or operation of any trailer or its equipment used for private pleasure purposes, providing that such trailer is not being towed by, attached to or carried on a motorized vehicle.

Business and Business Property. You are insured against claims arising out of:

1. your work for someone else as a sales representative, collector, messenger or clerk provided that the claim does not involve injury to a fellow employee;
2. your work as a teacher, provided the claim does not involve physical disciplinary action to a student or injury to a fellow employee;
3. the occasional rental of your residence to others; rental to others of a one or two-family dwelling usually occupied in part by you as a residence, provided no family unit includes more than 2 roomers or boarders;
4. the rental of space in your residence to others for incidental office, school or studio occupancy;
5. the rental to others, or holding for rent, of not more than 3 car spaces or stalls in garages or stables;
6. activities during the course of your trade, profession or occupation which are ordinarily considered to be non-business pursuits;
7. the temporary or part time business pursuits of an insured person under the age of 21 years.

Claims arising from the following business pursuits are insured only if the properties or operations are declared on the Policy Declaration page:

1. the rental of residential buildings containing not more than 6 dwelling units;
2. the use of part of your residence by you for incidental office, school, or studio occupancy.

LOSS OR DAMAGE NOT INSURED

You are not insured for claims arising from:

(1) war, invasion, act of a foreign enemy, declared or undeclared hostilities, civil war, rebellion, revolution, insurrection or military power;
(2) (a) loss or damage caused directly or indirectly by any nuclear incident as defined in the Nuclear Liability Act or any other nuclear liability act, law or statute, or any law amendatory thereof or nuclear explosion, except for ensuing loss or damage which results directly from fire, lightning or explosion of natural, coal or manufactured gas;
    (b) loss or damage caused directly or indirectly by contamination by radioactive material.
(3) your business or any business use of your premises except as specified in this policy;
(4) the rendering or failure to render any professional service;
(5) bodily injury or property damage caused by any intentional or criminal act or failure to act by:
    (a) any person insured by this policy; or
    (b) any other person at the direction of any person insured by this policy;
(6) the ownership, use or operation of any aircraft or premises used as an airport or landing strip, and all necessary or incidental operations;
(7) the ownership, use or operation of any motorized vehicle, trailer or watercraft except those for which coverage is provided in this form;
(8) the transmission of communicable disease by any person insured by this policy.
(9) (a) sexual, physical, psychological or emotional abuse, molestation or harassment, including corporal punishment by, at the direction of, or with the knowledge of any person insured by this policy; or
    (b) failure of any person insured by this policy to take steps to prevent sexual, physical, psychological or emotional abuse, molestation or harassment or corporal punishment;

continued

5085 (05/2001) BC

(11) Sound and electronic communication equipment, including radios, tape players/decks, compact disc players, telephones, cellular telephones, CB radios, ham radios, televisions, facsimile machines, computers and items of a similar nature including their tapes, discs and compact discs, up to $500 in all if stolen from an automobile;
(12) Bicycles, including their parts, equipment and accessories, for not more than $500 any one bicycle;
(13) Collectible cards, sports memorabilia and comic collectibles up to $250 any one item with a maximum of $2,000 in all.

Specified Perils

Subject to the exclusions and conditions in this policy, Specified Perils means:

1. fire;
2. lightning;
3. explosion;
4. smoke due to a sudden, unusual and faulty operation of any heating or cooking unit in or on the premises;
5. falling object which strikes the exterior of the building;
6. impact by aircraft or land vehicle;
7. riot;
8. vandalism or malicious acts, not including loss or damage caused by theft or attempted theft;
9. freezing of any part of a plumbing, heating, sprinkler or air conditioning system or domestic appliance;
10. rupture of a heating, plumbing, sprinkler or air conditioning system or escape of water from such a system, or from a swimming pool or equipment attached, or from a public watermain; or damage caused by melting of ice and snow and resulting interior water damage from the roof;
11. windstorm or hail;
12. transportation meaning loss or damage caused by collision, upset, overturn, derailment, stranding or sinking of any automobile or attached trailer in which the insured property is being carried. This would also apply to any conveyance of a common carrier.

COVERAGE D -- Additional Living Expenses The amount of insurance for Coverage D is the total amount payable for any one or a combination of the following coverages. The periods of time stated below are not limited by the expiration of the policy.

1. **Additional Living Expense**: If an Insured Peril makes your dwelling unfit for occupancy, or you have to move out while repairs are being made, we insure any necessary increase in living expenses, including moving expenses incurred by you, so that your household can maintain its normal standard of living. Payment shall be for the reasonable time required to repair or rebuild your dwelling or, if you permanently relocate, the reasonable time required for your household to settle elsewhere.

2. **Fair Rental Value**: If an Insured Peril makes that part of the dwelling or detached private structures rented to others or held for rental by you unfit for occupancy, we insure its Fair Rental Value. Payment shall be for the reasonable time required to repair or replace that part of the dwelling or detached private structure rented or held for rental. Fair Rental Value shall not include any expense that does not continue while that part of the dwelling or detached private structure rented or held for rental is unfit for occupancy.

If a civil authority prohibits access to your dwelling as a direct result of damage to neighbouring premises by an Insured Peril under this form, we insure any resulting Additional Living Expense and Fair Rental Value loss for a period not exceeding two weeks.

We do not insure the cancellation of a lease or agreement.

FIRE DEPARTMENT SERVICE CHARGE

We will pay up to $1,000 for your liability assumed by contract or agreement for fire department changes incurred when the fire department is called to save or protect your property from an Insured Peril.

Any deductible specified in the policy does not apply to these charges.

LOCK REPLACEMENT

We will pay up to $500 to replace or re-key, at our option, the locks on your principal residence if the keys are stolen during a burglary, robbery or in conjunction with theft of other property.

Any deductible specified in the policy does not apply to this coverage.

REWARD COVERAGE

We will pay up to $500 to any individual or organization for information leading to the arrest and conviction of any person(s) who robs, steals, or burglarizes any covered personal property from any insured. We will also pay $1,000 for information which leads to a conviction for arson in connection with a fire loss to property insured by this form. This coverage may increase the amount otherwise applicable, however, the $500 or $1,000 limit will not be increased regardless of the number of persons providing information. This coverage is not subject to a deductible.

INFLATION PROTECTION

During the term of this policy, we will automatically increase the limit of insurance on your Dwelling Building (Coverage A) by an amount which is solely attributable to the inflation increase since the inception date of this policy or the latest renewal or anniversary date.

We will also automatically increase the limits of insurance on your Detached Private Structures (Coverage B), Personal Property (Coverage C) and Additional Living Expenses (Coverage D) by the same proportion.

On renewal date, we will automatically increase the limits of insurance shown on the Policy Declaration Page in the same way and adjust the premium.

If, at your request, we change the limit of insurance on your Dwelling Building (Coverage A) shown on the Policy Declaration Page, we will apply this Inflation Protection on the changed limits of insurance from the date the change is made.

continued

5109 (08/90)

RENT AND RENTAL VALUE ENDORSEMENT

If this coverage is shown on the Policy Declaration Page, we insure Rent and Rental Value of the dwelling building indicated in the Schedule of Additional Coverages and/or Endorsements in accordance with the terms and conditions of this endorsement.

We will not pay more than the amount shown in the Policy Declaration Page for this coverage at each location indicated.

COVERAGES

We insure the reduction in "gross rent and rental value" which is a direct result of the dwelling building being unfit for occupancy as a result of damage caused by an Insured Peril. Payment shall be for the reasonable time required to repair or replace the dwelling building but not exceeding twelve (12) months from the date of damage. The insurance shall not include any expense that does not continue while the dwelling building held for rental is unfit for occupancy.

"Gross Rent and Rental Value" is defined as:

(1)   the actual total annual gross rent or rental value of the occupied portion(s) of the dwelling building.
(2)   the estimated annual rental value of the unoccupied portion(s) of the dwelling building; and
(3)   a fair rental value of any portion of the dwelling building occupied by the Insured.

If a civil authority prohibits access to the dwelling building as a direct result of damage to neighboring premises by an Insured Peril, we insure any resulting Rent and Rental Value loss for a period not exceeding two weeks.

Co-Insurance Clause: In return for the rate of premium charged for this endorsement, you are required to maintain insurance similar in form and wording to a limit of at least 100% of the annual "gross rent and rental value" (as defined) of the building(s) to which this insurance applies. Failing this, you will only be entitled to recover the portion of any loss that the amount of insurance in force bears to the amount of insurance required by this clause.

This clause applies separately to each location where a separate amount of insurance is shown in the Policy Declaration Page.

LOSS OR DAMAGE NOT INSURED

We do not insure:

(1)   loss or damage as stated in the "Loss or Damage Not Insured" Clause under Section 1 of the Homeowners Form or the "Loss or Damage Not Insured" Clause under the Residential Building and/or Contents Rider (AB).
(2)   any increase of loss due to interference at the location(s) specified in the Policy Declaration Page by strikers or other persons with rebuilding, repairing or replacing the property.
(3)   loss due to the suspension, lapse or cancellation of any lease or license or contract which may affect your gross rent and rental value after the period following any loss during which indemnity is payable.

BASIS OF CLAIM PAYMENT

Any loss hereunder shall not reduce the amount(s) of insurance provided by this endorsement.

Subrogation: We will be entitled to assume all your rights of recovery against others and may bring action in your name to enforce these rights when we make payment or assume liability under this endorsement. Your right to recover from us is not affected by any release from liability entered into by you prior to loss.

Insurance Under More Than One Policy: Our policy will pay its rateable portion of the loss.

All other terms and conditions of the policy to which this endorsement applies remain unchanged.

Life Insurance

objectives

1. Explain the function of life insurance in enhancing financial security.

2. Relate the need for life insurance to changing life cycle requirements.

3. Evaluate the use of life insurance as a savings vehicle.

4. Explain the following principles: pooling risk, the pure cost of life insurance, the level premium, term insurance, whole life insurance, and universal life insurance.

5. Demonstrate how the two basic types of life insurance policies differ with respect to policy reserves, duration of insurance protection, and insurer's liability.

6. Explain how the following policy variations serve specific needs: decreasing term, limited-payment life, family policy, family income policy, and universal life.

7. Assess the merits of renewability, convertibility, waiver of premium, guaranteed insurability, accidental death benefit, cash surrender value, dividends, and mortgage insurance.

8. Ascertain from an insurance policy the main features of the agreement.

Introduction

The intent of this chapter is to help you take control of another aspect of your financial affairs. Most Canadians believe they ought to have some life insurance, but many are bewildered by the process of making a choice. Besides experiencing a natural reluctance to think about their own mortality, many people are dubious about insurance agents and feel unable to evaluate the sales presentation. Their perplexity stems from a lack of understanding of life insurance principles and concepts and is compounded by the sometimes confusing terminology used within the industry. Since there is unfortunately no established standard nomenclature for life insurance policies, companies adorn their offerings with a wide variety of names. Much of the confusion felt by buyers can be traced to the naming of policies, to the existence of various financing methods, and to the multiplicity of renewal provisions. You may find it encouraging to learn that in fact there are only two fundamental types of life insurance. The confusion arises because of the numerous modifications and combinations of the basic types, named as companies see fit. By gaining an understanding of basic principles and terms, you will put yourself in a better position to determine your own life insurance requirements and to make rational choices about these matters.

The Economic Risk of Dying Too Soon

If you died tomorrow, would your death create economic hardship for anyone? If the answer to that question is yes, you will want to consider insuring your life as one way of improving financial security for your dependents. If, as far as you can foresee, the answer is no, you probably do not need life insurance. The primary purpose of life insurance is to protect an income stream for dependents should the breadwinner die prematurely. Another use of insurance, important in certain cases, is to provide liquidity for an estate at death. When ready cash is needed by the survivors but most of the assets are tied up in property or securities that take time to sell, a lump-sum insurance settlement can be helpful. This chapter concentrates on the use of life insurance to protect a family's income stream and does not address other possible uses.

Financial Responsibility of Parents

Raising children creates a financial risk that peaks on the day the last one is born; at that time, the family has its maximum number of children with the longest period of dependence ahead. (See Personal Finance in Action Box 6.1, "When Insurance Is Needed.") As the children grow and the time left to support them decreases, this economic risk lessens. That is, the amount of money that would be needed to support children until they become independent becomes less each year. This changing risk is represented in Figure 6.1 by a hypothetical curve; for comparison, the average profiles of family income and wealth over the life cycle are superimposed.

For many families, the financial risk associated with parenthood does not correspond very well with their economic resources. Their financial risk tends to peak before their income or assets reach their highest levels. On average, a family can expect their income to increase until at least middle age and their assets to grow until retirement or after, with the period of greatest wealth occurring after the children have left home. This discrepancy, which can pose a significant threat to the financial security of young families, may be minimized by life insurance.

FIGURE 6.1   RESOURCES AND ECONOMIC RISKS OF PARENTHOOD BY LIFE CYCLE
STAGE

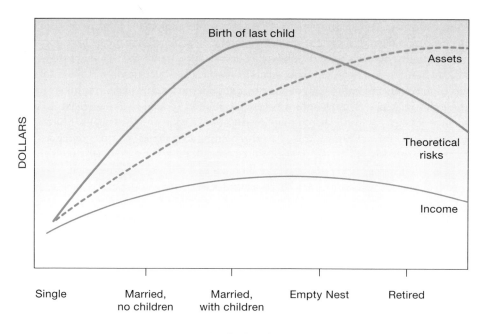

LIFE CYCLE STAGES

When Insurance Is Needed

Neither Tara nor Ravi had any life insurance when they married, but after baby Daphne's arrival, they became aware of their responsibility to support her for at least 18 years. Since both were employed, they decided that each should have some life insurance coverage, and they bought two policies. The birth of Adam two years later increased their financial commitments. Now that they were responsible for supporting Daphne for at least 16 more years and Adam for 18, or the equivalent of 34 child-years, they needed to increase their insurance coverage.

Will Tara and Ravi need to carry the same amount of life insurance throughout their lives? Assuming that they have no more children, the economic risk of parenthood will decline each year, going from the peak of 34 child-years to 32 at the end of the next year, then to 30, and so on to zero when they stop supporting the children. After the child support years and before their retirement, they should be building their net worth in anticipation of their non-earning years. Thus, their need for life insurance may slowly decline, eventually reaching a point where they need very little or even none.

Basic Concepts and Principles

Terminology

When you buy life insurance, the company provides an agreement or contract, called a **policy,** that states which risks the company has agreed to assume. The policy specifies in detail all aspects of the agreement, including the maximum liability that the company will assume, known as the face amount or face value. A policy with a **face amount** of $100 000 is an agreement that the insurance company will pay your beneficiary or beneficiaries $100 000 on your death. A **beneficiary** is the person named in the policy to receive the proceeds. The regular payments that are required to keep the policy in force are called **premiums.** Insurance premiums may be paid monthly, semi-annually, or annually, depending on the arrangement with the company, and are generally paid throughout the period during which the coverage is in force.

As with any type of insurance, a policy cannot be purchased unless there is an **insurable interest,** or a relationship between the insured and the event being insured against. You do not have an insurable interest in the life of another person unless that person's death would have a financial impact on you. Usually, a person is considered to have an insurable interest in his or her own life and in the life of a spouse, child, grandchild, employee, or any person on whom he or she may be wholly or partially dependent. For example, a creditor has an insurable interest in the lives of his or her debtors.

Basic Principles

Three basic principles of life insurance will be discussed here:

(a) pooling risk,

(b) the pure cost of life insurance,

(c) the level premium.

POOLING RISK Life insurance, like general insurance, is a method of pooling small contributions from many people to create a fund that will be able to compensate those who experience a loss. Actuaries use mortality tables drawn from death records collected over many

---

Pooling the Risk

Population of men aged 30. . . . . 200 000
Amount to be paid per deceased $50 000
Mortality rate for males aged 30 . . . 2.13/1000

Number of deaths expected in the year in this population:

$$200\ 000 \times \frac{2.13}{1000} = 426$$

Fund for dependents:
$426 \times \$50\ 000 = \$21\ 300\ 000$

Cost per man:

$$\frac{21\ 300\ 000}{200\ 000} = \$106.50 \text{ for the year}$$

At the end of the year, the fund would be exhausted; more contributions would then be needed.

years to predict the number of persons of any given age who can be expected to die within the year. These predictions, although quite accurate for large numbers, cannot forecast which persons will die in a given year—only how many. Once the number of expected deaths is known for a specific population, as well as how much money is to be given to the dependents of each, it is possible to determine the size of fund required to make the payments. The over-simplified example in the box "Pooling the Risk" illustrates this point.

THE PURE COST OF LIFE INSURANCE   As you can see from Figure 6.2, the one-year mortality rate rises with age and is higher at any given age for males than females. The cost of insuring a life for one year is based on the mortality rate for persons of the same age and gender and is called the pure cost of life insurance. Therefore, the **pure cost of life insurance** follows the mortality curve, becoming more expensive each year as one ages, but is less costly for females.

THE LEVEL PREMIUM   In response to resistance from buyers, who dislike having to pay higher premiums each year, insurance companies have devised the level premium. Rather than charge enough to cover the pure cost of insurance each year, they establish a constant or **level premium** when a life insurance policy is bought; the policyholder pays this amount regularly for

FIGURE 6.2   PROBABILITY OF DYING WITHIN THE YEAR, BY AGE AND GENDER

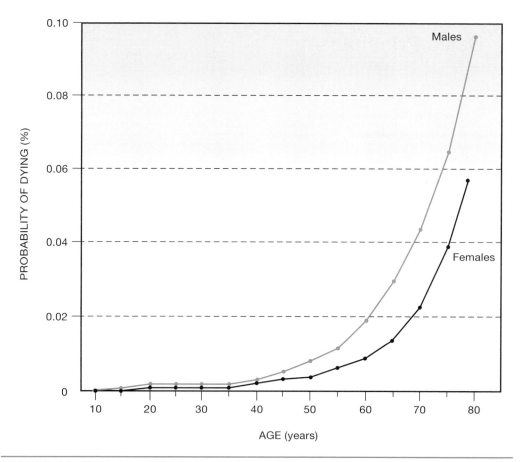

SOURCE: Statistics Canada, *Selected Mortality Statistics, Canada, 1921–1990.* Catalogue No. 82-548, Table 5, pp. 59–60.

FIGURE 6.3 OVERPAYMENT AND UNDERPAYMENT TO SUSTAIN A LEVEL PREMIUM

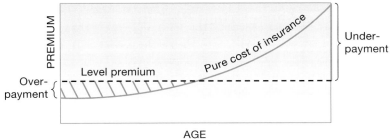

the duration of the policy, whether that is 5 years or 50 years. If we superimpose the amount of the level premium on the curve of risk, or the pure cost of insurance, it is obvious that in the early years of the contract the premium is higher than the pure cost, but in later years it is lower (Figure 6.3). The reserve accumulated from the overpayment at the beginning, together with the interest generated by that reserve, helps to meet the higher cost of coverage in the later period.

A company that writes an insurance policy to cover an individual for his or her entire life has assumed a liability that is certain. It has promised to pay a specified sum when the insured person dies—a situation with 100 percent probability; this is an important feature distinguishing life insurance from other forms of insurance. Many policies on homes, cars, and personal liability do not result in claims, and of those that do, few require payment of the maximum coverage. When an insurer establishes the premium for a policy to cover a person for life, it must be set at a level that will accumulate enough reserves in the early years to pay the certain claim later on.

The level premium and the policy reserves are established in order to ensure that there will be enough money to pay the face amount to the beneficiary or beneficiaries at some future date. However, if the policyholder decides to cancel the policy, the insurance company is relieved of the promise to pay this amount, and the reserve fund will not be needed; it can therefore be refunded to the policyholder.

Unfortunately, much of the life insurance literature (and sales pitch) refers to policy reserves as the savings feature. The policy reserves are available to the policyholder only if the policy is cancelled or the coverage reduced; it is impossible to have both full life insurance coverage and access to the policy reserves at the same time. (See Personal Finance in Action Box 6.2, "Alec and Katrina Cancel Their Policies.") Life insurance will be easier to understand if you remember that a policy's cash value is the reserve required to cover the certain liability that the company has assumed.

Factors Affecting Cost

A number of factors affect the cost of life insurance, including mortality rate, loading charges, the frequency of premium payments, whether or not it is a participating policy, and the type of policy.

Mortality Rate

Mortality rate is the primary determinant of the price you will pay for life insurance. To estimate your mortality risk, an actuary would need to know your age and gender, the state of your health, your and your family's medical history, and whether you engage in any hazardous

---

Personal Finance in Action 6.2

Alec and Katrina Cancel Their Policies

When Alec and Katrina first got married they followed the advice of her father and purchased whole life insurance policies on both their lives. (See "Whole Life Insurance" later in the chapter for more details.) The face values were $150 000 each, and they paid premiums of $64 and $62 a month each.

By the time Alec and Katrina were 48, they had paid off their mortgage and their two daughters had moved out. With no other dependents and no debts, they decided to cancel the policies and use the money they invested monthly in life insurance for saving for their retirement. They informed the insurance company of their plan, and the policy reserves of $8 650 and $7 950 were returned to them. By cancelling the policies, their life insurance company had no further liability to Alec and Katrina. They did, however, both have life insurance policies through their employers.

---

activities. Your cost will be raised by anything that increases the risk of death (for instance, smoking or skydiving). If the insurance company considers the probability of your dying soon to be too high, the company will not insure your life. Fortunately, the proportion of applicants who are rejected is very small (only about 2 percent); but people who are classified as higher-than-average risks do sometimes have to pay larger premiums.

Loading Charges

In addition to the pure cost of insuring a life, an amount called the loading charge is included in the premium. The company's **loading charge** includes administrative costs, commissions to salespeople, and profit for shareholders. The largest component in loading charges is a commission to life insurance agents, which may range from 13 percent to 110 percent of the first year's premium. The commission on renewals may range from 2 percent to 15 percent. Individual life insurance policies are sold by sales agents who depend on commissions for income and must therefore search energetically for clients, a very expensive method of selling. Other financial institutions—especially banks—are also involved in selling insurance. With the recent collaboration among banks and life insurance companies, such as CIBC with Great West Life and TD with Sun Life in the areas of joint marketing loan insurance, it will be interesting to see the future landscape of the insurance industry.

Offsetting these loading costs to some extent is the interest that may be earned on the pooled funds, which the company can invest until claims are made. Life insurance companies, as managers of the pooled insurance funds, usually collect more than they expect to pay out in claims, not just to establish policy reserves, but also to set up special reserve funds in case their estimates are too low.

Frequency of Premium Payments

Your total cost per year will vary slightly depending on the frequency with which the premiums are to be paid. If you pay annually, the total cost is lower than if you were to pay either semiannually or monthly. These differences reflect the amount of interest the company knows that it can obtain by investing the premium funds.

Participating and Non-Participating Policies

The difference between participating and non-participating policies lies in the way the premiums are calculated. Premiums for **non-participating policies** are estimated as accurately as possible and cannot be increased by the company. If the company turns out to have underestimated or overestimated the cost, the difference is met from the company's funds or by changing the premium rates on policies sold in the future. For **participating policies,** the premiums are usually set somewhat higher than for non-participating ones, but the policyholder will receive a refund on any excess. These refunds are called **dividends;** but the term is confusing since, unlike stock dividends, these are not a form of income. Because they are refunds, they are not subject to income tax. In other words, insurance dividends are a return of after-tax dollars.

In any one year, the dividend amount will depend on such factors as the company's efficiency, its return on investments, the amount that has been paid out in claims, and the number of policies that have been cancelled. Dividends may be taken in cash, used to pay the next premium, used to buy more insurance, or left on deposit to earn interest. Although the dividends themselves are not considered taxable income, any interest they generate will be taxable.

Basic Types of Life Insurance

Distinguishing Features

A life insurance policy, however it may be labelled to interest prospective buyers, is almost always one or a combination of two basic types—term or whole life. The inventiveness of companies in naming their many elaborations has led to unnecessary confusion. Despite the lack of uniform terminology, it is usually possible to identify the fundamental policy type if you have a good understanding of the distinguishing features of each. Two important characteristics to consider are whether or not

(a) the coverage is for life,

(b) the policy accumulates a cash value.

Term insurance is coverage for a specific period, without cash value, while whole life provides lifelong protection, with cash value.

Term Insurance

Like fire or auto insurance, **term insurance** provides protection against a specified risk for a definite period of time. At the end of that time, or term, the insurance lapses unless it is renewed. The important characteristic of term insurance is that it represents protection for a designated period—not for life. Term insurance may be purchased for periods of various length: one, five, and ten years are common. It is also possible to buy term to age 65, or even to age 100. A product called "term to 100" adds to the confusion by offering coverage for life with no cash value.

Because most buyers of term insurance have a fairly low probability of dying in the near future—they are usually under 65 years of age—and because the company does not assume coverage for life, the cost of term insurance is lower than for other types. The premium is made level for the term of the policy; any reserves accumulated are relatively small and will be used up during the term. For these reasons, no cash value is available to the policyholder. As with all life insurance, the face value will be paid to the beneficiary or beneficiaries if the insured dies while the policy is in force. However, from the company's point of view, the probability of paying claims on term insurance is low; the company has not taken on the sure liability that it assumes in policies with lifelong coverage.

Although the premium for term insurance is level for the specified term, at the next renewal the premium must necessarily be raised, since the insured has aged and the probability of his or her dying has therefore increased. Figure 6.4 illustrates the changes in premium at each renewal as the pure cost of life insurance rises. By age 65, the pure cost of life insurance becomes very high, and few term policies are offered because of the limited market at that price.

Term insurance offers the most face value per premium dollar of any type of life insurance, because it does not give protection at advanced ages (when the cost of insurance is high). As illustrated in Figure 6.5, for every $100 that you can afford to spend each year on life insurance, you will obtain more face amount (life insurance coverage) with term insurance than other types of policies. Although this is a useful comparison, there are two caveats. First, the insurer's liability is not the same with each type of policy shown, varying from five years to life. Second, the premiums shown in this comparison have been made level for different periods, involving varying amounts of reserve funds. Looked at in another way, for a given amount of life insurance, the annual cost will be lowest for term coverage.

DECREASING TERM INSURANCE Thus far we have discussed term insurance with a face amount that is constant throughout the term. However, it is also possible to buy term insurance with a decreasing face amount. This variant is useful when the risk being covered is expected to diminish. It is often used as mortgage insurance by people who wish to leave their

FIGURE 6.4 PREMIUM LEVELS FOR FIVE-YEAR RENEWABLE TERM INSURANCE BY GENDER AND AGE

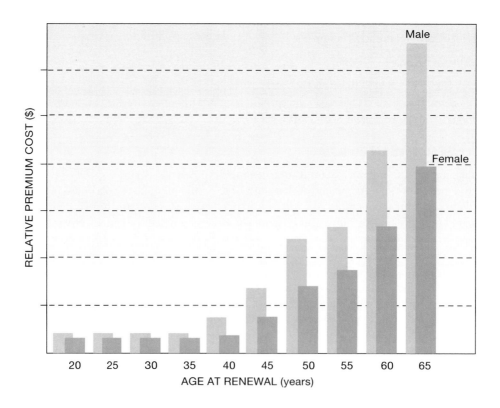

FIGURE 6.5   FACE AMOUNT BY POLICY TYPE FOR A GIVEN PREMIUM

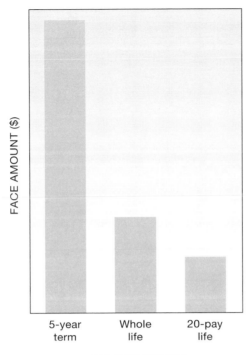

dependents a debt-free home in the event of their death. At the outset, the policy's face amount is equal to the outstanding debt on the house, but the face amount decreases at a rate roughly equal to that at which the debt is expected to be reduced. If the insured dies during the term, the policy's face amount should be adequate to pay the outstanding balance on the mortgage. The beneficiary is, of course, under no obligation to use the death benefit for this purpose. It is simply a life insurance policy that will pay a certain sum to the beneficiary when the insured dies. One may argue that special mortgage insurance is unnecessary if overall life insurance coverage is adequate.

Another use for decreasing term insurance is to provide income protection for a young family. Many people feel that it is wise to arrange their insurance coverage to match the period of highest financial risk, so that coverage is at a maximum when the children are very young. As the children grow, the risk decreases, and so may the need for life insurance. Reducing term insurance is appropriate for such a situation.

The face amount of a decreasing term policy falls to zero at the end of the term, with downward adjustments monthly or annually. Premiums, however, are level for the term, probably to discourage policyholders from cancelling the policy when the coverage becomes low. Some companies set a level premium for a period shorter than the entire term; for instance, the premiums on a 20-year decreasing term policy might be paid up in 16 years. Term and decreasing term insurance are compared in Figure 6.6.

GROUP LIFE INSURANCE   Life insurance may be purchased by individuals or groups. In its most common form, group insurance is bought by employers to cover the lives of a large group of employees. Payment for this insurance may be shared by employer and employee; alternatively,

FIGURE 6.6 TERM AND DECREASING TERM INSURANCE

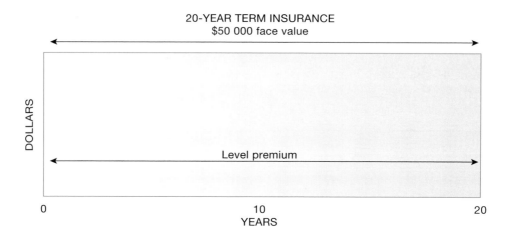

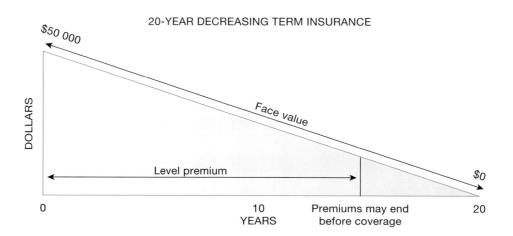

one or the other may pay the entire amount. In either event, one policy covers a group of lives. Usually no medical examinations are required as evidence of insurability, but there are some rules. These rules are intended to avoid a selection of risks that might be adverse to the insurance company. For instance, all employees may be required to join the group plan; or, if there is a choice, employees may be required to join at a specific time, perhaps when they begin employment. In any case, such a plan will be arranged so that most employees cannot avoid being insured. The amount of coverage will also depend on a rule: the face amount may be some multiple of the employee's annual salary, or all employees may be covered for the same amount. There may be an option to purchase more coverage.

Group insurance is most often one-year renewable term, but it may also be whole life insurance. Since employees of all ages pay the same premium, group coverage can be a bargain for the older worker. The coverage usually ends whenever an employee terminates employment, but there may be an option of converting, within a month, from the group policy to individual term or whole life. The premiums for group policies are usually lower than for similar insurance bought individually, because selling and administration costs are decreased when a single policy covers a large group of lives. The employer collects the premiums and pays the insurer for the group.

CREDIT LIFE INSURANCE   A specialized version of group term insurance, known as **credit life insurance**, is purchased by lenders to cover the lives of a group of borrowers. If a borrower should die with a debt still outstanding, the insurer will reimburse the creditor for the balance owing. Ultimately, the cost of such insurance is borne by the borrower, who may or may not be given a choice about having the loan life insured. This type of insurance is certainly of interest to creditors, who are not keen to see debt repayments cease when a borrower dies; it can also be useful to anyone who is anxious not to leave a debt that must be paid out of his or her estate.

Home owners frequently purchase from their lending institution a common form of group term insurance—that is, **mortgage insurance**. As the principal owing on the mortgage decreases, so too does the amount that would be paid to the lending institution should one of the home owners die prematurely. This is an easy method of insuring your mortgage, but may be more expensive than buying a straight term policy; it definitely offers less flexibility for the survivors, who may need more coverage than merely having the mortgage paid off.

Whole Life Insurance

A type of insurance commonly bought by individuals is **whole life insurance** (also called straight life or ordinary life). It provides insurance protection from the time of purchase until death (Figure 6.7). To maintain this lifelong coverage, premiums must be paid each year as long as the insured lives—unless the premiums are prepaid. Some companies terminate the policies at very advanced ages, such as 95, and pay the policyholder the face amount. The premium, which is established at the time of purchase, is level for life.

In addition to its long duration, another distinguishing feature of whole life insurance is the accumulation of policy reserves, also known as **cash reserves** or **cash surrender value.** From Figure 6.3, you will recall that in order to have a level premium, the policyholder overpays during the early years and underpays later. Because the early payments exceed the pure cost of insurance, they create a reserve that in turn grows over time as more premiums are paid and the reserve funds earn interest.

Any cash reserves created in the first year or two are used for the company's selling and issue expenses, including commissions, and therefore the policy has no cash value at first. A sample whole life policy is reproduced in Appendix 6A. This policy has a table showing cash values for each year that the insurance is in force. To read the table, find the column headed by the policyholder's age at the time of purchase, which in this case is 30. Assume that you wish to know the cash value five years later. This policy was for $50 000; therefore the cash value after five years would be $715. The reserves continue to grow each year until around age 100, when the cash value will equal the face amount (Figure 6.7).

It is impossible to have the use of the cash reserves while also maintaining full insurance coverage. The policy states that if the insured person dies, the policy's full face amount will be paid to the beneficiary. Whenever that happens, the policy terminates— and so does the cash value. However, during the insured person's lifetime, he can make use of the cash reserves if he is willing to diminish the coverage accordingly. A number of uses for the cash reserves will be outlined under "Uses for the Cash Reserves," later in this chapter.

FIGURE 6.7 TYPES OF LIFE INSURANCE

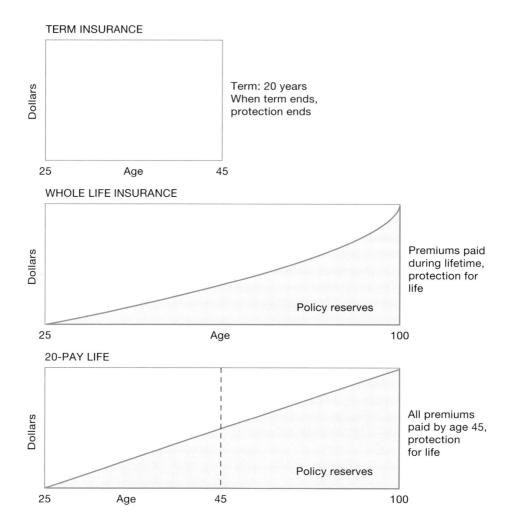

LIMITED PAYMENT LIFE INSURANCE A variation on whole life insurance is the **limited payment policy,** which, as the name indicates, is completely paid for during a specified period. Instead of paying premiums for life, the insured pays higher premiums for a shorter time, usually 20 years or to age 65. After it is paid up, the policy remains in force for the rest of the insured's life. This type of policy is selected when the insured expects to be able to pay for insurance more readily early in life, and thus may be appropriate for people who expect high incomes for a short time, such as professional athletes. However, for most families this type of policy cannot provide sufficient coverage when it is most needed.

The more rapid rate of payment with limited payment insurance causes the cash surrender value of such a policy to increase faster than with whole life. After the payment period ends, the cash surrender value continues to grow (Figure 6.7). Except for the shorter payment period, limited-pay life is similar in most respects to whole life insurance; the cash surrender value can also be used in the same ways.

Combination Policies

There are too many variations and combinations of the two basic types of life insurance to consider them all here. As well, the industry is constantly inventing new versions. The four combination types selected for discussion here are endowment life, universal life, family income policy, and family policy.

Universal Life Insurance

The rigidity of having to face a fixed premium for life with an inflexible face amount to be paid many years later has not always been attractive to insurance buyers. For instance, in inflationary periods, insurance coverage once thought to be sufficient for dependents may become inadequate because of lost purchasing power. Those who want to invest their savings with an insurance company may prefer to have insurance coverage and savings kept separate. **Universal life insurance,** invented to offer buyers such flexibility, is a combination of term insurance and a savings account.

The distinctive features of universal life are (i) the flexibility in payments, (ii) the opportunity to withdraw funds, (iii) the freedom to alter the amount of insurance coverage at any time, and (iv) the regular disclosure of fees, interest earned, and other information. These features contrast with traditional policies, where the buyer does not know how the premiums are divided among the pure cost of insurance, the policy reserves, and the loading charges, or what rate of interest is being credited on the reserves.

FLEXIBLE PAYMENTS The payment of money into a universal life policy is voluntary within prescribed limits. The money is used to create a fund from which the company deducts the cost of insurance protection—which is rather like term coverage—and a loading charge. The balance is credited with interest and treated as a sort of investment fund from which the policyholder may make withdrawals. The policyholder can choose how much to put in each year, but if no payment is made for a time, the insurance cost will be deducted from any balance in the fund. If the company is deducting the pure cost of insurance each year, you can expect this amount to increase as you grow older.

WITHDRAWAL PRIVILEGES The funds in the cash account are available for you to withdraw or borrow against as you wish. If you leave the money in the account, you will draw interest at current rates. A minimum rate may be guaranteed for a year.

FLEXIBLE COVERAGE There may be possibilities for changing your coverage, within limits, as your needs change. However, the flexibility in premiums sometimes lead buyers to forget payments, with consequent loss of coverage.

REGULAR STATEMENTS You will receive regular statements showing all the transactions in your account. These statements will keep you informed about your coverage and its cost, the loading charges, and the return on the cash account.

CAVEATS FOR BUYERS Prospective buyers of universal life insurance need to become informed about all the charges that will be assessed—for example, one-time administrative fees, loading charges, and surrender charges. Buyers should also know how the loading charges will be distributed. Some companies deduct loading charges before depositing the premium in the account, while others first credit the premium and then deduct charges. Some may charge an initial fee and then add a loading charge of 5 percent to 10 percent, as well as a fee for each withdrawal. Loading charges may be a constant proportion of each premium, front-loaded, or back-loaded. If in the early years of the policy a larger share of the premium is used for loading charges, the policy is referred to as **front-loaded.** When little is deducted from the premiums at the outset for loading charges, but a disproportionate share is added when a policy is surrendered, the policy is **back-loaded.** Some companies may impose very high surrender charges if the policy is cancelled within a few years. However, if the policy remains in force for some time, the surrender charges diminish.

Other aspects to investigate include the tax treatment of interest, buried fees, and the costs and benefits of having insurance coverage combined with a savings account. The tax treatment of interest and the payments to beneficiaries should be inquired into, along with the nature of the various fees. It is also possible that some charges may be buried in changed rates for the "pure cost of insurance." Companies may use high interest rates to attract buyers, but decrease them later, or project unrealistic future interest rates. Thought should be given to the wisdom of combining a term life policy and an investment fund in one contract, instead of separate arrangements for each.

Family Income Policy

Term and whole life insurance are combined in various ways to make a **family income policy** (Figure 6.8). The insured person is usually the family's principal income earner. The whole life portion of the policy covers the insured for life, paying a specified amount on his or her death, whenever it may occur. The term portion provides coverage for a definite period—for example, 20 years. If the insured dies during the term, the policy will provide an income for dependents

FIGURE 6.8   FAMILY POLICY AND FAMILY INCOME POLICY

FAMILY POLICY

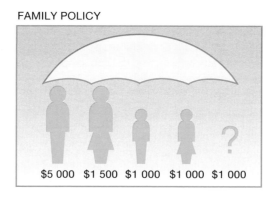

FAMILY INCOME POLICY

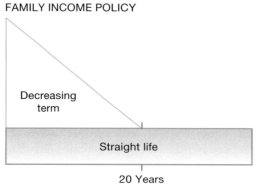

that will continue for the remainder of the term. If the insured lives more than 20 years after buying the policy, the term coverage will have expired, but the whole life insurance will continue.

Family Policy

Some insurers may offer a **family policy,** which is a package with separate coverage for the husband, the wife, and each present and future child. This policy may involve term insurance only, or a combination of term and whole life. In the latter instance, the whole life coverage would probably be on the life of the principal earner. If any family member should die during the term of his or her coverage, the insurer will pay the coverage for that individual, but the package will continue to cover the lives of the survivors. The buyer should evaluate the risks to the family's economic situation of the death of each family member.

The Insurance Policy

A life insurance policy is a contract between the insuring company and the policyholder. Some aspects of this complex legal document will be outlined here. A life insurance contract is not a contract of indemnity—unlike property insurance, where the insured is to be indemnified or returned to the financial position he or she would have been in had the loss not occurred. With a life insurance policy, a predictable sum of money is payable by the insurer— an important distinction. For a sample whole life policy, see Appendix 6A.

Description of Policy

Near the beginning of the policy, there should be such basic information as the face amount, the type of policy, the name of the insured person, the insured's age, the date the coverage begins, the period during which the insurance is to be effective, and the amount of the premium.

Grace Period

The policyholder is usually given a **grace period** of one month after the date the premium is due, during which the insurance remains in force and the premium may be paid without penalty. If the insured should die during the grace period, the beneficiary or beneficiaries will receive the face value less the amount of the unpaid premium.

Dividends

The dividend clause in a participating policy covers the details of the company's payment of dividends and describes the various options available to the policyholder. The insured may take the dividends in cash, use them to reduce the premium, use them to purchase paid-up additions to the life insurance in force or one-year term additions, or leave them on deposit with the company to earn interest. The range of options available is determined by the company.

Incontestability

To protect themselves from future legal actions arising from alleged misrepresentations by the insured, life insurance companies have instituted an **incontestability clause,** which states that after the policy has been in force for two years, it will not be invalidated by any non-disclosure or misrepresentation that may be discovered, with the exception of fraud. During these two years, the company can seek to be released from the contract if it discovers that the applicant made false statements.

Policy Loans

In any policy with cash reserves, the conditions under which policy loans are available will be stated somewhere in the policy. Related to these conditions is the automatic premium loan, which provides that if a policyholder fails to pay the premiums or take certain other actions (such as requesting a grace period for delayed payments), the company will use the cash surrender value to pay the premium, repeating the process as required until the cash value has been exhausted.

Ownership Rights and Assignment

The rights of the life insurance policy owner include the right to name and change the beneficiary or beneficiaries, to use the cash value, to receive any dividends, and to dispose of any of these rights. If one person holds all of these rights, that person is the sole owner of the policy; if the policy's ownership is shared with one or more other people, each becomes a part or joint owner. Usually the person insured and the owner are the same. Like other contracts, a life insurance policy is assignable—that is, its ownership may be transferred. For example, when a policy is used as collateral for a loan, the policy is assigned to the creditor.

Beneficiary

The beneficiary clause identifies the person(s) or organizations intended to receive the proceeds of the insurance on the policyholder's death. In most cases, the insured may alter the designation of beneficiary by signing a declaration to be filed with the insurance company. Sometimes people forget to do this when family conditions change, leaving the insurance payable to an estranged, divorced, or deceased spouse. Insurance proceeds payable to a named beneficiary are not distributed through the deceased's will, but go directly to the person designated, free from claims that creditors or others may have on the estate, including Revenue Canada.

   If the primary beneficiary dies before the person whose life has been insured, and no alternative (secondary) beneficiary has been named, the company may pay the proceeds to the estate of the deceased. Only rarely will a policyholder name a beneficiary irrevocably, which means that the designation of beneficiary cannot be changed without the consent of the beneficiary. In such instances, the policyholder cannot assign the cash surrender value of the policy to a third party without the consent of the named **irrevocable beneficiary.**

Settlement Options

The way in which the proceeds of a life insurance policy will be paid to the beneficiary may be settled by the insured, prior to death, or may be left to the beneficiary's discretion. Some of the ways in which life insurance can be paid, other than as a lump sum, will be outlined here. The interest option involves leaving the principal sum on deposit with the insurance company and receiving the interest regularly. In the instalment option, the proceeds are paid in instalments over a selected period of time by various arrangements, all involving payment of principal and interest. The proceeds can be used to purchase a single-payment annuity (life income), with payments to begin either immediately or at a later date; this is sometimes referred to as the life income option. (Annuities are explained in the chapter on retirement income.)

Uses for the Cash Reserves

The policy reserve, also known as cash value or cash surrender value, has a number of possible uses during the policyholder's lifetime; five of them will be reviewed here:

(a) Surrender of the policy

(b) Policy loan

(c) Automatic premium loan

(d) Collateral for a loan

(e) Paid-up policy

Surrender of the Policy

One obvious use of the cash value involves cancelling or surrendering the policy and taking the cash value, effectively terminating the insurance coverage. The table of cash values in the policy shows how much the cash value is according to the number of years the policy has been in force (Appendix 6A).

Policy Loan

It is possible to arrange a **policy loan,** or to borrow from the cash surrender value, usually at an interest rate that is lower than the rate on loans from other sources. (See Personal Finance in Action Box 6.3, "Mimi Takes Out a Policy Loan.") There is no pressure to repay a policy loan, but in the meantime the interest continues to accumulate. If the insured should die before the loan is repaid, the unpaid balance and outstanding interest will be deducted from the face value of the policy before the proceeds are paid to the beneficiary or beneficiaries.

Personal Finance in Action 6.3

Mimi Takes Out a Policy Loan

As she reviewed her finances in preparation for buying a new car, Mimi remembered that she had a whole life insurance policy, purchased 20 years previously. Since her children were now independent and her need for life insurance protection had therefore declined, it occurred to her that a policy loan might be appropriate. On calling her insurance agent, she discovered that the current rate on policy loans was 6 percent, with interest calculated annually on the policy's anniversary date. The maximum cash value available for a loan on this policy was $13 700.

Mimi decided to request a policy loan and to let the interest accumulate as a claim against the policy. Five years later, when Mimi died, the insurance company paid her beneficiary the policy's face value minus the outstanding debt. The amount was determined as follows:

Face amount of policy:. $50 000.00

Amount of loan:. 13 700.00

Compound interest factor:
  (6%, for 5 years). 1.3382

Principal + interest due:
  $13 700 x 1.3382 = $18 333.34

Amount payable to beneficiary:
  $50 000 – 18 334.34 = $31 666.66

Choose a Paid-Up Policy

Assume that you own the insurance policy that is enclosed as Appendix 6A. At age 60 you decide that you no longer require the life insurance as your investments have done quite well and your children are grown and have left home. After looking at the table of Guaranteed Values in your policy, you realize that your paid-up value of life insurance is $35 750. This reflects the ability to convert your current policy into a new policy of $35 750 and not have to pay any further premiums for life. Alternatively, you could take the cash value of $18 480 and cancel your life insurance.

Automatic Premium Loan

The cash surrender value may be used to pay the premiums if for some reason the policyholder does not do so. Such an arrangement is essentially the same as a policy loan, because the face value will be reduced by the amount used for this purpose. It is called an **automatic premium loan,** because the company will use the cash value to pay the premiums rather than let the policy lapse if the policyholder takes no action. Policyholders who have assumed that their policy has lapsed because they have stopped paying premiums might be surprised to learn how much longer their coverage extends. If the insured should die, the face amount would be diminished by the amount of any such loan.

Collateral for a Loan

The cash surrender value may also be used as collateral for a loan. To use the cash value this way, the insured must transfer the right to the cash surrender value to the creditor until the loan is repaid. If the insured defaults on the loan, the creditor can cash in the policy and retain whatever is owed. Such an event would effectively terminate the policy. Should the insured die during the term of the loan, the outstanding balance would have to be paid either from insurance proceeds or from the estate.

Paid-Up Policy

Instead of cancelling the policy and taking the cash surrender value, another option is to use the cash value to purchase a **paid-up policy** with a smaller face value. (See Personal Finance in Action Box 6.4, "Choose a Paid-Up Policy.") This approach is, in effect, a single-premium purchase of life insurance. The amount of the face value will depend on the amount of the cash surrender value at that time. Policies usually include tables that show the cash value for each year the policy is in force and the amount of paid-up insurance that the cash value will purchase. Alternatively, the policyholder could use the cash surrender value to purchase term insurance with a larger face value.

Endorsements or Riders

An insurance policy may be modified by the addition of **endorsements** or **riders,** which specify various supplementary benefits to be included or omitted without affecting the rest of the policy. Such additions can be worthwhile, but they may change the risk to be covered, thus adding to the cost. Some riders in common use are guaranteed renewability, waiver of premium, guaranteed insurability, conversion privilege, and accidental death benefit. These features may be available as riders in some instances, or they may be written directly into the policies, depending on the company's practices.

Guaranteed Renewability

Term insurance buyers may find it desirable to have the option of renewing the policy at the end of the term without providing evidence of insurability with another medical examination. Guaranteed renewability adds another risk for the life insurance company, but the extra cost may be worthwhile to the insured.

Waiver of Premium

A waiver-of-premium rider usually releases the policyholder from paying premiums when disabled, while keeping the policy in force. A precise definition of what constitutes disability is generally included, and there is often a waiting period of several months. Inspect the definition of disability very closely.

Guaranteed Insurability

A rider that permits the policyholder to purchase additional life insurance at specified future dates, without evidence of insurability, can be useful. This option may be restricted to younger persons, and the maximum face amount that may be added will probably be specified. This approach is highly recommended for younger people who do not currently have dependents but who may desire additional coverage when they start a family and increase their financial obligations.

Conversion Privilege

With a term policy, a rider may be added that gives the insured the option of converting the policy to another type of insurance at any time before the end of the term without having to provide evidence of insurability. There may be an age limit on this privilege, such as age 60 or 65.

Accidental Death Benefit

Another rider that is frequently added to basic policies is the accidental death benefit. Such a rider provides an additional benefit, which may be as much as the face amount of the policy, if the insured dies as a result of an accident before some specified age, such as 65 or 70. The additional premium for this rider is usually small, because the majority of deaths are not considered accidental. A buyer of life insurance needs to remember that the amount of insurance bought should be determined by the expected needs of dependents, not by the cause of death. Also, careful note should be taken of the definition of accidental death as far as the life insurance company is concerned. Accidental death coverage, like travel insurance, should not be necessary if the insurance program is carefully planned.

Buying Life Insurance

National Trends

How much life insurance do Canadians buy; do they prefer individual or group policies; and who buys life insurance? National life insurance industry data provides a general picture of coverage, of the characteristics of the insured, and of their policy preferences.

REASONS FOR TERMINATION It is well known that some buyers of life insurance change their minds and either surrender policies or let them lapse. From the limited information available, it is obvious that many people buy insurance that they are unable, or do not want, to keep in force. Some whole life policies are surrendered by policyholders who prefer to take the cash value and cancel the coverage. Other policies are allowed to lapse through non-payment of premiums. The surrender and lapse rates are climbing and far exceed the rate for termination by death and maturity. For instance, in 1987 less than 1 percent of face value was terminated by death, maturity, disability, or expiry, but about 12 percent was terminated because of surrender or lapse. The obvious question is why is this so? It is interesting to consider to what extent this problem is related to the way life insurance is sold.

LIFE INSURANCE OWNERSHIP Canadians are among the most life-insured people in the world, with total coverage in 1997 amounting to more than $1.7 trillion dollars (an average per capita coverage of about $55 000). As Figure 6.9 shows, the increase in coverage between 1960 and 1998 was quite significant, although inflation and Canada's growing population can explain some of the increase.

We have been examining the trends in life insurance ownership, but not every individual needs or owns coverage. In 1997, 83 percent of all Canadian households had some form of life insurance. It is important to look also at the average amounts owned per policyholder and per household. In 1997, the average per insured individual was $107 900, with about $181 000 per household. Although these figures may seem high, many families are not adequately covered: too often, the wrong amounts of the wrong kinds of insurance are bought on the lives of the wrong people. The combination of uninformed buyers and high-pressure sales techniques can be disastrous for some families.

FIGURE 6.9 PERCENTAGE DISTRIBUTION OF INDIVIDUAL AND GROUP LIFE INSURANCE OWNED, 1960–1998

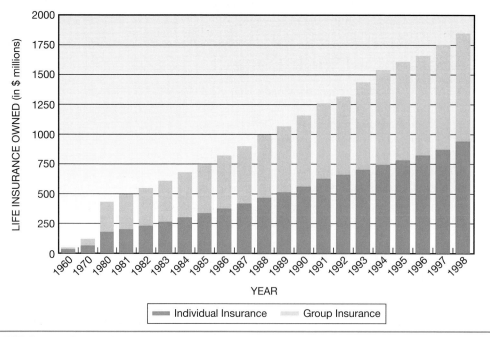

SOURCE: Reprinted from the "Canadian Life and Health Insurance Facts, 1999 edition," with the permission of the Canadian Life and Health Insurance Association Inc.

INDIVIDUAL OR GROUP POLICIES On examining the total value of life insurance owned in Canada, it becomes evident that the long-term trend, until recently, has been toward an increasing share for group insurance (Figure 6.9). Group insurance represented nearly 60 percent of all insurance owned in 1980, but that proportion had dropped somewhat by 1997.

CHARACTERISTICS OF THE INSURED The decision to buy life insurance is influenced by a number of variables, but most logically by the presence of dependents. The available industry data do not mention dependents, but do include the insured's gender, age, and income. Each pie graph in Figure 6.10 represents a different perspective on how the total face value of the individual life insurance policies purchased in 1994 was distributed, by selected characteristics. For instance, there was more coverage on the lives of males (64 percent) than on females (36 percent). With regard to age, the largest proportion of the coverage was on those between the ages of 25 and 34. Buyers of life insurance tended to have incomes between $30 000 and $50 000. One might conclude, therefore, that young males with average incomes are most likely to buy life insurance.

TYPE AND SIZE OF POLICY Although whole life policies have historically been the leading type sold to individuals (as opposed to groups), it is interesting to note that by 1997

FIGURE 6.10 PERCENTAGE DISTRIBUTION OF TOTAL FACE AMOUNT OF INDIVIDUAL LIFE POLICIES PURCHASED, BY SELECTED FACTORS, CANADA, 1998

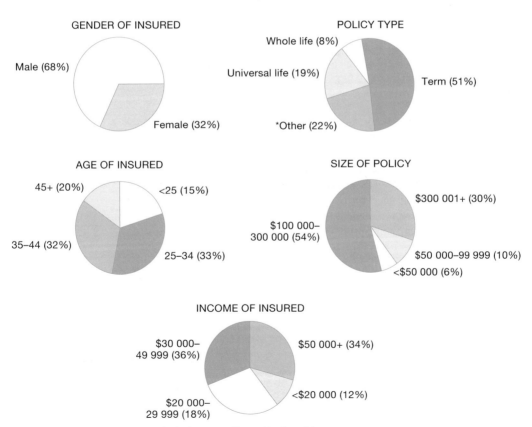

* Includes other combination policies, limited payment life, and family policies.

SOURCE: Reprinted from the "Canadian Life and Health Insurance Facts, 1999 edition," with the permission of the Canadian Life and Health Insurance Association Inc.

whole life represented less than one-tenth of face value purchased individually (Figure 6.10). There was more term coverage (46 percent) than any other type, with the balance spread among universal life and various other combination policies. A full 84 percent of the coverage was for policies with a face value of $100 000 or more.

How Much to Buy

The following five steps provide a simplified way of estimating how much life insurance you may need. First, assume that your death could occur tomorrow. Who would need financial support and for how long? Refer to Table 6.1 for an example.

TABLE 6.1   CURRENT LIFE INSURANCE NEEDS

AS OF MAY 7, 2001

1. *Available Assets*

Liquid assets (Table 1.1 Subtotal A)	$15 250	
Other financial assets, including pensions and RRSPs (Table 1.1 Subtotal B)	45 000	
Personal assets to be liquidated		
Lump-sum benefits (CPP, RPP, etc.)	4 000	
Group life insurance	25 000	
Mortgage life insurance	—	
Personal life insurance	200 000	
TOTAL ASSETS AVAILABLE		**$289 250 (A)**

2. *Financial Expenses*

Funeral and medical expenses	8 000	
Debts, excluding mortgage	54 500	
Short-term living expenses (50% of annual salary)	21 250	
Income taxes due including capital gains	11 746	
Mortgage principal outstanding	125 000	
Post-secondary education of children	80 000	
TOTAL FINANCIAL ASSETS REQUIRED		**$300 496 (B)**
CAPITAL AVAILABLE (INSURANCE REQUIRED) (A – B)		**$–11 246 (C)**

3. *Annual Required Income*

Income replacement (60% of annual salary if mortgage is paid off or is covered elsewhere; otherwise 75% of current salary)		31 875 (D)	
Less extra annual income from:			
Spouse's income		—	
CPP/QPP pension	3 890		
RPP		—	3 890 (E)
ANNUAL REQUIRED INCOME (D – E)			**$ 27 985 (F)**

4. *Capital Required to Generate Income (F / 0.10)*   **$279 850 (G)**

5. *Total Required Insurance (G – C)*   **$291 096**

1. Estimate your total available assets. Call this total A.

2. List the financial expenses that will need to be covered, including debts and future obligations (such as children's education). Call this total B.

3. The difference between A and B is the capital available, or C.

4. Calculate a percentage of your annual income or salary: 60 percent if your mortgage is paid off and 75 percent of it is not. If you are a stay-at-home parent who is the primary caregiver for a child or children, estimate the value of the services you provide (generally considered to be at least $20 000 per year) to cover the cost of housekeeping, day care, and so on. This amount is D. Deduct from this amount the increase in income for the household from a spouse returning to work or from pension income such as CPP. This amount is E, and the difference between D and E is the annual increase in income that the household will need to generate from investments that derive from the life insurance; this increase is F.

5 The net amount of annual income required is divided by a discount figure to determine the gross amount of money that will be needed in order to generate that annual income. Table 6.1 uses 10 percent, to account for the declining need for money over time as dependents mature and leave the home and to generate the sum of additional or unneeded insurance as G.

6. The total required insurance for immediate needs is deducted from the total required for long-term needs in the final calculation. This number is the starting point for discussion and for determining whether you have adequate coverage to maintain the lifestyle that the household would require and prefer should the breadwinner(s) die prematurely and leave dependents.

Selecting a Policy

Buyers of life insurance are advised to first define their needs and then obtain quotations from several companies. (See Personal Finance in Action Box 6.5 "Term or Whole Life"). It may be difficult to make meaningful comparisons, because different companies are offering dissimilar insurance packages that protect against different risks. The more clearly you can specify your requirements before approaching an insurance agent, the greater the probability that you will be able to get comparable quotations.

Selling Methods

Individual life insurance policies are sold by salespeople who depend on commissions for their livelihood, thus creating a possible conflict of interest when they act as advisors to buyers. When companies pay higher commissions on certain types of policies, salespeople may attempt to sell those kinds rather than others. Generally, it has been possible to earn higher commissions by selling cash value policies than by selling term policies. A recent development is that agents are presenting themselves more as general financial planners than as insurance agents. If the planner's remuneration comes from commissions rather than from fees, conflicts of interest are bound to arise.

Another difficulty for consumers is the rapid turnover among life insurance salespeople; after three years, only 20 percent of agents remain in the business. Although some do make a career in insurance sales, the large number of new entrants lowers the overall knowledge and skill level. This situation, combined with the pressure on agents to sell, makes it essential that prospective buyers of life insurance be as well informed as possible.

Personal Finance in Action 6.5

Term or Whole Life?

Tina, who is 30 years old and has two dependents, has decided that she requires $100 000 of life insurance coverage; but she wonders which type of policy to buy. With the information she has collected from agents, she plotted the annual premium costs (Figure 6.11). She was surprised to find that five-year term insurance, although much cheaper than whole life initially, would increase in cost at each renewal. This graph clarified for her the difference between the level premium for whole life and the increasing premiums for term. It also illustrated that until she turns 55, even the increasing premiums for term coverage will be significantly less than those for whole life. She now realizes that since her children should be independent in 15 years, she does not need whole life coverage. She has decided to buy five-year renewable term insurance.

FIGURE 6.11 ANNUAL PREMIUMS FOR FIVE-YEAR RENEWABLE TERM AND WHOLE LIFE INSURANCE, BY AGE

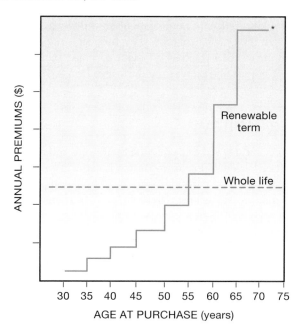

* Five-year renewable term insurance is no longer available after age 65.

Protection for Buyers

Although there have been few instances of life insurance companies that have gone out of business and left policyholders unprotected, the industry has set up a compensation fund to provide for such a contingency. For holders of RRSPs with life insurance companies, the fund provides protection to a maximum of $60 000, as the Canada Deposit Insurance Corporation does for banks, trust companies, and credit unions. Insurance policyholders are protected to a maximum of $200 000, and annuitants to $2000 per month. This plan is similar to an insurance plan initiated to protect the clients of general insurance companies should one of these companies go out of business.

Summary

Life insurance, which may appear very confusing at first glance, is based on a few fundamental principles, such as pooling risk, the pure cost of insurance, and the level premium. By sharing or pooling the risk of an untimely death with many people, individuals can obtain life insurance protection at reasonable cost. The pure cost of life insurance is determined by the mortality curve, which rises with age. Premiums are made level for the term of the policy in order to provide lifelong insurance protection at a predictable cost.

Like most other financial sectors, the insurance industry uses some specific vocabulary that a competent consumer must understand; but in this field, the problem is compounded by a lack of common terminology for naming policies. Companies may add numerous special features to the few basic types of insurance policies and then call the combinations whatever they wish. It is necessary to understand the fundamental types and principles of insurance in order to make an informed choice.

Before making any market comparisons, identify your need for life insurance, remembering that it is primarily a method of risk management. Rarely is life insurance needed as a form of savings. Unfortunately, uninformed buyers tend to make poor choices. The sums of money involved are not small, so the need for greater awareness on the part of consumers is great.

Key Terms

automatic premium loan (p. 144)

back-loaded (p. 140)

beneficiary (p. 129)

cash reserve (cash surrender value) (p. 137)

credit life insurance (p. 137)

dividend (p. 133)

endorsement (rider) (p. 144)

face amount (face value) (p. 129)

family income policy (p. 140)

family policy (p. 141)

front-loaded (p. 140)

grace period (p. 141)

incontestability clause (p. 141)

insurable interest (p. 129)

irrevocable beneficiary (p. 142)

level premium (p. 130)

limited payment policy (p. 138)

loading charge (p. 132)

mortgage insurance (p. 137)

non-participating policy (p. 133)

paid-up policy (p. 144)

participating policy (p. 133)

policy (p. 129)

policy loan (p. 143)

premium (p. 129)

Problems

1. Bert, a 33-year-old Marketing Representative, is wondering whether he has enough life insurance, especially since a second child is due to arrive in a few months. His wife, Mira, who is 31, is busy looking after young Jake, the couple's first-born, and does not work outside the home. Reviewing his financial situation has led Bert to estimate that if he should die tomorrow, he would need to leave a sum of $300 000 in his estate in order to support his children until they become independent, and to support his wife for her lifetime. His list of assets and debts is as follows:

    Life insurance, five-year renewable term........$100 000

    Deposits in bank 2 700

    Equity in home 44 000

    Registered Pension Plan 6 000

    Mutual funds 3 500

    Consumer debts 12 400

    Funeral expenses 4 500

    RRSPs...15 500

    (a) If Bert were to die tomorrow, what would be the net worth of his estate? Would it be sufficient to provide the support he desires for his family? Should the equity in the house be included in this analysis? Give your reasons.

    (b) What recommendation would you make to Bert regarding amount and type of life insurance?

    (c) Assuming that Bert could purchase five-year renewable term insurance for $2.40 per $1000 and whole life for $6.50 per $1000, how much would your recommendation cost him per year?

    (d) Assume that Mira acquires a full-time job. Should she have life insurance also? Would this change Bert's need for life insurance?

    (e) Assume that Mira stays home. Should she have life insurance also? Would this change Bert's need for life insurance?

2. Tony, a 35-year-old tool and die maker owns his own small business in a small town near a major automotive city. He is an active coach in minor sports and enjoys mountain climbing and other outdoor activities. His wife, Alicia, is 33 years old. She worked as an insurance underwriter before their family arrived, but now stays home with their two small children. At this stage in their life, Tony has placed most of his savings into the business and paying off the house. His current income is more than adequate for their growing family, and the business loans are insured through the bank

where they received their financing. Beyond this amount of loans, Tony has not purchased any other life insurance on himself or his wife. He believes that should anything happen to him, the business, which is paid off, could be sold to provide for the family. If necessary, his wife could always return to work in the insurance industry to support the family.

(a) Do you think Tony needs any more life insurance? Consider the family's immediate needs for money should anything happen to Tony. How would they get money to survive in the short and long term?

(b) What would you recommend to Tony and Alicia? Do you have any specific measures that they should undertake? (Hint: use the spreadsheet.)

3. When you bought the policy shown in Appendix 6A, you had been convinced that whole life insurance was the correct way to go. You had researched the alternatives, consulted various advisors, and considered the future you face in your current job and family situation. When applying for the policy, your agent required that you complete a detailed application form that requested information about your job, finances, family health history, your own health history, hobbies, and life style among other concerns.

(a) Why does the life insurance company need the information?

(b) How does each kind of information affect your policy or premium?

4. Decide whether you AGREE or DISAGREE with the following statements:

(a) If Tony and Bert applied to the same company for the same type of life insurance policy and both were accepted, they would pay the same annual premiums.

(b) If they chose whole life, both would pay level premiums for life, or until they reached an age limit such as 85.

(c) If Bert purchases decreasing term insurance, his premiums will decrease each year during the term of the contract.

(d) If Bert changes his job, his present group insurance coverage will continue as long as he pays the premiums.

(e) If Tony chooses a participating policy, he can expect to receive dividends.

(f) Five-year renewable term insurance means that the contract can be renewed at the same premium after five years.

(g) If Tony's health deteriorates, his term policy premium would increase.

(h) A dividend may be regarded as interest earned by the money you paid the insurance company.

(i) A group policy is the same as a participating policy.

5. In the case of a couple where one of the spouses stays home, should both spouses be insured, why? And what factors would warrant the different treatment?

6. What difference does it make in the distribution of property after the death of a policyholder whose life insurance is payable to her estate rather than to a named beneficiary, if (a) she dies intestate, or (b) she leaves a will?

7. Analyze each of the following situations and decide whether you AGREE or DISAGREE with the conclusions:

(a) A single woman of 35, without dependents, who has $35 000 of group insurance in association with her employment, has been called on by a life insurance agent. He encourages her to take out a whole life policy of $100 000. His arguments are as follows: (i) the premium will increase if she postpones buying insurance, and (ii) she should have permanent insurance and not depend on the group policy, which covers her only as long as she stays with that employer. She decides that he is right.

(b) A woman who is widowed at 35 returns to work as a professional librarian to support her four school-age children because her husband's estate was small. She asks an insurance agent for a renewable term policy. The agent recommends that she buy permanent whole life insurance instead, so that she will have something for her old age. She tells the agent that she doesn't want a small amount of permanent life insurance, but a large amount right now.

(c) A young couple with three small children wonders what kind of life insurance to buy. He earns $45 000 a year, and she stays at home to look after the children, while working part-time for another $12 000 per year. They are thinking of taking out a family policy that would put $10 000 on his life, $3 000 on hers and $4 000 on the life of each child. That way the couple would cover the major risks.

(d) A retired couple of 75 and 73, who have a whole life policy for $25 000 on the husband's life, wonder whether to keep paying the annual premium of $175 or to cash in the policy and take the cash surrender value of $12 200. They are living on Old Age Security, Canada Pension, an employer's pension, and the income from their modest investments. They decide not to cash in the policy now but to keep it for the wife's protection in case she should be widowed.

8. Review the life insurance policy in Appendix 6A and decide whether you AGREE or DISAGREE with each of the following:

(a) It is a limited-pay whole life policy.

(b) The insured should have requested an accidental death rider as better protection for his/her family.

(c) It is a participating policy.

(d) If the insured decided to cancel the policy one year after purchasing it, he/she would receive a cash value.

(e) If they decided to surrender the policy 10 years after purchase, they could apply for the cash value plus accumulated dividends.

(f) The insured could buy a paid-up policy if he/she surrendered his or her policy after 10 years.

(g) If the insured could not make a payment, the policy would be cancelled.

(h) The insured should select a lump-sum settlement option for the beneficiary, because this will leave him/her free to select the settlement option that best suits his or her situation at the time.

(i) Who selects how the proceeds are to be paid?

(j) If the policy is cancelled, can it be reinstated? If so, under what terms?

9. Examine the following statements, and identify those that are myths or that involve faulty reasoning. Explain the error.

(a) Buying life insurance is a good way to build up savings.

(b) A policyholder's savings in a whole life insurance policy drop to zero when the policyholder dies.

(c) You should buy life insurance while you are young, when the premiums are lower.

(d) The cash surrender value of a whole life policy is your own money, and the company should not charge interest when you borrow your own money.

(e) Term insurance is not a good buy, because the coverage is temporary but the problem is permanent.

(f) At your death, your beneficiary should receive your policy's cash value as well as its face value.

(g) Only wage earners need life insurance.

10. Why is it said that "life insurance is sold but not bought"?

11. At retirement, a person needs to review his or her insurance coverage in the light of future needs. What are some reasons for either (a) cashing in or cancelling all life insurance, (b) retaining some coverage, or (c) buying more life insurance?

12. Proceed to the industry Web site, **www.clhia.ca,** and determine the code of conduct for members when dealing with consumers. What would you expect the typical insurance salesperson to do to help you with buying insurance? What other concerns would you want addressed? What else can a life insurance agent do for you?

References

BOOKS AND ARTICLES

BALDWIN, BEN. *The Complete Book of Insurance: The Consumer's Guide to Insuring Your Life, Health, Property and Income.* Revised Edition. Toronto: Irwin Professional Publishing, 1996. A guide that helps you explore and determine for your actual insurance needs and costs for all facets of your life.

BULLOCK, JAMES, and GEORGE BRETT. *Insure Sensibly: A Guide to Life and Disability Insurance.* Toronto: Penguin, 1991. Offers practical tips on different kinds of life and disability insurance and on how to determine the right policy and best price.

CANADIAN LIFE AND HEALTH INSURANCE ASSOCIATION INC. *Canadian Life and Health Insurance Facts.* Toronto: Canadian Life and Health Insurance Association, annual. A booklet that provides industry data on purchases and ownership of life insurance, health insurance, and annuities. (Available from the Association at Suite 2500, 20 Queen Street West, Toronto, ON M5H 3S2.)

DELOITTE and TOUCHE. *Canadian Guide to Personal Financial Management.* Scarborough: Prentice Hall Canada, annual. A team of accountants provides guidance on a broad range of topics, including planning finances, estimating insurance needs, managing risk, and determining investment needs. Instructions and the necessary forms for making plans are also included.

PRASKEY, SALLY, and HELENA MONCRIEFF. *The Insurance Book: What Canadians Really Need to Know Before Buying Insurance.* Toronto: Pearson Education Canada Inc., 2000. A thorough coverage of all the insurance options available to Canadians.

Personal Finance on the Web

Canadian Life and Health Insurance Association Inc.

www.clhia.ca An industry body representing the 100 life and health insurance companies in Canada. An overview of the industry and the role it plays as well as the self-established rules of the industry.

Insurance Canada

www.insurance-canada.ca A consumer-focused site with information regarding the needs and intricacies of the industry. It is co-sponsored by the Consumers Council of Canada and the Consumers Association of Canada.

Appendix 6A

Sample Life Insurance Policy

SAMPLE

Basic insurance benefit

London Life will pay $50,000 on the death of the life insured.

Premiums

The agreements made by London Life are conditional on payment of premiums as shown in the policy summary. The first premium is payable on February 12, 2001.

Premiums are payable monthly under London Life's Pre-authorized payment agreement (PPA). If the agreement stops and is either re-started or a different method of paying premiums is selected, increased premiums may become payable due to higher administration charges then in effect.

If any premium other than the first is not paid within thirty-one days after it is due, the contract ceases to be in force, except as provided in Premium loans. If proceeds become payable within the thirty-one days, unpaid premiums will be deducted.

If any premium is paid by cheque or other promise to pay which is not honoured, the premium will be considered unpaid.

Premium Vacation
Premium Vacation is an arrangement that permits the policyowner to apply available dividends and/or existing values (dividend acquired values) to pay part or all of each premium due under the contract, as described in the Use of dividends provision, for a selected period of time. The policy does not become paid-up if Premium Vacation is chosen.

Dividends are not guaranteed and may vary from time to time. Changes in the dividends credited or actions by the policyowner, such as taking a policy loan, may cause the dividends credited and/or existing values (dividend acquired values) to be insufficient to pay the amount selected for Premium Vacation. In that event, other arrangements must be made to pay that part of the premium which can no longer be paid under Premium Vacation. Payment of the full premium, regardless of payment method selected, remains at all times the responsibility of the policyowner.

The policyowner may discontinue Premium Vacation at any time by notifying London Life, though income tax considerations may restrict flexibility when making other premium payment arrangements. London Life may also discontinue Premium Vacation at any time.

Guaranteed values

The guaranteed values at certain dates are shown in the policy summary. Values at other dates will be calculated by London Life on the same basis. There are no values before the first date for which an amount greater than zero is shown.

Dividends

Dividends apportioned by the directors of London Life will be credited to the contract at each anniversary of February 12, 2001. A dividend will not be credited at the first anniversary unless the premium then due is paid.

Policy number - B000030-3   London Life   12 Feb 01   page 1

SOURCE: London Life Insurance Company, London, Canada.

Appendix 6A (continued)

Sample Life Insurance Policy

SAMPLE

Econolife

Dividends credited provide an Econolife insurance benefit, subject to the Use of dividends provision. The Econolife insurance amount is guaranteed not to be less than $50,000, provided no part of the Econolife insurance benefit is surrendered under the Use of dividends provision. The Econolife insurance benefit will be paid in the same event and subject to the same terms as the basic insurance benefit.

Use of dividends

Part or all of the Econolife insurance benefit may be surrendered for its cash value less any indebtedness. On written request and with the agreement of the policyowner and London Life, part of the dividends credited, and/or part or all of the cash value of the Econolife insurance benefit may be

- applied towards payment of premiums (Premium Vacation),
- applied to reduce any indebtedness, or
- paid in cash.

These uses of dividends may result in decreases to the Econolife insurance amount.

If part of the dividends credited are used for purposes other than purchasing the Econolife insurance benefit, and/or part or all of the Econolife insurance benefit is surrendered, the Econolife insurance amount of $50,000 will no longer be guaranteed.

Conversion

The policyowner may exchange the Econolife insurance benefit for

- paid-up additions under this contract, plus
- a new contract on the life insured

by giving written notice to London Life not later than thirty-one days after February 12, 2036 and paying the first premium under the new contract. The total amount of paid-up insurance under this contract after the exchange plus the basic insurance amount of the new contract will be equal to the death benefit under this Econolife insurance benefit.

The application for the new contract includes the application for this contract and any application for change or reinstatement of this contract received before the new contract is made.

New contract after conversion

The policy date will be the date of exchange. The plan of insurance, subject to London Life's issue limits, may be any plan issued by London Life at the date of exchange, other than term insurance.

The premium will be determined according to

- the plan and amount of insurance,
- additional insurance benefits included in the new contract,
- the attained age of the life insured at the date of exchange, and
- the class of risk applicable to this Econolife insurance benefit.

Subject to London Life's issue limits and evidence of insurability satisfactory to London Life, additional insurance benefits issued by London Life at the date of exchange may be included in the new contract.

The beneficiary under the new contract will be the beneficiary under this contract. The policyowner may change or revoke the beneficiary as permitted by law.

page 2   12 Feb 01   London Life   Policy number - B000030-3

London Life

SAMPLE

Use of policy values

The cash value of the contract is the cash value of the basic insurance benefit plus the cash value of the Econolife insurance benefit.

Premium loans

If any premium is not paid, and if the contract has a cash value, London Life will keep the contract in force until the indebtedness exceeds the cash value of the contract. Unpaid premiums become indebtedness. The policyowner may start paying premiums again at any time while the contract is in force.

Cash loans

If the basic insurance benefit has a cash value, on written request London Life will make a loan on the security of the contract. The maximum loan available at any time will be

- the cash value of the contract at the next anniversary of the policy date, discounted to the date of the loan at the interest rate then applicable to the loan
- less existing indebtedness at the time of the loan.

The loan will be made within ninety days after receipt of the request for the loan.

Indebtedness

The indebtedness at any time is

- premium loans plus cash loans,
- less payments made to reduce indebtedness
- with interest to that time.

London Life sets the rate of interest and the times when interest is compounded, and may change them. Payments to reduce indebtedness may be made at any time while the contract is in force.

If the indebtedness becomes greater than the cash value of the contract, the contract will cease to be in force.

Indebtedness will be deducted in determining the proceeds under the contract.

Paid-up insurance

On written request to London Life, this contract will be changed to a paid-up contract. If there is indebtedness, it is first deducted from the cash value of the Econolife insurance benefit. Any remaining cash value of the Econolife insurance benefit will continue to provide an Econolife insurance benefit. The amount of the Econolife insurance benefit will be determined by London Life according to its rules at that time. Any remaining indebtedness is deducted from the cash value of the basic insurance benefit. The amount of paid-up insurance will be

- the amount of paid-up insurance determined from the table of guaranteed values in the policy summary for the date the contract is changed to paid-up (values for dates not shown will be calculated by London Life on the same basis),
- multiplied by the cash value of the basic insurance benefit after deducting any indebtedness, as described above, and
- divided by the cash value of the basic insurance benefit before deducting any indebtedness.

There will be no other benefits in the paid-up contract.

continued

Appendix 6A (continued)

Sample Life Insurance Policy

Surrender for cash
On written request, London Life will pay

SAMPLE

- the cash value of the contract
- less any indebtedness.

Payment will be made within ninety days after surrender of all rights under the contract.

Claims

Death claim
London Life must be provided with proof of death. London Life may also require proof of the truth of the information in the application for the contract and for any amendment or reinstatement of the contract.

Exceptions

Suicide
If the life insured commits suicide, while sane or insane, the amount of proceeds payable with respect to that portion of any insurance benefit that has been continuously in force with respect to that life insured, for less than two years immediately before the death of that life insured, will be limited to the greater of the cash value of that portion and the sum of the premiums paid for that portion during that period.

Settlement options

The payee may elect to have any proceeds that are payable under the contract in one sum applied to provide one or more of the following, subject to the rules and rates London Life is using at that time:

- a deposit account earning interest,
- periodic payments for a selected number of years up to 30,
- periodic payments for life, with payments guaranteed 10, 15 or 20 years as selected,
- periodic payments as long as either of two persons lives, with payments guaranteed 10, 15 or 20 years as selected, and
- any other settlement option London Life is issuing at that time.

London Life will issue a new policy if the proceeds are applied to provide periodic payments.

General provisions

Contract
The contract is the agreement between the policyowner and London Life. It consists of

- this policy,
- any amendment to the contract, and
- the application for the contract and for any amendment or reinstatement of the contract.

page 4   12 Feb 01   London Life   Policy number - B000030-3

SAMPLE

The contract comes into force if

- the first premium has been paid,
- the policy has been delivered to the policyowner or the beneficiary, and
- there has been no change in the insurability of the life insured since the application was completed.

The contract ceases to be in force when the basic insurance benefit ceases to be in force.

The signature of a London Life registrar is required to amend the contract or to waive any of its terms.

Giving facts to London Life
London Life makes the contract on the basis of facts disclosed in the written application for

- the contract,
- any amendment to the contract, and
- any reinstatement of the contract.

It is not sufficient that an agent, employee or medical examiner has knowledge of a fact. If a fact that is material to the insurance benefits was not disclosed in the written application, the contract may be declared void.

Proof of birth date
If the date of birth of the life insured was not correctly disclosed, London Life may

- adjust the amount of the insurance benefits for the correct date of birth,
- adjust any starting and expiry date of the insurance benefits and the date to which premiums are payable, and
- cancel any insurance benefit not available because of age.

Beneficiary
The policyowner may designate a beneficiary to receive the proceeds and may revoke or change the designation as permitted by law.

Reinstatement
London Life will put the contract back into force if

- application for reinstatement is made within two years after the contract ceased to be in force,
- the good health and insurability of the life insured are proved to the satisfaction of London Life,
- overdue premiums with interest at a rate determined by London Life are paid, and
- indebtedness is paid to London Life.

Place of payment and currency
All payments to or by London Life will be made in Canada in lawful money of Canada.

Policy number - B000030-3   London Life   12 Feb 01   (last page) 5

continued

Appendix 6A (continued)

Sample Life Insurance Policy

SAMPLE

Secretary's Office - Terminal 467

Information about your voting privileges

As the owner of one or more London Life participating policies or one or more policies to which voting rights are attached, you are entitled to attend and vote at meetings of the company. This includes the right to vote for policyholder directors. Your right to vote can be exercised either in person or by proxy.

If you complete and return the *Request for meeting notification* form below, you will receive notices of, and forms of proxy that may be used to appoint a proxyholder for, meetings of policyholders and shareholders of the company during the three-year period commencing on the date the form is received by the Corporate Secretary of London Life.

The Request for meeting notification form should be mailed to:

The Corporate Secretary, Terminal 467
London Life Insurance Company
Head Office, 255 Dufferin Avenue
London, Ontario, Canada, N6A 4K1

Request for meeting notification (completion is optional)

I am the owner of one or more London Life participating policies or one or more policies to which voting rights are attached. I request London Life to send me notice of the time and place of, and a form of proxy that may be used to appoint a proxyholder for, each meeting of policyholders and shareholders of the company held or begun during the three-year period commencing on the date the Corporate Secretary of London Life receives this request. I understand that notice will be sent not later than twenty-one days and not earlier than fifty days before any meeting is held.

Month	Day	Year	Signature of LIFE INSURED 30

Policy number	Policyholder's name
B000030-3	LIFE INSURED 30

SAMPLE

Premiums

The total premium payable on the 12th day of each month consists of the following benefit premiums:

Benefit	Premium	Prior to
Basic insurance	$82.98	February 12, 2071

Mode of payment is monthly (PPA).

Guaranteed values

Basic insurance benefit

Date	Age	Cash value - $	Paid-up value - $
Feb 12, 2001	30	0.00	00
Feb 12, 2002	31	0.00	00
Feb 12, 2003	32	50.00	250
Feb 12, 2004	33	100.00	400
Feb 12, 2005	34	170.00	700
Feb 12, 2006	35	715.00	2,700
Feb 12, 2007	36	1,285.00	4,700
Feb 12, 2008	37	1,870.00	6,700
Feb 12, 2009	38	2,470.00	8,600
Feb 12, 2010	39	3,090.00	10,500
Feb 12, 2011	40	3,730.00	12,350
Feb 12, 2012	41	4,385.00	14,100
Feb 12, 2016	45	7,190.00	20,750
Feb 12, 2021	50	10,650.00	26,850
Feb 12, 2026	55	14,375.00	31,650
Feb 12, 2031	60	18,480.00	35,750
Feb 12, 2036	65	22,845.00	39,100
Feb 12, 2041	70	27,370.00	41,900
Feb 12, 2046	75	31,720.00	44,050
Feb 12, 2051	80	35,610.00	45,650
Feb 12, 2056	85	38,945.00	46,850
Feb 12, 2061	90	41,715.00	47,750
Feb 12, 2066	95	44,015.00	48,400
Feb 12, 2071	100	50,000.00	50,000

The guaranteed cash values shown above apply to the basic insurance benefit only. Total value at any time includes the guaranteed cash value plus any dividend acquired values.

continued

Appendix 6A (continued)

Sample Life Insurance Policy

Policy summary

SAMPLE

Data

Life insured..David Gerald Hill

Insuring age 30

Policyowner...David Gerald Hill, the life insured

Beneficiary..BENEFICIARY 30

Plan ....Jubilee Whole Life
with annual dividends

Dividend option ....Econolife

Policy number B000030-3

Policy date..February 12, 2001

Benefits

On death of the life insured

    Basic insurance...............................$50,000

    Econolife insurance.........................$50,000 initially

    Total basic plus Econolife ....$100,000 initially

---

Policyowner - LIFE INSURED 30

Life insured - LIFE INSURED 30

Policy number - B000030-3
Issue date - February 12, 2001
SAMPLE OFFICE - 99999-9

Retirement Income

1. Outline the three sources of retirement income, public and private pensions, and investment income.

2. Define the terms used with the Canada and Quebec Pension Plans: year's basic exemption, year's maximum pensionable earnings, and contributory earnings.

3. Define the terms used with private pension plans: defined contributions, defined benefits, portability, and indexing.

4. Define the annuity principle and the terms used with annuities.

5. Differentiate between the various types of annuities.

6. Outline the costs of buying an annuity.

7. Show how an RRSP can help to provide for a financially secure retirement.

8. List the six criteria for selecting an RRSP.

9. Define the following terms associated with RRSPs: spousal plan, contribution limits, and maturity date.

10. Define segregated funds, RRIFs, and LIFs.

11. Understand the costs and benefits of universal life policies as a means of creating an estate.

Introduction

Retirement is not likely to be on the minds of students as they select courses and make plans for their future careers. Neither is it an important priority for many working people, who put the thought of retirement, like that of death itself, out of their minds. This head-in-the-sand approach is foolish, however, because without a plan for one's retirement, what are popularly called the "golden years" can be very grey indeed. The purpose of this chapter is to raise your awareness of the importance of financial planning for retirement and to emphasize that the earlier this planning starts, the better off you'll be.

Everyone faces two questions when planning for retirement:

(a) Where will I find the money for my retirement?

(b) Will I have enough to live comfortably?

The biggest financial change facing newly retired people is the replacement of their employment income with income from pensions and investments. The level of both types of replacement income depends on investment decisions made many years earlier. Retirees may have no control over employment-related pensions, but they do have control over their own investments and RRSPs. It is important that they pay careful attention to these private investments in order to best meet their retirement needs. While determining these needs may be very difficult when you are young, failing to think about them can have serious consequences. References given at the end of the chapter outline methods of estimating your retirement needs.

Techniques for saving and investing to meet your retirement needs will be discussed in Chapters 9 through 11. In this chapter, we will identify sources of retirement income, discuss private and public pensions, and examine annuities, segregated funds, RRSPs, RRIFs, and LIFs.

Financial Planning for Retirement

Retirement planning requires a long-term perspective on personal finances. As explained in Chapter 1 (under the heading "Lifetime Perspective") over a lifetime your income is likely to be more variable than your living costs, and the positive gap between your income and expenditures will probably be largest during your middle years (see Chapter 1, Figure 1.1). When you retire, your earnings cease; from then on, pensions and investments will be your main sources of income. What you do about pensions and investments during your working years will have a significant bearing on the amount of retirement income available to you.

The basic rule in planning for retirement income is to begin saving early. To achieve financial independence and be able to maintain your preferred lifestyle in retirement, you must ensure that your net worth grows steadily during your working years. It is truly amazing how, due to the magic of compounding, small amounts saved regularly over a long period of time can result in a substantial sum (see Chapter 9, Figure 9.1). Generally, saving gradually in this way is preferable to attempting to save a great deal during the last few years of your working life (see Chapter 1, Figure 1.2). Since it is difficult to predict the exact time you will retire (illness or a decision to retire early could affect the event's timing), it can be unwise to leave saving for retirement until your last few working years.

Sources of Retirement Income

A number of potential sources of retirement income exist. People who have been working can expect to receive benefits from the Canada Pension Plan (or, in Quebec, the Quebec

Pension Plan), and perhaps also from a plan established by their employer. At age 65, they may also become eligible for the Old Age Security pension and for the Guaranteed Income Supplement. In addition, many people will be able to use their RRSPs and other personal investments to generate income. The major sources of retirement income include the following:

Public Pensions
    Old Age Security (OAS)
    Guaranteed Income Supplement (GIS)
    Canada Pension Plan (CPP) or Quebec Pension Plan (QPP)

Private Pensions
    Employment-related pensions

Investment Income
    Funds from RRSPs
    Registered retirement income funds (RRIFs)
    Life income funds (LIFs)
    Annuities
    Segregated funds
    Bond interest and stock dividends
    Rent
    Business income

To qualify for benefits from both public and private pension plans, you must meet certain eligibility requirements, including age, residence, and, for employment-related plans, membership in the plan. Members of a private plan may be able to opt for early retirement with a reduced pension. The Canada and Quebec Pension Plans are not available until age 60, and retirees must be 65 to collect the OAS or the GIS. Old Age Security and the Guaranteed Income Supplement are part of Canada's *Social Safety Net* for seniors. They provide monthly benefits payable to Canadians over 65. Those who wish to receive them must apply.

To qualify for OAS a person must have lived in Canada for 10 years after the age of 18. Those who have lived in the country for 40 years after they have turned 18 qualify for the full amount. In the fall of 2000, the maximum OAS payment per month was $428.79. Once a person's income reaches $53 960, payments begin to be *clawed back*. They are completely eliminated for anyone earning $87 025 and above. Payments are indexed to inflation based on the Consumer Price Index and adjusted four times a year.

The GIS is a monthly payment to those who receive OAS and have little other income. The payment for a single person in the fall of 2000 was $509.59 per month. Anyone earning more than this amount does not qualify.

Income Patterns

What are the major sources of income for those who have already retired? The data presented in Figure 7.1, collected from 1996 taxation statistics, illustrate the income pattern by age and gender for people aged 60 and over. Each bar represents the percentage distribution of the total income for one age and gender group. These data reflect a bias toward higher-income individuals, however, because only those who filed income tax returns and had taxable income in 1994 are represented.

Although the 1996 pattern on income sources for men and women differed by age and gender, there were also some noticeable similarities. For the youngest group, those between 60-64, employment was still the major source of income, 42 percent for men and 33 percent for women. Many of both sexes had not yet retired. For the remaining age groups, public pensions (CPP/QPP, OAS, and GIS) became the largest source of income. Income from these sources increased to between 30 percent and 40 percent as income from employment dropped and was slightly higher for women than men. Investment income for those over 65 also increased with age, reaching a high of 32 percent for males over 75 and 35 percent for females over 75.

We will review some highlights of public and private pension plans before looking more closely at two ways to create retirement income from investments: (i) annuities, which convert funds into a lifetime income, and (ii) registered retirement savings plans (RRSPs), which accumulate funds in a tax shelter.

FIGURE 7.1   INCOME COMPOSITION OF PERSONS AGED 60 AND OVER, BY GENDER AND AGE, CANADA, 1996 TAXATION YEAR FROM TAX STATISTICS ON INDIVIDUALS 1998 EDITION

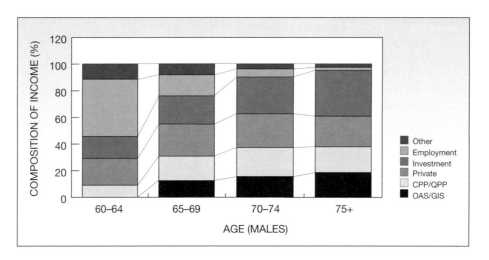

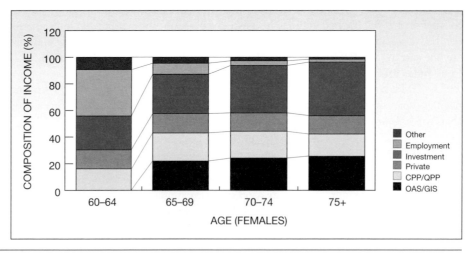

SOURCE: Adapted from Canada Customs and Revenue Agency. www.rc.gc.ca, Table 4, 2000.

Public Pensions

The federal, provincial, and municipal governments provide a variety of social security programs, some of which are intended to provide benefits for older or retired persons. Federal programs are the major source of public retirement pensions, but most provinces and the territories provide income supplements for people who are in financial need.

Public Retirement Pensions

Federal	**Eligibility Criteria**
Old Age Security	age, residence, need
Guaranteed Income Supplement	age, residence, need
Spouse's Allowance	age, residence, need
Canada Pension Plan	age, contributions
Provincial	
QPP for Quebec residents	age, contributions
Income support programs	need

Canada Pension Plan (CPP)

This federal plan was established in 1966 to provide a measure of economic security for three categories of people: the retired, the disabled, and the dependent survivors of contributors. The Province of Quebec decided not to participate in the Canada Pension Plan, setting up the companion Quebec Pension Plan (QPP) instead. There is complete portability between the two plans for those who move into or out of Quebec.

CONTRIBUTIONS Employees and employers are both required to contribute to either the CPP or the QPP. On retirement, the employee will receive a lifetime pension. The amount of the pension depends on the length of time the employee spent in the labour force and on the amount contributed to the plan. The information that follows applies to the Canada Pension Plan; those who live in Quebec are advised to investigate the specific details of the Quebec Pension Plan.

Employers must match their employees' contributions. Self-employed people must make both contributions themselves. To calculate contributions, earnings are divided into three parts. The first part, known as the **year's basic exemption,** is excluded from the calculations. In 1999, this amount was $3500. The second part, the portion on which the employee's contribution rate is based, is called **contributory earnings** and includes any income between $3500 and $37 400. The third part, which is also exempt from the calculations, is any income above the year's **maximum pensionable earnings** ($37 400 in 1999). See Figure 7.2 for a graphic summary of these terms.

In 1996, the federal government indicated that unless changes are made to CPP funding, the fund will be exhausted by 2015. In order to prevent a financial calamity and a major political embarrassment, the government proposed some major funding changes. The 1997 contribution rate was 5.85 percent of contributory earnings, with half of that amount paid by the employer and half by the employee. In 1998, Parliament passed legislation (Bill C-2) to gradually increase the contribution rate until it reaches a combined rate of 9.9 percent. At that point it will be frozen.

Another change is the recent establishment of the **CPP Investment Board**. It will invest funds as they are received in equities. By 2001, 20 percent to 35 percent of the funds will be in equities, the balance in **treasury bills** and **derivatives** that "replicate direct investments in stock indices" through **stock index funds**. Twenty percent may be invested outside of Canada.

The maximum pensionable earnings figure has been increasing annually in recent years. Using 1999 figures, the Personal Finance in Action Box 7.1, "Contributions to Canada Pension," shows how an employee's contributions are calculated.

BENEFITS The size of an individual's CPP benefit depends on the contributions made by that person while employed. In 1999, the average CPP retirement pension was $412.27 per month. The maximum monthly pension was $762.92. CPP benefits are adjusted for inflation and are taxable. Those who qualified received the OAS benefit of $405.44 per month in addition.

FIGURE 7.2 TERMINOLOGY ASSOCIATED WITH CPP/QPP CONTRIBUTIONS (2001 AMOUNTS)

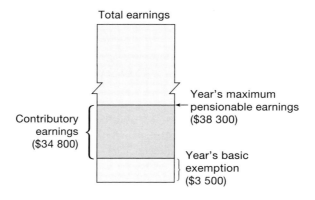

Personal Finance in Action 7.1

Contributions to Canada Pension

Tatiana's earnings in 2000 . . . . $60 000

Year's basic exemption 3 500

Year's maximum
pensionable earnings 38 300

Contributory earnings
($38 300 – 3 500) 34 800

In 2001, Tatiana paid 4.3 percent of $34 800, or $1 496.40, into the CPP; her employer paid the same amount on her behalf.

Long-Term Viability of the CPP

Considerable controversy surrounds the Canada Pension Plan and its ability to provide pensions, even after the contributory rate is raised to 9.9 percent. The Office of the Superintendent of Financial Institutions claimed in December 1998 that "the CPP is on a sound financial footing." [1] But the Association of Canadian Pension Management disagrees. *Dependence or Self-reliance: Which Way for Canada's Retirement Income System*, a study released in January 2000, argues that "unless we begin to institute changes soon, the ratio of working taxpayers to non-working pensioners will halve from 4:1 now to 2:1 by 2030." The study concludes "the current system will provide too little retirement income at too high a cost in an unfair manner 20 to 30 years hence."[2]

Private Pensions

Private retirement pensions may be arranged from personal savings, but generally when we speak of private pensions we mean employment-related ones. The following terms can be considered synonyms: registered pension plans (RPPs), company pension plans, private pension plans, and employer-sponsored pension plans. Essentially, private pension plans represent a way of deferring a portion of your wages until retirement. There is, however, no uniformity in the benefits provided by private pension plans, nor are all of Canada's paid workers covered by such a plan. Almost all medium and large companies have RPPs for their employees. Companies contribute and administer the funds. Employees are not obligated to contribute. Many workers are not members of private pension plans and will therefore have to depend on public pensions and on their own savings when they retire.

Defined Contributions or Defined Benefits

Contributory pension plans require employees to pay a percentage of their wages to the plan in addition to whatever the employer contributes. Some employers offer noncontributory plans—that is, plans in which the employer provides all funds.

There are two main types of private pension plans: defined contribution plans and defined benefits plans. A **defined contribution** (or money purchase) **pension plan** has rules about the amount to be contributed by the employer and employee, but makes no promises about the size of the retirement pension. The contributions credited to an employee's pension account, plus interest, will be available at retirement to purchase an annuity. A **defined benefits pension plan**, by contrast, has a formula for calculating a retirement pension; the formula usually depends on the employee's years of service and on the average wages earned during the last five years of the employee's working life. With such a plan, the employer promises a certain level of retirement benefits. For the long-service employee, a defined benefits plan is usually preferable to a defined contributions plan. Not surprisingly, some employers prefer defined contributions plans, because under such plans they have no pension liability to fund (as they would with a defined benefits plan): that is, they have not promised employees a certain level of pension income.

Although the majority of private pension plans have been of the defined-benefit type, the trend is changing. Some employers, finding the new pension regulations onerous, are shifting the risk to employees by setting up defined contribution plans or group RRSPs. Thus, contributions are made to a retirement fund for employees, but the employer does not promise any particular level of pension. The employer also has less of an obligation to compensate for the effects of future inflation rates or to maximize the yield from the invested pension funds.

---

[1] "CPP Premiums to Stay Below 10 percent," Report on Business, *The Globe and Mail*, December 17, 1998.

[2] "Dependence or Self-reliance: Which Way for Canada's Retirement System," *The Association of Canadian Pension Management*, January 2000, pp. 2–5.

Pension Terminology

Important issues related to pensions involve vesting, portability, survivor benefits, and indexation. We will examine each in turn.

VESTING It is usual for employees not to be granted vesting rights until they have worked for the employer for a specified number of years (traditionally 10, but this specification is being reduced in many places). **Vesting** refers to the time when employees have the right to receive a future pension or when they become entitled to receive the contributions paid into the plan on their behalf by their employer. For instance, vesting occurs after one year in Saskatchewan; after two years in Quebec, in Ontario, and for federal employees; and after five years in Alberta and Manitoba. Employees who leave a job before acquiring vesting rights will receive a refund of their contributions to the pension fund with interest, but will not have rights to the amounts that were contributed by their employer. If they leave their job after they have vesting rights, however, they may have a choice between receiving a refund or collecting retirement benefits, as explained in the next paragraph.

PORTABILITY Formerly, employees who changed jobs could not take their pension credits with them. **Pension portability** is the right to transfer pension credits from one employer to another. The lack of portability in private pensions has long been a serious problem. Recent legislation has, however, brought about some improvement. Workers with vesting rights now have three options when they change jobs: they may (i) leave their pension credits with their former employer and receive a pension at retirement; (ii) transfer their credits to their new employer's pension plan if that plan permits such a transfer; or (iii) transfer their benefits to a locked-in registered retirement savings plan (RRSP). But if they do not stay long enough with an employer for vesting to kick in, all too often a change of job will cause a loss of pension rights and will require them to start over in another pension plan. Some of the options listed above for handling the pension credits for those with vesting rights offer a partial solution to the portability problem. If you change jobs, analyze the costs and benefits of the various options to see which would make a better contribution to your retirement income.

SURVIVOR BENEFITS When one member of a married couple dies, the surviving spouse, if he or she is 65 or older, will receive benefits equal to 60 percent of the calculated retirement pension. If the surviving spouse is disabled, the survivor's pension is equal to the above plus 37.5 percent of the calculated retirement pension. There are many private pension plans. The pension paid to surviving spouses aged 65 and older from such plans varies.

INDEXATION Although public pensions have been fully indexed, many occupational plans do not have either full or partial indexing. A **fully indexed** pension is adjusted regularly to reflect changes in the Consumer Price Index. **Partial indexation** means that the pension is adjusted for part of the change in the Consumer Price Index. There has been more partial or full indexation of pensions in the public sector than in the private sector. The limiting factor is the unknown cost. Employers have been reluctant to promise fully indexed pensions to retirees because of uncertainty about future pension liabilities. Many employees, who are often more oriented to the present than to the future, may also be reluctant to reduce their current take-home pay by making contributions to the pension plan that are large enough to cover future indexing. Those who have not yet retired often display a lack of awareness about the ways in which inflation can erode a fixed pension. For example, with inflation of only 4 percent per year, an unindexed pension will lose about a third of its purchasing power in 10 years, and about half its purchasing power in 18 years. If inflation is 6 percent, purchasing power will be reduced by half in only 12 years. However, at the low levels of inflation currently enjoyed in Canada, pension indexation has become less of a public issue than it once was.

Know Your Plan

An employee may not have much influence on the benefits offered by an employment-related pension plan. Nevertheless, it is in the employee's interest to be informed about the plan. Pension benefits vary so widely that it is wise to ask the following questions:

(a) Is the plan a defined-benefit plan or a defined-contribution plan?

(b) If it is a defined-benefit plan, what formula will be used to calculate pension benefits?

(c) If it is a defined-contribution plan, who makes the investment decisions, and what retirement options are offered?

(d) Are there provisions for early retirement?

(e) What happens if an employee should become disabled?

(f) What are the survivor benefits?

(g) Will the employee's estate receive any of the employer's contributions?

(h) Is it possible to split pension credits in the case of marriage breakdown?

Life Annuities

At retirement, you may need to transform your life savings into an income stream. One way to do so involves purchasing an annuity. For instance, pension funds or RRSPs may be invested in annuities that will produce a monthly income for life. The following discussion of annuities will explain the basic annuity principle and the various ways in which annuities may be bought and paid out to the **annuitant.**

Because none of us knows how long we will live, retirees face the question of whether to use some of their capital for living expenses. If they do decide to use their capital, they must decide at what rate to spend it. If they spend too rapidly, they could outlive their resources; if they are too cautious, they could be forcing themselves to scrimp unnecessarily. So a method has been devised for ensuring that your savings last for a lifetime: it is called a life annuity. Any system that involves liquidating a sum of money through a series of regular and equal payments is called an **annuity.** To annuitize a sum of money means to convert it into a monthly income. Annuity payments were originally made annually (hence the name *annuity*), but these days they are often made monthly or semi-annually instead. It is usually safe to assume that an annuity income payment will be made monthly, unless stated otherwise.

The Annuity Principle

There are two possible ways of protecting against the risk of outliving your savings: (i) acquiring sufficient net worth to support your desired lifestyle indefinitely, or (ii) buying a life annuity. Like insurance, a life annuity is a way of pooling resources with others to ensure that all members of the pool will be protected against a given risk—in this case, that of outliving the income generated by one's savings. Life insurance companies, the only financial institutions currently authorized to sell life annuities, accept the savings of many people; in return, the company promises each annuitant a life income. Those who live a very long time will receive more from the pooled funds than will those who die sooner, but all annuitants will receive an income for as long as they live. As Figure 7.3 emphasizes, though, insurance companies do not promise annuitants that they will receive as much as they have contributed. A life annuity can be useful for a person with modest means who is concerned more about protecting his or her level of living than about creating an estate for heirs. Some misconceptions about annuities stem from not understanding the annuity principle. Do not think of an annuity as a way of making money, but rather as *a way of converting a sum of money into a lifetime income*. This principle is at work in Personal Finance in Action Box 7.2, "Should He Use Some of His Capital?"

FIGURE 7.3   EXPERIENCES OF TWO LIFE ANNUITANTS

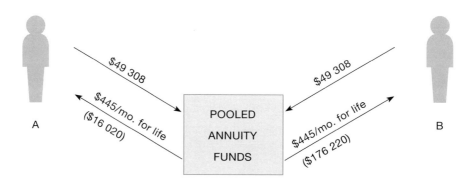

ACCUMULATION PERIOD: At age 65, both A and B purchased immediate, straight life annuities with lump sums of $49 308.

LIQUIDATION PERIOD: Immediately A and B began receiving payments of $445 a month, which would continue for life.

A died at age 68 after receiving payments for 3 years, or a total of 36 × $445 = $16 020.

B died at age 98 after receiving payments for 33 years, or a total of (33 × 12) × $445 = $176 220.

Personal Finance in Action 7.2

Should He Use Some of His Capital?

You are a financial planner. Eric comes to you for advice. He will be retiring next month, when he turns 65. Over the course of his life, he has managed to save $500 000, and he wants to know what to do with this money. He is healthy and has never had a major illness. His wife, Ina, died recently. He has two grownup children, both of whom are married and have good jobs; he also has three grandchildren.

You explain to Eric that what he ought to do with his money depends on his financial goals. Does he want to leave an estate for his heirs, or does he want to use up the capital himself? If he decides to protect the capital and thereby leave some money for his children and grandchildren, he has several options. You point out, however, that no investment can guarantee to protect the purchasing power of his money.

In order to preserve his capital, you suggest to Eric that he divide his money between conservative stocks with growth potential and bonds or GICs. You recommend $100 000 in blue chip stocks and $400 000 in GICs. The

continued

stocks will pay him dividends and allow his portfolio to grow to keep up with inflation. Also, income tax on dividends is less than that on interest income. Stocks can, of course, decline in value, but should appreciate over time. GICs do not fluctuate and will provide Eric with an income.

At the time of his visit, chartered banks are offering 5.35 percent interest for 5 years on non-redeemable deposits of between $250 000 and $999 999.99. The rate is 5.1 percent for redeemable deposits. At 5.35 percent, Eric would earn $1783.33 per month on his GIC. He would earn $1700 a month at the lesser rate of 5.1 percent. No one knows what will happen to interest rates in the future. If Eric locks in the 5.35 percent rate, he may miss out on a rate increase in the future. You point out that the long-range forecast for the Canadian economy is very good. Unemployment is still higher than in the U.S., and inflationary pressures are benign. There is therefore not much likelihood that the Bank of Canada would want to see interest rates climb.

Another option open to Eric is a **segregated fund**, a special type of mutual fund sold only by life insurance companies (see Chapter 11 for a discussion of mutual funds). Sold like an annuity with a maturity of at least 10 years, segregated funds are kept separate from the insurance company's other assets and therefore offer a guarantee of principal. When the annuitant dies, the fund must provide a minimum death benefit of 100 percent of the funds invested minus withdrawals. In addition, on the annuitant's death, the money in the fund can pass directly to a beneficiary and avoid probate fees.

You can also tell Eric that if he doesn't want to leave an estate, he can buy a life annuity from an insurance company; this approach will guarantee him an income for life. The problem with such an annuity is that the insurance company will keep his capital once he dies, even if his death occurs just weeks after he buys the annuity.

The options Eric is considering are diagrammed in Figure 7.4.

FIGURE 7.4   OPTIONS FOR GENERATING RETIREMENT INCOME

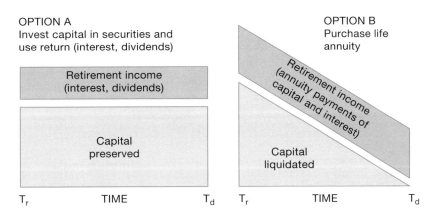

OPTION A
Invest capital in securities and use return (interest, dividends)

Retirement income (interest, dividends)

Capital preserved

T_r TIME T_d

OPTION B
Purchase life annuity

Retirement income (annuity payments of capital and interest)

Capital liquidated

T_r TIME T_d

T_r = date of retirement
T_d = date of death

Characteristics of Annuities

Annuities have several important characteristics that should be clearly understood:

(a) the distinction between the accumulation period and the liquidation period,

(b) the method of paying the purchase price,

(c) when the liquidation period will start,

(d) the number of lives covered,

(e) the refund features.

ACCUMULATION AND LIQUIDATION PERIODS Every life annuity comprises two stages: (i) the **accumulation period**—that is, the interval during which the annuitant pays the insurance company for the annuity; and (ii) the **liquidation period**—that is, the time span during which the insurer makes payments to the annuitant (see Figure 7.5). The accumulation period may last for many years if the annuity is bought by instalment; it may be very brief if the annuity is purchased with a lump sum. Regardless of the method chosen for buying an annuity, the accumulation period must be completed before the liquidation period may start.

METHOD OF PAYING If an annuity is purchased with a lump sum, it will be a **single-payment annuity.** The other alternative is to buy the annuity gradually, over a number of years, by making a series of regular instalment payments or premiums. The instalment method is useful for a person who finds saving difficult and therefore needs a contractual savings plan, but others may prefer the flexibility of accumulating capital on their own and then deciding later whether to buy an annuity.

STARTING THE LIQUIDATION PERIOD The payout from an annuity may begin immediately after the annuity is purchased, or it may be deferred until a later date. An **immediate**

FIGURE 7.5 PAYMENT OPTIONS DURING THE ACCUMULATION AND LIQUIDATION PERIODS OF A LIFE ANNUITY

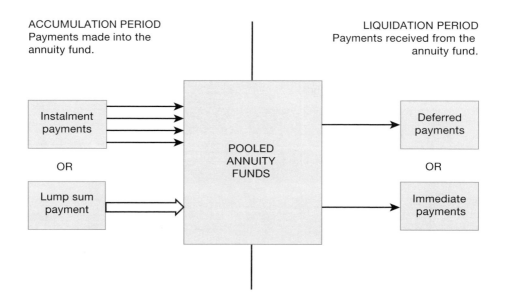

annuity will start making regular payments to the annuitant at once. By definition, an immediate annuity must be bought with a single payment, since all payments for an annuity must be completed before the liquidation period begins. With a **deferred annuity,** the liquidation period begins some time after purchase, and the annuity may be bought either with a single payment or with a series of premiums. For instance, a young person who has inherited a sum of money could decide to buy a single-payment deferred annuity that will begin payments when he or she is older.

NUMBER OF LIVES COVERED The simplest and cheapest form of life annuity is the **straight life annuity,** which pays an income for the life of the annuitant and ceases at death, with no further payments to beneficiaries. But an annuity may also be designed to produce a life income for more than one person—commonly for two. A couple, for example, may buy a **joint-life-and-last-survivorship annuity.** The name of such an annuity is derived from "joint life," which pays as long as both are alive, and from "last survivor," meaning that the annuity will continue during the lifetime of the survivor. These points are illustrated in Figure 7.6.

Not surprisingly, a **joint-and-survivor annuity** (its abbreviated name) is the most expensive of all annuities. The rates for a couple are based on the woman's age when the annuity is purchased, because of her longer life expectancy and the possibility that she may be younger than her husband. The purchaser must decide whether, after the death of the first spouse, the survivor will continue to receive the full payment or will receive only some proportion of it, such as half or two-thirds. The cost of a joint-and-survivor annuity can be reduced if the payments are planned to decrease after the first death. Another possibility is to buy two separate life annuities, one on each life. Table 7.1 illustrates the costs of both alternatives.

ANNUITY CONTRACT Appendix 7A presents a sample annuity contract. What type of annuity is it?

REFUND FEATURES An annuitant may be interested in the refund features available during either the accumulation period or the liquidation period of the annuity. If the annuitant should die during the accumulation period, or decide to discontinue payments, it would be desirable to have the amount that has already been paid, plus interest, refunded. Or, an annuitant who does not wish to continue payments may be given the option of converting to a smaller paid-up annuity.

FIGURE 7.6 LIQUIDATION PAYMENTS BY NUMBER OF LIVES COVERED

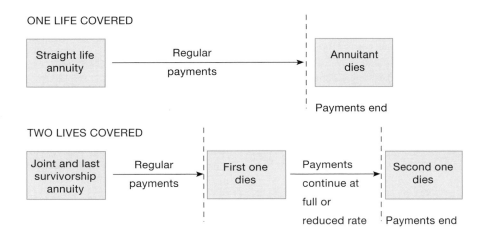

TABLE 7.1   TWO LIFE ANNUITY OPTIONS FOR A COUPLE

A.   STRAIGHT LIFE ANNUITY—20-year guarantee

Annuitant	Purchase price	Income per month
Husband, age 65	$399 922.44	$2 500

B.   JOINT-LIFE-AND-LAST-SURVIVORSHIP-ANNUITY—20-year guarantee
(Survivor to receive 50% of monthly income)

Annuitant	Purchase price	Income per month
Husband and wife	$300 000	1 242.27
Survivor		621.13

Refund features during the liquidation period are very popular with buyers who worry that they may not live long enough to receive as much as they contributed. In response to this concern, life insurance companies have created annuity plans that include payments for a guaranteed length of time, or to a guaranteed minimum amount, regardless of whether the annuitant lives or dies. Because of these provisions, these plans are called **refund annuities.**

A very popular type of refund annuity is one with a minimum number of instalments guaranteed. A life annuity with 10 years "certain," for example, promises to make payments as long as the annuitant lives, but for a minimum of 10 years even if the annuitant dies. If the annuitant should die within the first 10 years of the payout period, a named beneficiary will receive a lump sum equivalent to the balance of payments the annuitant would have received if he or she had lived until the end of the 10-year period. Note that the certain period refers to the minimum payment period, not the maximum. These ideas are summarized below.

Refund Features During the Accumulation and Liquidation Periods of an Annuity

Situation	Refund
Accumulation Period:	
Annuitant decides to stop paying.	Contributions refunded.
Annuitant dies before completing purchase of annuity.	Contributions refunded.
Liquidation Period:	
Annuitant has policy with 10 years certain but dies before 10 years.	Sum equivalent to balance of payments remaining in the 10-year period is paid to the annuitant's beneficiary or to the annuitant's estate.

The Cost of an Annuity

Six factors influence the cost of an annuity:

(a) the size of the monthly payments desired,

(b) the annuitant's life expectancy (as influenced by age, gender, and health),

(c) interest rates,

(d) the length of the accumulation period,

(e) whether the annuity has either refund features or inflation protection features,

(f) the number of lives covered.

SIZE OF PAYMENTS There are two ways to approach purchasing an annuity: either (i) put a certain amount of money into an annuity, and then accept the income it will generate; or (ii) determine the specific monthly income desired, and then pay the necessary amount to generate this. Most buyers of annuities fall into the first group: they buy as much monthly income as their limited funds permit, and are well aware of the relationship between cost and expected income.

LIFE EXPECTANCY Although an annuity's price is based on a number of factors, life expectancy is a critical one. Three variables commonly used to predict life expectancy are gender, age, and health. Since females, younger people, and healthy people are expected to live longer than are males, older people, or sickly people, the insurance company can expect to have to make annuity payments to someone who falls into one or more of the first three categories for a longer time. And because this situation is more costly for the insurance company, individuals in the former group will receive a smaller monthly income from a given amount that they put into an immediate life annuity. The difference gender makes is shown in Figure 7.7.

FIGURE 7.7 MONTHLY ANNUITY INCOME BY AGE AT PURCHASE AND GENDER (SINGLE-PAYMENT, IMMEDIATE, STRAIGHT LIFE ANNUITY; ALL PURCHASERS PAY THE SAME PRICE)

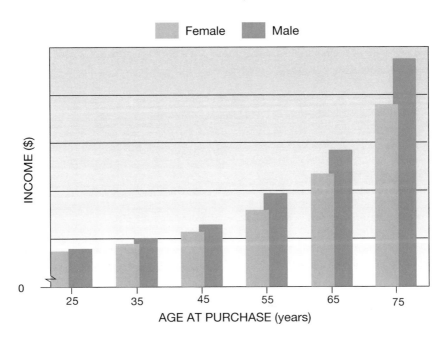

INTEREST RATES An annuity's cost is greatly influenced by the expected return that can be earned on the annuity's funds while they are held by the insurance company. When interest rates are high, a sum of money can be turned into a higher level of annuity income than it can become when interest rates are low. For this reason, financial advisors suggest carefully choosing the time when you will convert your capital into an annuity.

LENGTH OF ACCUMULATION PERIOD Compared with an immediate annuity, an annuity that is bought with instalments over many years will cost less, because of the additional interest the insurance company earns during the longer time the premiums are on deposit. Table 7.2, which compares the total cost of two ways of buying a certain level of annuity income, shows that a single-payment, immediate annuity costs more than an instalment annuity that is bought over 30 years. Instalment annuities have largely been replaced by segregated funds. These are discussed later in this chapter.

TABLE 7.2   PURCHASE PRICE AND MONTHLY INCOME BY METHOD OF PURCHASE

METHOD OF PURCHASE*	PURCHASE PRICE	MONTHLY INCOME
Single-payment, immediate annuity bought at age 65	$300 000	$1 378.38
Instalment annuity; premiums paid from age 30 to age 60. ($2100/yr.)	63 000	2 000

*Straight life annuity bought by a female with income, to start at age 65.

REFUND FEATURES An annuity with a guaranteed period will cost you more, because the guarantee changes the probable number of years the insurance company will have to make payments to you (see Table 7.3). The cost differences reflect the certainty of having to make payments for 10 years, regardless of the annuitant's life expectancy. Few insurance sales people now sell annuities with no certain period.

TABLE 7.3   PURCHASE PRICE BY GUARANTEED PERIOD

TYPE OF ANNUITY*	PURCHASE PRICE
Straight life; no certain period	$71 805
Life annuity; 10 years certain	$75 845

*Immediate annuity to provide a life income of $650 per month for a male, aged 65.

Figure 7.8 makes the same point, showing that, in general, a lump sum that is used to buy an immediate annuity will produce a lower monthly income if the annuity has is a refund feature (see also Personal Finance in Action Box 7.3, "Buying an Annuity"). However, if the annuity is bought before age 45, the difference is small.

FIGURE 7.8 ANNUITY INCOME BY AGE AT PURCHASE AND GUARANTEED PERIOD (SINGLE-PAYMENT, IMMEDIATE LIFE ANNUITY)

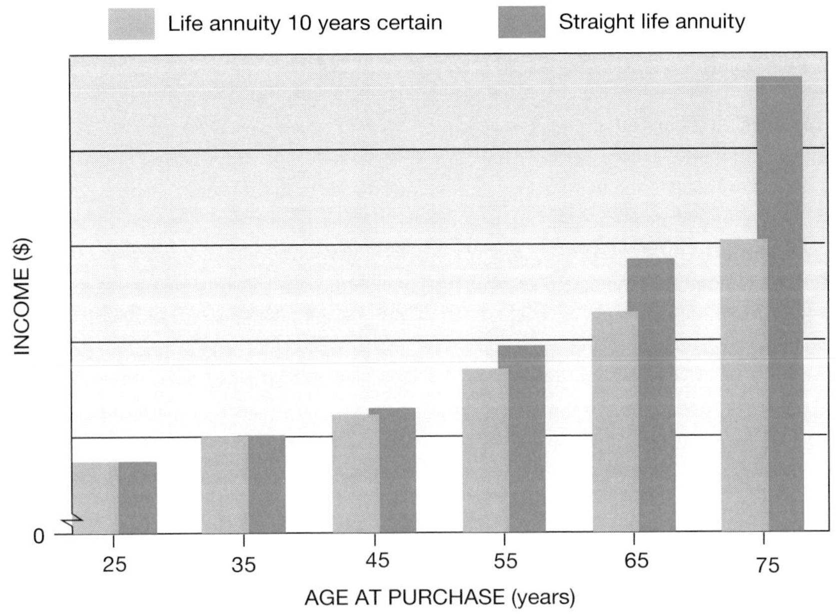

Personal Finance in Action 7.3

Buying an Annuity

In preparation for her forthcoming retirement, Mrs. Alvarez is thinking of converting her three RRSPs to a life annuity to generate a dependable income. Because she has no dependents and has a distaste for investment management, she believes that an annuity is her best option. Her first thought is to ask her life insurance agent to make all the arrangements. But Mrs. Alvarez talks about her plans to several friends, who advise her to consult an insurance broker for help. An insurance broker can obtain quotations from many life insurance companies for a client, and since brokers get commissions from the companies that issue the annuities, the client is not normally charged for this service.

On talking to a broker, she discovers that there is more to buying an annuity than she has supposed. The broker first familiarizes himself with Mrs. Alvarez's financial situation, considering such aspects as other sources of retirement income, her predicted marginal income tax rate, and the potential needs of any dependents. Then he presents several options for her consideration. He mentions that if a person's health is poor, she might, with the support of medical evidence, qualify for an impaired-health annuity, which would pay a higher income for the same premium. When Mrs. Alvarez asks why, the broker explained that the insurer's liability is reduced if the annuitant is not expected to live for a long time, making it possible for the company to pay a higher rate.

The broker presents Mrs. Alvarez with two potential ways of preserving purchasing power. She can investigate the escalating

continued

annuities offered by some insurance companies, or she can plan to buy a series of annuities in various years. The escalating annuity will initially pay a lower monthly income, but that income will be adjusted annually according to prevailing interest rates. Since an inflationary period normally causes interest rates to rise, she would therefore receive higher annuity payments to offset the inflation. If interest rates were to fall, the company would not lower payments, but would instead increase them more slowly. Such escalating annuities are one example of the ways in which insurers have modified annuities to help preserve clients' purchasing power in inflationary times.

Some brokers suggest that a client buy a series of annuities in different years to take advantage of changing interest rates. The premiums for annuities are very sensitive to the interest rates that companies expect to receive on invested funds. Mrs. Alvarez could deregister one of her RRSPs to buy an annuity now, and do likewise with the other two in later years. (She must have all her RRSPs deregistered by the time she is 69 in order to comply with the income tax laws.) In a period of rising interest rates, buying a series of annuities could be advantageous, but if rates were falling, the reverse could be true.

Mrs. Alvarez knows that she wants an immediate annuity, but she is undecided about the refund feature. She discovers that for a given premium, she can obtain a somewhat larger annual income with a straight life annuity than with one that has a 10-year guarantee. The broker asks her whether she would rather have (i) the higher income, or (ii) the assurance that should she die before the 10 years elapse, her estate will receive payments for the balance of the decade.

The broker advises her to decide what kind of annuity she wants before he starts obtaining quotations for her, since annuity prices change rapidly—sometimes even daily. For this reason some companies will guarantee their quotations for only one to three days. Because rates vary not only from time to time but also among companies, the broker will seek quotations from quite a number of firms for Mrs. Alvarez.

NUMBER OF LIVES COVERED You will pay more to buy a life annuity that will provide an income for the lifetimes of two people than if the annuity must provide an income for just one person. In the case of a couple, the cost is related to the gender and age of the younger partner. A woman is expected to outlive her husband even if they are the same age; a woman who is younger than her husband can be expected to live proportionately longer than he does.

Variable Annuities

Segregated funds have replaced variable annuities. This type of fund is discussed later in this chapter (see "Segregated Funds").

Annuities and Income Tax

The income tax treatment of annuity payments depends on whether the annuity was bought with before-tax or after-tax dollars. Each payment includes both capital and interest, and these components may be treated separately for tax purposes. If the annuity was purchased with before-tax dollars (which would have been in a tax shelter, such as an RRSP) both the capital and the interest components of the income payments will now be exposed to income tax. But if the annuity was purchased with after-tax dollars (i.e., the annuity was not in a tax

Buying a Segregated Fund

Margie had always been a shrewd investor. After graduating from university, she landed a good job with a major fibre optics manufacturer. She earned much more than she required to meet her meager needs, and so she invested on a regular basis in some of the leading information technology companies. Her investments did very well.

When she was 45, on the advice of her insurance agent, she decided to take some of her gains and put $300 000 into segregated funds. This would provide security for her retirement. She arranged to make monthly payments of $100. Since her contribution was more than $10 000, she could make automatic withdrawals if she wished. She could also make annual withdrawals of up to $60 000, or 20 percent of her original contributions without paying a withdrawal fee. She believed her retirement was secure no matter what happened to the stock market.

If Margie continued to make contributions of $100 a month and made no withdrawals at age 65, her fund would be worth at least $1 006 273. The insurance company told her a return of 6 percent was possible (see Table 8A.5).

$1 200 per year x 36.786 = $ 44 143.6
$300 000 x 3.2071   = $ 962 130
                              $1 006 273

shelter), the capital portion is not taxable when received. The issuing company will provide the annuitant with annual statements that separate the capital and interest portions he or she has received. Income tax rules require that during the accumulation period of a deferred annuity, the owner report the accrued interest at least every three years.

Whether to Buy an Annuity

Before deciding to buy an annuity, you should review various costs and benefits of annuities. A major advantage of an annuity is that it provides a guaranteed, usually fixed, lifetime income without the concern of having to manage any investments. But by the same token, you lose the flexibility to manage your own money; once funds are put into an annuity, they are committed, and their management is out of your hands. If a more beneficial investment opportunity should arise, you will not be able to take advantage of it. Conversely, an annuity offers protection against a depressed investment climate. In an inflationary period, a fixed income loses purchasing power, but a fixed income would be an advantage if prices should fall. There is no way to guarantee that an annuitant will receive as much as or more than was paid into an annuity, but that should be of little concern. The annuitant will have a guaranteed life income, even if his or her heirs do not receive an estate. Of course, it is also possible to put only a portion of one's capital into an annuity, leaving part of it available to be bequeathed to others.

Annuities are not for everyone, but they are a useful way to make a small estate last for a lifetime. Those who are in poor health, those who want to leave an estate for heirs, and those who have the time and inclination to manage their own investments may all be wise to put their money elsewhere. But a deferred annuity is a reasonable option for anyone who needs a contractual savings plan to ensure that money is saved for his or her retirement. Please note that this discussion of annuities is intended only to illustrate the basic principles involved, not to describe all the possible variations of annuities that may become available. Financial institutions are quite inventive in constantly creating new services for consumers, so you will need to familiarize yourself with the options that are currently available before making your own decision.

Registered Retirement Savings Plans

What Is an RRSP?

A **registered retirement savings plan** (an RRSP) is a method used to shelter savings from income tax. When you invest savings outside a tax shelter, you are using after-tax dollars; any income earned by those investments, such as interest or dividends, is taxable. But if you put that same money into an RRSP, no tax is payable when the investment is made, nor is the yield taxable while it remains within the RRSP. Tax-exempt funds that go into an RRSP are referred to as before-tax dollars. Chapter 2 contains a diagram that illustrates this point (see "Contributions to Retirement Plans"). Note that having an RRSP does not mean that you need never pay tax on this income: sheltering money in an RRSP merely *defers* (postpones) having tax on that money. All funds become taxable when they are removed from the tax shelter. The ideal strategy is to put money into an RRSP when you are being taxed at a high marginal tax rate, and then take it out later when your income (and therefore your rate) is lower—for example, after you have retired. An example in Chapter 2 (Personal Finance in Action Box 2.3, "Should She Use a Tax Shelter?") demonstrates how income tax may be deferred by an RRSP.

Two widely held misconceptions associated with RRSPs are (i) that everyone needs an RRSP, and (ii) that an RRSP is a specific type of investment. Because Canadians are exposed to such energetic promotion of RRSPs, investors may forget that income tax deferment is a major reason for putting money into an RRSP. It is a way of sheltering savings from tax to allow them to grow at a faster rate than they otherwise would, and thus to accumulate a fund for retirement or for another purpose. If your financial circumstances are such that you already pay little or no income tax, you probably do not need an RRSP; you can invest your savings on your own without having to obey the restrictions imposed on RRSPs. *An RRSP is not a specific type of investment, but a way of registering one or more of a variety of types of investments in order to shelter the invested funds and to defer paying income tax both on the original funds and on any income generated by investing those funds.* As we will see, many kinds of investments may be put in an RRSP.

To repeat, the chief reason for putting money into a registered retirement savings plan is to defer income tax. Your savings will grow faster inside a tax shelter than they could grow outside it, and if you take the money into income in future years, when your marginal tax rate is lower, you may pay less income tax on it than you would have paid on the same amount had it been taxable the year in which you earned it. (Refer to Chapter 2, under "Federal Income Tax Rates," for an explanation of the marginal tax rate.) Remember, though, that the money in your RRSP will be taxable eventually, when you deregister the plan. Since RRSP funds are not quite as accessible as other savings, such plans may help some people build a retirement fund, especially those people who normally have a hard time holding onto their savings.

Putting money into an RRSP does involve investing, so you should take as much care in choosing an RRSP as you would in selecting any investment. It can be a mistake to become so caught up in the prospect of deferring income tax that you pay little attention to the quality and appropriateness of your RRSP investments. The principles of investing that we will discuss in Chapters 9 through 11 apply equally well to RRSP decisions.

Types of RRSPs

Canada's federal *Income Tax Act* allows you to register a broad range of investments as RRSPs. Although some of these types may be unfamiliar to you, that should not matter at this stage. This chapter focuses on the tax shelter aspect of RRSPs, not on the specifics of the various types of investment, each of which is treated in some detail in later chapters. The major types of investments currently acceptable for RRSPs may be categorized as follows:

A. **Guaranteed funds**   These funds promise the return of the principal with a guaranteed rate of return; they are available from most banks, trust companies, credit unions, and life insurance companies.

 1. savings accounts
 2. term deposits or guaranteed investment certificates

B. **Mutual funds**   These funds make no promises about rate of return or safety of principal; they are available from mutual funds companies and agencies, trust companies, life insurance companies, investment dealers, and banks.

 1. equity funds
 2. bond funds
 3. balanced funds
 4. money market funds
 5. clone funds

C. **Self-administered RRSPs**   Plans in which the investor makes the investment decisions. Self-administered RRSPs, which are available from various financial institutions, may include any combination of the following:

 1. cash
 2. treasury bills
 3. bonds, including Canada Savings Bonds
 4. mortgages
 5. mutual funds
 6. stocks

D. **Life insurance or life annuity**   These products are sold by life insurance companies.

GUARANTEED FUNDS   A guaranteed fund is the safest place to put RRSP money, as long as you are prepared to accept the lower return associated with the low risk. The institutions that market such funds promise a return of the principal with interest, and your deposits (up to $60 000 per institution) are insured against loss. It is wise to inquire whether the plan is covered by deposit insurance, since there may be some exclusions.

Savings accounts in an RRSP, like any savings account, pay interest regularly at the prevailing rate without locking in the funds for a certain term. Higher interest is usually paid on term deposits or guaranteed investment certificates, which promise a given interest rate in exchange for locking up your money for a stated term.

When choosing a guaranteed plan, check the following features:

(a) the interest rate,

(b) how often interest is compounded,

(c) when interest rates may be adjusted,

(d) the minimum deposit,

(e) the annual fees,

(f) any registration, withdrawal, or other fees.

Many banks and trust companies have discontinued fees on guaranteed funds RRSPs. It is worthwhile to do some comparison shopping before selecting a plan and an institution.

MUTUAL FUNDS Without going into a detailed explanation of mutual funds here (see Chapter 11 for an extensive discussion of this topic), suffice it to say that mutual funds pool the funds of many investors. Instead of actually buying stocks, bonds, or mortgages, the investor just buys one or more shares in the mutual fund, which in turn invests in such securities. Professional fund managers make the investment decisions for the fund's investors. Over 2000 different mutual funds are sold in Canada, and each is designed to achieve a range of investment objectives. Some funds are invested in common stock or equities, some in bonds or mortgages, and yet others, called money market funds, in treasury bills and other debt instruments.

Mutual funds are sold directly by the fund companies, financial advisors, investment dealers (stock brokers), and financial planners. The banks and insurance companies also sell their own funds. Fund buyers face certain costs. The management expense fee varies with funds' values. Sales fees may be front-load or deferred (back-end load). Special fees may also be charged.

Use mutual funds for your RRSP only if you are prepared to accept more risk than with guaranteed funds. Mutual funds do not give you any assurance that you will get back either your original investment or any income you earn from it; but they do offer the prospect of greater gain (or loss) if you are willing to accept the risk. Even so, mutual funds represent a wide spectrum of risk levels, so it is usually possible to find an appropriate fund for almost any objective.

SELF-ADMINISTERED PLANS For those who have the time, expertise, and enough money to make it worthwhile, a self-administered RRSP has the advantage of allowing the investor to make the investment decisions. A wider range of investment types may be held in a self-directed plan, such as Canada Savings Bonds, other bonds, stocks, treasury bills, or mortgages. You can shift funds from one form of investment to another as desired, and you can decide how much risk to assume. Institutions that handle self-directed RRSPs—which include most investment dealers and some banks, trust companies, and life insurance companies— usually charge an annual administration fee, as well as commissions on some transactions.

LIFE INSURANCE PLANS Besides offering guaranteed funds and mutual funds, life insurance companies provide a combination of life insurance coverage and retirement saving, whereby a policy's cash value is registered as an RRSP. Think carefully before tying your RRSP money to your life insurance coverage, though. The contract may require fixed annual payments that limit your flexibility in annual contributions and in moving RRSP money around. Since the fees and commissions tend to be heaviest in the early years, an investor who cancels such a contract after only a short time will lose money.

Various types of annuities available from life insurance companies are eligible as RRSP investments. The schedule of payments may be fixed or flexible. As with life insurance, there will be commissions payable in the early years.

Criteria for Selecting an RRSP

The stiff competition among the financial institutions that sell RRSPs has been a boon to consumers, resulting in considerable variety in the characteristics of RRSP offerings. As with any investment, you should be clear about your objectives before selecting your RRSP(s). Here are six important questions to ask yourself:

1. **Does the RRSP fit with my investment objectives?**

    How well will this RRSP complement my other investments with regard to risk, return, and liquidity?

2. **How much flexibility in contributions do I want?**

Some RRSPs are contractual: they require that you agree at the outset to contribute a set amount at regular intervals. Such a plan permits no changes in the level of your contribution if your circumstances change. Other plans require a minimum payment to keep the plan open, but are otherwise flexible; still others may not require any payment in a given year. When considering flexibility, remember that there is a maximum limit on annual RRSP contributions. If your income changes, your contribution limit will also change. Having only contractual RRSPs could restrict your flexibility too much.

3. **Will the plan accept transfers of lump sums?**

   If you should change jobs and receive a refund of your pension contributions, you might be interested in "rolling over" this lump sum into an RRSP in order to postpone paying income tax on it (in addition to the tax payable on your regular income) during the year in which you receive it.

4. **Will there be a penalty if the fund is cashed in before maturity?**

   Suppose you find a fund's performance unsatisfactory and wish to transfer the money to another RRSP. You need to know in advance whether this will be possible—and if so, whether the institution will exact a penalty or charge a fee.

5. **How much risk and return can be expected?**

   There is usually a trade-off between risk and return, with less risk associated with a lower return. What level is appropriate for you? Generally, the more distant your expected retirement date, the more risk you can safely handle. As you near retirement, you will want to reduce risk.

6. **What will the administrative charges be?**

   Is there a sales charge taken off contributions, or a management fee that is charged initially, annually, or at maturity? Are there redemption fees, or any other charges? What is the relationship of the charges to the predicted yield? Looking for the lowest administrative charges may not always be the wisest move.

Contribution Limits

Anyone with earned income (salary, wages, royalties, business income, rental income, alimony) may contribute to a RRSP. But you are allowed to contribute no more than a certain maximum each year. Your maximum annual contribution depends on whether you are also a member of an employer-sponsored registered pension plan (RPP). If you are not in an RPP, you can contribute 18 percent of your previous year's earned income, up to a specified maximum. The contribution limit is currently frozen at $13 500 until 2003. It is then scheduled to increase to $14 500 in 2004, and to $15 500 in 2005. In subsequent years, the maximum limit will be indexed to increases in the Consumer Price Index.

You are allowed to exceed your limit by $2000 without incurring a penalty. The penalty for contributing anything beyond that is 1 percent per month; Revenue Canada will bill you for the overcontribution until you take the extra money out of your plan, or until enough time passes so that the overcontribution can been applied to the following year's limits. Overcontributing is a common mistake, since calculating your precise limits is hard to do (and even the statement that Revenue Canada sends with your annual tax assessment can be incorrect). Many people find that the penalty is compensated for by the growth in the fund, so they just leave the extra money in the fund and treat it as part of the following year's contribution. You do not receive any tax deduction for overpayments.

If you are a member of an employer-sponsored RPP, your maximum annual contribution is 18 percent of your previous year's earned income—up to the limits described above, less a pension adjustment. The pension adjustment is calculated by employers and by Revenue Canada Taxation; notification of this amount is sent to employees late in each year. The calculation differs for defined benefit plans and defined contribution plans. These rules are aimed at adjusting RRSP limits to ensure equity for employees of different firms who participate in different kinds of pension plans. Members of plans with generous benefits are not allowed to contribute as much to their RRSPs as members of plans with more restricted benefits.

RRSP CARRY FORWARD If you cannot use your RRSP maximum in a particular year, you are allowed to "carry forward" the allowance indefinitely. This way, you will experience no penalty if you want to invest in RRSPs, yet are short of money one year while having more the next.

Spousal Plans

As we have seen, having an RRSP lets you reduce your taxable income during your working years while simultaneously accumulating funds for your retirement. You may also contribute to a spousal plan, provided that your total contributions (to your own plan and to your spousal plan together) do not exceed your maximum limit. Spousal RRSPs have become very popular, particularly where one spouse is anticipating very little pension income—as a result, for example, of having spent a number of years outside the paid work force while raising children (see Personal Finance in Action Box 7.5, "Income Splitting on Retirement"). Such plans are now also available to common-law couples. The benefits of contributing to a spousal plan are twofold. The contributing spouse lowers his or her taxable income for the year in which the contribution is made. In addition, the spouse with the plan will have a lower marginal tax rate on retirement when the funds are withdrawn. Note that if funds are withdrawn from a spousal plan either in the year of the contribution or during the next two calendar years, they are taxed in the hands of the contributor. If a couple with a spousal plan divorces, the assets in the plan become the property of the spouse in whose name the plan is registered (not the contributing spouse).

Personal Finance in Action 7.5

Income Splitting on Retirement

Omar will be retiring this year when he turns 65. Unlike many men his age, he is not worried about his financial future. He will have an excellent pension from his employer, the Ford Motor Company. He also has considerable income from his investments, and he will receive the Canada Pension.

Sarah, his wife, is 63 and has not worked outside their home since the birth of their first son, John, 30 years ago. As a result, she will get very little from the CPP, but she does have $200 000 in a spousal RRSP. Omar has contributed to this plan for many years in order to reduce his taxable income and to income-split

with Sarah on his retirement. Since her taxable income will be less than his, they stand to realize considerable tax savings as a result of the spousal RRSP.

Upon retirement, Omar and Sarah plan to travel, work in their garden, and pay more attention to their investments. Sarah has six years before she needs to close the spousal RRSP and wants to change the investments in the plan to significantly increase its value. She would like to have enough money once she turns 69 so that she is not dependent on Omar.

It is generally not possible to transfer funds retroactively from your own RRSP to your spouse's RRSP, so you must contribute to a spousal RRSP from current income. Funds can be transferred from one spouse's RRSP(s) to the other's RRSP without attracting income tax in only two situations: (i) when one spouse dies, if the surviving spouse is named as beneficiary, and (ii) after a marriage breakup, if the court orders a division of the RRSPs accumulated during the marriage.

Other RRSP Rules

A LOCKED-IN RRSP   To help make pensions more portable, new pension rules use locked-in RRSPs. One of the options becoming available to employees who leave an employer is to transfer pension credits to a locked-in RRSP. Also, some employers are sponsoring locked-in RRSPs rather than RPPs for their employees. When the employee retires, the funds in a locked-in RRSP will be used to purchase an annuity.

MORE THAN ONE RRSP?   There is no limit to the number of RRSPs a person may have. Because of the variation in the types of plans and their yields, you might be wise to establish more than one RRSP in order to diversify your assets.

BORROWING FROM AN RRSP   Generally, it is not possible to borrow from your RRSP. An exception is the home purchase plan that was introduced in 1993–94, which allows you to withdraw RRSP funds in order to buy a home. You pay no tax on the withdrawn funds when they are used for this purpose, but you must repay what you have "borrowed" back into your plan within 15 years. But RRSP funds may be used as security for a loan; the exact procedure for doing so is complex, however, because of the way the transaction must be reported on your income tax return.

WITHDRAWALS BEFORE MATURITY   You may withdraw funds from your RRSP before maturity (that is, before the plan is collapsed, when you turn 69), but they will be subject to income tax; tax will also be payable on any interest or dividends earned by the plan to date.

DEATH OF THE RRSP OWNER   If you die before your RRSP matures, all contributions to the plan, along with any accumulated yield, will be refunded to the beneficiary you've named for the plan or, if you did not name a beneficiary, to your estate. The income tax treatment of such a refund varies depending on the beneficiary. A spouse who is named as beneficiary has two options: rolling the refund over into his or her own RRSP without incurring any income tax, or accepting the refund as a lump sum and paying the tax. If you name any beneficiary other than your spouse or certain categories of dependents, RRSP refunds will be treated as if they were part of your income in the year of your death and taxed accordingly. Your estate will be required to pay the taxes.

Who Needs an RRSP?

An RRSP is a good idea for anyone who has earned income and is paying a significant amount of income tax. On the other hand, if you have money to invest but pay very little income tax, you can forgo the restrictions of an RRSP. The financial press regularly publishes articles on RRSPs that emphasize the amount of tax deferred and the increase in savings possible with RRSPs. Whether these advantages will hold true for your particular case depends on your marginal tax rate and on the yield from your RRSP. (See Personal Finance in Action Box 7.6, "Is an RRSP Worthwhile?")

Maturity Options

All of your RRSPs must be deregistered at some point before the end of the year in which you turn 69. Deregistering means changing from accumulating savings to either (i) removing the funds from the tax shelter and paying the required income tax on them, or (ii) initiating a liquidation plan to provide income. You can choose one or any combination of the following six options:

Removal from the tax shelter

(a) withdraw the funds and pay the income tax,

Income plan

(b) purchase a single-payment life annuity,

(c) purchase a fixed-term annuity,

(d) set up a registered retirement income fund (RRIF),

(e) set up a life income fund (LIF),

(f) set up a segregated fund.

WITHDRAW THE FUNDS The first of these options differs from the others in that you are moving funds from the RRSP tax shelter and into your control. Money taken out of an RRSP is always subject to tax in the year of its withdrawal. But once you have paid the tax, no more restrictions are imposed by Revenue Canada. Unfortunately, withdrawing all your RRSP funds at one time could result in an enormous tax bill. To minimize your tax burden, you can either make a series of withdrawals over a number of years or withdraw all the funds during a year in which your income is considerably lower than usual.

The other five options represent various ways of converting RRSP funds into income gradually, over a number of years, thus spreading out your income tax liability. With any of these options, your RRSP funds do not come into your hands as a lump sum, but are instead transferred

---

Personal Finance in Action 7.6

Is an RRSP Worthwhile?

Meena lives in Saskatchewan. She plans to save $3 000 a year in anticipation of her retirement in 30 years' time. She decides to compare the results of putting her money inside a tax-sheltered RRSP with investing it outside a tax shelter. For comparison purposes, she makes the following assumptions:

Average interest rate 6%
Combined marginal tax rate 38.48%
After-tax interest rate 6% – (6% x .3848)
          = 3.69%
Annual investments for 30 years of
          a) $3 000 before-tax dollars in the RRSP

b) $1 845.60 after-tax dollars outside an RRSP
          3 000 – (3 000 x .3848) = 1 845.6

Using the formula for the "Future Value of a Series of Deposits" (see Personal Finance in Action Box 8.2) Meena learns why RRSPs are so popular. The $3 000 inside the RRSP grows to $237 174. (3 000 x 79.058). Assuming that she pays the maximum tax rate upon withdrawing the funds, the tax would be $237 174 x .3848 = $91 264.55, leaving her with $145 909.45. The $3 000 invested outside the plan only grows to $98 399. Meena will therefore do much better if she invests inside an RRSP.

directly into an income plan. When an RRSP matures, there is no restriction in moving the funds to other firms, if desired. It is wise to do some comparison shopping before choosing an income plan and the company to handle it.

LIFE ANNUITY With a single-payment life annuity, your funds are transferred directly from your RRSP to a life insurance company from which you are buying a life annuity. You can choose among a variety of annuity products, some of which were described earlier in this chapter (under "Life Annuities"). An annuity converts funds into a lifetime income, with income tax payable each year only on the amount received in that year. This approach effectively spreads the tax burden over the annuitant's lifetime.

FIXED-TERM ANNUITY Fixed-term annuities, which are available from life insurance companies and from trust companies, allow you to gradually convert your RRSP funds into income. A fixed-term annuity differs from a life annuity in that it is unrelated to life expectancy; it involves no pooling of funds with others. Your funds are simply converted into an income stream that will continue until you reach a specific age. But if you do not live that long, the balance in the account will be refunded either to your beneficiary or to your estate. Your monthly payment will depend on the term, the amount invested in the annuity, and interest rates. With life or fixed-term annuities, you have the option of cancelling the contract and taking the commuted value (see Chapter 8, under "Uniform Series of Payments Received") of the remaining payments. You can then take these amounts out of the tax shelter and pay the tax, or you can roll the amounts over into a RRIF.

REGISTERED RETIREMENT INCOME FUND A **registered retirement income fund** (a RRIF: the abbreviation is pronounced to rhyme with "stiff") is similar to a self-directed RRSP; with a RRIF, you can make your own investment decisions if you wish to do so. RRIFs may also be set up so that little management is required—by, for instance, investing all funds in fixed-income securities. The same firms that handle RRSPs also look after RRIFs. Your choice of possible RRIF investments includes savings accounts, term deposits, bonds, stocks, and mutual funds. It is a good idea to do some comparison shopping when deregistering your RRSPs, in order to find a RRIF with the most suitable terms.

After you purchase a RRIF, income from the fund may start at any time. But Revenue Canada requires that you withdraw a minimum amount each year (there is no ceiling or maximum withdrawal). Your minimum withdrawal depends on your age. The formula for determining your minimum withdrawal until you turn 71 is as follows:

$$\frac{\text{RRIF balance at January 1}}{90 \text{ minus age at January 1}} = \text{the minimum annual payment}$$

After you turn 71, your minimum withdrawal payments are based on a percentage of the fund's balance.

Since it is possible to have more than one RRIF, you can diversify your RRSP funds by using different firms or financial products. For instance, you could put some funds into bank deposits and others into equity mutual funds that are held elsewhere. You can transfer funds from one RRIF to another, but it would be wise to find out whether any restrictions or fees will be involved. The advantage of a RRIF over an annuity is that RRIFs leave you free to choose your preferred type of investment and to determine the amount you will withdraw beyond the required minimum each year.

Figure 7.9 shows a sample RRIF contract. In this example, the RRIF was started by a 65-year-old man with an investment of $300 000 on October 12, 2000. A monthly payment of $2 000

FIGURE 7.9   A SAMPLE RRIF CONTRACT

Annuitant: Mr. Average Canadian	**Date of purchase:** Oct. 12, 2000
Date of birth: Oct. 15, 1935	**First payment date:** Nov. 12, 2000
Investment amount: $300 000.00	**Payment frequency:** Monthly
Source of funds: RRSP	**Assumed interest rate:** 10.00%
Payment option: Increasing payment – 3.00%	

Year	Age	Jan. 1 fund value	Gross payment	Withholding tax	Net payment
2000	65	*$302 438	$2 000	$200	$1 800
2001	66	302 364	2 060	105	1 955
2002	67	306 632	2 122	106	2 016
2003	68	310 546	2 185	106	2 079
2004	69	314 048	2 251	106	2 145
2005	70	317 078	2 319	106	2 213
2006	71	319 556	2 388	106	2 282
2007	72	321 405	2 460	48	2 411
2008	73	322 536	2 534	52	2 481
2009	74	322 852	2 610	57	2 553
2010	75	322 239	2 688	62	2 626
2011	76	320 578	2 768	67	2 701
2012	77	317 734	2 852	74	2 778
2013	78	313 562	2 937	81	2 856
2014	79	307 891	3 025	89	2 936
2015	80	300 542	3 116	98	3 018
2016	81	291 314	3 209	109	3 101
2017	82	279 989	3 306	121	3 185
2018	83	266 313	3 405	135	3 270
2019	84	250 020	3 507	151	3 356
2020	85	230 809	3 612	170	3 442
2021	86	208 355	3 721	193	3 528
2022	87	182 286	3 832	219	3 613
2023	88	152 202	3 947	251	3 696
2024	89	117 661	4 066	289	3 776
2025	90	78 177	4 188	336	3 852
2026	91	33 298	2 898	252	2 646

Subject to the death benefit guarantee, any of the premium or other amount that is allocated to a segregated fund investment option is invested at the risk of the policy owner and may increase or decrease in value according to the fluctuations in the market value of the assets of the segregated fund.

*In the first year, fund value is shown at Nov. 12, 2000, prior to payment.

started on November 12, 2000. Payments are indexed at 3 percent and increase to age 90. If Mr. Average Canadian had purchased an annuity instead of a RRIF, it would have provided him with an income for life. The funds in this RRIF are invested in a segregated fund and are assumed to earn a return of 10 percent per year. This is well within the historic return on such investments.

LIFE INCOME FUND (LIF) If you terminate your membership in a registered pension plan, you can buy a **life income fund (a LIF, pronounced to rhyme with "stiff")** with the lump-sum payment you receive. A LIF is also an option if you have transferred pension funds into a locked-in RRSP. LIFs are available in all provinces except Prince Edward Island. The minimum deposit necessary for starting one is $10 000. A LIF is treated like a RRIF for tax purposes. You must withdraw a minimum amount each year. There is also a maximum amount that you may withdraw annually until you turn 80. This amount will change from year to year depending on interest rates and on the investment returns available. In addition, you may withdraw a lump sum each year, but this sum may not exceed your maximum withdrawal amount. The balance of the funds in your LIF must be used to purchase a life annuity before December 31 of the year in which you turn 80. If you die before the LIF matures, the funds in the LIF are paid to your designated beneficiary.

SEGREGATED FUNDS Segregated Funds have replaced the variable annuity. In 2000, there were over 1 000 such funds. They have many popular features. Contributions, in most cases, are protected from creditors. Upon the death of the contributor, the beneficiary receives the money in the fund without paying a probate fee. A plan may be opened for as little as $25 per fund along with a minimum pre-authorized payment agreement (PPA). With a PPA, automatic monthly payments of a minimum of $25 may be made to the fund. A minimum withdrawal of $500 per fund may be made at any time for a fee. Without a PPA, a minimum of $300 must remain in each fund.

There are no contribution fees. Withdrawal fees are a percentage of the amount withdrawn and vary according to when contributions were made to the fund. For example, one insurance company (London Life) charges 5 percent in years one and two but nothing in year seven and after.

Universal Life Policies

Universal life policies have become a popular retirement planning vehicle (see Chapter 6). Unlike whole life insurance, part of the universal life premium pays for insurance, and part is invested to provide for retirement. The amount a person can invest is determined by his or her age and the amount of the insurance coverage. What makes this kind of policy so popular is that the investment portion of the policy is tax-sheltered and can be used to create an income in retirement. Up to 75 percent of the investment portion of the policy can be lent tax-free to the policyholder (see Personal Finance in Action Box 7.7, "Investing Outside a Plan Versus Investing in Universal Life to Create a Tax-Deferred Estate").

Investing Outside a Plan Versus Investing in Universal Life to Create a Tax-Deferred Estate

Fernando has just turned 52. Chloe, his wife, is 48. They have three children ranging in age from 15 to 25. Like many baby boomers, they made a lot of money in the 1990s from their investments. Fernando works for one of Canada's leading telecommunications firms and earns a three-figure salary. Chloe, a trustee in bankruptcy with one of Canada's leading firms, earns even more. They have much more income than they need in order to maintain their lifestyle. Both are concerned about high taxes and what will happen to the value of their estates when they die. Their investment advisor suggests universal life to them as a means of protecting their wealth and leaving it to their children, tax-free. She shows them what will happen to money invested inside a universal life plan compared to the same money invested outside a universal life plan.

A. $150 000 is invested each year for five years outside a plan. The income is not protected. Capital gains average 7 percent per year. One-third of the investments are realized each year, and taxes paid on all income are at the highest marginal tax rate. Rolling over portfolios every three years is typical behaviour for clients in their investment advisor's firm.

B. $150 000 is invested each year for five years. The money is used to purchase a *joint universal last-to-die life* policy of $4.3 million with benefits payable on the death of the last spouse. After 30 years, the insurance portion of their plan has grown to $7 540 717. No capital gains tax or probate is payable on the insurance left to their children.

	A		B	
	ANNUAL DEPOSIT	VALUE OF INVESTMENT	ANNUAL INVESTMENT	CASH VALUE
Year 1	$150 000	$ 157 875	$150 000	$ 87 728
Year 2	$150 000	$ 324 038	$150 000	$ 213 654
Year 3	$150 000	$ 498 925	$150 000	$ 334 905
Year 4	$150 000	$ 682 993	$150 000	$ 466 674
Year 5	$150 000	$ 876 724	$150 000	$ 642 483
		$ 922 751		$ 673 463
		$ 971 195		$ 735 789
		$1 022 182		$ 800 625
		$1 075 845		$ 868 161
		$1 132 326		$ 943 269
		$1 191 772		$ 993 085
		$1 254 339		$1 046 922
		$1 320 191		$1 105 103
		$1 389 500		$1 167 979
		$1 462 448		$1 235 930
		$1 539 225		$1 309 364
		$1 620 033		$1 388 724
		$1 705 083		$1 474 489

ANNUAL DEPOSIT	A VALUE OF INVESTMENT	B ANNUAL INVESTMENT	CASH VALUE
	$1 794 598		$1 567 175
	$1 888 813		$1 667 340
	$1 987 974		$1 775 589
	$2 092 341		$1 892 574
	$2 202 187		$2 018 999
	$2 317 800		$2 155 627
	$2 439 483		$2 303 280
	$2 567 553		$2 462 850
	$2 702 348		$2 635 296
	$2 844 219		$2 821 659
	$2 993 538		$3 023 062
	$3 150 696		$3 240 717

As the table indicates, money invested inside a universal life plan performs slightly better than money invested outside a plan. There are several possible reasons for this. Money invested in such a plan is used to purchase units of index-based mutual funds. Money invested outside a plan faces no such restriction and may be subject to greater risk. As well, capital gains inside a plan are not subject to tax as are the funds outside a plan.

It should be pointed out that the management expense ratios or MERs are very high with universal life. These weaken the growth of the investments. It should also be stressed that a universal life policy is primarily a means of creating a tax-free estate for one's beneficiaries and only secondarily as an investment vehicle.

Summary

This chapter was intended to increase your awareness of the possible sources of retirement income and of the need to begin preparing for your retirement early in your working life. At present, public pension programs, such as Old Age Security and the Guaranteed Income Supplement, provide benefits to eligible people from the federal government's general revenues. If you have been in the labour force, you have contributed to either the Canada Pension Plan or the Quebec Pension Plans, which pay benefits to retirees and to the survivors of contributors, as well as a lump-sum death benefit. About half of all full-time employees are members of employment-related private retirement pension plans, which vary widely in their benefits.

Life annuities allow you to stretch a sum of money over your lifetime, providing protection against the risk of outliving your savings. By gradually liquidating the principal and interest, a life annuity creates a lifetime income for you, but will leave no estate for your heirs. Various modifications of the basic life annuity exist—for example, some cover several lives, and some provide a refund if the annuitant dies shortly after starting to receive payments.

At retirement, most people will find public and private pensions inadequate to support the lifestyle to which they have become accustomed. They need to supplement their pension with income from their own investments. RRSPs allow you to invest tax-sheltered funds, permitting the income to compound tax-free until the plan is deregistered. Because most people have a lower marginal tax rate after they retire, most people find it beneficial to accumulate retirement funds in RRSPs. Universal life policies are another popular retirement planning vehicle.

Key Terms

accumulation period (p. 176)

annuitant (p. 173)

annuity (p. 173)

contributory earnings (p. 169)

CPP Investment Board (p. 170)

deferred annuity (p. 177)

defined benefits pension plan (p. 171)

defined contribution pension plan (p. 171)

derivatives (p. 170)

full indexation (p. 172)

immediate annuity (p. 176)

joint-life-and-last-survivorship annuity (joint-and-survivor annuity) (p. 177)

life income fund, or LIF (p. 193)

liquidation period (p. 176)

maximum pensionable earnings (p. 169)

partial indexation (p. 172)

pension portability (p. 172)

refund annuity (p. 178)

registered retirement income fund, or RRIF (p. 191)

registered retirement savings plan, or RRSP (p. 184)

segregated fund (p. 175)

single-payment annuity (p. 176)

stock index funds (p. 170)

straight life annuity (p. 177)

Treasury Bills (p. 170)

vesting (p. 172)

year's basic exemption (p. 169)

Problems

1. A common problem for many people who are planning retirement is who to turn to for advice. How would you find a reliable financial planner you could trust?

2. Axel is 40. He wants to have $2 million by the time he is 60. How much does he need to invest each year at 5 percent to achieve his goal?

3. Find out what the expected ratio of working people to retirees will be in 2015. Will it be sufficient to keep the CPP financially secure or will employer/employee contributions have to increase? What unknown factors can influence the employee/retiree ratio?

4. Compare the pros and cons of having CPP contributions invested in equities and derivatives.

5. Considerable publicity is given to RRSPs each winter during RRSP season. It has become a given that everyone must have one. Is this true? Does everyone need to open an RRSP?

6. Discuss the strengths and weaknesses of the following as vehicles for retirement planning: RRSPs, Segregated Funds, and Universal Life. Should anyone have money in all three?

7. Sean is 59 and plans to retire when he turns 60. His company pension will be $40 000. His assets consist of a $30 000 GIC earning 4.5 percent as well as the following:

800 shares of Bell Canada	$27 000
100 shares of Nortel	$12 200
600 shares of Canada Life	$21 000

BCE pays a dividend of 3.6 percent, Nortel 0.1 percent, and Canada Life 1 percent. How much does Sean earn from his investments? How can he increase his investment income?

8. If, as many critics believe, the present and future funding of the CPP is insufficient to meet the needs of future retirees, should the benefits be clawed back from more affluent Canadians as OAS payments are? With reference to income patterns in 1996, at what income would such a claw back be realistic?

9. Allison has just retired from her job as CFO of a small Internet software company. She has a diversified investment portfolio of $1.5 million which originally cost her $500 000. Assuming that she is in the highest tax bracket, what are the tax implications if she retires to a Caribbean island to tax-shelter her investments?

10. Explain what is meant by the following and their relevance to retirement planning: OAS, GIS, annuity, RRIF, LIF.

11. True or False

   (a) Men, at every age, receive more money from OAS than women.

   (b) CPP is a major income source for retirees aged 60-65.

   (c) Retired women have less investment income than men.

   (d) Retired men earn more from employment than women.

   (e) Retired women earn more from private pension plans than men.

   (f) Segregated Funds are less secure than regular mutual funds.

12. Referring to the income tax rates in Chapter 2, how much would a person now earning $100 000 save by putting $13 500 into an RRSP?

13. Which will cost an individual more, an immediate annuity or one that is bought in instalments? How do you account for the difference?

14. Joseph retired with an annual pension of $40 000 indexed to inflation. Ingrid retired with the same sized pension but hers was only indexed to inflation over 2 percent. If inflation averages 3 percent per year, compare the purchasing power of their pensions after 20 years.

15. Pick Sing earned $60 000 in 1997 and $65 000 in 2000. In 1997 she paid 2.925 percent of $32 300 (her contributory earnings) to the CPP. In 2000 she paid 4.95 percent of her contributory earnings, assumed to be $36 400. By how much did her contribution increase?

16. Are the income guarantees of Canada's public pension system too high? If the system is unsustainable at the combined contribution rate of 9.9 percent, is it reasonable to assume that Canadians will be happy to continue to pay more and more?

17. What are the consequences to the economy when the combined employer/employee CPP contribution rate rises from 5.85 percent to 9.9 percent?

18. Assume that you are opening an RRSP with the maximum contribution allowed. You earned $100 000 last year, and you are 30 years old. Realizing the devastating effect even a small amount of inflation can have on purchasing power, what investments will you put in the plan to maximize its growth?

19. Your parents took out a universal life policy in their 50s. Both have died recently and, as a result, you have received $3 million from their policy. Go to the Canada Customs and Revenue Agency Web site, www.rc.gc.ca. Click on Tax Individuals, then hit 2000 General Income Tax & Benefit Package, then Province, then General Income Tax & Benefit Guide, then Main Table of Contents and finally Lines 120, 121 and 127. Check the tax rates on investment income, and decide how you would invest this money in order to pay the least amount of tax.

References

BOOKS AND ARTICLES

BAREHAM, STEVE. *The Last Resort: A Retirement Vision for Canadians and How to Achieve It.* Toronto: HarperCollins, 1997. This is a topical book with useful advice.

CANADIAN ASSOCIATION OF RETIRED PERSONS (CARP). *CARP's Black and Blue Book: The Bruising of Seniors in Canada.* Toronto: CARP, 1997. This book looks at how Canadian governments have reduced seniors' benefits over the past 25 years.

CANADIAN LIFE AND HEALTH INSURANCE ASSOCIATION. *Retirement as You Like It.* Toronto: Canadian Life and Health Insurance Association, 1994. With updated insert. Prepared by a leading insurance-industry association, this booklet contains useful information.

CIMORONI, SANDY, BETH GRUDINSKI, and PATRICIA LOVETT-REID. *Retirement Strategies for Women: Turning Your Dreams into Reality.* Toronto: Key Porter Books, 1997. A well-written review of the subject by several knowledgeable authors.

COHEN, DIAN. *The New Retirement: Financial Strategies For Life After Work.* Toronto: Doubleday Canada Limited, 1999. This is a must read for anyone planning to retire as it covers all the basic topics on finances and retirement.

DAGYS, ANDREW. *The Ontario Retirement Handbook: A Guide to Programs and Services for Retirees.* Toronto: ECW Press, 1996. A valuable source for Ontario residents.

DYCHTWALD, KEN, and JOE FLOWER. *Age Wave: The Challenges and Opportunities of an Aging North America.* Los Angeles: J.P. Tarcher, 1988. Slightly dated, but the challenges remain the same.

FIDELITY DIRECTIONS. *Real-Life Strategies for Retirement Planning.* Toronto: Fidelity, 1977. Fidelity is a major mutual fund company. This report may be obtained by calling 1-888-203-4778 (toll-free). Fidelity's web site is listed under "Personal Finance on the Web," below.

THE FINANCIAL POST. *Retirement Planning.* Guides to Investing and Personal Finance, No. 8. Toronto: *The Financial Post*, 1998. Part of a series of newspaper supplements, this guide is current and interesting.

FOSTER, SANDRA E. *You Can't Take It with You: The Common-sense Guide to Estate Planning for Canadians*. Toronto: John Wiley & Sons, 1996. Useful advice for those with little knowledge of the subject.

THE GERONTOLOGY RESEARCH CENTRE. *Canada Pension Plan Reforms: Issues For Women*. Vancouver: Simon Fraser University, 1996. A useful resource for women.

GRAY, DOUGLAS A. *A Canadian Snowbird's Guide: Everything You Need To Know About Living Part-time in the USA*. Toronto: McGraw-Hill-Ryerson, 1997. Will interest the many elderly Canadians who vacation in the United States.

HUNNISETT, HENRY S. *Retirement Guide for Canadians: An Overall Plan for a Comfortable Future*. Vancouver: Self-Counsel Press, 1993. Similar to other books on retirement.

KELM, WALTER. *The Seniors Benefit—A Flawed Proposal: An Analysis of the Proposed Seniors Benefit*. Toronto: Canadian Association of Retired Persons. 1997. The criticism of Kelm, CARP, and other seniors groups convinced the government not to proceed with the Seniors Benefit.

KERR, ROBERT JOHN. *The Only Retirement Guide You'll Ever Need*. Toronto: Penguin, 1997. Despite its misleading title (you will need other retirement guides as well), this is still a valuable resource.

McDOUGALL, BRUCE. *The Complete Idiot's Guide to a Great Retirement*. Scarborough: Prentice Hall Canada, 1996. Well written and easy to understand.

MIDLAND WALWYN. The following reports are available from Midland Walwyn's Retirement and Estate Services department or from its Private Client Investing department. They are all useful and informative and may be obtained by calling 1-800-563-6623.

Estate Friendly Investing Through Life Company Products

Estimating the Costs of Settling Your Estate

Giving Someone the Power to Act on Your Behalf

Investment at the Retirement Stage: More Important Than Ever

Maximize Your Estate by Reducing It for Probate Purposes

Offshore Planning Strategies

RRSP Contribution Checklist

RRSP Maturity Options: Creating Retirement Income with your Registered Plan Assets

RRSP Planning: Retirement Savings Guide

Seven Steps to Building a Successful RRIF Portfolio

Strategies for Dealing with an Early Retirement Package

PERRY, FRED A. *Charting a New Course: A Positive Guide and Sourcebook for the "Early Retiree."* Gloucester, ON: Perry, 1995. A valuable reference.

POLSON, KIRK, and GEORGE BRETT. *Retire Right: The Practical Guide to RRIFs, Annuities and Pensions*. Toronto: Penguin, 1997. One of the very few books ever written on these specific topics.

RESTAK, RICHARD M. *Older and Wiser*. New York: Simon and Schuster, 1997. Another valuable reference for seniors.

STARCHILD, ADAM. *Tax Havens for Canadians: Ingenious Ways to Preserve Your Wealth (and Have Fun Doing It!)*. Toronto: Productive, 1995. No longer especially relevant, since Canadians must now report their worldwide assets to Revenue Canada.

TAFLER, DAVID. *Fifty-plus Survival Guide: Winning Strategies for Wealth, Health, and Lifestyle.* Toronto: ITP Nelson, 1998. Tafler, the editor of *CARP News*, has become a leading spokesman on retirement issues.

———. *Everything You Always Wanted to Know About RRIFs…But Were Too Young to Ask.* Toronto: ITP Nelson, 1997. Answers all the most common questions about RRIFs.

TOWNSON, MONICA. *Independent Means: A Canadian Woman's Guide to Pensions and a Secure Financial Future.* Toronto: Macmillan, 1997. A *Financial Post* staffer, Townson is one of Canada's most highly qualified financial writers; she also appears frequently on television.

WATTERS, GRAYDON G. *Financial Pursuit—Canada's Working Guide to Personal Wealth: How to Retire with Financial Dignity.* North York, ON: Financial Knowledge, 1996. A valuable and interesting book.

WYLIE, BETTY JANE. *The Best is Yet to Come.* Toronto: Key Porter Books, 1996. Points out how good retirement can be.

———. *Planning Ahead for a Financially Secure Retirement.* Toronto: Key Porter Books, 1996. Emphasizes the importance of planning for retirement.

Personal Finance on the Web

MISCELLANEOUS RETIREMENT SITES

Altavista
www.altavista.ca This site allows users to calculate asset allocation and to track their investments on graphs.

American Association of Retired Persons (AARP)
www.aarp.org AARP is the largest seniors' organization in the United States.

Benefits Canada
www.benefitscanada.com *Benefits Canada* is a magazine that deals with employee benefits and pension investments.

A.M. Best Canada Ltd.
www.trac.com A.M. Best provides an insurance information service.

The Big List
insurance.about.com/industry/insurance This site has the Big List of insurance company home pages.

Canada Pension Plan
www.cpp-rpc.gc.ca Provides current information on the CPP.

Canadian Association of Financial Planners
www.cafp.org A complete list of organization members across Canada, along with questions to help people select a planner.

Canadian Association of Retired Persons (CARP)
www.fifty-plus.net CARP is Canada's largest organization for those over the age of 50. It covers many topics of interest to those who have retired and those considering retirement.

Capital Estate Planning
www.capitalestateplanning.com Offers retirement planning advice.

CAPP Ontario
> **www.retirementplanners.net/cap** CAPP is The Canadian Association of Pre-retirement Planners.

Department of Finance
> **www.fin.gc.ca** Helps retirees by showing any changes to taxation.

Elder Web
> **www.elderweb.org** Financial topics are popular on this senior citizens' chat line.

The Fund Library
> **www.fundlibrary.com** The Fund Library is a useful site for information on RRSPs.

The Globe and Mail's Mutual Fund Web site.
> **www.globefund.com**

Government of Canada
> **Canada.gc.ca/main-e.html** Provides information on all federal government programs.

Human Resources Development Canada
> **www.hrdc-dhrc.gc.ca** Information on the CPP and the Old Age Security program are available on this site.

InfoSeniors
> **www.infoseniors.com** Provides information about programs and services available to retirees.

Insurance Canada
> **www.insurance-canada.ca** Insurance Canada provides information on many insurance related topics.

The Last Resort
> **www.kootenaytrader.com/lastresort** This site introduces a new book on retirement, *The Last Resort*, by Steve Bareham.

Money
> **www.pathfinder.com/money** This American magazine has articles on retirement.

The RRSP Planner
> **www.quiken.ca** Contains a useful retirement planning tool.

RetireWeb
> **www.retireweb.com** This site has advice for those who are planning to retire, those who are in the process of retiring, and for those who have retired.

Superintendent of Financial Institutions
> **www.osfi-bsif.gc.ca** The Office of the Superintendent of Financial Institutions has a mandate to regulate pension plans.

CANADIAN LIFE INSURANCE COMPANIES

Canada Life Individual
> **www.canadalife.com/individual** A major Canadian company that specializes in life insurance.

Clarica

> **www.clarica.com** Clarica was formerly Mutual Life.

Equitable Life of Canada

> **www.equitable.ca** Equitable Life offers life insurance, employee benefits, savings products, and mortgages through independent producers and group representatives.

Great-West Life Assurance

> **www.gwl.ca** A Canadian shareholder-owned life insurance company that specializes in group and disability insurance.

Imperial Life Financial

> **www.canlink.com/imperial** A life insurance company that provides financial information.

London Life Insurance Company

> **www.londonlife.com** London Life offers individual and group insurance, retirement savings plans, and investment advice that focuses on mutual funds.

Manufacturers Life

> **www.manulife.com** Manufacturers Life is a major insurance company.

MetLife Canada

> **metlife.com** A company that offers a full range of insurance services.

Norwich Union

> **www.norwich-union.ca** Norwich Union provides information on savings and retirement.

Sun Life of Canada

> **www.sunlife.com** Sun Life, a major Canadian insurance firm, runs many company fringe benefit plans.

Western Life Assurance Company

> **www.westernlife.com** This site provides on-line quotes and also offers a library of financial- and estate-planning information. It also features interactive on-line questionnaires that will help you generate a last will and testament, as well as a power of attorney.

Appendix 7A

Sample Annuity Policy

C℞ *the co·operators*

Policy Data

POLICY NUMBER   181206

POLICY DATE   January 8, 1998

ANNUITANT   Ed Gallos
JOINT ANNUITANT   Ramona Gallos

AGE OF ANNUITANT   65
AGE OF JOINT   65
ANNUITANT

BENEFICIARY   as stated in the application unless subsequently changed

PLAN   Joint & Last Survivor Annuity Guaranteed 10 Years,
                        Immediate Annuity

AMOUNT OF ANNUITY $ 474.74 payable on the 1st day of each month
                        commencing January 1, 1998. These payments will
                        continue monthly until the later of December 1, 2007
                        or death of the last Annuitant.

PREMIUM   Amount $ 75,000.00

Policy Data   **SPECIMEN**

PROVISIONS

The Contract

The policy and the application are part of the contract. The contract also includes documents attached at issue and any amendments agreed upon in writing after the policy is issued. The policy may not be amended nor any provision waived except by written agreement signed by authorized signing officers of the Company.

Participation

This policy participates in the surplus distribution of the Company. Any distribution of excess charges or surplus shall remain at the credit of the contract and be used to increase the annuity.

Payment of Premium

The premium is payable either at the Head Office or at any Branch Office or through an authorized representative of the Company.

Currency

All payments to be made in connection with this policy shall be in the lawful money of Canada.

Age

The Company shall be entitled to proof of age of the annuitant before making any payment under this policy. If the age has been misstated, any amount payable hereunder shall be that which the premium would have purchased at the correct age.

Beneficiary

The annuitant may appoint a beneficiary. The annuitant may change the beneficiary unless the appointment was irrevocable. The interest of any legally designated beneficiary who shall die before the Annuitant, or before the surviving Annuitant or Annuitants, if there be more than one Annuitant, shall vest in the Annuitant or the surviving Annuitant or Annuitants, as the case may be, in the absence of any statutory provision as to the disposition thereof and if there be no other legally designated beneficiary.

No Assignment

The policy or annuity payments thereunder cannot be assigned.

SPECIMEN

(01/82) 504

SOURCE: Co-operators Life Insurance Company. Reprinted with permission of Co-operators Life Insurance Company.

Chapter 8

Interest

1. Define the concept of interest and show how it relates to the time value of money.

2. Distinguish between simple and compound interest and demonstrate how to calculate each.

3. Distinguish between the nominal interest rate and the effective annual yield.

4. Outline the process of calculating a repayment schedule for a loan to be repaid in equal instalments, with each payment a blend of interest and principal.

5. Show how frequency of compounding interest affects the effective annual yield.

6. Show how the total interest charge on loan contracts for either simple or compound interest is determined.

7. List the five factors that influence the total interest charged on a loan.

8. Distinguish between the concepts of future value and present value.

9. Using either formulas or compound interest tables, compute the future and present values of a single payment.

10. Calculate the future and present values of an identical series of deposits made or an identical series of payments received.

11. Define the following terms: principal, maturity date, the term of a loan, sinking fund, blended payment, and amortization.

Introduction

Interest is important both to lenders and to borrowers. Contrary to popular belief, not all lenders are wealthy. When children open bank accounts with money they earn from paper routes or lawn mowing jobs, they are actually lending money to the bank. In return, the bank pays them interest. This chapter discusses some basic principles of interest and the time value of money, and demonstrates a number of ways to calculate interest.

The **time value of money** is important to the concept of interest. As a result of this principle, a dollar invested for 10 years will grow in value. However, a dollar promised to someone in 10 years will be worth less. Loans increase in value because of the interest or "rent" paid to the lender by the borrower. A knowledge of interest and of how to calculate the future value of money will be of value to both borrowers and lenders and will help them make wise financial decisions.

This chapter deals with interest and with the present and future values of money. Understanding the basic principles of interest and methods of calculation will help you solve the problems in the upcoming chapters on credit, mortgages, and investments. The ability to calculate compound interest and to deal with the future and present values of money can also be very valuable.

In addition, the chapter explains interest, defines basic terms, and illustrates the calculations for simple and compound interest. Borrowers are frequently confused by repayment schedules for loans and mortgages that feature blended payments for principal and interest. Illustrations explain how this approach works. Formulas and compound interest tables show how to calculate the future and present value of money.

The Concept of Interest

Interest, the payment for the use of someone else's money, is like rent. To the lender, interest is income; to the borrower, it is an expense. A loan allows a borrower to do today what he or she would otherwise have to postpone because of a lack of money. Interest compensates the lender for postponing having the use of his or her money. It also pays the lender for the risk involved in lending and for the administrative costs associated with the loan.

The **interest rate** is defined as the ratio of the interest payable at the end of the year to the money owed at the start of the year. The boxed example "Annual Interest Rate" illustrates how to calculate the interest rate. This bare-bones definition will be clarified when the concepts of nominal rate and effective annual yield are explained. (Unless stated otherwise, when an interest rate is quoted in this chapter, it is assumed to be the annual rate.)

A most important component of any loan transaction, the total interest charge, is the amount that must be repaid in addition to the **principal,** or the amount borrowed. The total

---

Annual Interest Rate

What is the interest rate on a $5 000 debt, with interest of $500 payable annually?

$$\frac{500}{5\ 000} = 0.10 \text{ (or 10\% per annum)}$$

interest charge represents the lender's total return and the borrower's total carrying cost. The five factors that determine the magnitude of the total interest charge are as follows: (i) rate of interest, (ii) frequency of compounding, (iii) term or length of time the loan is outstanding, (iv) principal, and (v) method of repayment. The effects of these factors will become apparent as various ways of calculating interest are explained in this chapter or illustrated in mortgage applications in Chapter 13.

Simple Interest

Simple interest is used when the total principal and all interest due are to be repaid as a lump sum at a specified time. The date when a loan is due is called the **maturity date,** and the length of time the loan is to be outstanding is the **loan term.** The amount of interest due may be calculated with the following formula:

Interest = principal × annual rate × time (in years)

Simple Interest

Principal: $3 000
Annual interest rate: 8%
Term of loan: 2 years

Interest = principal × rate × time
         = $3 000 × 0.08 × 2
         = $480

At maturity, the borrower will pay the lender:

$3 000   (principal returned)
   480   (total interest charge)
$3 480   (total payment)

Compound Interest

Compound interest is paid on most savings accounts and charged on many loans, including home mortgages. **Compounding** simply means that at specified intervals, the accumulated interest is added to the principal; in the next period, interest is earned on the new balance (that is, the previous principal *and* the interest earned in the previous period). In this way, interest is reinvested to earn more interest. Compounding may be done as often as daily, monthly, semi-annually, or annually. Naturally, the more frequently interest is compounded, the faster the investment grows. Assuming that there is no repayment of principal or interest on a regular basis, the calculation of compound interest is exactly like simple interest, but it is repeated at each compounding interval, using a larger principal each time.

    Compound interest is important to the saver, because income (interest) is being reinvested regularly and begins earning additional interest. Banks calculate interest on savings accounts at different intervals, depending on the type of account. With a traditional savings account, interest may be calculated monthly on the minimum balance that was in the account during the month, but this interest is not added to the principal until the compounding date, which may be every six months. If you are planning to make a large withdrawal from such an account, consider doing so just after the end of a calendar month to avoid losing a month's interest. If you withdraw your money too soon, it will not earn any interest for that month.

Compound Interest

Principal: $3 000
Interest rate: 8%, compounded semi-annually
Term of loan: 2 years

(a) **At the end of the first six months,**

$$interest = principal \times rate \times time$$
$$= \$3\,000 \times 0.08 \times 0.5$$
$$= \$120.00$$

$$new\ balance = principal + interest$$
$$= \$3\,000 + \$120$$
$$= \$3\,120.00$$

(b) **At end of the second six-month period,**

$$interest = principal \times rate \times time$$
$$= \$3\,120.00 \times 0.08 \times 0.5$$
$$= \$124.80$$

$$new\ balance = \$3\,120.00 + \$124.80$$
$$= \$3\,244.80$$

To summarize compound interest calculations over the two-and-a-half-year period:

TIME PERIOD (MONTHS)	BALANCE OF PRINCIPAL AND INTEREST AT BEGINNING OF PERIOD	INTEREST AT END OF PERIOD	OUTSTANDING BALANCE AT END OF PERIOD
6	$3 000.00	$120.00	$3 120.00
12	3 120.00	124.80	3 244.80
18	3 244.80	129.79	3 374.59
24	3 374.59	134.98	3 509.58

At maturity, the borrower pays $3 000.00 (principal returned)
+ 509.58 (total interest charge)
$3 509.58 (total payment)

With a daily interest account, interest is calculated daily on the minimum balance and then perhaps compounded monthly. Although the interest on such accounts is usually slightly lower than that on the traditional savings account, a daily interest account can be worthwhile if you have a fluctuating balance in your account. Understandably, the interest rates paid by deposit institutions vary with the type of account: the interest rate may be depressed somewhat by chequing privileges, by having ready access to the deposit, or by compounding more frequently.

RULE OF 72 If you would like to know how fast your money will double, you can use the Rule of 72, which gives an approximation of annual compounding. Divide 72 by the compound interest rate to find the number of years it will take to double your money. Alternatively, the compound interest rate can be approximated by dividing 72 by the number of years necessary to double your money.

COMPOUND INTEREST TABLES To determine how much a sum of money will increase at various rates of interest, compounded annually, and left on deposit for various lengths of time, you may consult a compound interest table such as the one shown in Table 8A.1 (see Appendix 8A).

Using Compound Interest Tables

What will be the value of $1 000 in 15 years, invested at 6% compounded annually?
From Table 8A.1 (see Appendix 8A), find the compound value of 1, at 6%, for 15 years. The compound value will be 2.40.

$1 000 × 2.40 = $2 400

So $1000 invested at 6% compounded annually will be worth $2 400 after 15 years.

FREQUENCY OF COMPOUNDING AND YIELD Whenever you lend or invest money, you expect some return. This return, which is called **yield,** may be expressed as an annual rate or as the total dollar amount received over some time period. The rate of return or **effective annual yield** is not necessarily the same as the quoted interest rate or nominal rate. The **nominal interest rate** is an annual rate that does not take the compounding effect into account. The more frequently interest is compounded, the faster your savings will grow and the higher the effective annual yield will be. To determine the effective annual yield, use the following formula:

$$\text{Effective annual yield (\%)} = \frac{\text{total annual interest}}{\text{principal}} \times 100$$

Working out the annual amount of interest for various compounding periods can become tedious, so it is helpful either to know the formula to use or to be able to refer to convenient tables. If the interest is compounded m times a year at a nominal rate of r, then the effective annual yield can be defined as follows:

$$\text{Effective annual yield} = \left(1 + \frac{r}{m}\right)^m - 1$$

Effective Annual Yield

If the nominal interest rate (r) is 7% and the frequency of compounding (m) is quarterly, then

$$\text{Effective annual yield} = \left(1 + \frac{.07}{4}\right)^4 - 1$$
$$= 0.0719$$
$$= 7.19\%$$

Examine Table 8A.2 (see Appendix 8A) to observe the effect of compounding frequency on effective annual yield. Would you prefer an investment paying 7.25 percent compounded monthly, or one paying 7.5 percent compounded semi-annually? Which has the higher effective annual yield?

Compound Interest on Instalment Loans

BLENDED PAYMENTS Loans are frequently repaid in equal monthly instalments that comprise both principal and interest. Each payment includes one month's interest on the outstanding principal, plus a return of some of the principal. In the succeeding months, as the principal gradually decreases, payments contain changing proportions of principal and interest. Figure 8.1 illustrates this process graphically. Notice that the first payment includes a larger share of interest than the later payments do. As time goes on, the payments' interest component declines, while their principal component increases. Such payments, which feature changing proportions of principal and interest, are called **blended payments.** The boxed example "Blended Payments" shows how the changing proportions of principal and interest are calculated, making the payments level.

FIGURE 8.1 PROPORTIONS OF PRINCIPAL AND INTEREST IN EACH PAYMENT OF A 24-MONTH CONTRACT

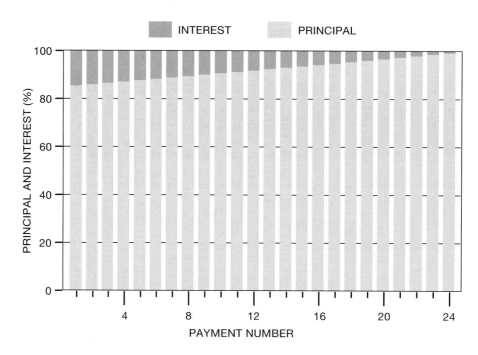

Blended Payments

Principal: $3 000
Annual interest rate: 8% compounded semi-annually
Amortization period: 2 years
Equal monthly blended payments

(a) **How much will each monthly payment be?**
The monthly payment on a loan of $3 000, at 8%, for two years is $135.51 (see Appendix 8A, Table 8A.3).

continued

(b) How much interest will be paid the first month?

Refer to a table of interest factors; such tools are used to calculate monthly interest on instalment loans (see Appendix 8A, Table 8A.4). In this example, the appropriate interest factor is 0.006 558 1970.

$$\begin{array}{lll} \text{interest for} \\ \text{1 month} \end{array} = \begin{array}{l} \text{outstanding} \\ \text{principal} \end{array} \times \begin{array}{l} \text{appropriate} \\ \text{interest factor} \end{array}$$

$$= \$3\ 000 \times .006\ 558\ 1970$$

$$= \$19.68$$

(c) How much principal will be repaid the first month?

Interest for one month must come out of the payment; the balance of the payment will be applied against the principal.

$$\begin{array}{l} \text{payment on} \\ \text{principal} \end{array} = \begin{array}{l} \text{monthly} \\ \text{payment} \end{array} - \begin{array}{l} \text{interest} \\ \text{for 1 month} \end{array}$$

$$= \$135.51 - \$19.68$$

$$= \$115.83$$

(d) What will be the principal balance outstanding after the first payment has been made?

$$\begin{array}{l} \text{principal} \\ \text{still owing} \end{array} = \begin{array}{l} \text{principal} \\ \text{owing} \\ \text{before} \\ \text{payment} \end{array} - \begin{array}{l} \text{payment} \\ \text{on principal} \end{array}$$

$$= \$3\ 000 - \$115.83$$

$$= \$2\ 884.17$$

(e) How much interest will be paid the second month?

$$\begin{array}{l} \text{interest for} \\ \text{one month} \end{array} = \begin{array}{l} \text{outstanding} \\ \text{principal} \end{array} \times \begin{array}{l} \text{appropriate} \\ \text{interest} \\ \text{factor} \end{array}$$

$$= \$2\ 884.17 \times .006\ 558\ 1970$$

$$= \$18.91$$

The process of calculating the monthly interest and then determining the size of the repayment on the principal will continue each month until the principal has been reduced to zero, as illustrated in the boxed example "Excerpts from Payment Schedule for a $3 000 Loan." You may note small discrepancies in amounts between the above calculations and the table in that boxed example because of differences in numbers of decimal points used in the calculations.)

(f) How much will the total interest be?

To find the total interest paid in a blended-payment contract, use the following formula:

$$\begin{array}{l} \text{monthly} \\ \text{payment} \end{array} \times \begin{array}{l} \text{number of} \\ \text{months} \end{array}$$

$$\$135.51 \times 24$$

$$= \begin{array}{l} \text{total} \\ \text{amount repaid} \end{array} - \begin{array}{l} \text{borrowed} \\ \text{principal} \end{array} = \begin{array}{l} \text{total} \\ \text{interest charge} \end{array}$$

$$= \$3\ 252.24 - \$3\ 000 = \$252.24$$

Finally, there are a couple of points to note regarding compounding and terminology. Although payments on instalment loans are remitted monthly, interest is typically compounded at some other interval—often semi-annually. You may encounter the term **amortization,** which simply means repayment of a loan over a period of time. For instance, a loans officer might say that your loan will be amortized over three years.

To review, a loan that is amortized using blended payments, as in the boxed example "Excerpts from a Payment Schedule for a $3 000 Loan," will include changing proportions of interest and principal in each payment. As you gradually reduce the principal that you owe, you gradually pay less interest each time, leaving an ever-increasing share of your payment that can be applied toward repaying the principal. The relation between the interest and principal portions of each payment will vary with such factors as interest rates, the term of the loan, and the size of the monthly payment. Home mortgages work the same way, but the rate of principal repayment can be discouragingly slow at first if the loan is large, the payments are modest, and the term is 25 years or longer.

Excerpts from Payment Schedule for a $3 000 Loan (8% for 2 years)

PAYMENT NUMBER	MONTHLY PAYMENT	PRINCIPAL OWING BEFORE PAYMENT MADE	INTEREST PAID PER MONTH	PRINCIPAL REPAID PER MONTH	PRINCIPAL OWING AFTER PAYMENT
1	$135.50	$3 000.00	$19.68	$115.82	$2 884.18
2	135.50	2 884.17	18.92	116.58	2 767.60
3	135.50	2 767.60	18.15	117.35	2 650.25
4	135.50	2 650.25	17.38	118.12	2 532.13
5	135.50	2 532.13	16.61	118.89	2 413.24
6	135.50	2 413.24	15.83	119.67	2 293.57
12	135.50	1 683.33	11.04	124.46	1 558.87
18	135.50	924.22	6.06	129.44	794.78
24	135.50	134.74	0.88	134.62	0.12

Total Interest Charges

The three previous examples used the same principal, interest rate, and time, but they differed in method of repayment and in whether or not interest was compounded. How do these two differences affect the total amount of interest paid? With an instalment loan that has blended payments, the total interest charge is less apparent than in the examples of simple and compound interest with a single repayment.

The total interest charge on each of the above examples is, respectively, as follows:

(a) simple interest $480.00

(b) compound interest   509.58

(c) compound interest, blended payments   252.24

Can you suggest reasons for the variation?

As indicated at the beginning of this chapter, the five factors that influence the total interest charge are as follows:

(a) rate of interest,

(b) frequency of compounding,

(c) term of the loan,

(d) principal borrowed,

(e) method of repayment.

It is fairly obvious that higher interest rates will increase the cost of borrowing. On a small, short-term loan, small differences in the interest rate do not affect the cost very much; but when the principal is very large and the term is long, as is typically the case with a home mortgage, a difference of a quarter of a percentage point in the interest rate can make a substantial difference in the total interest charge.

The second factor, the frequency of compounding, is important for the borrower to keep in mind. If the interest on a mortgage is to be compounded quarterly instead of semi-annually, the difference in the total interest charge will be significant. The effect of the third factor, the term of the loan or the amortization period, is also fairly obvious; the longer your loan is outstanding, the more total interest you will have to pay. Likewise, the larger the principal borrowed, the higher the total interest charge.

Finally, the method of repayment affects the total interest charge. If you have the use of the total principal for the whole term of the loan, you will have to pay more interest than if you start repaying the principal right away. Most mortgages and consumer loans are instalment loans with blended payments—payment that comprise both principal and interest. Since the very first payment includes some return of the principal to the lender, this approach will reduce the total interest charge. Essentially, the method of payment affects the amount of principal outstanding at various times during the term of the loan. Did you notice that the total interest charge was lowest for the boxed example that featured an instalment loan with blended payments? The reason is that the borrower did not have the use of the total principal for the entire term.

Future Values and Present Values

Investors frequently ask the following kinds of questions: How much will I have if I invest $5 000 at 8 percent for five years? How much will I need to invest at 8 percent in order to have $5 000 in five years? The first question deals with the **future value** of money—that is, what the total of principal and interest will be in five years. The second deals with the **present value** of money. How much will you have to invest at 8 percent to have $5 000, in five years?

The two examples above assumed that a lump sum would be invested and a single payment received at a later date. These are fairly simple situations. Sometimes, though, investments are made in a series of deposits, or receipts may be received in a series of payments. For instance, what is the future value of depositing $500 a year for 10 years? And what is the present value of an annuity of $800 a month that will continue for seven years? For the sake of simplicity, we will examine instances of single payments first, and will later explain how to determine future and present values when serial payments are involved.

Single Payments

FUTURE VALUE OF A LUMP SUM What will a present sum of money (P) be worth (i.e., its future value, F) if the money is to be deposited at interest rate i for a period of n years? A time line may help you visualize such a problem. On the time line, receipts are shown by the upward-pointing arrow and payments by the downward-pointing arrow.

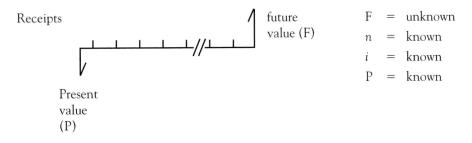

Receipts   future value (F)   F = unknown n = known i = known   P = known

Present value (P)

Payments

The unknown future value (F) can be found using the following formula, which is applicable to a single-payment compound amount:

$$F = P(1 + i)^n$$

Another way of expressing $(1 + i)^n$ is F/P at a given rate (i) and number of years (n), where F/P is the compound amount factor. Conveniently, there are tables of compound amount factors (F/P) for various combinations of interest rates and number of interest periods. Excerpts may be found in Tables 8A.5 and 8A.6 (see Appendix 8A). When tables are used to solve a problem, the equation may be expressed as follows:

$$F = P(F/P, i\%, n)$$

Future Value of $1 000

You have $1 000 and wish to know its future value, if invested for five years, at 10% compounded annually.

Set up a time line that indicates the knowns and unknowns.

Receipts

F   F $=$ unknown
      n $=$ 5
      i $=$ .10
      P $=$ 1 000

P

Payments

Calculate F, using the formula:

$F = P(1 + i)^n$
$F = 1\ 000(1 + 0.10)^5$
$ = 1\ 000 \times 1.6105$
$ = 1\ 610.51$

Or, use Table 8A.6 (see Appendix 8A) to find the value for F/P:

$F = P(F/P, 10\%, 5)$
$ = 1\ 000 \times 1.6105$
$ = 1\ 610.51$

Therefore, the future value of $1 000 in five years' time will be $1 610.51.

PRESENT VALUE OF A LUMP SUM   In this case, we want to know the present value (P) of a future sum of money (F) if it can be invested at interest rate i for a period of n years. By cross-multiplying the formula used for future values, we get the following:

$$P = \frac{F}{(1 + i)^n}$$

Or, using tables:

$P = F\ (P/F, i\%, n)$
$ = F \times \text{present worth factor (P/F) (see Appendix 8A, Table 8A.5 or 8A.6)}$

Present Value of $30 000 in Five Years

Mario plans to buy his first house with a down payment of $30 000 in five years. He wants to know how much he needs to invest now (P) in order to have the money for the down payment if the interest rate is 6%, compounded annually.

F = 30 000

n = 5

i = 0.06

P = unknown

Using the formula: $P = \dfrac{F}{(1 + i)^n} = \dfrac{30\ 000}{(1 + .06)^5} = \dfrac{30\ 000}{1.338225} = 22\ 417.75$

If Mario invests $22 417.75 now at 6%, in five years, he will have the $30 000 needed for his down payment. Expressed in another way, the present value of $30 000, invested at 6%, is $22 417.75.

Uniform Series of Deposits

An interesting challenge involves finding the *future* value of a series of deposits. For example, if you know how much you can afford to save each year (P) and for how many years (*n*), you can find out the future value (F) of this savings program.

A practical method of saving for a trip or for a down payment on a house would be to make regular deposits for several years. If you know how much will be needed (F) and how long you have to save (*n*), you can calculate the present value (P) in terms of the amount to be deposited each year. This second type of problem requires determining the present value of a series of deposits.

FUTURE VALUE OF A SERIES What will be the future value (F) of a series of annual deposits (A) for *n* years at interest rate *i*? The time line will be as follows:

Receipts

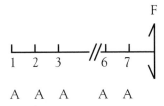

$F = $ unknown

$n = $ known

$i = $ known

$A = $ known

Deposits

The appropriate formula is as follows:

$$F = A\left(\frac{(1 + i)^n - 1}{i}\right)$$

Or, using compound interest tables:

F = A × compound amount factor (F/A)

  = A(F/A, i%, n)

Future Value of a Series of Deposits

Harold wants to establish an education fund for his new granddaughter, Evelyn. If he puts $3 000 into the fund for the next 18 years when she will be ready for college, how much money will she have if interest is 6%, compounded annually (assuming no taxes)?

F = unknown
n = 18
i = 6
A = 3 000

$$F = 3\ 000 \times \left(\frac{(1.06)^{18} - 1}{.06}\right) = 3\ 000 \times 30.906 = 92\ 718$$

Or, using Table 8A.5

F = A(F/A, 6%, 18) = 3 000 x 30.906 = 92 718.

Therefore, the future value of $3 000 deposits invested at 6% will be $92 718.

PRESENT VALUE OF A SERIES   How much must be deposited in a uniform series in order to accumulate a future sum of money at a given date? This question, which is relevant for those planning to retire a debt, is often referred to as a sinking fund problem. A **sinking fund** is a sum that is being accumulated to retire a debt. The formula is as follows:

$$A = F\left(\frac{i}{(1 + i)^n - 1}\right)$$

Using compound interest tables:

$$A = F \times \text{sinking fund factor (A/F)}$$
$$= F(A/F, i\%, n)$$

Present Value of a Series of Deposits

Since Ed wants to pay off his mortgage as fast as possible, he has decided to make a lump-sum payment of $5 000 in four years' time. At 6% interest, how much should he put aside annually for the next four years to reach his objective?

The time line will be as follows:

Receipts

F = 5 000
n = 4
i = 0.06
A = unknown

Deposits

$$A = 500\left(\frac{.06}{(1 + .06)^4 - 1}\right)$$
$$= 5\ 000 \times 0.2286$$
$$= \$1\ 142.95$$

Or, using tables:
$$A = F(A/F, 6\%, 4)$$
$$= 5\ 000 \times 0.22859$$
(from Appendix 8A, Table 8A.5)
$$= \$1\ 142.95$$

If Ed invests $1 142.95 a year at 6%, he will be able to reduce his mortgage debt by $5 000 in four years' time.

Uniform Series of Payments Received

The previous two examples involved the present and future values of a uniform series of *deposits*. Now we will consider the present and future values of a uniform series of *payments*. Often a financial institution faces the question of converting a series of future payments into an equivalent lump sum, known as the **commuted value.** One instance of this situation occurs at the death of an annuitant who had an annuity with a guaranteed period. A lump sum may be paid to the beneficiary instead of making payments for the balance of the guaranteed period.

Another common problem involves deciding how much you can spend each year if you wish to exhaust a known sum in a certain length of time. This is called recovery of capital in a uniform series of payments.

PRESENT WORTH OF A SERIES OF FUTURE PAYMENTS What is the present worth of a property that is now renting at (A) each year, at a given interest rate (*i*)? The time line will be as follows:

Receipts

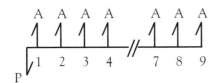

A = known
n = known
i = known
P = unknown

Payments

The appropriate formula is:

$$P = A \left(\frac{(1 + i)^n - 1}{i\,(1 + i)^n} \right)$$

Or, if using compound interest tables:

P = A × present worth factor (P/A)

Personal Finance in Action 8.4

Present Value of a Series of Annuity Payments

After Ted's death, the insurance company representative called on his widow, Magda, to tell her that she would receive a lump sum that would be equivalent to the annuity payments due to her husband. He had been receiving annual payments of $8 000 from an annuity that was guaranteed for six more years. When commuting the series of payments to a lump sum, the company assumed an interest rate of 10%. The time line would be as follows:

Receipts

A A A A A A
1 2 3 4 5 6
P

A = $8 000
n = 6
i = 0.10
P = unknown

Payments

continued

Using the formula:
$$P = A\left(\frac{(1 + i)^n - 1}{i(1 + i)^n}\right)$$

$$= 8\,000\left(\frac{(1 + .10)^6 - 1}{.10\,(1 + .10)^6}\right)$$

$$= \$34\,840$$

Using Table 8A.6 (see Appendix 8A):

$$P = A(\,P/A,\,10\%,\,6)$$
$$= 8\,000 \times 4.355$$
$$= 34\,840$$

Magda received a lump sum of $34 840 instead of six annual payments of $8 000. Why did she not receive $48 000?

CAPITAL RECOVERY IN A UNIFORM SERIES OF PAYMENTS   How much can be withdrawn each year (A) from a capital fund that has a present value of P, if the capital fund is invested at interest rate *i* so that the fund will be exhausted in *n* years? The time line will be as follows:

Receipts

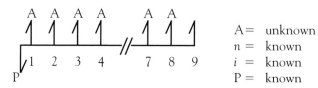

A = unknown
n = known
i = known
P = known

Payments

The appropriate formula is:

$$A = P\left(\frac{i(1 + i)^n}{(1 + i)^n - 1}\right)$$

Or, using compound interest tables:

$$A = P \times \text{capital recovery factor (A/P)}$$
$$= P(A/P,\,i\%,\,n)$$

Personal Finance in Action 8.5

Gradual Withdrawal of Capital

Stephanie has an education fund of $100 000 established in trust by her grandfather. She would like to study for her master's and possibly her Ph.D degree, and wants to know how much she can use each year over the next seven years if her money is invested at 10%.

Using Appendix 8A.6

A = unknown
n = 7

i = .10
P = 100 000
A = P(A/P, i%, n)

= 100 000 x 0.20541 = 20 541

Therefore, Stephanie can withdraw $20 541 from the fund each year for her education.

Multiple Compounding Periods per Year

Thus far, we have explained how to calculate present and future values when interest is compounded annually, but very often interest is compounded more frequently. There is a simple way to adapt the formulas and procedures given in this chapter to accommodate various frequencies of compounding. Simply change the annual interest rate to the semi-annual rate (or the quarterly rate, or whatever rate is appropriate), and change the number of years to the number of compounding periods. For example, if the interest rate is 10 percent per year for six years, compounded quarterly, it will be expressed as 2.5 percent per quarter. The number of compounding periods will be 4×6 years = 24. When you are using the formula or tables, $i = 0.025$ and $n = 24$.

Semi-Annual Compounding

You wish to know the future value of $1 000 in three years if the interest rate is 12%, compounded semi-annually.

First, put the interest rate into the same time frame as the compounding period. Thus, the rate will be 6% per half-year. The total number of compounding periods will be 2 per year x 3 years = 6. Therefore $n = 6$, and $i = 0.06$.

$$F = P(F/P, i\%, n)$$
$$= 1\ 000 \times 1.4185$$
$$\text{(Appendix 8A, Table 8A.5)}$$
$$= \$1\ 418.50$$

The future value of $1 000, compounded semi-annually at 12% for three years, is $1 418.50.

Summary

This chapter has demonstrated the concept of interest as applied to a variety of situations, including compound interest with either a single payment or a series of blended payments. An important consideration in many transactions is the total interest charge, which depends on the interest rate, the frequency of compounding, the term of the loan, the principal borrowed, and the method of repayment.

The next time you encounter a problem that involves future or present values, you should first draw a time line and then list your knowns and unknowns. This approach will permit you to clarify the problem and to classify it as one involving either single payments or a series of payments, and to decide whether your unknown is a present value or a future value. By comparing your problem statement and time line with the examples given in this chapter, you can find the appropriate formula to use in solving your problem.

Key Terms

amortization (p. 211)	maturity date (p. 207)
blended payments (p. 210)	nominal interest rate (p. 209)
commuted value (p. 217)	present value (p. 213)
compounding (p. 207)	principal (p. 206)
effective annual yield (p. 209)	simple interest (p. 207)
future value (p. 213)	sinking fund (p. 216)
interest rate (p. 206)	time value of money (p. 206)
loan term (p. 207)	yield (p. 209)

Problems

1. (a) How much will a $1 000 Canada Savings Bond be worth in seven years at 5 percent interest, compounded annually?

    (b) Would you prefer a bank account that paid compound interest annually or semi-annually? Explain.

    (c) What does a character in a Shakespearean play mean when he says, "neither a borrower nor a lender be?"

2. How can the Rule of 72 be of value to someone contemplating retirement?

3. Explain what is meant by the present value of money.

4. Josee is 40 and has $75 000 in her RRSP. How much will this be worth when she is 69 and must collapse the plan if it is compounded annually at 6%?

5. You have a piece of antique furniture that you are thinking of selling. You have received two offers from an interested buyer: $1 500 now or $2 000 in two years' time. Assuming an interest rate of 9 percent compounded annually, which offer would you accept? Did you make your comparison based on present values or future values?

6. Recently, André won $10 000 in a lottery. He would like to spend this sum on holidays, over a five-year period, and is wondering how much he can withdraw annually to make his winnings last five years. Assume an interest rate of 10 percent, compounded annually.

7. As the owner of a company that rents office furniture, you have received two offers from one of your clients: $3 000 per year for the use of the equipment over the next three years, or $9 000 at the end of three years. Which offer will you accept, assuming 6 percent interest, compounded annually?

8. John wants to know what sum of money he must save each year in order to have $15 000 available in five years' time to buy a new car.

    (a) Assume that the money will be invested at 6 percent interest, compounded annually.

    (b) Assume that the money will be invested at 9 percent interest, compounded semi-annually.

9. If you are receiving $3 000 a year in rent from 50 acres of farmland, what is the present worth of this contract if the interest rates are 10 percent, compounded annually? (Assume that the rent will be paid at the beginning of the year for each of the next three years.)

10. Lou has determined that his young family should have an educational fund of $10 000 to become available in eight years' time. If he were to die tomorrow, how much money would be needed from an insurance settlement in order to provide this sum if the money could be invested at 8 percent, compounded annually?

11. Go to the CANNEX Web site www.cannex.com. Then go to CANNEX Canada and click on Annuities. Using the example given, compare the income guaranteed by the companies listed. Which has the highest monthly income? The lowest?

    Go back to Welcome to CANNEX Canada. Scroll down and click on List of Canadian Financial Institutions. Check out the size of the assets of the companies whose annuities are shown above. (You can access the home pages of these companies from this site.) By comparing the guaranteed monthly incomes and the financial health of these companies, which company would you prefer to deal with?

References

BOOKS AND ARTICLES

Before personal computers become widely available, people who wanted to calculate loan repayments and other matters discussed in this chapter had to refer to books of mortgage tables. Several sample tables of this sort are reproduced in Appendix 8A to enable you to follow the formulas presented in the chapter and to help you solve the end-of-chapter problems. One book of tables is referenced below. But be aware that few people nowadays refer to such books; computer software (e.g., spreadsheets, financial calculators) serves as a much more effective tool for this purpose.

GRAY, DOUGLAS A. *Mortgage Payment Tables Made Easy: A Complete Canadian Guide.* Toronto: McGraw-Hill Ryerson, 1994.

Personal Finance on the Web

Bank of Canada
> **www.bankofcanada.ca** The Bank of Canada has responsibility for Canada's monetary policy including interest rates.

CANNEX
> **www.cannex.com** This site has a large list of comparative interest rates for GICs and term deposits.

CANOE
> **www.canoe.ca** Offers a comparative list of term deposit and savings account rates.

Department of Finance
> **www.fin.gc.ca** Provides information related to interest rates and the economy.

Statistics Canada
> **www.statcan.ca** This site has some useful Canadian statistical resources.

Appendix 8A

Interest Rate Tables

TABLE 8A.1 COMPOUND VALUE OF $1 AT VARIOUS INTEREST RATES FROM 1 TO 40 YEARS (COMPOUNDED ANNUALLY)

YRS.	4%	5%	6%	7%	8%	9%	10%	11%	12%	13%	14%	15%	16%
1	1.04	1.05	1.06	1.07	1.08	1.09	1.10	1.11	1.12	1.13	1.14	1.15	1.16
2	1.08	1.10	1.12	1.14	1.17	1.19	1.21	1.23	1.25	1.28	1.30	1.32	1.35
3	1.12	1.16	1.19	1.23	1.26	1.30	1.33	1.37	1.40	1.44	1.48	1.52	1.56
4	1.17	1.22	1.26	1.31	1.36	1.41	1.46	1.52	1.57	1.63	1.69	1.75	1.81
5	1.22	1.28	1.34	1.40	1.47	1.54	1.61	1.69	1.76	1.84	1.93	2.01	2.10
6	1.27	1.34	1.42	1.50	1.59	1.68	1.77	1.87	1.97	2.08	2.19	2.29	2.44
7	1.32	1.41	1.50	1.61	1.71	1.83	1.95	2.08	2.21	2.35	2.50	2.61	2.83
8	1.37	1.48	1.59	1.72	1.85	1.99	2.14	2.30	2.48	2.66	2.85	2.98	3.28
9	1.42	1.55	1.69	1.84	2.00	2.17	2.36	2.56	2.77	3.00	3.25	3.40	3.80
10	1.48	1.63	1.79	1.97	2.16	2.37	2.60	2.84	3.11	3.39	3.71	3.87	4.41
11	1.54	1.71	1.90	2.10	2.33	2.58	2.85	3.15	3.48	3.84	4.23	4.45	5.12
12	1.60	1.80	2.01	2.25	2.52	2.81	3.14	3.50	3.90	4.33	4.82	5.12	5.94
13	1.67	1.89	2.13	2.41	2.72	3.07	3.45	3.88	4.36	4.90	5.50	5.89	6.89
14	1.73	1.98	2.26	2.58	2.94	3.34	3.80	4.31	4.89	5.53	6.26	6.77	7.99
15	1.80	2.08	2.40	2.76	3.17	3.64	4.18	4.78	5.47	6.25	7.14	7.79	9.27
16	1.87	2.18	2.54	2.96	3.43	3.97	4.59	5.31	6.13	7.07	8.14	8.96	10.75
17	1.95	2.30	2.69	3.16	3.70	4.33	5.05	5.90	6.87	7.99	9.28	10.30	12.47
18	2.03	2.41	2.85	3.38	4.00	4.72	5.56	6.54	7.69	9.02	10.58	11.85	14.46
19	2.11	2.53	3.03	3.62	4.32	5.14	6.12	7.26	8.61	10.20	12.06	13.62	16.78
20	2.19	2.66	3.21	3.87	4.66	5.60	6.73	8.06	9.65	11.52	13.74	15.67	19.46
21	2.28	2.79	3.40	4.14	5.03	6.11	7.40	8.95	10.80	13.02	15.67	18.02	22.57
22	2.37	2.93	3.60	4.43	5.44	6.66	8.14	9.93	12.10	14.71	17.86	20.72	26.19
23	2.46	3.07	3.82	4.74	5.87	7.26	8.95	11.03	13.55	16.63	20.36	23.83	30.38
24	2.56	3.23	4.05	5.07	6.34	7.91	9.85	12.24	15.18	18.79	23.21	27.40	35.24
25	2.67	3.39	4.29	5.43	6.85	8.62	10.83	13.59	17.00	21.23	26.46	31.51	40.87
26	2.77	3.56	4.55	5.81	7.40	9.34	11.92	15.08	19.04	23.99	30.17	37.24	47.41
27	2.89	3.73	4.82	6.21	7.99	10.25	13.10	16.74	21.32	27.11	34.39	41.78	55.00
28	3.00	3.92	5.11	6.65	8.63	11.17	14.42	18.58	23.88	30.63	39.20	47.93	63.80
29	3.12	4.12	5.42	7.11	9.32	12.17	15.86	20.62	26.75	34.62	44.69	55.12	74.01
30	3.24	4.32	5.74	7.61	10.06	13.27	17.45	22.89	29.96	39.12	50.95	63.38	85.85
31	3.37	4.54	6.09	8.15	10.87	14.46	19.19	25.41	33.56	44.20	58.08	72.89	99.59
32	3.51	4.76	6.45	8.72	11.74	15.76	21.11	28.21	37.58	49.95	66.21	83.82	115.52
33	3.65	5.00	6.84	9.33	12.68	17.18	23.23	31.31	42.09	56.44	75.48	96.40	134.00
34	3.80	5.25	7.25	9.98	13.69	18.73	25.55	34.75	47.14	63.78	86.95	110.86	155.44
35	3.95	5.52	7.69	10.68	14.79	20.41	28.10	38.57	52.80	72.07	98.10	127.48	180.31
36	4.10	5.80	8.15	11.42	15.97	22.25	30.91	42.82	59.14	81.44	111.83	146.61	209.16
37	4.27	6.08	8.64	12.22	17.25	24.25	34.00	47.53	66.23	92.02	127.49	168.60	242.63
38	4.44	6.39	9.15	13.08	18.63	26.44	37.40	52.76	74.18	103.99	145.34	193.89	281.45
39	4.62	6.70	9.70	13.99	20.12	28.82	41.14	58.56	83.08	117.51	165.69	222.97	326.48
40	4.80	7.04	10.29	14.97	21.72	31.41	45.26	65.00	93.05	132.78	188.88	256.42	378.72

TABLE 8A.2 EFFECTIVE ANNUAL YIELD BY NOMINAL RATE AND FREQUENCY OF COMPOUNDING

NOMINAL RATE %	SEMI-ANNUALLY %	QUARTERLY %	MONTHLY %	WEEKLY %	DAILY %
3	3.02	3.03	3.04	3.04	3.05
3.25	3.28	3.29	3.30	3.30	3.30
3.50	3.53	3.55	3.56	3.56	3.56
3.75	3.79	3.80	3.82	3.82	3.82
4	4.04	4.06	4.07	4.08	4.08
4.25	4.30	4.32	4.33	4.34	4.34
4.50	4.55	4.58	4.59	4.60	4.60
4.75	4.81	4.84	4.85	4.86	4.86
5	5.06	5.09	5.12	5.12	5.13
5.25	5.32	5.35	5.38	5.39	5.39
5.50	5.58	5.61	5.64	5.65	5.65
5.75	5.83	5.88	5.90	5.92	5.92
6	6.09	6.14	6.17	6.18	6.18
6.25	6.35	6.40	6.43	6.45	6.45
6.50	6.61	6.66	6.70	6.71	6.72
6.75	6.86	6.92	6.96	6.98	6.98
7	7.12	7.19	7.23	7.25	7.25
7.25	7.38	7.45	7.50	7.51	7.52
7.50	7.64	7.71	7.76	7.78	7.79
7.75	7.90	7.98	8.03	8.05	8.06
8	8.16	8.24	8.30	8.32	8.33
8.25	8.42	8.51	8.57	8.59	8.60
8.50	8.68	8.77	8.84	8.86	8.87
8.75	8.94	9.04	9.11	9.14	9.14
9	9.20	9.31	9.38	9.41	9.42
9.25	9.46	9.58	9.65	9.68	9.69
9.50	9.73	9.84	9.92	9.96	9.96
9.75	9.99	10.11	10.20	10.23	10.24
10	10.25	10.38	10.47	10.51	10.52
10.25	10.51	10.65	10.74	10.78	10.79
10.50	10.77	10.92	11.02	11.06	11.07
10.75	11.03	11.19	11.29	11.33	11.34
11	11.30	11.46	11.57	11.61	11.63
11.25	11.57	11.73	11.84	11.89	11.90
11.50	11.83	12.00	12.12	12.17	12.19
11.75	12.10	12.28	12.40	12.45	12.47
12	12.36	12.55	12.68	12.73	12.74
12.25	12.62	12.82	12.96	13.01	13.03
12.50	12.89	13.10	13.24	13.29	13.31
12.75	13.15	13.37	13.52	13.58	13.60
13	13.42	13.65	13.80	13.86	13.88
13.25	13.69	13.92	14.08	14.15	14.18
13.50	13.95	14.20	14.36	14.43	14.45

continued

TABLE 8A.2 EFFECTIVE ANNUAL YIELD BY NOMINAL RATE AND FREQUENCY OF COMPOUNDING (CONTINUED)

NOMINAL RATE %	SEMI-ANNUALLY %	QUARTERLY %	MONTHLY %	WEEKLY %	DAILY %
13.75	14.22	14.47	14.65	14.72	14.74
14	14.49	14.75	14.93	15.01	15.02
14.25	14.75	15.03	15.22	15.30	15.31
14.50	15.02	15.30	15.50	15.58	15.60
14.75	15.29	15.58	15.79	15.87	15.89
15	15.56	15.87	16.08	16.16	16.18
15.25	15.83	16.14	16.36	16.44	16.47
15.50	16.10	16.42	16.65	16.74	16.76
15.75	16.37	16.70	16.94	17.03	17.00
16	16.64	16.98	17.23	17.32	17.34

TABLE 8A.3 AMORTIZATION TABLE: MONTHLY PAYMENT NECESSARY TO AMORTIZE A LOAN AT 8%

TERM AMOUNT	1 YEAR	2 YEARS	3 YEARS	4 YEARS	5 YEARS	6 YEARS	7 YEARS	8 YEARS	9 YEARS	10 YEARS	11 YEARS	12 YEARS	13 YEARS	14 YEARS	15 YEARS
$100	8.70	4.52	3.13	2.44	2.03	1.75	1.56	1.41	1.30	1.21	1.14	1.08	1.03	.99	.96
200	17.39	9.04	6.26	4.88	4.05	3.50	3.11	2.82	2.60	2.42	2.27	2.16	2.06	1.98	1.91
300	26.08	13.56	9.39	7.31	6.07	5.25	4.66	4.23	3.89	3.62	3.41	3.23	3.08	2.97	2.87
400	34.78	18.07	12.52	9.75	8.09	6.99	6.21	5.63	5.19	4.83	4.54	4.31	4.11	3.97	3.82
500	43.47	22.59	15.64	12.18	10.11	8.74	7.77	7.04	6.48	6.04	5.68	5.38	5.13	4.96	4.78
600	52.16	27.11	18.77	14.62	12.13	10.49	9.32	8.45	7.78	7.24	6.81	6.46	6.16	5.95	5.73
700	60.85	31.62	21.90	17.05	14.15	12.23	10.87	9.85	9.07	8.45	7.95	7.53	7.19	6.94	6.69
800	69.55	36.14	25.03	19.49	16.18	13.98	12.42	11.26	10.37	9.66	9.08	8.61	8.21	7.93	7.65
900	78.24	40.66	28.15	21.92	18.20	15.73	13.97	12.67	11.66	10.86	10.22	9.68	9.24	8.92	8.61
1 000	86.93	45.17	31.28	24.36	20.22	17.47	15.53	14.08	12.96	12.07	11.35	10.76	10.26	9.91	9.56
2 000	173.86	90.34	62.56	48.71	40.43	34.94	31.05	28.15	25.91	24.13	22.70	21.51	20.52	19.83	19.11
3 000	260.79	135.51	93.83	73.06	60.65	52.41	46.57	42.22	38.86	36.20	34.04	32.26	30.78	29.74	28.67
4 000	347.72	180.68	125.11	97.41	80.86	69.88	62.09	56.29	51.81	48.26	45.39	43.02	41.04	39.65	38.23
5 000	434.65	225.84	156.39	121.76	101.08	87.35	77.61	70.36	64.76	60.33	56.73	53.77	51.30	49.57	47.78
6 000	521.57	271.01	187.66	146.12	121.29	104.82	93.13	84.43	77.71	72.39	68.08	64.52	61.55	59.48	57.34
7 000	608.50	316.18	218.94	170.47	141.50	122.29	108.66	98.50	90.66	84.45	79.42	75.28	71.81	69.39	66.90
8 000	695.43	361.35	250.22	194.82	161.72	139.76	124.18	112.57	103.62	96.52	90.77	86.03	82.07	79.31	76.45
9 000	782.36	406.52	281.49	219.17	181.93	157.23	139.70	126.64	116.57	108.58	102.11	96.78	92.33	89.22	86.01
10 000	869.29	451.68	312.77	243.52	202.15	174.70	155.22	140.71	129.52	120.65	113.46	107.54	102.59	99.13	95.57

continued

TABLE 8A.3 AMORTIZATION TABLE: (CONTINUED)
MONTHLY PAYMENT NECESSARY TO AMORTIZE A LOAN AT 8%

TERM AMOUNT	16 YEARS	17 YEARS	18 YEARS	19 YEARS	20 YEARS	21 YEARS	22 YEARS	23 YEARS	24 YEARS	25 YEARS
$100	.92	.90	.87	.85	.83	.82	.80	.79	.78	.77
200	1.84	1.79	1.74	1.70	1.66	1.63	1.60	1.58	1.55	1.53
300	2.76	2.68	2.61	2.54	2.49	2.44	2.40	2.36	2.33	2.29
400	3.67	3.57	3.47	3.39	3.32	3.25	3.20	3.15	3.10	3.06
500	4.59	4.46	4.34	4.24	4.15	4.07	3.99	3.93	3.87	3.82
600	5.51	5.35	5.21	5.08	4.98	4.88	4.79	4.72	4.65	4.58
700	6.43	6.24	6.07	5.93	5.80	5.69	5.59	5.50	5.42	5.35
800	7.34	7.13	6.94	6.78	6.63	6.50	6.39	6.29	6.19	6.11
900	8.26	8.02	7.81	7.62	7.46	7.32	7.19	7.07	6.97	6.87
1 000	9.18	8.91	8.68	8.47	8.29	8.13	7.98	7.86	7.74	7.64
2 000	18.35	17.82	17.35	16.94	16.57	16.25	15.96	15.71	15.48	15.27
3 000	27.52	26.72	26.02	25.40	24.86	24.37	23.94	23.56	23.21	22.90
4 000	36.70	35.63	34.69	33.87	33.14	32.49	31.92	31.41	30.95	30.53
5 000	45.87	44.53	43.36	42.33	41.42	40.62	39.90	39.26	38.68	38.17
6 000	55.04	53.44	52.03	50.80	49.71	48.74	47.88	47.11	46.42	45.80
7 000	64.22	62.34	60.70	59.26	57.99	56.86	55.86	54.96	54.15	53.43
8 000	73.39	71.25	69.37	67.73	66.27	64.98	63.84	62.81	61.89	61.06
9 000	82.56	80.15	78.04	76.19	74.56	73.11	71.81	70.66	69.62	68.69
10 000	91.74	89.06	86.72	84.66	82.84	81.23	79.79	78.51	77.36	76.33

TABLE 8A.4 MONTHLY INTEREST FACTORS AT NOMINAL ANNUAL RATES, INTEREST COMPOUNDED SEMI-ANNUALLY

RATE %	FACTOR			RATE %	FACTOR			RATE %	FACTOR		
4	.003	305	8904	8.875	.007	262	6831	13.75	.011	143	2522
4.125	.003	408	3260	9	.007	363	1231	13.875	.011	241	7802
4.25	.003	510	7094	9.125	.007	463	5130	14	.011	340	2602
4.375	.003	613	0406	9.25	.007	563	8530	14.125	.011	438	6923
4.50	.003	715	3196	9.375	.007	664	1431	14.25	.011	537	0764
4.625	.003	817	5466	9.50	.007	764	3832	14.375	.011	635	4128
4.75	.003	919	7215	9.625	.007	864	5735	14.50	.011	733	7014
4.875	.004	021	8445	9.75	.007	964	7141	14.625	.011	831	9423
5	.004	123	9155	9.875	.008	064	8049	14.75	.011	930	1355
5.125	.004	225	9347	10	.008	164	8461	14.875	.012	028	2811
5.25	.004	327	9021	10.125	.008	264	8377	15	.012	126	3791
5.375	.004	429	8178	10.25	.008	364	7797	15.125	.012	224	4297
5.50	.004	531	6818	10.375	.008	464	6722	15.25	.012	322	4327
5.625	.004	633	4941	10 1/5	.008	564	5152	15.375	.012	420	3883
5.75	.004	735	2549	10.625	.008	664	3089	15.50	.012	518	2966
5.875	.004	836	9642	10.75	.008	764	0532	15.625	.012	616	1575
6	.004	938	6221	10.875	.008	863	7482	15.75	.012	713	9712
6.125	.005	040	2285	11	.008	963	3940	15.875	.012	811	7377
6.25	.005	141	7837	11.125	.009	062	9906	16	.012	909	4570
6.375	.005	243	2875	11.25	.009	162	5381	16.125	.013	007	1292
6.50	.005	344	7401	11.375	.009	262	0365	16.25	.013	104	7543
6.625	.005	446	1416	11.50	.009	361	4858	16.375	.013	202	3325
6.75	.005	547	4919	11.625	.009	460	8863	16.50	.013	299	8636
6.875	.005	648	7912	11.75	.009	560	2378	16.625	.013	397	3478
7	.005	750	0395	11.875	.009	659	5404	16.75	.013	494	7852
7.125	.005	851	2369	12	.009	758	7942	16.875	.013	592	1758
7.25	.005	952	3834	12.125	.009	857	9993	17	.013	689	5196
7.375	.006	053	4791	12.25	.009	957	1557	17.125	.013	786	8166
7.50	.006	154	5240	12.375	.010	056	2634	17.25	.013	884	0670
7.625	.006	255	5182	12.50	.010	155	3225	17.375	.013	981	2708
7.75	.006	356	4617	12.625	.010	254	3331	17.50	.014	078	4280
7.875	.006	457	3546	12.75	.010	353	2952	17.625	.014	175	5387
8	.006	558	1970	12.875	.010	452	2088	17.75	.014	272	6030
8.125	.006	658	9889	13	.010	551	0740	17.875	.014	369	6208
8.25	.006	759	7303	13.125	.010	649	8909				
8.375	.006	860	4214	13.25	.010	748	6596				
8.50	.006	961	0622	13.375	.010	847	3799				
8.625	.007	061	6527	13.50	.010	946	0522				
8.75	.007	162	1929	13.625	.011	044	6762				

Interest for one month on any amount may be obtained by multiplying that amount by this factor.

TABLE 8A.5 6% COMPOUND INTEREST FACTORS

	SINGLE PAYMENT			UNIFORM SERIES			
	COMPOUND AMOUNT FACTOR	PRESENT WORTH FACTOR	SINKING FUND FACTOR	CAPITAL RECOVERY FACTOR	COMPOUND AMOUNT FACTOR	PRESENT WORTH FACTOR	
n	F/P	P/F	A/F	A/P	F/A	P/A	*n*
1	1.0600	0.9434	1.00000	1.06000	1.000	0.943	1
2	1.1236	0.8900	0.48544	0.54544	2.060	1.833	2
3	1.1910	0.8396	0.31411	0.37411	3.184	2.673	3
4	1.2625	0.7921	0.22859	0.28859	4.375	3.465	4
5	1.3382	0.7473	0.17740	0.23740	5.637	4.212	5
6	1.4185	0.7050	0.14336	0.20336	6.975	4.917	6
7	1.5036	0.6651	0.11914	0.17914	8.394	5.582	7
8	1.5938	0.6274	0.10104	0.16104	9.897	6.210	8
9	1.6895	0.5919	0.08702	0.14702	11.491	6.802	9
10	1.7908	0.5584	0.07587	0.13587	13.181	7.360	10
11	1.8983	0.5268	0.06679	0.12679	14.972	7.887	11
12	2.0122	0.4970	0.05928	0.11928	16.870	8.384	12
13	2.1329	0.4688	0.05296	0.11296	18.882	8.853	13
14	2.2609	0.4423	0.04758	0.10758	21.015	9.295	14
15	2.3966	0.4173	0.04296	0.10296	23.276	9.712	15
16	2.5404	0.3936	0.03895	0.09895	25.673	10.106	16
17	2.6928	0.3714	0.03544	0.09544	28.213	10.477	17
18	2.8543	0.3503	0.03236	0.09236	30.906	10.828	18
19	3.0256	0.3305	0.02962	0.08962	33.760	11.158	19
20	3.2071	0.3118	0.02718	0.08718	36.786	11.470	20
21	3.3996	0.2942	0.02500	0.08500	39.993	11.764	21
22	3.6035	0.2775	0.02305	0.08305	43.392	12.042	22
23	3.8197	0.2618	0.02128	0.08128	46.996	12.303	23
24	4.0489	0.2470	0.01968	0.07968	50.816	12.550	24
25	4.2919	0.2330	0.01823	0.07823	54.865	12.783	25
26	4.5494	0.2198	0.01690	0.07690	59.156	13.003	26
27	4.8223	0.2074	0.01570	0.07570	63.706	13.211	27
28	5.1117	0.1956	0.01459	0.07459	68.528	13.406	28
29	5.4184	0.1846	0.01358	0.07358	73.640	13.591	29
30	5.7435	0.1741	0.01265	0.07265	79.058	13.765	30
31	6.0881	0.1643	0.01179	0.07179	84.802	13.929	31
32	6.4534	0.1550	0.01100	0.07100	90.890	14.084	32
33	6.8406	0.1462	0.01027	0.07027	97.343	14.230	33
34	7.2510	0.1379	0.00960	0.06960	104.184	14.368	34
35	7.6861	0.1301	0.00897	0.06897	111.435	14.498	35
40	10.2857	0.0972	0.00646	0.06646	154.762	15.046	40
45	13.7646	0.0727	0.00470	0.06470	212.744	15.456	45
50	18.4202	0.0543	0.00344	0.06344	290.336	15.762	50

TABLE 8A.5 6% COMPOUND INTEREST FACTORS (CONTINUED)

	SINGLE PAYMENT				UNIFORM SERIES		
55	24.6503	0.0406	0.00254	0.06254	394.172	15.991	55
60	32.9877	0.0303	0.00188	0.06188	533.128	61.161	60
65	44.1450	0.0227	0.00139	0.06139	719.083	16.289	65
70	59.0759	0.0169	0.00103	0.06103	967.932	16.385	70
75	79.0569	0.0126	0.00077	0.06077	1 300.949	16.456	75
80	105.7960	0.0095	0.00057	0.06057	1 746.600	16.509	80
85	141.5789	0.0071	0.00043	0.06043	2 342.982	16.549	85
90	189.4645	0.0053	0.00032	0.06032	3 141.075	16.579	90
95	253.5463	0.0039	0.00024	0.06024	4 209.104	16.601	95
100	339.3021	0.0029	0.00018	0.06018	5 638.368	16.618	100

TABLE 8A.6 10% COMPOUND INTEREST FACTORS

	SINGLE PAYMENT				UNIFORM SERIES		
	COMPOUND AMOUNT FACTOR	PRESENT WORTH FACTOR	SINKING FUND FACTOR	CAPITAL RECOVERY FACTOR	COMPOUND AMOUNT FACTOR	PRESENT WORTH FACTOR	
n	F/P	P/F	A/F	A/P	F/A	P/A	n
1	1.1000	0.9091	1.00000	0.10000	1.000	0.909	1
2	1.2100	0.8264	0.47619	0.57619	2.100	1.736	2
3	1.3310	0.7513	0.30211	0.40211	3.310	2.487	3
4	1.4641	0.6830	0.21547	0.31547	4.641	3.170	4
5	1.6105	0.6209	0.16380	0.26380	6.105	3.791	5
6	1.7716	0.5645	0.12961	0.22961	7.716	4.355	6
7	1.9487	0.5132	0.10541	0.20541	9.487	4.868	7
8	2.1436	0.4665	0.08744	0.18744	11.436	5.335	8
9	2.3579	0.4241	0.07364	0.17364	13.579	5.759	9
10	2.5937	0.3855	0.06275	0.16275	15.937	6.144	10
11	2.8531	0.3505	0.05396	0.15396	18.531	6.495	11
12	3.1384	0.3186	0.04676	0.14676	21.384	6.814	12
13	3.4523	0.2897	0.04078	0.14078	24.523	7.103	13
14	3.7975	0.2633	0.03575	0.13575	27.975	7.367	14
15	4.1772	0.2394	0.03147	0.13147	31.772	7.606	15
16	4.5950	0.2176	0.02782	0.12782	35.950	7.824	16
17	5.0545	0.1978	0.02466	0.12466	40.545	8.022	17
18	5.5599	0.1799	0.02193	0.12193	45.599	8.201	18
19	6.1159	0.1635	0.01955	0.11955	51.159	8.365	19
20	6.7275	0.1486	0.01746	0.11746	57.275	8.514	20
21	7.4002	0.1351	0.01562	0.11562	64.002	8.649	21
22	8.1403	0.1228	0.01401	0.11401	71.403	8.772	22
23	8.9543	0.1117	0.01257	0.11257	79.543	8.883	23
24	9.8497	0.1015	0.01130	0.11130	88.497	8.985	24
25	10.8347	0.0923	0.01017	0.11017	98.347	9.077	25
26	11.9182	0.0839	0.00916	0.10916	109.182	9.161	26
27	13.1100	0.0763	0.00826	0.10826	121.100	9.237	27
28	14.4210	0.0693	0.00745	0.10745	134.210	9.307	28
29	15.8631	0.0630	0.00673	0.10673	148.631	9.370	29
30	17.4494	0.0573	0.00608	0.10608	164.494	9.427	30
31	19.1943	0.0521	0.00550	0.10550	181.943	9.479	31
32	21.1138	0.0474	0.00497	0.10497	201.138	9.526	32
33	23.2252	0.0431	0.00450	0.10450	222.252	9.569	33
34	25.5477	0.0391	0.00407	0.10407	245.477	9.609	34
35	28.1024	0.0356	0.00369	0.10369	271.024	9.644	35
40	45.2593	0.0221	0.00226	0.10226	442.593	9.779	40
45	72.8905	0.0137	0.00139	0.10139	718.905	9.863	45
50	117.3909	0.0085	0.00086	0.10086	1 163.909	9.915	50

TABLE 8A.6 10% COMPOUND INTEREST FACTORS (CONTINUED)

	SINGLE PAYMENT			UNIFORM SERIES		
	COMPOUND AMOUNT FACTOR	PRESENT WORTH FACTOR	SINKING FUND FACTOR	CAPITAL RECOVERY FACTOR	COMPOUND AMOUNT FACTOR	PRESENT WORTH FACTOR	
n	F/P	P/F	A/F	A/P	F/A	P/A	*n*
55	189.0591	0.0053	0.00053	0.10053	1880.591	9.947	55
60	304.4816	0.0033	0.00033	0.10033	3034.816	9.967	60
65	490.3707	0.0020	0.00020	0.10020	4893.707	9.980	65
70	789.7470	0.0013	0.00013	0.10013	7887.470	9.987	70
75	1 271.8952	0.0008	0.00008	0.10008	1 2708.954	9.992	75
80	2 048.4002	0.0005	0.00005	0.10005	2 0474.002	9.995	80
85	3 298.9690	0.0003	0.00003	0.10003	3 2979.690	9.997	85
90	5 313.0226	0.0002	0.00002	0.10002	5 3120.226	9.998	90
95	8 556.6760	0.0001	0.00001	0.10001	8 5556.760	9.999	95
100	13 780.6123	0.0001	0.00001	0.10001	13 7796.123	9.999	100

Saving and Investing

1. Distinguish between the following pairs of terms: saving and investing; investing and speculating; liquidity and marketability; debt and equity securities; income and capital gain; total and liquid assets; nominal and real interest rates; and, income and wealth.

2. Give four reasons for saving and explain how these reasons affect the choice of investments.

3. List three reasons why people find saving difficult and two reasons why they find investing overwhelming.

4. Examine the trends in the savings rate in Canada and analyze the effects of age and income on the amount that Canadians save.

5. Define the following terms: portfolio, term, and investment pyramid.

6. Distinguish among the different types of risks to which investments are exposed and give examples of the four types of risk associated with various kinds of investments.

7. Explain why there are trade-offs between risk and return, return and liquidity, term and return, and current income and capital gain.

8. Explain the principle of diversification and why it is important in investment planning.

9. Examine three ways of handling risk in an investment portfolio.

10. Identify conflicting investment objectives and explain how to make an investment plan.

Introduction

One of the keys to successful financial planning is investing wisely. In order to invest, you first need to save. But investing and saving do not mean the same thing. A saver merely reduces spending and allows surplus funds to accumulate. An investor puts savings to work to generate income. This income is usually referred to as the yield. You are an investor if you have a savings account, a Canada Savings Bond (CSB), or a guaranteed investment certificate (GIC). If you simply keep your savings in a metal box in your desk, you are not an investor.

The extensive range of investments available today can be quite confusing. Possible investment vehicles include everything from the simple savings account to the more complex mutual funds and derivatives. Each investment is chosen because it holds the promise of a gain. No one invests with the intention of losing money. Each investment also carries a risk. Generally, the greater the risk, the greater the chance of a significant gain. There is little risk in a savings account, but also very little chance for gain. There is considerable risk in an emerging-markets mutual fund, but also the possibility of a large gain. Each investor must decide his or her own level of risk tolerance. How much risk you are comfortable tolerating will depend on your age, financial well-being, family circumstances, and investment objectives.

To become an investor, you must first become a saver. This chapter therefore begins by looking at ways to encourage saving and then introduces you to the world of investing. It also examines the characteristics of various investments, discusses investment objectives, and describes how to prepare an investment plan and create a portfolio of investments. Much of this information will be discussed in greater detail in Chapters 10 and 11.

Saving

Why Save?

As mentioned earlier, you must save before you can invest. Everyone with an income faces frequent decisions about whether to spend or save. In our market-driven economy, the desire to spend is often far greater than the desire to save. Spending, for many people, is exciting, because it provides instant gratification. Saving, on the other hand, seems dull, since it provides no immediate reward. But unless you start saving at an early age, your retirement years could be very unpleasant.

To put the need for savings in perspective, it may be helpful to project income and economic needs over a life span (see Chapter 1, Figure 1.1). On average, earnings can be expected to increase until about age 55 or 60, after which they typically level off or start to decline. During your working years, your wages will probably increase to reflect your growing skill and experience as well as to accommodate price changes, but in late middle age your circumstances may shift: you may choose early retirement, or you may need to leave the labour force because of ill health or job loss. At retirement, which often occurs by age 65, earnings stop and must be replaced by pension and investment income. Whether you have investment income will depend on whether you first had some savings and then invested them wisely.

Your spending needs over a lifetime probably will not coincide with your level of income (see Chapter 1, Figure 1.1). Early in your working life, you may need more money than you are earning. But this imbalance will probably shift after you have been employed for some time. At that point, many people are well established, own a house and other assets, and earn an income that exceeds their cost of living. Then, after retirement, incomes decline. Without some investment income, you may have difficulty maintaining the standard of living to which you have become accustomed.

It would certainly be more convenient if income increased gradually throughout a person's life and did not decline in later years. If this were a typical earning pattern, many people could maintain their financial independence relatively easily. But you can reach this goal by another route—that is, by creating a long-term financial plan with retirement in mind. To do so, you must invest some of your income on a regular basis, thereby creating an estate. Your estate can then be used when you retire to help you remain financially independent. You will also need some savings during your working years in order to meet short-term and emergency needs.

There are at least four important reasons to save. Funds are needed for (i) emergencies, (ii) liquidity, (iii) short-term goals, and (iv) long-term goals. We will consider each in turn.

EMERGENCY FUND Since most people start out their working lives with very little net worth, the first need is to create an emergency fund—readily accessible money that can be used to handle the unexpected expenses that we all have. It is often suggested that several (perhaps three) months' take-home pay should be set aside as the emergency fund. Expect that you will need some time to achieve this goal. Emergency funds can be kept in a savings account, term deposits, Canada Savings Bonds, or any savings instrument that pays interest without locking in the money. In addition, you should give serious consideration to obtaining adequate insurance to cover risks to your property or dependents, as was discussed in Chapters 4 through 6.

LIQUIDITY NEEDS You will need to have some funds available to cope with any unevenness in your cash flow and to pay for infrequent large expenses. Ready access to about one month's take-home pay may be adequate. Put these funds where they will earn as much interest as possible but remain easily accessible—for example, in an interest-bearing deposit account that permits chequing.

SHORT-TERM GOALS How can you distinguish a short-term goal from a long-term goal? When you review your financial goals, you will find some that can be accomplished within the next five years and others that will take longer. You can decide what time frame best fits your situation, but do make a distinction between short-term and long-term goals. It is best to segregate the funds for short-term goals from those for longer-term goals, either on paper (in your accounting records) or by actually keeping the funds in separate accounts. The money being saved for next year's holiday should not get mixed with that being saved for retirement.

Short-term goals might include holidays and trips, vehicles, furniture, appliances, and education for you or your children. If your children are very young, planning for their postsecondary education will be a long-term goal. People who hope to own a home some day may want to start saving for a down payment; if you already have a house, you may want to reserve funds for mortgage prepayments.

Home ownership is the single most important investment for most Canadian families. In general, house prices change in response to both the prevailing inflation rate and the demand for housing. During periods of rapid inflation, the prices of houses tend to appreciate as much as or more than the inflation rate, making property an effective and tax-free storehouse of value. At other times, house prices may fall, to the disadvantage of people who must sell during those periods.

Despite some uncertainty about future house prices, home ownership has advantages. Any capital gain realized on your home has long been excluded from taxation. From an investment perspective, buying a house is a form of forced saving. The discipline of regular mortgage payments results not only in a place to live now but also in the eventual ownership of an asset.

Depending on how soon you will need them, funds being saved for short-term goals may be invested in low-risk securities with appropriate maturities. The discussion that follows in this and later chapters should give you some ideas.

LONG-TERM GOALS Many people share the key long-term goal of increasing their net worth in such a way that they enhance their financial security, achieve financial independence, and ensure financial support for their retirement years. To be certain of having a comfortable lifestyle during retirement, you must start planning early in your working years (for example, see Personal Finance in Action Box 9.1, "How Much Capital Will She Need?"). The magic of compounding will cause small amounts to grow to large sums if left invested for long periods. For instance, if you invest $1 000 each year at an average annual compound rate of only 3 percent, your deposits of $30 000 will grow to $47 575 in 30 years. At 5 percent interest, your money will double in the same three decades, to $66 439; at 7 percent, it will nearly triple, to $94 461 (see Figure 9.1). But if you put off saving for your retirement until you have only a few working years remaining, your savings will not have enough time to grow (see Chapter 1, Figure 1.2). Acquiring capital to fund your retirement is a long-term savings goal, and such funds can be invested with a longer time horizon than those intended for short-term goals. That is, you can invest them in securities that, while not readily accessible, have prospects for long-term growth.

How to Save

Despite the widely held belief that everyone should save some money, many of us give these good intentions low priority. Saving can be hard to do, easy to postpone, and not much fun. To ensure success, you must have a firm commitment and definite plans. There will always be

FIGURE 9.1 COMPOUND VALUE OF ANNUAL INVESTMENTS OF $1 000, INVESTED AT 3%, 5%, AND 7%

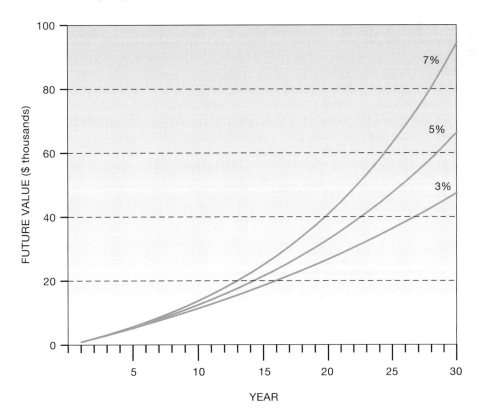

Personal Finance in Action 9.1

How Much Capital Will She Need?

Deirdre estimates that she will need an income of about $600 a month ($7 200 a year) from her investments to supplement her pensions when she retires. She wonders how much capital (principal) she will need, based on a conservative return of 5 percent on average. She makes her calculations using the following formula:

Interest = principal × rate × time

$$Principal = \frac{interest\ (required\ income)}{rate \times time}$$

$$= \frac{600 \times 12}{0.05 \times 1}$$

$$= \$144\ 000$$

Deirdre has made no adjustments for inflation, because she anticipates that a higher inflation rate will push interest rates up correspondingly. Now that she has a long-term goal of building up a net worth of $144 000, she will make plans for saving and investing.

---

demands on your income that seem urgent and tempt you to postpone saving. You may reason that you will find saving easier at some later point, when you will have no unexpected expenses. But eventually you will discover that this pattern tends to become repetitious: no time ever seems to be the right time to save. The only solution is to set up an automatic savings plan now and follow it determinedly.

There are two basic approaches to saving—taking savings off the top of each paycheque before spending anything, or waiting to see what will be left at the end of the pay period. People who follow the first system will accumulate savings and will therefore have funds to invest; the others will never get around to it. Which approach will you take? The best plan is to establish a certain amount or percentage—e.g., 5 to 10 percent—that you will set aside from each pay.

When developing a savings strategy, be aware of your strengths and weaknesses. If you are an impulsive spender, you will need a system that makes your savings unavailable. Look into payroll savings plans and automatic saving methods at financial institutions; arrange for a certain portion of your income to be directed into such a plan before it ever reaches you. (See Personal Finance in Action Box 9.2, "An Automatic Savings Plan.") For example, each autumn Canada Savings Bonds become available by payroll deduction, some credit unions have automatic savings plans, and a number of mutual funds offer regular investment plans.

RULES FOR SAVING The three key rules for becoming a successful saver are as follows:

(a) have a purpose or goal for which you are saving,

(b) make a plan for accomplishing your goal,

(c) save regularly.

You must be committed to a plan for increasing your net worth, or nothing will be accomplished. It would be ridiculous, of course, to go to the other extreme and become a miser; letting saving become an end in itself is also a mistake. Your objective should be a balance between present and future consumption. Some financial experts suggest that if you save 10 percent of your salary throughout your working years and invest it carefully, you can become financially independent by the time you retire.

An Automatic Savings Plan

Peter finds saving very difficult. He always intends to bank whatever money is left at the end of the month—but more often than not, nothing is left. His friend Ayeesha, who belongs to a credit union, tells him about an automatic savings plan by which she saves $400 a month. She has authorized the credit union to deduct funds on each payday from the account into which her employer deposits her pay, and to transfer these funds to her savings account.

Peter decides that he will give this plan a try, but when he inquires at his bank, he finds that they have no such system in effect. An alternative, they suggest, is for Peter to write a year's supply of postdated cheques and, at the appropriate time, the bank will transfer funds from his chequing account to his savings account. Peter tries this method, and is very pleased at the end of the year to find that he has saved $4800.

How Much Do Canadians Save?

The Importance of Saving

Saving is essential in a modern, vibrant economy. As previously mentioned, without it, it is impossible for people to reach their financial goals. Without savings, a person's retirement years could be bleak indeed. Also, without savings it is impossible for businesses to find the money necessary to modernize and expand their capital. Banks will have nothing to lend. Capital markets will be unable to raise money for investment. It then becomes difficult for them to provide the goods and services demanded by a growing population or for export to foreign markets.

Without savings, it also becomes difficult for governments to borrow to finance their deficits when spending exceeds revenue. The Canadian government no longer has deficits but must continue to borrow to manage the national debt. The money for these purposes can always be found abroad, but a healthy rate of domestic savings is important for the survival of a strong, vibrant economy. If money is raised outside the country, the economy may grow. The income earned on the investments may, however, be repatriated by the investors and leave the country. In Canada in the 1990s, many Canadian subsidiaries of foreign firms closed as a result of corporate downsizing. When this happened, more investment funds left the country.

The actual rate of saving in Canada in the last 50 years has been lower than that in many other industrialized nations. While comparable to savings rates of the United States, it is much lower than Japan's and less than most of European countries.[1] Because the savings rate in Canada has been traditionally low and the population small, Canadian governments have long encouraged foreign investment. This was a policy of the first government of Canada headed by Sir John A. Macdonald and continues to be popular today with both the federal and provincial governments. Without foreign investment, Canada would be less industrialized. The consequence is that many of the firms doing business in Canada are foreign owned.

From 1993 to 2000 the rate of saving in Canada does not show any specific trend (see Figure 9.2). The biggest factor in the earlier years was the negative effect on private investment caused by the combination of federal and provincial deficits. Governments had to borrow

---

[1] Joseph E. Stiglitz and Robin W. Broadway, *Principles of Macroeconomics and the Canadian Economy*, Second Edition (New York: WW. Norton and Company, 1997), p. 402.

FIGURE 9.2   SAVINGS BY PERSONS AND UNINCORPORATED BUSINESS, CORPORATIONS AND GOVERNMENT BUSINESS, AND GOVERNMENT

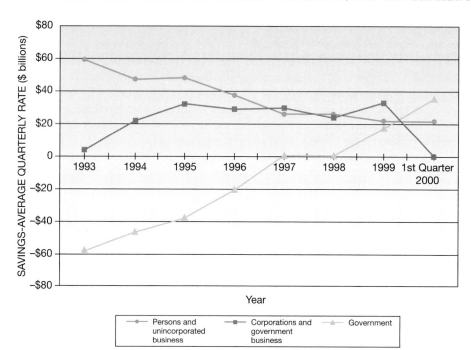

SOURCE: Adapted from Statistics Canada "Income and Expenditure Accounts: Sector Accounts," Catalogue No. 13-001, First Quarter, pages 26, 28, or 36.

large amounts from the private sector, thereby leaving less available for private business. Only in the third quarter of 1997 did government borrowing drop, as the federal deficit declined. By 1998, the federal government actually recorded a surplus, the first in 28 years. Program spending had declined, and tax revenue had increased as the economy prospered. This is shown on the bottom line of the chart of Figure 9.2.

Corporate investment increased from 1993 to 1999 and then dropped significantly. This is shown in the middle line. The most consistent saving was done by persons and unincorporated business, which averaged around $60 billion in 1993. However, it too has declined steadily since then until it averaged only $20 billion a quarter by 2000. While the economy grew at a healthy rate at this time, and employment rose, incomes for many Canadians remained stagnant or grew only slightly. People therefore dipped into their savings in order to maintain the lifestyle they had become accustomed to. Throughout the 1990s, total household debt also increased as the cost of borrowing declined.

Realizing the importance of saving, the federal government provides a tax incentive to anyone who opens an RRSP. The main purpose of an RRSP is to encourage saving for retirement. Funds inside an RRSP accumulate tax-free. This "tax shelter" has become extremely popular with some Canadians. There are two good reasons for opening an RRSP: as well as providing a tax shelter for income, investments from tax contributors also receive a tax deduction.

The financial industry has praised the government for this innovative approach to saving. Until the 2000 federal budget, 20 percent of the funds in an RRSP could be in foreign investments. This was seen as a way of improving the long-term potential of RRSPs. The Canadian stock market had long underperformed other major markets. Foreign content allowed Canadians to benefit from rapid growth elsewhere. Critics argued that the 20 percent limit was too low and had long encouraged the government to raise the ceiling on foreign content. It finally listened. The 2000 budget increased the foreign content level to 25 percent for 2000 and 30 percent for 2001.

In spite of the obvious benefits of investing in an RRSP, contributions began to fall in the late 1990s after six years of almost 6 percent annual growth. This came at a time of strong economic growth when people should have had more money available for investment. In addition, Canadians who do have an RRSP have not been taking full advantage of the contribution room available. While it is possible to carry forward indefinitely and make up the shortfall later, this has proven to be very difficult to do. If someone initially finds an excuse for not investing in an RRSP, it is even easier to postpone topping up one's contribution in the future.

Recent research indicates that the majority of RRSP contributors are university graduates ranging in age from 25 to 49. The 35 to 49 age group is the largest contributor.[2] It stands to reason that more highly educated Canadians whose incomes are generally higher, make greater use of RRSPs than less educated Canadians. A study by Statistics Canada, however, also indicated that some low-income earners have also taken advantage of the incentives to save offered by RRSPs. Many of these were younger people between the ages of 25 and 29 who were probably influenced by the major advertising campaigns launched by the fund companies each winter. Some companies are also willing to make loans available for investing in RRSPs. Several, for example, offer loans up to $13 500, the maximum allowable contribution, interest free for 120 days. Some lower income people may have taken advantage of such incentives. The sad thing is, according to Statistics Canada, that a large number of eligible Canadians between the ages of 25 and 64 often make no contribution to an RRSP.

The amount a person saves will depend on a number of things. These include age, occupation, marital status, and the number of dependents. It will also depend on one's level of income as well as interest rates. Little research has been done recently on the saving habits of Canadians. However, with the baby boom segment of the population fast approaching retirement, it would be realistic to assume that at least some Canadians are saving a larger proportion of their incomes than in the past.[3] If, to the baby boom population we add the growing number of people who are self employed and forced to provide for their own pensions, then the savings rate of Canadians should soon start to increase. A recent survey indicated that planning for retirement is the major reason Canadians invest. An Angus Reid poll several years ago found that retirement topped the list at 22 percent, followed by investing for children's education at 18 percent, and financial comfort at 16 percent.

The economic climate in Canada at the start of the new millennium should also set the stage for an increased rate of saving. The economy is healthy. Incomes are rising. Unemployment is at its lowest level in years. The federal government and some provincial governments are also cutting taxes. The taxation of capital gains was reduced to 66.67 percent from 75 percent in February 2000 and to 50 percent in October. Many people therefore will have more money in which to invest. In addition, the media has been filled with articles about the importance of saving and investing. The decision to save, of course, has to compete with the power of the

---

[2] David K. Foot with Daniel Stoffman, *Boom, Bust and Echo: How to Profit from the Coming Demographic Shift* (Toronto: Macfarlane Walter and Ross, 1996), p. 19.
[3] "A Marketing Profile of RRSP Contributors," www.marketingmag.ca Available by subscription.

marketplace and the advertising for goods and services, which is often very slick and could jeopardize all but the most committed investment plans.

Investing

Why Invest?

The primary reason for investing is self-evident: your savings must grow in order to make reaching your financial goals possible. A secondary reason may be that you enjoy investing and see the possibilities for an interesting hobby. Some people are excellent savers, but have no idea how to invest their money profitably. They may be quite cautious and apprehensive about investing; instead, they may simply deposit their money at the credit union, bank, or trust company—or, at best, buy Canada Savings Bonds—because they want safety and ready access to their funds at all times. These cautious people probably do not realize that by taking this approach, they may be sacrificing a great deal in the way of yield, inflation protection, and tax reduction—and that all investments are exposed to some risk.

In many cases, though, fear of the unknown and lack of information are the chief impediments to wise investing, rather than unwillingness to assume some risk. Do not confuse fear of investing with risk. If you let anxiety, confusion, and uncertainty keep you from investing, your inaction can be costly—that is, it can be risky *not* to invest. You may pay more income tax than necessary, forgo higher yields, and see your savings eroded by inflation.

Investing Versus Speculating

Assuming that you have been successful at saving, what can you do to make your net worth grow? First, you must have (or cultivate) patience. Wise investing does not involve speculating or gambling. You do not want to risk your hard-earned savings: rather, you want them to increase gradually. Although many people erroneously believe that investing involves putting your money in a safe place, while speculating involves buying stocks, **investing** can be defined as committing funds in a way that minimizes risk yet at the same time protects capital, while also earning a return that is satisfactory for the degree of risk. You can achieve this combination of aims in a variety of ways.

Investors are not in a hurry; speculators, on the other hand, look for large profits from a small layout of funds within a short time. **Speculation** tends to be based on a shorter time horizon and to involve more risk than investing. Speculators use money with the expectation of capital gain through a change in market value and are primarily motivated by short-term gains.

Unless you have several hundred thousand dollars in assets and can afford to hire an investment counsellor, you will have to manage your own investments. The choices are either to become knowledgeable and devote some time to monitoring your portfolio, or to choose investments that require minimal attention. Having a portfolio may sound very grand, but a **portfolio** is simply a list or collection of assets. If you would rather not have to deal with financial matters, put your savings into less risky investments that require little attention, such as Canada Savings Bonds or guaranteed investment certificates. Most of the discussion that follows is based on the assumption that you are interested in learning more about investing.

When you have finished reading this book, you will have been introduced to the basics of investing and should have a vocabulary that allows you to understand the articles in the financial press that you need to read to keep up-to-date. As mentioned before, lack of knowledge and fear of the unknown deter many people from making wise investment decisions. Since you need an understanding of the basic characteristics of investments before you can make a personal investment plan, these will be examined next.

Debt and Equity Investments

Debt Securities

There are two basic ways to invest: (i) by lending money, or (ii) by acquiring ownership. Lenders become creditors and are said to possess **debt securities.** The income from debt instruments is called interest (see Chapter 8). The borrower promises to repay the principal with interest at some specified time. Perhaps you had not realized that you become a creditor whenever you deposit funds at a bank, trust company, or credit union. And did you know you are lending money to a government or corporation whenever you buy a bond or a treasury bill? Deposit accounts, term deposits, guaranteed investment certificates, mortgages (when you are the lender), bonds, and treasury bills are types of debt securities. Their characteristics will be reviewed in the next chapter.

Equity Securities

You acquire **equity** when you own investments. A house is an investment; other types of investments include goods such as art, jewellery, and antiques for which there is a market. They may also include stocks, or shares, in publicly traded companies. Ownership gives you certain rights regarding the management of your equity, but does not guarantee any gain or income. Investment income depends on market forces over which you have no control. Equity securities are usually riskier than debt securities. A few equity securities, however, are less risky. Shares in telephone companies or chartered banks, for example, are less risky than mortgage loans to unreliable people. They are also often less risky than shares in many other types of companies. Shares in gold mining companies, for example, are usually quite speculative. Investors buy equities because of the expectation of a greater gain than they could obtain from debt securities.

To see the difference between the return of debt investments and that typical of equity investments, compare the graphs in Figures 9.3 and 9.4. Figure 9.3 shows the average annual rate of return on three-month treasury bills from 1975 to 2000. The interest rate fluctuated considerably across these two decades, reaching a high of close to 16 percent in 1981 and a low of just under 5 percent in 1993. These are, of course, only the nominal returns; they do not take inflation into account. Since inflation was 13.6 percent in 1981, the investor whose nominal return was 16 percent had a real rate of return of only 2.6 percent. It is also important to point out that with debt securities, the investor's principal would not have increased in value unless the interest was reinvested. There was no capital gain. Given the gap between inflation and the real rate of return, even when the principal plus interest came back to the investor, that total amount no longer bought as much as the principal alone would have bought when it was originally invested.

Anyone who had bought shares in the companies that make up the TSE 300 Index, on the other hand, would have seen his or her investments gradually increase in value during these years (see Figure 9.4). A $1 000 purchase of units in a mutual fund that tracked the shares in this index would have increased in value to $4 500 over this 20-year period. While this increase is not particularly dramatic, it does show the superiority, over a long period, of equity investments.

Investment Returns

INCOME   The return on an investment may take one of two basic forms: (i) income (interest, dividends, rent, profit) or (ii) capital appreciation (capital gain). The type of return received will vary with the investment. Those who lend money expect interest; those who own shares in a business expect to earn dividends when the business makes a profit; and those who own

FIGURE 9.3 AVERAGE ANNUAL RATES OF RETURN ON THREE-MONTH TREASURY BILLS, 1975–1999

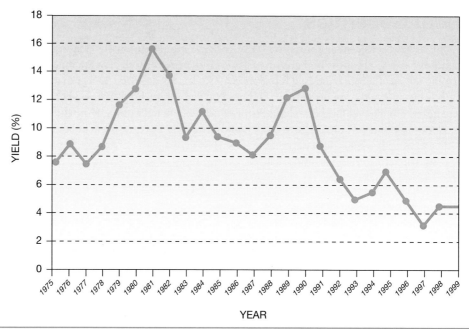

SOURCE: Nesbitt Burns Quantitative Research

FIGURE 9.4 AVERAGE ANNUAL PRICE IN THE TORONTO STOCK EXCHANGE INDEX, 1975–1999

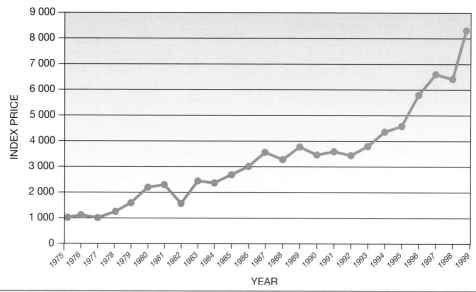

SOURCE: Nesbitt Burns Quantitative Research

property and rent it to others will receive rent. In addition to the income generated by ownership, the purchase itself (for example, the rental property) may increase in value, thereby generating capital gain.

TYPE OF INVESTMENT	FORM OF RETURN
Debt investments	
Deposits, loans	interest
Mortgage loans	interest
Canada Savings Bonds	interest
Treasury bills	interest
Bonds	interest, capital gain (loss)
Equity investments	
Real property	rent, capital gain (loss)
Business	profit, capital gain (loss)
Stocks (shares)	dividends, capital gain (loss)
Gold, silver	capital gain (loss)

CAPITAL GAIN The difference between an asset's purchase price and the same asset's selling price represents capital gain. For example, something purchased at $2700 and sold for $3500 would produce a capital gain of $800. **Capital gain** is the windfall that accrues to an investor, by virtue of owning the investment, during a change in prices that is caused by increased demand or inflation. Note that when you improve an asset (for example, when you renovate a house) and then sell it, the value added by the improvements does not count as capital gain. Remember, too, that the expectation of capital gain always carries with it the possibility of capital loss.

Current Income or Capital Gain?

Investments with a high yield, such as bonds and preferred shares, have little potential for a capital gain. If there is a gain, it is usually low. Bonds with a high yield will gain slightly in value if interest rates fall. Growth oriented companies with potential for capital gain, on the other hand, have a very low yield. They may not pay any dividends. If they do, the dividends are low. Instead, profit is reinvested in the company to fuel future growth. There is therefore an inverse relationship between the objectives of capital gain and high yield or current income. This is shown in Personal Finance in Action 9.3, "Income with Inflation Protection."

Personal Finance in Action 9.3

Income with Inflation Protection

Anwar owned a Halal butcher shop. When he and his wife, Fatima, came to Canada from Egypt 15 years ago, they had few resources. At the suggestion of their neighbours, Anwar took out a life insurance policy after buying the butcher shop, naming Fatima as his beneficiary. Suddenly last March, Anwar was stricken with a heart attack and died almost immediately.

continued

Now Fatima has $2 million from his life insurance but has no idea what to do with it. She is 45. Her son, Hosni, who is now running the shop, suggests she talk with their cousin who works for a discount broker.

The cousin explains some basic investment concepts such as risk/return, capital gains, and inflation. He points out, that while $2 million is a large sum of money, inflation could erode its value unless she invests in something with capital gains potential. Since Fatima also needs to live on the income from her investments, he recommends that her money be split between common and preferred shares in some of Canada's leading public companies. The combined after-tax return on her dividend income will be 4 percent, or $80 000. In the future, her cousin says that she could realize some of her capital gains and invest in high yielding preferred shares to increase her income.

Characteristics of Investments

Six characteristics of investments are particularly relevant to investors as they try to decide among alternatives:

(a) the risk/return trade-off,

(b) liquidity,

(c) marketability,

(d) term,

(e) management effort required,

(f) income tax treatment.

Risk, the most important factor in investment decisions, will be examined in more detail here than the others and will be discussed further in Chapter 11. The significance of the other five factors will be considered next.

Liquidity

In the strictest sense, **liquidity** means the ability of an investment to be converted into cash readily and without loss of principal. Investments vary in their degree of liquidity: cash is the most liquid asset, while property tends to be the least liquid. Because savings accounts, term deposits, and Canada Savings Bonds can be liquidated during banking hours without loss of principal, they are considered very liquid. Corporate bonds, stocks, and real estate are not very liquid, because it may take time to sell them without a loss. Since very high liquidity is asso-

FIGURE 9.5   THE LIQUIDITY/RETURN TRADE-OFF

Low					RETURN					High
0	1	2	3	4	5	6	7	8	9	10
10	9	8	7	6	5	4	3	2	1	0
High					LIQUIDITY					Low

ciated with an expectation of lower yield, investors must decide what compromise to make (see Figure 9.5). As an investor, what is the relative importance to you of having your investment provide high liquidity versus high return? If you decide to put your money in a savings account, you have chosen high liquidity and low return; if you invest in a business or in property, you may have reversed the situation.

Marketability

The popular usage of the term liquidity when marketability is what is really meant, can be confusing. Marketable assets are those for which there is an active market. Certain stocks are in greater demand and trade more often than others, and thus are more marketable. Some houses are easier to sell than others, and thus are more marketable. An asset may be highly marketable but not very liquid because of price fluctuations. At the time you wish to sell the asset, the prices of, for example, all houses or all stocks may be in a slump, making it impossible to recover your capital totally. Although any asset can be sold if the price is lowered enough, that is not what is meant by marketability; your aim when selling is to get at least a fair market price.

Term

Investments that mature at a specified date are said to have a **term,** which is the time until maturity. Some kinds of investments are not accessible until maturity; others can be sold before the term ends. You can find investments with terms that range from a few days to many years. Choose investments appropriate to your savings goals. Term and return tend to be directly related, because the further away the maturity date, the higher the uncertainty. Investors demand a higher return in exchange for making a longer-term commitment of their funds. Short-term investments therefore tend to yield less than long-term ones, although this relationship does become inverted at times.

Personal Management Effort

How much time and attention are you prepared to give to your investments? This is an important consideration in choosing securities. If you would prefer not to put time and effort into supervising your investments, select investment vehicles that require minimal attention: choose debt securities rather than equities, for example, or buy mutual funds. If you decide not to become involved with investing, however, you may have to accept a lower return. Effort and return tend to be directly related: the people who get the highest returns are those who invest their time as well as their money. On the other hand, management effort and liquidity are inversely related. The most liquid investments usually require the least attention, whereas more attention may be required for less liquid investments.

Tax Considerations

When comparing the potential yield from two or more investments, you should think in terms of after-tax dollars, because the various types of investment return are taxed differently: interest is taxed at a higher rate than dividends, and capital gains are taxed at a lower rate than both income and dividends. If income can be deferred until a time when you expect to have a lower marginal tax rate, two advantages can be gained. Not only will the total tax be less, but funds put in a tax shelter (an RRSP, for instance) grow faster, since the tax on the yield is also deferred. Later chapters will provide more information about income tax in connection with investments.

Investment Risks

Every investor wants maximum return with minimum risk, but unfortunately there are no risk-free investments. Any investment carries some risk: the possibility of (i) losing all or part of the principal, (ii) losing some of the principal's purchasing power, or (iii) receiving a return that is less than anticipated. Moreover, these risks are generally not insurable. Nevertheless, you can attempt to reduce risk by being as well-informed as possible about investment alternatives and by building some diversity into your choice of assets, so that a single setback will not result in your losing everything. Since investments are not risk-free, it is essential to understand the different types of risks and to know which assets are most subject to which kinds of risks.

Types of Risks

Four classes of risk are associated with investments:

(a) **inflation risk**—the possibility that invested funds will lose purchasing power,

(b) **interest rate risk**—the likelihood that interest rates will fall, adversely affecting either the return or the price of the asset,

(c) **market risk**—the chance that the demand for the asset will drop, lowering its value,

(d) **business risk**—the possibility that the firm you invest in will do poorly or fail entirely.

Inflation is measured by the annual percentage change in the **Consumer Price Index**. Canada had very high inflation, by Canadian standards, in the early 1980s. To put this inflation in perspective, look at the trend in the inflation rate from 1981 to 2000 (see Figure 9.6). Inflation was over 12 percent in 1981 but by 1994 it had fallen to less than 2 percent annually.

FIGURE 9.6 THE RATE OF INFLATION, 1981–2000

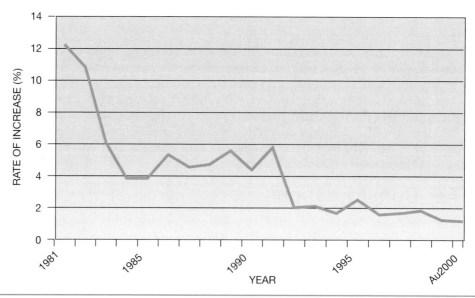

SOURCE: Adapted from Statistics Canada, The Consumer Price Index, "The Rate of Inflation, 1981–2000," Catalogue No. 62-001-XPB.

FIGURE 9.7 GOVERNMENT OF CANADA BONDS, REAL LONG-TERM INTEREST RATES, 1975–2000

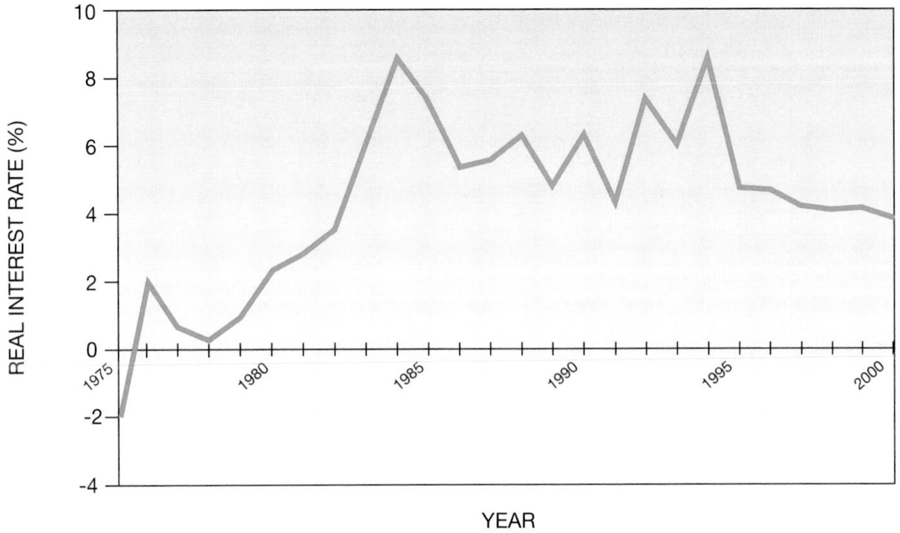

SOURCE: Data from Bank of Canada. Reproduced with the permission of the Bank of Canada.

Therefore, in 1981, the **real rate of return** on Government of Canada Bonds was negative because the rate of inflation was greater than the rate of interest (see Figure 9.7). At that time, investors who owned these government bonds earned a **negative rate of return** on their investment. In other words, these investors lost money.

As can be seen, only looking at the interest earned on an investment can be quite misleading. The gains from interest may be illusory because of inflation. To be sure, one must look at the real rate of return and not just the nominal rate of interest. Another factor to consider is the taxation of interest income. This is higher than either the tax on dividend income or that from capital gains. Therefore, unless the rate of interest is very high, bonds are a poor form of investment.

Interest rates rise as a result of uncertainty in the economy. When this happens, neither businesses nor consumers have much interest in borrowing. When interest rates are low, confidence returns; businesses and consumers borrow and spend more, and the economy expands. This sequence of events took place in the winter of 1997. Inflation was at its lowest level in a generation, and consumer confidence hit a nine-year high.

Personal Finance in Action 9.4

The Importance of Comparing Interest Rates

Mario, when hearing that Canada Savings Bonds carry an interest rate averaging 5.69 percent for the first three years, tells his grandson, Geno, of the good old days when he earned over 18 percent. "But Grandpa," says Geno, "wasn't your mortgage close to 25 percent? Now, I can find a variable rate mortgage for under 8 percent."

FIGURE 9.8 THE REAL VALUE OF MONEY

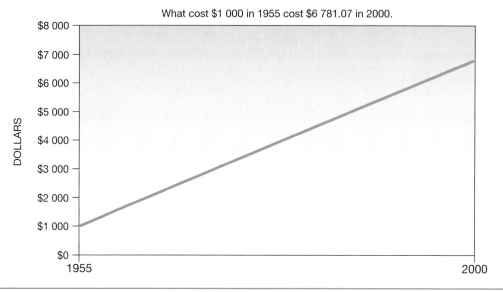

What cost $1 000 in 1955 cost $6 781.07 in 2000.

SOURCE: Formula used to calculate this figure was found at www.bankofcanada.ca/en/inflation_calc.htm, 2000.

Inflation's destructive effects are shown even more dramatically in Figure 9.8. This graph shows what happened to the purchasing power of $1000 over the 45-year period from 1955 to 2000. The annual decline in the value of Canadian money over this time was 4.16 percent. The basket of goods that cost $1000 in 1955 cost $6781.07 in 2000. Such declines in the real value of money make any kind of financial planning very difficult.

INTEREST RATE RISK Any change in interest rates can affect investments. The value of a long-term bond paying 6 percent will drop, for example, if interest rates rise. Under these circumstances, investors will prefer to buy new bonds that pay higher interest. (See Personal Finance in Action Box 9.5, "Time and Money," for an example of what happens when interest rates fall.) If you must sell the bond prior to maturity, you will sustain a capital loss. If you buy a five-year GIC paying 6 percent and interest rates rise, you will be unable to earn the higher rate, if your money is locked in. If the interest you earn does not exceed the inflation rate, your investment's value declines. To protect yourself, you must therefore have debt securities in your portfolio with a broad range of maturities. (See also Personal Finance in Action Box 9.6, "A Choice between Two Conservative Investments.")

Personal Finance in Action 9.5

Time and Money

In 1955, when Gerry was 20 years old, he inherited $100 000 from his grandfather. A busy man who knew little about investing, he put the whole sum into a five-year GIC and rolled the money over into a new GIC when the certificate matured. He used the interest he had earned to pay for skiing holidays and

continued

summer vacations. This became his pattern over the next 42 years. After he retired in 1997, Gerry decided that it would be a good idea to increase the income from his investment. What had seemed like a lot of money in 1955 no longer went very far. But when he called an investment dealer for advice, he was surprised to learn just how far interest rates had fallen. He had not paid much attention to financial matters over the years. The dealer told him to stay away from bonds and GICs since interest rates were low. Instead, she suggested some units in a new real estate investment trust her company was underwriting. These units would yield 9 percent, and tax on the income would be deferred for five years. She also told him that he should not have spent the interest from his GICs; instead, he should have reinvested it. If he had done so at an average of 5 percent, **compounding** would have made his $100 000 inheritance grow to over $700 000 by 1997, leaving him with fewer financial worries (see Appendix 8A, Table 8A.1).

Common stocks can also be influenced by changes in interest rates. A high rate will discourage business investment, encouraging investors to switch from stocks to bonds. Conversely, low rates stimulate the economy, causing investors to move from bonds to stocks.

Although interest rates and inflation do not follow each other exactly, they are linked. Generally, lenders require interest rates that are high enough to more than compensate for inflation. A lack of stability in interest rates complicates investing. When interest rates are volatile, it is difficult to make wise investment decisions, because there is so much uncertainty about future rates. And when investors feel uncertain, they demand higher real interest rates as compensation.

MARKET RISK Economic conditions may cause the value of your assets to fall. During a period of robust economic activity, the demand for houses, and as a result, house prices, will be high. Suppose you buy a house during such a period; five years later, though—when you must sell because you are moving to another city—the economy is in the midst of a recession. Because workers are being laid off and factories closed, the demand for houses has fallen, and you will have to sell your house at a loss. Similarly, shares in many companies can fall in value when the investment climate turns bearish and stock prices start to decline. When such a sequence of events takes place, many investors will want to sell their shares and invest in something less risky.

Personal Finance in Action 9.6

A Choice Between Two Conservative Investments

When Geraldine and Sylvie were four years old, their grandmother gave them each $2 000 for Christmas. Their parents decided to invest the money, but in different ways. Geraldine's was invested in Canada Savings Bonds, the value of which doubled in seven years when the interest was compounded. Sylvie's was invested in common shares of a bank. With the $2 000, they bought her 80 shares at $24 per share and still had enough to pay the broker's commission. The shares yielded 4.8 percent. As a result of the bank's dividend reinvestment plan, Sylvie had 100 shares after seven years. In that time, the value of the shares had risen to $45, so her original $2 000 had grown to $4 500. Geraldine's more conservative CSBs were now worth $4 000.

BUSINESS RISK   There is a risk to every business. The risk can range from an occurrence that is as serious as bankruptcy and failure to an event that is as mild as a decline in earnings. Investors need to be aware of this risk before they buy stocks or bonds. As an economy progresses through business cycles, company earnings rise and fall. Sometimes companies collapse, wiping out the investments of many people. But the most common risk that investors face is a decline in a company's earnings. When this happens, the value of the company's shares may decline. Investors look for companies with either good prospects for growth or increased earnings, or both, and may sell shares in a company that does poorly. There is no insurance available for investors who suffer a capital loss.

How to Reduce Risk

Uncertainty about the future creates investment risk, and the further into the future you try to predict the quality of an investment, the greater the uncertainty—hence, the greater the risk. Risk is thus related to both time and knowledge. This relationship is summarized in Figure 9.9, which shows that risk exposure increases as knowledge about the future decreases. The best defence against risk in your investment portfolio is an understanding of current economic conditions, knowledge of particular investments, and diversification.

KNOWLEDGE   There is a wide range of investment alternatives to consider, some of which will be discussed in later chapters.

A successful investor should be well-informed about the securities he or she holds. Anyone who plans to invest in real estate must learn a great deal about the real estate market; to make money in the stock market, you will need take an interest in the market in general and in some specific stocks in detail. Leaving money in deposits requires less learning on the investor's part. A compromise might be to buy mutual funds and then leave investment decisions to the funds' managers.

FIGURE 9.9   DEGREE OF RISK AND KNOWLEDGE ABOUT THE FUTURE

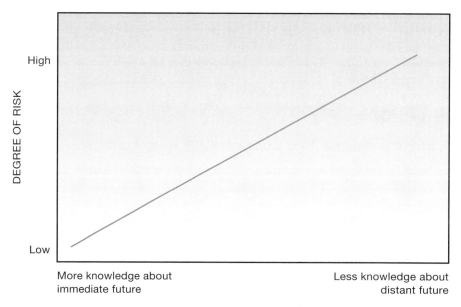

THE RISK/RETURN TRADE-OFF Everyone wants the highest return and the lowest risk, but most will accept somewhat more risk if the expected return is greater. This fact brings up the risk/return trade-off. How much safety will you give up in anticipation of an additional unit of return? The inverse relationship between these two investment characteristics is illustrated in Figure 9.10.

Once you know your priorities with respect to risk and return, look for investments that provide the desired qualities. It is difficult to generalize about classes of investments and risk, because there are always exceptions and qualifications. Figure 9.10 is intended as a general illustration of the relationship between risk and return.

Risk Management

What Are Your Risks?

Analyze the various kinds of assets you have, or might acquire, to identify which risks apply to them. Plan to avoid concentrating on investments that fall into one risk category. If most of your assets are fixed-income debt securities, you are more exposed to interest rate and inflation risks, but much less exposed to market and business risks. Try to diversify by choosing investments that expose you to different kinds of risks. A portfolio that reflects a balance between debt and equities should protect against a broad range of risks.

Balance Investment and Other Risks

LIFE CYCLE AND RISK The amount of risk that will be acceptable to you will likely vary with your life cycle stage. A young single person who has an adequate income and no dependents may be in a position to handle more risk than will be advisable a few years later, when the person is starting a family. The middle years, when income is typically more than enough to handle expenses, permit a higher proportion of risk than is wise to accept during retirement. A young

FIGURE 9.10 EXPECTED RETURN AND ESTIMATED RISK OF SELECTED INVESTMENTS

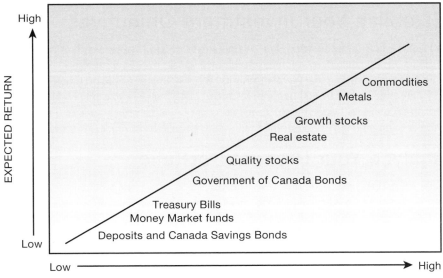

person will have time to recoup a loss, but retirees should not put their retirement income at risk unless their net worth is very large.

INCOME AND RISK Some people have more risk associated with income than others. A civil service employee can usually count on more security than either a self-employed person or one who is in a cyclical industry that often lays off workers. Farmers and other self-employed people often invest in their businesses instead of in the stock market. To balance the high risk associated with their equity-based income, they may put some savings in very low-risk debt securities.

At this first level of diversification, look at your total net worth as well as at your income source or sources. If, for instance, your income depends on the real estate market, you will not want to put your savings into the same sector. Besides planning for a balance among a broad range of risks, you should also spread the risk within your investment portfolio by diversifying the types of assets you own.

Diversify Investments

A basic principle in portfolio management is **diversification,** which means reducing total risk by choosing securities that are not subject to the same types of risk. If you have enough money to work with, you can reduce the risk to your whole portfolio by spreading the risk over a variety of investments. Small investors can diversify by using mutual funds (see Chapter 11). Since you cannot maximize safety, yield, and growth in any one portfolio, decide which of these qualities is your highest priority; but do not neglect the other two. Expect to adjust your portfolio from time to time as needs and economic conditions change (see Personal Finance in Action Box 9.7, "Diversity in Portfolios").

Summary of Investment Characteristics

Despite the difficulties of classifying investments by various characteristics, the summary chart in Table 9.1 is presented as a general guide.

Creating a Personal Investment Plan

Establish Your Investment Objectives

Within the general framework of an overall aim of maximizing investment return while minimizing both risk and effort, you must establish personal priorities with respect to your total portfolio before considering specific investments. What is your personal preference for risk, and for spending time and effort managing investments? At your life cycle stage, what are your needs for current income? Use Table 9.2 to record your preferences, on a scale of 0 to 10. With each pair of characteristics, the combined values must equal 10 to reflect the trade-off involved.

Analyze Your Present Portfolio

Make a list of the assets you now own, showing their values, their share of the total, and their annual rate of return. Use Table 9.3 to classify each according to its prime investment objective.

Compare your investment priorities with this asset analysis, but do not be surprised if you find that your expressed preferences do not exactly correspond to your current holdings. You might have indicated that you give a high priority to inflation protection, but then discover that you have mostly fixed-income assets. Analyzing your objectives and your current situation will help you plan changes to your portfolio and choose additional investments.

Diversity in Portfolios

Three investors, Ann, Mohammed, and Carl, are at different stages in life and have different attitudes toward investments, as you can see from the following summary of their portfolios.

Investment	Ann	Mohammed	Carl
	%	%	%
Canada Savings Bonds	0	50	15
Guaranteed Investment Certificates	0	25	10
Mutual fund (balanced)	0	25	30
Corporate bonds	0	0	15
Common stocks	60	0	25
Gold	40	0	5
TOTAL	**100**	**100**	**100**

Which of the three investors is probably young, single, and not averse to risk? Who probably spends the least time looking after his or her portfolio? Who seems to have spread the risk most widely?

Mohammed, who appears to be the most conservative in this group (since three-quarters of his portfolio is in debt securities), is exposed to interest rate and inflation risks. But these are offset by the balanced mutual fund (invested in stocks and bonds), which offers some opportunity for growth and protection from inflation without very high risk. Perhaps he is retired, has a lower marginal tax rate, and needs income-producing securities.

Ann, who owns no debt securities, has the most risk in her portfolio. She is very heavily exposed to market and business risks, but should be protected against inflation. Still, what will she use for emergency funds or short-term goals? If she happens to need funds when the market is low, she might be forced to take a capital loss.

Carl, the seasoned investor, may have the largest net worth. At any rate, he has diversified his holdings more than the others, and has thereby protected his assets against a range of risks.

Draw an Investment Pyramid

A widely used guide to investment planning is the investment pyramid, which summarizes an individual's portfolio (for an example, see Figure 9.11). As the pyramid rises, so does the risk; the investments at the base of the pyramid carry the least risk. If you drew the figure to scale, each slice of the pyramid would represent the distribution within the portfolio of investments that fall into the various risk categories. The best order of priority is from bottom to top. First, ensure that you have put money aside for emergencies, liquidity needs, and short-term goals in secure but accessible investments. For those who choose home ownership, investment in a home property will be the next priority. After taking care of these needs, you can invest in good-quality securities with a view toward funding long-term goals. The pyramid's top slices contain high-risk securities: such investments should not represent a significant share of most portfolios and should be considered only when all other investment goals have been adequately funded.

Make a drawing of your own portfolio pyramid to see how well you have implemented your priorities. There is no one right way to divide the pyramid; the best arrangement will depend on your stage in the life cycle, your personal objectives, and your financial situation. People who are very young or very wealthy may be more aggressive than older or retired investors. Nevertheless, everyone needs a safety cushion of funds for short-term needs before moving into other types of investments. The pyramid exercise helps you become more aware of portfolio planning and to avoid haphazard investing, which is not usually the most effective way to achieve your financial goals.

FIGURE 9.11 THE INVESTMENT PYRAMID

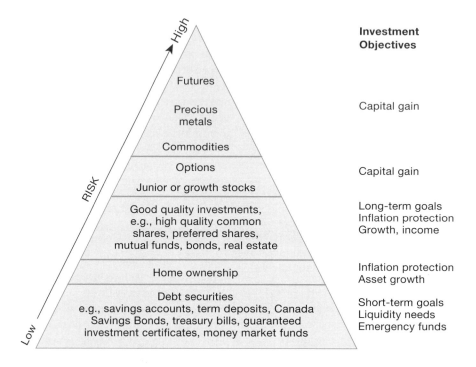

TABLE 9.1   INVESTMENT CHARACTERISTICS BY ASSET CATEGORY

| ASSET CATEGORY | INVESTMENT CHARACTERISTICS | | | | |
	SAFETY	LIQUIDITY	INCOME/ CAPITAL GAIN	MGT. EFFORT	INFLATION PROTECTION
Deposits: (savings accounts, CSBs, term deposits)	Excellent	Excellent	Fixed income	Very little	None
GICs	Excellent	Poor	Fixed income	Very little	None
Treasury bills, money market funds	Excellent	Very good	Fixed income	Little	None
High-quality bonds	Excellent to good	Varies	Fixed income, gain possible	Not much	Not much
High-quality preferred shares	Good to fair	Varies	Both possible	Some	Some
Common stock	Good to poor	Poor	Both possible	Some to much	Good in long run
Real estate (income property)	Good to poor	Poor	Both possible	Necessary	Usually good
Mutual funds	Good to poor	Poor	Both possible	Not much	Varies

TABLE 9.2 PRIORITIES FOR YOUR TOTAL PORTFOLIO

Objectives Priorities (combined value = 10)

1.	Return	0	1	2	3	4	5	6	7	8	9	10
	Safety	10	9	8	7	6	5	4	3	2	1	0

(combined value = 10)

2.	Current income	0	1	2	3	4	5	6	7	8	9	10
	Capital gain (growth)	10	9	8	7	6	5	4	3	2	1	0

(combined value = 10)

3.	Liquidity	0	1	2	3	4	5	6	7	8	9	10
	Return	10	9	8	7	6	5	4	3	2	1	0

(combined value = 10)

4.	Inflation protection	0	1	2	3	4	5	6	7	8	9	10
	Safety	10	9	8	7	6	5	4	3	2	1	0

5.	Management effort	0	1	2	3	4	5	6	7	8	9	10
6.	Tax reduction	0	1	2	3	4	5	6	7	8	9	10

TABLE 9.3 ANALYSIS OF PRESENT PORTFOLIO

PRESENT VALUE	% OF TOTAL	ANNUAL RATE OF RETURN	INVESTMENT OBJECTIVE
Savings account			
GIC			
Term deposits			
Canada Savings Bonds			
RRSPs			
Mutual funds			
Bonds			
Stocks			
Real estate			

Decide on Your Next Investment

Once you have a clear picture of your overall objectives, you will be in a position to determine the specific objectives of an additional investment. If your portfolio comprises largely low-risk, low-return fixed-income securities, you will probably want your next investment to offer more inflation protection, more return, and somewhat less safety.

Design an Investment Plan

A well-designed plan for saving and investing is crucial for setting you on the road to financial independence. As we saw in Chapter 4, financial security is the assurance that you can maintain your desired level of living now and in the future. Despite the existence of public income security programs and personal insurance, a significant component of your financial security still depends on your individual net worth. If you hope to retire early from the labour force to pursue other interests, or to have a comfortable life after you reach the conventional retirement age, the size of your net worth will be a determining factor in whether you can achieve these goals. Furthermore, a saving and investment plan is a good defence against impulse spending or spending that is motivated by social pressure to buy things.

Earlier in this chapter, we discussed the need to save for emergency funds, liquidity needs, and short-term and long-term goals. This money should be invested in securities with appropriate maturities and with characteristics that match your priorities. Your investment plan will include a forecast of the total amount required, the amount to be saved each pay period, and indications as to how these savings will be invested.

Banking and Financial Services

How Canadians handle their money has changed considerably in recent years. Much has been made in the press about how banking services have deteriorated. But contrary to what some newspapers have said about the decline in personal, or one-on-one, service with tellers, Canadians are obviously thrilled with the changes. According to the Canadian Bankers Association, only 15 percent of banking transactions are now done in banks with tellers. The remaining 85 percent of transactions are done via bank machines, over the telephone, or on-line. Of the three options, the use of ABMs tops the list with 1,159.2 million transactions in the fiscal year, which ended October 31, 1999. This compares with 27.2 million on-line transactions during the same period and 63.5 million transactions over the telephone. As a result of changes in technology, customers now have much more opportunity to deal with their banks.

Summary

This general discussion of investment provides an introduction to the upcoming chapters, which focus on the specifics of debt securities and stocks. This chapter emphasized that you must save money if you wish to invest. You should devise ways to give saving a high priority, examine your reasons for investing, and learn how to make an investment plan. All investors want to maximize their return and minimize risk, the effects of inflation, and income tax. To accomplish these objectives, you must have clear investment goals and some knowledge about securities, and you must be prepared to invest time as well as money in the process. Although there are no risk-free investments, the wise investor understands the risk inherent in various types of securities and uses diversification to reduce overall risk.

Key Terms

business risk (p. 246)

capital gain (p. 243)

compounding (p. 249)

Consumer Price Index (p. 246)

debt securities (p. 241)

diversification (p. 252)

equity (p. 241)

inflation risk (p. 246)

interest rate risk (p. 246)

investing (p. 240)

liquidity (p. 244)

market risk (p. 246)

negative rate of return (p. 247)

portfolio (p. 240)

real rate of interest (p. 248)

real rate of return (p. 247)

speculation (p. 240)

term (p. 245)

Problems

1. Do you agree or disagree with the following statements? Explain the reasons for your decision.

    (a) Stocks are not suitable investments to have in a RRSP.

    (b) RRSPs are something only the very wealthy can afford.

    (c) Because of all the risks involved, investing is very foolish.

    (d) There is very little difference between investing and speculating.

    (e) People with RRSPs would be wise to invest only in Canadian securities.

    (f) Most stocks are just as liquid as Canada Savings Bonds.

    (g) There is never any risk when you invest in Government of Canada bonds.

2. Discuss the following:

    (a) Why do many people find saving money very difficult?

    (b) A young person starting his/her first job doesn't really need to think about retirement.

    (c) The longer one lives, the more one realizes that money is a very poor investment.

    (d) GICs are one of the best hedges against inflation.

3. Explain how diversification can be used to minimize the four types of investment risk.

4. Explain why you agree or disagree with the following statements.

    (a) There are some risks you can never avoid.

    (b) It is not possible to have investments that grow in value and provide an income at the same time.

    (c) Wealthy people need not concern themselves with risk.

    (d) The real rate of interest means the same thing as the nominal rate.

    (e) Every investor should own Canada Savings Bonds.

    (f) Adding foreign investments to your RRSP reduces risk.

    (g) All investment income is treated the same for tax purposes.

    (h) The investment return on bonds is the same as that on stocks.

    (i) All saving should be for the long term.

    (j) You can never lose money on a good corporate bond.

5. (a) Explain why many people prefer to invest money in their homes rather than in shares of publicly traded companies.

    (b) Do you think many people equate buying stocks with speculating?

6. (a) List four factors that are inversely related to return on investments.

    (b) Why is there usually an inverse relation between income and capital gain?

    (c) Why is more risk generally associated with equity than with debt investments?

7. Which investment in each of the following pairs is more liquid:

    (a) a Canada Savings Bond or a five-year guaranteed investment certificate?

    (b) a common stock or a term deposit?

8. In Personal Finance Box 9.5, "Time and Money," which outlines how Gerry invested his $100 000 inheritance, safety of principal was apparently given the highest priority.

   (a) Identify some risks Gerry failed to protect against.

   (b) How would you have invested such a sum if you wanted it to be a source of retirement income?

9. Refer to Figures 9.5 and 9.6. This investor locked in funds in 1980, when interest rates were at a historic high, a decision that seemed very rational at the time.

   (a) Did the investor receive enough return during this period to compensate for inflation and also to gain from having lent the money?

   (b) If you planned to invest several thousand dollars in debt securities, would there be any way to hedge against a sudden change in interest rates?

10. Why do we say that stocks are not liquid investments?

11. Assume that a friend, who has just inherited $40 000, asks your advice on investing it. Before you can offer any ideas, you need to know something about your friend's situation. Write out five essential questions you would ask your friend.

12. **What Are His Investment Objectives?**

    Lee usually spends all of his income. He loves to shop and, until recently, had no reason to save. He is 28 and has worked as a welder-fitter since his graduation from a community college six years ago. For three years he has had a girlfriend, Tina; he wants to marry her as soon as he has a few thousand dollars in the bank. At Tina's suggestion, Lee recently bought a lottery ticket and won $100 000. Having learned about investments in an economics course he took at college, he has several goals for this money. He knows all about inflation and wants to invest this money so that it earns a capital gain. He also wants the money to be both secure and quite liquid. Tina would like to buy a house, and Lee would like to be able to afford the one she has been admiring in a new subdivision.

    (a) From this limited information, make a list of Lee's investment priorities.

    (b) How would you suggest he should invest this money to achieve all of his goals?

    (c) If you were Lee's investment advisor, what advice would you have for him?

13. **Investment Priorities**

    Sid, a widower of 45, has two adult children who both have good full-time jobs. He owns a prosperous hardware store and recently paid off the mortgage on his house. He earns a good salary and has few expenses. Several years ago, he began to invest for his retirement: he owns a self-directed RRSP and a diversified portfolio of common stocks and bonds worth over $150 000. Recently he sold some shares in a high-tech stock and made a capital gain of $25 000. Yesterday his broker called with some suggestions for this money. Sid told him that income, capital gains, and security of the principal are his main priorities. He also said that liquidity and inflation protection are far less important. If he has another capital gain, he told the broker that he wants to invest in some mining stock and a second mortgage.

    (a) Examine Sid's investment objectives in view of what you know about his financial situation.

(b) Identify any inconsistencies between his stated objectives and his plans.

(c) It is not uncommon to find such inconsistencies. Why is that?

14. How Much Risk?

Claude and Janet are in their mid-forties and live in Calgary. They have two teenage daughters and a large mortgage on their house. Claude is a multimedia developer who works for a very successful advertising agency; Janet is a high-school teacher. Their combined incomes total $105 000. The only investments they have are some Canada Savings Bonds and a $40 000 GIC. One recent night they were at a dinner party with their friends Frank and Chelsea. When the conversation turned to investing, Chelsea told them that she had invested in the shares of some Alberta energy companies. Recently these had appreciated considerably in value. She convinced Claude and Janet that they should also buy common stocks in energy companies with some of their savings. You are a financial planner. When they come to your office for some suggestions, you learn that their priority is inflation protection. They also want investments that require little attention and that have the potential for some capital gain. They are nervous about risk and want their investments to be quite liquid.

(a) What would you say to this couple about their investment goals?

(b) What kind of investment would you suggest for them?

15. Go to the Web site www.canoe.ca/Money. Click on banking and scroll down to GIC. Compare the rate of interest offered on five-year GICs by the following companies: Clarica Trust, CIBC, Effort Trust, Great West Life, and Home Trust. Why do you think the rates vary? Search out these companies' Web sites. Compare the size of the assets under administration. Would you buy a GIC solely on the amount of interest you can earn? Which of these five companies' GICs would you feel most comfortable buying?

References

BOOKS AND ARTICLES

ALTAMIRA. *Welcome to Altamira*. Toronto: Altamira, updated regularly. While it deals specifically with Altamira's mutual fund products, this package provides useful advice about building an investment proposal and setting up a Registered Education Savings Plan (RESP). Available by calling 1-800-263-2824 (toll-free) or 416-507-7050 in the Toronto area.

BUDD, JOHN, CLAUDE RINFRET, RICHARD DAW, and DANIELLE BRIEN. *Canadian Guide to Personal Financial Management*. Scarborough: Prentice Hall, annual. A team of accountants provides guidance on a broad range of topics, including planning finances, estimating insurance needs, managing risk, and determining investment needs. Instructions and the necessary forms for making plans are also included.

CANADIAN ASSOCIATION OF RETIRED PERSONS (CARP). *Financial Guide for the Fifty-plus*. Toronto: *CARP News*, January 1998. The third edition of this useful guide, which appears annually as a special issue of *CARP News*, published by the Canadian Association of Retired Persons, 27 Queen St. East, Toronto, ON M5C 2M6. Telephone: 416-363-5562.

CHAKRAPANI, CHUCK. *Financial Freedom on Five Dollars a Day*. Sixth Edition. Vancouver: Self-Counsel Press, 1994. This book has proven popular with investors.

CHILTON, DAVID. *The Wealthy Barber: The Common Sense Guide to Successful Financial Planning*. Toronto: Stoddart, 1992. In its 59th printing, this is one of the most popular books on investing ever written.

COSTELLO, BRIAN. *Money Talks!: Multi-Dimensional Investing*. Toronto: ECW Press, 1997. Helpful advice from one of Canada's best-known financial writers.

DOMINGUEZ, JOE, and VICKI ROBIN. *Your Money or Your Life: Transforming Your Relationship with Money and Achieving Financial Independence*. New York: Viking, 1992. A unique perspective on saving, which is the first step toward investing.

THE FINANCIAL POST. *Getting Started*. Guides to Investing and Personal Finance, No. 1. Toronto: The Financial Post, 1998. A valuable aid to novice investors.

THE FINANCIAL POST MAGAZINE. "The Money Issue: The Breadwinner's Guide to Starting the Year." January 1998. This special supplement to *The Financial Post Magazine* contains excellent articles on investing and other personal finance topics. Indexed online through Canadian Business and Current Affairs, available on QL Systems, DIALOG, CAN/OLE, IST InformathÀque.

FRIEDLAND, SEYMOUR, and STEVEN G. KELMAN. *Investment Strategies: How to Create Your Own and Make It Work for You*. Toronto: Penguin, 1996. Novice investors will find this book useful.

LYNCH, PETER, and JOHN ROTHCHILD. *One Up on Wall Street: How to Use What You Already Know to Make Money in the Market*. Toronto: Penguin, 1990. Previously with Fidelity, the world's largest mutual fund company, Lynch is one of North America's best-known investors.

PAPE, GORDON. *Low Risk Investing in the Nineties*. Scarborough: Prentice Hall Canada, 1994. The author of many books on investing and a frequent radio commentator, Pape always offers timely and helpful advice.

SOVEREIGN. *Can You Get Better Returns Without Playing the Odds?: The Remarkable Effect of Strategic Asset Allocation on Investment Performance*. Toronto: Frank Russell Company, 1995. Available from RBC Dominion Securities. Asset allocation has become a popular way of trying to reduce the risks associated with investing.

VAZ-OXLADE, GAIL. *The Money Tree Myth: A Parent's Guide to Helping Kids Unravel the Mysteries of Money*. Toronto: Stoddart, 1996. This book provides activities that help children age 10 and older learn about investing.

WYATT, ELAINE. *The Money Companion: How to Manage Your Money and Achieve Financial Freedom*. Toronto: Penguin, 1997. A guide to personal financial management that focuses on planning, investment strategy, and retirement needs.

Personal Finance on the Web

Bank of Montreal
  www.bmo.com

Canada Trust
  www.canadatrust.com

Canada WealthNet

www.nucleus.com/wealthnet Features an index of financial and investment news available on the Internet.

Canadian Financial Network

www.canadianfinance.com Provides information and resources of value to investors.

Canadian Imperial Bank of Commerce

www.cibc.com

Canadian Investor Protection Fund (CIPF)

www.cipf.ca CIPF, which is managed by the Canadian investment industry, provides coverage for people who purchase investments through fund members. This site provides information about how to make a claim.

Canadian Oil and Gas Financial Database

www.mossr.com Offers news and analysis of this important sector of the economy.

Canadian Western Bank

www.cwbank.com

Carlson On-Line Services

www.fin-info.com Provides investors with access to all Canadian public companies as well as bond-issuing Crown corporations that have Web sites.

Canadian Venture Exchange

www.cdnx.ca The Web site for Canada's venture exchange, the amalgamated Alberta and Vancouver stock exchanges.

E*Trade Canada

www.canada.etrade.com Offers on-line stock trading and mutual fund sales.

Financial Pipeline

www.finpipe.com An independent source of investment information.

The Fund Library

www.fundlibrary.com Features a questionnaire that helps investors determine their investment objectives.

mbanx

www.mbanx.com Discusses the Bank of Montreal's on-line banking services and explains how to open an account, pay bills, transfer funds, or arrange a loan over the Internet. Will interest anyone who wants to learn about on-line banking.

Money

www/canoe.ca/Money/home.html Provides the interest rates offered at all Canadian banks and trust companies. Also suggests ways in which Canadians can avoid paying more tax than necessary.

Morningstar.ca

www.morningstar.ca/main/index.asp The Web site of a leading investment fund research firm that markets the mutual funds software products, PALTrak and Bell Charts.

Gordon Pape's Building Wealth on the Net
> **www.gordonpape.fiftyplus.net/** A very useful reference for investors; contains a great deal of financial information. Pape is one of Canada's best known and most highly regarded investment advisors.

Royal Bank Financial Group
> **www.royalbank.com**

Scotiabank
> **www.scotiabank.ca**

Screaming Capitalist
> **www.screamingcapitalist.com** Boasts angst-free investment schemes and answers such questions as "What if I die?" and "What investments should I buy?"

Stock Quotes
> **www.canoe.ca/Investment/home.html** Can be used to find quotations for any stock traded in Canada or the United States.

Toronto-Dominion Bank
> **www.tdbank.ca**

Toronto Stock Exchange
> **www.tse.com**

Chapter 10

Debt Securities

objectives

1. Understand the following features of debt securities: term, interest rate and frequency of compounding, minimum, deposit, and accessibility of funds.

2. Explain the purpose of deposit insurance.

3. Define the following: term deposits, guaranteed investment certificates, commercial paper, treasury bills, money market funds, and mortgage backed securities.

4. Outline the process of bringing a bond issue to market and determining interest rates on new issues.

5. Distinguish between the various types of bonds and the difference between a principal and an agent in the bond market.

6. Define the special feature of bonds.

7. Calculate the yield to maturity on a bond and show how the changing of a bond's price affects the yield.

8. Understand the accrual process.

9. Explain the different tax treatment of bond interest and capital gains.

10. Show why Canada Savings Bonds are more like savings certificates than bonds.

Introduction

This chapter is about debt securities, a kind of investment in which the investor becomes a lender rather than an owner. As a result, there is generally less risk assumed and less management required. Five groups of debt securities will be discussed:

(a) deposits,

(b) money market securities,

(c) mortgage-backed securities,

(d) bonds and debentures,

(e) Canada Savings Bonds.

Most of these items are low-risk, very liquid investments, appropriate as a base for any portfolio. Deposits and Canada Savings Bonds are not transferable to other investors, but money market securities, mortgage-backed securities, and bonds may be traded in the financial markets. It is important to distinguish between Canada Savings Bonds, which are more like savings certificates, and other types of bonds.

This chapter provides an introduction to some of the basic principles and terminology associated with debt securities, but does not address portfolio management strategies. To learn more about debt securities further, you may wish to consult the other references and resources listed at the end of the chapter.

Deposits

The easiest and simplest way to invest is to lend capital to financial institutions by placing it in deposit securities. Savings accounts, term deposits, and guaranteed investment certificates are all examples of deposit securities. Although these savings vehicles may differ in interest rates, terms, minimum deposits, and accessibility, most involve a very low level of risk, pay interest regularly, and require minimal attention from the investor.

Savings Accounts

Banks, trust companies, and credit unions (*caisses populaires* in Quebec) offer a great variety of accounts. Some permit chequing; others do not. These financial institutions pay a higher rate of interest on savings accounts where the money is left for long periods of time. If you do not need your money soon and you decide that you want such an account, look for one that pays a high interest rate and that compounds interest frequently. If you expect to use some of your money occasionally, consider a daily interest account instead. While the interest rate on such accounts is lower, it is paid on the daily balance and is compounded monthly. Interest on regular savings accounts is paid only on the minimum monthly balance and is compounded semi-annually. Competition for customers is so strong today that financial institutions make frequent changes to their account offerings, with a view toward attracting and keeping customers. A wise consumer should therefore check with a number of institutions before opening an account. Some things to look for when comparing companies are shown in the box titled "Criteria for Comparing Banking Services."

Criteria for Comparing Banking Services

General Service Charges
Stop payment on cheques
Bill payment at branch
Transfer between accounts

Cheque-Related Charges
Certification
Chargeback (wrong date, etc.)
Not sufficient funds

Chequing/Savings Account
Minimum balance required

Cost per cheque
Cost per withdrawal at ATM

Savings Account
Minimum monthly balance required
Cost per withdrawal at counter
Penalty for account closed within 90 days of opening

Other
Packaged services

Term Deposits

As the name implies, **term deposits** are deposits taken by a financial institution for a specified term at a guaranteed interest rate—and, in some cases, they require a minimum investment. Savings accounts, by contrast, have no guaranteed interest rate, no minimum deposit, and no set term during which the funds must stay on deposit. The rate of return on term deposits is usually higher than that on savings accounts, and although the money is invested for a specified term, funds can usually be withdrawn before maturity by sacrificing some interest. Since the frequency of interest payments affects the interest rate, you can expect a lower rate if interest is to be paid monthly.

Guaranteed Investment Certificates (GICs)

Until quite recently, GICs were one of the most uninteresting investments. Money was locked in for a specific term and earned a very low rate of return. This has all changed. In order to compete with Canada Savings Bonds, which are redeemable on any business day and pay an attractive rate of interest, GICs with a number of new features are now available. They are available in both redeemable and non-redeemable varieties with competitive interest rates. Some have rising rates of interest similar to CSBs. Interest may be received annually or compounded and paid at maturity. They are also available in U.S. dollars. Some denominations in U.S dollars may be purchased with Canadian funds. The most interesting new feature appeals to investors who are more risk tolerant. They may purchase non-redeemable GICs indexed to a Canadian stock market index or to the S&P 500, a major U.S. stock market index. Therefore, if the stock market rises, so does the value of their GIC.

Before the addition of the new features, money invested in GICs could be eroded by inflation. To avoid this problem, some investors purchased certificates with different maturity dates known as "ladder GICs." An investor might buy five GICs, with one maturing in each of the next five years. As they matured, they would be reinvested for a five-year term allowing the investor to take advantage of any increase in interest rates.

Deposit Insurance

Funds deposited in a bank, trust company, or credit union are insured against loss if the institution should become insolvent. In 1967, the federal government established the Canada Deposit Insurance Corporation (CDIC) as a Crown corporation to insure deposits in member institutions. Signs indicating CDIC membership are often displayed in the windows of banks and trust companies.

The CDIC insures savings and chequing accounts, money orders, deposit receipts, guaranteed investment certificates, debentures, and other obligations issued by the member institutions. The maximum coverage is changed from time to time; currently, the limit is $60 000 per depositor for each institution (that is, the combined total of your deposits at all branches of a given institution must be $60 000 or less in order to be covered by CDIC). One restriction is that term deposits, to be insurable, must be redeemable no later than five years after deposit. Joint accounts are insured separately from individual accounts, meaning that it is possible to have both a personal and a joint account in the same bank, with the maximum coverage of $60 000 on each account. Credit unions, through their provincial organizations, offer similar deposit insurance.

Money Market Securities

From time to time, governments and corporations need to borrow money. The federal government accomplishes its required borrowing in a variety of ways. The best-known of these ways, and one that is popular with many thousands of Canadians, is the Canada Savings Bond that is issued each October. The government also borrows money by selling treasury bills (often called T-bills) and Government of Canada bonds. Provincial and municipal governments raise money by selling bonds or debentures. Corporations often borrow from banks, of course, but they may also raise money by issuing bonds, debentures, and short-term commercial paper. The people who invest in these vehicles are loaning their money to the corporation that issues them. These loans are classified as either short-term or long-term. Money market securities are short-term loans; bonds and debentures are long-term loans. This section examines money market securities, including T-bills, commercial paper, and money market funds.

The Money Market

A large pool of cash moves from lenders to borrowers for short periods through a mechanism known as the **money market.** The major actors in this market are banks, trust companies, investment dealers, corporations, governments, and the Bank of Canada. The lenders are usually corporations or institutions with spare cash that can be invested for a short period, and the borrowers are those who temporarily need extra funds. There is no physical site where money market transactions take place; the "market" consists only of a communication system. Because of the large minimum investment required, few individual investors are aware of all this money market activity.

The money market, as has been mentioned, deals strictly with short-term loans—mostly for 30, 60, 90, or 365 days, but occasionally for as long as three to five years. Commercial paper and treasury bills are two of the money market's most widely used instruments. **Commercial paper** (discounted paper) is the name used for short-term loans or promissory notes. Instead of lending the borrower a principal sum and expecting the borrower to repay the principal and the accumulated interest at maturity, the lender may invest a discounted sum, expecting to receive at maturity an amount equivalent to the loan plus interest. For instance, a 30-day note for

$50 000 might be purchased for $49 600 by the lender, who would receive $50 000 at maturity. The $400 difference between the amount invested and the amount received is the interest on the loan, which in this instance is 9.6 percent.

Treasury Bills

Treasury bills are short-term promissory notes that are issued mainly by the federal government, but also by other levels of government. They are purchased by financial institutions (such as banks and trust companies) and have terms to maturity of 91, 182, or 364 days. Retail clients wishing to invest in high-quality, low-risk, very liquid securities often purchase T-bills from investment dealers. Each dealer has a specific minimum purchase requirement. T-bills do not have a specific interest rate; instead, they sell at a discount and mature at par. The yield on a T-bill, which is determined by the difference between its purchase price and its maturity value, is higher than savings account interest (see Table 10.1). Investors may sell T-bills before maturity, at a price determined by current interest rates.

Each Tuesday, Government of Canada treasury bills are auctioned in Ottawa by the Bank of Canada. Prior to the auction, the Bank of Canada announces the amounts and maturities of the bills to be auctioned, and interested investors (e.g., banks and investment dealers) submit bids. At the auction, bills are sold to the highest bidders. Most T-bills are bought by banks (to be kept as part of their reserves) or by investment dealers (who sell them on the secondary market).

Until recently the Bank of Canada, could, in theory, announce a change in the Bank Rate on any business day. In September 2000 it announced the introduction of a new system. Any changes to the Bank Rate will now be made on eight pre-specified dates. Announcements will be made at 9 a.m. on either a Tuesday or Wednesday in specific weeks from January to November.

Investment dealers provide an active secondary market, offering outstanding T-bills with shorter maturities than the Bank's new issues. In recent years, some investment dealers have made T-bills available to small investors with a minimum purchase of $1000, in increments of $1000. Anyone who wishes to invest for the short term in a top-quality, low-risk, very liquid investment, might consider treasury bills (for example, see Personal Finance in Action Box 10.1, "Buying a T-Bill"). To buy treasury bills, you may need to open an account with a stockbroker. Usually treasury bills pay somewhat higher interest than savings accounts or term deposits, as noted in Table 10.1.

TABLE 10.1 COSTS AND BENEFITS OF SEVERAL DEBT SECURITIES OCTOBER 19, 2000

DEBT SECURITY	INTEREST RATE %	COSTS AND BENEFITS
Chequing Account	.10	Liquid, little interest $3–4 999
Investment Savings Account	.25	Liquid, little interest to $4 999.99
Money Market Fund	3.48	Liquid, minimum $2 500
GIC	4.75	Locked in 270–364 days, minimum $5 000
Treasury Bill 6 months	5.77	Liquid, minimum purchase required
NHA Mortgage backed securities	6.11	Maturity April 1, 2001 $5 000 required

Buying a T-Bill

When Ivan inherited $27 000, he needed a short-term investment until he made other plans. His broker offered him a 36-day treasury bill, quoted at a price of 99.627. Note that the quoted price is the amount he will pay for each $100 that he buys. The amount he invested was 270 x 99.627 = $26 899.29. When the T-bill matures, Ivan will receive $27 000, including interest of $100.71.

To calculate the yield on his T-bill, Ivan used the following formula:

$$\text{Yield} = \frac{100 - \text{price}}{\text{price}} \times \frac{365 \times 100}{\text{term}}$$

$$\text{Yield} = \frac{100 - 99.627}{99.627} \times \frac{365}{36}$$

$$\text{Yield} = \frac{0.373}{99.627} \times \frac{365}{36}$$

$$\text{Yield} = .0037439 \times 1\ 013.888 = 3.8\%$$

If Ivan had needed to sell the treasury bill before it matured, the return would have been recalculated to reflect the current T-bill rate at the time of the sale.

Money Market Funds

Savings accounts are not the only low-risk, highly liquid, interest-earning securities available for small sums. When you do not have enough money to buy treasury bills directly from a broker, you can still put your savings into the money market through a **money market fund,** which is a way of pooling contributions from many small investors. A money market mutual fund accepts small amounts from many people. A paid manager invests these funds in a portfolio of treasury bills and commercial paper. The return from money market funds, in the form of interest, may be received regularly by the investor, or reinvested in additional shares of the fund. The investor's shares in a money market fund can be sold at any time.

Money market funds differ in selling practices and commission fees. Some funds are sold directly to customers, while others are available through brokers. Some funds do not charge a fee, but require a large initial deposit; others charge an acquisition fee of 2 to 9 percent, depending on the size of the investment (the larger the deposit, the smaller the rate). Most money market funds charge annual management fees, which are deducted before any return is paid to the investor (see Personal Finance in Action Box 10.2, "Caitlin Invests in a Money Market Fund"). Fees for mutual funds will be discussed in detail in Chapter 11.

Caitlin Invests in a Money Market Fund

Caitlin has $5 000 in her savings account but is thinking instead of investing in a money market fund. The higher interest and liquidity of such funds appeal to her. She recently read in the newspaper's business section that her bank offers a number of such funds. This pleases her because she believes that the bank is well run and that her money will be safe. The bank manager is also a friend of her

continued

father's. A bank employee explains that the fund she likes earned 2.5 percent last year and had an average return for the past five years of 4 percent. To invest in the money market fund, Caitlin must pay a one-time acquisition fee of $100. Also, a yearly management fee of 0.5 percent will be deducted before her interest is paid. Even after these fees have been explained to her, Caitlin decides to invest in the fund. The interest she earns on her savings account is very low, and she will earn more in the fund. She understands that the interest the bank pays is low because of the Bank of Canada's monetary policy. Inflation is at a historic low as a result of the Bank's policies, and her money will therefore retain its value better than it would have in the past. The cost of borrowing has dropped as well. She is also afraid of riskier investments, such as stocks, where she could possibly make a capital gain.

Caitlin's investment will earn $125 per year with interest of 2.5 percent. During the first year, she will pay that same amount ($125) in fees. After that, she will clear $100 each year, and can have the interest automatically reinvested so that her money will grow inside the fund.

Mortgage-Backed Securities

Investing directly in home mortgages requires expertise, time, and willingness to accept risk. But you can overcome these difficulties by using mortgage-backed securities. When you buy **mortgage-backed securities,** you acquire a share in a large pool of residential mortgages that are secured by the Canada Mortgage and Housing Corporation (CMHC). Each pool of mortgages has its own interest rate and maturity date, which could be as short as six months. Mortgage-backed securities are available from stockbrokers in units of $5000 and are traded on the public market, where they may be sold before maturity. Generally, the yield on this investment vehicle is higher than that for treasury bills.

There are two types of mortgage-backed securities: open and closed (terms that will be more meaningful to you after you study Chapter 13, "Home Mortgages"). In essence, the terms mean that some mortgage pools permit home buyers to make prepayments in order to repay their mortgages faster. Investors in mortgage-backed securities are affected by this type of arrangement, because they may find their principal being repaid faster than they anticipated; investors must therefore reinvest their capital at a faster rate. But there may be a bonus of some extra money for investors, because of penalties paid by those making prepayments.

The holders of mortgage-backed securities need not be concerned either with managing this investment or with its safety. Each month, they simply receive a cheque, which includes a combination of interest and principal. They do have to remember, however, that some of their capital is being returned in each cheque; if they want to preserve their capital, they need a plan for continual reinvestment. But if their goal is to gradually spend some of their capital, this is one way to accomplish that goal.

Bonds

Bonds and Debentures

Debt securities with longer-term maturities include bonds and debentures, which may have terms up to 25 years or more. Technically, there is a distinction between bonds and debentures, although the terms are often used interchangeably: **bonds** are secured with property, while

debentures are unsecured loans. To further confuse matters, Government of Canada bonds are really debentures. In this chapter, bonds will be used as a generic term that includes both bonds and debentures. Bonds are issued by the federal, provincial, and municipal governments, by public utilities, and by private corporations when they need to borrow money. Those who buy their bonds become their creditors, receiving a promise that interest will be paid on specific dates and that the principal will be repaid at maturity.

How Bonds Are Issued

A government or corporation that wishes to float a new bond issue usually uses an investment dealer as an underwriter. The **underwriter** agrees to purchase all of the bonds offered at a stated price, and then tries to sell them at a slightly higher price. With large bond issues, a group of investment dealers may act as underwriters. In the initial stages, the underwriter will be consulted for advice on terms (interest rate, maturity, etc.). After an agreement is reached, the bonds will be printed and transferred by the issuer (the borrower) to the underwriters. Thus, underwriters are involved in designing the terms of the issue as well as in its sale and distribution. The **par value** is the face value of the bond or other security and is printed on the bond itself (the bond's par value might, for example, be $1 000). Investment dealers advertise each new issue of bonds and sell them to buyers at a price that may be either at par or slightly below, depending on the market at the time.

A NEW BOND ISSUE When a new bond is issued, a copy of a prospectus giving detailed information about the bond is sent to interested people. The first page of one such prospectus is shown in Figure 10.1. It shows the name of the issuer (Sears Canada Inc.) and the value of the issue ($125 000 000), along with other pertinent information. This bond will pay 6.55 percent per year for 10 years in semi-annual instalments on November 5 and May 5 of each year, beginning on May 5, 1998, and ending on May 5, 2007. Sears may redeem the bonds at any time before the maturity date by paying the lender a price equal to the greater of par and the Canada Yield Price[1] plus any accrued and unpaid interest.

FACTORS AFFECTING INTEREST RATES The three significant factors that affect the interest rate on a new bond issue are (i) the general level of interest rates in the country at the time, (ii) the length of time to maturity, and (iii) the issuer's credit rating. If general interest rates happen to be high, bond issuers will have to offer equivalent rates in order to attract investors. Recall from Chapter 8 that money has a time value. The longer the term, the more uncertainty about the future—and consequently, the higher the rate needed to interest investors in very long-term bonds.

A bond issuer's credit rating depends on the issuer's financial status and revenue base. The federal government, which is considered to have the highest credit rating, can borrow more cheaply than the provinces can. Municipalities are considered to be in the third level of safety and must therefore pay somewhat more interest than the two senior levels of government do. Generally, corporations rank below all governments and must pay somewhat higher interest rates on their bonds. But corporations vary considerably in their credit ratings: some have a much better rating than others. Moreover, this ranking of credit status—from the federal government at the top to corporations at the bottom—is a useful generalization, but it does not cover all cases.

---

[1] "The Canada Yield Price means a price equal to the price of the Debentures calculated, on the business day preceding the date on which the corporation gives notice of redemption pursuant to the Trust Indenture, to provide a yield from the date fixed for redemption to the maturity date equal to the Government of Canada Yield plus 0.20%" (*Preliminary Short Form Prospectus*, October 27, 1997, p. 5).

FIGURE 10.1 ANNOUNCEMENT OF A BOND ISSUE

Preliminary Short Form Prospectus Dated October 27, 1997

This short form prospectus constitutes a public offering of these securities only in those jurisdictions where they may be lawfully offered for sale and therein only by persons permitted to sell such securities. No securities commission or similar authority in Canada has in any way passed upon the merits of the securities offered hereunder and any representation to the contrary is an offence. These securities have not been and will not be registered under the United States Securities Act of 1933. Accordingly, except pursuant to an exemption from registration under the United States Securities Act of 1993, these securities may not be offered or sold within the United States, and this prospectus does not constitute an offer to sell or a solicitation of an offer to buy any of these securities within the United States. See "Plan of Distribution".

Information has been incorporated by reference in this short form prospectus from documents filed with securities commissions or similar authorities in Canada. Copies of the documents incorporated herein by reference may be obtained on request without charge from the Secretary of the Corporation, 222 Jarvis Street, Toronto, Ontario, Canada, M5B 2B8 (Telephone: (416) 941-4418). For the purpose of the Province of Québec, this simplified prospectus contains information to be completed by consulting the permanent information record. A copy of the permanent information record may be obtained from the Secretary of the Corporation at the above-mentioned address and telephone number.

New Issue

Sears Canada Inc.
$125,000,000

6.55% Debentures due November 5, 2007
(unsecured)

To be dated November 5, 1997   To mature November 5, 2007

The 6.55% Debentures due November 5, 2007 (the "Debentures") will be direct unsecured obligations of Sears Canada Inc. (the "Corporation") and will bear interest at the rate of 6.55% per annum, payable in semi-annual instalments on November 5 and May 5 in each year, commencing May 5, 1998. The Corporation will be entitled, at its option, to redeem the Debentures, in whole or in part, at any time prior to maturity at a redemption price equal to the greater of the Canada Yield Price (as defined herein) and par, together in each case with accrued and unpaid interest to, but excluding, the date fixed for redemption. See "Details of the Offering — Redemption and Purchase".

In the opinion of counsel, the Debentures will qualify for investment under certain statutes as set out under "Eligibility for Investment".

	Price to the Public	Underwriters' Fee and Discount [1]	Net Proceeds to the Corporation [2][3]
Per $1,000 principal amount of Debentures..........	Non-fixed price	$9.17	$990.83
Total	Non-fixed price	$1,146,250	$123,853,750

(1) Consists of the underwriting fee of $7.50 and a discount of $1.67 per $1,000 principal amount of Debentures. The Underwriters' overall compensation will increase or decrease by the amount by which the aggregate price paid for the Debentures by the purchasers exceeds or is less than the aggregate price paid by the Underwriters to the Corporation.

(2) Plus accrued interest, if any, from November 5, 1997 to the closing date.

(3) Before deducting expenses of this offering estimated to be $200,000 which, together with the Underwriters' fee, will be paid from the general funds of the Corporation.

The Underwriters have agreed to purchase the Debentures from the Corporation at 99.833% of their principal amount plus accrued interest, if any, from November 5, 1997 to the closing date, subject to the terms and conditions of the Underwriting Agreement referred to under "Plan of Distribution", and will receive a fee of $937,500.

The Debentures will be offered to the public at prices to be negotiated by the Underwriters with purchasers. Accordingly, the price at which the Debentures will be offered and sold to the public may vary as between purchasers and during the period of distribution of the Debentures. The Underwriters' overall compensation will increase or decrease by the amount by which the aggregate price paid for the Debentures by purchasers exceeds or is less than the aggregate price paid by the Underwriters to the Corporation.

The Underwriters, as principals, conditionally offer the Debentures, subject to prior sale, if, as and when issued by the Corporation and accepted by the Underwriters in accordance with the conditions of the Underwriting Agreement referred to under "Plan of Distribution" and subject to the approval of certain legal matters on behalf of the Corporation by Tory Tory DesLauriers & Binnington and on behalf of the Underwriters by Blake, Cassels & Graydon.

Subscriptions for the Debentures will be received subject to rejection or allotment in whole or in part and the right is reserved to close the subscription books at any time without notice. It is expected that the closing of this offering will take place on November 5, 1997 or on such other date as the Corporation and the Underwriters may agree, but not later than November 19, 1997. The definitive Debenture will be delivered on closing.

(side text, rotated): This is a preliminary short form prospectus relating to these securities, a copy of which has been filed with the securities commission or other regulatory authority in each of the provinces and territories of Canada, but which has not yet become final for the purpose of a distribution to the public. Information contained herein is subject to completion or amendment. These securities may not be sold to, nor may offers to buy be accepted from, residents of such jurisdictions prior to the time a receipt for the final short form prospectus is obtained from the appropriate securities commission or other regulatory authority.

BOND RATINGS Bond ratings, which are published in Canada by the Canadian Bond Rating Service or the Dominion Bond Rating Service, may be consulted to find the credit rating of a government or corporation. Moody's and Standard and Poor's are two American agencies that rate Canadian bond issues sold in the United States. In descending order of creditworthiness, the ratings range from AAA (often called "triple-A") at the top to AA, A, BBB, and so on.

Bond Certificates

A bondholder receives a bond certificate that states the terms of the issue and the bond's **denomination** or par value, which may be $500, $1000, $10 000 or more. The smallest denomination is usually $1000. The terms of the bond issue include the maturity date, the interest rate, and how the interest will be paid. The maturity date is the date when the issuer promises to repay the principal, a process known as **bond redemption.** Interest payments are usually made twice a year on the dates indicated on the bond. A typical bond certificate is shown in Figure 10.2.

INTEREST PAYMENTS   Interest on bonds may be paid either by cheque or by coupon. A **coupon bond** features a series of coupons attached to the bond certificate. Each coupon has a value printed on it, along with the date on which it may be cashed. For example, a bond with a 10-year term will have 20 coupons, dated at six-month intervals; each coupon will be worth half a year's interest. Either the coupons or the certificate will state which financial institutions will cash the coupons. When the specified date arrives, the bondholder cuts off the coupon and exchanges it for cash at the bank or brokerage house. Cash in your coupons promptly and reinvest the interest, since no interest is earned on uncut coupons. Bond coupons are the equivalent of cash, so you should take care to safeguard them.

BOND REGISTRATION   Some bonds have registered owners, while others do not. Where ownership is concerned, three types of bonds exist: (i) bearer bonds, (ii) bonds registered as to principal, and (iii) fully registered bonds. **Bearer bonds**, which used to be printed on paper, had no name or proof of ownership on them. The bonds and the coupons attached to them could, as a result, be cashed by anyone. Printed bearer bonds have been replaced, much like stock certificates, by entries in a computer. They can now be sold more quickly and are more secure. **Bonds registered as to principal** have the name of their owner typed on them, but they also carry coupons that, if detached, may be cashed in by anyone. Other bonds are **fully registered,** meaning that not only is the owner's name on the bond certificate but also the interest is paid directly to the owner by cheque. Coupons are therefore not required. When bonds are sold by one owner to another, bearer bonds can simply be handed over, but with the two registered types of bonds, a transfer-of-ownership form must be signed and witnessed. It is therefore difficult for anyone but the registered owner to redeem a registered bond.

Bond Issuers

GOVERNMENT OF CANADA   Debt securities issued by the federal government are considered to be of the highest quality and to be safer than those of any other Canadian borrower. With its broad taxing powers, the government is unlikely to fail to pay interest on or to redeem the "Canadas," as Government of Canada bonds are often called. Since the federal government's need for borrowed money has declined in recent years, fewer "Canadas" have been issued. They are, as a result, very marketable. In addition to its own bonds, the Government of Canada guarantees bonds issued by various Crown corporations. Although the federal government also issues Canada Savings Bonds, these investments are more like savings certificates than bonds; they will therefore be considered separately (see "Canada Savings Bonds," later in this chapter).

PROVINCIAL GOVERNMENTS The provinces also issue bonds in their own right; as well, they guarantee the bond issues of those commissions, hydro-electric corporations, and school boards under their jurisdiction. As previously mentioned, provincial bonds are usually considered to be a notch or two below the "Canadas" in security. Quebec and Ontario are currently the largest bond issuers in Canada.

MUNICIPALITIES Local governments issue debentures to pay for costly but long-lasting public projects such as streets, waterworks, schools, and hospitals. By issuing bonds, the municipality can spread the cost over a number of years. The provinces usually exert some regulatory control over the borrowing done by their municipalities, a fact that may be a comfort to investors. Because municipal debentures do not trade as frequently as the more senior provincial and federal debentures do, they are generally less marketable. The quality of a municipality's securities depends on its tax base: municipalities with a broader range of industries are preferable to single-industry towns or regions. The bond rating agencies usually rank municipal debentures below provincial and federal issues; but generalizing is difficult, because the budgets of some large Canadian cities exceed those of the smallest provinces.

CORPORATIONS When long-term funding is needed, corporations issue a variety of bonds and debentures; a few types will be mentioned here. If a corporation's credit rating is high enough, unsecured debentures may be issued; otherwise, corporate bonds must be backed by some type of security. As a loan that is secured by property, a **mortgage bond** is similar to any mortgage. But because corporations borrow such large sums, each such loan is divided into smaller units, enabling a number of investors to be involved. Property that is put up as security will be used to compensate bondholders if the corporation should default. Among mortgage bonds, as with home mortgages, there are first-mortgage bonds and second-mortgage bonds; the "first" and "second" designations indicate the order in which creditors would rank in the case of compensation claims.

If a corporation does not have a high enough credit rating to borrow with unsecured debentures, but also has no property to offer as security, it may issue **collateral trust bonds,** which are secured with financial assets held by the company, such as bonds and stocks.

Special Features

Bonds and debentures are often issued with special characteristics. They may be callable, convertible, extendible, or retractable. Some of these features are intended to make an issue more attractive to investors.

CALLABLE Some bond certificates state that the issuer can recall the bond before the maturity date: such instruments are known as **callable bonds.** When borrowers wish to reserve the right to pay off bond debt before maturity, they issue callable bonds. The call or redemption feature usually includes an agreement to give the bondholder a month's notice of the intention to call them in. The issuer may agree to pay the owner somewhat more than the bond's face value as compensation for the early recall, although the Government of Canada usually does not do so. Bonds are assumed to be non-callable unless otherwise designated. With a call feature, the initiative remains with the issuer; bondholders do not have the option of redeeming a callable bond whenever they wish. Unless the bond is called by the issuer, investors who want to sell a callable bond must either find a buyer or wait until the maturity date. Personal Finance in Action Box 10.3, "A Bond Redemption," illustrates the recall of a bond issue.

CONVERTIBLE Bonds with a clause that gives the bondholder the option of exchanging the security for a specified number of the issuing company's common shares are called **convertible**

Personal Finance in Action 10.3

A Bond Redemption

On January 31, 2001, the financial press carried an announcement that on March 30, the Province of Alberta would be redeeming its 12.5 percent callable bond, due to mature July 31, 2010. The bonds pay interest annually on July 31, so the bondholder, in addition to receiving $1 000 for each bond, would receive accrued interest of $83 on March 30.

Personal Finance in Action 10.4

Conversion Terms

On November 30, 2000, Frontier Welding issues a convertible debenture. Up until the close of business on January 29, 2021, the debenture owner may convert the debenture to common shares of the company at a price of $12.50, receiving 80 shares for each $1 000 debenture. If the shares have risen before the conversion date, the debenture owner will have earned a capital gain.

---

bonds. The terms of the conversion, which are established when the bonds are issued, do not change. This feature gives the holder of a debt security the possibility of capital gain. The investor would profit if, in the future, the price of the borrowing company's common stock should rise above the set conversion price. The option of converting to common stock may help support the price of a bond, which might otherwise drop. The terms of one series of convertible debentures are shown in Personal Finance in Action Box 10.4, "Conversion Terms."

EXTENDIBLE Sometimes bonds or debentures with short maturities carry an extendible feature, which allows the bondholder to extend the maturity date, perhaps for 10 years, at the same or a slightly higher interest rate.

RETRACTABLE Long-term bonds that carry an option permitting the holder to shorten the maturity are called **retractable bonds.** This feature may attract investors who are willing to accept a slightly lower interest rate in exchange for this flexibility. An example of a debenture series with a retraction privilege is shown in Figure 10.2.

FLOATING RATE A **floating interest rate bond** is issued during a period of rapidly changing interest rates. The interest rate on such bonds is periodically adjusted in relation to the treasury bill rate. With this feature, neither the lender nor the borrower is locked into a set interest rate. Which of the parties—that is, the lender or the borrower—benefits in the long run depends on which way interest rates move. The price of floating rate bonds fluctuates very little, but their rate normally varies every six months.

SINKING FUND PROVISION Many debt securities carry a **sinking fund** provision, meaning that the issuer will be setting aside sums of money each year to provide for their redemption. These funds are held in trust by a trustee—usually a trust company—until needed. A sinking fund provision is useful to the corporation as a way of reducing debt, but not particularly helpful to the investor, who may not want to have the bonds recalled before maturity. Note that the bond announcement in Figure 10.1 carries a sinking fund provision.

BUYING AND SELLING BONDS A new bond issue is announced in the financial press through a notice like the one shown in Figure 10.2. Such advertisements are referred to in the industry as **tombstones.** The issue mentioned in this ad has already been sold, and the notice appears in the press for information purposes only. A typical tombstone gives some details about the bond issue and also lists the underwriters, the investment dealers who financed the issue. Normally, these firms buy the whole issue for their own accounts or for later resale to clients.

Suppose you are holding a bond that will not mature for many years, but you need the cash now: in this situation, you must find a buyer for your bond. Bonds are bought and sold on the **bond market** or "over the counter." Neither the market nor the counter is a physical place,

FIGURE 10.2 ANNOUNCEMENT OF A RETRACTABLE DEBENTURE

This advertisement is not to be construed as a public offering in any province of Canada unless a prospectus relating thereto has been accepted for filing by a Securities Commission or similar authority in such province. The offering is made by prospectus only, copies of which may be obtained from the undersigned.

New Issue

UNION GAS LIMITED

$75,000,000
10⅝% Debentures, 1986 Series
(unsecured)

To be dated February 26, 1986   To mature December 15, 2005

Multiple Retraction Privilege and Interest Rate Adjustment
The Debentures will be retractable at the option of the holder on December 15, 1995 and on December 15 each year thereafter at par plus accrued interest thereon to the date of retraction. Prior to each retraction date, Union Gas Limited may, at its option, increase the interest rate. Any increase in interest rate will be effective for a period of one year from such retraction date.

Price: 100

Nesbitt Thomson Bongard Inc.	Gordon Capital Corporation	Merrill Lynch Canada Inc.
Midland Doherty Limited	Dominion Securities Pitfield Limited	McLeod Young Weir Limited

February 1986

Spread in Bond Prices

Consider the following bond quotation:

"Bell Canada 7.0 percent due 24 September 2007, bid 106.472, ask 107.472."

Until you are familiar with bond quotations, this little paragraph may not mean much to you. Here's what it says, in English: Bell Canada is issuing a $1 000 bond that may be either sold to a broker for $1 064.72 or purchased for $1 074.72. The spread between these two prices represents the broker's commission. The amount of the spread depends on both the trading activity in a particular bond and the size of the transaction. If a certain issue of bonds trades thinly, the broker may have more difficulty finding a buyer or seller and thus may take a larger spread. Investors who place large bond orders are able to negotiate a smaller spread per bond than a small investor can. The minimum spread is generally around $10.

though: like "money market," these terms refer to a communication system—in this case, one that links investment dealers and brokers. When you, the investor, inform your broker that you have a bond to sell, your broker, in turn, sends this information to other brokers, one of whom may have a client who is interested in buying that very bond. Alternatively, an investment dealer may purchase the bond from you. In the distribution of bonds, investment dealers may act either as principals or as agents. They are said to be acting *as principals* when they buy bonds for resale to the public. Conversely, they are said to be acting *as agents* when, rather than buying the bonds for their own account, they just try to link would-be buyers with would-be sellers.

Commission is not charged on bonds; instead, investment dealers add their profit to the buying or selling price. The difference between the base price and the dealer's marked-up price is sometimes called the **spread.** The spread is greater for bonds that are less frequently traded and for small orders of bonds.

BOND PRICE FLUCTUATION When a bond is issued, the interest rate is fixed for the entire term, which may be 10, 20, or more years. But economic conditions generally cause interest rates to change during that period. This fluctuation creates a problem for anyone who wishes, for instance, to sell a bond that is paying 5 percent when rates on other, more recently issued debt securities are closer to 10 percent. To interest a purchaser, the seller will have to lower the price of the bond below par—a process known as selling it **at a discount.** Likewise, if interest rates have fallen since this bond was issued, it can be sold for a price greater than par— or sold **at a premium.**

YIELD TO MATURITY In the financial world, yield usually means the annual return from an investment expressed as a percentage of its market price. In the case of bonds, the time value of future interest and the time value of the principal payments are taken into account. Payments received in the near future are worth more to the investor than those received in the uncertain, distant future. A precise calculation of bond yield to maturity takes into account the present value of coupon payments and the present value of the principal repayment at maturity. Bond traders use a complex formula to make this calculation. The simple method used in the Personal Finance in Action Box 10.5, "Bond Prices and Yields," serves to show how the

Personal Finance in Action 10.5

Bond Prices and Yields

Danielle received a $20 000 Government of Canada bond as part of her divorce settlement from Andrew. It pays 10 percent interest and matures on June 1, 2008. Now that her son and daughter have left home, she decides to use the money as a down payment on a cottage on a nearby lake. She thinks this will encourage her children and grandchildren to visit her. She learns that if she sells the bond, she will make a capital gain of $5 214. Interest rates have come down since she acquired the bond, and each $1 000 bond is now worth $1 260.70. If, not wanting to pay capital gains tax, she keeps the bond, she will continue to earn interest of $2 000 per year.

Paolo bought a Domtar bond for $22 494 with the money from his early retirement buy-out. The yield he will earn on this bond can be determined as follows:

Face Value	$20 000
Purchase Price	$22 494
Nominal rate of interest	10%
Maturity Date	15 April 2011
Time to maturity	11 years
Date of purchase	29 Nov. 2000

The average annual return from this bond, if held to maturity, will consist of the interest paid on the bond minus the capital loss.

Annual interest	$2 000
Capital loss over 11 years	$2 494
Average annual capital loss	$2 494/11 = $226.72
Total average annual return	$2 000 – $226.72 = $1 773.27
Annual yield to maturity	$= \dfrac{\text{ave. annual return} \times 100}{\text{purchase price}}$
	$= \dfrac{1\ 773.27 \times 100}{22\ 494}$
	$= 7.8\%$

Why is Paolo's yield to maturity less than Danielle's?

nominal interest rate and the potential capital gain or loss can influence the yield. (The results from calculations made using this method will be somewhat different from those found in bond yield quotations, since here we have made no adjustment for the time value effect.)

If you hold a bond until maturity, you can expect to receive the bond's face value regardless of the price you paid for it. But if you sell the bond prior to maturity, you may experience either a capital gain or a capital loss. So when buying a bond, you must take into account the possibility of capital gain or loss, in addition to the amount of interest the bond will pay.

ACCRUED INTEREST Bond interest is paid on fixed dates, usually every six months from the date of issue. This situation presents problems for people who buy and sell bonds, who may transfer ownership at any time. Whoever owns the bond on the interest payment date will receive six months' interest, but this person may have held the bond for only two months. The seller should not lose four months' interest because the bond was sold to someone else. The solution is to charge the buyer **accrued interest,** which is the amount that is owing but that has

Personal Finance in Action 10.6

Accrued Interest

Margo bought a $1 000 Government of Canada bond for $1 536.50 on January 1. While the nominal rate of interest was 11.25 percent, she did not realize that she would only earn 5.75 percent because the bond had appreciated in value. The bond pays interest once a year on June 1. When Margo bought the bond, she learned that she had to pay accrued interest to the previous owner. At the time of the purchase, seven months' interest was owing. She therefore had to pay 1 000 x 0.1125 x 7/12, or $65.62, in interest. On June 1, Margo will receive five months' interest ($46.88).

not yet been paid. Bonds are therefore sold at a certain price plus accrued interest. The buyer pays the seller for the interest due to date, and recovers that amount in the next interest payment. Personal Finance in Action Box 10.6, "Accrued Interest," clarifies this process.

BOND QUOTATIONS Financial papers do not provide as much information about bond quotations as they do about stock prices, because of the difficulty of collecting these data; bond trades are not concentrated on a few exchanges, the way stock transactions are. Bond quotations may be found in *The Financial Post* or in the "Report on Business" section of each Monday's *Globe and Mail*. In these quotations, bond prices are given in hundreds, and bonds from the same issuer are distinguished by the interest rate and the maturity date. Therefore, the quote "8 percent Canadas of 1 June 2027" means that this issue of Government of Canada bonds carries an interest rate of 8 percent and will mature on June 1, 2027. The quotation will also give a recent price at which these bonds traded, and the yield to maturity (see Table 10.2).

Strip Bonds

Strip bonds are another way of investing in debt securities. Investment dealers buy large-denomination bonds that are issued either by federal or provincial governments or by Crown corporations, and strip off the coupons. Long-term bonds with maturities of at least 20 years are usually selected for coupon stripping. With a **strip bond,** the interest has been separated from the principal (bond residue); interest and principal are sold separately. Each coupon, with its fixed payment date, becomes a little bond that may be sold at a discount; its price will depend on the prevailing interest rates. In 1997, a $10 000 strip bond maturing in 2007 cost an

TABLE 10.2 BOND QUOTATIONS, OCTOBER 19, 2000

ISSUER	MATURITY	COUPON	QUOTE	YIELD
Canada	1 June 29	5.75	102.65	5.56
Ontario	8 March 29	6.50	103.68	6.62
Loblaw	8 Nov 27	6.65	95.00	7.07
Domtar	15 April 11	10.00	114.57	7.93
IPL	15 Feb 24	8.20	114.10	6.97
3-month T-bills				5.60

investor $5717. If the bond is held to maturity, the investor will receive $5717 plus interest of $4283, for a yield of 5.72 percent.

Dealers usually pool the strip bond funds and give a deposit receipt or certificate. These go by a variety of names, depending on who issues them: examples include TIGRs (term investment growth receipts), Cougars, and Sentinels. In the latter case, the investor has a share in a pool of coupons or residuals that are held in trust. These certificates are registered in the name of the investor, who may sell them at any time on the secondary market. The sale price, which changes with general interest rates, will generally fluctuate more than bond prices. The purchase price of strip bonds reflects current interest rates and the time value of money, or the time the investor has to wait to receive the yield. The market offers investors discounted coupons that mature every six months.

Taxation of Bond Yield

Bond yield consists of interest income and the possibility of capital gain or loss if the bond is traded before maturity. Interest and capital gains are taxed differently. Interest is added to taxable income and taxed accordingly. Only 50 percent of a capital gain is taxed (see Personal Finance in Action Box 10.7, "What Has Happened to Our Income?").

The differential tax treatment of interest and capital gain provides an incentive for some investors to prefer to receive their bond return in the form of capital gain rather than in interest.

Personal Finance in Action 10.7

What Has Happened to Our Income?

Jan and Paul took early retirement in 1985. At the time, all of their savings were in bonds and GICs, earning interest at an average rate of 10 percent per year. This arrangement seemed excellent at the time they retired. But by 1997, interest rates had fallen to their lowest level in 30 years. As a result, the couple's income had seriously declined. Jan and Paul now wondered whether they could continue to support themselves in the future.

When they retired, they owned $500 000 in GICs and government bonds. These securities had provided them with a healthy income of $50 000 a year, quite adequate in 1985. By 1997, however, since they were earning interest of only 5.25 percent, their income had dropped to $26 250 a year. Jan and Paul became very worried. Their friend Vince, a financial planner they had known since their university days, told them that in order to increase their capital and have a healthier financial future, they should invest in common

stocks. Banks and utilities were his favourites: they pay good dividends, and their shares tend to increase in value. While capital gains are never guaranteed, Vince pointed out that bank stocks had been excellent performers in recent years because of Canada's low inflation. The stock of one bank he liked had appreciated by 45 percent in one year. The economy was healthy and both inflation and interest rates were low. In addition, because of the favourable treatment of dividend income by Revenue Canada, Jan and Paul would pay less income tax. Whatever capital gains they made would not be taxed until they sold their investments. Vince suggested that they not sell these stocks unless absolutely necessary, since stocks perform best over the long term. He also pointed out that unless they switch a large portion of their investments to stocks, the purchasing power of their capital would decrease in value as time passed, as a result of inflation.

The yield from stripped bonds is considered by Revenue Canada Taxation to be interest, not capital gain; for this reason, such bonds are often selected as a component in self-administered RRSP accounts, where the return is tax-sheltered. If strip bonds are not held inside a tax shelter, accrued interest must be reported annually, even if it is not received.

Canada Savings Bonds

Although they are called bonds, Canada Savings Bonds (CSBs) are actually very different from bonds and debentures. They are more like savings certificates. Since they cannot be traded but can only be redeemed, their value does not fluctuate. Canada Savings Bonds developed from Victory bonds, which were issued between 1940 and 1944 to help Canada fight World War II. Although they were an important part of the federal government's borrowing for over 50 years, they have become less so in recent years as the government's need for funds has declined.

Terms of the Issues

A new issue of CSBs goes on sale once each year, in October, and only for a limited time. Available only to Canadian residents, they are bought at face value in denominations of $100, $300, $500, $1 000, $5 000, and $10 000. Interest is paid every November 1. Investors can elect to receive their interest every year or to have it compounded. Compound bonds start at $100, while regular interest bonds start at $300. Holders of regular interest bonds receive interest cheques by mail in November. The Bank of Canada will also deposit cheques directly into a bondholder's bank account. CSBs may be purchased from banks, trust companies, credit unions, and investment dealers. Compound interest bonds may also be purchased through payroll deduction plans. You pay no commission either when you purchase CSBs or when you redeem them. The bonds cannot be transferred, except after the bondholder dies, but they may be redeemed for their face value on any business day. They represent low-risk and very liquid investments. (See Personal Finance in Action Box 10.8, "Canada Savings Bonds versus Common Shares," for a comparison between CSBs and common shares.)

Until 1997, the maximum amount of CSBs someone could purchase was $200 000 per year. It is now possible to purchase up to $200 000 worth of bonds in each type of ownership registration. This means that a person may buy $200 000 for an individual account, another $200 000 for a joint account, and another $200 000 for an RRSP or a RRIF.

CSBs are bought by people who want security combined with liquidity. Many are redeemed when a better rate becomes available. If the bond is redeemed within three months of its purchase, however, no interest is paid. On redemptions that occur at any time after the first three months, interest is paid up to the end of the previous month.

At the time of writing, there were 23 CSB issues outstanding. The most recent, CSB Series 67 was issued on December 1, 2000. It has a 10-year term and an interest rate of 4.85 percent for the first year. This rate will increase if "market conditions warrant." Rates for subsequent years will be announced.

The Bank of Canada also issues **Canada Premium Bonds**. Previously known as Canada RRSP Bonds, they have a higher coupon, i.e., a higher rate of interest. Series 16, issued on December 1, 2000 has a 10-year term. Interest for the first year is 5.50 percent. The compound interest rate for the first three years is 5.69 percent. These bonds are only redeemable on the anniversary date and for 30 days thereafter. At the time of writing all 16 issues were still outstanding.

Canada Savings Bonds versus Common Shares

You have $5 000 to invest this October. Should you buy the new CSBs, which are paying 3 percent interest, or shares in Telus, the Alberta telephone company, which are yielding 2.76 percent? On the surface, this may look like a simple question to answer, because of the higher yield on the CSBs. But in order to encourage investment in Canadian-owned businesses, the federal government taxes dividends from such corporations at a special rate. As a result of the dividend tax credit (explained in Chapter 11), the equivalent yield on Telus shares is actually 3.59 percent. Interest income is taxed at a higher rate than dividend income. Assuming a combined federal and provincial tax rate of 44 percent, the tax on the $150 CSB interest will be $66. Therefore, the actual yield of $84 will represent only 1.68 percent. In addition, shares in public utility companies like Telus have gained significantly in value in recent years. They may do so again, and are therefore considered by some to be a better investment than CSBs.

Income Tax

Before 1991, holders of compound interest bonds were allowed to choose one of two possible ways of reporting interest: (i) as received (that is, on a cash basis), or (ii) as earned (that is, on a receivable basis). As a result of revisions to the *Income Tax Act*, interest on bonds purchased since 1990 must be reported annually, whether or not it has been received.

Savings Bonds Versus Other Bonds

Despite their name, Canada Savings Bonds lack many of the attributes of bonds. Instead, think of them as a type of savings certificate. The unique features of CSBs are listed below:

(a) **Sale**—They are sold directly to investors, are not traded on the bond market, are not transferable, and carry no commission charges.

(b) **Eligibility**—Distribution is limited to Canadian residents.

(c) **Redemption**—Face value is available on any business day.

(d) **Denominations**—CSBs are available in smaller denominations than other bonds.

(e) **Types**—There are two types: regular interest bonds (interest mailed annually), and compound interest bonds (interest paid at redemption or maturity).

(f) **Annual interest**—Interest is paid each November on regular interest CSBs.

Summary

Debt securities represent not only a very large share of the financial transactions in this country, but also a significant portion of the portfolios of individual investors. Because the investor is lending the funds, he or she does not acquire either the opportunity to influence management decisions or the potential for gain that is possible with equities. On the other hand, there is generally less risk with debt securities, which are considered senior to equity in the case of company failure. Deposits, money market instruments, Canada Savings Bonds, mortgage-backed securities, and bonds and debentures promise regular interest payments and the return of the principal at some specified time. Capital gain or loss is a possibility with bonds and debentures if you trade them prior to maturity, but that is not the case with the other debt securities discussed in this chapter.

Canada Savings Bonds are very secure, liquid investments. They have more of the attributes of savings certificates than of bonds: that is, they do not trade on the bond market, they are redeemable at par at any time, they do not carry an interest rate that is fixed for the term, they are available in small denominations, and they are sold only to Canadian residents.

Key Terms

accrued interest (p. 277)	fully registered bond (p. 272)
at a discount (p. 276)	floating interest rate bond
at a premium (p. 276)	(p. 274)
bearer bond (p. 272)	money market (p. 266)
bond (p. 269)	money market fund (p. 268)
bond market (p. 275)	mortgage bond (p. 273)
bond redemption (p. 272)	mortgage-backed security
bond registered as to principal	(p. 269)
(p. 272)	par value (p. 270)
callable bond (p. 273)	retractable bond (p. 274)
Canada Premium Bonds (p. 280)	sinking fund (p. 274)
collateral trust bond (p. 273)	spread (p. 276)
commercial paper (p. 266)	strip bond (p. 278)
convertible bond (p. 273)	term deposit (p. 265)
coupon bond (p. 272)	tombstone (p. 275)
debenture (p. 270)	treasury bill (p. 267)
denomination (p. 272)	underwriter (p. 270)

Problems

1. On November 30, 2000 *FP Investing* reported the following information about interest rates:

   Canadian-Administered Rates

Bank of Canada	6.00
Prime	7.50

   Money Market Rates

3-month treasury bills	5.61
1-month commercial paper	6.51
2-month commercial paper	6.52
3-month commercial paper	6.59

   (a) Look in the financial section of a recent paper to find current interest rates, and update the above table.

(b) Why is the Bank Rate lower than the prime rate?

(c) Why is the rate higher on commercial paper than on treasury bills?

(d) Do the interest rates on commercial paper increase as the term increases? If not, why not?

(e) What is commercial paper, and who would buy and sell it?

(f) If you had $5000 to invest in the money market, would the interest rate quoted be the same as those above? Explain.

(g) How would you go about investing the $5000 in the money market?

2. Try to find a newspaper advertisement announcing a new bond issue. (These are usually found in the financial section, but they occur irregularly.) Otherwise, analyze the announcement in Figure 10.1.

Look for the following information in the advertisement:

(a) the name of the bond issuer,

(b) the name(s) of the underwriter(s),

(c) the offering price,

(d) the maturity date,

(e) the interest rate,

(f) any special features (for example, whether the bonds are callable, retractable, extendible, convertible, or none of these),

(g) the denominations available,

(h) the size of the issue (the amount to be borrowed).

3. Examine the following two bond quotations:

Issuer	Maturity	Coupon	Quote	Yield
Canada	1 Jun 2027	8.00	127.659	5.990
Suncor	7 Aug 2007	6.10	92.269	6.20

(a) Are these bonds selling at par, at a premium, or at a discount? Suggest the reasons why.

(b) What is the probable minimum denomination available in these bonds?

(c) Calculate the yield to maturity if you had purchased these bonds in 1997 at the quoted price on June 1 and August 7, respectively. How does your result compare with the published yield?

(d) Explain why the Canada bond has a lower yield to maturity than the Suncor bond does.

4. Assume that on March 24, 1997, you bought a $1000 Bell Canada 7 percent bond maturing 24 September 2027.

(a) How much accrued interest would you have paid?

(b) Will you get this interest back? If so, when?

(c) Why did you have to pay accrued interest?

(d) If you could buy this bond at a price of $106.472, how much capital loss would you suffer at maturity?

5. The following questions refer to Figure 10.3.

(a) How do dealers distinguish between the various issues of Canada bonds, only a few of which are listed here?

(b) Why is one Ontario Hydro bond quoted at 98.96 and another at 125.68?

(c) Suggest two reasons for the wide range of interest rates on these bonds.

(d) One Canada bond maturing May 01/02 has a coupon of 10 percent. A MstrCr (Mastercard) bond maturing a few months later on August 21/02 has a coupon of only 5.760. Can you suggest a reason for this?

FIGURE 10.3 EXCERPTS FROM BOND QUOTATIONS, NOVEMBER 29, 2000

Bonds

Benchmark issues, as designated by the Bank of Canada, are listed in boldface.
(N)—new benchmark, (O)—old benchmark   c—callable
Supplied by Securities Valuation Co. from RBC Dominion Securities Inc./International from Reuters

Canada

	Coupon	Mat. date	Bid $	Yld %
OMHC	6.00	Dec 1/98	100.63	5.30
OMHC	8.25	Aug 3/99	104.27	5.44
OMHC	8.50	Dec 1/99	105.47	5.49
OMHC	8.80	Mar 1/00	106.72	5.49
OMHC	8.20	Jun 30/00	106.10	5.57
OMHC	7.75	Dec 1/00	105.85	5.56
Canada	6.25	Feb 1/98	100.14	4.79
Canada c98	3.75	Mar 15/98	99.80	4.59
Canada c98	3.75	Mar 15/09	99.80	4.59
Canada (N)	**6.00**	**Mar 15/08**	**100.29**	**4.63**
Canada	10.75	Mar 15/98	101.35	4.61
Canada	6.50	Sep 1/98	100.92	5.11
Canada	9.50	Oct 1/98	103.22	5.17
Canada (N)	**8.00**	**Nov 1/98**	**102.28**	**5.23**
Canada	10.25	Dec 1/98	104.54	5.23
Canada	5.75	Mar 1/99	100.55	5.26
Canada	7.75	Sep 1/99	103.72	5.40
Canada	9.00	Oct 15/99	106.06	5.43
Canada	9.25	Dec 1/99	106.93	5.43
Canada	13.50	Dec 1/99	114.65	5.43
Canada	8.50	Mar 1/00	106.23	5.44
Canada	13.75	Mar 15/00	117.15	5.45
Canada	9.75	May 1/00	109.36	5.46
Canada	10.50	Jul 1/00	111.72	5.46
Canada	15.00	Jul 1/00	122.10	5.50
Canada (O)	**7.50**	**Sep 1/00**	**105.01**	**5.47**
Canada	11.50	Sep 1/00	114.84	5.48
Canada	9.75	Dec 15/00	111.45	5.53
Canada	15.75	Feb 1/01	128.95	5.48
Canada (N)	**7.50**	**Mar 1/01**	**105.81**	**5.48**
Canada	10.50	Mar 1/01	114.41	5.50
Canada	13.00	May 1/01	122.55	5.53
Canada	9.75	Jun 1/01	113.16	5.49
Canada	9.75	Jun 1/01	113.16	5.49
Canada	9.50	Oct 1/01	113.36	5.52
Canada	9.50	Oct 1/01	113.36	5.52
Canada	9.75	Dec 1/01	114.76	5.52
Canada	9.75	Dec 1/01	114.76	5.52
Canada	8.75	Feb 1/02	111.75	5.51
Canada	15.50	Mar 15/02	137.05	5.54
Canada	8.50	Apr 1/02	111.17	5.52
Canada	10.00	May 1/02	117.01	5.54
Canada	11.25	Dec 15/02	124.54	5.54
Canada	11.75	Feb 1/03	127.22	5.55
Canada	7.25	Jun 1/03	107.83	5.56
Canada	7.25	Jun 1/03	107.83	5.56
Canada	9.50	Oct 1/03	119.15	5.57
Canada	7.50	Dec 1/03	109.56	5.58
Canada	10.25	Feb 1/04	123.82	5.59
Canada	6.50	Jun 1/04	104.80	5.60
Canada	13.50	Jun 1/04	142.30	5.58
Canada	10.50	Oct 1/04	127.13	5.62
Canada	9.00	Dec 1/04	119.17	5.62
Canada	12.00	Mar 1/05	137.19	5.63
Canada	12.25	Sep 1/05	140.65	5.65
Canada (O)	**8.75**	**Dec 1/05**	**119.59**	**5.65**
Canada	12.50	Mar 1/06	144.20	5.67
Canada	14.00	Oct 1/06	156.65	5.70

Provincial

	Coupon	Mat. date	Bid $	Yld %
AGT	9.60	Jul 7/98	102.47	4.89
AGT	11.70	Nov 15/99	110.70	5.65
AGT c00	11.50	May 31/03	113.04	5.69
AGT	9.50	Aug 24/04	119.09	5.98
Alberta	7.75	Feb 4/98	100.31	4.84
Alberta	6.00	Mar 1/99	100.77	5.31
Alberta	8.50	Sep 1/99	104.78	5.48
Alberta	8.00	Mar 1/00	105.07	5.50
Alberta	9.25	Apr 1/00	106.93	5.93
Alberta	10.25	Aug 22/01	115.41	5.54
Alberta	6.37	Jun 1/04	103.75	5.67
Alta MF c00	12.25	Dec 15/02	117.61	5.73
B C Hydro c04	13.50	Jan 15/11	138.65	5.83
British Columb	8.25	Apr 9/98	100.94	4.90
British Columb	9.85	May 1/98	101.72	4.84
British Columb	7.00	Jun 9/99	102.20	5.41
British Columb	11.25	Aug 16/00	113.87	5.54
British Columb	9.75	May 15/01	145.32	6.23
British Columb	10.15	Aug 29/01	114.97	5.59
British Columb	10.15	Aug 29/01	114.97	5.59
British Columb	9.00	Jan 9/02	112.04	5.63
British Columb	9.00	Jun 21/04	117.70	5.70
British Columb	9.50	Jan 9/12	132.25	6.06
British Columb	10.60	Sep 5/20	153.45	6.18
British Columb	9.50	Jun 9/22	141.35	6.19
British Columb	8.75	Aug 19/22	131.75	6.21
Ont Hydro	10.00	Feb 10/98	100.65	4.82
Ont Hydro	7.25	Mar 31/98	100.63	4.79
Ont Hydro	10.37	Jun 16/98	102.57	4.87
Ont Hydro	10.25	Jul 12/98	102.86	4.91
Ont Hydro	9.62	Aug 3/99	106.34	5.45
Ont Hydro	9.37	Jan 31/00	107.61	5.49
Ont Hydro	11.20	Aug 8/00	113.60	5.56
Ont Hydro	10.00	Mar 19/01	112.79	5.61
Ont Hydro c99	17.00	Mar 3/02	113.17	5.41
Ont Hydro	9.00	Apr 16/02	112.55	5.67
Ont Hydro	9.00	Jun 24/02	112.96	5.69
Ont Hydro	9.00	Jun 24/02	112.96	5.69
Ont Hydro c00	12.50	Nov 30/02	117.87	5.79
Ont Hydro c01	13.50	May 1/03	123.30	5.75
Ont Hydro c01	14.25	Apr 21/06	125.35	5.75
Ont Hydro c01	10.25	Apr 4/09	113.14	5.78
Ont Hydro c05	10.50	Jan 15/10	126.23	5.90
Ont Hydro c03	13.37	Mar 25/10	133.53	5.86
Ont Hydro c03	13.25	May 14/10	134.16	5.78
Ont Hydro c04	13.00	Jan 29/11	135.70	5.93

Corporate

	Coupon	Mat. date	Bid $	Yld %
Alta Nat Gas	8.40	Jul 15/03	111.00	6.04
Avco Fin	8.75	Mar 15/00	105.98	5.84
Avenor +	10.85	Nov 30/14	129.46	7.71
B C Gas	11.80	Sep 30/00	156.22	6.44
B C Gas	8.50	Aug 26/02	110.48	5.90
B C Gas	8.50	Aug 26/02	110.48	5.90
B C Gas	8.15	Jul 28/03	109.93	6.03
Bell Can	8.95	Apr 1/02	111.45	5.87

	Coupon	Mat. date	Bid $	Yld %
Emco CV +	8.00	Dec 31/00	100.75	7.72
Emco CV +	7.25	Apr 30/02	99.00	1.00
Enfield CV +	8.00	Mar 31/02	96.50	1.00
Gaz Metro	11.75	Nov 15/05	125.71	7.39
Gaz Metro	10.75	Dec 15/06	130.77	6.22
Gaz Metro	10.45	Oct 31/16	142.98	6.47
Hammerson	10.25	Apr 1/02	114.87	6.22
Household EXT 01	11.35	Apr 16/01	115.88	5.98
I B M	10.90	Feb 15/00	131.11	7.04
ICG Util c01	10.62	Jul 14/06	107.38	8.48
IPL Energy c96	8.20	Feb 15/24	121.00	6.52
Imasco	10.50	Apr 28/98	101.78	5.13
Imasco	10.25	Dec 18/01	115.26	5.89
Imperial Oil	9.87	Dec 15/99	107.69	5.70
Inco	9.87	Jun 15/19	106.71	7.37
Inland Nat Gas	9.75	Dec 17/96	111.87	6.33
Inland Nat Gas	10.55	Jun 8/99	135.69	6.30
Inter-City Gas	10.75	Jun 31/09	127.04	7.26
Interhome c03	10.80	Apr 15/08	121.63	5.98
Interprov NW c96	13.40	Apr 1/04	104.10	11.42
Interprov NW c96	12.70	Nov 15/04	103.90	11.36
Investors Grou	10.65	Jun 15/99	106.80	5.77
Island Tel	11.45	Jul 20/08	123.19	6.86
K Mart +	11.40	Sep 22/98	103.48	6.57
Laurentian Bk	10.25	Jul 4/01	113.02	6.09
Loblaws	9.75	Sep 30/01	104.16	5.77
Loblaws	10.00	Mar 31/06	109.00	6.95
Loblaws c02	10.00	Apr 15/07	115.08	5.97
Mac Bld	10.12	Jan 23/02	113.48	6.32
Mac Bld CV +	5.00	May 1/07	82.50	7.65
Mar Rlty	10.30	Aug 10/99	105.53	6.65
Maritime Tel c00	10.95	Dec 15/05	114.32	6.28
Maritime Tel c01	10.25	Aug 1/06	106.82	8.49
Maritime Tel c06	10.45	Mar 1/13	127.31	6.23
N B Tel	10.37	Oct 16/99	107.80	5.76
N B Tel	10.00	Jun 15/02	116.03	5.87
N B Tel c01	10.00	Sept 16/06	111.26	6.80
N B Tel c06	11.12	Jul 19/13	133.11	6.18
NS. Power c97	9.45	Dec 1/02	105.65	1.41
NS. Power c00	13.50	Dec 1/02	120.61	5.77
NS. Power c98	9.37	Jan 10/03	100.18	5.27
NS. Power	7.70	Oct 15/03	108.05	6.03
NS. Power c01	12.50	Dec 20/03	123.54	5.80
NS. Power c02	12.12	Feb 14/05	122.67	5.87
NS. Power c00	11.50	Jul 15/05	113.20	5.87
NS. Power	10.87	Nov 15/12	146.21	6.10
NS. Power	11.25	Apr 27/14	151.88	6.16
NS. Power	10.25	Jan 10/20	146.17	6.33
National Bk c98	10.87	Jun 1/98	102.42	5.18
National Bk	10.50	Apr 5/01	113.41	5.93
National Trust	10.70	Oct 30/99	108.53	5.76
National Trust	11.60	Jul 4/01	117.94	5.89
Nfld Lt Pwr	10.55	Aug 1/14	141.38	6.45
Nfld Lt Pwr	10.12	Jun 15/22	142.32	6.61
Nfld Tel c01	9.75	May 6/06	104.90	8.24
Nfld Tel	11.40	Jul 5/10	143.26	6.34
Nfld Tel	10.75	Jun 12/14	142.97	6.47
Noranda CV +	5.00	Apr 30/07	92.00	6.14

SOURCE: *The National Post* November 29, 2000

6. Are these statements true or false?

(a) Canada Savings Bonds should be renamed because they are not really bonds.

(b) The tax on bond interest is less than the tax on stocks.

(c) The prices of bonds, unlike stocks, never change in value.

(d) GICs trade on the bond market.

(e) Only savings accounts are covered by deposit insurance.

(f) There is no actual exchange or building where the money market operates.

(g) T-bills have a high rate of interest because they are so risky.

(h) Small investors, as well as institutions, often buy T-bills.

(i) Stockbrokers are not allowed to sell mortgage-backed securities.

7. Explain why you must pay more than the face value if you buy a Canada Savings Bond by payroll deduction. Is this extra sum called interest? Can it be used as an income tax deduction?

8. Assume that you decide to redeem three $1 000 Canada Savings Bonds on March 1. You will receive the face value and accrued interest. These bonds are paying 5 percent interest at the moment. Calculate the amount of accrued interest you will receive.

9. Look at bond quotations in a recent newspaper.

(a) How do bond yields compare with the current rate on treasury bills?

(b) Are most bonds selling at a discount or at a premium? Why?

10. In 1997, Kase invested $5 000 in a compound series of Canada Savings Bonds. For income tax purposes, should he report interest on a receivable basis?

11. If you wanted to invest $5 000 in bonds, what special features would you want your bonds to have?

12. Why would a corporation issuing a bond be interested in callable bonds? In covertible bonds?

13. Why are bond certificates expected to soon become extinct? Will this move be of value to the financial services industry or the investor?

14. (a) Go to www.cbrs.com, the Canadian Bond Service/Standard & Poor Web site. Compare the credit rating of the following Canadian corporations: Air Canada, Alcan Aluminum, Bombardier, Hollinger Inc., and Talisman. Find out how these credit ratings were determined.

(b) Find out what CBRS means by A, A-, A-1, CreditWatch negative.

(c) At the time of writing, CBRS put out a very negative rating on forest industry giant Weyerhaeuser. Why did Weyerhaeuser receive this poor rating? What effect will a negative rating have if the company plans to issue a new bond? If Weyerhaeuser is no longer featured, find out why CBRS has a special rating on any highlighted company.

References

BOOKS AND ARTICLES

BOREHAM, GORDON F., and RONALD G. BODKIN. *Money, Banking and Finance: The Canadian Context*. Fourth Edition. Toronto: Dryden Canada/Holt, Rinehart and Winston, 1993. A respected survey of the field.

NEUFELD, E.P., ed. *Money and Banking in Canada*. Ottawa: Carleton University Press, 1964. One of the classic texts on these topics.

SIKLOS, PIERRE L. *Money, Banking and Financial Institutions: Canada in the Global Environment*. Toronto: McGraw-Hill Ryerson, 1997. Very relevant in view of the proposed Canadian bank mergers.

PERIODICALS

The Financial Post. Daily. Toronto: The National Post, 300 Don Mills Road, Don Mills, ON M3B 3R5. www.nationalpost.com. This is a very valuable source for financial and economic information.

Report on Business. Daily. Toronto: *The Globe and Mail*, 444 Front Street W., Toronto, M5V 2S9. Toll Free 1-800-461-3298. Toronto area 585-5500. www.globeandmail.com The ROB is a major source of financial information.

Personal Finance on the Web

The Bank of Canada
   www.bankofcanada.ca Gives current market rates and weekly financial statistics.

Bank of Montreal
   www.bmo.com

the BOND market a Canadian perspective.
   www.bondcan.com Access to some of their information is by subscription.

Canadian Bond Rating Service
   www.cbrs.com

Canada Trust
   www.canadatrust.com

Canadian Financial Network
   www.canadianfinance.com Provides access to valuable investment information and resources.

Canadian Imperial Bank of Commerce
   www.cibc.com/index.html

Canadian Western Bank
   www.cwbank.com

Dominion Bond Rating Services
   www.dbrs.com

eBOND
> **www.ebond.ca** Canada's on-line investment dealer for Canadian fixed-income securities.

Department of Finance
> **www.fin.gic.ca** Provides information of value to investors on the federal government's macroeconomic policies.

Fitch ICBA
> **www.dcro.com** A full-service bond rating agency.

Found Money International
> **www.foundmoney.com** Helps people to find the location of forgotten bank accounts.

Moody's Investors Services
> **www.moodys.com**

Royal Bank Financial Group
> **www.royalbank.com**

Scotiabank
> **www.scotiabank.ca**

Statistics Canada
> **www.statca.ca** Provides access to statistics of interest to investors but charges for most information.

Toronto-Dominion Bank
> **www.tdbank.ca**

11

Stocks and Mutual Funds

objectives

1. Understand the rewards of stock market investing.

2. Interpret stock quotations in the daily press.

3. Discuss the characteristics of common and preferred shares.

4. Understand the many terms associated with stock market investing.

5. Explain the features of the various kinds of mutual funds.

6. Discuss the pros and cons of mutual fund investing.

7. Understand the different tax treatment of interest, dividend, and capital gains income.

8. Understand the investment risk and the value of diversification as a means of reducing this risk.

Introduction

This chapter introduces you to the fascinating and sometimes confusing world of investing in stocks and mutual funds. You will learn how stocks are bought and sold, and about the differences between common and preferred shares. You will also learn about the many features and types of mutual funds. This chapter should help you understand articles in the financial press, books about investing, the many investment newsletters available, and other information you may encounter on the Internet or on television broadcasts about investing. You will not learn how to evaluate the quality of stocks and other types of investments: this complex subject is one that you must research on your own. Making wise decisions in this field depends on a number of constantly changing factors, including the economy's general health, the management of companies you might be interested in, events in the global economy, and the luck and skill of mutual fund managers.

Investing in the Stock Market

You should not invest in stocks if you cannot afford to lose the invested money. Investing in publicly traded shares is too uncertain an activity to risk money that you may need. While share prices generally rise over the long term, the investment world can sometimes be like a minefield to both the experienced and the novice investor. It has not been uncommon, for example, to see the book value of an individual's fortune wiped out because share prices declined drastically and unexpectedly within a just a few hours. Share prices have, of course, often rebounded just as dramatically. But such a rebound cannot be counted on: stock prices may remain depressed for long periods. As mentioned in Chapter 9, investing in stocks comes with no guarantee either of capital or of income. No one can predict when an event may occur in some remote corner of the world that may cause investors to panic. All investments come with risk. Stocks and mutual funds are no exception. But there are various degrees of risk. When investing, you should look for investments that match your own tolerance for risk.

Comparative Returns

Over the long term, stocks have proven a better hedge against inflation than have debt securities. For instance, between 1975 and 1992, when consumer prices increased an average of 6.7 percent a year, treasury bills paid 10.4 percent interest on average. This 3.7 percent real rate of return, less income tax, did not leave a great deal for the investor. During the same period, stocks in the Toronto Stock Exchange 300 Composite Index (often referred to simply as the "TSE Composite") produced an average annual return of 15.7 percent, which translated into an annual real return of 9 percent. Since income from stocks is taxed at a lower rate than is interest (as will be explained later in the chapter—see especially "The Dividend Tax Credit," under the heading "Income Tax"), the after-tax return on stocks was quite attractive. But this higher return was associated with more risk and more price volatility. The greater variability in the yield from common stocks compared to that from treasury bills is illustrated in Chapter 9, Figures 9.3 and 9.4.

Price Volatility

Even though stocks have been more profitable over the long term than debt securities have been, stocks' price fluctuations can be a drawback. Stock prices are affected by business cycles that may last for years. During a business cycle, business activity tends to expand and then contract, causing stock prices to move up and then down. It is normal for stock prices to fluctuate, but the result can be low liquidity for the investor, who cannot be sure of selling without a loss on any given day. But genuine investors (as opposed to speculators: see Chapter 9's "Investing Versus Speculating" section), view stocks as relatively long-term investments, carefully choosing when to buy and when to sell.

Need for Knowledge

To invest successfully in the stock market, you need to become reasonably well-informed. Two common problems arise when investors fail to understand price volatility and the breadth of choice within the stock market. Inexperienced investors may become pessimistic when stock prices are low and be reluctant to invest in the market. Conversely, rising prices lead to optimism; thus, these people often decide to buy just as the market reaches a high level. Later, when stock prices fall (as they invariably do), the inexperienced investor may panic and sell, vowing never to invest in the market again. Unfortunately, you cannot make money by buying high and selling low. These people have made the mistake of viewing stocks as short-term investments. Another difficulty arises for those with limited knowledge of investment alternatives. They may feel that their choices are restricted either to depositing their funds in safe, low-yielding debt securities (see Chapter 10) or to speculating in the stock market. They fail to realize that many intermediate possibilities exist.

Stock Analysis

The major concerns of all investors are the direction of stock exchange indices and the performance of the individual stocks in their portfolios. In order to determine the latter, investment analysts have devised a number of different methods. One method, **quantitative analysis,** is based on information included in a company's financial statements. Another, **qualitative analysis**, is much more subjective and looks at such things as the skill of top managers. A third, **technical analysis**, looks at past performance of a stock in conjunction with overall market performance in order to try to detect a recurring pattern.

A major component of the TSE 300 is Nortel Networks. Recently, its every move has caused great fluctuations in the 300 index. Following are analyses of Nortel using the above methods:

Quantitative:

	1999	2000E	2001E	2002E
Earnings Per Share	$0.52	$0.72	$0.95	$1.14
Price/Earnings		50.0x	38.6x	32.2x
Rev ($mm)	$21 287	$30 230	$39 900	$47 880

Nortel issued a press release following a recent drop in its share price saying that revenue forecasts were on target. This forecast was revised downward by the company in February, 2001. The negative news caused a major drop in the price of the stock as well as the TSE 300. The analyst's conclusion is: no change in the market perform rating. The stock is viewed as a long-term hold. Price declines are seen as buying opportunities.

Qualitative:
We have the utmost trust in Nortel management. It has built the company into an industry leader. Nortel shares are a hold and any decline in price is considered a buying opportunity.

Technical:

A technical analyst's report in July 2000, based on historic support and resistance levels, had an upside target for the stock in the $145 to $165 range over the next three to six months. The price at the time was $117.50. A drop in price to $105 was considered a buying opportunity. The analyst also recommended selling the stock if it reached $101.85. In the first week of January 2001 it had fallen to $49.30.

Stock Trading

Stock Exchange

A **stock exchange** is an organized marketplace for buying and selling shares in corporations. Businesses that require working capital can obtain it by selling shares to investors—who, by purchasing the shares, become part owners of the corporation. Companies that have undergone this process are called publicly owned corporations. A new offering of shares may be put on the market when a business is new or whenever the company requires additional capital. After the new offering has been sold, the shares usually begin trading in the secondary market, where they change owners frequently. Investors cannot sell their shares back to the corporation whenever they wish. For instance, if you own some Canadian Pacific shares and you no longer wish to keep them, you must find a buyer for them. Stockbrokers and stock exchanges exist to link would-be sellers and would-be buyers of securities, and to facilitate transactions between them.

Stocks may be traded either at stock exchanges or on the **over-the-counter market,** which is not a physical place but rather a communication system. Generally, stocks that do not meet the listing requirements for a major stock exchange (referred to as unlisted stocks) are traded on the over-the-counter market. On the stock exchange, only members can execute orders for clients. Each member of an exchange has purchased one of a limited number of seats or member trading permits that entitle their owners to trade securities that are listed on that exchange. A firm of investment dealers that wishes to trade on a certain stock exchange must either purchase one of these seats or work through a dealer who owns one.

The advent of computer technologies has brought about a move toward electronic selling through a communication system rather than requiring that representatives of buyers and sellers be physically present on the "floor" of an exchange (the place where trading takes place). The Toronto, Venture, and Montreal Stock Exchanges have already converted to computerized trading, whereas the New York Stock Exchange still prefers traditional floor trading. If the exchange is computerized, the order to buy shares is handled by traders in offices, who can see bids and ask quotations on their computer screens, and can then execute a trade by touching a button.

Another victim of the computer is the share certificate. In the past, anyone who purchased shares received an elaborately engraved certificate of share ownership in the mail. While this is still possible for those who wish to have them, the vast majority of shares are now held in **street form.** This means that all the shares owned by a securities dealer's clients are registered in the dealer's name, and the dealer keeps a record for each client in its computer. This approach is more convenient both for the investment dealer and for the dealer's clients. Now, when a client wishes to sell some shares, no certificate needs to be signed over to the dealer. Instead, the shares are transferred from dealer to dealer via the computer—or simply from one file to another file if both clients use the same dealer. (See Personal Finance in Action Box 11.1, "Capital Versus Preferred Shares.")

Whether a trade is executed on the exchange floor or electronically, information about the transaction is transmitted immediately to the stock exchange's computer, which makes

Common Versus Preferred Shares

Dag learned from his broker that her firm was creating a new company to invest in a portfolio of resource company shares. This new company would issue both common and preferred shares. The former would pay a low dividend but have the potential for consider- able capital appreciation. The preferred shares would pay a dividend of over 5 percent but have little potential for growth. Dag decided to buy some of both shares since she liked the idea of combining growth with income.

it widely available across the nation and the world. Details of the trade are quickly sent to the investor's broker, who in turn can inform the client of the results. All this activity may be accomplished within just a few minutes. After an order has been executed, the client has three business days to pay for the shares.

Trading Quantities

Just as "one dozen" is the basic unit for buying eggs, shares can be purchased in convenient quan- tities known as **board lots.** Board lots make trading easier, because it is more difficult to match buy and sell orders for odd numbers of shares. The number in a board lot is related to the share price, as shown below, but most shares are priced to sell in board lots of 100.

Price of Shares	Number in a Board Lot
Under 10 cents	1000
From 10 to 99 cents	500
From $1 to under $99	100
$100 and over	10

When fewer shares than a board lot are traded, they are referred to as an **odd lot.** Since it is more difficult to find buyers or sellers for odd lots, the price may be somewhat higher or the trade less quickly executed than for board lots.

Kinds of Orders

Various kinds of orders may be placed with a broker. A **market order** is executed immediately at the best available price. Any order without a specific price is handled as a market order; the trader is responsible for getting the best price. An **open order** specifies a price; the order then remains open until it is either executed (because the share price reached the specified amount) or cancelled. If you want to buy a specific stock, but only if its price falls to a certain level, you give your broker an open order, which will be executed only if and when that price is reached. A **stop loss order** works in reverse, giving your broker the authority to sell your shares if their price falls to a named level. A stop loss order is used to ensure that the shares will be sold at a set price should prices fall, but makes it unnecessary to sell if the price keeps rising.

Stockbrokers

Stockbrokers—or registered representatives, as they are often called—may be classified as ei- ther full-service brokers or discount brokers. **Full-service brokers** charge higher commission

Janine and Her On-line Broker

Until recently, Janine used a full-service broker. She realized, after talking with her girlfriend, that her commissions were quite high. A seasoned investor, who followed the market closely, she decided to deal with her broker on-line. Realizing that the demand for natural gas was very high, she purchased 300 shares of BC Gas. The transaction cost was determined as follows:

Buy 300 shares BC Gas	
@ $30.00	$9 000.00
Commission	30.00
Total	$9 030.00

Janine was pleased with herself. With her full-service broker the commission would have been over $300.

rates, but also offer advice, research reports on companies, and other information. By contrast, **discount brokers** charge less than full-service brokers do but may offer very little, if any, information. An increasing number of Canadians now trade on-line through a discount broker. See Personal Finance in Action Box 11.2, "Janine and Her On-line Broker."

Stockbrokers charge a commission for arranging either a sale or a purchase of securities. Each firm sets its own fee schedule, usually on a sliding scale, with lower rates for larger orders. If you plan to place a small order, you should inquire about the minimum commission charge, which are about $50.

Transactions involving large sums of money are carried out by verbal agreement, depending solely on trust. The client simply telephones an order to the broker, who then executes it. Consequently, a broker will not conduct business for a client until an account has been opened. Doing so usually involves a meeting between the client and the broker to discuss the investor's objectives and financial status. The broker may also check with the credit bureau (see Chapter 14) to verify the client's creditworthiness.

Stock Quotations

Considerable information about the previous day's stock trades appears in the financial press. Stock quotations give the price range within which the stock traded, the share price at the closing of the exchange, and how many shares traded. In addition, the stock's high and low prices for the past year and the amount of the most recent dividend are usually included. (The income from a stock is known as a **dividend**.) Some newspapers provide even more information in their weekly summaries. Newspapers differ somewhat in the way they present stock quotations; see the box "Reading Stock Quotations" for a representative example. Some newspapers quote bid and ask prices. The **bid price** is what a buyer is willing to pay, and the **ask price** is what the seller is willing to accept. Unless buyer and seller can reach an agreement, there will be no transaction. Stock prices are quoted in dollar amounts, except in the case of those that are trading for less than $5: these are quoted in cents. Those with prices around $3 or less are often referred to as **penny stocks.**

Stock Exchange Indices

Every day, some stocks go up while others fall. The overall behaviour of the market can be learned by watching the performance of a **stock exchange index**. Such an index is a statistical

Reading Stock Quotations

On July 25, 1998, Royal Bank common stock
was quoted in the *Globe and Mail*'s "Report
on Business" section as follows:

52-week								
high	low	Stock	Sym.	Div	Hi/bid	Lo/ask	Chg	Vol(h)
92.20	60.85	Royal Bank	RY	1.84	86.80	85.00	-0.10	8 873

Reading from left to right, this quotation
means that over the previous 52 weeks, common shares of the Royal Bank of Canada have
traded at prices ranging from a high of $92.20
to a low of $60.85 per share. The company is
referred to in the stock quotation pages by the
short form "RY." The stock currently pays a
dividend of $1.84 per share per year. On the
previous day (July 24, 1998), these shares
traded at prices ranging between $86.80 and
$85.00; at the close of trading, they were down
$0.10 (i.e., 10 cents) from the previous day's
closing price. A total of 88 730 Royal Bank
shares were traded on the day in question.

measurement of the percentage change in the prices of a select group of common stocks.
Changes in an index give an indication of the overall performance of the stock market and how
investors in general feel.

There are many stock indices. The Toronto Stock Exchange has seven. The most widely followed is the TSE 300, which tracks the performance of Canada's 300 largest publicly traded companies. It contains 14 groups and 41 sub-groups, which represent the major sectors of the
economy. A graph showing recent changes in the TSE 300 is included in the business section of most newspapers. (See Figure 11.1.)

The value of the TSE 300 Index on a particular day is calculated using the following formula:

$$\text{Index value} = \frac{\text{Aggregate Quoted Market Value}}{\text{Base Value}} \times 1\ 000$$

The **Aggregate Quoted Market Value** = Current market price × total shares − control
blocks. QMV is available from the TSE at marketdata@tse.com.

The **Base Value** = $38.002.1 million which is the Aggregate Quoted Market Value Weighted
Average for 1975.↓

↓TSE MARKET MATTERS, August 1985.

The TSE 100 includes 100 of the largest and most liquid of the TSE 300 companies. The
TSE 200 represents the 200 smaller companies in the TSE 300. The TSE 35 is made up of
Canada's largest companies. To be included, companies must first be in the TSE 300. In addition,
there are now three indices associated with Standard & Poor's, the large U.S financial services company. The S&P 60 includes 60 companies from the TSE 300 which cover all TSE 300
sub-groups such as financials, utilities, and communications services. The S&P Canadian

FIGURE 11.1 TORONTO STOCK EXCHANGE 300 COMPOSITE INDEX, MONTHLY CLOSE, DECEMBER 1999–NOVEMBER 2000

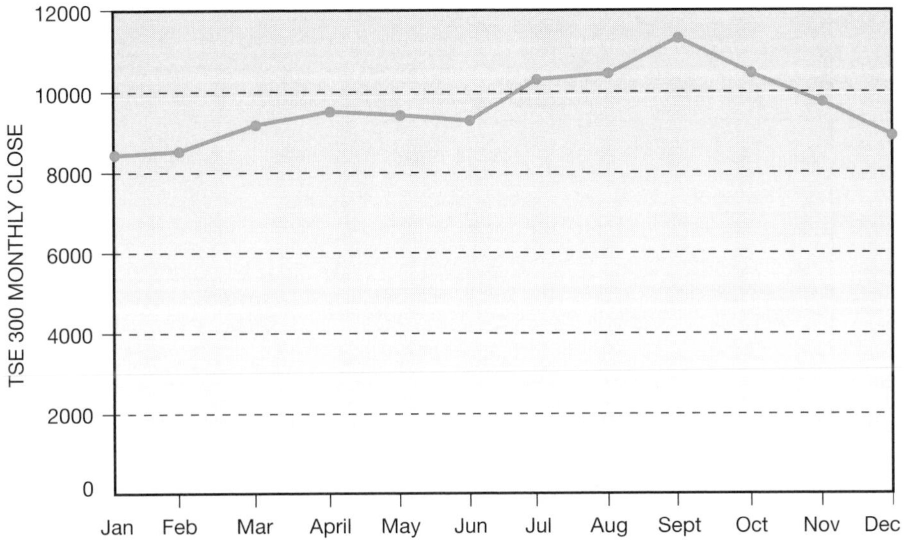

SOURCE: Nesbitt Burns Quantitative Research.

Small-Cap Index is made up of the smallest companies in each sector of the TSE 300. The S&P Mid-Cap Index tracks 60 highly liquid stocks.

The DJIA is the world's most-watched stock market index. Several others—for example, the Standard and Poor's 500—are also popular, but the Dow symbolizes stock trading for investors globally. The 30 stocks that make up the DJIA include some of the largest and most successful U.S. companies: names like Coca-Cola, Walt Disney Co., Exxon, and GE are recognized worldwide.

Fluctuations in the DJIA can be misleading. Since the average is calculated by adding the prices of the 30 stocks and then dividing that sum (usually by 4), the more expensive stocks receive a higher weighting. With so few stocks in the index, dramatic fluctuations occasionally occur. A major change in a heavily weighted stock can skew the average, affecting it far more than changes in the broader market really warrant. On the other hand, the Dow may underperform the market as a whole, since it comprises only "blue chip" stocks, which are usually less volatile than others.

The TSE Composite Index, like all stock indices, fluctuates frequently. This is more obvious if a shorter period is covered than the one in Figure 11.2. As this graph shows, though, over a long period the stock market generally rises. As can be seen, "bear markets" (the common term for markets in which price trends are travelling downward over a considerable period; the opposite situation is called a "bull market") eventually recover. The message for investors therefore seems clear: do not be overly concerned by periodic bear markets. The best advice from some of the world's most successful investors is to buy and hold. Since nobody can consistently outguess the market, your wisest approach is to become fully invested and then to ignore the periodic declines in the stock market indices. Over the long term, your investments will gain as the entire market rises.

FIGURE 11.2 TORONTO STOCK EXCHANGE 300 COMPOSITE INDEX, YEARLY CLOSE, 1925–2000

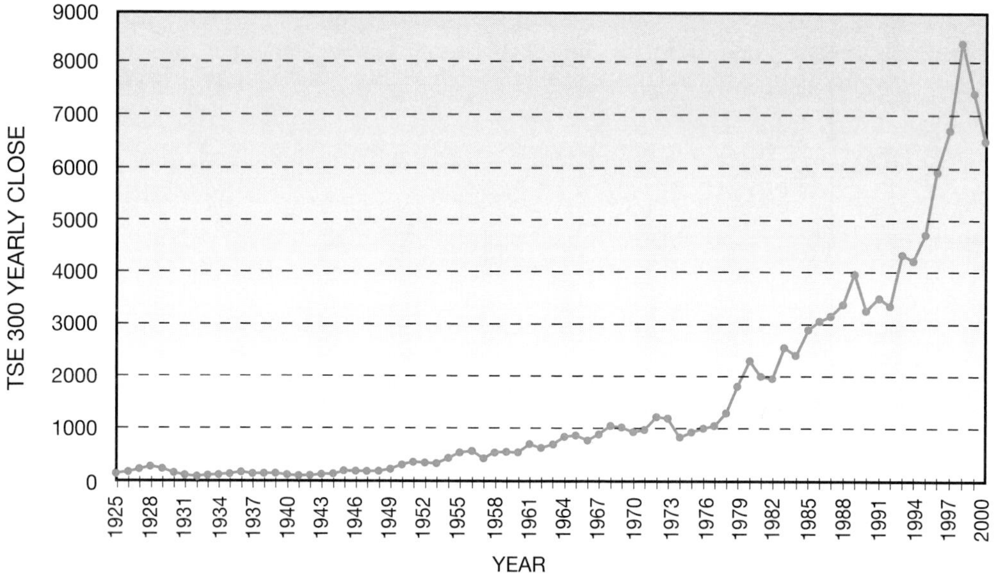

SOURCE: Nesbitt Burns Quantitative Research.

Day Traders

Changes in technology, combined with rapid increases in the prices of technology shares, have resulted in a new breed of investor, the **day trader**. Day traders profit from rapid fluctuations in the stock market during the day. Like other investors try to do, day traders buy when stock prices are low and sell when the prices rise. They can also make money by selling short when the market falls. Unlike other investors, however, day traders close or sell all positions by the end of the day. This can be done in a split second on the Internet. With the rapid rise in the prices of tech stocks like the **dot-coms** in 1999-2000, many day traders made a great deal of money. Such behaviour, it should be noted, is extremely risky because stock market volatility can be dramatic and unpredictable and prices can drop just as quickly as they can rise. No one should use money he or she needs in order to become a day trader. Each successful trade also results in a capital gain and therefore an increase in income tax.

Common Shares

Corporations, especially large ones, often have many owners who provide capital for the business. These owners, or shareholders, may hold either common or preferred shares. Common shareholders take a greater risk; their investment may gain or lose more than that of preferred shareholders. Owners of preferred shares usually accept a smaller voice in the management of the enterprise in exchange for greater safety of principal and assurance of income. The characteristics of common shares will be examined first.

Characteristics of Common Shares

An investment in common stock has two attributes that differentiate it from a debt security: (i) equity (ownership), with its associated rights, and (ii) uncertainty of return. **Common shareholders** become part owners in a corporation. As such, they enjoy certain rights, which include the following:

(a) a vote at annual meetings,

(b) an opportunity to share in the company's profit (dividends or capital gain),

(c) regular financial statements from the company,

(d) a claim on the company's assets in case of dissolution.

Today, quarterly statements and press releases, which were traditionally mailed to all shareholders, are sent only to those who request them; this approach helps with cost control (always a concern, since lowering a firm's costs contributes to increasing its profitability). Shareholders must notify the company each year if they wish to remain on the mailing list. Most companies will now send statements electronically if you prefer. All publicly owned corporations also post their financial reports and other related information on the Internet for the perusal of shareholders and other interested persons, who can print out and keep the information they find most useful. Quarterly reports are also usually published in the press.

Most voting at annual meetings is done by proxy, since relatively few shareholders attend in person. Traditionally, proxies were sent in by mail. Now, in both Canada and the United States, shareholders may register their votes either by mail or by telephone. The convenient, efficient Toll-Free Telephone Proxy Voting Service has proven very popular with shareholders.

Some companies offer several types of common shares. These may be designated Class A or Class B. Holders of Class B shares typically have fewer rights. They may not have voting rights at all, or they may be allowed to vote only in certain circumstances. Such shares may not be distinguishable from normal shares in the newspaper, but an investment dealer can identify them for you.

Buying common stock represents a decision to give up some measure of safety in favour of prospects for greater return. As mentioned earlier, an equity investment carries neither a promise that your capital will be returned to you nor a guarantee that your investment will earn income. When a company does well, its shareholders benefit; but when it does poorly, some or all of each shareholder's investment can be lost. Fortunately, a shareholder has a limited liability for the corporation's losses: if the firm goes bankrupt, each shareholder's maximum loss is limited to the funds that he or she has invested.

Rights and Warrants

Sometimes shareholders are offered **rights,** which are privileges that allow them to buy additional shares directly from the company. Rights can be an effective way for a firm to raise more capital while also offering the shareholder the chance to obtain more shares (often at a price below what is being paid on the open market) without paying commission. The recipient of rights has the choice either of exercising them to buy more shares or of selling the rights on the market. There is usually a short period during which rights may be exercised before they expire and become valueless (see Personal Finance in Action Box 11.3, "A Rights Offer").

The term **warrant** has more than one application: most commonly, it refers to a certificate that can be attached to bonds and to new issues of common or preferred shares to make

Personal Finance in Action 11.3

A Rights Offer

Acme Corporation has been cleared for a rights offering to shareholders of record July 28 on the basis of one right for each share held. Five rights and $2.25 will be needed to purchase three additional shares. The offer expires August 25.

Personal Finance in Action 11.4

Managed Money

Hans is a retired mining engineer. Prior to the collapse of Bre-X in the 1990s, he made a lot of money investing in mines around the world. Now 75, he no longer wants to manage his investments himself and decides to open an equity WRAP account. He understands the benefits of owning equities for both income and capital gains, even for someone of his age. His father was still alive at 102. He puts $1.5 million in the account for an annual fee of 1.5 percent. For this fee he gets unlimited trades and exceptional advice.

them more appealing to investors. A warrant allows the owner to buy shares of the issuing company at a set price within a specified period of time (see Personal Finance in Action Box 11.4, "Managed Money"). Warrants do not usually expire as quickly as rights; but like rights, they may be detached and sold separately.

Personal Finance in Action Boxes 11.3, "A Rights Offer," and 11.4, "Managed Money" illustrate that rights and warrants are similar in some ways. Both arrangements, for example, offer the holder the opportunity to buy shares from the company under certain conditions. But whereas rights may be offered to existing shareholders with a limited time to exercise them, warrants tend to be attached to new issues of bonds or stocks and do not expire as quickly. Since warrants cost less than shares do, an investor can buy warrants as an inexpensive way to make a capital gain (see Personal Finance in Action Box 11.5, "Buying Warrants"). If the underlying stock rises in price, so will the warrants; the warrants can then be sold at a profit.

Personal Finance in Action 11.5

Buying Warrants

Joe thinks he should invest in the Zenith Pipe Line company. Currently the firm's common shares are trading at $19.00, while its warrants are at $3.40. Each warrant gives its holder the right to purchase one common share at $19.25 before July 25, 2005, when the warrants will expire. Joe is prepared to forgo the dividends he would receive as a Zenith common shareholder in expectation of capital gain from this small investment in warrants. If the common shares' price rises, the warrants will also increase in price. Joe can then make a capital gain by selling the warrants without exercising them. But if Zenith prices fail to rise above $19.25 before the warrants expire, Joe will lose his investment.

Stock Splits

Corporations sometimes split their stock: that is, they offer several shares in exchange for each existing share. For example, when Bank of Nova Scotia common shares were trading at around $70, the bank's board of directors decided to split the stock on a two-for-one basis. A shareholder who previously owned 200 shares therefore became the owner of 400 shares, each of which was now trading at around $35. The new lower price made the stock more attractive to investors: instead of paying $7000 to buy a board lot of 100 shares, they needed only to come up with a more manageable $3500. Essentially, by doubling the number of outstanding shares, the bank increased the possibility that its shares would be more widely held.

Preferred Shares

Characteristics of Preferred Shares

In addition to common stock, companies often issue a class of shares called **preferred shares,** which represent limited ownership in a corporation. Investors may choose preferred shares over common shares because the former involve lower risk and greater assurance of income. (In recent years, however, the number of preferred issues has decreased. Such offerings are more expensive for a company, because the dividends paid are not treated as a tax-deductible expense.) Because such a broad spectrum of both common and preferred shares exists, it is possible to find common shares that are less risky than some preferred shares. Nevertheless, if the company prospers, its common shares typically rise in price more than its preferred shares do. Most preferred shares promise a certain rate of return—in contrast to common shares, which have no set dividend rate. Issues of preferred shares can vary considerably, but in general their characteristics may be summarized as follows:

(a) part ownership in the company,

(b) no voting rights,

(c) a set dividend rate,

(d) a risk level that is lower than that of the company's common shares.

When a company experiences financial difficulties, its first obligation is to pay interest on its bonds; second, it must pay dividends on any preferred shares. Only then can dividends be declared on the common shares. This arrangement puts the security of preferred shareholders midway between that of bondholders and that of common shareholders. Investors will regard any company that does not pay dividends on its preferred shares with disfavour. If a company closes down, bondholders (who are creditors, not owners) have claims on assets that take precedence over those of both preferred and common shareholders.

Special Features

Issues of preferred shares often carry features that are intended to attract investors. Preferred shares may be cumulative, redeemable, retractable, or convertible.

CUMULATIVE Most Canadian preferred shares are **cumulative preferred shares,** meaning that if the company does not pay the dividends that are due each quarter, the unpaid dividends accumulate in arrears. All arrears of cumulative preferred shares must be paid before any common dividends are paid. Whenever the company's financial condition improves, dividends in arrears are paid to the current shareholders without any interest for the period they were in arrears. In stock quotations, companies with dividends in arrears are shown with an "r" or some equivalent designation. The existence of unpaid dividends usually causes the shares' market price to drop.

Dividends on non-cumulative preferred shares are not paid automatically, instead, these must be "declared" each quarter by the board of directors. If the board decides not to declare a dividend in some particular quarter, the shareholder has no future claim.

REDEEMABLE **Redeemable** or **callable preferred shares** give the issuer the right to redeem them at a future date. Like callable bonds, redeemable preferred shares may be called in by the company at its discretion, usually at a price slightly higher than the par value.

Sometimes redeemable preferred shares come with a **purchase fund** (also known as a **sinking fund**) included in their terms. Under such an arrangement, the company agrees to buy or redeem a certain number of preferred shares in the market if the trading price reaches or drops below a specified level. If the fund cannot buy enough shares, no redemption takes place.

RETRACTABLE If the shareholder has the right to sell the shares back to the company at a specific date, those shares are called **retractable preferred shares.** The option to exercise this privilege belongs to the shareholder. This contrasts with the redeemability feature, under which only the issuing company has the right to call in shares.

CONVERTIBLE **Convertible preferred shares** give the investor the option of converting the shares into other stock of the company—often common stock—at a specified price and within a certain period. The shareholder thus has the opportunity to decide at a later date which type of stock—common or preferred—will be more beneficial to hold.

A New Issue of BCE Inc. Preferred Shares

Issued in December 1997, these shares came with the following features:

Cumulative, with a par value of $25.

Dividends of $1.15 per share per year, to be paid quarterly on the first day of March, June, September, and December, with the first dividend in the amount of 0.23 payable, if declared, on March 1, 1998. From that point forward, shareholders will be entitled to floating, adjustable, cumulative cash dividends, which will accrue beginning December 1, 2002, and be payable on the 12th of each month beginning in January 2003. The dividend will float in relation to changes in the prime rate.

Redeemable at the company's option at $25 per share plus any accrued and unpaid dividends on December 1, 2002. From that date forward, the company may redeem the shares at any time for cash at $25.50 plus accrued and unpaid dividends.

Convertible into CR First Pfd Series Z shares (that is, into another class of shares) of BCE Inc. on December 1, 2002, and thereafter every five years.

Investment Return

Investors in the stock market expect a return on their capital in one or more forms: cash dividends, stock dividends, or capital gain. The return from ownership of common shares will be examined first; then we will look at that of preferred shares.

Common Share Dividends

Unlike interest on debt securities, common stock dividends are neither promised in advance nor paid automatically. The corporation's board of directors decides whether a dividend will be paid, when it will be paid, and how large the dividend will be. As may be expected, the amount paid out in dividends varies with the company's profitability. At times, the directors may decide not to declare any dividend at all, because of (i) low profits in the past quarter, (ii) a decision to invest most of the profits back into the business, or (iii) the need to conserve cash flow. When dividends are declared, they are usually paid every quarter.

Some companies—particularly younger, more growth-oriented firms—do not issue dividends. Instead, they reinvest any earnings in the company, with a view to helping it grow. Growth companies exist in a broad range of industries. Some companies that adopt this approach are resource-based firms like Pangea Goldfields, a Toronto company that explores for and develops gold mines in Canada, South America, and Africa. Others, like Vancouver's QLT PhotoTherapeutics, may be involved in research in science and technology (QLT is developing light-activated drugs to be used in the treatment of cancer). Shares in these and other young companies are more speculative, and therefore riskier, than are shares in more established, dividend-paying companies. They are purchased for the prospect of capital gains, rather than for any current income they might provide.

Since common shares are continually trading, there must be a way to determine who is entitled to receive a dividend cheque. Whenever a dividend is declared, a record date is set to determine ownership. For instance, notices often appear in the financial press stating that a dividend will be paid to **shareholders of record,** or those who owned shares at the close of business, as of a certain date (see Personal Finance in Action Box 11.6, "Dividend Notice"). This date may be set two weeks before the payment date, thereby giving the company time to prepare dividend cheques. During this two-week interval, the stock will continue to trade, but the corporation will send dividends only to those who were shareholders on the dividend record date.

Personal Finance in Action 11.6

Dividend Notice

The board of directors of ABC Corporation has declared the following dividends, payable on December 2, to the company's shareholders of record as at the close of business on October 31:

Class A common shares	10 cents per share
Class B common shares	12.5 cents per share

By Order of the Board
John A. Doe, Secretary
Dated this 17th day of October.

The stock exchange sets a date, known as the ex-dividend date, on or after which the stock sells **ex-dividend,** or without a dividend for that quarter. During this time, the shares' sellers, not its buyers, receive the dividend. For example, if you purchase 100 shares of Noranda that are trading ex-dividend, you would not receive the next dividend; the shares' seller would. From the buyer's viewpoint, the advantage of ex-dividend shares is that they cost less than usual: the price of a share drops right after a dividend is paid, since there will be no further dividends for at least three months.

STOCK DIVIDENDS Instead of cash dividends, companies may offer shareholders new shares in the company, known as **stock dividends.** Such new shares are allotted in proportion to the number of shares already held by each shareholder. Recipients of stock dividends may add them to the shares already owned or sell them on the market. The tax treatment of stock dividends is the same as that of cash dividends.

AUTOMATIC DIVIDEND REINVESTMENT PLANS Some major companies have **automatic dividend reinvestment plans,** known as **DRIPs,** whereby dividends are not paid in cash but instead are reinvested in more of the firm's stock. This can be arranged directly with the company, without a broker's assistance. One advantage for the investor is not having to pay commission on the new shares; another is the possibility of purchasing new shares below the current market price. Such plans are not only a useful way to increase net worth with little effort; they are also a disciplined way of reinvesting dividend income, rather than spending it.

Preferred Share Dividends

Investors who buy a new issue of preferred shares pay the face or **par value.** After the initial offering has been sold, the shares trade in the market, where the price may fluctuate. Preferred share dividends are expressed either as a percentage of the par value or as a specified amount per share.

Interest rates declined so dramatically in the 1990s that it was not uncommon to see preferred shares issued at $20 and yielding 10 percent selling for much higher than their face value. Investors were willing to pay a premium for the high interest rate. When rates decline in this fashion, companies often redeem their high-yielding shares; they can then raise more money if necessary by offering new issues at lower yields.

Preferred shares are identified in newspaper stock quotations by the letters "pf" or "PR." For example, Bell Canada's preferred ("p") shares are labelled "BCEpfP" in one newspaper and "BCE.PR.P" in another. Despite the different labels they're using, both newspapers are referring to the same stock.

Further evidence that these are preferred shares can be found by looking at the dividend yields, which are higher for preferred shares than for common shares.

Capital Gains

Most investors in common stock are looking for capital gains (also known as capital appreciation) in addition to dividends—or, in the case of growth stocks, in lieu of dividends. They hope ultimately to sell each share at a higher price than they originally paid for it, but they must also face the possibility of a capital loss. Capital gain (loss) is calculated as follows:

$$\text{Total receipts from sale} - \left(\text{selling commission} + \text{purchase cost} \right) = \text{capital gain (loss)}$$

The term **growth stocks** is usually applied to shares from companies that are thought to have very good prospects for increasing their business and thus their profits. As mentioned above, under "Common Share Dividends," growth companies tend to invest any profits back into the business instead of paying large dividends to shareholders. Investors who choose growth stocks are hoping that the shares' price will eventually rise, so that they can make a capital gain. If you want current income and low or moderate risk, do not choose growth stocks.

Investment Funds

Some people experience two obstacles to investing in the stock market. One is the management effort required. The other is the impossibility of achieving an appropriate level of diversity within a small portfolio. One solution to both problems involves investing in pooled funds, known collectively as **investment funds.** Such funds gather together the moneys of many investors; investment fund companies then, in turn, hire professional managers to invest the pooled funds in a portfolio comprising many securities. Each investor acquires units in the investment fund, rather than shares in the individual companies whose securities make up the fund's portfolio (see Figure 11.3). The fund itself owns the shares it buys on its unitholders' behalf. The investor pays fees to the investment funds company to make the investment decisions; in return, the investor receives whatever interest, dividends, or capital gain the securities held by the fund collectively earn.

FIGURE 11.3 BUYING AN INVESTMENT FUND

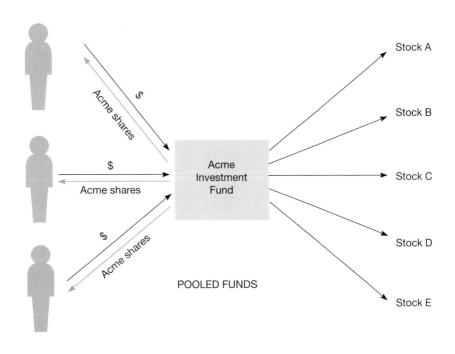

INVESTORS

FUND PORTFOLIO

Closed-End and Open-End Funds

Investment funds fall into one of two classes:(i) closed-end funds, or (ii) open-end funds (see Figure 11.4). **Closed-end investment funds** issue a fixed number of units. After the initial offering, anyone who wishes to invest in a closed-end fund must find someone who has units to sell. At the time of writing, the units of 17 closed-end funds, such as the United Corporation were trading on the TSE and were listed in the daily stock quotations of the financial press. A few others, such as the Altamira Closed End Fund, were listed with the mutual funds, under the subheading "Canadian Mutual Funds—Other Funds" or some equivalent. You will pay the usual broker's commission[1] if you buy or sell a closed-end fund, but you will not need to pay any entry or exit fees, as you would with open-end funds. Management fees for closed-end funds also tend to be less than those of open-end funds, since the latter spend more on marketing.

Open-end investment funds, commonly known as **mutual funds,** are much more numerous than closed-end funds. These funds do not have a fixed number of units; they will accept as much money as investors wish to put into them. Therefore, the total assets in a mutual fund portfolio are constantly changing; thus, such funds are referred to as open-ended. Investors buy units directly from the mutual funds company, which usually promises to redeem them at any time. Mutual funds differ from closed-end funds and from both common and preferred stock in that mutual fund units are never sold to one investor by another investor. A mutual fund, then, is an ever-changing common pool of funds that belongs to many investors, who have arranged for professional managers to invest in a portfolio on their behalf.

FIGURE 11.4 CLOSED-END AND OPEN-END FUNDS

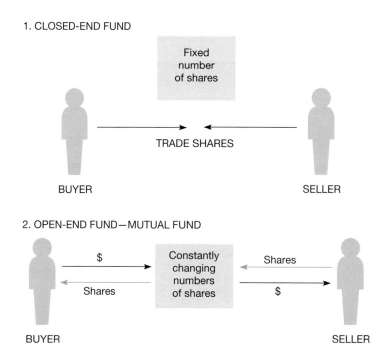

---

[1]The commission charged by today's brokers is quite flexible: it depends on such factors as the number and value of the shares, as well as the amount of advice and help given to the client.

Net Asset Value per Share

The value of an investment fund's individual shares, which is called the **net asset value per share** (NAVPS), is based on the net worth of the fund's total portfolio on any given date. The NAVPS is calculated by subtracting liabilities and management costs from the estimated value of the total portfolio, and then dividing the answer by the number of outstanding units. The calculation is as follows:

$$\text{Net asset value of portfolio} = \text{Total fund value of portfolio} - \left(\text{Liabilities} + \text{Management charges} \right)$$

$$\text{Net asset value per share} = \frac{\text{Net asset value of portfolio}}{\text{Total number of shares outstanding}}$$

The net asset value per share of a mutual fund is determined frequently (daily for most funds, but weekly or quarterly in some cases) and published regularly in the financial papers. While mutual funds are bought and sold at their NAVPS, closed-end funds trade on the stock market at prices that may be either at a premium or at a discount to their net asset value; the price depends on the demand for the shares. For instance, Central Fund of Canada, with a net asset value per share of $5.89, may be trading at $6.63 (that is, at a premium) on the same day that BGR Precious Metals, with a NAVPS of $12.49, is trading at $11.63 (that is, at a discount). The NAVPSs of closed-end funds are published occasionally in the financial papers.

Mutual Funds

Types of Mutual Funds

In 2000, Canadians had over 2000 mutual funds to choose from. These funds fall into various categories, each with different goals and approaches; the current categories are described briefly below and are also summarized in Table 11.1. There is probably a fund available to suit the needs of every investor, from the most conservative to the most venturesome. The number of such funds increases frequently as the funds companies seek to attract new investors. In 2000, Canadians had invested a total of over $400 billion in such funds. Clearly, they are a popular investment vehicle.

MONEY MARKET FUNDS The goal of a money market fund is income and liquidity. Income is usually distributed to unitholders each month, either as cash or as new units. As a result, there is no chance for capital gain.

MORTGAGE FUNDS The objective of a mortgage fund is income combined with safety. Since the mortgage terms are for five years or less, such funds are not very volatile, and thus they are considered less risky than bond funds.

BOND FUNDS A bond fund also has safety and income as goals; but because bond prices can fluctuate, investors in such funds may also have capital gains or losses. Such funds invest in high-yielding government and corporate bonds.

TABLE 11.1   CLASSIFICATION OF MUTUAL FUNDS

CATEGORY	DESCRIPTION
1. *Money market funds*	Invested in treasury bills, commercial paper, and short-term government bonds.
2. *Mortgage funds*	Invested in mortgages.
3. *Bond funds*	Invested in bonds.
4. *Dividend funds*	Invested in preferred shares and in good-quality common shares.
5. *Balanced funds*	Invested in both common shares and fixed-income investments.
6. *Asset allocation funds*	Similar to balanced funds, but the shift between asset classes is more frequent.
7. *Equity funds*	Invested in common shares for the purpose of capital gains.
8. *Specialty funds*	Invested in common shares either in one specific industry or in one geographic location.
9. *Global funds*	Invested in markets outside Canada that are considered to have the best chance of gain.
10. *Real estate funds*	Invested in real estate companies for the purposes of gain.
11. *Ethical funds*	Invested in companies that do not make goods considered immoral or harmful to people, to animals, or to the environment.
12. *Segregated funds*	Sold by insurance companies as an alternative to the other types of mutual funds. Such funds are kept separate from all other funds controlled by the insurance company (see Chapter 7).
13. *Labour-sponsored (Venture Capital) funds*	For investors who are interested in long-term capital gain; invested in companies that organized labour views as likely to help the economy grow (e.g., by creating jobs). Investors receive a federal tax credit.

DIVIDEND FUNDS   Because the income from a dividend fund is paid in dividends, investors receive a dividend tax credit. And since they invest in stocks, these funds may also have capital gains or losses.

BALANCED FUNDS   A balanced fund seeks a combination of safety, income, and capital appreciation. Fixed-income securities provide the stability, while common stocks provide income and the chance for capital gains.

ASSET ALLOCATION FUNDS   Managers of asset allocation funds shift the weighting of their investments between equity, money market, and fixed-income securities, with a view toward maximizing the advantage to their investors by, for example, responding to what is happening with interest rates. Some such funds use computer models to determine the best moment for making changes in their asset allocation. Note, however, that whenever the assets in such a fund are reallocated, unitholders must pay tax on any capital gain.

EQUITY FUNDS   While an equity fund's managers may purchase fixed-income securities for purposes of income and liquidity, most of the money in such a fund is invested in common shares. As a result, the values of equity fund units tend to fluctuate.

SPECIALTY FUNDS The purpose of a specialty fund is capital gain. To achieve this goal, the specialty fund's managers invest in the shares of companies in one particular industry (such as high-tech companies) or in one geographical area, such as Latin America. The idea is to invest in a rapidly growing industry or area or in one that is viewed as being about to take off. As a result of their investment strategy, specialty funds are often more speculative than equity funds.

GLOBAL FUNDS A global fund is a type of specialty fund that invests in those global markets seen as best suited to the fund's objectives—which always involve growth and long-term capital gains. These funds do not specialize in a single geographic area; instead, they concentrate on emerging markets located anywhere in the world. Some global fund managers invest in bonds; others concentrate on equities; and still others aim to create a balanced fund.

REAL ESTATE FUNDS A real estate fund's managers are interested in long-term growth; to achieve this result, they invest in income-producing real estate (that is, land and/or buildings that are rented to others at a profit, such as an apartment building, a shopping centre, or an office building).

ETHICAL FUNDS An ethical fund is designed to appeal to people who are averse to investing in firms that produce socially and morally offensive products (such as tobacco or alcohol) or products that harm the environment; such funds concentrate instead on companies whose products are above reproach. They also invest in firms that have reputations for good employee relations.

SEGREGATED FUNDS As described in Chapter 7 (under "Segregated Funds"), segregated funds have a variety of objectives. Some invest in equities, while others choose bonds, and others aim for a balanced approach. In this way, they are like other mutual funds. The difference is that segregated funds are sold only by insurance companies and come with a guarantee of principal when the fund matures.

LABOUR-SPONSORED (VENTURE CAPITAL) FUNDS A venture capital fund is one that is sponsored by organized labour (i.e., a trade union); its interests lie in long-term gain. Such funds invest in small and mid-sized companies to help promote economic growth and jobs. Investors who buy units in a venture capital fund receive a tax credit.

Risk Levels

Before investing in a particular mutual fund, you can estimate its risk level by examining the type of securities held in its portfolio and by comparing its past performance with that of others from the same fund category. The financial press rates mutual funds according to their risk or volatility based on the stability of the rates of return of the stocks in the fund's portfolio. The various financial papers use somewhat different measures of volatility, which are explained in the report each paper publishes on mutual funds. For instance, the *Globe and Mail*'s "Report on Business" section reports volatility on a scale of 1 (low) to 10 (high). Volatility data show how a fund's monthly return has fluctuated in recent years, compared to that of other funds within the same category. When one category of funds is compared against another, money market funds are usually at the low end of the scale, while growth funds are at the high end. High-variability funds make great gains when the stock market is rising—but conversely, they lose rapidly in a falling market. Low-risk funds will neither make nor lose as much money.

Fees

The fees charged for investing in mutual funds not only vary considerably among funds but have also become increasingly difficult for investors to assess. The sales commissions charged when shares are either purchased or redeemed are made quite explicit. But annual fees for management and other expenses tend to be less well explained.

ACQUISITION FEES   A sales fee that is imposed when you purchase mutual fund units is called an **acquisition fee** or a **front-end loading charge;** such charges may range from 1 to 5 percent of the amount you are investing. This type of fee tends to be higher for funds managed by companies that hire their sales force directly. Independent brokers, who handle the funds of many companies, may be willing to negotiate a lower commission fee.

REDEMPTION FEES   Another way of covering sales commissions is to charge a **redemption fee** or **rear-end loading charge,** which is paid when you withdraw money from the fund. Redemption fees may be a set amount per transaction (e.g., $15 to $25), or they may be calculated as a percentage (e.g., 1 to 8 percent) of either your initial investment or your holding's current market value. Redemption fees often have a sliding-scale structure: the longer you hold the funds, the lower the redemption fee you will pay when you do withdraw money. After nine years or so, the fee may fall to zero. Some investors are attracted by redemption fees as a way of postponing costs. But you should not select a mutual fund only by the timing of its fees; you will need to consider other factors, such as risk and performance, as well. Nevertheless, the length of time you expect to hold your shares is an important consideration when choosing between a front-load fund and a back-load fund.

NO-LOAD FUNDS   Funds that do not charge sales fees are called **no-load funds.** Be careful, though: such funds may simply disguise their fees. Some supposedly no-load funds impose a "distribution fee" of 1 percent a year, which is added to the management fee for the first few years as a way of compensating salespeople. Genuine no-load funds, most of which have no sales force, use other methods of finding investors, such as advertising, direct mail, and arrangements with stockbrokers. Sometimes, a system of reciprocal commissions will be arranged, whereby mutual funds managers who need the services of stockbrokers will agree to send business to a particular broker—who, in return, will promote sales of that particular mutual fund. In such instances, the investor pays no sales fee, but may receive somewhat biased advice.

MANAGEMENT FEES   Management fees represent a significant cost for both closed-end and mutual funds. While acquisition and redemption fees are visible, management fees are less so. Charges of between 1 and 3 percent a year are deducted directly from the fund's assets before calculating return to investors. Management fees cover a variety of costs, including investment advice, annual reports, legal services, brokerage commissions, sales commissions, and the federal goods and services tax (GST). A useful means of comparing the management fees of various funds is the **expense ratio.** This ratio, expressed as a percentage, is an annual ratio of all fees (excluding sales fees) and expenses to the fund's average net assets. A cursory examination of newspaper reports on mutual funds indicates how widely funds vary in their expense ratios, even within a similar group of funds. Some of the factors that affect fund expense ratios are the marketing and distribution costs of a fund, and whether or not the fund pays trailer fees. Some funds pay their agents annual commissions, called **trailer fees,** in addition to the initial sales commission. A broker receives trailer fees on an ongoing basis as encouragement to continue to provide services to the client. The **Management Expense Ratio (MER)** averages between 1 percent to 2.5 percent in Canada.

Buying Mutual Funds

Buying units in a mutual fund is easy. When you want to invest, you either contact the fund company directly, or contact a mutual funds agent, and indicate how much money you wish to invest. Your cost will be the net asset value per unit plus any sales fees (see Personal Finance in Action Box 11.7, "Investing in a Mutual Fund"). Likewise, when you want to sell mutual fund units, you need only inform one of the fund's representatives. You will receive the current net asset value per unit less any exit fees.

Because the market is very competitive and many agents are anxious to sell mutual fund units, you must consider your choices carefully. As a guide, here are four steps to take when you are thinking of investing in mutual funds (each will be discussed in further detail below):

(a) Determine your objectives for this investment.

(b) Find a fund that matches your objectives.

(c) Investigate the fees that will be charged.

(d) Analyze the past performance of several possible funds.

OBJECTIVES The names of mutual funds often indicate their different objectives—for example, growth, income, dividend, and money market funds. You can find more information about a fund's objectives in its prospectus, which lists the securities currently held in the portfolio. Since many mutual fund companies operate a number of funds with different objectives, you can contact a few companies, state your objectives, and request the prospectuses of any appropriate funds. You will find the Web addresses of mutual funds companies under "Personal Finance on the Web" in the "References" section at the end of this chapter.

FEES The various fees already described can have a significant effect on the gains you will make from your mutual fund investment. Compare the fees (both obvious and hidden) carefully before choosing a fund.

Personal Finance in Action 11.7

Investing in a Mutual Fund

With $1 000 to invest and no time to look after it, Aya decides to buy units in a mutual fund. The fund she chooses has a 5 percent sales fee and a net asset value per unit of $6.53. How many units can she buy?

Sales commission	$1 000 × 0.05 = $50.00
Sum to invest	$1 000 – $50 = $950.00
Number of units bought	$950/$6.53 = 145.482

Some months later, a dividend of 0.30 per unit is declared.

| Dividends received | 145.482 × 0.30 = $43.64 |

Aya has arranged to have her dividends automatically reinvested in more units of the mutual fund, which now has a net asset value per unit of $7.04. This will give her 6.199 more units.

Dividends to reinvest	= $43.64
Number of units received	$43.64/$7.04 = 6.199
Total units owned	145.482 + 6.199 = 151.681

PERFORMANCE Information about a mutual fund's past performance can be useful to prospective mutual fund buyers. How does this fund's historical return compare to that of similar funds? The financial papers publish regular surveys of mutual fund performance over a number of years. The yield figures are based on annual compound rates of return, assuming that dividends and capital gain are reinvested in the fund. But the reported returns exclude direct charges, such as acquisition or redemption fees. Hidden fees for management costs have been taken into account, but you must also consider the effect of sales fees on reported investment return. Of course, past performance is not a sure indication of future success; still, it is one factor that is worth considering.

ADVANTAGES AND DISADVANTAGES To conclude this discussion of mutual funds, we will summarize the four advantages and the four disadvantages of such investment vehicles. The advantages of mutual funds are as follows:

(a) professional management,

(b) the wide variety of funds available,

(c) the opportunity to diversify,

(d) the units' marketability.

Mutual funds may also present disadvantages for investors; generalizing is difficult, though, because of the great variety of funds. The following factors do not apply to all funds, but the list suggests the matters you might wish to consider:

(a) low liquidity,

(b) high fees,

(c) the long-term nature of the investment,

(d) the variable skill of fund managers.

Equity mutual funds are low in liquidity, because their unit values fluctuate as the whole stock market rises and falls. The optimum time for selling your units may therefore not coincide with your need for funds. The substantial fees attached to mutual funds may, at least in the short term, reduce the net yield on your investment. With the exception of money market funds, most mutual funds make for poor short-term investments; they are best selected with a view toward remaining invested over the long term. And of course, the success of a particular fund depends greatly on the skill of its managers.

Wrap Accounts

To reduce the confusion caused by the great variety of mutual fund accounts and by the complexities of the funds' elaborate fee structures, the investment industry has developed a new product. Known as a **wrap account,** this investment vehicle has the maintenance-free appeal of a mutual fund, along with some added benefits. A wrap account features none of the front-end or rear-end load charges that many mutual fund investors find so confusing. In addition, no commission is charged on each transaction (as is the case with equities). Instead, wrap account clients are charged an annual management fee, which ranges from 1.5 percent to 3 percent of the amount invested; and unlike standard mutual fund fees, this charge is tax deductible. To open a wrap, you do need a minimum investment of at least $50 000. For your management fee, however, you do get individual service from a professional asset manager, and you will have more input into how your funds are invested than is possible with a mutual fund.

Investment Risk

Types of Risk

All investments are exposed to some degree of risk, but the kind of risk varies with the type of investment. It is essential that you be aware of and be willing to accept the risks associated with any investment you are considering. As explained in Chapter 9 (under "Investment Risks") investors face risks caused by (i) inflation, which causes the value of cash and that of debt securities to fall; (ii) interest rates, which have differential effects on various investments; (iii) the stock market, where the demand for a security rises and falls; and (iv) the poor performance or outright failure of a particular business. When you own stocks, your investment is subject to three kinds of risk: market risk, business risk, and interest rate risks.

MARKET RISK An asset may lose favour among investors because of factors other than either the company's profitability or the prevailing economic conditions. The price of an equity asset also depends on demand in a stock market that is variable (Figure 11.1). It is normal for stock prices to fluctuate for many reasons, some of which may be unrelated to earnings or dividend changes. Since a great deal of emotion is associated with stock ownership, irrational factors influence prices. It is therefore extremely difficult to predict the direction or magnitude of change in stock prices in the short run; over the long run, however, stock prices have produced real gains (that is, gains in excess of inflation).

BUSINESS RISK Although the business in which you have invested could fail totally, the more likely risk is that the firm's earnings could decline. Lower earnings often result in lower dividends and a drop in the security's price. You also risk paying too much for a stock. One example many Canadians will not soon forget concerned the price of gold. On the morning of November 14, 1997, gold's price per ounce fell to U.S.$299.25. In January 1997, gold had been valued at over U.S.$380 an ounce. Its price had not dropped below U.S.$300 since February 1985. Because this price decrease meant that some gold producers would have a difficult time making money, their share prices fell accordingly. Shares of Agnico Eagle, a Canadian gold mine, for example, that had been worth $20.25 a year earlier fell to $7.05 at this news. By April 24, 1998, however, the per-ounce price of gold in Europe had rebounded to U.S.$314. This did not mean that the U.S.$380 price was again within reach, but at least the prospects for some gold producers were no longer quite so grim. Agnico Eagle shares, reflecting the more positive outlook, closed at $10.25 that day. Shares of Barrick Gold, a major producer, whose value had plunged to $25.80 on November 14, had climbed to $33.00 by April 24.

The reality every investor has to face is that no one, not even the shrewdest investment professional, knows when share prices will rise or fall. You could conceivably find two opposite forecasts for the same stock on the same day in the same newspaper. That is just the nature of the market: investing is a very imprecise business. At any given time, some analysts will be bullish (that is, they will believe that market prices will continue to travel generally upward, perhaps with minor "corrections," for a considerable time to come) and others will be bearish (that is, they will expect market prices to fall). As already mentioned, the best investment advice is to buy and hold stocks in good companies. When you do this, you avoid the market's periodic ups and downs in the market and will likely come out ahead, since stocks generally rise over the long-term. Practise patience, and operate with a long-term investment horizon.

INTEREST RATE RISK Rising interest rates, which are beneficial for people who have invested in debt securities, are not helpful for shareholders. High interest rates restrict business activity and tend to affect both profits and share prices adversely. When interest rates are low, people decide to buy cars and houses, and businesses borrow to expand. This increased activity is reflected in rising stock prices.

Risk Reduction

Since there is no way to pick investments that will do well under all circumstances or to avoid experiencing a certain number of bad results, the rational approach is to take steps to reduce the risk you are exposed to. Some risk will always remain, because the future may not turn out as we expected. Some people are more averse to risk than others—that is, they are less comfortable with uncertainty. The most risk-averse people are uneasy with any but the most secure fixed-income investments. They prefer certainty to the possibility of greater yield.

Knowing that it is impossible to avoid all risk, wise investors decide on an acceptable risk level and then try to spread this risk by diversification. Diversification can be applied at several levels: to the investor's total portfolio, and to individual elements within in it. For example, a portfolio might be balanced between debt investments and equity investments. Within both the debt portion and the equity portion, however, further diversity is possible as well as desirable. A well-constructed stock portfolio, for instance, does not concentrate solely on any one sector. Instead of buying shares in, say, oil companies only, some portfolios would be invested in transportation, utilities, or industrial products. A diversified portfolio, increases the odds that while some securities will not do as well as you hope, others will do better than expected, thereby balancing out the portfolio's performance on the whole. In a well-balanced portfolio, the overall risk will be less than the risk associated with any particular investment. Diversity reduces risk by allowing successes in one sector to offset poor performance in another, since individual companies react in different ways to economic and other conditions.

But like nearly any good thing, even diversification can be carried to a problematic extreme. No one investor can effectively monitor a portfolio that contains too many kinds of assets. For a small stock portfolio, six to ten stocks may be appropriate. A workable guideline is until your investments exceed $50 000 (excluding the value of your residence), you should limit any given asset to roughly 10 percent of the total. People with a larger net worth may be able to handle 20 securities.

Income Tax

Investment return may consist of interest, dividends, or capital gain. Generally, these three types of income are taxed differently. Each will be reviewed in turn.

Interest

All interest must be added to your taxable income, and will be taxed as such. This requirement makes debt securities less attractive than equities for some investors, as will be illustrated in the following examples.

Marginal federal tax rate	=	25%
Provincial tax rate (which varies)	=	52%
Total interest earned	=	$2 000.00
Federal income tax	$2 000 × 0.25 =	$500.00

Provincial income tax (which varies) $500.00 × 0.52 = $260.00

Total income tax $500.00 + $260.00 = $760.00

After-tax return $2 000.00 − $760.00 = $1 240.00

The Dividend Tax Credit

When corporations pay dividends, they do so with after-tax income. To prevent this money from being taxed twice, dividends received from Canadian corporations are taxed in a special way. Shareholders receive a dividend tax credit, which in effect means that dividend income is taxed at a lower rate than either interest income or income from capital gains. To calculate the dividend tax credit, the actual dividend is *grossed-up* or increased by a certain percentage. The *gross-up* indicates the amount of pre-tax income the corporation has paid. In 2000, the gross-up rate was 25 percent. The following example shows how the dividend tax credit is calculated:

Marginal federal tax rate		= 25%
Provincial tax rate (which varies)		= 52%
Gross-up rate		= 25%
Tax on grossed-up dividends		= 13.33%
Total dividends received		= $2 000.00
Grossed-up by 25%	$2 000.00 × 1.25	= $2 500.00
Federal income tax (25%)	$2 500 × 0.25	= $625.00
Dividend tax credit		
(*13.33% × grossed-up amount*)	$2 500 × 0.1333	= $333.25
Federal tax payable		
(*federal tax − dividend credit*)	$625.00 − $333.25	= $291.75
Provincial tax		
(*52% of federal tax*)	$291.75 × 0.52	= $151.71
Total tax (*federal + provincial*)		= $443.46
After-tax return	$2 000 − 443.46	= $1 556.54

The above examples show that the after-tax return from $2 000 in dividends is $316.54 greater than that from $2 000 in interest income. To calculate the after-tax difference between interest and dividend income, multiply the dividend rate by 1.3. An investor trying to choose between two investments, one of which pays 6 percent interest while the other pays a 5 percent dividend will find by doing this that the after-tax return for the dividend is equal to interest of 6.5 percent, or 1.3 (0.05 × 1.3 = 6.5), while the after-tax return for the interest is only 6 percent .

Capital Gains

As of October 2000, 50 percent of capital gains must be included in income.

Alternative Ways to Invest

Cash Management Account (CMA)

A recent addition to the services offered by some investment dealers is the **cash management account**. For a minimum balance ranging from as low as $20 000 to as high as $250 000, clients can have all of their financial needs handled through their broker. CMAs allow clients to combine bank accounts, investment accounts, and credit-card accounts. Using their ABM card, customers can pay bills, write cheques, and even borrow on margin to purchase securities. In addition, the interest rates on CMA deposits are high and the annual fee low, usually about $200.

Equity Derivatives

No discussion of stocks and mutual funds would be complete without some mention of **equity derivatives,** which have received considerable publicity in the financial press. While these instruments have been used mainly by institutional investors, they also show up in the portfolios of private or retail investors with a fondness for risk. They are not for the faint of heart.

An option to buy the underlying security is a call. An option to sell is called a put. Call options increase in value as the security on which they are derived rises in value. Holders of calls are bullish. A put option increases in value when the market falls. Holders of puts are bearish. Those who sell options are said to be writing an option. Those who buy options are called holders. (They are both investors but the term is not used in this case.)

Bearish investors (those who expect the market to fall) will be sellers of call options or buyers of put options. Those with contracts to sell call options are obligated to sell the shares from which the call is derived at a specified price before a specified time. Those with contracts to buy put options are obligated to buy the shares from which the put is derived at a specified price before a specified time. If they have speculated correctly, the market will have fallen and they will come out ahead in both cases.

Investment Trusts

Investment trusts are another new type of investment. Also classified as derivatives (because the income they generate "derives" from the assets they buy), these instruments allow individuals to invest with relative ease in things like natural resource assets and real estate. Such trusts are sold as units, listed on exchanges, and traded as if they were equities. The money raised from selling the units is used to buy natural resource or real estate assets, which generate a cash flow. The income is paid to the unitholders either monthly or quarterly.

Many of the resource trust units are able, at the start, to pay out cash distributions which are non-taxable. The distributions are treated as a return on capital and reduce the unitholder's cost base. If there is a capital gain on distribution it will be taxed. Any dividend or interest payments to unitholders are taxed in the usual way.

Investments in real estate trusts are also taxed in a special way. Capital cost allowances and other deductions are allowed to flow through into the hands of unitholders. One such fund, for example, as a result of this treatment, paid $1.30 per unit in 1997 on which investors only paid tax on $.34.

Summary

This overview of stocks and mutual funds introduced the specific vocabulary of the stock market and outlined the process of stock trading. Now that you understand the basics, you should find the newspaper's financial section easier to understand. Some knowledge of the stock market and of the risks involved is essential for anyone who plans to invest in stocks. The differences between common and preferred shares were explained, as were rights, warrants, stock splits, and certain special features that may be attached to preferred shares. Investors in the stock market may receive various kinds of returns, including cash dividends, stock dividends, and capital gain

Investment funds may be closed-end or open-end, but the vast majority are of the latter type, also known as mutual funds. The net asset value per unit is the price of mutual funds, but not of closed-end funds. Mutual funds, of which there are currently 13 categories, offer enough diversity to suit a wide range of investment objectives. It is important to choose a fund to match personal objectives, and to be aware of the various sales and management fees.

The discussion of investments concluded with a look at the three kinds of risk associated with equity investing—that is, market, business, and interest rate risks—and at the importance of portfolio diversification. Taxation of investment return varies with the type of income earned; it is therefore wise to compare yield on an after-tax basis.

Key Terms

acquisition fee (front-end loading charge) (p. 308)

ask price (p. 293)

automatic dividend reinvestment plan (DRIPs) (p. 302)

bid price (p. 293)

board lot (p. 292)

cash management account (p. 314)

closed-end investment fund (p. 304)

common shareholders (p. 297)

convertible preferred share (p. 300)

cumulative preferred share (p. 299)

discount brokers (p. 293)

dividend (p. 293)

day trader (p. 296)

dot-coms (p. 296)

equity derivatives (p. 314)

ex-dividend (p. 302)

expense ratio (p. 308)

full-service broker (p. 292)

growth stock (p. 303)

investment fund (p. 303)

investment trust (p. 314)

Management Expense Ratio (MER) (p. 308)

market order (p. 292)

net asset value per share (p. 305)

no-load fund (p. 308)

odd lot (p. 292)

open-end investment fund (mutual fund) (p. 304)

open order (p. 292)

over-the-counter market (p. 291)

par value (p. 302)

penny stock (p. 293)

preferred share (p. 299)

purchase (sinking) fund (p. 300)

Problems

1. Use stock quotations from a recent newspaper to answer the following questions. Look at the legend (usually at the top of the relevant page or section in the newspaper) for an explanation of the footnotes.

   (a) How much was the most recent dividend per share, in annual terms, on Noranda common stock? On Bell Canada Enterprises (BCE)?

   (b) Try to find an example of a preferred share for which the dividend is in arrears.

   (c) Look at the volume figures and find a stock that traded very actively.

   (d) Find a quotation for stock warrants. (It may be indicated by a "w" after the name of the corporation.)

   (e) Examine the quotations for Bank of Nova Scotia preferred shares to find out how many issues are listed.

   (f) Look for a stock that has issued stock dividends recently.

2. Answer true or false.

   (a) Mutual funds are less risky than stocks.

   (b) Preferred shares do not change in value like their common share cousins.

   (c) Mutual fund fees and expenses are always clearly explained.

   (d) When you sell units in a mutual fund, the fund manager does not need to find a client who wants to buy them.

   (e) Stock market volatility is a phenomenon that will never cease.

   (f) Canadian stock exchanges still process orders in the traditional way on the floor of the exchange.

   (g) Investors can protect their investments with stop-loss orders.

   (h) Movement on the Dow is an accurate indication of the health of the U.S. economy.

   (i) The TSE 35 is Canada's most influential stock exchange index.

   (j) It is not possible for an investor to know when bull markets will turn to bear markets.

(k) There is no way for investors to protect themselves over the long term from stock market fluctuations.

(l) Corporations never have more than one type of common share.

3. Examine the Rights Offering below and answer the following questions:

Rights Offering

A news report states that Consolidated Trustco plans to raise approximately $80 million in new capital through an issue of rights to shareholders, who will receive one right for every four common shares held. With one right and $12, the holder can buy another share of Consolidated Trustco. The offer will be mailed to shareholders in late October, and will expire 21 days later. With this new issue, rights will be offered to shareholders of record on October 15.

At the time of this announcement, Consolidated Trustco shares are trading at $12. By November 1, they are up to $13. Over the previous year, the shares had been trading between $7.25 and $14.

(a) As a shareholder, would you be interested in this offering? Comment.

(b) If you were a shareholder, what choices would you have with regard to this rights offering?

(c) If you buy Consolidated Trustco stock on October 30, will you be eligible for rights? Explain whether you would be considered a shareholder of record as far as this offering is concerned.

4. Now that you know something about RRSPs, debt securities, stocks, and mutual funds, what kind of investment would you suggest a 23-year-old college graduate put in her RRSP?

5. Imagine that you are a financial advisor and a client asks you to help her select a mutual fund. Her investment goals are income, capital gains, and security of capital. After analyzing the various classifications of mutual funds, which category/ies would you recommend in order to help her achieve her goals?

6. Identify the type of investment risk that seems to predominate in each of the following cases:

(a) A lumber company's shares drop in price after news that the United States plans to impose a duty on wood products.

(b) Stock market prices, which have been rising for several years, start falling; they continue to fall for months.

(c) An investor who inherits $100 000 invests it all in five-year GICs at 4 percent; interest rates then move to 6 percent.

7. A survey of mutual funds published in the financial press is shown on the following page.

Mutual Funds

	AGF CANADIAN EQUITY FUND	ALTAMIRA BALANCED FUND
Assets	$614 000 000	$78 000 000
Fees	F 0-6%	No load fund
Management	D 4.9% *	
Expense Ratio	2.95%	2.00%
Volatility **	4	2
Rate of Return %		
1 month	–4.7	0.07
Year to date	2.2	6.6
1 year	0.7	11.3
3 years	9.5	10.0
5 years	7.4	7.1

	TD GREENLINE CANADIAN EQUITY FUND	FIDELITY CANADIAN ASSET ALLOCATION
Assets	$950 000	$3 017 000 000
Fees	No load fund	F 0-2% or 0-4% R 4.9%
Management		
Expense Ratio	2.10	2.48
Volatility	3	2
Rate of return %		
1 month	–4.5	0.7
Year to date	2.5	9.9
1 year	11.3	20.0
3 years	18.3	21.4
5 years	13.3	The fund is not 5 years old

* "F" means Front-end load. A fee is charged when units are purchased.

"D" means the fee is deferred until the units are redeemed and it is a declining fee based on the original capital invested.

"R" means the fee is deferred until redemption and it is a declining fee based upon the market value.

The longer you own units in funds where the fee is deferred, the smaller the fee charged.

** Volatility refers to the variability in a fund's monthly rate of return over three years compared with all other funds listed in the paper. The lower the number, the more stable the monthly rate of return.

Rates of return include management fees and expenses, but not sales charges; assume reinvestment of dividends.

Management Expense Ratio reflects the annual fee charged to the fund by the fund manager.

Source: *The Financial Post*, August 8-10, 1998, pp. 39, 41, 43.

(a) Which fund has the largest amount of money invested?

(b) Does there appear to be any relationship between the management expense ratio, the fees, and the volatility?

(c) How much is the management paid to manage these funds? Which fund charges the most? Does the high fee result in a better performance?

(d) Is past performance a good indicator of how a fund will do all of the time?

(e) Are the funds which do not charge either a front-end or a back-end fee better funds in which to invest from a performance point of view?

8. AGF, AIM (formerly Trimark), CI, Fidelity, and Templeton are mutual fund companies operating in Canada. Their Web sites are as follows:

www.agf.com

www.aimfunds.ca

www.cifunds.com

www.fidelity.ca

www.templeton.ca

Find out the size of the following funds, what Management Expense Rations (MERs) they have, and what this worked out to in dollar terms for the fund managers in 1999. Find out as well what front-end or rear-end fees these funds have. Then research the past five-year history of one of these funds. Do you feel that its performance justifies these fees and charges?

AGF Canadian Dividend Fund

BPI Canadian Resource Fund

Fidelity Far East Fund

Templeton Growth Fund

Trimark Canadian Fund

References

BOOKS AND ARTICLES

ADEGBOYEGA, JOSEPH: *Money: Smart Investor Handbook*. Adegboyega, 1996.

ALTAMIRA. *Altamira Investor Workbook*. Toronto: Altamira, Prepared by one of Canada's leading mutual fund companies, this 13-page workbook has some excellent advice for all kinds of investors. Available by calling 1-800-263-2824 (toll-free).

ANDERSON, HUGH. *Bulls and Bears: Winning In the Stock Market in Good Times and Bad*. Toronto: Penguin, 1997.

_____. *Investing For Income*. Toronto: Penguin, 1997.

ARMSTRONG, CHRISTOPHER. *Blue Skies and Boiler Rooms: Buying and Selling Securities In Canada, 1870-1940*. Toronto: University of Toronto Press, 1997.

BROOKS, JOHN, and BRENDA BROOKS. *Catching the Wave: How To Profit From Canada's Four Prosperity Waves*. Ottawa: Rumington, 1995.

CANADIAN SECURITIES INSTITUTE. *How to Invest in Canadian Securities.* Scarborough: Prentice Hall, 1994.

CARLOS, MIGUELITO. *Stock Market Discoveries: Avoiding Pitfalls [and] Learning Secret Investing Strategies.* Richmond, B.C: Carlos, 1996.

CARROLL, JIM, and RICK BROADHEAD. *Mutual Funds and RRSPs Online: A Financial Guide for Every Canadian.* Scarborough: Prentice Hall, 1997.

CARTER, TED E. *Successful Stock Market Speculation: A Speculator's Manual.* Calgary, Alberta: Mistaya, 1991.

CHAKRAPANI, CHUCK. *Financial Freedom On Five Dollars a Day.* Sixth Edition. North Vancouver, B.C.: Self-Counsel, 1994.

CHAND, RANGA. *Ranga Chand's Getting Started With Mutual Funds.* Toronto: Stoddart, 1995.

CHEVREAU, JONATHAN, STEPHEN KANGAS, and JOHN PLATT. *The Financial Post Smart Funds 1998: A Fund Family Approach to Mutual Funds.* Toronto: Key Porter Books, 1997.

CHEVREAU, JONATHAN, MICHAEL ELLIS, and KELLY ROGERS. *The Wealthy Boomer: Life After Mutual Funds. Low Cost Alternatives in Managed Money.* Toronto: Key Porter Books, 1998.

COOPER, SHERRY. *The Cooper Files. A Practical Guide to Your Financial Future.* Toronto: Key Porter Books, 1999.

COSTELLO, BRIAN. *Money Talks! Multi-dimensional Investing.* Toronto: ECW Press, 1997.

CROFT, RICHARD. *A Beginner's Guide to Investing: A Practical Guide to Putting Your Money to Work for You.* Toronto: HarperCollins, 1997.

_____, and ERIC KIRZNER. *The Fundline Advisor.* Toronto: HarperCollins, 1997.

CRUISE DAVID and ALLISON GRIFFITHS. *Fleecing the Lamb: The Inside Story of the Vancouver Stock Exchange.* Toronto: Penguin, 1991.

DAGYS, ANDREW. *Common Sense Investing in Real Estate Investment Trusts.* Scarborough: Prentice Hall, 1998.

ELLMEN, EUGENE. *Canadian Ethical Money Guide: The Best RRSPs, Mutual Funds, and Stocks for Ethical Investors.* Toronto: Lorimer, annual.

ENNIS, DALE L. *Guide to Making Money: How To Do It Yourself.* Bath, ON: Canadian Money Saver, 1987.

THE FINANCIAL POST. *Money and Investments.* Toronto: Key Porter Books, 1993.

_____. The following guides to investing and personal finance: were first published by The Financial Post in early 1998; they contain some very useful information.
Understanding Equities (No. 2)
Beyond Equities (No. 3)
Mutual Funds (No. 5)
Investment Planning (No. 6)

FRIEDLAND, SEYMOUR and STEVEN G. KELMAN. *Investment Strategies: How To Create Your Own and Make It Work For You.* Toronto: Penguin, 1996.

GERLACH, DOUGLAS, JAMES GRAVELLE, and TOM McFEAT. *The Complete Idiot's Guide to Online Investing for Canadians.* Scarborough: alpha books, 1999.

HEADY, CHRISTY, and STEPHEN NELSON. *The Complete Idiot's Guide to Making Money in the Canadian Stock Market.* Scarborough: Prentice Hall, 1997.

HEINZL, MARK J. *Stop Buying Mutual Funds. Easy Ways to Beat the Pros Investing On Your Own*. Toronto: John Wiley & Sons, Inc., 1999.

KAN, JOE, ed. *Handbook of Canadian Security Analysis: A Guide to Evaluating the Industry Sectors of the Market, From Bay Street's Top Analysts*. Toronto: John Wiley & Sons, Inc., 1997.

KELMAN, STEPHEN G., NED GOODMAN, and JONATHAN GOODMAN. *Investing In Gold: How To Buy It, How To Profit From It*. Toronto: Key Porter Books, 1992.

KENNEDY, GAIL. *You're Worth It! Investment Strategies for Women*. Etobicoke, ON: Raintree, 1995.

KIM, CHARLES. *Swift Trader: Perfecting the Art of Day Trading*. Toronto: Prentice Hall, 2000.

KOCH, EDWARD T., DEBRA DeSALVO, and JAMES LANGTON. *The Complete Idiot's Guide to Investing Like a Pro for Canadians*. Scarborough: alpha books, 1999.

LASSONDE, PIERRE. *The Gold Book: The Complete Investment Guide to Precious Metals*. Toronto: Penguin, 1994.

MACBETH, HILLIARD. *A Canadian Guide to Investment Traps and How to Avoid Them*. Scarborough: Prentice Hall, 1999.

MAUDE, TIMOTHY J. *The Internet Investor: A Practical and Time-Saving Guide To Finding Financial Information On The Internet*. Toronto: HarperCollins, 1997.

NESBITT BURNS. *Nesbitt Burns Guide to Equity Derivative Products*. Toronto: Nesbitt Burns, n.d. Nesbitt Burns is one of Canada's leading investment dealers. This 48-page book gives a thorough introduction to the often confusing world of equity derivatives. Nesbitt Burns may be reached by calling 1-800-263-2286 (toll-free).

_____. *Canadian Banks: Looking A Lot Like Utilities*. Toronto: Nesbitt Burns, April 1995.

_____. *Funds For Income. A Summary of a Recent Research Report*. Toronto: Nesbitt Burns, 1997

_____. *The Stock Book*. Toronto: Nesbitt Burns. This is a good introduction to the stock market.

_____. *U.S. Equity Research Monitor*. Toronto: Nesbitt Burns, April 1997.

ORMAN, SUZE. *The Courage to Be Rich. Creating a Life of Material and Spiritual Abundance*. New York: Riverhead Books, 1999.

OTAR, CEMIL. *Commission Free Investing: The Handbook of Canadian DRIPs and SPPs*. Etobicoke, ON: Uphill, 1997.

PAPE, GORDON. *Gordon Pape's 2000 Buyer's Guide to Mutual Funds*. Scarborough: Prentice Hall, 2000.

_____. *Making Money in Mutual Funds: A Pape Starter's Guide*. Scarborough: Prentice Hall, 1996.

SANDER, JENNIFER, BAYSE, ANNE BOUTIN, and JANICE BIEHN. *The Complete Idiot's Guide to Investing for Women in Canada*. Scarborough: alpha books, 2000.

SARLOS, ANDREW, and PATRICIA BEST. *Fear, Greed, and the End of the Rainbow: Guarding Your Assets in the Coming Bear Market*. Toronto: Key Porter Books, 1997.

SCHWARTZ, MARTIN "BUZZY." *Pit Bull: Lessons from Wall Street's Champion Trader*. New York: HarperCollins, 1998.

SEASE, DOUGLAS, and JOHN PRESTBO. *Barron's Guide to Making Investment Decisions*. Paramus, NJ: Prentice Hall, 1994.

SHARPE, WILLIAM, F., GORDON J. ALEXANDER, and DAVID JOHN FOWLER. *Investments*. Toronto: Prentice Hall, 1996.

STANLEY, THOMAS J., and WILLIAM D. DANKO. *The Millionaire Next Door. The Surprising Secrets of America's Wealthy*. Atlanta: Longstreet Press, 1996.

STENNER, GORDON, and WILLIAM ANNETT. *Stenner on Mutual Funds: The Complete and Authoritative Guide to Mutual Fund Investment in Canada*. Toronto: HarperCollins, 1997.

STEWART, SAMUEL BLACK. *It's That Easy: A Proven Strategy for the Individual Investor*. Toronto: Copp Clark, 1995.

STILES, PAUL. *Riding the Bull: My Year in the Madness at Merrill Lynch*. Toronto: Random House, 1998.

TADICH, ALEXANDER. *Rampaging Bulls: Outfox Promoters at Their Own Game on Any Penny Stock*. Calgary: Elan, 1995.

WISE, MICHAEL H. *Canadian Asset Allocation Strategies*. Calgary: WiseWords, 1993.

WOODS, SHIRLEY E. *Through the Money Labyrinth. A Canadian Broker Guides You to Stock Market Success*. Toronto: John Wiley & Sons, Inc., 1994.

YOUNG, DUFF. *Duff Young's Fund Monitor 2000. An Expert's Guide to Selecting Outstanding Mutual Funds*. Scarborough: Prentice Hall, 1999.

PERIODICALS

The Investment Reporter. MPL Communications Inc., 133 Richmond Street West, Toronto, ON M7Y 3P6. Fax 416-869-0456. Telephone: 1-800-430-1897 (toll-free), or 416-869-1177 in Toronto area. Fax: 416-869-0456.

Investor's Digest of Canada. 133 Richmond Street West, Toronto, ON M5H 3M8.

Personal Finance on the Web

MUTUAL FUND COMPANIES

The following companies all sell a full range of mutual funds:

AGF Management
www.agf.com

AIM
www.aimfunds.ca (formerly Trimark)

Altamira Investment Services
www.altamira.com

Assante
www.assante.com

C.I. Mutual Funds
www.cifunds.com

Canada Trust Mutual Funds
www.canadatrust.com

Dynamic Mutual Funds
www.dynamic.ca

Fidelity Investments
www.fidelity.ca

First Canadian Funds (Bank of Montreal)
www.bmo.com/mutualfunds/

GLOBEfund
www.globefund.com

GT Global Mutual Funds
www.gtglobal.ca

Guardian Mutual Funds
www.guardianfunds.com

Hirsch Funds
www.hirschfunds.com

Mackenzie Financial Corporation
www.mackenziefinancial.com

MAXXUM Group of Funds
www.maxxumfund.com/

Merrill Lynch
www.atlasfunds.ca

Royal Mutual Funds
www.royalbank.com/english/fund/index/html

Saxon Mutual Funds
www.saxonfunds.com/~saxon

Scotiabank Investment Centre
www.scotiabank.ca

Scudder Funds of Canada
www.scudder.ca

Spectrum United Mutual Funds
www.spectrumunited.ca

Talvest Fund Management
www.talvest.com

Templeton Management Association of Canada
www.templeton.ca

Working Venture Canadian Fund
www.workingventures.ca

FULL-SERVICE BROKERS

These firms sell a complete range of investment products, including mutual funds.

C.I.B.C. Wood Gundy
www.cibc.com

Levesque Beaubien Geoffrion
www.lbg.ca/lbgmenua.html

Merrill Lynch
www.ml.com

Nesbitt Burns
ww.nesbittburns.com

Philips, Hager and North
www.phn.ca

RBC Dominion Securities
www.rbcds.com/

ScotiaMcLeod
www.scotiamcleodpei.com

Yorkton Securities
www.yorkton.com

DISCOUNT BROKERS

Bank of Montreal: InvestorLine
www.investorline.com

CIBC Investor's Edge Discount Brokerage
www.investorsedge.cibc.com

*E*Trade Canada*
ww.canada.etrade.com

HSBC Invest Direct
nettrader.hkbc.ca

Charles Schwab
www.schwabcanada.com/

Scotia Discount Brokerage (Scotiabank): StockLine
www.sdbi.com

TD WATERHOUSE
www.tdwaterhouse.ca

INVESTMENT NEWSLETTERS

Canadian Mutual Fund Advisor
133 Richmond Street W., Toronto, ON M5H 3M8 416-869-1177

The Canadian Speculator
www.specstock.com

Capital Ideas
www.capitalideas.com

IE: Money
   www.iemoney.com

Stock Letter Positioning: Unique Investment Club
   www.stockletter.com

The Successful Investor
   www.thesuccessfulinvestor.com

OTHER USEFUL SOURCES

Bloomberg
   www.bloomberg.com Provides a wealth of financial information.

Canadian Securities Administrators
   www.osc.gov.on.ca

Canadian Securities Institute
   www.csi.ca

The Canadian Shareholders Association (CSA)
   www.shareowner.ca

Canadian Venture Exchange
   www.cdnx.ca

Chicago Board of Options Exchange
   www.cboe.com

Chicago Board of Trade
   www.cbot.com One of the few sites that provides information on futures.

Chicago Mercantile Exchange
   www.cme.com/ A major commodities exchange where futures contracts are traded.

CNN Financial-US Stock Markets
   www.cnnfn.com/ Provides quotations from the various U.S. stock markets.

CNN Financial-World Stock Market Indices
   www.cnfn.com/markets/world_markets.html Offers information on world stock market indices.

Day Traders
   www.daytraders.com Provides a full list of day-trader Web sites.

Directions
   www.ndir.com Provides a lot of educational material.

Fortune
   pathfinder.com/fortune A leading American business magazine famous for creating the "Fortune 500" rating system for U.S. corporations.

FundWatch Online Services
   www.fundwatch.ca Offers a great deal of mutual fund information.

Globe and Mail "Report on Business"
   www.globeandmail.ca Considered one of Canada's leading sources of financial news; the *Globe and Mail*'s "Report on Business" is always of interest to investors. *The Report on Business Magazine*, published once a month, contains in-depth articles on related subjects.

Gordon Pape's Building Wealth on the Net
   www.gordonpape.com Through his books and radio broadcasts, Gordon Pape has become one of Canada's best-known investment commentators. This site gives his opinions of the many mutual funds available.

Guide for Starting an Investment Club
   24929 Warden Avenue, Keswick, ON L4P 3E9

Investing for Kids
   http://tqd.advanced.org/3906/

Investment Funds Institute of Canada
   www.ific.ca IFIC publishes many booklets on mutual funds, which are available free of charge.

The Investor Learning Centre of Canada
   www.investorlearning.ca

Morningstar.ca
   www.morningstar.ca Filled with information on mutual funds.

National Association of Investors Clubs
   www.better-investing.org

Online Canadian clubs
   www.computerland.net/

Quicken
   www.intuit.com Allows you to obtain current stock and mutual fund values.

Quote.Com
   www.quote.com Provides quotes on stocks, bonds, mutual funds, and commodity futures. Also offers company profiles and access to stock exchange information.

ROB Top 1000 Companies
   www.robmagazine.com/top1000/ Provides information on Canada's largest and most profitable companies.

Stock Quotes
   www.canoe.ca/Investment/home.html Allows you to search for quotes for any Canadian or U.S. stock.

Stock Research Group
   www.stockgroup.com Specializes in small-cap companies with growth potential.

StockSmart
   www.stocksmart.com Lets investors set up an alert so that they are notified by e-mail or pager if a stock price drops below a certain level.

Wall Street Journal

www.public.wsj.com/home.html Widely viewed as the leading financial newspaper in the United States, the *Journal* is considered essential reading by many investors. It provides on-line stock quotes.

What's New in Ethical Investment?

www.web.apc.org/ethmoney/new.htm Provides current information about investments which qualify as ethical.

Yahoo! Finance

http://ca.quote.yahoo.com Considered by many to be the best free site on the net.

Duff Young

www.fundmonitor.com Young is one of Canada's mutual fund experts.

Credit

This section presents a thorough discussion of consumer and mortgage credit, beginning with trends in the use of consumer credit in Canada. Chapter 12 also discusses consumer loans and vendor credit; some of the institutions that provide credit; and the terminology they use, and provides some samples of the contracts used by lenders. These samples will help familiarize you with the contracts and help you understand these documents.

Following the convention of treating mortgage credit separate from consumer credit, Chapter 13 discusses home mortgages. Chapter 14 explains credit reporting and debt collection proceedings, which can confuse most people. That chapter also discusses an unpleasant topic: the options and strategies available for debtors who find themselves overcommitted.

Chapter 12

Consumer Credit and Loans

objectives

1. Distinguish among consumer debt, mortgage debt, and total debt.

2. Explain some of the trends in the use of consumer credit.

3. Formulate generalizations that apply at the household level about relations between the following variables: income and the probability of having consumer debt; income and average consumer debt; stage in the life cycle and incidence of consumer debt; and, age and average consumer debt.

4. Examine four major reasons for using credit.

5. Distinguish between enforcement of security and other ways of collecting debts.

6. Explain how a promissory note, wage assignment, chattel mortgage, and lien differ from one another and identify a situation where each might be used.

7. Ascertain the following by examining a chattel mortgage: the security pledged; the repayment conditions; the penalties for late payments; and the conditions under which a creditor may enforce security and the means that may be used.

8. Compare the costs of various types of consumer loans and suggest reasons for the interest rate spread.

9. Distinguish among debit cards, charge cards, credit cards, conditional sales contracts/agreements, and chattel mortgages.

10. Explain the main provisions of the legislation regarding the following matters: disclosure of information about credit transactions; supervision of itinerant sellers; repossession of goods when the borrower defaults; advertising credit; and unsolicited credit cards and unsolicited goods.

Introduction

To set the foundation for the discussion of consumer credit, we will first examine some information on the amount and types of consumer credit used in Canada. Both national data and some micro surveys of households will further the discussion of the variables concerned with consumer credit. This chapter also discusses consumer loans, with a focus on how consumers arrange for a loan from a financial institution (as opposed to point-of-sale-credit, which is arranged when an item or service is purchased). In the former situation, the purchase is separate from the arranging of the loan. We will briefly discuss debit cards, and finally we will review some issues and problems that are of concern to credit users; in particular, we will provide sample credit contracts that will help you understand such documents.

What Is Credit?

Credit and Debt

Every borrowing transaction involves two actors. The lender (the creditor) supplies money for a loan in exchange for a credit, and views the transaction in terms of the amount of credit that has been extended. The borrower (the debtor) receives the money, and views the transaction as an accumulation of debt. That which is *consumer debt* to you, the borrower/debtor, is *consumer credit* to the lender/creditor. Information about this transaction may be reported either as debt or as credit, depending on the reporter's perspective. Although it is really the same phenomenon, data obtained from households about their borrowing are usually reported as consumer debt, while statistics gathered from lenders are referred to as consumer credit. This chapter examines both kinds of data.

The debtor in a credit/debt transaction accepts a commitment to repay the debt at some time in the future, and thus must be prepared to give up future purchasing power in order to have extra resources available at present. In deciding that it is more important to have extra funds now than to wait until the money can be saved, the debtor should realize that a cost of using credit is the commitment of future income to interest payments; these funds will not be available for other uses. The borrower/debtor promises to repay not only the principal (that is, the sum borrowed) but also the interest(that is, the charge for borrowing). Thus, the lender/ creditor holds a claim that the borrower/debtor will repay interest and principal as promised.

It is conventional to distinguish between consumer debt and mortgage debt: **total debt** is the sum of these two. **Consumer debt** is defined as all the personal debt incurred by households, excluding mortgage debt or business debt. **Mortgage debt** is any debt that is secured by real property, such as buildings and land. To summarize:

consumer debt + mortgage debt = total debt of households

Mortgage debt generally involves much larger amounts and for much longer terms than consumer debt does; combining these statistics would obscure trends in consumer debt. From the household's perspective, mortgage debt can be viewed as the ongoing cost of housing—a regular expense—in contrast to short-term debt. Also, borrowing to invest in property can be an effective way to accumulate assets, but borrowing for current consumption is not. For a discussion of mortgages, see Chapter 13.

National Consumer Credit Data

Sources of Information

Lenders are required to report regularly to Statistics Canada about the amount of credit they have extended; when gathered together, these data are called the **total consumer credit outstanding.** These statistics, collected at the national level (macro data), show the amounts of credit held by various lenders, but they provide no information about individual borrowers. Still, macro data are quite useful for giving a picture of national trends. Such data were not available before 1951; the shift toward collecting them probably indicates the increasing significance of consumer credit in our society.

How Much Credit Do We Use?

You may have heard that Canadians now use more consumer credit than ever before. To verify this statement, examine the trends in the total consumer credit outstanding since 1970 (Figure 12.1). Clearly, the increase in total credit outstanding over this time span has been dramatic. Look at one decade at a time to find when the rate of increase (slope of the line) changed significantly. What are some possible explanations for the great increase in the use of consumer credit? It may be that (i) the population grew rapidly and thus more credit was needed in Canada, or (ii) the prices of goods rose substantially, necessitating larger loans, or (iii) each person used more credit. We will examine each of these possibilities in turn.

POPULATION CHANGES The data shown in Figure 12.1 make no allowance for any changes in Canada's population. To correct this problem, we can divide each year's total

FIGURE 12.1 TOTAL CONSUMER CREDIT OUTSTANDING, CANADA, 1970–1998

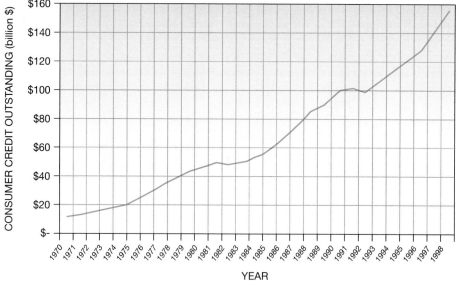

SOURCE: Data from *Bank of Canada Review* (Ottawa: Bank of Canada), Winter 1980/81, Table 50, p. S100; Winter 1989/90, Table E2, p. S72; Winter 1993/94, Table E2, p. S48; Winter 1997/98, Table E2, p. S50; *Weekly Financial Statistics* (Ottawa: Bank of Canada), February 16, 2001, Table E2, p. 13.

credit figures by Canada's population for that year. Examine the line in Figure 12.2 labelled "constant credit outstanding," showing the amounts of consumer credit outstanding per capita. The slope of this line generally matches that in Figure 12.1, indicating about the same rate of increase. Apparently, then, the rapid increase in total consumer credit outstanding cannot be explained by a change in Canada's population.

INFLATION Perhaps prices caused people to use increasing amounts of consumer credit. For example, as the prices of cars rose, the size of each car loan necessarily increased. Thus, inflated prices increased loan amounts, rather than more people buying more cars. To check whether the rapidly rising amounts of consumer credit were caused by inflation, we must adjust the credit outstanding per capita to reflect changes in consumer prices. The statistical procedure for doing so involves converting the values that were in **current dollars** (that is, the dollar amounts recorded in each year) into **constant dollars** (which estimate the values if prices had remained constant). The numbers plotted in Figure 12.1 reflect current dollars, but these may be converted to constant dollars by using the following formula:

$$\frac{\text{Value in current dollars in Year X}}{\text{Consumer Price Index in Year X}} \times 100 = \begin{array}{c} \text{Constant \$} \\ \text{in Year X} \end{array}$$

This is a way of eliminating, statistically, the effect of changes in prices. In other words, if consumer prices had remained unchanged since 1971, the amount of consumer credit extended would be approximately that shown in constant dollars in Figure 12.2.

If the increase in consumer credit outstanding had been entirely due to population changes and rising prices, the constant dollar line in Figure 12.2, which has been corrected to reflect

FIGURE 12.2 CONSUMER CREDIT OUTSTANDING PER CAPITA, CANADA, 1970–1998
(IN CURRENT AND CONSTANT 1970 DOLLARS)

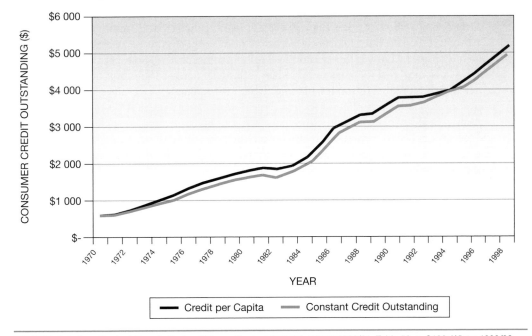

SOURCE: Data from *Bank of Canada Review* (Ottawa: Bank of Canada), Winter 1980/81, Table 50, p. S100; Winter 1989/90, Table E2, p. S72; Winter 1993/94, Table E2, p. S48; Winter 1997/98, Table E2, p. S50; *Weekly Financial Statistics* (Ottawa: Bank of Canada), February 16, 2001, Table E2, p. 13.

both, would be perfectly horizontal. Since instead it shows a rising trend, we can conclude from these data that regardless of any changes in population or in consumer prices, Canadians' use of consumer credit did increase during the years in question. Much of the difference between the two lines in Figure 12.2 can be attributed to the effects of inflation; as prices of goods and services rose, so did the amounts borrowed.

These data clearly show that the recessions of 1982–83 and 1991–92 were turning points in Canadians' use of consumer credit. The slowdown in the economy, escalating interest rates, and high unemployment combined during each of those periods to create uncertainty and a natural reluctance to incur more debt. Many people who already had debts found it very difficult to maintain their payment schedules, and bankruptcies were common. For a while, attitudes toward using consumer debt became more cautious. How long did these effects last? To answer this question, we need only look at what happened to the trend from 1982 through 1990, and at what the trend has been since 1992.

By 1985, Canadians had begun once again to increase their use of consumer credit, and the trend resumed its climb—slowly at first, and then more rapidly between 1987 and 1990. Predictably, the 1990–92 recession resulted in another downturn in consumer credit outstanding. But in 1994, the trend had returned to its previous steady ascent.

Debt Burden/Personal Use

Another way of analyzing the use of consumer credit involves relating it to income levels. If people commit about the same proportion of income to repaying debts year after year, their burden of debt does not change, even though the actual level of debt rises. **Debt burden** is often measured as a ratio of debt or credit to income. Continuing to use macro data, we will now compare the ratio of total consumer credit outstanding to total personal disposable income in each of the years since 1978. (**Personal disposable income** is defined as all the income received by Canadians after income tax was paid.)

Debt burden, which was less than 10 percent in 1951, had by 1980 more than doubled, to 22 percent; it then declined for a few years before rising again (Figure 12.3). To understand debt burden, consider what was happening to family incomes in the same period. After World War II Canadians' **real incomes** (adjusted for inflation) increased substantially, leaving most families with more **discretionary income,** which is income left over after paying for such necessities as food, clothing, and shelter. This new prosperity made it possible to buy more consumer durables (items that are expected to last for some time, such as appliances or stereos) and recreational goods, which at the time were the types of items most frequently bought on credit. People's steadily rising incomes made repaying their debts easier, because incomes tended to increase annually while most debt contracts remain fixed for several years. Thus, the combination of fixed debt commitments and rising incomes was beneficial for borrowers. But in times of slower economic growth, wise people reduce their debt burden. By 1990, the ratio of debt to income had dropped somewhat. After the recession of the early nineties, the debt burden began once again to increase steadily each year.

Consumer Debt Use at the Household Level

Thus far, we have been examining macro statistics that give a general picture of credit use in Canada over a number of years. Another source of information about credit or debt is micro data, obtained by interviewing householders. Statistics Canada conducts occasional surveys of

FIGURE 12.3 RATIO OF TOTAL CONSUMER CREDIT OUTSTANDING TO PERSONAL DISPOSABLE INCOME, CANADA, 1970–1998

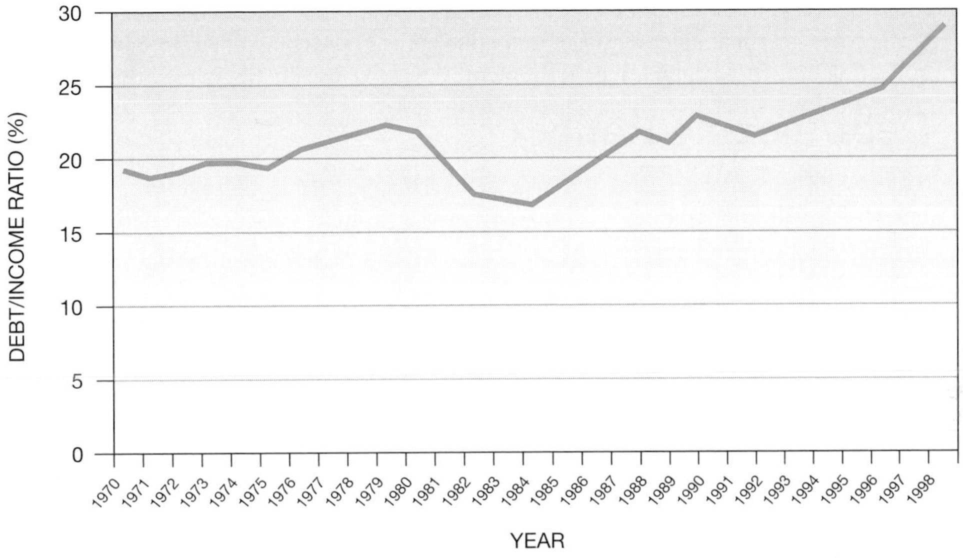

SOURCE: Data from *Bank of Canada Review* (Ottawa: Bank of Canada), Winter 1980/81, Table 50, p. S100; Winter 1989/90, Table E2, p. S72; Winter 1993/94, Table E2, p. S48; Winter 1997/98, Table E2, p. S50; *Weekly Financial Statistics* (Ottawa: Bank of Canada), February 16, 2001, Table E2, p. 13.

consumer debt. Asking people about their debts, incomes, and other variables allows researchers to explore the relationships, if any, between debt levels and other characteristics such as income, age, education, and occupation. Let us examine the connections between the use of consumer debt and both income and age, based on studies conducted in the past by Statistics Canada. Because the most recent data are from 1984, we will review consumer debt in a general way. (We will not report the old data in detail.)

When reviewing research reports, make sure you know exactly how a particular study defines credit and debt. Although debt is generally classified as either consumer debt or mortgage debt, somewhat different terms are used in Statistics Canada household surveys, where "personal debt" refers to all non-mortgage debt. For our purposes, we will consider personal debt and consumer debt to be the same.

Income and Consumer Debt

Are people with higher incomes more likely to incur consumer debt than those with lower incomes? Low-income families may wish to use credit, but are usually denied it because they lack the ability to repay their debts. Previous Statistic Canada studies (as mentioned above) allow us to generalize that if 1984 patterns have remained unchanged, a household's probability of having consumer debt increases with the household's income.

Stage in the Life Cycle and Consumer Debt

Is a person's stage in the life cycle (or age) associated with the probability of having certain kinds of debt? A curvilinear relation (which reflects an increasing, then decreasing, probability of two events or variables occurring together) between age and the incidence (probability) of personal and mortgage debt was clearly shown in past studies. People who are 35 to 44 years old appear most likely to have both kinds of debt (this age group also has the highest average levels of consumer debt), while those over 65 appear most likely to have neither. This pattern is consistent with people's needs at different stages in the life cycle. Younger families start buying houses and collecting household durables; by retirement, they have usually discharged these debts.

Debt/Income Ratio

So far we have seen how income and stage in the life cycle (that is, age) affect the likelihood that households will carry consumer debt. Another way to analyze the use of consumer debt is to look at the ratio of consumer debt to income—that is, to look at debt burden. Here again, no recent data are available, but past researchers have found that middle-income households have a higher propensity for incurring a heavy debt burden. This pattern is quite understandable, considering that the heads of low-income families are often very young or very old, and are therefore not usually seen as good candidates for consumer credit. People with high incomes, while they are heavy users of credit, have incomes that are large enough to make the burden manageable.

Why Do We Use Credit?

People no doubt use credit for many reasons, but most can be classified into four main categories. We use credit (i) for convenience; (ii) to obtain something before we have saved enough to pay for it; (iii) to bridge the gap when our income is insufficient, infrequent, or irregular; and occasionally (iv) to consolidate debts. Each of these reasons may have costs as well as benefits.

Convenience

Many of us find it very handy to use a credit card instead of carrying cash, as well as to be able to pay a number of bills using just one cheque (to the credit card company). As long as you pay the outstanding amount monthly, a credit card is an interest-free convenience. Some charge accounts require you to pay your total bill each month, but others, such as bank credit cards and retail revolving accounts, offer you a choice: you may pay all or only a portion of the debt. Having this option makes it quite easy to let bills accumulate, and the interest rates charged on unpaid balances are usually high. A credit card also tends to encourage impulsive shopping; having to pay in cash is a more effective restraint.

Immediacy

As advertisers eagerly point out, credit allows us to have things immediately and pay later. Offering credit is a very successful way to sell high-priced goods and services: buyers need not consider whether they can afford the selling price, but merely whether they can manage the monthly payments. Each individual must decide whether or not credit's benefits outweigh its costs. Sometimes, the chance to have a good or service immediately can be worth the cost. When you take into account the costs of being without a car or certain equipment, you may discover monetary benefits in using credit.

But most of the benefits of using credit for this reason are not monetary. Many of us find it very appealing to have something we want as soon as we see it, but whether the resulting satisfaction offsets the cost must be a personal decision. Some people find it almost impossible to save enough to accumulate the purchase price of certain expensive items; using credit is thus the only way they can acquire such things. In such instances, credit becomes a form of forced saving, albeit an expensive one.

Two costs of using credit to obtain immediate satisfaction are (i) the interest to be paid, and (ii) the loss of financial flexibility. Interest is a direct monetary cost that varies directly according to the time taken to repay the debt. Another cost—which can be very significant, although it may be less visible—is the flexibility cost of having committed some future income to debt repayment. When you use credit, you are accepting an obligation to make future payments; those payments may curtail your freedom to spend in other ways. If something happens to your income stream—if, for example, you become ill or lose your job—debt payments can become a substantial burden. If unexpected emergencies occur, you will have less money available for large expenses. When you buy consumer durables or vehicles on credit, you must consider not only the flexibility cost but also whether you will be able to handle the recurring expenses of operating and maintaining the item you are buying.

To Bridge the Gap

People who have an irregular income (such as many self-employed persons) may require loans in order to pay regular expenses until the arrival of their next income cheque. Until a sufficient reserve fund is built up, loans that will bridge this gap may be necessary. Even with a regular income, people sometimes find themselves without enough money to cover reasonable needs. When your income prospects appear good, you may consider it worthwhile to incur debt to furnish your first home, to support a growing family, or to obtain an education.

Consolidation Loans

When their bills and debts exceed their income, some people borrow enough to repay all outstanding debts. With a consolidation loan, they then owe one large amount to one lender for a longer time. Such loans may reduce the financial pressure temporarily, but this approach tends to lock people into continual debt. We will discuss this topic in more detail in Chapter 14, under "Alternatives for the Overcommitted Debtor."

Inflation

In inflationary periods, borrowers tend to benefit at the expense of lenders. As prices rise and incomes tend to increase, a borrower pays back loans that have fixed payments. This makes it comparatively easy to handle debt. The lender, on the other hand, is paid back in dollars that will buy less than when they were lent. Another aspect of very rapid inflation is the advantage to the borrower of being able to make a purchase before the price goes up any further. Under such conditions, it may be quite rational to use credit rather than to accumulate savings. But doing so may leave you vulnerable if economic conditions change, as they did for Canada in the early 1980s and the early 1990s.

The Two Forms of Consumer Credit

As mentioned earlier, we can classify consumer credit transactions according to the source of the funds. You may obtain a **consumer loan** from a financial institution. Alternatively, you may arrange for financing to be extended at the time you make a purchase; this approach (which may involve a credit card, a charge card, or a conditional sales contract) is known as **point-of-sale credit.** We will discuss consumer loans next; later, we will examine point-of-sale credit (sometimes called vendor credit), as well as debit cards.

Major Consumer Lenders

Funds can be borrowed from a number of places, but four types of financial institutions are particularly active in providing consumer loans: banks, credit unions, trust companies, and small loans companies. You may also borrow against the cash value of your life insurance if you happen to own the right kind of policy—see Chapter 6, especially the sections "Policy Loan" and "Collateral for a Loan" under the heading "Uses for the Cash Reserves." (Other possible sources of borrowed funds, which will not be discussed here, are family, friends, pawnbrokers, and loan sharks.)

Market Shares

Earlier in this chapter, we saw that the long-term trend in Canada has been toward an increase in the use of consumer credit. We will now examine how the consumer credit market is shared by various creditors. In Figure 12.4, each bar represents all the consumer credit

FIGURE 12.4   SHARE OF TOTAL CONSUMER CREDIT OUTSTANDING BY SOURCE,*
CANADA, 1970–1997

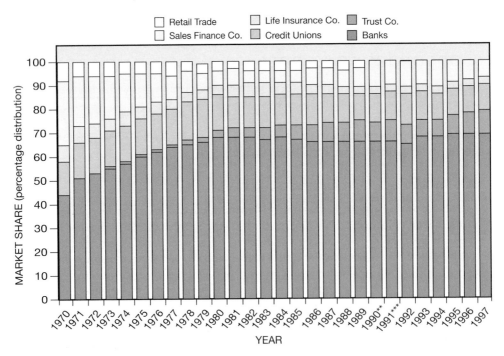

* These data show estimated amounts of consumer credit on the books of selected lenders. The data collected have not been completely consistent over the 40-year period shown. From 1978 on, the data have not included credit held by TV and appliance stores, other retail outlets, motor vehicle dealers, public utilities, credit card issuers not included elsewhere in the data, and oil companies' charge card accounts.

** Retail trade no longer shown separately.

*** Before 1992, the "finance companies" category comprised only sales finance and small loans companies; the 1992 category includes retail trade institutions as well as finance companies.

SOURCE: Data from *Bank of Canada Review* (Ottawa: Bank of Canada), various issues; *Canada Year Book* (Ottawa: Statistics Canada), various issues (Catalogue No. 11-402). Reproduced with the permission of the Bank of Canada and the Minister of Industry, Science and Technology, 1998.

outstanding in Canada in a given year; the divisions within the bar show how the business was divided among major lenders. These data include both consumer loans and point-of-sale credit (both of which are explained in detail later in this chapter); since some creditors offer both, the data are difficult to separate. Bank consumer lending, which includes personal loans and credit cards, represents a mixture of loan and point-of-sale credit.

As Figure 12.4 clearly shows, significant changes in market shares occurred during the latter half of the century. The most striking shift involves the banks' steadily increasing role as the major creditors; they have taken market share from retail trade, as well as from sales finance and small loans companies. Credit unions slightly increased their share of the consumer credit business, while life insurance policy loans showed a decline. Trust companies, which entered the consumer credit business more recently than the other types of institutions, gained an increasing market share. We will review the major consumer lenders and think about possible reasons for the changes.

Financial Institutions

At one time banks, credit unions, trust companies, and small loans companies were distinctly different in their structures and in the services they provided, but now the trend is toward greater similarity. Legislative changes have removed many of the barriers that once kept banks, brokers, trust companies, and insurers operating independent and different businesses. Although consumers may find that little has changed on the surface, behind the scenes things are very different. Banks have bought much of the brokerage industry, have become active in mutual funds, are dominating the trust business, and are trying to get into the life insurance industry. What does all this change mean for consumers? For one thing, there is less competition in the marketplace, which is now dominated by a few giant companies. Whether these changes will affect service and prices remains to be seen, but the possibility that they would do so was frequently considered when the proposed mergers were denied in 1999.

In the present period of rapid change, it is difficult to find clear distinctions among financial institutions. Soon, we may go to just one place to do our banking, buy insurance, order mutual funds, and set up trusts. Credit unions have changed, too, but so far they have not merged with other financial institutions.

Banks

The chartered banks, many of which have large systems of branch offices, borrow from depositors in order to lend to those who need money. They charge enough interest on the money they lend so that they are, in turn, able to pay interest to their creditors (the depositors). The difference between the interest rate charged on loans and the interest rate paid on deposits, which is called the **spread,** covers the bank's operating costs and also provides profit for the bank's shareholders. Chartered banks are regulated by the federal Bank Act, which is revised about once a decade. Until its 1967 revision, the Act restricted banks in their consumer loan activity. Afterward, banks became very active in consumer loans (see Figure 12.4). Although they once concentrated on banking, chartered banks are now Canada's most powerful financial institutions.

Trust Companies

Trust companies, which have been active in Canada since the latter part of the nineteenth century, provide financial and trustee services to individuals and corporations. A **trustee,** which may be a person or a trust company, manages the financial affairs of others—either during their lifetime or after death. Some people stipulate in their wills (see Chapter 3) that a trust fund must be set up on their death; they name a person or trust company as trustee to handle the funds. In Canada, trust companies have been the only corporations that may act as trustees. Previously, banks and other financial institutions were not permitted to conduct **fiduciary** business—that is, to act as trustees—but this distinction has been loosened somewhat as many banks own trust companies.

Trust companies have certain advantages over individuals who are acting as trustees: a company can provide continuous service over a long period of time. A trust company's expertise may be invaluable with a complex trust that involves large sums of money. In exchange for their services, trust companies charge an annual fee—usually a percentage of the capital being managed. For individuals, trust companies handle both **living trusts,** which have been established by people who are still alive, and **testamentary trusts,** which are created by a will, on a person's death. A large part of a trust company's business involves acting as a trustee for other corporations in handling pension funds, bond issues, and the like.

A trust company's charter does not limit it to fiduciary business, so trust companies are active financial intermediaries, taking in deposits and making loans of various kinds. Generally, only the larger trust companies are in the consumer loan business, but mortgage lending is a different matter. In recent years, trust and mortgage loan companies have provided significant amounts of mortgage funds. As many small trust companies are bought by larger ones or by banks, we see fewer and larger trust companies dominating the scene. The survivors compete directly with the banks in the services they offer, even with the banks that own them.

Small Loans Companies

Many small loans companies and money lenders are affiliated with other financial institutions; this is especially true of sales finance companies. It is not uncommon for a firm to operate both a small loans company and a sales finance business from the same premises; because of this close affiliation, the statistics of such businesses are often combined. The principal distinction is that small loans companies and money lenders make cash loans, while sales finance companies buy credit contracts arranged by retailers. The cost of credit at a small loans company tends to be high, reflecting such factors as their willingness to accept higher-risk borrowers, the cost of processing small loans, and the fact that they themselves are not deposit-taking institutions but must instead borrow from other sources in order to have money to lend. Before 1975, such firms had a significant share of the consumer credit business, but that share subsequently diminished (Figure 12.4). As a result, there are fewer small loans companies or sales finance companies in business these days.

Life Insurance Policy Loans

Loans may be made against life insurance policies that have a cash surrender value, such as whole life policies, but not against term policies or against most group policies, which have no cash value. It takes two or three years for a policy's cash surrender value to build up enough to make the policyholder eligible for a loan. The policy's cash value grows each year that the policy is in force, and the amounts are shown in the policy. Generally, policies permit about 90 percent to 100 percent of the cash value to be borrowed.

The interest rate on life insurance policy loans is usually lower than that available from other commercial sources. Before 1968, the maximum loan rate was 6 percent, but policies written since that time have not been so restricted; the usual practice now is not to state a lending rate in the policy. There is no difficulty in obtaining the loan, because the policyholder is borrowing from the cash value of his or her own policy. Nor is there a time limit for repaying the loan; any interest that is due will automatically be added to the loan. A loan on a policy does not invalidate life insurance coverage. When the policyholder dies, the policy remains intact, but any outstanding debt is subtracted from the payment to the beneficiary. The terms of the loan are stated in the life insurance policy. Look at the sample life insurance policy in Chapter 6 (see Appendix 6A, "A Sample Life Insurance Policy") to find out what the terms are for a policy loan.

As a share of all consumer credit outstanding in Canada, life insurance policy loans are not very significant; in fact, they have been decreasing. In 1955, policy loans represented less than 9 percent of all consumer credit, but by 1997 this share was down to 3 percent. Some possible reasons for this change are (i) that the demand for consumer credit has increased at a much faster rate than the purchase of life insurance has, (ii) that more life insurance without cash value is being sold now than previously, and (iii) loans are readily available elsewhere. It is quicker and simpler to charge things on a credit card than to negotiate a life insurance loan. Life insurance companies do not especially promote policy loans, and many people have so little understanding of their life insurance coverage that they may not be aware of this source of credit.

Credit Unions

The financial cooperatives in the consumer lending and saving business are the **credit unions,** originally created to offer services to low-income families whose only other option was to borrow from a loan shark. By pooling the funds of savers, a credit union allows money to be lent at reasonable rates to those who need to borrow, resulting in an arrangement that is advantageous to both savers (who receive dividends from the interest paid on the loans) and borrowers. Early credit unions were small: their members knew one another, and personal needs received careful attention. A debt to one's credit union was seen as a personal obligation to friends or associates, so social pressure to repay loans was strong and losses were thus minimized; sadly, the growth of credit unions has meant a shift in the attitudes of some borrowers, who now default on loans nearly as often as people who borrow from other kinds of financial institutions.

History

The credit union movement began in 1847 when, Friedrich Raiffeisen, who was a mayor and a lay preacher, became concerned about the peasants of southern Germany, who were hopelessly in debt following a series of crop failures. The only sources of loans available to them were banks, which required gilt-edged security, or loan sharks, who exacted punitive interest rates. Raiffeisen was instrumental in establishing credit societies, using the small savings of members to create funds that could be borrowed by others. By the time Raiffeisen died, in 1888, 423 credit unions were flourishing in Germany.

As the twentieth century dawned, Alphonse Desjardins of Lévis, Quebec, a legislative reporter, noted the high rates being charged by money lenders to the region's poor people. Using some of Raiffeisen's ideas, Desjardins started *La Caisse Populaire de Lévis* with an initial membership of 80 people and assets of $26. This venture met a widespread need so successfully that credit unions were organized in many Quebec parishes. As the credit union idea spread, first from Lévis to Boston, and then to Nova Scotia, Saskatchewan, and across the continent, people adapted it to meet local requirements. Few credit unions were established in Ontario before 1945, when the move toward industrial credit unions began.

Organization

COMMON BOND To do business with a credit union, you must be a member of the cooperative. Moreover, legislation requires that a credit union's members share a **common bond:**

they may all work for the same company; belong to the same church or synagogue, labour union, or volunteer organization; or live in the same community or on the same military base. Potential members must meet the common bond requirement; they must also buy a share in the credit union, which may cost as little as $5. Recently, as a result of mergers, larger credit unions with residential common bonds have replaced small credit unions with very specific common bonds (such as place of employment or church membership).

MEMBER INVOLVEMENT As part of a non-profit cooperative, a credit union's members have a say in its operation through the elected board of directors, which determines general policy and either handles operating decisions or delegates them to a paid manager. The credit union's net earnings are returned to members, whether those members are borrowers or depositors or both, in a variety of ways, such as dividends on the share accounts, higher interest rates on deposits, lower charges for loans, or additional services.

PROVINCIAL DIFFERENCES In Canada, the credit union movement is strongest in Quebec (where over 60 percent of the population are members) and in Saskatchewan (where more than half of the population are members). In most other provinces, credit union members represent less than a third of the population. The Quebec credit unions, or *caisses populaires*, have nearly half of all the Canadian credit union assets. Saskatchewan and Quebec far outrank the other provinces in credit union assets per capita.

NETWORK All credit unions are linked into regional, provincial, and national networks. Starting at the top, the World Council of Credit Unions comprises national associations such as the Credit Union Central of Canada. In Canada, the three-tiered structure consists of provincial chapters or centrals, regional groupings within the province, and local credit unions. This arrangement leaves credit unions with a great deal of local autonomy but with connections to the larger organization. Local credit unions, with their separate boards of directors, are more independent from the larger umbrella organizations than are the branches of large banks with respect to the banks' head offices. Nevertheless, there is a move to coordinate services so that a member of one credit union can conduct business at another credit union.

The provincial centrals offer important assistance to credit unions, including investing their surplus funds or lending them additional money; supplying legal assistance, lobbying power, and educational services; and helping them save money through central purchasing of supplies. Deposit insurance, which is very important to savers, is arranged through the provincial centrals.

SECURITY Borrowers at credit unions may be asked to provide several forms of security. For example, they may be required to maintain the equivalent of 10 percent of the outstanding balance on their loans in a deposit account; in addition, they may be expected to sign a promissory note, a wage assignment, and, if appropriate, a chattel mortgage. In some instances a co-signer may be required. These terms will all be explained later in this chapter under "Security for Loans."

Recent Trends

NUMBERS OF CREDIT UNIONS Historically, most credit unions were operated by volunteers in premises that were often rent-free. These small amateur operations were low-cost and intimate, but eventually they became unable to compete with the larger-scale and more professional activities of banks and trust companies. As a consequence, many small credit unions merged to form fewer, larger unions, hiring staff to run them and making them into more efficient and impersonal institutions. Figure 12.5 illustrates the pattern of change in the numbers of credit union locals,

FIGURE 12.5   NUMBER OF CREDIT UNIONS IN CANADA, 1947–1995

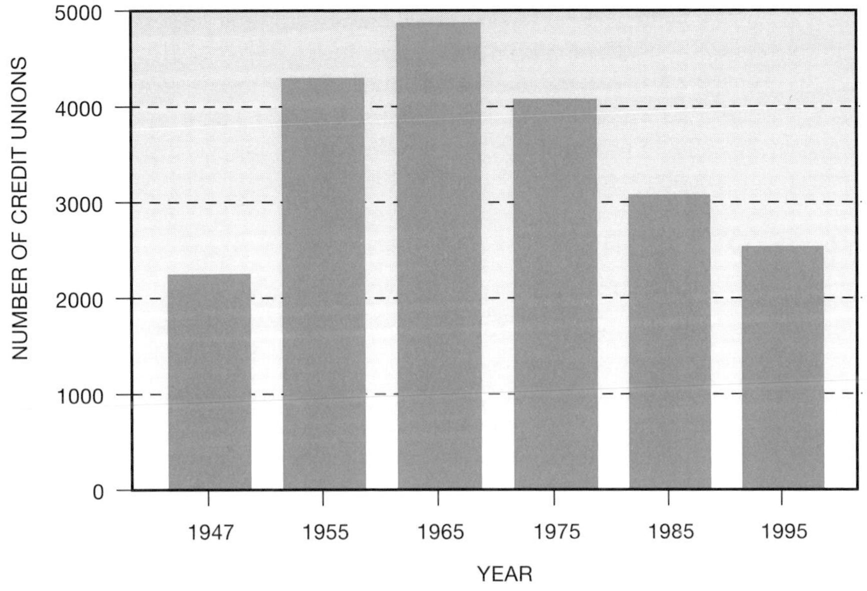

SOURCE: Statistics Canada, *Canada Year Book* various issues: 1948–49 (p. 1051); 1961, Table 18 (p. 1130); 1962, Table 18 (p. 1108); 1972, Table 17 (p. 1245); 1990, Table 18.14, (p. 18-6); 1997 (Catalogue No. 11-402). Reproduced with the permission of the Minister of Industry, Science and Technology, 1998.

showing the gradual growth of credit unions in the early years, their rapid expansion during the 1950s and 1960s, and the effects of the mergers beginning in the 1970s.

SERVICES   Credit unions vary considerably in size and in the range of services they provide. All receive deposits and make loans, but some also offer a variety of deposit accounts and savings vehicles, chequing services, mortgage loans, and automatic tellers. The larger credit unions have become quite competitive with banks and trust companies in interest rates and services offered.

As larger credit unions were created, volunteer staff were replaced with paid professional managers, loans officers, and independent auditors. Such changes were necessary if credit unions were to become competitive with other financial institutions. Interestingly, credit unions were the first financial institutions to offer such innovations as weekly-payment mortgages and daily interest savings accounts, and to explore the use of debit cards (see the "Debit Cards" section later in this chapter, under "Economic Significance"). To increase the competition among financial institutions, British Columbia revised its *Financial Institutions Act*, making credit unions subject to the same rules as other institutions and giving them the right to sell equity shares to their members. In 1992, the credit unions' national trade association, the Credit Union Central of Canada, introduced a new group of ethical mutual funds across the country.

Obtaining a Loan

Applying for a Loan

The procedure for obtaining a loan is about the same at any lender. The credit manager (sometimes called a loans officer) will ask you to complete a loan application form which requires considerable detail about your past financial activities. On the basis of this and other information that may be obtained in a credit report, the loans officer decides whether or not to approve the loan. (Chapter 14 discusses credit reports, credit bureaus, and how lenders evaluate a customer's creditworthiness.) If the decision is favourable, the next step is to settle the main **terms of the loan:** the principal to be lent, the interest rate, the length of time to repay, and the security required. The date by which the loan must be completely repaid is known as the **maturity date**, and the maximum length of time that the loan is to be outstanding is called the **term of the loan.** (Notice the distinction between the "terms" of the loan and the "term" of the loan.)

Types of Loans

The kinds of loans available to individuals at financial institutions differ in their terms and conditions. Interest rates depend on the risk level represented by the borrower and on the services provided. Some arrangements provide funds on an ongoing basis; others are contracts drawn up for a specific instalment loan. Examples of the ongoing types of loans are (i) a line of credit, (ii) overdraft protection, and (iii) cash advances on a bank credit card. All of these give the borrower advance permission to borrow within set limits if the need arises. The advantage of these arrangements is that the funds are available to you if you need them, but you pay no interest charges if you do not use them. At other times, a sum may be borrowed for a specific purpose with a set repayment schedule; examples of such arrangements include (i) a demand loan or (ii) an instalment loan.

PERSONAL LINE OF CREDIT Banks, trust companies, and credit unions may offer their creditworthy customers a personal line of credit as a convenient substitute for personal loans. A personal line of credit is a flexible way to use credit; the financial institution makes funds available to you up to a set limit, whenever you need the money. You pay no interest charge until you use some or all of the available funds.

Once your line-of-credit application has been approved, the financial institution supplies you with a line of credit up to a specified maximum amount. You will usually be required to make a minimum monthly payment in addition to interest on any outstanding monthly balance. Your line of credit could involve an amount as low as $2500 or $5000; payments must generally cover at least 3 percent to 5 percent of the outstanding balance. The interest rate on a line of credit is related to the prime rate (defined below, under "Demand Loan") and is adjusted monthly. Sometimes you can arrange a line of credit that requires interest payments only. If you are eligible for one, a line of credit may cost less than a personal loan.

OVERDRAFT PROTECTION The difference between a personal line of credit and overdraft protection may be blurred by some financial institutions. Overdraft protection, which is available at banks, trust companies, and credit unions, allows deposit accounts to become overdrawn to a set limit—for instance, $1000. The overdraft becomes a loan that is subject to interest rates as high as or higher than those charged on credit card loans. The rates on a personal line of credit may be 6 percent to 7 percent lower than those on overdraft protection; clearly, then, it is worthwhile to check this.

CREDIT CARD CASH ADVANCES Anyone with a credit card issued by a financial institution (bank, credit union, trust company) has the option of obtaining a loan, called a cash advance, without making a special application each time funds are needed. The original contract and the previously established loan limit cover the situation. Interest, calculated daily, begins at once—usually at rates that are higher than those charged for either a line of credit or a personal loan.

Applying for a Personal Loan

Sarah and Devon want to buy a sailboat. When they apply at their bank for a $10 000 personal instalment loan for this purpose, they know that they will need to list outstanding balances on several credit and charge cards, but they also know that their credit rating is well established. After the loans officer hears about their debts—$1100 to MasterCard, $500 to American Express, and $950 to Sears—she strongly recommends that they consolidate these debts into one bank loan, so that they will have only one payment to make. The bank will be happy to lend them the $10 000 they are asking for—and, in addition, enough to pay off all their other debts.

Sarah and Devon are not keen to consolidate their credit card debt with the bank loan, but they have the impression that the bank will look more favourably at their loan application if they agree to do so.

What factors should they consider before deciding to consolidate their debts?

DEMAND LOAN Rather than flexible credit, customers with a good credit rating may arrange for a demand loan by signing an agreement to repay the loan in full at a certain date, with interest due monthly. The lender has the right to recall a demand loan at any time. Holders of demand loans often renegotiate them at maturity. Interest charges will be set slightly above the prime rate and will fluctuate according to the prevailing rate. The **prime rate** is the lowest interest rate that financial institutions charge: offered to their best corporate customers, the prime rate also serves as a guide for setting other interest rates. (Thus, you may be charged "prime plus two," meaning that you will pay interest set at two percentage points higher than the prime rate. So if the prime rate is 6 percent, then you will pay 8 percent.)

INSTALMENT LOANS Instalment loans usually have a set interest rate, a maturity date, a repayment schedule, and certain security requirements, as will be explained shortly under "Security for Loans." The contract you will sign varies with the kind of security you are pledging. Personal Finance in Action Box 12.1, "Applying for a Personal Loan," illustrates part of the decision-making process for one couple who are applying for an instalment loan.

Security for Loans

Lenders must consider the risk of not being repaid and take steps to minimize the consequences. Some lenders do so by accepting as borrowers only those who appear to be good risks; others lend to a wider range of people, but ask each borrower for certain assurances. It is common practice to require a borrower to sign documents that give the lender permission in advance to take over specified possessions or assets belonging to the borrower if the latter fails to make all payments as agreed. These various claims on the borrower, which are arranged when the loan is taken out, are referred to as the security for the loan.

SECURITY AND COLLATERAL Distinguishing clearly between security and collateral can be difficult. It may help to consider security as a claim or right that the borrower has voluntarily assigned to the lender in order to reduce the lender's risk. The term collateral applies only to tangible assets that are used as security, such as financial assets or durable goods. So the signature of a guarantor or co-signer is a form of security for the lender; but because the signature is not a tangible object, it is not collateral. Promises may have some security value, but they do not qualify as collateral.

Fully and Partly Secured Loans

Loans may be fully or partly secured. If the borrower signs over to the lender assets that are equal in value to the total loan, that loan is said to be **fully secured.** Naturally, very few consumer loans are fully secured, because people who have enough assets to do so would probably buy the goods for cash. But requesting a fully secured loan can occasionally be a reasonable decision. For instance, if you need funds for only a few months, you might prefer to use your assets as security rather than to sell the assets so that you can pay in cash. If the assets in question are already invested and are producing a higher yield than would be possible in the current market, you might be wiser to retain the assets and instead to take a short-term loan. When you use bonds or similar financial assets as security for a loan, you can expect to be charged a very favourable interest rate, because the lender is taking no risk at all.

More often, loans are only **partly secured,** because borrowers rarely have sufficient assets to obtain a fully secured loan. A car buyer may use the car as security for the car loan, but this debt is not fully secured, because cars and certain other durables depreciate faster than loans are repaid.

Signature Loans

A borrower who is considered to present little risk to the lender may be asked for nothing more than a signature on a **promissory note,** which is an unconditional promise to repay the loan. Such a loan, also called a signature loan, is considered by the lender to be unsecured. In other words, if the borrower does not repay the loan as promised, the lender has nothing of value belonging to the borrower that can be liquidated to pay the debt. The legal contract used for a signature loan is the promissory note, which, as noted above, is simply a promise to repay the loan. Figure 12.6 shows a sample promissory note used for a personal loan.

FIGURE 12.6   PERSONAL LOAN PROMISSORY NOTE

Many people are not eligible for signature loans, and even those who are may instead choose the greater flexibility offered by a personal line of credit. If you are a longtime customer of a financial institution, and if its credit managers judge your character and credit record to be exemplary, you may be permitted a signature loan with no other security; otherwise, like most borrowers, you will probably be required to provide a tangible form of security in addition to your promise. For this reason, promissory notes are often incorporated into more complex credit contracts of the sort we will discuss below. Four frequently used forms of security for loans are (i) co-signers, (ii) future wages, (iii) financial assets, and (iv) durable goods.

Co-Signers

A lender may require that the borrower find another person to sign the loan agreement. By signing, the **co-signer** (also called the guarantor) is agreeing to repay any outstanding balance on the loan if the borrower fails to do so. People sometimes agree to co-sign loans as a gesture of friendship, without fully realizing the commitment they are making. The extent of their responsibility becomes evident to them only when the lender requires them to make restitution on behalf of the friend or relative who cannot repay or who has disappeared without repaying the loan. People who can't be found are referred to in the credit business as skips.

Future Wages

Sometimes borrowers sign an agreement that if they do not maintain the repayment schedule, the lender has permission to collect a portion of their wages directly from their employers. This type of contract is called a **wage assignment.** To protect borrowers from certain abuses of this system that occurred in the past, the use of wage assignments has been curtailed. For instance, in Ontario credit unions are the only creditors that are permitted to use wage assignments. Figure 12.7 shows a sample wage assignment. By signing this document, the borrower is voluntarily agreeing that if he does not repay the debt, the Guelph and Wellington Credit Union may collect a percent of his wages—in this case, his net wages, after the standard payroll deductions for income tax and CPP—directly from his employer until the loan is repaid. (Whether the percent figure is based on gross or net wages varies according to jurisdiction.)

In practice, the credit union would not enforce a wage assignment until other, less drastic collection measures had failed. The debtor would also be informed that the wage assignment was about to be enforced, giving him time either to repay the debt or to petition for a reduction in the amount of wages to be taken. (Note that a wage assignment differs from the wage garnishment discussed in Chapter 14 under "Debt Collection": a wage garnishment requires a court order, while a wage assignment—as a contract that is signed in advance by the borrower—can be initiated by a credit union as a result of its own internal decision.) Either the credit union's loans officer or its board of directors decides when and whether to enforce a wage assignment; they may also grant an exemption or reduction if the borrower's situation seems to warrant doing so.

Financial Assets

To secure a loan, a lender may require a borrower to lodge in the lender's possession some form of **collateral,** such as bonds, stock certificates, life insurance policies, or deposits. These types of collateral are financial assets that can be readily converted to cash, which is what the lender will do if the borrower fails to maintain the terms of the loan agreement. With each form of collateral offered, the borrower will be asked to sign an appropriate agreement giving the lender the power to realize these assets if the borrow defaults on the loan. Different types of contracts are used depending on the nature of the asset being pledged.

FIGURE 12.7 ASSIGNMENT OF WAGES

ASSIGNMENT OF WAGES

TO: Guelph and Wellington .... CREDIT UNION LIMITED
(hereinafter called the "Credit Union")

I...
(Name of Assignor)

for Valuable Consideration hereby assign, transfer and set over unto the Credit Union, (i) 20 per cent of all wages, (as defined in the Wages Act of Ontario), but excluding any amount that an employer is required by law to deduct from any such wages and (ii) all other monies owing to me, or hereafter to become owing to me by my employer: ....

....

or any other person, firm, corporation or entity by whom I may be hereafter employed.

AND I HEREBY AUTHORIZE AND DIRECT my said employer or any future employer to pay the said 20 per cent of all such wages and all such other monies to the Credit Union, and I hereby irrevocably authorize the Credit Union to take all proceedings which may be proper and necessary for the recovery of any amount or amounts above assigned and to give receipts for same, or any part thereof, in my name and I hereby release and discharge my said employers and each of them from all liability to me for or on account of any or all monies paid in accordance with the terms hereof. Nothing herein shall prevent the Credit Union from exercising any other right of recovery available in law of any amount lawfully owing to the Credit Union in excess of the amounts assigned above.

THIS ASSIGNMENT OF WAGES is irrevocable by the Assignor, and shall remain a valid and enforceable security in respect of all debts owing by the Assignor to the Credit Union until delivery of notice in writing signed by the Credit Union to the contrary.

Signed, Sealed and Delivered this .... day of ...., ...

....at... Ontario in the presence of:

Witness

(FORM # 021923)

....
(Signature of Assignor)

Rev. 10/98

Reproduced with the permission of the Guelph and Wellington Credit Union.

A borrower who has a life insurance policy with an adequate cash surrender value may assign the policy to a lender as security for a loan. This process was discussed in Chapter 6, under "Collateral for a Loan" in the "Uses for the Cash Reserves" section. Essentially it means that the policy is held by the lender until the debt is cleared, but the policyholder must continue to pay the premiums. If the borrower defaults on the loan, the lender can cash in the policy.

Durable Goods

When consumer durables such as vehicles, appliances, and furniture are bought with credit, the articles themselves are usually offered as security. If you obtain a loan from a bank, a credit union, a small loans company, or a trust company, you will be required to sign a **chattel mortgage** or **security interest,** a document that transfers ownership of the goods to the lender (Figure 12.8). Note that the term **chattel** applies to moveable goods, but not to land or buildings (which are called real property); the latter are used as security in home mortgages (see Chapter 13). As the borrower, you have possession and full use of the goods, but through the chattel mortgage you are agreeing to maintain them in good condition and in most cases to insure them.

During the term of the chattel mortgage, which is the time until the debt is repaid, you do not have the right to sell the pledged goods without the lender's permission. If you default on the loan, the lender has your written prior permission to repossess and sell the goods. In some provinces—Ontario, for instance—the creditor (the lender) may also have the right to sue for any balance outstanding if the proceeds from the sale of the repossessed

FIGURE 12.8 SECURITY AGREEMENT

SECURITY AGREEMENT - CONSUMER CREDIT

DATE:_____

ACCOUNT NO.:_____

TO: _____ *(the "Credit Union")*
(Name of Credit Union)

FROM: _____   AND: _____
(Surname) (First Name) (Middle Initial)   (Surname) (First Name) (Middle Initial)

Date of Birth: _____ (Day) _____ (Month) _____ (Year)   Date of Birth: _____ (Day) _____ (Month) _____ (Year)

_____   _____
(Number and Street)   (Number and Street)

_____   _____
(City, Town) (Province) (Postal Code)   (City, Town) (Province) (Postal Code)

(Collectively referred to hereinafter as the "Debtor")

1. Security Interest

The Debtor for valuable consideration hereby assigns, transfers, sets over, mortgages, charges and grants to the Credit Union a security interest in the following motor vehicle(s):

Make	Year	Model	Style	Vehicle Identification Number	Colour	Ontario Plate Number

and the property, if any, described in Schedule A attached hereto and any and all substitutions or replacements thereof, increases, additions or accessions thereto and any interest of the Debtor therein (all of which shall hereinafter be referred to as the "Collateral").

In this Agreement, any reference to the word "Collateral" shall, unless the context otherwise requires, refer to "Collateral or any part thereof". In this Agreement, the word "Collateral" shall include the proceeds thereof. Until default, the Debtor may have possession of the Collateral and enjoy the same subject to the terms hereof.

2. Obligations Secured

The fixed and specific mortgages, charges and security interests granted hereby:

(CHECK AND INITIAL AS APPROPRIATE)

☐ (a) secure payment to the Credit Union of all debts and liabilities, present or future, direct or indirect, absolute or contingent, matured or not, at any time owing by the Debtor to the Credit Union or remaining unpaid by the Debtor to the Credit Union, whether arising from dealings between the Credit Union and the Debtor or from other dealings or proceedings by which the Credit Union may be or become in any manner whatever a creditor of the Debtor and wherever incurred, and in any currency, and whether incurred by the Debtor alone or with another or others and whether as principal or surety, including expenses under paragraph 5 of this Agreement and all interest, commissions, legal and other costs, charges and expenses (all of the foregoing being herein called, and included in, the "Obligations");

☐ (b) secure payment to the Credit Union of the principal amount of

$_____ and interest on the unpaid principal amount at the rate of _____% per year calculated daily and payable monthly, as well after as before maturity, default and judgment and interest on overdue interest at the rate aforesaid (the principal amount and accrued and unpaid interest being herein called, and included in, the "Obligations");

3. Representations and Warranties

The Debtor represents and warrants as follows:

(a) the Debtor is, or is to become, the beneficial owner of the Collateral;

(b) the Collateral is, or will be when acquired, free and clear of all security interests, mortgages, hypothecs, charges, liens, encumbrances, taxes and assessments; and

(c) the Debtor's name, address and the date of birth shown at the beginning of this agreement are correct.

4. Covenants

The Debtor hereby agrees that:

(a) Maintain, Use, etc. - the Debtor shall diligently maintain, use and operate the Collateral in a proper and efficient manner so as to preserve and protect the Collateral and the earnings, incomes, rents, issues and profits thereof;

(b) Insurance - the Debtor shall cause all of the Collateral to be properly insured and kept insured with reputable insurers against loss or damage by fire or other hazards and shall maintain such insurance with loss if any payable to the Credit Union and shall deliver to the Credit Union evidence of such insurance satisfactory to the Credit Union and if the Debtor fails to obtain satisfactory insurance, the Credit Union shall have the right to obtain it at the Debtor's expense;

(c) Rent, Taxes, etc. - The Debtor shall pay all rents, taxes, rates, levies, assessments and government fees or dues lawfully levied, assessed or imposed in respect of the Collateral or any part thereof as and when the same shall become due and payable, and shall exhibit to the Credit Union, when required, the receipts and vouchers establishing such payments;

(d) Observe Law - the Debtor shall duly observe and conform to all valid requirements of any governmental authority relative to any of the Collateral and all covenants, terms and conditions upon or under which the Collateral is held;

(e) Information - the Debtor shall furnish to the Credit Union such information with respect to the Collateral and the insurance thereon as the Credit Union may from time to time

Page 1 of 2
(Form O.L.-D 1922/7-95)

FIGURE 12.8 SECURITY AGREEMENT (CONTINUED)

require and the Credit Union may examine and inspect the Collateral at any time upon reasonable notice.

(f) Other Encumbrances - the Debtor shall not, without the prior consent in writing of the Credit Union, create any security interest, mortgage, hypothec, charge, lien or other encumbrance upon the Collateral of any part thereof;

(g) Defend Title - the Debtor shall defend the title to the Collateral against all persons and shall, upon demand by the Credit Union furnish further assurance of title and further security for the Obligations and execute any written instruments or do any other acts necessary, to make effective the purposes and provisions of this Agreement;

(h) Dealings with the Collateral - the Debtor shall not sell, exchange, assign or lease or otherwise dispose of the Collateral or any interest therein without the prior written consent of the Credit Union;

(i) Motor Vehicle - the Debtor shall, if any part of the Collateral is a motor vehicle, not remove the motor vehicle from the Province of Ontario; and

(j) Change of Name - the Debtor shall not change its name.

5. Immediate Possession

Upon failure by the Debtor to perform any of the agreements described in paragraph 4 hereof, the Credit Union is authorized and has the option to take immediate possession of the Collateral and, whether it has taken possession or not, to perform any of the agreements in any manner deemed proper by the Credit Union, without waiving any rights to enforce this Agreement. The expenses (including the cost of any insurance and the amount of taxes or other charges and reasonable solicitors' costs and legal expenses) incurred by the Credit Union in respect of the custody, preservation, use or operation of the Collateral shall be repaid forthwith by the Debtor to the Credit Union immediately after they are incurred, shall bear interest at the rate of 20% per annum and the repayment of such expenses and interest thereon shall be secured by this Agreement.

6. Events of Default

At the option of the Credit Union, the Obligations shall immediately become due and payable in full upon the happening of any of the following events:

(a) if the Debtor shall fail to pay or perform when due any of the Obligations;

(b) if the Debtor shall fail to perform any provisions of this Agreement or of any other agreement to which the Debtor and the Credit Union are parties;

(c) if any of the representations and warranties herein is or becomes incorrect in any respect at any time;

(d) if the Debtor or any guarantor of any of the Obligations dies, commits an act of bankruptcy, assigns or is petitioned into bankruptcy, becomes insolvent, or proposes a compromise or arrangement to its creditors;

(e) if any execution, sequestration or any other process of any court beomes enforceable against the Debtor or any guarantor of any of the Obligations or if any distress or analogous process is levied upon the Collateral or any part thereof;

(f) if the Credit Union in good faith believes that the prospect of payment or performance of any of the Obligations is impaired.

7. Remedies

If pursuant to paragraph 6 hereof, the Credit Union declares that the Obligations shall immediately become due and payable in full, the Debtor and the Credit Union shall have, in addition to any other rights and remedies provided by law, the rights and remedies of a debtor and a secured party respectively under the Personal Property Security Act, 1989 and those provided by this Agreement. The Credit Union may take immediate possession of the Collateral and enforce any rights of the Debtor in respect of the Collateral by any manner permitted by law and may require the Debtor to assemble and deliver the Collateral or make the Collateral available to the Credit Union at a reasonably convenient place designated by the Credit Union. The Credit Union may take proceedings in any court of competent jurisdiction to sell, lease or otherwise dispose of the whole or any part of the Collateral at public auction, by public tender or by private sale, either for cash or upon credit, at such time and upon such terms and conditions as the receiver may determine.

Page 2 of 2

(Form O.L.-D 1922/7-95)

DATE: _____

ACCOUNT NO.: _____

TO: _____
(Name of Credit Union)

FROM: _____
(Surname)   (First Name)   (Middle Initial)

8. Expenses

Any proceeds of any disposition of any of the Collateral may be applied by the Credit Union to the payment of expenses incurred in connection with the retaking, holding, repairing, processing, preparing for disposition and disposing of the Collateral (including solicitors' fees and legal expenses and any other expenses), and any balance of such proceeds may be applied by the Credit Union towards the payment of the Obligations in such order of application as the Credit Union may from time to time effect. All such expenses and all amounts borrowed on the security of the Collateral under paragraph 7 hereof shall bear interest at 20% per annum and shall be Obligations under this Agreement. If the disposition of the Collateral fails to satisfy the Obligations and the expenses incurred by the Credit Union, the Debtor shall be liable to pay for any deficiency on demand.

9. Miscellaneous

The Debtor and the Credit Union further agree that:

(a) the Debtor shall not be discharged by any extension of time, additional advances, renewals and extensions, the taking of further security, releasing security, extinguishment of mortgages or charges or the security interest as to all or any part of the Collateral, or any other act except a release or discharge of the mortgages or charges or security interest upon the payment in full of the Obligations including charges, expenses, fees, costs and interest;

(b) any failure by the Credit Union to exercise any right set out in this Agreement shall not constitute a waiver thereof; nothing in this Agreement or in the Obligations shall preclude any other remedy by action or otherwise for the enforcement of this Agreement or the payment or performance in full of the Obligations secured by this Agreement;

(c) all rights of the Credit Union hereunder shall be assignable and in any action brought by an assignee to enforce such rights, the Debtor shall not assert against the assignee any claim or defence which the Debtor now has or may hereafter have against the Credit Union;

(d) the Debtor agrees that all proceeds of the Collateral shall be held in trust by the Debtor for the Credit Union;

(e) all rights of the Credit Union hereunder shall enure to the benefit of its successors and assigns and all obligations of the Debtor hereunder shall bind the Debtor, his heirs, executors, administrators, successors and assigns;

(f) if more than one person executes this Agreement as Debtor, their obligations under this Agreement shall be joint and several;

(g) this Agreement shall be governed in all respects by the laws of the Province of Ontario;

(h) the Debtor hereby acknowledges receipt of an executed copy of this Agreement; and

(i) this Agreement shall become effective when it is signed by the Debtor.

SIGNED, SEALED AND DELIVERED as of the date first above written.

```
                                    )
                                    )
_____  ) _____(seal)
Witness                             ) Debtor
                                    )
                                    )
                                    ) _____(seal)
                                    ) Debtor
                                    )
                                    )
```

SOURCE: Reproduced with the permission of the Guelph and Wellington Credit Union.

goods are insufficient to extinguish the debt. Elsewhere (in British Columbia, Alberta, and Newfoundland), there has been a trend toward "seize or sue" laws, which give the creditor the option of either repossessing the goods or suing the debtor, but not both.

It is important to take careful note that chattel mortgages are the contracts used by lenders when taking the title to goods as security. Vendors of goods, who already have title to the goods they are selling, are in a position to retain the title until the total cost is paid; for these transactions a different contract, called a conditional sales contract, is used. If you default on one of these agreements, the vendor will enforce security by repossessing the goods (see "Enforcing Security" and "Conditional Sales Contracts," later in this chapter).

Lien

In popular usage, the term **lien** is often used as a synonym for a chattel mortgage, but there is a distinction in law. A lien is a claim registered against certain property, generally in cases where the goods or services provided cannot be seized. For example, if a contractor has already paved a driveway, but payment is now overdue, the creditor may register a lien against the house. This claim against the property would have to be settled before the owner could ever obtain a clear title (so a lien on the house prevents its owner from selling the house without paying off the debt represented by the lien). If a service station has not been paid for repairing a car, a mechanic's lien can be registered against the car. The proprietor of the garage would then have the right to keep the car until the debt is satisfied—or, if the default continues, to sell the car.

Cost of Borrowing

Insurance

When you sign a credit contract, you assume not only the responsibility of repaying the debt, but also the risk that something will happen to make it impossible or difficult for you to carry out this intent. Unexpected illness, unemployment, disability, or death may disrupt a payment schedule. Insurance can protect against two of these risks—death or disability.

CREDIT LIFE INSURANCE Lenders often require that their consumer loans be life insured. The lender arranges for this coverage by having a group life insurance policy that covers the lives of its borrowers against the risk that any given borrower will die before his or her debts have been repaid. This insurance on the life of the borrower is often called credit life insurance. When an insured borrower dies, the insurance company pays the lender the outstanding balance due on the debt. The borrower's estate does not receive anything, but the survivors may be relieved that the debt has been paid.

Some lenders automatically include credit life insurance without an additional charge; others offer it as an option with a specific cost. Either way, the borrower ultimately pays for this service. Even if it is optional, you might give some thought to whether purchasing it would make sense. When a borrower with an outstanding debt dies without credit life insurance, the balance of the debt becomes a charge on the debtor's estate; this charge must be paid before any funds are distributed to the heirs. If the estate is adequate, such a situation may cause no difficulty; but if the family has many needs and few assets, a large debt could create hardship for the survivors.

DISABILITY INSURANCE Not all lenders offer disability insurance, but credit unions often do. For an additional fee, disability insurance covers the borrower for the risk of being unable to make payments because of a personal disability. It is important to find out the conditions of such insurance as well as what it will cost. How does the insurance company define disabled? How long must one be disabled before the insurance will take effect? If the borrower meets the criteria for disability, the insurance company will assume responsibility for the debt payments as long as the disability lasts.

Interest Charges

The cost of borrowing depends on the lender's cost of money (how much it costs the lender to acquire the funds it lends), the lender's assessment of the risk that the loan might not be repaid, and the services offered by the lender. Deposit-taking institutions, which have a ready supply of funds to lend, can charge lower rates than small loans companies, which must borrow the funds they plan to lend. To cover their costs, banks, trust companies, and credit unions allow a spread of between 1 percent and 3 percent between the interest rate they pay to depositors and the interest rate they charge borrowers.

When you submit a loan application, the creditor assesses the degree of risk involved in lending money to you. Some lenders—notably small loans companies, which will lend to higher-risk borrowers—charge higher rates aimed at covering their losses on bad debts. Most lenders establish the level of risk they will accept, and then refuse loans to those who do not qualify.

INTEREST RATES   At present, financial institutions vary little in the rates they charge for the same type of loan; but there are significant differences in the rates charged for different types of loans.

Enforcement of Security

In Arrears

When a debtor does not adhere to the repayment schedule originally agreed on, the account is first considered to be **in arrears** (delinquent), because the payments are somewhat behind. But if the borrower contacts the lender and explains the problem, it is usually possible to make some adjustments. If the borrower is ill or unemployed, the lender may agree either to freeze the loan payments or to allow the borrower to pay only interest until able to begin making full payments again. An account that is in arrears, provided that the situation does not last too long, is not as serious a blot on the debtor's credit record as an account that is in default.

In Default

The difference between an account in arrears and one in default is largely a matter of degree. In both cases, the borrower has not maintained the regular payment schedule. An account is **in default** if payments are hopelessly behind and if the lender is having no success in collecting the debt. Such an account may be turned over for collection to a special department within the firm or to an outside collection agency. Default has a negative effect on your credit record. Lenders' leniency varies; in recessionary times, creditors may take action more quickly than in periods of prosperity and high employment.

Enforcing Security

When a debtor defaults, the lender is in a position to **enforce security**—that is, to realize funds from whatever the borrower put up for security before the loan was granted. If there was a co-signer, the lender will first try to collect from that person, using various amounts of pressure. If the creditor is a credit union, a decision may be made to exercise the wage assignment, which means directing the debtor's employer to deduct up to 20 percent of wages due on each payday and send the amount to the creditor. If financial assets—such as bonds, stocks, deposits, and life insurance—were used as security, the lender can now convert these into cash to cover as much of the debt as possible. If consumer durables were the security, the lender can repossess them and offer them for sale.

Enforcement of security is limited to whatever the particular credit contract specifies; it means taking steps to obtain funds from goods, assets, or co-signers according to the pledges made when the loan was initially arranged. At this stage, the creditor cannot seize goods unless they were listed as security in the credit contract. A creditor may choose not to enforce his or her security, especially in the case of chattel mortgages or conditional sales contracts, if the pledged goods have been in use for some time. Whether exercised or not, the possibility of repossession serves as a powerful threat to debtors.

ENFORCEMENT OF SECURITY VERSUS COURT ACTION There is a distinction between enforcing security and using the courts to collect debts. In the first instance, the lender exercises a right given by the borrower when the loan was arranged; as explained above, the creditor can take any of the steps specified in the contract without resorting to the courts. If the creditor does not realize enough from the sale of the pledged assets, or if a decision is made not to enforce the security, the debtor can be sued in the appropriate court. The court will determine the validity of the creditor's claim on the debtor and make a decision about how much is owed to the creditor. If the creditor wins the case, there are ways to coerce the debtor to make payment. Court collection of debts is discussed in Chapter 14, under the heading "Using the Courts to Collect Debts."

Regulations and Policies

Consumer credit practices are governed by federal laws and by provincial statutes, as well as by the policies of lenders. It may be difficult at first to distinguish among these. Laws can be changed only by legislatures, and regulations can be changed only by an order-in-council; but lender policies can be altered much more readily and are therefore often modified in response to the pressures of competition. For instance, firms make policy decisions about determining levels of acceptable risk or when a loan is in default.

Federal Regulation

The power to regulate consumer credit is shared between the federal and provincial governments. The federal government has jurisdiction over banks, promissory notes, bills of exchange, interest, and bankruptcy. In general, there is no legislated ceiling on interest rates on consumer loans. The *Small Loans Act* does state that it is an indictable offence to charge more than the criminal rate of interest, which is 60 percent.

Provincial Regulation

All provinces have consumer credit laws requiring that borrowers be informed about the cost of credit, with the amount expressed both as an annual rate and as a total dollar cost. Also, all provinces have an *Unconscionable Transactions Relief Act*, which permits a debtor to apply to court for a review of a loan contract. If the court finds, considering the circumstances, that the cost of the loan is excessive and the contract harsh and unconscionable, the transaction may be reopened and all or part of the contract set aside. There is more about the regulation of consumer credit later in the chapter (see "Credit Regulation").

Point-of-Sale Credit

As mentioned earlier (under "The Two Forms of Consumer Credit"), consumer loans are not the only type of consumer credit. Rather than having to apply for a consumer loan from a financial institution, you can often arrange to have credit by the retailer from which you make a purchase: credit cards, charge cards, and conditional sales contracts are the three major methods for doing so.

Economic Significance

Canadian society depends on credit for much economic activity; the studies discussed earlier in the chapter (see the sections "National Consumer Credit Data" and "Consumer Debt Use at the Household Level") show clearly that our use of consumer credit has been accelerated quite rapidly. In recent times, we have come to depend quite heavily on credit cards: approximately two-thirds of Canadians have at least one credit card, and it is not at all uncommon to have more than one. This trend toward greater use of consumer credit cards is reflected in the increasing value of sales charged to cards issued by Visa and MasterCard between 1977 and 1999 (Figure 12.9). In 22 years, sales increased about 20 times; even when converted to constant dollars, sales have risen around 6.0 times. During this same period, the number of MasterCard and Visa

FIGURE 12.9   DOLLAR SALES USING MASTERCARD AND VISA, CANADA, 1977–2000 (IN CURRENT DOLLARS)

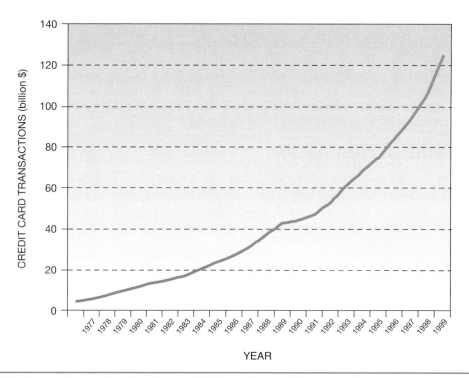

SOURCE: Data from Mastercard and Visa Statistics DB 38 Public, Web site of the Canadian Bankers' Association, www.cba.ca, February 2001.

cards in circulation tripled, to about 24.3 million cards. The Canadian credit card market is dominated by these two cards: together, they account for more than 50 percent of all the credit cards in circulation and for 75 percent of the total outstanding balances on credit cards.

Debit Cards

Although debit cards are not used for credit, they are included in this chapter to prevent confusion with credit cards. A **debit card,** also called a payment card, differs from a credit card in that the costs of any purchases made using this type of card are immediately deducted from the cardholder's chequing or savings account, possibly with a line of credit to handle overdrafts. Debit cards may also be used as a means of access to automatic teller machines.

Credit unions initiated the use of debit cards, most often at the local level. Other financial institutions, especially banks, eventually established a nationwide electronic system that allows their customers to pay for goods and services without using either cash or a cheque. With this electronic payments system in place, you can now use a plastic card to instantly debit your bank account for the week's groceries right at the supermarket's checkout counter, the gas station for your fill up, and even at some restaurants. The ease of use makes these cards widely accepted, but as with all other cards, the risks of loss to unscrupulous persons can be of concern. Still, the use of the personal identifier prior to the user receiving either cash at the Automated Teller or paying a bill requires the user to protect the security number at all times. Businesses also benefit from this system as the money is immediately transferred to their account, earning interest or paying down loans. Debit card use also eases bank service charges for businesses that would have paid for the bank to process the deposit and any associated documents such as cheques or credit card slips.

Personal Finance in Action 12.2

Ivana Considers Using a Line of Credit

When Ivana moved for a promotion, she had to set up new banking arrangements. Moving her credit card and chequing account from the old branch was no problem. The bank officer did, however, offer her a line of credit that would be tied into the credit card and provide unsecured credit up to $15 000 whenever she needed the money. At the same time, the account would be linked to her chequing account and debit card, so that any time the account was overdrawn, the money would be automatically advanced for a transaction fee of $3. This sounded excellent to Ivana as there was significant travel involved in her new position, and she frequently found banking difficult to conduct when far from home.

The interest rate on the line of credit would be the same as her credit card for balances under $2 500 and prime plus 3 percent for any balances over $2 500. However, any advances would be charged interest from the date of the advance and not from the date of the statement. To make matters even more complicated, the whole banking arrangement would be accessible via the Internet or over the telephone. In this way Ivana could pay bills or make transfers from wherever the job demanded her presence. The convenience was enticing, but Ivana was concerned about the increased availability of such a large amount of credit, the interest charges, and the possibility of losing her access card and someone else running up a large balance for which she would be responsible.

Point-of-Sale Credit Arrangements

Whenever you obtain credit in connection with a purchase, you are obtaining point-of-sale credit (or vendor credit)—in contrast to loan credit, which is obtained separately from purchases. We will focus on three of the most common kinds of point-of-sale credit: charge cards, credit cards, and conditional sales. Note the distinction between a **charge card,** which is used for accounts that require payment in full each month, and a **credit card,** which is used for accounts that permit instalment payments.

Charge Cards

Charge cards are provided for short-term credit (about a month), primarily by oil companies and by travel and entertainment clubs such as American Express or Diner's. They offer charge accounts requiring full payment within a specified **grace period**—the number of days after the statement date before a late-payment penalty becomes effective. The grace period varies, but may range from 21 days to 45 days. After that, late payments will attract a penalty at a fairly high rate of interest.

Credit Cards

REVOLVING ACCOUNTS Credit cards are used for **revolving charge accounts,** so named because it is possible to continue charging purchases to the account as long as a portion of the bill is paid each month. There are two major types of credit cards: (i) those issued by banks, trust companies, credit unions, and other financial institutions (often called "bank cards") and (ii) those issued by retailers. Credit card accounts at financial institutions differ from retailers' credit card accounts in two respects: (i) in the former case, the institution is providing a loan, while in the latter, the institution is selling goods, and (ii) in the way that credit charges are calculated.

To open a revolving charge account (referred to in legislative documents as **variable credit**), you must complete an application form similar to the one in Figure 12.10 or one on the Net. The institution's credit department evaluates the information provided in the application and sometimes obtains your credit report from the credit bureau (explained in Chapter 14). On the basis of your current financial situation and previous credit record, the credit manager assesses your creditworthiness and establishes a ceiling on the amount of credit that you may have outstanding at any one time.

Once you have opened the account, you may make credit purchases within the set limit. You will receive monthly statements reporting the account's status, including the minimum payment you are required to make that month, your outstanding balance, and how much credit you still have available. Whenever your balance reaches the account's established limit, you are supposed to stop using the card until the debt has been reduced. In some instances, though, the credit card issuer may simply increase the limit, without consulting the cardholder; the new credit limit will just be shown on the next statement.

GRACE PERIOD Most credit card issuers offer the cardholder a certain number of days after the statement date, called a grace period, in which to make full payment without interest charges. Some low-interest-rate accounts, however, have no grace period. Generally, bank, trust company, and credit union accounts have a grace period of 21 days, while retailer accounts offer between 21 days and 30 days. There is no grace period on amounts carried over from previous months, or on cash advances.

FIGURE 12.10 CREDIT CARD APPLICATION

CIBC CREDIT CARD APPLICATION

BRANCH TRANSIT

1. YOUR CHOICE OF CIBC VISA CARD CHECK ONE ONLY ☑

☐ USS UC ☐ Gold GO ☐ Aerogold AF ☐ Vacationgold TO

2. PLEASE TELL US ABOUT YOURSELF

☐ 1 MR. ☐ 2 MS. ☐ 3 MISS ☐ 4 MRS. ☐ 5 OTHER

LEGAL NAME (MAXIMUM 19 CHARACTERS)

FIRST NAME/INITIAL/LAST NAME (INCLUDE TITLE IF APPLICABLE)

HOME ADDRESS (YOUR VISA CARD WILL BE MAILED HERE)
ADDRESS | APT. NO.
CITY, PROVINCE | POSTAL CODE

HOW LONG HAVE YOU LIVED AT CURRENT HOME ADDRESS? YEARS MONTHS HOME TELEPHONE ( )

☐ OWN YOUR HOME ☐ BOARD ☐ RENT ☐ LIVE WITH PARENTS

PREVIOUS ADDRESS (IF LESS THAN 3 YEARS AT CURRENT ADDRESS)
ADDRESS | APT. NO.
CITY, PROVINCE | POSTAL CODE

WHEN APPLYING FOR AEROGOLD, IF CURRENTLY A MEMBER, PLEASE PROVIDE AEROPLAN MEMBER NUMBER. IF NOT, A NEW AEROPLAN MEMBER NUMBER WILL BE ASSIGNED.

WHEN APPLYING FOR CLUB Z, IF CURRENTLY A MEMBER, PLEASE PROVIDE MEMBER CARD NUMBER. IF NOT, A NEW CLUB Z MEMBER NUMBER WILL BE ASSIGNED.

SIN NUMBER (OPTIONAL) | DATE OF BIRTH (REQUIRED) DAY MONTH YEAR

SPOUSE'S FIRST NAME/INITIAL/LAST NAME (INCLUDE TITLE IF APPLICABLE)

MOTHER'S MAIDEN NAME (FOR SECURITY PURPOSES)

3. YOUR SOURCES OF INCOME

SELF-EMPLOYED? ☐ YES ☐ NO IF YES, PLEASE ENCLOSE FINANCIAL STATEMENTS FOR STUDENTS ONLY ☐ PART TIME ☐ PERMANENT ☐ SUMMER ONLY

EMPLOYER'S NAME | EMPLOYER'S TELEPHONE ( )

HOW LONG? YEARS MONTHS GROSS MONTHLY INCOME $ | POSITION/OCCUPATION

SPOUSE NOW EMPLOYED BY
EMPLOYER'S NAME | GROSS MONTHLY INCOME $

OTHER INCOME AND AMOUNTS (PLEASE SPECIFY SOURCE, USE SEPARATE PAGE IF NECESSARY) STUDENTS REPORT SCHOLARSHIPS, PARENTS CONTRIBUTION, BANK BALANCES.
| GROSS MONTHLY INCOME $

WHICH INSTITUTION DO YOU BANK WITH? | NAME | ☐ CHEQUING ☐ SAVINGS
| LOCATION

☐ Club Z UA ☐ Classic CL ☐ Dividend UI ☐ Select LC
☐ Club Z Student UH ☐ Classic Student ST ☐ Dividend Platinum DV 144

4. YOUR FINANCIAL OBLIGATIONS AND CREDIT REFERENCES

MONTHLY PAYMENTS

TOTAL RENT/HOUSING PAYMENTS $ | (MORTGAGE ISSUED BY)
PERSONAL/CAR LOAN $ | ISSUED BY
OTHER MORTGAGE $ | ISSUED BY
CIBC VISA CARD $ | ACCOUNT NUMBER 4 5 0
OTHER CREDIT CARD $ |
OTHER CREDIT CARD $ |

HAVE YOU DECLARED PERSONAL BANKRUPTCY IN THE PAST 7 YEARS? (IF YES, YOUR VISA APPLICATION WILL NOT BE APPROVED.) ☐ YES ☐ NO

LANGUAGE PREFERRED ☐ ENGLISH ☐ FRENCH

5. YOUR CHOICE OF ADDITIONAL CARDS

PLEASE SEND ME AN ADDITIONAL CARD FOR USE BY THE FOLLOWING INDIVIDUAL(S) WHO I AM DESIGNATING AN AUTHORIZED USER(S) AND WHO IS (ARE) SIGNING THIS APPLICATION BELOW.

AUTHORIZED USER NO.1 FIRST NAME/INITIAL/LAST NAME (MAXIMUM 19 CHARACTERS)

AUTHORIZED USER NO.2 FIRST NAME/INITIAL/LAST NAME (MAXIMUM 19 CHARACTERS)

6. PLEASE READ AND SIGN HERE

☐ YES, please add Payment Protector Insurance to my CIBC VISA card. (See back panel for details)

I AGREE TO BE BOUND BY THE TERMS AND CONDITIONS ON THE REVERSE. IF I AM APPLYING FOR A CIBC DIVIDEND PLATINUM CARD AND DO NOT QUALIFY, PLEASE CONSIDER ME FOR A CIBC DIVIDEND CARD. IF I AM APPLYING FOR A CIBC SELECT VISA CARD AND DO NOT QUALIFY, OR IF I DID NOT INDICATE MY CHOICE OF CARD IN SECTION 1, PLEASE CONSIDER ME FOR A CIBC CLASSIC CARD.

SIGNATURE OF APPLICANT X | DATE
SIGNATURE OF AUTHORIZED USER NO. 1 X | DATE
SIGNATURE OF AUTHORIZED USER NO. 2 X | DATE

Grace Period for Payment of Purchase Balance.............No less than 17 days from statement date
Method of Computing the Balance for Purchases............ Average Daily Balance
Annual Interest Rate................................ For current rate, call 1 800 465-CIBC (2422).
Card interest rates depend on an Applicant's credit history and personal financial situation.
Additional cards (maximum of 2) available as an added benefit.

CASH ADVANCES Credit cards issued by financial institutions permit cash advances, within limits, as well as retail purchases. These advances are treated as small daily loans, with daily interest charged from the date on which the funds are advanced.

COMPARATIVE INTEREST RATES It is instructive to compare the relation between the Bank Rate (defined in Chapter 10) and the rates charged on retail and bank cards over the decade between 1981 and 1991 (Figure 12.11). During most of that time, there was a substantial spread between credit card rates and the Bank Rate; note that interest rates for retail cards were the highest and the most infrequently adjusted. One reason for high interest rates on credit cards is the substantial risk associated with them; credit card issuers lose millions of dollars each year through uncollectible debts and fraudulent use of these cards.

Note also that credit card rates changed slowly in response to changes in the Bank Rate. Two contributing factors that make credit card rates "sticky" are (i) the requirement that issuers give their cardholders at least a month's notice (six months in some provinces) of a change and (ii) the large fixed costs of running a credit card operation. Before concluding that it will cost more to use a retail card than to use a bank card for instalment credit, you should examine the different methods of calculating interest charges, which will be demonstrated later in this chapter (see "Interest Charges").

LOST OR STOLEN CREDIT CARDS If a credit card is lost or stolen, the owner's responsibility tends to vary with the policy of the company issuing the card. In Alberta, Manitoba, or Quebec, however, cardholders have no legal obligation for any debts incurred after they have notified the company of the loss. If any bills are charged after the loss and before notification, the cardholder's responsibility in Alberta and Manitoba is limited to about $50. All banks limit the cardholder's liability to $50 after notification. Some firms offer insurance protection against lost or stolen credit cards in return for an annual fee.

FIGURE 12.11 REPRESENTATIVE CREDIT CARD RATES VERSUS THE BANK RATE, CANADA, 1973–1991

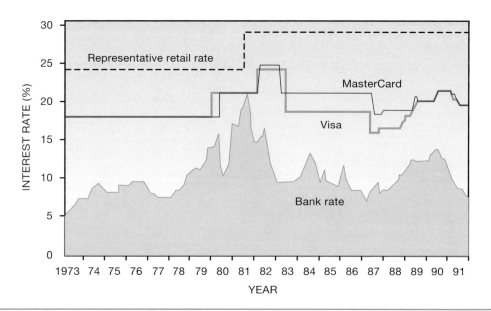

SOURCE: Data from *Credit Cards in Canada in the Nineties* (Report of the Standing Committee on Consumer and Corporate Affairs and Government Operations, Ottawa, 1992), p. 5.

Lost and Stolen Credit Cards

In 1991, of the roughly 25 million bank credit cards then in use in Canada, more than 600 000 were reported lost or stolen. Of the 37 000 that were used fraudulently, 8 000 were taken from an unattended purse, jacket, or locker, and 6 000 from automobiles. Some were stolen from lockers at recreational facilities, and about 5 000 lost cards were left behind in restaurants and bars. A few cards are also pilfered from the mail every year.

Before reporting a card as lost, it is wise to check with family members. When a credit card is reported as lost or stolen and someone uses it, this becomes a criminal matter. If a family member should inadvertently use your lost card, you may be surprised to find yourself caught up in the justice system.

PREMIUM CREDIT CARDS Nowadays, you can get more than credit with a credit card. For an additional fee, it is possible to have a kind of super credit card, called a premium card, that provides such features as a higher credit limit, travel insurance, guaranteed hotel reservations, collision insurance on rental cars, health insurance, a credit card registry, airline points, and travellers' cheques. To determine whether or not you would benefit from having such a card, you must evaluate your need for these additional services in relation to the extra cost involved. The annual fee may be in the range of $100 to $150.

Do You Need a Credit Card?

Consumer and Corporate Affairs Canada has developed a set of questions to help you decide (i) whether or not you need a certain credit card and (ii) whether you can afford it. A slightly adapted version of these questions appears below.

(a) Why do you want this credit card?

(b) What inconveniences are you experiencing by not having this credit card?

(c) When and why would you use this credit card rather than cash, a debit card, a cheque, a personal line of credit, or your existing credit card(s)?

(d) What types of purchases would you be making with this credit card, and how often would you be using it?

(e) How much new credit do you feel you require, and why?

(f) What portion of your current average monthly expenses is related to the use of existing credit cards?

(g) How would the use of this credit card affect your monthly expenses?

(h) Would you expect to pay your monthly balance in full? If not, what repayment schedule would you meet?

(i) Can you afford new debt, and how will you budget for it?

(j) Should you be trying instead to cut back on your use of credit cards?

Conditional Sales Contracts/Agreements

For the sale of high-priced items—such as vehicles, appliances, and furniture—that are paid for in instalments, the retailer may use a conditional sales contract rather than a revolving charge account in order to increase the vendor's security in case of default. With a credit card sale, the vendor has no security claim on the merchandise purchased; instead, the vendor has only the borrower's signature with a promise to repay. A **conditional sales contract** (sometimes referred to as a conditional sales agreement), however, permits the creditor to retain title of the goods until they are paid for, with the option of repossessing them if the buyer defaults. For more information, see the heading "Conditional Sales Contracts" later in this chapter.

Rates for Point-of-Sale Credit

There is no regulation of the rates charged either on revolving charge accounts or on conditional sales, because it is expected that competition among creditors will keep rates in line with other forms of consumer credit. At present, a comparison between lenders shows interest rates to be about the same for similar forms of credit. There is, however, variation among types of credit at any given source (Figure 12.12). Although the interest rates move up and down, the relationship among rates for different types of credit remains fairly stable.

FIGURE 12.12 CREDIT AND CHARGE CARD INTEREST RATES, CANADA, 1992

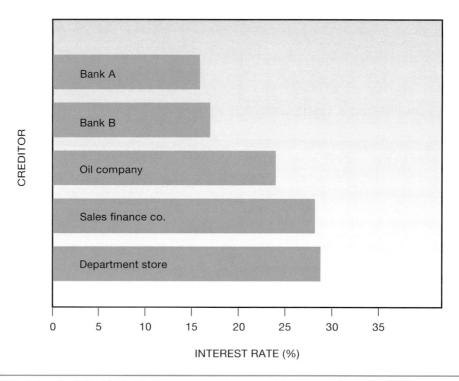

SOURCE: Data from *Credit Card Costs* (Ottawa: Consumer and Corporate Affairs Canada, September 1992).

Credit and Charge Card Costs

Holders of credit cards may be charged for two types of costs: (i) transaction or annual fees, and (ii) interest. Each will be examined in turn.

Transaction or Annual Fees

Some financial institutions, such as banks, trust companies, and credit unions, may impose either an annual fee (between $8 and $15) or a transaction fee (15 cents per transaction). Travel and entertainment cards (which, as we have seen, are charge cards, not credit cards) have much higher annual fees, perhaps in the range of $30 to $55 for a basic card, with additional fees charged for some of the optional add-on services. As mentioned earlier, fees for premium cards typically run much higher, sometimes totalling well over $150 per year. Retailers usually do not charge fees for their credit cards. With this much variation in costs, it is worthwhile to check out the fees before applying for a credit card.

Interest Charges

Interest charges are not a concern for the 50 percent of credit cardholders who pay their total outstanding balance each month, but they may well be of some significance to the rest of us. Two important factors affect interest costs on partial or instalment payments: (i) how often interest is calculated, and (ii) timing, or when the interest charges are applied. Lenders can change their methods of calculating interest at any time, making it difficult to generalize about these matters. The essential point of this section is to make you aware that methods of determining interest charges can be quite complex and that consumer information about these charges is often hard both to obtain and to understand.

FREQUENCY OF INTEREST CALCULATION Banks, trust companies, and credit unions calculate interest on the daily outstanding balance. For example, suppose you use a bank card to charge three purchases that are posted to your account on March 2, March 12, and March 23, respectively, and you make a partial payment after receiving the first statement. Daily interest charges on Purchase A begin March 2; those on Purchase B begin March 12, and those on Purchase C begin March 23. This approach makes it virtually impossible for cardholders to figure out the interest charges on bank cards. Retailers, on the other hand, are more apt to charge interest on the monthly balances.

TIMING OF APPLICATION OF INTEREST CHARGES When you receive a credit card statement, you have the option of (i) paying the balance in full without interest, or (ii) making a partial payment. If you choose the latter option, you may be surprised to find that some financial institutions charge interest for three periods: (i) from the date the credit card office posts the transaction to the next statement date, (ii) from one statement date to the next, and (iii) from the second statement date to the payment date (called **residual interest**). The amount of residual interest due appears on the second statement.

Retailers, on the other hand, generally charge interest on a monthly basis, starting from the statement date, not from the purchase date (except in Quebec, where all interest must be calculated daily). Usually, retailers do not charge residual interest; interest charges apply only to the balance outstanding after partial payment is made, accruing from the previous statement date. One example of such complexity is described in Personal Finance in Action Box 12.3, "Gina's Charge Accounts," and illustrated in Figure 12.13. However, by changing the assumptions about the proportion of the debt repaid each month, a different result may be

Gina's Charge Accounts

Soon after she starts her first job, Gina applies for and is given two credit cards—a bank card and a department store card. She makes purchases using each card that are posted to her accounts on March 2, 12, and 23. Soon after the end of the month, statements arrive from both the bank and the retailer: both statements are dated March 30.

When Gina settles down to pay a batch of bills on April 11, she knows that if she pays these credit card bills in full, there will be no interest charges. But she is a bit short of funds at the moment, so she decides to pay only half of each bill. Each statement indicates the minimum payment due, but neither shows any interest charges.

In May, new statements (both dated April 30) arrive for both credit cards, showing how much she has paid and how much interest has accrued.

Gina knows that there is a difference in interest rates (16.75 percent on the bank card and 28.8 percent on the store card), but she does not understand how the interest is calculated. After some investigation, she learns that the retailer has charged interest on the unpaid portion of her bill for the month between statement dates. On the other hand, the bank card's interest charges began from the date her purchases were posted. Moreover, each charge is divided into three periods—(i) from the posting date to the statement date, (ii) from one statement date to the next, and (iii) from the second statement date to the payment date (residual interest)—as shown in Figure 12.13. After her partial payment on April 11, the bank charged her interest on the new balance.

FIGURE 12.13 BANK AND RETAIL CREDIT CARD INTEREST CHARGES ON ACCOUNTS WITH PARTIAL PAYMENTS

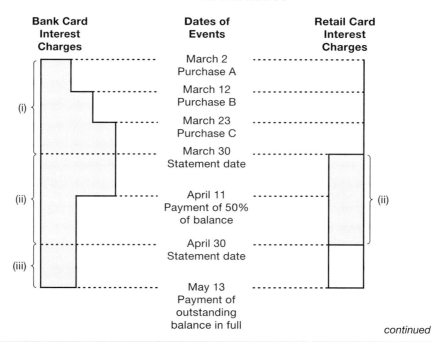

continued

On May 13, Gina pays the total outstanding balance shown on each of her April 30 statements. Although she has not charged any other purchases to her bank card in the meantime, she is surprised to find another interest charge on the May 30 statement. That charge, she learns, represents residual interest for the period between April 30 (the last statement date) and May 13 (the payment date).

obtained. The point of this example is to illustrate the complexity involved in interest charges on credit cards rather than to present a model that is generally applicable.

EFFECT OF SUBSTANTIAL PAYMENT If your partial payment represents 50 percent or more of the balance you owe, credit card issuers differ in when they apply interest charges. Retailers usually subtract the partial payment from the outstanding balance before calculating the new interest charges. Financial institutions, however, calculate interest on the previous total balance and then subtract the partial payment. When the partial payment is less than 50 percent of the balance, retailers do not subtract the payment before calculating the interest.

NOMINAL AND EFFECTIVE INTEREST RATES Nominal interest rates on revolving charge accounts can vary significantly; recently the range extended from 16.75 percent to 28.8 percent. (Recall from Chapter 8 that the nominal interest rate is the quoted rate, but that this rate may not be the same as the more significant effective rate—that is, the real rate of interest.) Unfortunately, the complex calculation methods make it quite difficult to compare effective annual interest rates on credit cards.

Conditional Sales Contracts

When you examine the sample contract in Figure 12.14, you will notice that a conditional sales contract is quite similar to a chattel mortgage: both state the terms of the credit agreement, describe the security pledged, and specify the penalties for failing to honour the contract's terms. The main difference is that the former document is a sales agreement rather than a loan agreement. The vendor retains title to the goods until complete payment has been received, reserving the right to repossess the pledged goods if the buyer does not make payments as scheduled.

Acceleration Clause

A statement indicating that the lender can demand immediate payment of the total outstanding debt if the borrower is late with one or more payments, or does anything else that makes the lender feel "insecure," is called an **acceleration clause.** Such a clause is often included in credit agreements for the benefit of the lender. By making the total balance due at once, the lender positions itself to initiate court proceedings to collect the debt, rather than having to wait for each monthly instalment to become in arrears.

Assignment of a Conditional Sales Contract to a Third Party

Signing a conditional sales contract gives you the chance to buy—and to begin enjoying the use of—a high-priced durable good sooner than you might otherwise have been able to afford it. Such contracts accomplish this by distributing the cost over a number of months or years. Retailers find that this approach encourages sales, but also ties up working capital that they need

FIGURE 12.14 CONDITIONAL SALES CONTRACT

CONDITIONAL SALE CONTRACT

SELLER: Keyboards Plus
Name

Address
Peterborough, Ont.
City　　Province　　P.C.

BUYER(S): JK Trawinski
Name(s)

Address
Peterborough, Ont.
City　　Province　　P.C.

Dear Customer:
We are writing this Contract in easy-to-read language because we want you to understand its terms. Please read your Contract carefully and feel free to ask us any questions you may have about it. We are using the words, *you, your* and *yours* to mean all persons signing the Contract as the Buyer. The words *we, us* and *our* refer to the Seller.

Contract Coverage: We sell and you buy the following Property and/or Services:

Description of Goods	Make	Model	Serial No.	Price
Piano	Yamaha	YH252	23Y3467	#3560

Disclosure of your credit costs:

Cash Price	$ 3560.00
Less Trade-In	$ —
Net Cash Price	$ 3560.00
Provincial Sales Tax +GST	$ 534.00
Fees for Registration	$ 10.00
Total Cash Price	$ 4104.00
Cash Down Payment	$ 304.00
Amount Financed	$ 3800.00
Scheduled Finance Charge	$ 1216.18
Total Amount of Contract	$ 5016.18
Annual Percentage Rate 28.22 %	

Payment Schedule: Your payment schedule is 24 payments of $ 209.03, except the last which shall be the balance owing. Each payment shall be due on the first day of each month beginning June 1, 19 XX, or one month from the date of this Contract if not otherwise specified.

Date of Contract May 18th, 19 XX

SEE REVERSE SIDE FOR TERMS OF THIS CONTRACT

Notice to Buyer: Do not sign this Contract before you read it, or if it contains any blank spaces.

1. Please note that in connection with this credit application a consumer report containing credit information or personal information may be obtained by the prospective creditor. If you so request the creditor will inform you of the name and address of the consumer reporting agency supplying the report. Any information obtained in connection with this credit application may be divulged to other credit grantors or to a consumer reporting agency. 2. When you sign this Contract, you acknowledge that you have read and agreed to all its terms. 3. Be sure and read the terms and conditions contained on the reverse side of this Contract as they are binding on you as well. 4. All copies must be individually signed in ink.

Seller's Signature

I hereby guaranty payment of the total of payments of this Contract:

Guarantor's Signature

You confirm receiving a completed copy of this Contract with disclosures of your credit costs.

Buyer 1's Signature

Buyer 2's Signature

AP 24 ONT. Ed. 9/89

FIGURE 12.14 CONDITIONAL SALES CONTRACT (CONTINUED)

TERMS AND CONDITIONS

1. Promise to Pay: You promise to pay the total amount of contract according to your payment schedule.

2. Interest Rate: The rate shown on the front page as Annual Percentage Rate shall be the rate agreed upon for the computation of pre-judgment and post-judgment interest and shall be used in the computation of any such interest by a Court of Justice when making an order or granting a judgment to enforce this contract.

3. Credit Statement: You certify that all statements in your credit statement are true and complete and were made for the purpose of obtaining credit.

4. Warranties: Unless you have been given a written warranty, there is no warranty on the goods purchased and no statements or promise made by any party shall be valid or binding.

5. Title: Title, and therefore legal ownership, to the goods which you have purchased by this Contract does not pass to you until payment in full of this Contract. You understand and acknowledge that the Seller, and any assignee of the Seller, retains a continuing security interest in the goods which you have purchased until payment in full of this Contract. Furthermore, you agree not to transfer possession or control of the property to any other person without first notifying us by registered mail of your intention to do so.

6. Location: You agree that the goods are to remain at the address indicated on the front of this Contract. If you wish to move the goods, you must notify us by registered mail before you do so. The registered letter can be sent to the same address where you send you payments If you move from the address shown on the reverse side, you must notify us of your new address without delay.

7. Insurance: It is your obligation to keep the property insured against fire and theft. You acknowledge that any loss, injury or destruction of the property covered by this Contract does not relieve you of your obligation to pay the full amount owed on the Contract.

8. Default: You will be considered in default under the terms of this Contract if:

a) you fail to make any payment on time;
b) you fail to meet any promise you have made in this Contract;
c) you become insolvent or bankrupt;
d) the property is lost or destroyed;
e) the property is seized in any legal proceeding.

9. Remember: *If you are in default under this Contract, we have certain legal remedies available to us. We may, at our election,*

a) *demand that the full balance owing be paid immediately;*
b) *take possession of the goods according to law;*
c) *commence legal proceedings for recovery of the balance owing.*

Where we have taken possesion of the goods, you will be sent the required notice which will explain how you may regain possession of the goods. If you do not do so, we will be entitled to dispose of the goods at a public or private sale, or at an auction. We may exercise our rights at any time. Where a deficiency has resulted from such a sale, we may commence legal proceedings for recovery of the deficiency, if permitted by law.

10. Additional Charges on Default: You agree to pay a delinquency charge of 5¢ per each $1.00 of any instalment which is not paid within 5 days after the instalment due date. You agree to pay interest at the same annual percentage rate as stated in this contract after maturity on any unpaid balance which remains.

11. Insufficient Funds Charge: In the event a cheque tendered for payment is returned for insufficient funds, we may collect a $10.00 charge as a reasonable charge for expenses incurred, over and above any other charges.

12. Refund: If you repay in full one month or more before the maturity date of this Contract, a portion of the Total Amount of Contract shall be refunded to you, calculated according to the Consumer Protection Act of Ontario and the regulations. We are entitled to retain an additional amount of $20 or one half of the refund, whichever is less. You are not entitled to the rebate if after deducting the amount we can retain, the rebate is less than two ($2.00) dollars.

13. Assignment: You understand that this Contract may be assigned by the Seller. The assignee will then be entitled to all the rights which the Seller may have had.

14. Applicable Law: Any part of this Contract which is contrary to the laws of any province shall not invalidate the other parts of this Contract.

THIS CONTRACT CONTAINS THE ENTIRE AGREEMENT BETWEEN THE PARTIES

---

to buy new stock. This difficulty is solved by sales finance companies and some banks, which make a business of buying conditional sales contracts from retailers—a transaction sometimes referred to as selling credit paper.

Careful examination of most conditional sales contracts may reveal a statement specifying that the contract may be assigned to a third party—a named financial institution. The blank contract forms that are often supplied to the retailer by the sales finance company may bear the name of that company. The arrangements made between retailers and sales finance companies vary, but the sales finance company usually buys the contract from the retailer for a sum equal to the item's purchase price; this makes it equivalent to a cash sale from the retailer's perspective. The purchaser now makes payments directly to the sales finance company that holds the contract.

The sales finance company makes its profit from the interest part of the contract. Depending on competition and economic conditions, the sales finance company may offer the retailer an additional premium, or it may charge a discount.

Credit Regulation

Historical Background

Consumer protection legislation began proliferating in the mid-1960s, continuing until all provinces had enacted one or more laws that confirmed consumers' rights in credit transactions. This surge of legislative activity reflected the fact that the use of consumer credit had increased fairly gradually in the 1950s but had accelerated in the 1960s. Many consumers, having little expertise in the credit market, were at a disadvantage in their dealings with large corporate creditors. Consequently, provincial governments tried to come to the consumer's aid with consumer protection legislation.

Until the middle of the twentieth century, most credit transactions had been conducted between businesses, and both businesses were typically experienced in the credit market; except for informal charge accounts at the local store, few consumers ever entered the credit market. This pattern changed after 1950, with the advent of mass production of high-priced consumer durables that were merchandised on a "buy now, pay later" basis. Unsophisticated buyers, unversed in credit or contracts, entered the market, enlarging the demand for both the durables and the credit; but unfortunately many consumers signed contracts they did not understand, waiving rights they did not know they held.

Not surprisingly, some borrowers got into difficult situations for which they had no legal defence. Provincial legislatures responded by entrenching certain rights of consumers in law and by setting up ministries of consumer affairs to oversee the regulation of credit. The provinces' aims were laudable, but the ministries' budgets were rarely sufficient to provide help on the required scale. Although consumers acquired rights that lawyers and creditors knew about, most consumers remained unaware of these rights. Insufficient resources were allocated either for public information or for law enforcement. Consumers still benefited from the legislation, however, because lenders knew the rules and tried to follow them.

The different provincial statutes that regulate credit contain many similar provisions. The following very general discussion is limited to some of the highlights; for greater detail or precision, consult the relevant legislation in your province. In most provinces, the statute in question is called the *Consumer Protection Act*; in New Brunswick and Saskatchewan, the equivalent laws are called the *Cost of Credit Disclosure Act*; and Alberta's residents are protected by the *Consumer Credit Transactions Act*.

Disclosure of Credit Charges

One of the main achievements of the consumer protection legislation was to require creditors to disclose all the costs of credit, both as annual percentage rates and as total dollar amounts. Because of divided federal–provincial jurisdiction regarding the regulation of consumer credit (interest is a federal matter, while trade is a provincial one), there was uncertainty about exactly which costs of borrowing could be called interest. Consequently, the provincial acts generally avoid using the word interest, substituting a broader term—credit charges—instead. Disclosing the full cost of credit, both as an amount and as a rate (an approach referred to as "truth in lending" in the United States), is now mandatory in all provinces and states.

After the disclosure laws had been in effect for a number of years, some research was done to determine whether consumers use this information in comparison shopping for credit. Many borrowers were found to be generally insensitive to interest rates and more concerned with the size of their monthly payments. Apparently, users of consumer credit are often more interested in shopping for the purchase than in shopping for the financing.

For variable credit or revolving charge accounts, the disclosure requirements stipulate that the borrower must be told in advance what the interest rate will be and that after extending the credit, the lender must provide a statement showing the outstanding balances at the beginning and end of the statement period, the amounts and dates of each transaction, and the cost of borrowing expressed in dollar amounts.

When a conditional sales contract is used for a consumer purchase, it is subject to provincial consumer protection legislation regarding disclosure of credit charges and the content of the contract. The statutes covering conditional sales contracts may refer to them as a type of **executory contract**—that is, one in which both parties have made promises regarding future action, but have yet to act.

The rules for disclosure of credit costs apply to conditional sales contracts whether they are signed at the vendor's premises or in the customer's home. The method of calculating credit charges on conditional sales is set forth in the regulations that accompany the various provincial acts. The disclosure legislation contains a list of information that must be included in an executory contract (e.g., a conditional sales contract) if the total cost of the purchase, excluding credit charges, is above a specified amount—typically around $50. Essentially, the contract must contain the full name and address of both the buyer and the seller, a description of the goods being purchased, and details about the financial transaction.

Supervision of Itinerant Sellers

Do door-to-door sellers exert undue pressure on people to buy their products? Perhaps. At any rate, each province has legislation that allows consumers time to change their minds about contracts signed in their own homes. In fact, the consumer's right to cancel the agreement can apply to any sales contract signed at a location other than the company's place of business. The length of this "cooling-off" period varies from province to province, but within the specified time, a consumer may cancel the contract simply by informing the company of his or her intention to do so. This is best done by registered mail, but verbal notice is acceptable in some provinces. The date on the letter's postmark is usually considered to be the time the notice was received by the company. When calculating the cooling-off period, do not include Sundays and statutory holidays (i.e., a standard seven-day calendar week would comprise only six days—Monday through Saturday—that would count as part of the cooling-off period). If you cancel a conditional sales contract during the cooling-off period, you are expected to return any goods that you received and possibly to pay compensation for having had the use of them; the seller is expected to return any down payment. A summary of the relevant legislation by province is shown in Table 12.1.

TABLE 12.1 COOLING-OFF PERIODS BY PROVINCE

PROVINCE	LEGISLATION	LENGTH OF COOLING-OFF PERIOD	NOTIFICATION OF CANCELLATION
Newfoundland	*Direct Sellers Act*	Within 10 days of date on which contract was signed.	Sent or delivered by means of proving the notice is sent, in which case it is deemed effective on the date it is sent.
Prince Edward Island	*Direct Sellers Act*	Within 7 days of date on which contract was signed.	In writing or by personal delivery, telegram, or registered mail to vendor's last known address. When sent by registered mail, it is deemed effective on the day after it is mailed.

continued

TABLE 12.1   COOLING-OFF PERIODS BY PROVINCE (CONTINUED)

PROVINCE	LEGISLATION	LENGTH OF COOLING-OFF PERIOD	NOTIFICATION OF CANCELLATION
Nova Scotia*	*Direct Sellers Licensing Act*	Within 10 days of date on which contract was signed.	Written or by personal delivery to direct seller or to one of the direct seller's sales representatives or by registered mail to address shown on contract, in which case it is deemed effective at time of mailing.
New Brunswick	*Direct Sellers Act*	Within 10 days of receiving a copy of the contract. Within 5 days of date on which contract was signed.	Written, to direct seller or to one of the direct seller's sales representatives or by personal delivery, fax, registered mail, or any other method that permits the purchaser to provide evidence of cancellation.
Quebec*	*Consumer Protection Act*	Not later than 10 days after buyer receives copy of contract.	By returning goods to vendor's address, by written notice, or by returning the contract.
Ontario*	*Consumer Protection Act*	Within 2 days after buyer receives duplicate original copy of contract.	Written, by personal delivery, or by registered mail to address stated in contract, in which case it is deemed effective at time of mailing.
Manitoba*	*Consumer Protection Act*	Within 10 days of date on which contract was signed.	Written, by personal delivery, by fax, or by registered mail to vendor, provided proof of date of cancellation is given when sent.
Saskatchewan	*Direct Sellers Act*	Within 10 days of date on which contract was signed.	Written, by personal delivery, fax, or registered mail to vendor's last known address. If sent other than by personal delivery, it is deemed effective on the date sent.
Alberta	*Direct Sales Cancellation Act*	Not later than 4 days after date on which buyer receives copy of contract by personal delivery or by mail.	Written, by personal delivery or mailed to vendor named in contract. If no contract, notice sent to any address of sales representative known to buyer. Deemed effective at time of mailing.
British Columbia*	*Consumer Protection Act*	Not later than 7 days after date on which buyer receives copy of contract.	Written, by personal delivery or mailed to seller's address as stated in contract or to any address of seller known to buyer.

* In these provinces, legislation is effective only when the purchase exceeds a minimum dollar price.

In Manitoba and Nova Scotia, if the contract does not include rescission rights, the cooling-off period is 30 days after the goods or services were delivered.

All provinces, except Ontario and Quebec, provide for cancellation after longer periods if certain conditions are not met.

Prepayment of Credit Contracts

Most creditors arrange the repayment of accounts by calculating the credit charges on the outstanding balance at the end of each month, as discussed in Chapter 8. Less frequently, a precomputed schedule of credit charges may be used. In both instances, the monthly payments are of equal size, comprising varying amounts of principal and interest. The difference is that the proportions of interest and principal are established in advance in the precomputed schedule, instead of being computed for each payment period. The monthly computation offers more flexibility to a borrower who may wish to repay the debt faster than scheduled. In such a case, the lender simply charges interest on whatever principal sum is outstanding at the end of the month, subtracts this amount from the payment, and uses the remainder to reduce the principal. (You may wish to review the section "Compound Interest on Instalment Loans" in Chapter 8.) Precomputed charges create more complexity if the borrower wishes to repay early; but since precomputed charges are becoming less common, we will not go into the details here.

Unsolicited Credit Cards and Goods

Provincial legislation sets limits on your responsibility for unsolicited goods or credit cards you may receive.

UNSOLICITED CREDIT CARDS   Five provinces prohibit the issuing of unsolicited credit cards (Table 12.2). Other provinces do not make it illegal to send out such cards, but they make it quite clear that if a credit card was not requested, the intended recipient has no legal responsibility for transactions made with it unless some indication of acceptance was made, such as signing the card and presenting it to a vendor.

TABLE 12.2   PROVINCIAL LAWS REGARDING UNSOLICITED CREDIT CARDS

THE LAW STATES THAT...	PROVINCES WHERE THIS LAW APPLIES
issuing of unsolicited credit cards is forbidden.	Alberta, Manitoba, New Brunswick, Prince Edward Island, Quebec
if an unsolicited credit card is received, the recipient has no legal obligation for transactions made with it, unless he or she writes to the card's issuer stating that he or she intends to accept it.	Alberta, British Columbia, Newfoundland, Nova Scotia, Ontario, Saskatchewan
signing and using an unsolicited credit card is considered to be acceptance of responsibility for the card.	Alberta, Newfoundland, Nova Scotia, Ontario
if an unsolicited credit card has not been accepted, the intended recipient has no responsibility if the card is lost or misused.	Alberta, British Columbia, Ontario, Newfoundland, Nova Scotia, Saskatchewan

UNSOLICITED GOODS   Prince Edward Island is the only province that prohibits sending unsolicited goods. In British Columbia, Newfoundland, Nova Scotia, Ontario, and Saskatchewan, the recipient of unsolicited goods has no responsibility to return, pay for, or take any special care of such goods. But if residents of British Columbia or Saskatchewan acknowledge having received such goods (e.g., by signing for them—but even simply using an unsolicited credit card constitutes acknowledgment of having received it), they lose their immunity from responsibility.

Advertising the Cost of Credit

All provinces regulate advertising the cost of credit. This became necessary because retailers and lenders had begun to deceive potential customers by advertising credit arrangements in such a way as to be misleading. For instance, an advertisement might have stated that there would be no down payment without telling the rest of the story. Lenders who advertise the cost of credit must indicate the cost of borrowing expressed as an annual percentage rate. If other information about the credit terms is to be advertised, lenders are required to present all relevant information, which includes the number of instalments, the amount of the down payment, and the size of each instalment.

Repossession of Secured Goods

If a debtor is in default, the creditor can usually seize the secured goods without a court judgment. However, provincial laws place some restrictions on this process. In practice, most creditors prefer to press for payment of the debt rather than become involved in the complications of repossession. Although threatening to repossess is a powerful weapon for encouraging borrowers to make payments, carrying out the threat is not worthwhile for creditors unless the pledged goods are of significant value. The creditor usually has the right to repossess the goods, sell them, and claim against the debtor for any balance not covered by the sale. But because some unscrupulous creditors would sell the goods at a lower price to friends and then sue the debtor for the difference, some provinces (Alberta, British Columbia, and Newfoundland) have "seize or sue" laws that allow the creditor either to repossess secured goods or to sue, but not to do both.

Promissory Notes on Conditional Sales Contracts

A promissory note is not only an unconditional promise to repay a debt, it is also a negotiable instrument. Like a cheque, it can be endorsed and made payable to a third party. A promissory note is generally implied in a conditional sales contract, but when such a contract is sold, there are some restrictions to protect borrowers. A person who holds the usual type of promissory note can demand payment regardless of any responsibilities for delivery, quality of goods, and so on. But anyone who buys a conditional sales contract from a retailer shares responsibility with the retailer for ensuring that the obligations associated with the goods are met. The vendor and the third party, usually a sales finance company or a bank, share the responsibility for ensuring that the goods or service are satisfactory for the intended purpose.

Issues and Problems

Credit Cards

NEED FOR STANDARDIZED DISCLOSURE   Despite the widespread use of credit cards, their costs are not well understood by many users. The available cards differ significantly in two kinds of costs: (i) non-interest costs (such as annual or transaction fees) and (ii) the terms and conditions associated with interest charges. In order to make rational choices, consumers must understand each credit card's terms and conditions. But the present state of information disclosure makes this level of understanding impossible. Although the nominal interest rates are readily available, they are not, as we have seen, an accurate basis for comparing costs.

Some of the information that card issuers do provide is not presented in an easily understandable form. For instance, many people believe that a partial payment will proportionately reduce the interest charges, but this is not the case with all credit cards. Consumers would be well served by having a standardized set of terms and conditions for calculating interest charges on credit cards, as is the case for consumer loans.

In 1987, in response to a demand for better information about credit card costs, Consumer and Corporate Affairs Canada began issuing a brief release called "Credit Card Costs" three times a year. It includes a chart comparing credit cards by fees, grace periods, interest rates, and the period to which interest charges apply. Contact the department if you wish to be on its mailing list for these updates.

DISPUTES WITH RETAILERS A complicating aspect of purchases made with bank cards is that if you need to dispute any goods or services you purchase with them, you must deal with a retailer who has already been reimbursed by your financial institution. The bank or other institution, which specifically states in your cardholder agreement that it takes no responsibility for merchandise or services you may purchase using its card, will not be interested in hearing about the dispute. While trying to resolve the dispute with the retailer, you must also keep your payments to the card's issuer up-to-date; withholding payment for the disputed transaction will not help resolve the dispute, and in fact will merely cause you further expense and trouble, since more credit charges will be added to the unpaid amount. Instead, you will need to handle the problem exactly as you would handle an unsatisfactory cash purchase.

Some consumers have faced a quite different problem: they have had the unfortunate experience of having a credit card rejected at the point of sale, despite a good payment record. The cause could be an employee error, or it could be that the card issuer's computer has detected unusual purchasing patterns of the sort that might reflect the use of a stolen card. When mix-ups like this occur, it is difficult to get the problem resolved in a store or hotel lobby. One alternative is to ensure that you always have another method of payment—such as cash, a debit card, or another credit card—available.

CREDIT CARD COSTS There is no restriction on the interest rates that issuers may charge on credit card debt. Legislators have apparently assumed that cardholders will be able to compare costs among various sources of credit and make rational choices based on the information they gather. An estimated 70 percent to 80 percent of cardholders pay interest charges at least some of the time. Banks claim that they need high interest rates to cover losses from fraud and default. Yet the delinquency rate on bank cards is only about 1.5 percent, compared to 2 percent on other bank personal loans.

Contracts

Two significant problems that consumers face when they sign credit contracts are their weak bargaining position and the difficulty of understanding the legal terminology used in the contracts. Chattel mortgages and conditional sales contracts are drawn up by lawyers who are hired to protect the creditors' interests, not those of consumers. As a borrower, your choices are limited: you can either accept the contract as it stands, or reject it and go elsewhere for credit. The salesperson or credit manager usually lacks the authority to renegotiate the credit contract's terms to suit you—and rarely understands the contract any better than you do. It is encouraging, however, to find that some creditors have started to rewrite their contracts in language that is much easier to understand.

Summary

Consumer debt and credit are synonyms: the term you choose will depend on your perspective. Over the past several decades, Canadians have significantly increased their use of consumer credit, even when we take inflation and population growth into account. Three measures of consumer credit were discussed: (i) the incidence of credit use, (ii) the household's average debt level, and (iii) the ratio of consumer debt to income. Many sources of loans or credit are available, though the banks have become the dominant players in the credit market. Differences among the institutions have decreased over time, as increased competition has encouraged all firms to provide similar services at similar rates. The relevant documentation and legal statutes are also becoming very similar throughout the country as business practices as well as the rates become virtually identical among the various lenders. The proliferation of credit cards and debit cards has given Canada one of the world's most electronically linked financial systems. Our point-of-sale-credit systems have enabled exact calculations of our debts, while the complexities of calculating interest remain even more complicated. Consumers rarely know about their rights with regard to credit laws or itinerant sales agents. This situation is frequently because of the perceived disadvantage consumers face compared to large firms and consumers' lack of knowledge of business law.

Key Terms

acceleration clause (p. 363)
charge card (p. 356)
chattel (p. 348)
chattel mortgage (security interest) (p. 348)
co-signer (p. 347)
collateral (p. 347)
common bond (p. 341)
conditional sales contract (agreement) (p. 360)
constant dollars (p. 333)
consumer debt (p. 331)
consumer loan (p. 337)
credit card (p. 356)
credit union (p. 341)
current dollars (p. 333)
debit card (p. 355)
debt burden (p. 334)
discretionary income (p. 352)

enforce security (p. 367)
executory contract (p. 340)
fiduciary (p. 346)
fully secured loan (p. 346)
grace period (p. 356)
in arrears (delinquent) (p. 352)
in default (p. 352)
lien (p. 351)
living trust (p. 340)
maturity date (p. 344)
mortgage debt (p. 331)
partly secured loan (p. 346)
personal disposable income (p. 334)
point-of-sale-credit (p. 337)
prime rate (p. 346)
promissory note (p. 334)
real income (p. 334)

Problems

Note: You may need to consult the appropriate consumer protection legislation for your province to find the information needed to answer these questions.

1. What are the four reasons for using consumer credit suggested in the chapter? Are there any other reasons you can suggest? What, in your opinion, is the primary reason for using consumer credit?

2. Have you observed any difference between your parents' or your own generation regarding the use of credit? Comment.

3. What changes have you faced in your own use of credit? Have you increased your usage? And if so, to whom? What are or will be your monthly payment, term, and total expected payments when the loan comes due? (Hint: Don't forget any student loans.)

4. What are the responsibilities of a person who co-signs a loan?

5. (a) Why did the Dubois pay a lower rate of interest on the fully secured loan?

   (b) Was the loan for the car fully or partly secured? How can you tell?

   (c) The loans officer at the bank told the Dubois that credit life insurance would be

Borrowing to Buy a Car

The Dubois have had two experiences with consumer loans. First they borrowed money from the bank to buy a washing machine. By using Chantal's Canada Savings Bonds as collateral, they were able to obtain a fully secured loan at a low interest rate.

A year later, Peter and Chantal realized that they needed a new car, but they knew that they could not pay cash for it. They thought about approaching the credit union in Brandon, Manitoba, where Peter worked, but since he had never joined it, he wasn't sure how their request would be received. Remembering how easy it had been to borrow at the bank, they went back for a larger loan. The loans officer asked them to sign a chattel mortgage on the car and gave them the loan.

included at no additional cost. Does that mean that if Peter or Chantal dies, the other will receive some money from insurance? Explain.

(d) There are real estate mortgages and chattel mortgages. What characteristics of the security that the Dubois pledged differentiate these mortgages?

(e) Must the Dubois carry insurance on this car? Does it matter to the bank?

(f) If the Dubois wish to trade in this car and get another before the debt is repaid, do they need to consult the bank, as long as they make their payments?

(g) If the bank's loans officer had reservations about the ability of the Dubois to repay the loan on schedule, would she

    i. offer them a signature loan?

    ii. offer them a loan without credit life insurance?

    iii. require more security before making the loan?

6. What factors would a loans officer consider if you or one of your friends walked in to a bank today to apply for a loan? Would these factors change as you age 10, 20, or 30 years? What would you expect to happen to the interest rate you pay over the same periods of time?

7. Shameem is frustrated because the lawn mower she purchased from Handy Appliances, using her Visa card, has been defective since she brought it home. She took it back to the store, but was unable to get satisfaction there. At first they said, "Bring it in; we'll look it over." But they turned out to be only a sales outlet and to have no service personnel. The store suggested that she try the mower again, as it appeared to them be in working order. Meanwhile, her Visa bill arrived. Since she was contesting the sale, she advised Visa that she would not pay the bill until she was either satisfied with the mower or provided with a replacement. In time, another Visa bill arrives: the mower remains on the bill, and now a credit charge for delayed payment has been added.

(a) Where can Shameem find out what her rights are in the dispute with Visa?

(b) What are these rights?

(c) What is your opinion of the situation? What would you recommend that Shameem do?

(d) What rights does Shameem have with the retailer?

(e) What interest rate would Shameem pay if she obtained a cash loan with her Visa card? How does this compare with the rates that banks charge for personal loans? (Refer to the business section of your newspaper or call a financial institution to gather the information you need before answering this question.)

8. What minimum monthly payment is required on a Visa account?

9. If you obtain a cash advance on your Visa card and repay it all when the bill arrives, will you pay any credit charges?

10. Suppose that you and a friend each want to own a particular computer game so that you can play against each other via modem. You buy the appropriate software using your debit card, while your friend makes a parallel purchase using a credit card. What differences would there be between the two transactions?

11. If you and a friend both purchased a set of living room furniture upon graduating from school at a large box store with a Don't-Pay-for-One-Full-Year deal, and one of you paid immediately when the debt came due and the other took an extra year to pay, how much more money would your friend have to pay for the furniture? If necessary, go to the Web site of a furniture store, or telephone or visit them to determine the actual financing arrangements.

12. Proceed to any of the financial institution's Web sites listed below in "Personal Finance on the Web" and explore the consumer credit area.

   (a) What credit facilities may you apply for?

   (b) What are the terms of the credit card?

   (c) What are the interest rates charged on the loan, line of credit or credit card?

   (d) What do you authorize the financial institution to do regarding your past?

   (e) Are there any specific services for students available at the site?

   (f) How comfortable do you feel placing your confidential information on the Web?

   (g) Would you use the Web to apply for credit? Why or Why Not?

References

BOOKS

BEARES, PAUL. *Consumer Lending. Third Edition*. San Francisco: American Bankers Association, 1997. An industry-specific training manual from the lender's perspective.

CONSUMER AND CORPORATE AFFAIRS CANADA. *Charge It: Credit Cards and the Canadian Consumer*. Ottawa: Consumer and Corporate Affairs Canada, 1989. Minutes and proceedings of a House of Commons Committee that reviewed the background regarding Canadians' problems with credit card costs, the extent of market competition, and current disclosure practices, and made proposals for legislation. Data in appendix.

———. *Credit Cards in Canada in the Nineties*. Ottawa: Consumer and Corporate Affairs Canada, 1992. Bilingual. Report of the Standing Committee on Consumer and Corporate Affairs and Government Operations. Reviews developments in the credit card market in Canada and the United States since 1987, identifies current issues, and makes recommendations for change.

———. *Discussion Paper on Credit Card Interest Charges*. Ottawa: Consumer and Corporate Affairs Canada, 1988. An analysis of the pricing of credit cards that examines how interest is calculated and recommends more standardization.

DYMOND, MARY JOY. *The Canadian Woman's Legal Guide*. Toronto: Doubleday, 1989. Includes a section on women and credit.

GRAHAM, TERRY, and PAMELA GRAHAM. *Credit Cure: A Guide to Improving Your Credit*. Aurora, CA: Credit Cure Publications, 1996. Two experienced lenders and credit bureau managers outline a step-by-step method for reviewing and improving your credit standing. Caution, however: since this is an American book, some of the authors' advice will not apply in Canada. Still, the general material is useful.

HO, KWOK, and CHRIS ROBINSON. *Personal Financial Planning*. Second Edition. North York, ON: Captus Press, 1997. A Canadian textbook presented by two York University finance professors.

PARKER, ALLAN A. *Credit, Debt, and Bankruptcy.* Eighth Edition. Vancouver: International Self-Counsel Press, 1990. A handbook on Canadian credit law for credit users.

STEVENSON, DEREK. "Playing Your Cards Right." *Canadian Consumer,* 1989, Vol. 19, No. 10. Explains the complexities of selecting credit cards and how the various charges are calculated.

WYLIE, BETTY JANE, and LYNN MACFARLANE. *Everywoman's Money Book.* Fourth Edition. Toronto: Key Porter, 1989. By a journalist and a stockbroker who have collaborated on a wide variety of personal finance topics.

PERIODICALS

Canadian Commercial Law Guide. Don Mills, ON: CCH Canadian, Topical Law Reports. Subscription service in two volumes on federal and provincial law regarding the sale of personal property and consumer protection.

Canadian Economic Observer. Ottawa: Supply and Services Canada, monthly. (Catalogue No. 11-010.) Published by Statistics Canada.

Credit Card Costs. Ottawa: Consumer and Corporate Affairs Canada, three times a year. Lists fees, interest rates, grace periods, and date from which interest is calculated by name of creditor. Free copy on request.

Personal Finance on the Web

Bank of Montreal
> **www.bmo.com** Provides full exposure to all aspects of bank operations, including both personal and commercial banking. You can even apply for a MasterCard on the Internet.

Canada Trust
> **www.canadatrust.com** Includes the trust company's online banking service, from investment services to a list of Canada Trust ATM locations.

Canadian Financial Network
> **www.canadianfinance.com** Solid information regarding personal finance for Canadians with extensive links to other relevant sites.

Canadian Imperial Bank Of Commerce
> **www.cibc.com/index.html** Allows you to apply online for loans and credit cards; also provides numerous financial tools for such tasks as calculating your mortgage or applying for insurance.

Citizens Bank of Canada
> **www.citizensbank.ca** This bank, owned by VANCITY Credit Union, has no branches; it does all its business over the telephone or via the Internet.

ING Bank of Canada
> **www.ingdirect.ca** This international bank is making significant inroads in Canadian financial markets. It possesses no branches, but has two offices in Toronto and Vancouver. The majority of its business is conducted via the Internet or over the telephone.

Royal Bank Financial Group
> **www.royalbank.ca** Incorporates all information on investments, mutual funds, loans, and so on, covering all facets of the bank's operation.

Scotiabank

www.scotiabank.ca A fully searchable site with significant information on most facets of financial planning.

Toronto-Dominion Bank

www.tdbank.ca Provides financial management tools and allows you to apply for loans, personal lines of credit, mortgages, and Visa credit cards.

Visa

www.visa.com Describes and offers worldwide services; be aware, though, of flagged material that applies only in the United States.

Chapter 13

Home Mortgages

objectives

1. Explain the opportunity costs in buying a house.

2. Compare the costs and benefits of the various means of mortgage funding.

3. Explain the differences between a conventional mortgage and an insured mortgage.

4. Explain how lenders determine whether a potential borrower qualifies for a loan.

5. Calculate the size of loan for which an applicant is eligible.

6. Distinguish between equal instalments of principal and blended payments.

7. Calculate the interest and principal in a mortgage payment.

8. Identify the components in a mortgage contract.

9. Explain how the total cost of buying a house is determined.

10. Understand the many terms associated with mortgages including the term, amortization period, and open and closed mortgages.

11. Explain how a reverse mortgage may be used to provide an income to the home owner.

12. Explain the relationship between the National Housing Act, the Canada Mortgage and Housing Corporation, and lenders in the mortgage business.

13. Explain the following terms: gross debt service, total debt service, closing costs, closing date, appraisal, mortgage discharge, interest penalty, prepayment privilege, capital gain, commitment period, equity, maturity date, amortization, mortgage broker, equity of redemption, high-ratio mortgage, non-money income, preapproved mortgage, interest adjustment date, interest-rate differential.

Introduction

This chapter explains the basic process of using credit to buy personal real estate; it is not about how to choose a house, but rather about how to understand mortgages. There is, of course, much more to buying a house than the financing: many books have been written on such topics as whether to buy or rent, and how to select a house. While these issues are important, they are beyond the scope of this book, which focuses on financial issues, rather than on all aspects of consumer decision making.

Sometimes prospective buyers are so enthusiastic about their new house that they leave all the financial arrangements to the real estate agent. They may feel overwhelmed by the terminology and mathematics associated with mortgages. After studying this chapter, you should be able to talk intelligently with mortgage officers, ask knowledgeable questions, and do some comparison shopping.

The Economics of Home Ownership

To Buy or Rent

For most families, the decision regarding whether to buy or rent is not strictly an economic one; rather, it involves choosing between two different lifestyles. But the economics of this question involve considering the opportunity costs of ownership as well as any differences in regular monthly expenses. (An **opportunity cost** is anything that was forgone in order to do something else.) Deciding to buy a house means tying up funds that could otherwise have been invested in an income-producing asset. To find the financial opportunity cost of buying a house, you must estimate how much interest you will forgo by not investing the money at current interest rates and then leaving it to compound. But remember that there are other opportunity costs of home ownership—such as the time you will be committing to home maintenance.

The house you live in does not usually generate money income; instead, it provides services or non-money income, in the form of shelter. **Non-money income** is a flow of services that are available for use as a result of our own efforts or gifts, but are not purchased in the market. For instance, a home owner gets a place to live without paying rent. In addition to a stream of non-money income, home ownership has the potential for capital gain. When a house is sold for more than it cost, the difference is called **capital gain.** In times of rising prices, houses may appreciate faster than they wear out, thus creating a potential capital gain.

Finally, you will want to consider the income tax implications of buying a house. If your savings are invested in a house, any capital gain you make when you sell that house will not be taxable because of the tax exemption on principal residences. If instead you invest your funds in deposits, bonds, or stocks, the income from your investments will be fully taxable.

How Much to Spend

How much should a family spend on a house? Some financial advisors suggest that a house should not cost more than two or three times one's annual salary, but these guidelines are much too imprecise to be helpful. Such a rule does not specify whether to base your calculations on gross income or take-home pay, and the difference can be quite significant. Families live so differently and have such varied financial goals that general rules are rarely applicable. It is preferable to work out what is affordable based on consideration of each unique situation.

One way to start is to determine how much you can spare for a down payment, and then add on the amount that can be borrowed; this will give you an approximation of the maximum purchase price that you can afford. (Note that if you hope to buy a newly constructed house, you will need to pay GST on its advertised purchase price, so your calculations here will need to take the tax into account as well.) The next step is to find out what your monthly costs would be if you owned a home that you purchased at that price.

Financing a Home

Most people who buy homes or other real estate need credit to finance the purchase, but because the loan is likely to be large and the repayment period long, the borrowing process is somewhat more complex than for the usual personal loan. To obtain such a large loan, the buyer must pledge security of some significance—usually the property being purchased.

When real estate (immoveable property) is used to secure a loan, the borrower signs a contract called a **mortgage**—not to be confused with a chattel mortgage (discussed in Chapter 12, under "Security for Loans"), which is used for moveable goods. The mortgage contract refers to the borrower as the **mortgagor,** because this person gives the mortgage to the lender, who in turn becomes the **mortgagee**—that is, the one who receives the mortgage as security for the loan. Sometimes chargor and chargee, respectively, are used as alternatives to these terms. The gradual repayment of a mortgage by periodic payments of principal and interest is referred to as **amortizing** the debt. (See Personal Finance in Action Box 13.5, "Interest and Principal Payments.")

MORTGAGE DEBT   Most of the total debt of households is mortgage debt, although the pattern varies somewhat with income level, occupation, marital status, and number of children. It is perhaps not surprising to find that, regardless of income level, mortgage debt represents the largest component of total family debt. There appears to be a tendency for mortgage debt to represent a larger proportion of total debt among higher-income households, which can afford more expensive houses and may also have vacation homes.

Equity in Real Estate

Equity, which refers to the value that the owner has in a property, can be estimated by finding a fair market price and then subtracting the outstanding mortgage debt. If house prices fall, equity falls too, as people who live in areas that have experienced severe economic downturns have discovered.

Types of Mortgages

First and Second Mortgages

A particular property may have more than one mortgage on it; the multiple mortgages will be ranked as first, second, and so on, according to the order in which they were recorded at the local Registry Office. If the first mortgage on a property is discharged, the second mortgage automatically becomes the first mortgage. This does not happen often, though, because first mortgages are usually for larger sums and longer terms than second mortgages.

What distinguishes a first mortgage from a second mortgage is its priority ranking in claims against the property. In the event that the buyer defaults on the mortgage payments and the property must be taken back and sold, the holder of the **first mortgage** has first claim on the proceeds from the sale. Only after this has been paid will the claims of the holder of the **second mortgage** be settled. If there are insufficient funds to pay all claims, the second mortgagee might have to accept a loss. Second mortgages are therefore considered to be riskier than first mortgages, and consequently carry higher interest rates.

Personal Finance in Action 13.1

Buying a House

Theo and Sarah are ready to buy a house. They have enough money to make a down payment on what they consider an ideal house, but the process of negotiating a mortgage frightens them. They have never owned a house or borrowed money, and do not know what questions to ask their banker. The banker simplifies things by asking the following questions:

Do you think interest rates will rise?

Do you want to pay down the mortgage quickly?

Do you want financial stability?

Theo and Sarah are unsure about the future of interest rates but recently read that they are on the way up, so answered yes to all three questions. The banker says this simplifies things because it means that they should choose a fixed-rate mortgage with an amortization period of less than 25 years. This will mean stability if interest rates rise. It also means that they can renegotiate without penalty and will have lower interest rate costs because of the shorter amortization period.

From the home owner's perspective, the number of mortgages on the property is not as important as the amount of equity he or she has in the property. For instance, on a property valued at $200 000, the owner's equity of $30 000 would be the same (i) with a first mortgage of $150 000 and a second mortgage of $20 000, or (ii) with a first mortgage of $160 000 and a second mortgage of $10 000. The interest rate paid on the second mortgage depends on the owner's equity. From the lender's point of view, if the first and second mortgages combined are less than 75 percent of the appraised value (that is, the owner's equity is 25 percent), the second mortgage is nearly as secure as the first; the interest rate should reflect this.

Security for the Lender

Mortgage money may be obtained either privately or from financial institutions such as banks, trust companies, and credit unions. Because a mortgage is a large loan, the lender must have assurance that it is a sound investment. To protect the lender, the mortgagor must either make a sizeable down payment or have the mortgage insured. When the down payment is less than 25 percent of the property's value, the buyer's equity might not be enough to cover costs if, in the case of default, the lender had to take back the property and sell it. When the buyer cannot provide a down payment of at least 25 percent of the property's value, an institutional mortgagee will not offer a loan without mortgage insurance.

Mortgage insurance covers the risk to the lender that the borrower will default on the loan. The Canada Mortgage and Housing Corporation (CMHC), a Crown corporation, provides full loan insurance to mortgage lenders. CMHC reimburses the lender for loss in cases of default—but correspondingly imposes a number of restrictions on the granting of the mortgage, as will be explained later (under "Qualifying for a Mortgage"). First, we will examine the differences between conventional mortgages and insured mortgages.

Conventional Mortgages

A **conventional mortgage** is not usually insured, but the down payment is at least 25 percent of the property's value. A number of financial institutions—notably banks, trust companies, and mortgage companies—offer conventional mortgages. Privately arranged mortgages are always conventional mortgages: that is, they are not insured, and the down payment can be whatever the parties involved agree on.

Insured Mortgages

At one time, all mortgages were conventional mortgages; but in 1954, the federal government established a system that guarantees mortgage loans made by approved financial lenders as a means of increasing the mortgage money available to home buyers and builders. The legislation is the *National Housing Act*. As already mentioned, the Crown corporation that administers it is the Canada Mortgage and Housing Corporation, usually known as CMHC. A lender making a mortgage loan that is CMHC-approved can extend a mortgage that is up to 95 percent of the property's value. These **insured mortgages** permit the buyer to obtain a mortgage with less than 25 percent of the property's value as a down payment. If the buyer defaults on the mortgage, the lender applies to CMHC for any losses incurred.

To finance this mortgage insurance program, the buyer pays a fee of between 0.5 percent and 2.5 percent of the total loan; the appropriate amount is added to the principal at the outset. The fee is based on a sliding scale, depending on the ratio of the down payment to the loan. The lender deducts the mortgage insurance premium and forwards it to the insurer (CMHC). This insurance, which protects the lender in case of default, may not seem to offer much benefit to the borrower. But without it, mortgages with low down payments would not be available at all, or purchasers would have to resort to a more expensive second mortgage. Insured first mortgages that represent a high proportion of the house's cost are sometimes referred to as **high-ratio loans.**

Finding a Mortgage

There are a number of ways to obtain a mortgage. It may be possible to arrange a private mortgage with a relative or other individual who has money to lend. In such a case, a lawyer would draw up a contract stating terms that are agreeable to both borrower and lender. Most mortgages, however, are obtained from financial institutions: banks, trust companies, and credit unions.

In some cases, it is possible to arrange a **vendor take-back mortgage** for all or part of the required financing, which means that the seller lends part of the selling price to the buyer. Perhaps the buyer has found a desirable house and the vendor offers to sell it for $150 000, with the arrangement that the buyer will pay $50 000 on closing and the rest in monthly instalments. Since the vendor is providing the loan of $100 000, it is called a vendor take-back mortgage. Sometimes this takes the form of a second mortgage.

Assumption of an Existing Mortgage

At times it is advantageous to take over a mortgage that already exists on the property. If the vendor has a mortgage with four years remaining in the term, and that mortgage has a lower interest rate than that currently available for a new mortgage, the buyer may wish to take over the vendor's mortgage. The buyer should investigate whether the mortgagee's approval is required for such a transfer and if so, whether that approval can be obtained. Mortgage contracts vary in this regard. If an existing mortgage is assumed, the buyer replaces the original mortgagor by taking responsibility for the agreements in the mortgage contract; in case of default, the original borrower may still be bound by the personal covenant, which is the promise to repay the debt. In practice, when the purchaser has been approved to assume the existing mortgage, the vendor often obtains a written release of this covenant from the lender as protection from this contingency.

Mortgage Brokers

Mortgage brokers specialize in making contact between those who have funds to invest in mortgages and those who need a mortgage. The rates charged for arranging a mortgage vary, depending on the amount of work involved, but are payable by the borrower at the time of closing. As with any mortgage, the property in question must be satisfactory to the lender. Home buyers will sometimes ask a broker to find them a mortgage because they do not qualify at the local bank or trust company. A borrower might need the services of a broker because of his or her poor credit rating, previous bankruptcy, very short employment history, or seasonally fluctuating income.

Qualifying for a Mortgage

The rules and procedures that govern the mortgage-granting process originate from three sources: (i) legislation, both federal and provincial, (ii) insurers' requirements for high-ratio mortgages, and (iii) the policies of each financial institution. Two basic criteria for determining whether or not to grant a mortgage relate to the quality of the property as security, and the borrower's creditworthiness.

The Property

Before agreeing to arrange a mortgage on a property, a lender will have it appraised to determine its **lending value** (appraised value)—that is, the value assigned to the property by the lender's appraiser, which is not necessarily the same as the selling price. It is conceivable that a buyer may be prepared to pay $300 000 for a much desired property that the lender considers to be worth $286 000. In such a case, the mortgage loan is based on the lending value, not the selling price.

CMHC has rules that vary from time to time and from place to place relating to the proportion of the lending value that may be lent for an insured mortgage. For example, CMHC-insured loans could be as large as 95 percent of the first $180 000 of the lending value, plus 80 percent of the remainder (for a first-time home buyer).

The Borrower

A potential lender will want a full report on the buyer's credit history, as well as complete details about the buyer's income, assets, and debts. The applicant will be asked to provide a statement from an employer verifying the current income and employment history of the applicant and spouse, and a statement from a banker about funds available for a down payment.

From these facts, the lender will calculate two ratios to determine the client's capacity to handle the proposed mortgage: the gross debt service and total debt service. **Gross debt service** (sometimes abbreviated GDS) is the percentage of the buyer's annual gross income needed to cover the mortgage payments and the municipal taxes (and sometimes also heating costs). If a condominium is to be purchased, 50 percent of the condominium fee is usually included in the calculation. Lenders have guidelines, which change from time to time, about the maximum gross debt service that is acceptable to them; it may range from 25 percent to 32 percent.

A quick way to determine the maximum mortgage that you can afford is to find 30 percent (or whatever the ratio is) of your gross annual income, subtract the estimated annual property taxes, and divide by 12. The resulting amount is the monthly payment that you can presumably afford for principal and interest. For a given interest rate and amortization period, the size of the loan can be found from an amortization table.

Gross and Total Debt Service

The Ghorises have three questions about financing the house they would like to buy: (i) How much is the gross debt service? (ii) How much is the total debt service? (iii) What is the largest mortgage they can afford?

In order to find the answers to these questions, they make the following assumptions:

Combined incomes	$75 000
Property taxes	$2 000/yr.
Heating costs	$600/yr.
Mortgage	$120 000
Interest	7.65%
Amortization Period	10 years
Payments	$765/mo.; $9 180/yr.
Consumer debt	$4 000/yr.
Lender's maximum TDS	38%

1. **How much will the gross debt service (GDS) be?**

$$GDS = \frac{\text{payments/yr.} + \text{taxes/yr.} + \text{heating/yr.}}{\text{gross annual income}} \times 100$$

$$= \frac{9\ 180 + 2\ 000 + 600}{75\ 000} \times 100$$

$$= \frac{11\ 780}{75\ 000} \times 100$$

$$= 15.7\%$$

2. **How much will the total debt service (TDS) be?**

$$TDS = \frac{\text{payments/yr.} + \text{taxes} + \text{heating} + \text{consumer debt}}{\text{gross annual income}} \times 100$$

$$= \frac{9\ 180 + 2\ 000 + 600 + 4\ 000}{75\ 000} \times 100$$

$$= \frac{15\ 780}{75\ 000} \times 100$$

$$= 21\%$$

3. **What is the largest mortgage for which the Ghorises are eligible?**

Since their total debt service is much lower than the lender's maximum, the Ghorises wonder how large a mortgage they could get if they had a TDS of 38 percent.

Transpose the formula for the total debt service to find the annual payment, and then insert 38 percent as the TDS.

$$\frac{\text{Payments} + \text{taxes} + \text{heating} + \text{consumer debt}}{\text{gross annual income}} \times 100 = TDS$$

$$\text{Payments} + (\text{taxes} + \text{heating} + \text{consumer debt}) = \frac{TDS \times \text{gross income}}{100}$$

$$\text{Payments} = \left(\frac{TDS \times \text{gross income}}{100}\right) - (\text{taxes} + \text{heating} + \text{consumer debt})$$

$$= \left(\frac{38 \times 75\ 000}{100}\right) - (2\ 000 + 600 + 4\ 000)$$

$$= 28\ 500 \qquad\qquad -\ 6\ 600$$

$$= \$21\ 900 \text{ per year (or } \$1\ 825 \text{ a month)}$$

With a TDS of 38 percent, the monthly payment would be $1 825. The next step is to find the principal of such a loan. Table 13.1 shows the monthly payment per $1 000 for mortgages at various rates. At 7.65 percent and with a 10-year amortization period, the monthly payment per $1 000 is about $11.90. Multiply this amount by the number of thousands of principal to find the monthly payment. The formula is as follows:

$$\text{Monthly payment} \quad = \quad \frac{\text{principal}}{1\ 000} \quad \times \quad \text{payment per \$1 000 (11.90)}$$

Transposing the formula,

$$\text{Principal} \quad = \quad \frac{\text{monthly payment} \times 1\ 000}{11.90}$$

Assuming monthly payments of $1 825

$$\text{Principal} \quad = \quad \frac{1\ 825.00 \times 1\ 000}{11.90}$$

$$= \$153\ 361.00$$

Based on a total debt service ratio of 38 percent, the Ghorises would be eligible for a maximum mortgage of $153 361.00 if the property qualified.

TABLE 13.1 MONTHLY PAYMENTS REQUIRED TO AMORTIZE A $1 000 LOAN, INTEREST COMPOUNDED SEMI-ANNUALLY

NOMINAL INTEREST RATE	AMORTIZATION PERIOD (YEARS)						
	5	10	15	20	25	30	35
%	(DOLLARS PER THOUSAND)						
6	19.30	11.06	8.40	7.12	6.40	5.94	5.65
6 1/4	19.41	11.19	8.53	7.26	6.55	6.10	5.82
6 1/2	19.53	11.31	8.66	7.40	6.62	6.26	5.98
6 3/4	19.64	11.43	8.80	7.55	6.85	6.42	6.15
7	19.75	11.56	8.93	7.69	7.00	6.59	6.32
7 1/4	19.87	11.68	9.07	7.84	7.16	6.75	6.49
7 1/2	19.98	11.81	9.20	7.99	7.32	6.91	6.66
7 3/4	20.10	11.94	9.34	8.13	7.47	7.08	6.83
8	20.21	12.06	9.48	8.28	7.63	7.25	7.01
8 1/4	20.33	12.19	9.62	8.43	7.79	7.42	7.18
8 1/2	20.44	12.32	9.76	8.58	7.95	7.58	7.36

continued

TABLE 13.1 MONTHLY PAYMENTS REQUIRED TO AMORTIZE A $1000 LOAN, INTEREST COMPOUNDED SEMI-ANNUALLY (CONTINUED)

NOMINAL INTEREST RATE	AMORTIZATION PERIOD (YEARS)						
	5	10	15	20	25	30	35
%	(DOLLARS PER THOUSAND)						
8 3/4	20.56	12.45	9.90	8.74	8.12	7.76	7.54
9	20.68	12.58	10.05	8.90	8.25	7.93	7.72
9 1/4	20.08	12.71	10.19	9.05	8.45	8.11	7.90
9 1/2	20.92	12.84	10.34	9.21	8.62	8.28	8.08
9 3/4	21.04	12.98	10.48	9.36	8.78	8.46	8.26
10	21.15	13.11	10.63	9.52	8.95	8.63	8.45
10 1/4	21.27	13.24	10.77	9.68	9.12	8.81	8.63
10 1/2	21.39	13.37	10.92	9.84	9.29	8.99	8.81
10 3/4	21.51	13.51	11.07	10.00	9.46	9.17	9.00
11	21.63	13.64	11.22	10.16	9.63	9.34	9.18
11 1/4	21.74	13.78	11.37	10.32	9.80	9.52	9.37
11 1/2	21.86	13.91	11.52	10.49	9.98	9.71	9.56
11 3/4	21.98	14.05	11.67	10.65	10.15	9.89	9.74
12	22.10	14.19	11.82	10.81	10.32	10.07	9.93
12 1/4	22.22	14.32	11.97	10.98	10.50	20.25	10.12
12 1/2	22.34	14.46	12.13	11.15	10.68	10.43	10.31
12 3/4	22.46	14.60	12.28	11.31	10.85	10.62	10.50
13	22.59	14.74	12.44	11.48	11.03	10.80	10.69
13 1/4	22.71	14.22	12.59	11.65	11.21	10.99	10.88
13 1/2	22.83	15.02	12.75	11.82	11.39	11.17	11.07
13 3/4	22.95	15.16	12.90	11.99	11.56	11.36	11.26

Another measure of capacity to handle a mortgage is **total debt service** (TDS): that is, the percentage of annual income needed to cover mortgage payments, taxes, heating costs, and consumer debt payments. This number should not exceed 37 percent to 38 percent of annual income, or 40 percent if heating costs are included. Lenders may use this rule for any type of mortgage, conventional or insured. (For an example of how one couple would calculate their GDS and TDS, as well as the largest mortgage for which they will be eligible, see Personal Finance in Action Box 13.3, "Gross and Total Debt Service.")

In addition to gross debt service and total debt service, a third requirement for most mortgages is that the buyer have enough personal funds to make a down payment that represents some minimum proportion of the selling price. For a conventional mortgage, this would be 25 percent; for a high-ratio mortgage, it might be as little as 5 percent. If the total available for a down payment combined with the maximum mortgage is less than the price of the house, a second mortgage might be a consideration. However, the cost of servicing the second mortgage would have to be included in the gross and total debt service ratios. In qualifying purchasers for a mortgage, some conservative lenders may wish to satisfy themselves that the down payment actually comes from the borrower's own resources and not from a gift or an undisclosed loan. To this end, the lender may require evidence of the source of the funds, such as the history of a savings account.

The Mortgage Contract

Equity of Redemption

In the mortgage document, the mortgagor agrees to transfer the ownership of the property to the mortgagee (a financial institution or an individual lender) as security for the loan until such time as it is repaid. The mortgagor receives a copy of the signed mortgage; the mortgagee retains the original. The mortgage leaves the mortgagor with an interest in the property called the **equity of redemption,** which is the right to redeem the property and have the ownership transferred back when the mortgage is discharged. The document states that the mortgagor will retain possession of the property and may enjoy the use of it, but must take good care of it and keep it insured, with the mortgagee as joint beneficiary of the insurance policy. If there is a fire while the mortgage is outstanding, the insurance money will be paid to the mortgagee, who will then decide what to do about the repairs.

The exchanges involved when using real property as security for loans are summarized in Figure 13.1. The purchaser briefly acquires title to and possession of the property, but on giving the first mortgage, legal title is surrendered to the first mortgagee; the mortgagor retains the equity of redemption. If the mortgagor gives a second mortgage on this property, the equity of redemption is transferred to the second mortgagee as security.

The Contract

The essential features of a mortgage are as follows:

(a) a description of the property,

(b) identification of the mortgagor and the mortgagee,

(c) specification of the amount of the mortgage and the terms of repayment,

(d) an agreement that the mortgagor will give a charge on the property to the mortgagee, but will keep the right of possession and the right to redeem the property when the mortgage is discharged,

(e) certain promises or covenants.

Some lenders give the borrower a mortgage contract written in legal language as well as a version in plain English.

Mortgage Covenants

Apart from the main contract, every mortgage contains a number of **covenants,** or binding promises made by the borrower (the mortgagor). Particularly important is the personal covenant, which is the mortgagor's promise to pay principal and interest. It is called a personal covenant because having obtained it, the mortgagee can then sue the mortgagor personally to obtain repayment in full or any payments that are in arrears. The mortgagee can also take a number of other actions to recover the loan (see "Breach of Mortgage Contract," below)

TAXES Other covenants bind the mortgagor to pay the taxes, to insure the property, and to maintain it in good repair. It is important to the mortgagee that taxes be paid on time because taxes are a prior claim on property, taking precedence over a first mortgage. If taxes are allowed to fall into arrears, the mortgagee's security may be impaired, as in the case of a property being sold for taxes. Some lenders require that the mortgagor pay one-twelfth of the annual taxes with each monthly mortgage payment, in order to build up a fund to pay the

FIGURE 13.1 EXCHANGES WHEN REAL PROPERTY IS SECURITY FOR A LOAN

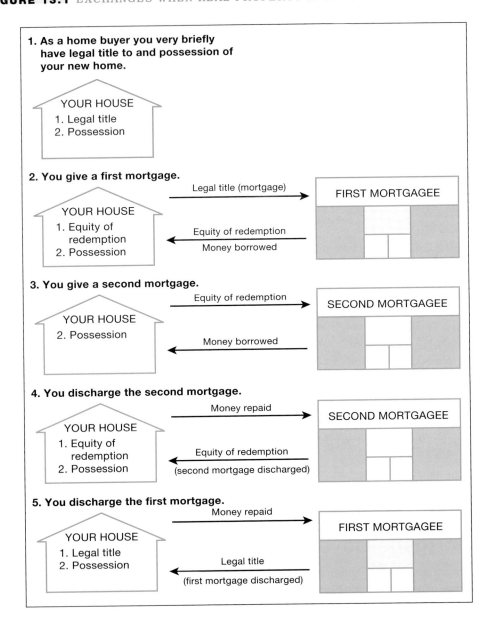

taxes when they become due. This approach saves the mortgagee the annual bother of finding out whether the taxes have been paid. Interest on this tax fund may or may not be credited to the mortgagor, depending on the agreement. Penalties for inadvertent late payment of taxes by the lender are usually debited to the borrower's account.

PROPERTY INSURANCE   Before mortgage money is advanced, the mortgagor may be required to insure the property against fire and other possible risks, and to have the policy made in favour of the mortgagee. The insurance policy will be endorsed to ensure that the insurer knows about the mortgagee's interest in the property.

Sale of Mortgages

A person or institution who holds a mortgage (a mortgagee) sometimes decides that they would prefer to have the cash at once instead of receiving a monthly income stream for the term of the mortgage. The mortgagee can sell the mortgage without asking the mortgagor's permission, although the mortgagor would be informed. Mortgages may be sold at their face value, or for more or less than their face value (i.e., at a premium or at a discount), depending on interest rates at the time. (Refer to Chapter 10 to review how changing interest rates affect the price of a security.) For the mortgagor, one of the risks of assuming a vendor take-back mortgage is that if the vendor sells the mortgage the mortgagor will have to deal with another person or institution. This is the principal reason why all of the terms of the loan should be written into the mortgage document.

Breach of Mortgage Contract

If the mortgagor fails to carry out any of the promises agreed to in the mortgage contract, this failure is considered a default. A mortgagor in default may be subject to a variety of penalties. The mortgage contract stipulates that the mortgagor must (i) make payments on time, (ii) pay the taxes, (iii) keep the property insured, (iv) keep the property in good condition, and (v) not sell the property without the mortgagee's written approval.

   If you ever find it impossible to make a mortgage payment on time, contact the mortgagee immediately to search for a solution to the problem before it gets worse. Under these circumstances, the mortgagor is usually liable for late interest charges, which would be added to the outstanding principal and thus cause interest to be paid on interest. A mortgagee has a number of options to force a defaulting mortgagor to pay: these may include taking possession of the property, suing the borrower under the personal covenant, exercising the acceleration clause, selling the property, and foreclosure. Before beginning any of these actions, the mortgagee would notify the mortgagor of the mortgagee's intentions, giving the mortgagor an opportunity to take some preventive steps if desired. The details of procedures that follow default are explained in several of the references listed at the end of this chapter.

Discharge of Mortgages

When a mortgage has been repaid in full, steps are taken to obtain a legal **mortgage discharge** and to transfer the property ownership back to the mortgagor. Either the mortgagor or the lawyer will take a signed statement, which indicates that the debt has been paid, from the mortgagee to the local land registry office. For a small fee, the claim against the property is removed and the title cleared.

Mortgage Repayment

Term and Amortization Period

Repaying a mortgage can take as long as 25 or 30 years. The time allowed for completely repaying a mortgage, which is established when the mortgage is arranged, is called the **amortization period.** The length of time before the lender can demand repayment of all the outstanding principal is the **mortgage term.** In most cases, the interest rate and monthly payments are fixed for the term. Although it has not always been so, nowadays mortgage terms are usually much shorter than amortization periods. Mortgage terms can now be as short as 6

Personal Finance in Action 13.3

Short Term, Long Amortization

When Tom and Vidya were buying a house, they were told that the mortgage would be amortized over 25 years, but that the term would be five years. That meant that the monthly payments were worked out so that, at current interest rates, the mortgage would be completely repaid in 25 years.

Since the lender did not want to be committed to a fixed interest rate for the next 25 years, when rates might move in any direction, the mortgage contract had a term of five years. During the term, the interest rate and monthly payments would be fixed; at maturity, the contract would terminate, and all of the outstanding balance would become due. This is an opportunity for Tom and Vidya to reduce their principal without penalty. Unless they could discharge the entire mortgage, they would have to renegotiate their mortgage at the prevailing interest rates. Their monthly payments could be adjusted at this time.

months or as long as 5 or more years. At the end of the term, or at the **maturity date,** the lender can legally demand full payment for all the outstanding balance; usually, though, the lender will offer to renew the mortgage at the prevailing rate. There have been times in the past when the term and amortization period were the same, but in recent years the high variability in interest rates has made lenders less likely to offer mortgages with interest rates that are fixed for 20 to 25 years. (See Personal Finance in Action Box 13.4, "Short Term, Long Amortization.")

Methods of Repayment

Mortgage loans may be repaid in a number of ways, as long as an agreement can be reached between the mortgagor and the mortgagee. Since it is not practicable for most people to repay an entire mortgage with interest in a lump sum, most mortgages are amortized—that is, the debt is extinguished by making regular payments of interest and principal over a period of time. Two methods of repayment will be explained here: (i) equal instalments of principal, and (ii) blended payments. The difference between them is in the proportions of interest and principal in each payment, as illustrated schematically in Figure 13.2. Each horizontal bar represents one payment, and shows the way that payment is divided between principal and interest. (These diagrams show the proportions in a general way only; an exact plot of blended payments would result in a curved line rather than a straight one dividing interest and principal.) As will be explained below, if a mortgage is repaid with equal instalments of principal, the amount of interest owing declines, making succeeding payments smaller. By contrast, if all payments are level, as is the case with blended payments, the proportions of interest and principal will vary over the repayment period.

Equal Instalments of Principal

In this repayment schedule, the principal is repaid at a constant rate, but each consecutive payment becomes smaller because, as the principal owing is reduced, the interest due also decreases (see Table 13.2 and Figure 13.2). This arrangement is used for various payment intervals—for instance, annually, semi-annually, or quarterly—but seldom monthly. Mortgages with equal instalments of principal are much less common than those with blended payments.

FIGURE 13.2 PROPORTIONS OF PRINCIPAL AND INTEREST PER PAYMENT, EQUAL INSTALMENTS OF PRINCIPAL, AND EQUAL BLENDED PAYMENTS

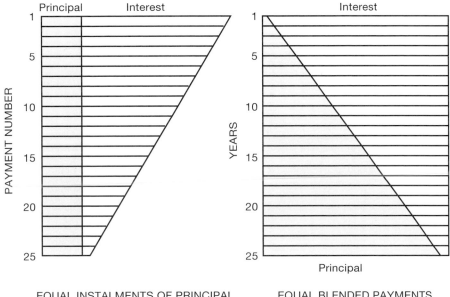

EQUAL INSTALMENTS OF PRINCIPAL   EQUAL BLENDED PAYMENTS

Equal Blended Payments

Repaying a loan in equal instalments of principal is quite easy to understand, but is not a widely used method because of the very large unequal payments. Most people prefer to repay loans with smaller and more frequent level payments that fit more easily into their budgets. To accomplish this, the arithmetic becomes somewhat complicated. Essentially, each payment will include one month's interest on the total outstanding balance, with the remainder of the payment used to reduce the principal. As the principal owing slowly drops each month, the interest component declines, allowing more of each payment to be used to reduce the principal, as is illustrated in Figure 13.2 and Table 13.3.

CALCULATING THE REPAYMENT SCHEDULE FOR EQUAL BLENDED PAYMENTS The procedure for calculating the repayment schedule for mortgages is identical to that used for instalment loans as described in Chapter 8. (Refer to Appendix 13A for a complete mortgage schedule.) The steps in calculating the interest and principal components in each payment are reviewed in the box titled "Calculations for Blended Payments."

Renewing a Mortgage

If a mortgage has a term of five years and an amortization period of 25 years, every five years the contract will have to be renewed. At the maturity date, all the outstanding balance on the principal is due and must be either repaid or renegotiated for a further term. At this time, the mortgage can be renewed with the same lender at the prevailing interest rate or changed to another lender. Changing lenders may result in a lower interest rate, but this gain may be offset by additional fees, such as for a new appraisal or title search. Currently, some lenders are

TABLE 13.2 MORTGAGE REPAYMENT SCHEDULE, EQUAL INSTALMENTS OF PRINCIPAL

PRINCIPAL	$100 000
TERM	20 YEARS
INTEREST	9% ANNUALLY ON OUTSTANDING BALANCE
ANNUAL PAYMENT	$5000 PLUS INTEREST

PAYMENT NUMBER	PAYMENT TO CONSIST OF		TOTAL PAYMENT	BALANCE OUTSTANDING
	PRINCIPAL	INTEREST		
1	$5 000	$9 000	$14 000	$95 000
2	5 000	8 550	13 550	90 000
3	5 000	8 100	13 100	85 000
4	5 000	7 650	12 660	84 000
5	5 000	7 200	12 200	75 000
6	5 000	6 750	11 750	70 000
7	5 000	6 300	11 300	65 000
8	5 000	5 850	10 850	60 000
...	...	...	...	...
19	5 000	900	5 900	5 000
20	5 000	450	5 450	nil

Total interest paid in 20 years = $94 500

TABLE 13.3 PORTION OF MORTGAGE REPAYMENT SCHEDULE, EQUAL BLENDED PAYMENTS

PRINCIPAL	$100 000
INTEREST RATE	9 PERCENT COMPOUNDED SEMI-ANNUALLY
AMORTIZATION PERIOD	20 YEARS
MONTHLY PAYMENT	$889.20

PAYMENT NUMBER	MONTHLY PAYMENT	PRINCIPAL PORTION	INTEREST PORTION	BALANCE OUTSTANDING
First year				
1	$889.20	$152.89	$736.31	$99 847.11
6	889.20	158.60	730.60	99 065.60
12	889.20	165.74	723.46	98 089.14
Final year				
230	889.20	820.33	68.87	8 533.49
239	889.20	876.32	12.88	873.33

Total interest = $113 392.30

Calculations for Blended Payments

Mortgage terms:

Principal	$120 000
Interest rate	7.25%
Compounding	semi-annual
Amortization period	25 years
Term	5 years
Monthly payment	$859.20
	(see Table 13.1)
Interest factor	.005 952 3834
	(see Table 8.4)

(a) Amount of monthly payment:

Consult an amortization table (Table 13.1) to find the monthly payment for a loan of $1 000, at 7.25 percent, for 25 years. Calculate the monthly mortgage payments for a loan of $120 000.

$$\text{Monthly payment} = \frac{\text{principal}}{1\ 000} \times \text{payment/\$1000 [7.25\%] (Table 13.1)}$$

$$= \frac{120\ 000}{1\ 000} \times 7.16$$

$$= 120 \times 7.16$$

$$= \$859.20$$

(b) Interest at end of first month:

$$\begin{aligned}\text{Interest for} \atop \text{one month} \quad &= \quad \text{outstanding} \atop \text{principal} \quad \times \quad \text{appropriate interest} \atop \text{factor (Table 8A.4)} \\ &= \quad 120\ 000 \quad \times \quad 0.005\ 952\ 3834 \\ &= \quad \$714.28\end{aligned}$$

(c) Principal component of the first month's payment:

$$\begin{aligned}\text{Repayment} \atop \text{of principal} \quad &= \quad \text{monthly} \atop \text{payment} \quad - \quad \text{interest for} \atop \text{one month} \\ &= \quad 859.20 \quad - \quad 714.28 \\ &= \quad \$144.92\end{aligned}$$

(d) Principal outstanding after first payment:

$$\begin{aligned}\text{Principal} \atop \text{outstanding} \quad &= \quad \text{principal owing} \atop \text{before payment} \quad - \quad \text{payment on} \atop \text{principal} \\ &= \quad 120\ 000 \quad - \quad 144.92 \\ &= \quad \$119\ 855.08\end{aligned}$$

continued

(e) Second month's interest:

$$
\begin{aligned}
\text{Interest for 1 month} &= \text{outstanding principal} \times \text{appropriate interest factor (Table 8A.4)} \\
&= 119\ 855.08 \times 0.005\ 952\ 3834 \\
&= \$713.41
\end{aligned}
$$

(f) Mortgage schedule for the first six months:

PAYMENT NUMBER	DATE OF PAYMENT	MONTHLY PAYMENT	INTEREST PORTION	PRINCIPAL PORTION	OUTSTANDING BALANCE
1	June 1	$859.20	$714.28	$144.92	$119 855.08
2	July 1	859.20	713.41	145.79	119 709.31
3	August 1	859.20	712.55	146.65	119 562.70
4	September 1	859.20	711.68	147.52	119 415.10
5	October 1	859.20	710.80	148.40	119 266.70
6	November 1	859.20	709.92	149.28	119 117.50

offering low or no-cost mortgage transfer promotions. The borrower needs to search out this information before deciding to change lenders.

At the end of a term, when the total outstanding balance becomes due, there is an opportunity to reduce the principal before renegotiating the mortgage. As illustrated in the boxed examples included throughout this chapter, any reduction in principal will result in considerable interest savings over the long run.

Prepayment of Principal

The difference between repayment and prepayment is that **repayment** means following the mortgage schedule in extinguishing the loan, while **prepayment** is a way of accelerating the reduction of the principal during the term. A mortgagor may wish to repay a mortgage faster than the original schedule, make lump-sum payments to reduce the principal, or discharge the mortgage when selling the property, but the mortgagor's chances of taking any of these actions will depend on the terms established when the original mortgage contract was drawn up.

Open and Closed Mortgages

There tends to be some confusion about open and closed mortgages, because of the degrees of openness and the fact that few are completely closed. A fully open mortgage permits prepayments without restriction or penalty; as well, the loan may be paid off completely at any time. A totally closed mortgage, on the other hand, permits no prepayments. In practice, most so-called closed mortgages permit some prepayments without penalty under certain conditions, and mortgages referred to as open may actually be only partly open. Some mortgage contracts permit limited amounts to be prepaid at specified times, while others are more liberal. In summary, prepayment may be totally unrestricted, or mortgagees may restrict either the amount of prepayment allowed or the timing of the prepayment.

Prepayment Penalties

When you make a prepayment, the lender may charge a fee called a prepayment penalty. Having to pay a penalty to make a prepayment of principal is not unusual and is based on the rationale that the mortgagee has invested money in this mortgage expecting to receive a regular income and is therefore inconvenienced by having to reinvest unexpected repayments. The penalty may be three months' interest on the amount of the prepayment. When interest rates are such that the lender must reinvest the prepaid funds at a rate of interest less than the contract rate of the mortgage, the lender may charge an amount, in addition to the prepayment penalty, representing the interest rate differential for the remainder of the term. Interest rate differential is discussed further in the section "Mortgage Features and Options" later in this chapter.

Since mortgage lenders change their policies about prepayment from time to time, it is important to find out the prepayment opportunities being offered by competing lenders. Regardless of verbal representations made by the lending officer, you must read a mortgage contract carefully in order to find out exactly what the prepayment conditions are. There may be a requirement not only to give the lender notice of intention to repay, but also to pay a penalty.

When prepayments are made, it is common practice for the lender to make no change in the size of the monthly payments, thus shortening the time that the loan will be outstanding. The reduced amortization period will result in less total interest.

To calculate the savings in making a prepayment, use an amortization schedule, which shows the principal and interest components of each payment (Appendix 13A). A prepayment eliminates a number of payments from the schedule, thus reducing both principal and interest for the mortgagor. Consequently, the mortgage will be repaid in less time than originally expected. (See Personal Finance in Action Box 13.4, "Costs and Benefits of a Prepayment.")

Personal Finance in Action 13.4

Costs and Benefits of a Prepayment

The Changs, who had a CMHC-insured mortgage for $100 000 at 9 percent, amortized over 20 years, were in a position to repay an additional $11 000 two years later. The mortgage stated that they could make a prepayment of 10 percent of the original loan at the end of the second year with a penalty of 3 months' interest. In their case, the maximum prepayment would be calculated as follows:

Prepayment = $100 000 × 0.10

  = $10 000

How much interest penalty would they have to pay?

Penalty = prepayment × interest rate × time

  = $10 000 × 0.09 × 3/12

  = $225

What are some of the costs and benefits of making this prepayment?

Costs

(a) *Penalty of three months' interest* = $225.

(b) *Forgone interest on prepayment:* The Changs had a choice of either leaving the $10 000 invested to earn interest or using it to reduce the principal outstanding on the mortgage. Assuming they could have earned interest at 6 percent on $10 000 for 18 years (the time remaining in their amortization period), what is the opportunity cost of this prepayment?

$10 000, invested at 6 percent and compounded annually for 18 years would grow as follows:

continued

Future value = principal × compound value of $1 [6%, 18 years]

= $10 000 × 2.85 (Table 8A.1)

= $28 500

Interest component = $28 500 – 10 000

= $18 500

Assuming a 30 percent average income tax rate:

Income tax = $18 500 × 0.30

= $5 550

After-tax income = $18 500 – 5 550

= $12 950

Total cost = $225 + 12 950

= $13 175

Benefits

(a) *Reduction in total mortgage interest:*

Use the Changs' amortization schedule (see Appendix 13A). Numbers taken from the schedule are marked with an asterisk in the following calculations.

Balance outstanding:

After payment #24 = $96 002.43*

After prepayment = 96 002.43 – 10 000

= $86 002.43

After payment #70 = $86 063.18*

Interest saved = accumulated interest at payment #70 – accumulated interest at payment #24

= $48 307.28* – 17 343.27*

= $30 964.01

(b) *Reduction in time:*

Number of payments eliminated = 70 – 24

= 46

Mortgage discharge is nearer by 46 months (3 years, 10 months).

Conclusion

The results will, of course, vary with the interest rates on mortgage loans and deposits, and with the mortgagor's marginal tax rate. In this case, looking at after-tax dollars, the prepayment would have saved the Changs $30 964, compared to a potential investment return of $13 175, and their mortgage would be discharged nearly four years sooner. In this example, no allowance was made for the opportunity to invest the interest savings resulting from the prepayment.

What are some other factors you would want to consider in making a decision to prepay or not?

Total Interest

Not infrequently the total interest paid during the life of a mortgage greatly exceeds the purchase price of the house. For example, a mortgage of $80 000 at 10 percent for 25 years would result in total interest charges of $134 677. Consult the mortgage schedule in Appendix 13A to find out the total interest on that $100 000 loan. Three influential and interrelated factors that affect total interest are (i) the principal, (ii) the interest rate, and (iii) the amortization period. If it is possible to reduce any of these factors, the total interest will be decreased. (You may wish to refer to Chapter 8 to review the method of calculating total interest.)

The first opportunity to reduce total interest is when the mortgage is being arranged. If you can lower the principal of the loan by making a larger down payment, you will pay less total interest (see Figure 13.3). A second factor is the interest rate. If you can find a loan at a lower rate, that will be to your advantage. What might appear to be quite a small difference in interest rates can have a significant effect on the total interest. Using the example in the previous paragraph, a 0.25 percent reduction in interest rate on the $80 000 loan would mean $4 026 less in total interest. Finally, the shorter the amortization period, the less total interest, as illustrated in Figure 13.3; it is, of course, necessary to make larger monthly payments to accomplish this.

Personal Finance in Action 13.5

Interest and Principal Payments

Steffan was able to make a down payment of 5 percent on a $200 000 house. His mortgage was amortized over 25 years with an initial term of five years. The interest on the mortgage was at 7.30 percent, compounded semi-annually. His payments were $1 366.17 monthly. This seemed a lot to Steffan, who had little knowledge of mortgages. He was surprised to find that after the initial five years he will have paid $81 970.20, but that only $16 370.68 of this money will be on the principal of his $190 000 loan.

FIGURE 13.3 TOTAL COST OF A HOUSE, VARYING DOWN PAYMENT AND AMORTIZATION PERIOD (PURCHASE PRICE AND INTEREST RATE HELD CONSTANT)

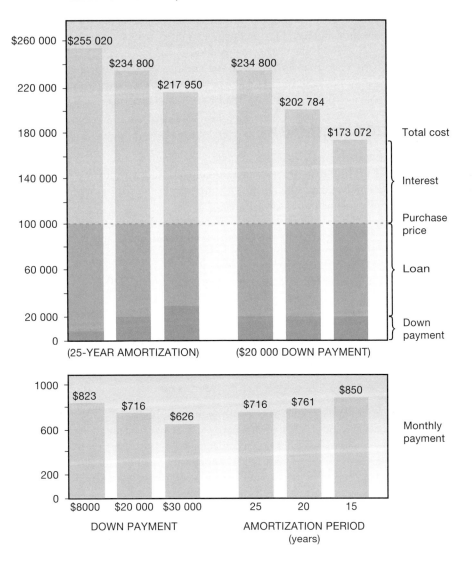

Closing Costs

When a property is purchased, the agreement to purchase is often signed some time before the date for closing the deal. When the closing date arrives, the buyer must pay (i) the seller for the property; (ii) the lawyer for services and disbursements, such as registration of the transaction at the registry office; (iii) taxes (where applicable), such as land transfer or property purchase tax, goods and services tax, and provincial sales tax; and (iv) adjustment costs. With or without a mortgage, there are sure to be closing costs when property is purchased.

Statement of Adjustments

Some time before the closing date for the house purchase, the lawyer sends the buyer a **statement of adjustments,** which sets forth the accounts between buyer and seller relating to this sale. It includes the purchase price, the deposit, and property taxes, as well as, possibly, insurance and fuel. Since the vendor has been paying property taxes and insurance, the buyer must reimburse the vendor for any prepaid taxes and insurance when ownership changes. For example, if a house is bought in June, the insurance may have been paid until September and the taxes until November. The buyer would pay the vendor three months' insurance and five months' taxes. Sometimes there is fuel oil in the tank to be paid for.

The new property must be insured against fire, as noted in the mortgage contract. At this stage, the buyer can decide whether to take over the vendor's property insurance policy, convert a previous policy to fit this new property, or take out a new one.

Legal Fees and Taxes

The lawyer's bill usually includes fees for services and any expenses paid on the buyer's behalf, such as fees for title searches and for the registration of various documents, as well as any federal or provincial taxes. The lawyer's fee itself depends on the complexity of the transaction and on the local guidelines for such fees.

Some provinces charge a land transfer or property transfer tax on real estate at the time that the deed is registered. In 2000, the Ontario **land transfer tax** rates were as follows:

- 0.5% on property worth up to and including $55 000
- 1.0% on amounts over $55 000, and up to and including $250 000
- 1.5% on amounts over $250 000
- 2.0% on amounts over $400 000

The 2000, British Columbia property transfer tax was as follows:

- 1.0% on property worth up to and including $200 000
- 2.0% on anything over $200 000.

A copy of an up-to-date land survey is usually required by all lenders. The vendor or the vendor's mortgagee may provide a copy of the survey. Otherwise, the purchaser may be liable for significant surveyor fees in conjunction with placing a new mortgage on the property.

The federal goods and services tax (GST)—along with any relevant provincial sales tax—is applied to some aspects of property purchases (e.g., mortgage insurance, legal fees, and certain disbursements), adding to closing costs.

Life Insurance and Mortgages

If they so wish, home buyers may arrange a decreasing term life insurance policy with their own insurance company to make provision for enough funds to discharge the mortgage in the event of their death. Initially, the life insurance policy will be for approximately the same amount as the mortgage loan, with periodic reductions in value to roughly correspond to the declining debt on the property. If the person whose life is insured dies before the mortgage is fully repaid, the beneficiary of the life insurance will have some funds to discharge the mortgage debt, but is not obligated to do so.

Some lenders maintain group policies covering the lives of a number of borrowers, and therefore offer mortgage life insurance as part of the mortgage package. If this coverage is selected, a deceased mortgagor's survivors have no choice in how to use the insurance money, since the policy is not a personal one. In such cases, the insurer repays the outstanding balance on the mortgage directly to the lender. If the income of two people purchasing a residence is required for debt servicing, it is important to determine whether the policy covers the lives of both wage earners. If not, purchasing additional private life insurance may be prudent. In any event, it is always wise to compare the cost of optional group life insurance offered by the mortgagee with that of similar coverage available in the open marketplace.

Decreasing term insurance is sometimes called mortgage life insurance, but it should not be confused with the mortgage insurance that lenders use to cover the risk of losing their money if the borrower defaults. The latter type of insurance is mandatory for CMHC-insured mortgages.

Mortgage Features and Options

From the previous discussion of basic mortgage principles, one might think that choosing a mortgage would not be too difficult. But keen competition among financial institutions has created a rapidly changing mortgage market that involves little variation in interest rates but intense competition in a fascinating and often confusing array of mortgage features and options. Because these variations are matters of company policy, they are readily changed, making it impossible to predict which special features or options will be available at any given time or place. We will discuss the following representative sampling of options here:

(a) preapproval,

(b) interest rate adjustments,

(c) early renewal,

(d) accelerated payment opportunities.

Preapproved Mortgages

It is not unusual for home buyers to select a property, sign an offer to purchase that is conditional on their being able to obtain financing, and then start looking for a mortgage. In the excitement of choosing a new house, they neglect to give as much attention to the financing as they do to finding the property. This approach has two significant disadvantages: the buyers must then do their mortgage shopping under time pressure, and they have made a commitment to a property before determining how large a loan they may qualify for.

Lenders are now offering **preapproved** (or prearranged) mortgages, which give tentative approval for a mortgage amount based on an assessment of the borrower, with final approval dependent on an appraisal of the property that the borrower hopes to buy. Applying for a prearranged mortgage allows buyers to shop around for the best financing terms before making

Negotiations

Tally was fascinated by mortgages and their ability to allow someone with little money to acquire the house of his or her dreams. In her finance class at college, she absorbed every bit of information she could and also searched in the library for more information. After working for several years, Tally had had enough of paying rent and decided to buy a condo. When she was ready to negotiate, she prepared the following questions:

Do you offer a discount on the quoted rate? (Lenders may be willing to offer from 50 basis points to one percentage point off the posted rate.)

Will you help pay something towards the legal cost of closing?

Will you waive the fee for an appraisal of the property?

Can I transfer my mortgage to another property if I decide to sell?

Do you offer air miles?

If I double up on payments, is there a penalty for skipping a month?

a commitment to a property, and at the same time find out how much lenders are willing to lend them. Armed with this knowledge, they will be in a position to make a more attractive offer on a property—one that is conditional not on obtaining financing, but rather only on obtaining a satisfactory appraisal.

Preapproved mortgages give the buyer an opportunity to apply to several lenders, usually with no fee for the assessment and no obligation to deal with any particular institution. But the period in which the lender will guarantee the interest rate in a preapproved mortgage may be quite short—usually no more than three months.

MORTGAGE SHOPPING STRATEGY Many borrowers tend to accept the first institution's terms rather than comparison shop for a mortgage. Applicants may feel so pleased to receive approval that they do not look any further. Such an approach works to the advantage of lenders who are trying to increase their market share, but it obviously works less well for borrowers. A better strategy for the prospective borrower is to first estimate how much debt can be handled, given current interest rates, and then visit multiple lenders to find out what terms and options are currently being offered. After determining which features are most desirable, list the most essential ones before applying for a preapproved mortgage from the lender that offers the best combination of preferred options. (see Personal Finance in Action Box 13.6, "Negotiations").

Interest Rate Adjustments

COMMITMENT PERIOD After a mortgage is approved, there is usually a period of weeks or months before the closing date. The day on which the purchase transaction is completed—that is, when the buyer pays the vendor and receives possession of the property—is known as the **closing date.** If interest rates are changing frequently, will the borrower be charged the rate prevailing at the time the mortgage is approved or at the closing date? Some lenders will commit to an agreed-upon rate at the time of approval with the option that if rates drop in the interim, the mortgage rate will be reduced accordingly. Find out the lender's policy and how long the commitment period is.

INTEREST ADJUSTMENT DATE Mortgage payments are usually made at the end of each month, "not in advance." As a result, if mortgage money is advanced on February 21, the first payment will be due a month later, on March 21. This may seem straightforward, but some institutional lenders prefer to collect all mortgage payments on the first of each month. Since a closing date can be set for any business day, the lender solves this problem by collecting interest for the period from closing to the beginning of the next month. When lenders refer to the **interest adjustment date,** they mean the day the mortgage starts.

VARIABLE RATE MORTGAGES Variable rate or floating rate mortgages were devised in the early 1980s to reduce uncertainty for lenders in a period of rapidly changing interest rates. Financial institutions had difficulty matching the interest rates and maturities of the deposits they accepted with those of the mortgage funds they were lending. With variable rate mortgages, lenders pass the risk of fluctuating rates on to the borrower, who has the compensating advantage of a fully open mortgage that can be discharged at any time. On this type of mortgage, the interest rate is adjusted frequently, usually monthly. A payment schedule, based on a 20- or 25-year amortization, is drawn up for a specified period, usually one year, during which the borrower is committed to making regular payments of a predictable amount. The rate quoted on variable rate mortgages, which may be 0.5 percent lower than that for other types, may look especially attractive, but remember that the interest is compounded monthly rather than semi-annually.

While reducing uncertainty for lenders, variable rate mortgages can create problems for borrowers by making it difficult for them to accurately predict their future liabilities. If interest rates rise, a mortgagor could find that the fixed monthly payment is composed entirely of interest, and therefore fails to reduce the principal. It is even conceivable that some payments will be insufficient to cover all the interest due; the balance of the interest owing for any such payments will be added to the unpaid principal. In such a case, the home buyer would actually be increasing liabilities rather than assets.

In times of more stable interest rates, borrowers are less interested in variable rate mortgages. Recently lenders have been offering short-term, fully open mortgages with an interest rate that is guaranteed for a period of, for example, six months. Few variable rate mortgages are now available.

Early Renewal

When interest rates are falling, mortgagors may be anxious to refinance their mortgages before the end of the term at the new lower rates. Mortgagees, of course, are not as keenly interested in receiving the smaller income stream; consequently, they may charge an interest rate differential. The **interest rate differential** is based on the present value of the difference between the lender's income stream under the old mortgage rate and the new lower rate; this is to compensate the lender for giving up future income. The mortgagor makes a lump-sum payment in return for a renegotiated mortgage at a reduced rate.

The amount of the interest rate differential depends on the spread between the existing contract rate and current mortgage rates, as well as the time remaining in the mortgage term. Predictably, the greater the spread and the longer the time, the greater the penalty. Also, lenders use different methods of calculating the interest rate differential. The wise mortgagor will do some calculations before deciding on refinancing. It may actually be better to make a prepayment to reduce the principal than to try to obtain a lower interest rate.

Accelerated Payment Opportunities

Repayment of the mortgage principal may be accelerated in one of three ways: (i) by making lump-sum prepayments (as was discussed earlier), (ii) by increasing monthly payments, or (iii) by making payments more often than once a month.

INCREASING MONTHLY PAYMENTS Lenders may permit mortgagors to increase their monthly payments, either once a year or on any payment date, by as little as 10 percent or as much as 100 percent.

MAKING PAYMENTS MORE FREQUENTLY Making mortgage payments either weekly or bi-weekly (i.e., every two weeks) shortens the amortization period. If the usual monthly payment is divided by four and paid each week, the borrower will make 52 weekly payments in a year, whereas the usual 12 monthly payments would be equivalent to only 48 weekly ones. The effect of making four extra weekly payments a year will be a reduction in total interest and in the time needed to repay the mortgage. The bi-weekly mortgage scheme is similar, except that payments are made fortnightly, or 26 times a year, instead of the equivalent of 24.

The mortgagor should be aware of the method being used to calculate the more frequent payments. If the monthly payment is divided either by four or by two and then paid either weekly or bi-weekly, the mortgage will definitely be reduced more quickly than by making 12 monthly payments. But if, instead, the annual amount of interest and principal is merely divided by either 52 or 26, the advantage of making more frequent payments will be lost.

Comparison Shopping for a Mortgage

Use the following chart to record the information you gather when shopping for a mortgage.

Item	Lender		
	1	2	3
Interest rates			
First mortgage			
Second mortgage			
Fixed for term or variable			
Frequency of payment			
Monthly, bi-weekly, or weekly			
Flexibility			
Charges			
Appraisal fee			
Application fee			
Qualification guidelines			
GDS			
TDS			
Prepayment privileges			
Amount			
Time			
Penalty			

Item	Lender		
	1	2	3
Flexibility			
Renewal conditions			
Fee			
Time before maturity			

After you select a mortgage, it is important to insist that any special features be written into the mortgage contract.

Reverse Mortgages

When interest rates drop, many senior citizens who depend on fixed-income investments find themselves short of cash. Most, however, do own their own homes—and typically the equity on those homes has been increasing steadily over the years. They are, in the words of a well-used cliché, *house rich but cash poor*. Until recently, their only option for obtaining cash was to sell their home and then either (i) buy something smaller, or (ii) rent. The **reverse mortgage** provides an alternative that many seniors find more palatable. It allows them to receive money for their home while still living in it. Instead of selling the house, they can apply to a bank or other financial institution for a loan that uses the house as collateral. The house's market value is determined. Then a payment schedule, similar to that for a mortgage, is arranged and monthly payments are made to the home owners. No payments of either interest or principal on the loan are made until the agreement ends and the home is sold.

The questions facing cash-poor seniors who are contemplating a reverse mortgage are the same as those facing anyone who buys an annuity. And these are questions that no one can answer. Will borrowers outlive the contract's term? If they do, how will they provide for themselves after it expires? This unavoidable uncertainty means that reverse mortgages are not for everyone. Such a device will be of no interest to people who wish to leave an estate to their heirs or to people with a strong attachment to their homes. (See Personal Finance in Action Box 13.7, "Reverse Mortgages.")

Personal Finance in Action 13.7

Reverse Mortgages

Billy Yeung is 65. His wife Waichi is 62. They have lived in the same house in Vancouver for 40 years. Having raised their four children in the house, they have a strong attachment to it. Unfortunately, the house is their only major asset. It has risen steadily in value from the $40 000 they paid for it to $700 000. All of Billy's income, while he worked in his cousin's grocery, was used to provide for his family.

Now that he is retired, their only income is what Billy gets from public pensions. They find out from a friend about reverse mortgages and how they can get up to 45 percent of the value of their house in cash or in a tax-sheltered income plan. They decide to take advantage of the latter and receive $315 000, which they invest in good quality bonds yielding 8 percent. Their money woes are over.

Summary

Although a mortgage is simply a large loan that is secured by real property, the magnitude of the sum being borrowed, the long repayment period, and the nature of the security create considerable complexity. There are two major types of mortgages, depending on the proportion of the property cost used for a down payment: conventional and insured. To qualify for a mortgage, a prospective home buyer must be considered a satisfactory credit risk and must also have selected a property that the lender's appraisers consider to represent acceptable security. Both the lender and the borrower sign a mortgage contract that sets forth the terms, conditions, and obligations associated with the loan. To safeguard their investment, mortgage lenders impose regulations regarding the size of the down payment, the need to insure the property, the need to insure against default, and prepayments.

The most common way of repaying a mortgage is with a series of equal blended payments that have changing proportions of principal and interest. Mortgage financing involves four interrelated factors: principal, interest rate, amortization period, and monthly payment. Often the total interest paid over the life of the mortgage is much greater than the original price of the house. But mortgagors may reduce this cost by decreasing the principal, the interest rate, or the amortization period. Whether and when the mortgagor gets the opportunity to do so, after the mortgage has been signed, depends on the rules of the lending institution. It is worthwhile to investigate the mortgage conditions offered by various institutions to find those best suited to your needs. Give special attention to prepayment privileges, payment frequency, and renewal policies.

- -

Key Terms

amortization period (p. 389)

amortizing (p. 380)

capital gain (p. 379)

closing date (p. 400)

conventional mortgage (p. 382)

covenant (p. 387)

equity (p. 380)

equity of redemption (p. 387)

first mortgage (p. 380)

gross debt service (p. 384)

high-ratio loan (p. 382)

insured mortgage (p. 382)

interest adjustment date
   (p. 401)

interest rate differential (p. 401)

lending value (appraised value)
   (p. 383)

maturity date (p. 390)

mortgage (p. 380)

mortgage broker (p. 383)

mortgage discharge (p. 389)

mortgage insurance (p. 381)

mortgage term (p. 389)

mortgagee (p. 380)

mortgagor (p. 380)

non-money income (p. 379)

opportunity cost (p. 379)

preapproved (prearranged)
   mortgage (p. 399)

prepayment (p. 394)

repayment (p. 394)

reverse mortgage (p. 403)

second mortgage (p. 380)

statement of adjustments
   (p. 398)

total debt service (p. 386)

vendor take-back mortgage
   (p. 382)

Problems

1. Assume that you buy a house for $135 000 with a $20 000 down payment and a $115 000 mortgage.

   (a) Some time later, when you are considering selling the house, your mortgage has an unpaid balance of $42 500. How much is your equity if you can sell the house for $153 000?

   (b) If you are making mortgage payments of $978 per month, do your payments add to your equity in the property? Explain.

   (c) Does the down payment represent part of your equity in the property?

2. Rick and Sari pay $187 000 for a house in Vancouver when prices are very high, financing the purchase with a $30 000 down payment and a $157 000 mortgage. Now that Rick has been transferred to a job in Calgary, they must sell the house. The outstanding balance on the mortgage is $135 000, and the best offer they get on the house is $125 000. Explain what has happened to Rick and Sari's equity.

3. Examine the sample mortgage contract, signed by Paul and Louise McCartney, that your instructor provides.

   (a) Who is the mortgagee (chargee) in this contract?

   (b) How long is the term of this mortgage? What will happen at the maturity date?

   (c) What are some of the property rights that the McCartneys have given up for the duration of the mortgage?

   (d) What is required of Paul and Louise by the insurance covenant?

   (e) Six months after they give this mortgage, the McCartneys win $5000 in a lottery, which they think that they would like to use to reduce their mortgage. When can they make a repayment? How much can it be? What will the penalty be?

   (f) If Paul dies before the mortgage is discharged, and Louise does not have enough income to maintain the payments, will she lose her equity in the house?

   (g) How much are Paul and Louise paying for mortgage insurance? If you can't find this figure in the contract, assume that they are paying 2 percent.

   (h) When is this mortgage insurance paid?

   (i) What protection does this insurance offer the mortgagors?

   (j) Do Paul and Louise have a choice about taking this insurance?

4. (a) Why would a person obtain a mortgage loan instead of a personal bank loan to buy a house?

   (b) Would you expect a bank to charge a higher interest rate on a loan that is secured by a chattel mortgage than on one that is secured by a real estate mortgage? Why?

5. A mortgage officer suggests to Duncan, a prospective client, that he can save on legal fees by engaging the same lawyer to look after his interests in the transaction as the lending institution is employing to look after its own interests. Would a possible conflict of interest be involved here? What would you do?

Their First House

After a lengthy search, Tiep and Vinh finally locate a house they really like. Its $145 000 asking price seems reasonable. They recognize that the house will require redecorating as soon as possible in two downstairs rooms, and that they will have to buy major appliances. Property taxes were $1 350 last year; heating costs for the same period amounted to $550. They offer to purchase the house for $135 000, on the condition that they can arrange adequate financing.

The bank's mortgage officer inquires about the family income and about how much money they have available as a down payment. Tiep explains that his annual income is $48 000, and Vinh's part-time earnings come to

$18 900; their only debt is for their car, and payments on that loan cost $280 a month. They have saved $16 000 for a down payment.

The mortgage officer calculates their gross debt service and their total debt service for a mortgage of $119 000 at 8.75 percent to be amortized over 25 years, and suggests that they apply for a CMHC-insured mortgage. They are told that the application will cost $100 and that an appraiser will look at the house they want to buy and will determine its lending value. The appraisal fee will be $150.

In a few days' time, they learn that the house has a lending value of $132 500 and that they are eligible for a $119 000 mortgage.

6. (a) List the criteria that the lender probably uses to determine the eligibility of (i) Vinh and Tiep, and (ii) the property.

    (b) Would this couple be eligible for a conventional mortgage?

    (c) How much would the monthly payments be on this mortgage?

    (d) Calculate the couple's gross debt service and the total debt service.

    (e) Work out the interest and principal components of the first payment.

    (f) How much total interest will this couple pay over 25 years, assuming that interest rates do not change and that the couple makes no prepayments?

    (g) How much would the total interest cost be reduced if they could get a mortgage for half a percent (0.5 percent) less?

    (h) How much interest could they save by amortizing this mortgage over 20 years instead of 25 years?

    (i) Use the chart below to estimate some of the costs (in addition to the down payment and mortgage) that Tiep and Vinh will probably encounter as they complete the house purchase and move from their apartment. What is the grand total?

SOME COSTS ASSOCIATED WITH HOME BUYING

Note: The numbers used here are estimates. Find out current costs.

Mortgage Fees		Totals
Appraisal fee	$ _____	
Mortgage insurance fee (added to mortgage; assume 2%)	$ _____	$ _____

Statement of Adjustments $ _____

    Tax adjustments (allow 6 months) $ _____

    Fire insurance $ 600.00

    Fuel oil (part of a tank) $ 300.00 $ _____

Goods and Services Tax (if applicable) $ _____

Lawyer's Account   _____

    Disbursements by lawyer for land transfer tax

    (if applicable) $ _____

    Deed registration $ 75.00

    Legal fees $ 1000.00 $ _____

Moving and Related Costs   _____

    Moving (two men and a truck for 5 hrs. @ $60/hr.) $ _____ $ _____

    Connection of utilities

    Telephone $ 58.50

    Cable TV $ 34.42

    Electricity $ 48.50

    Others $ 25.00 $ _____

Appliances, Repairs

    Purchase of major appliances $ 2900.00

    Decorating supplies $ 600.00

    Repairs $ 1000.00 $ _____

Grand Total   _____ $ _____

What are some other costs that might be anticipated but that are not included here?

7. The Valenzuelas' offer to purchase a house has been accepted. Now they are considering ways of financing it. The purchase price is $187 000, and they have $18 000 for a down payment. They are considering the following alternatives:

Down payment	First mortgage	Second mortgage
(i) $18 000	$169 000 @ 9%, 25 yrs.	none
(ii) $18 000	$169 000 @ 9%, 20 yrs.	none
(iii) $10 000	$169 000 @ 9%, 25 yrs.	$8000 @10% for 5 yrs. ($169.19/mo.)

(a) Which of these alternatives would result in the lowest monthly cost?

(b) Which of these alternatives would result in the lowest total interest?

(c) What are some factors the Valenzuelas should consider when making their choice?

8. Answer true or false.

(a) Capital gains apply only to stocks and bonds, not houses.

(b) An opportunity cost of buying a house could be a smaller pool of assets available at retirement.

(c) It is foolish to take over an existing mortgage since you can always negotiate better terms yourself.

(d) Second mortgages are less risky than first mortgages.

(e) The only thing that matters in applying for a mortgage is satisfying the lending institution.

(f) In addition to promising to pay principal and interest, mortgagors also usually promise to pay the taxes on the property, to insure it, and to maintain the property.

(g) Mortgage terms are generally the same length as amortization periods.

9. A reverse mortgage allows you to have both a home and money. What are the advantages and disadvantages to someone whose only asset is their home and who wants to leave an estate to their heirs? Is there any other solution to someone who is "house rich and cash poor?"

10. Use the Changs' amortization schedule (see Appendix 13A) to answer this question.

(a) How much principal and how much interest will the Changs pay in the first five years?

(b) How much principal and how much interest will they pay in the last five years?

(c) Compare the difference in total interest cost, and the effect on the time to repay the mortgage, if the Changs make a prepayment of $10 000 after five years.

(d) Compare the difference in total interest cost, and the effect on the time to repay the mortgage, if the Changs make a prepayment of $10 000 after 10 years.

(e) If they make two prepayments of $10 000—one after 5 years and the other one after 10 years—when will the mortgage be extinguished?

11. (a) Make a list of all the possible closing costs a mortgagor may face.

(b) What amount of land transfer tax will a resident of British Columbia pay when buying a $750 000 house?

12. Would you recommend a new home buyer select a monthly payment or a weekly payment schedule? Why?

13. Go to the Canada Mortgage and Housing Corporation Web site, www.cmhc-schl.gc.ca. Click on Buying a Home and then Information for Home Buyers. Compare the rate for both open and closed mortgages. Why are there differences in the quoted rates when anyone can compare and choose the company with the lowest interest? What is the range of rates for a five-year closed mortgage? Go to Information for Lenders and click on Borrower Eligibility Guide. What questions do mortgage lenders ask of potential customers? Can you suggest any others?

(a) What is the minimum amount of documentation required?

(b) What concerns regarding a prospect's income are raised?

(c) What income categories given here are not likely to excite the lender?

(d) What is the maximum Total Debt Service Ratio any client is likely to get?

(e) What does CMHC consider a "proven asset"?

References

BOOKS

As is true in several other areas of the burgeoning body of literature on personal finance topics, books about home mortgages constitute a large and constantly increasing subgenre. A sampling of some of the more recent entries in this field, along with some classic references, follows.

British Columbia Mortgages Practice Manual. Continuing Legal Education, 1996.

COSTELLO, BRIAN. *Making Money from Your Mortgage*. Toronto: Random House, 1991.

GOLDENBERG, DAVID. *Mortgages and Foreclosures: Know Your Rights*. Vancouver: Self-Counsel Press, 1993.

GRAY, DOUGLAS A. *All You Need to Know About Reverse Mortgages*. Toronto: McGraw-Hill Ryerson, 1994.

———. *Mortgage Tables Made Easy: A Complete Canadian Guide*. Toronto: McGraw-Hill Ryerson, 1994.

Monthly Mortgage Payments. Willowdale, ON: Computofacts, 1994.

Monthly Mortgage Tables. Willowdale, ON: Computofacts, 1971.

Mortgage Wise: A Guide for Home Buyers. Toronto: Canadian Bankers Association, 1998.

MACKENZIE, WARREN. *Canadian Association of Retired People's Financial Planning Guide*. Toronto: Stoddart, 1998.

PAPE, GORDON, and BRUCE McDOUGALL. *The Canadian Mortgage Book*. Scarborough: Prentice Hall Canada, 1997.

RAYNER, W.B., and R.H. McLAREN. *Falconbridge on Mortgages. Fourth Edition*. Aurora, ON: Canada Law, 1977.

RECEVEUR, LUIS W. *Real Estate in Saskatchewan: Mortgage Payment Tables*. Prince Albert, SK: United Real Estate, 1994.

ROACH, JOSEPH E. *The Canadian Law of Mortgages of Land*. Toronto: Butterworths, 1993.

SILVERSTEIN, ALAN. *Alan Silverstein's Perfect Mortgage: Cutting the Cost of Home Ownership*. Toronto: Stoddart, 1996.

———. *Hidden Profits in Your Mortgage: The Smart Move Guide to Home Ownership*. Toronto: Stoddart, 1995.

———. *Save!: Alan Silverstein's Guide to Mortgage Payment Tables*. Toronto: Stoddart, 1993.

TYERS, PAUL, and PIERCE NEWMAN. *Fiscal Fitness: A Guide to Personal Finance for All Strategies of Life*. Scarborough: Prentice Hall Canada, 1999.

WADE, P.J. *Have Your Home and Money Too: The Canadian Guide to Reverse Mortgages, Home Equity Conversion and Other Creative Housing Options. Second Edition*. Toronto: John Wiley & Sons, Inc., 1999.

Weekly, Bi-Weekly and Semi-Monthly Mortgage Payments. Willowdale, ON: Computofacts, 1985.

Personal Finance on the Web

Canada Mortgage .com
www.canadamortgage.com Mortgages on-line.

Canada Mortgage and Housing Corporation (CMHC)
www.cmhc-schl.gc.ca Home page of Canada's federal housing agency: a useful site for anyone interested in mortgages.

Canada Wide City and County Real Estate Search
www.web.onramp.ca/ipearcy Provides help in locating a home anywhere in Canada. Viewers can fill out a form and have real estate agents start a search.

Canadian Home Income Plan
www.chip.ca The site for reverse mortgages. 1-800-563-2447.

Canadian Real Estate Association
www.realtors.mls.ca/crea/ Contains a directory of all real estate boards.

MLS Online
www.mls.ca Contains all residential and commercial MLS (Multiple Listing Service) property listings in Canada, including special features and prices of properties.

The Mortgage Centre
www.mortgagecentre.com/index Lenders to compete for mortgages in an electronic bidding process.

Mortgage for less
www.mortgageforless.com Mortgages on-line.

Mortgage Made Easy
www.mortgage-made-easy.com/ Everything you need to know about mortgages.

Provincial Mortgage Brokers
www.provincialmortgage.com

Quicken.ca
www.quicken.ca/eng/bankingrates/index Provides a comparison of mortgage rates.

RealtyLink
www.realtylink.org MLS property listings for the Greater Vancouver area.

Your Mortgage.ca
www.YourMortgage.ca/ Mortgages on-line.

CANADIAN FINANCIAL INSTITUTIONS

All of the chartered banks and trust company sites provide information on mortgage rates and on calculating mortgage payments. It is also possible to apply for a mortgage on-line from these sites.

Bank of Montreal
www.bmo.com

Canada Trust
> **www.canadatrust.com** This site still existed in October 2000 even though the company had been taken over by the TD Bank.

Canadian Imperial Bank of Commerce
> **www.cibc/index.html**

Canadian Western Bank
> **www.cwbank.com**

Citizens Bank of Canada
> **www.citizensbank.ca**

Laurentian Bank of Canada
> **www.lbcdirect.laurentianbank.ca**

National Bank of Canada
> **www.nbfinancial.com**

Royal Bank Financial Group
> **www.royalbank.com**

Scotiabank
> **www.scotiabank.ca**

Toronto-Dominion Bank
> **www.tdbank.ca**

Appendix 13A

Mortgage Amortization Schedule

Principal	$100 000
Interest rate	9%
Amortization	20 years
Monthly payment	$889.20
Interest factor	007 363 081

PAYMENT NUMBER	PAYMENT AMOUNT	INTEREST PAID	PRINCIPAL PAID	ACCUMULATED INTEREST	OUTSTANDING BALANCE
1	889.20	736.31	152.89	736.31	99847.11
2	889.20	735.18	154.02	1471.49	99693.09
3	889.20	734.05	155.15	2205.54	99537.94
4	889.20	732.91	156.29	2938.45	99381.65
5	889.20	731.76	157.44	3670.21	99224.21
6	889.20	730.60	158.60	4400.81	99065.60
7	889.20	729.43	159.77	5130.24	98905.83
8	889.20	728.25	160.95	5858.49	98744.88
9	889.20	727.07	162.13	6585.56	98582.74
10	889.20	725.87	163.33	7311.43	98419.41
11	889.20	724.67	164.53	8036.10	98254.88
12	889.20	723.46	165.74	8759.56	98089.14
13	889.20	722.24	166.96	9481.80	97922.18
14	889.20	721.01	168.19	10202.81	97753.99
15	889.20	719.77	169.43	10922.58	97584.56
16	889.20	718.52	170.68	11641.10	97413.88
17	889.20	717.27	171.93	12358.37	97241.94
18	889.20	716.00	173.20	13074.37	97068.74
19	889.20	714.73	174.48	13789.10	96894.27
20	889.20	713.44	175.76	14502.54	96718.50
21	889.20	712.15	177.05	15214.69	96541.46
22	889.20	710.84	178.36	15925.53	96363.09
23	889.20	709.53	179.67	16635.06	96183.42
24	889.20	708.21	180.99	17343.27	96002.43

continued

PAYMENT NUMBER	PAYMENT AMOUNT	INTEREST PAID	PRINCIPAL PAID	ACCUMULATED INTEREST	OUTSTANDING BALANCE
25	889.20	706.87	182.33	18050.14	95820.10
26	889.20	705.53	183.67	18755.67	95636.43
27	889.20	704.18	185.02	19459.85	95451.41
28	889.20	702.82	186.38	20162.67	95265.02
29	889.20	701.44	187.76	20864.11	95077.27
30	889.20	700.06	189.14	21564.17	94888.12
31	889.20	689.67	190.53	22262.84	94697.59
32	889.20	697.27	191.93	22960.11	94505.66
33	889.20	695.85	193.35	23655.96	94312.31
34	889.20	694.43	194.77	24350.39	94117.54
35	889.20	693.00	196.20	25043.39	93921.34
36	889.20	691.55	197.65	25734.94	93723.69
37	889.20	690.10	199.10	26425.04	93524.59
38	889.20	688.63	200.57	27113.67	93324.02
39	889.20	687.15	202.05	27800.82	93121.97
40	889.20	685.66	203.54	28486.48	92918.43
41	889.20	684.17	205.03	29170.65	92713.40
42	889.20	682.66	206.54	29853.31	92506.86
43	889.20	681.14	208.06	30534.45	92298.80
44	889.20	679.60	209.60	31214.05	92089.19
45	889.20	678.06	211.14	31892.11	91878.06
46	889.20	676.51	212.69	32568.62	91665.36
47	889.20	674.94	214.26	33243.56	91451.09
48	889.20	673.36	215.84	33916.92	91235.25
49	889.20	671.77	217.43	34588.69	91017.82
50	889.20	670.17	219.03	35258.86	90798.79
51	889.20	668.56	220.64	35927.42	90578.15
52	889.20	666.93	222.27	36594.35	90355.88
53	889.20	665.30	223.90	37259.65	90131.98

continued

Appendix 13A *(continued)*

Mortgage Amortization Schedule

PAYMENT NUMBER	PAYMENT AMOUNT	INTEREST PAID	PRINCIPAL PAID	ACCUMULATED INTEREST	OUTSTANDING BALANCE
54	889.20	663.65	225.55	37923.30	89906.42
55	889.20	661.99	227.21	38585.29	89679.21
56	889.20	660.32	228.88	39245.61	89450.33
57	889.20	658.63	230.57	39904.24	89219.76
58	889.20	656.93	232.27	40561.17	88987.49
59	889.20	655.22	233.98	41216.39	88753.50
60	889.20	653.50	235.70	41869.89	88517.80
61	889.20	651.76	237.44	42521.65	88280.36
62	889.20	650.02	239.18	43171.67	88041.18
63	889.20	648.25	240.95	43819.92	87800.22
64	889.20	646.48	242.72	44466.40	87557.51
65	889.20	644.69	244.51	45111.09	87313.00
66	889.20	642.89	246.31	45753.98	87066.69
67	889.20	641.08	248.12	46395.06	86818.56
68	889.20	639.25	249.95	47034.31	86568.61
69	889.20	637.41	251.79	47671.72	86316.82
70	889.20	635.56	253.64	48307.28	86063.18
71	889.20	633.69	255.51	48940.97	85807.68
72	889.20	631.81	257.39	49572.78	85550.28
73	889.20	629.91	259.29	50202.69	85290.99
74	889.20	628.00	261.20	50830.69	85029.79
75	889.20	626.08	263.12	51456.77	84766.68
76	889.20	624.14	265.06	42080.91	84501.61
77	889.20	622.19	267.01	52703.10	84234.59
78	889.20	620.23	268.97	53323.33	83965.62
79	889.20	618.25	270.95	53941.58	83694.68
80	889.20	616.25	272.95	54557.83	83421.72
81	889.20	614.24	274.96	55172.07	83146.76
82	889.20	612.22	276.98	55784.29	82869.78

continued

PAYMENT NUMBER	PAYMENT AMOUNT	INTEREST PAID	PRINCIPAL PAID	ACCUMULATED INTEREST	OUTSTANDING BALANCE
83	889.20	610.18	279.02	56394.47	82590.76
84	889.20	608.12	281.08	57002.59	82309.68
85	889.20	606.05	283.15	57608.64	82026.53
86	889.20	603.97	285.23	58212.61	81741.30
87	889.20	601.87	287.33	58814.48	81453.97
88	889.20	599.75	289.45	59414.23	81164.52
89	889.20	597.62	291.58	60011.85	80872.94
90	889.20	595.47	293.73	60607.32	80579.21
91	889.20	593.31	295.89	61200.63	80283.31
92	889.20	591.13	298.07	61791.76	79985.25
93	889.20	588.94	300.26	62380.70	79684.99
94	889.20	586.73	302.47	62967.43	79382.52
95	889.20	584.50	304.70	63551.93	79077.81
96	889.20	582.26	306.94	64134.19	78770.88
97	889.20	580.00	309.20	64714.19	78461.68
98	889.20	577.72	311.48	65291.91	78150.19
99	889.20	575.43	313.77	65867.34	77836.41
100	889.20	573.12	316.08	66440.46	77520.34
101	889.20	570.79	318.41	67011.25	77201.93
102	889.20	568.44	320.76	67579.68	76881.16
103	889.20	566.08	323.12	68145.76	76558.03
104	889.20	563.70	325.50	68709.46	76232.53
105	889.20	561.31	327.89	69270.78	75904.65
106	889.20	558.89	330.31	69829.66	75574.33
107	889.20	556.46	332.74	70386.13	75241.59
108	889.20	554.01	335.19	70940.13	74906.40
109	889.20	551.54	337.66	71491.68	74568.74
110	889.20	549.06	340.14	72040.74	74228.60
111	889.20	546.55	342.65	72587.28	73885.95

continued

Appendix 13A *(continued)*

Mortgage Amortization Schedule

PAYMENT NUMBER	PAYMENT AMOUNT	INTEREST PAID	PRINCIPAL PAID	ACCUMULATED INTEREST	OUTSTANDING BALANCE
112	889.20	544.03	345.17	73131.31	73540.78
113	889.20	541.49	347.71	73672.81	73193.06
114	889.20	538.93	350.27	74211.74	72842.79
115	889.20	536.35	352.85	74748.09	72489.94
116	889.20	533.75	355.45	75281.84	72134.49
117	889.20	531.13	358.07	75812.97	71776.41
118	889.20	528.50	360.70	76341.47	71415.71
119	889.20	525.84	363.36	76867.31	71052.35
120	889.20	523.16	366.04	77390.47	70686.31
121	889.20	520.47	368.73	77910.94	70317.58
122	889.20	517.75	371.45	78428.69	69946.13
123	889.20	515.02	374.18	78943.71	69571.95
124	889.20	512.26	376.94	79455.97	69195.00
125	889.20	509.49	379.71	79965.46	68815.29
126	889.20	506.69	382.51	80472.15	68432.78
127	889.20	503.88	385.32	80976.03	68047.46
128	889.20	501.04	388.16	81477.07	67659.30
129	889.20	498.18	391.02	81975.25	67268.28
130	889.20	495.30	393.90	82470.55	66874.38
131	889.20	492.40	396.80	82962.95	66477.58
132	889.20	489.48	399.72	83452.43	66077.86
133	889.20	486.54	402.66	83938.96	65675.21
134	889.20	483.57	405.63	84422.53	65269.58
135	889.20	480.59	408.61	84903.12	64860.97
136	889.20	477.58	411.62	85380.71	64449.35
137	889.20	474.55	414.65	85855.25	64034.70
138	889.20	471.49	417.71	86326.74	63616.99
139	889.20	468.42	420.78	86795.16	63196.21
140	889.20	465.32	423.88	87260.49	62772.32

continued

PAYMENT NUMBER	PAYMENT AMOUNT	INTEREST PAID	PRINCIPAL PAID	ACCUMULATED INTEREST	OUTSTANDING BALANCE
141	889.20	462.20	427.00	87722.69	62345.32
142	889.20	459.05	430.15	88181.74	61915.17
143	889.20	455.89	433.31	88637.62	61481.86
144	889.20	452.70	436.50	89090.33	61045.36
145	889.20	449.48	439.72	89539.81	60605.64
146	889.20	446.24	442.96	89986.05	60162.68
147	889.20	442.98	446.22	90429.02	59716.46
148	889.20	439.70	449.50	90868.72	59266.96
149	889.20	436.39	452.81	91305.12	58814.15
150	889.20	433.05	456.15	91738.16	58358.00
151	889.20	429.69	459.51	92167.85	57898.49
152	889.20	426.31	462.89	92594.16	57435.60
153	889.20	422.90	466.30	93017.06	56969.30
154	889.20	419.47	469.73	93436.53	56499.57
155	889.20	416.01	473.19	93852.54	56026.38
156	889.20	412.53	476.67	94265.07	55549.71
157	889.20	409.02	480.18	94674.09	55069.53
158	889.20	405.48	483.72	95079.57	54585.81
159	889.20	401.92	487.28	95481.49	54098.53
160	889.20	398.33	490.87	95879.82	53607.65
161	889.20	394.72	494.48	96274.54	53113.17
162	889.20	391.08	498.12	96665.62	52615.05
163	889.20	387.41	501.79	97053.02	52113.26
164	889.20	383.71	505.49	97436.74	51607.78
165	889.20	379.99	509.21	97816.72	51098.57
166	889.20	376.24	512.96	98192.97	50585.60
167	889.20	372.47	516.73	98565.44	50068.87
168	889.20	368.66	520.54	98934.09	49548.33
169	889.20	364.83	524.37	99298.92	49023.96

continued

Appendix 13A *(continued)*

Mortgage Amortization Schedule

PAYMENT NUMBER	PAYMENT AMOUNT	INTEREST PAID	PRINCIPAL PAID	ACCUMULATED INTEREST	OUTSTANDING BALANCE
170	889.20	360.97	528.23	99659.89	48495.73
171	889.20	357.08	532.12	100017.00	47963.61
172	889.20	353.16	536.04	100370.10	47427.57
173	889.20	349.21	539.99	100719.30	46887.58
174	889.20	345.24	543.96	101064.60	46343.62
175	889.20	341.23	547.97	101405.80	45795.65
176	889.20	337.20	552.00	101743.00	45243.65
177	889.20	333.13	556.07	102076.10	44687.58
178	889.20	329.04	560.16	102405.20	44127.42
179	889.20	324.91	564.29	102730.10	43563.13
180	889.20	320.76	568.44	103050.80	42994.69
181	889.20	316.57	572.63	103367.40	42422.06
182	889.20	312.36	576.84	103679.80	41845.22
183	889.20	308.11	581.09	103987.90	41264.13
184	889.20	303.83	585.37	104291.70	40678.76
185	889.20	299.52	589.68	104591.20	40089.08
186	889.20	295.18	594.02	104886.40	39495.06
187	889.20	290.81	598.39	105177.20	38896.67
188	889.20	286.40	602.80	105463.60	38293.86
189	889.20	281.96	607.24	105745.60	37686.63
190	889.20	277.49	611.71	106023.10	37074.92
191	889.20	272.99	616.21	106296.10	36458.70
192	889.20	268.45	620.75	106564.50	35837.95
193	889.20	263.88	625.32	106828.40	35212.63
194	889.20	259.27	629.93	107087.70	34582.70
195	889.20	254.64	634.56	107342.30	33948.14
196	889.20	249.96	639.24	107592.30	33308.90
197	889.20	245.26	643.94	107837.50	32664.96
198	889.20	240.51	648.69	108078.10	32016.27

continued

PAYMENT NUMBER	PAYMENT AMOUNT	INTEREST PAID	PRINCIPAL PAID	ACCUMULATED INTEREST	OUTSTANDING BALANCE
199	889.20	235.74	653.46	108313.80	31362.81
200	889.20	230.93	658.27	108544.70	30704.54
201	889.20	226.08	663.12	108770.80	30041.42
202	889.20	221.20	668.00	108992.00	29373.42
203	889.20	216.28	672.92	109208.30	28700.50
204	889.20	211.32	677.88	109419.60	28022.61
205	889.20	206.33	682.87	109625.90	27339.74
206	889.20	201.30	687.90	109827.20	26651.84
207	889.20	196.24	692.96	110023.50	25958.88
208	889.20	191.14	698.06	110214.60	25260.82
209	889.20	186.00	703.20	110400.60	24557.62
210	889.20	180.82	708.38	110581.40	23849.24
211	889.20	175.60	713.60	110757.00	23135.64
212	889.20	170.35	718.85	110927.40	22416.79
213	889.20	165.06	724.14	111092.50	21692.65
214	889.20	159.72	729.48	111252.20	20963.17
215	889.20	154.35	734.85	111406.50	20228.32
216	889.20	148.94	740.26	111555.50	19488.06
217	889.20	143.49	745.71	111699.00	18742.35
218	889.20	138.00	751.20	111837.00	17991.15
219	889.20	132.47	756.73	111969.40	17234.42
220	889.20	126.90	762.30	112096.30	16472.12
221	889.20	121.29	767.91	112217.60	15704.21
222	889.20	115.63	773.57	112333.20	14930.64
223	889.20	109.94	779.26	112443.20	14151.38
224	889.20	104.20	785.00	112547.40	13366.38
225	889.20	98.42	790.78	112645.80	12575.60
226	889.20	92.60	796.60	112738.40	11779.00
227	889.20	86.73	802.47	112825.10	10976.53

continued

Appendix 13A *(continued)*

Mortgage Amortization Schedule

PAYMENT NUMBER	PAYMENT AMOUNT	INTEREST PAID	PRINCIPAL PAID	ACCUMULATED INTEREST	OUTSTANDING BALANCE
228	889.20	80.82	808.38	112906.00	10168.15
229	889.20	74.87	814.33	112980.80	9353.82
230	889.20	68.87	820.33	113049.70	8533.49
231	889.20	62.83	826.37	113112.50	7707.12
232	889.20	56.75	832.45	113169.30	6874.67
233	889.20	50.62	838.58	113219.90	6036.09
234	889.20	44.44	844.76	113264.30	5191.33
235	889.20	38.22	850.98	113302.50	4340.35
236	889.20	31.96	857.24	113334.50	3483.11
237	889.20	25.65	863.55	113360.10	2619.56
238	889.20	19.29	869.91	113379.40	1749.65
239	889.20	12.88	876.32	113392.30	873.33

Final Payment 873.34

Chapter 14

Credit, Debt, and Bankruptcy

objectives

1. Outline the role of credit bureaus in the establishment of credit ratings and risk assessment.

2. Define consumer rights according to the relevant legislation.

3. Show how collection agencies assist creditors and how they are controlled by provincial legislation.

4. Discuss the ways in which debts may be collected without going to court as well as by suing a debtor.

5. Discuss the role of garnishments and execution orders in debt collection.

6. Distinguish between the various kinds of garnishment.

7. Define the various terms associated with credit reporting such as credit file, credit scoring, and third-party collection.

8. Identify six major causes of overindebtedness.

9. Discuss the process of negotiating with creditors and when doing so may be appropriate.

10. Explain the costs and benefits of a consolidation loan and the process of a debt repayment program.

11. List seven reasons for the high rate of consumer bankruptcies.

12. Distinguish between a consumer proposal and a bankruptcy.

13. Explain the duties of five actors in the insolvency process.

14. Outline the results of bankruptcy for both creditors and debtors.

15. Evaluate the possible benefits of a consumer proposal for an insolvent debtor.

16. Define the following terms: overindebtedness, debt management, bankrupt, and discharged bankrupt.

Introduction

This chapter deals with the use and abuse of credit, with credit reporting, and with debt. It also deals with the roles of credit bureaus in the establishment of credit as well as with those of collection agencies in dealing with debt. It is a sad fact that many Canadians get into financial difficulties and have to declare bankruptcy. We will examine some of the causes of overindebtedness and what forces some people to become bankrupt. We will then look at what those who are in great debt can do to deal with the problem, including consumer proposals and bankruptcy.

Credit Reporting

When you apply for credit, the lender must estimate the probability that you will be able to repay the debt as scheduled. What does a lender need to know in order to predict your reliability and your capacity to repay this debt? The creditor starts by assessing your application for credit, in which you provide quite a bit of information about yourself—for instance, your residence, occupation, bank, salary, mortgage, and consumer debts (see Figure 12.10, "Credit Card Application"). In addition, the lender may want to know how you have handled previous credit transactions; such information can be obtained from the local credit bureau.

The Credit Bureau

A **credit bureau** is a business that sells information about credit transactions to its subscribers, who are mostly creditors and other businesses. The credit reporting business in Canada is currently dominated by a large multinational company and a few smaller ones that are in competition with each other.

Credit bureaus obtain funds by selling memberships to firms that extend credit—especially financial institutions and retailers—as well as to a variety of other businesses that need information on the credit histories of customers. Employers and landlords have an interest in subscribing to the credit bureau, as do life insurance companies; however, in order to become a member, each must have a legitimate business interest in such credit information.

Credit bureau subscribers pay an annual membership fee in addition to a charge for each credit report that they obtain. These days, most credit reports are transferred electronically from the credit bureau to the member, instead of by telephone as would have been the case in the past. Now, with electronic transmission of information, credit bureaus can easily send reports nearly anywhere in the world. The service contract signed by members binds them to using the information obtained from the credit bureau for strictly *bona fide* business purposes only, and also requires that they give the credit bureau any relevant credit information they have about their customers.

The Credit File

Anyone who has credit cards or charge accounts, has ever obtained a mortgage or another type of loan, has rented accommodation, or is connected to utilities such as telephone or hydro, probably has a file at a credit bureau. Most of the information in the file comes from three major sources: the individual, the individual's creditors, and public records. Each time you apply for credit, the facts supplied on the application form are transferred to your credit bureau file by the credit grantor when a credit report is drawn.

Current Manner of Payment

(North American Standard)

Abbreviations for Type of Account:

O   Open account (30 or 90 days)

R   Revolving or option (open-end account)

I   Instalment (fixed number of payments)

Current Manner of Payment

(Using payments past due or age from due date)

0   Too new to rate; approved but not used.

1   Pays (or paid) within 30 days of payment due date or not over one payment past due.

2   Pays (or paid) in more than 30 days from payment due date, but not more than 60 days, or not more than two payments past due.

3   Pays (or paid) in more than 60 days from payment due date, but not more than 90 days or not more than three payments past due.

4   Pays (or paid) in more than 90 days from payment due date, but not more than 120 days, or four payments past due.

5   Pays (or paid) in more than 120 days but not yet rated 9.

7   Making regular payments under a consolidation order or similar arrangement.

8   Repossession.

9   Bad debt; placed for collection; skip.

In addition, it is common practice for major credit grantors, such as bank credit card companies, large retailers, and financial institutions, to send their entire credit files to the credit bureau every month. These computer files, which report the status of all their credit accounts, are electronically merged with those already in the credit bureau files; new files are set up for anyone who does not already have one. The information in a credit bureau file includes the account number, the outstanding balance, and whether payment has been made on time. Items of public record, such as chattel mortgages and conditional sales agreements registered with provincial authorities, and reports on court judgments or bankruptcies, are obtained by the credit bureau and added to the files.

Credit bureaus store their files in computers, where they are immediately accessible to other bureaus. The sample credit report shown in Figure 14.1 illustrates the types of information that may be kept in a credit bureau file.

The Credit Check

Whenever you apply for a loan or a credit card, to open a charge account, or to purchase an appliance with a conditional sales contract, you will be asked to complete an application form and then await the credit grantor's decision. The credit officer at the bank, trust company, or store contacts the credit bureau. Two conditions must be met before the credit officer can receive information about your credit history: (i) the inquiring firm must be a member of the credit bureau, and (ii) the file that the credit bureau retrieves must apply to you and not to anyone else.

FIGURE 14.1 SAMPLE CREDIT REPORT

EQUIFAX

CONSUMER RELATIONS P.O. BOX 190 STATION JEAN TALON
MONTREAL QUEBEC H1S 2Z2

JANE DOE
10 PLEASANT ST.
TORONTO ONTARIO
M2N 1A2

CONFIDENTIAL INFORMATION
NOT TO BE USED FOR CREDIT PURPOSES
RE: EQUIFAX UNIQUE NUMBER: 3140123054

Dear JANE DOE,

Further to your request, a disclosure of your personal credit file as of **03/27/01** follows:

PERSONAL IDENTIFICATION INFORMATION:

The following personal identification information is currently showing on your credit file.

DATE FILE OPENED: 07/04/92

NAME: Doe, Jane
CURRENT ADDRESS: 10 PLEASANT ST. TORONTO,ON
DATE REPORTED: 12/96
PREVIOUS ADDRESS: 2 AVENUE ST,TORONTO,ON
DATE REPORTED: 12/93
PRIOR ADDRESS: 3 DU BOULEVARD,MONTREAL,PQ
DATE REPORTED: 07/92

BIRTH DATE/AGE: 10/05/1968/33
SOCIAL INSURANCE NUMBER: 123-456-789

OTHER REFERENCE NAMES:
CURRENT EMPLOYMENT: EDITOR
PREVIOUS EMPLOYMENT: TRANSLATOR
PRIOR EMPLOYMENT: CHEF
OTHER INCOME:

SPOUSES NAME: JOHN
SPOUSES EMPLOYMENT: CHEF

CREDIT INQUIRIES ON YOUR FILE:

Following is a list of Equifax members who have received a copy of your credit file for credit granting or other permissible purposes. Addresses are available by calling Equifax at 1-800-465-7166.

DATE	REQUESTOR NAME	TELEPHONE
03/02/00	CANADA TRUST MTG	(416) 361-8518
02/22/00	TD BANK	(800) 787-7065
01/16/00	BQE NATIONALE	(450) 677-9122

The following inquiries are for your information only and are not displayed to others. They include requests from authorized parties to update their records regarding your existing account with them.

DATE	REQUESTOR NAME	TELEPHONE
03/23/00	SOC ALCOOLS (not displayed)	(514) 873-6281
03/22/00	CANADA TRUST MTG (not displayed)	(416) 361-8518
02/16/00	CMHC SCHL (not displayed)	(888) 463-6454
01/16/00	AMERICAN EXPRESS (not displayed)	(416) 123-4567

CONSUMER INTERVIEWS AND OTHER SERVICES:
You contacted our office in 12/98 to request a review of your credit file.

CREDIT HISTORY AND/OR BANKING INFORMATION:

The following information was reported to us by organizations listed below.
Information is received every 30 days from most credit grantors.

GMAC last reported to us in 01/01 rating your installment account as I1, meaning paid as agreed and up to date. The reported balance of your account was $1000. Your account number: 23456789012345. The account is in the subject's name only. Date account opened: 04/99. Credit limit or highest amount of credit advanced: $4400. **DATE OF LAST ACTIVITY meaning the last payment or transaction made on this account was in 12/00.** Additional comments: auto loan. Monthly payments.

CANADA TRUST MC last reported to us in 01/01 rating your revolving account as R1, meaning paid as agreed and up to date. At the time the reported balance of your account was $285. Your account number: 12345678901234. Date account opened: 06/99. Credit limit or highest amount of credit advanced $2000. **DATE OF LAST ACTIVITY meaning the last payment or transaction made on this account was in 12/00. PREVIOUS PAYMENT STATUS:**
30 DAYS: 1 time (s) account previously R2 meaning one payment past due

PUBLIC RECORDS AND OTHER INFORMATION:

The following information was reported to your file on the date indicated.

A COLLECTION was **assigned** in 10/96 to Commercial Credit by Transamerica Financial in the amount of:$2675. Date reported paid: 07/97. Collection status: PAID. **DATE OF LAST ACTIVITY was in 04/96.** Collection agency reference number: 222222.

A JUDGEMENT was **FILED IN 01/96** in Min Govt Serv. Plaintiff and/or case number: Chrysler Canada 4444. Defendant/other info: joint with Dossier. Amount reported: $7525. Status reported: Satisfied. Date satisfied: 09/97.

continued

FIGURE 14.1 SAMPLE CREDIT REPORT (CONTINUED)

A BANKRUPTCY was **FILED IN 08/97** in SC Newmarket. Case number and/or trustee: 5555555 SYNDIC & ASS. Liabilities: $250000.Assets: $8900000.Item classification: individual. Information reported on: The subject only. The item is reported as: DISCHARGED. **DATE SETTLED: 05/98.** Additional comments: absolute discharge from bankruptcy.

THE CONSUMER PROVIDED A PERSONAL STATEMENT to us in 12/98. The statement has been recorded as follows:

RE: BANKRUPTCY, CONSUMER DECLARED BANKRUPTCY DUE TO DIVORCE
This statement is to be removed from the file in: 12/04.

RETENTION PERIOD OF DATA:

Trade reference information is retained in our database for not more than 6 years from the date of last activity reported to us. All inquiries made on your credit file are recorded and retained for a minimum of 3 years and are identified by requestors name and telephone number.

Public record information is retained in our database for a maximum of 7 years from the date filed, except in the case of multiple bankruptcies which results in retention of bankruptcy information for 14 years from the date of discharge of each bankruptcy. (Exception: P.E.I. Public records: 7 to 10 years, Bankruptcies: 14 years.

These purge rules are in compliance with provincial legislation governing consumer reporting agencies and are used as a standard across Canada. They are intended to reflect an accurate historical and current summary of your credit obligations and payment patterns reported to us.

The attached Reference Update Form is included for your convenience. If you wish to update your file with more current information or to request a change in the information provided above, please complete this form and return it to Equifax Canada. We will ensure that appropriate measures will be applied if corrections are required.

Please be advised that the file you have received is for your information only and may not be used for credit purposes.

Consumer Department

SOURCE: Equifax Canada Inc. Reproduced with the permission of Equifax Canada Inc.

Safeguards are built into the credit reporting system to ensure that access to credit information is restricted to members of the credit bureau. This is done electronically or with a code for telephone requests. To be sure that the retrieved file is the right one, a comparison is made between the information on your application form and that in the credit bureau file. In addition to name and address, other pieces of information that may be used to identify people are birth date, social insurance number, credit card account numbers, and place of employment.

Assuming that your credit application matches the credit bureau file, the lender and the credit bureau will exchange information. The credit bureau file will be updated with any new facts from your application, and the creditor will find out how you have handled credit in the past.

Credit Rating

The decision regarding whether or not to extend credit is made by the credit grantor, not the credit bureau. Credit bureaus merely collect and sell information; they do not make assessments of anyone's capacity to handle credit. In the interests of efficiency and of keeping costs down, large retail firms are coming to depend heavily on an automatic assessment system, called **credit scoring,** whereby points are given for certain characteristics. The weight given to these characteristics may vary somewhat from company to company—as well as from time to time, as the retail firm makes credit easier or harder to obtain. There is general agreement that the traditional three Cs—capacity, character, and collateral—play an important part. Higher scores are assigned to those who own property, who show stability in where they live and in their jobs, who possess several credit cards, who have paid past obligations on time, who do not write bad cheques, and who have a low debt/income ratio.

Lenders have programmed their computers to score the information on the application form quickly and to indicate whether the applicant is a good risk, a bad risk, or an uncertain risk. In the first two instances, the decision regarding whether to grant credit or not is fairly obvious and may be made without contacting the credit bureau. A firm may decide, for example, that all applicants whose scores rank in the top 10 percent to 15 percent will be considered good risks and will be automatically accepted, while the bottom 30 percent will be considered bad risks and will be automatically rejected. About half the applicants thus fall into the "uncertain" category: more information is needed about these applicants in order to reach a decision; credit bureau reports (which cost the credit grantor money) will then be drawn only for this group of people.

Since the assessment of your creditworthiness depends on the creditor, you may find that at any one time some lenders will grant credit while others will not. Obviously, this is more apt to be true if you fall into the uncertain category, because creditors vary in the levels of risk they are willing to accept. Nevertheless, whether or not credit will be granted may be influenced by factors other than personal history. Lenders' policies are affected by conditions in the economy and by the situation in the lender's own business. Sometimes a lender has surplus funds and is very anxious to lend, but at other times scarce funds or poor economic conditions (such as high unemployment) may discourage lending.

The Consumer and the Credit Bureau

Many users of consumer credit are unaware that some of their financial transactions are on file at the credit bureau; in fact, they may never even have heard of the credit bureau. Often, they discover its existence only when there is a mixup over their files or when they are refused credit. It is the policy of the Associated Credit Bureaus of Canada, and a legal requirement in all provinces, that consumers be permitted to know what is in their files, if they ask.

Regulation of Credit Bureaus

Except for Alberta, New Brunswick, and the two territories, Canada's remaining provinces have passed laws that regulate consumer reporting agencies, which include credit bureaus. The two basic concerns reflected in these laws are (i) the consumer's privacy with regard to credit information and (ii) the consumer's right not to suffer from inaccurate credit or personal information.

INFORMATION IN FILES Provincial laws make a distinction between **consumer information** (which includes such details as name, address, age, occupation, residence, marital status, education, employment, estimated income, paying habits, debts, assets, and obligations) and **personal information** (which has little to do with financial transactions, and includes, for example, character, reputation, and personal characteristics). Credit bureaus are restricted to consumer information only. Although the details differ, all of these acts limit the type of information that can be included in a consumer report; generally such reports must be restricted to consumer information. In addition, there are limits on the inclusion of detrimental information in a credit report. For example, in Ontario, the time limit for reporting that a bankruptcy occurred is seven years from the discharge date for the first bankruptcy. After two bankruptcies, the information is never deleted from a person's file. In Saskatchewan, the time limit is 14 years from the filing date for the first bankruptcy. Disclosing other detrimental information that is more than seven years old is also prohibited. Restrictions are set on the situations in which consumer reporting agencies may make reports. Acceptable circumstances include being required to do so by a court order and receiving a request from a person or organization who is concerned with extending credit, with renting, with employment, or with insurance.

PERMISSION FOR CREDIT REPORT Consumer reports, also known as credit reports, may not be requested unless a consumer either has given written consent or is sent written notice that the report was obtained. Ontario and Newfoundland require that notice be given before the report is obtained; in Manitoba, notice must follow within 10 days of granting or refusing credit. A request for permission to obtain a report may be included in a credit application, as in Figure 12.10.

If you have not applied for credit, the credit bureau cannot give a credit report to a third party without informing you of the request and providing you with the third party's name and address.

ACCESS TO OWN FILE As a consumer, you have the right to know what is in your credit bureau file. You can arrange with the local bureau to tell you the record's contents. If you find

Credit Reporting Legislation

Province	Title
British Columbia, Ontario, Nova Scotia, Prince Edward Island	*Credit Reporting Act*
Saskatchewan, Newfoundland	*Credit Reporting Agencies Act*
Manitoba	*Personal Investigations Act*
Quebec	*Consumer Protection Act*

that the information found there seems inaccurate, the agency must make every effort to verify the record and to correct any errors.

Other Credit Reporting Agencies

Although this chapter focuses primarily on credit bureaus, brief mention should be made of two other types of reporting agencies. **Information exchanges** are formed by groups of creditors, such as small loans companies and sales finance companies, to share information about their debtors as a way of preventing the occurrence of bad debts. Information exchanges and credit bureaus are interested in the same kinds of information, though they differ in their organizational structure. **Investigative agencies,** on the other hand, collect a wider range of information, including very personal data about family relations, addictions, and so on; they may even visit an individual's neighbours for opinions on his or her character.

Debt Collection

When a debt is in arrears or in default, the creditor is initially concerned with retrieving the money owed as quickly and cheaply as possible, with minimal destruction of the debtor's goodwill. If the first phase of debt collection—notices and reminders—is unsuccessful, difficult-to-collect debts may be handled more aggressively. They may be referred to a special collection division of the creditor's firm or to an independent collection agency. Finally, the debtor may be sued in court.

Who Does the Collecting?

From among the various possible approaches, creditors will choose whichever debt collection procedure is suitable for them and seems most likely to be successful for the particular debt. Firms in the finance business, such as banks, small loans companies, or credit unions, tend to have collection facilities to collect their own overdue accounts. Large retailers also do much of their own collecting. Smaller companies, along with independent professionals, typically prefer to devote their energies to their specialties and tend to turn delinquent accounts over to a collection agency. Some firms will pursue overdue accounts for a time, referring only the very difficult ones for further action. For simplicity, a distinction will be made between (i) a creditor's internal debt collection practices and (ii) third-party collecting.

INTERNAL COLLECTION PRACTICES Collection practices vary, but it is usual to begin with polite reminder notices or telephone calls. At this stage, most overdue accounts are collected without resorting to harassment, and without even requiring much personal contact. Debtors who remain resistant will find the collection techniques used becoming progressively more aggressive, since after a point, the creditor becomes more concerned with collecting the debt than with maintaining goodwill. Though the debt may eventually be written off in the accounts of the business, it may yet be possible to collect a portion of the debt by referring the matter to a lawyer or to an independent collection agency.

Collection Agencies

A **collection agency** is a provincially licensed business that specializes in collecting overdue accounts for others. Its income depends on its success in collecting, since the collector typically retains between 30 percent and 50 percent of the amounts collected, but earns no fees if unsuccessful. Not surprisingly, then, collection agencies are quite energetic in their efforts to collect.

In recent years, some collection agencies have started calling themselves "collection services" and have begun offering a wider range of services to creditors. A collection service might take over doing a company's credit approvals; alternatively, a bank credit card company or a large utility might arrange for the collection services to send out the usual monthly statements to card-holders or households. The collector's computers are programmed to identify anyone who is more than one day late with a payment: this way, the person can be called to ask whether a cheque has been sent. If payment is not on the way, collection procedures can then be put in place immediately. This approach saves money for the card company or utility since it means that they will have outstanding receivables for a shorter time.

THIRD-PARTY COLLECTION PRACTICES   Since the collection agency's staff work on commission, they are under pressure to get funds coming in as soon as possible. As a result, they usually demand immediate receipt of the amount owed—or at least evidence that it will be coming very shortly. Failing that, they will threaten to sue the debtor. In practice, the collector will sue only if there is a good chance of getting a return—for instance, if they find that there are wages that may be garnisheed or assets that can be seized. Creditors who refer debts to collectors expect to recover an average of 20 percent to 25 percent of the funds in question within three months. Collectors who cannot meet this target will lose business to those who can.

Collection procedures often depend heavily on psychological tactics, particularly in the early stages, before the collector takes the debtor to court. Measures are chosen with the aim of intimidating debtors to some degree: for example, using legal-looking forms and letterheads, referring the debt to a lawyer or a collection agency, or making threats that may not be enforceable but that will go unchallenged by uninformed debtors. At any time, the debtor can slow down or stop the collection process by making some payments.

No technique—however persuasive or intimidating—will be effective if the debtor cannot be found. Nowadays, reporting networks of credit bureaus make it much more difficult for debtors to disappear. An alert is placed on the file of a missing debtor. Whenever or wherever that person next applies for credit, his or her credit history will be examined; the creditor making the inquiry will provide the applicant's most recent address, which will then be forwarded to the creditor who is looking for the defaulter. Not all defaulters skip deliberately; some have merely moved, forgetting to inform their creditors.

ENFORCEMENT OF SECURITY   Normally, a creditor will enforce any security considered worthwhile before beginning aggressive collection processes. When the creditor holds security in the form of assets, durables, or promise of future income, the creditor also has the debtor's prior permission to realize on any of these in the case of default. But sometimes the security is not sufficient to cover the balance owing, and alternate procedures are needed.

REGULATION OF COLLECTION AGENCIES   The legislation regulating collections does not apply to all those who collect debts; in the main, it is directed at third-party collections—that is, situations in which the collector is not the creditor. It is chiefly concerned, therefore, with regulating collection agencies. The professions and institutions that are exempted from the requirements of this legislation vary among provinces. In British Columbia and Ontario, for instance, credit unions, banks, trust companies, barristers, real estate agents, and insurance agents, among others, are exempt. Refer to the appropriate provincial legislation to determine which collectors are regulated.

The Criminal Code of Canada prohibits indecent, threatening, or harassing telephone calls. This applies to all collection endeavours; thus, it provides some recourse for the con-

Legislation Regulating Collection Agencies

Province	Title
British Columbia	*Debt Collection Act*
Alberta	*Collection Practices Act*
Saskatchewan	*Collection Agents Act*
Manitoba	*Consumer Protection Act*
Ontario	*Collection Agencies Act*, and *Debt Collectors Act*
Quebec	*Act Respecting the Collection of Certain Debts*
New Brunswick, Nova Scotia, Prince Edward Island	*Collection Agencies Act*
Newfoundland	*Collections Act*

sumer who is being pursued for payment by someone whose activities are not regulated under provincial legislation. Initiative in lodging a complaint with provincial authorities would rest with the consumer. Another difficulty may arise in determining what constitutes harassment.

Using the Courts to Collect Debts

As mentioned earlier, the creditor who has an account in default has the right to enforce security and use reasonable collection procedures. If these are not sufficient, the next alternative is to sue the debtor. The details of the procedure vary from province to province, but a general summary of the process will indicate the procedure for collecting debts through the courts.

The creditor files a claim at the appropriate court (this depends on the amount of the claim), giving the names and addresses of both debtor and creditor, and the creditor's reasons for suing. The court clerk sends the claim and a summons to the debtor, who has three alternatives:

(a) try to settle the matter out of court (for instance, by repaying the debt),

(b) file a defence if there seem to be grounds for dispute,

(c) do nothing.

When the debtor selects the first alternative, the debtor and creditor may reopen negotiations about payment of the debt; if they reach an agreement, the creditor drops the claim. Should the debtor choose the second alternative, he or she must file a defence in the same court within a specified number of days, stating his or her reasons for disputing the creditor's claim. Anyone who decides to ignore the summons may be surprised to discover that failure to file a defence may result in a judgment against the debtor by default.

When the debtor files a defence, there may be a trial to hear both sides of the matter. On the trial date, all witnesses, the creditor, the debtor, and any lawyers for either party appear before the judge. Small claims courts are meant to be informal courts where legal counsel is not required. After hearing both sides of the story, the judge announces the decision. On very small claims, no appeal may be permitted. The judge's decision or judgment has two possible outcomes: either the debtor does not owe the money and the case is dismissed, or the debtor does owe some or all of the money claimed by the creditor. In the latter instance, the debtor is responsible for paying the amount owing, which becomes a **judgment debt.**

ENFORCEMENT OF JUDGMENT   If the debtor either cannot or will not repay the debt, the creditor has several possible courses of action to attempt to enforce the judgment. The creditor may choose either to garnishee the debtor's wages or bank account or to seize some of the debtor's goods under an execution order.

GARNISHMENTS   Wages or bank accounts may be garnisheed to satisfy a judgment debt. A **wage garnishment** is a court order that instructs an employer to pay into the court's trust some percentage of the debtor's wages. (Note that the terms can be slightly confusing. The word garnish*ment* applies to the court order itself; the debtor named in that document is called a garnish*ee*. The act of garnishment can be referred to by either of two verbs: to garnish*ee*—the form used in this book—or simply to garnish.) If a debtor has more than one garnishment order outstanding, the court will send them out one at a time. The debtor will not be taken by surprise, but will receive a statement from the court that the creditor has requested a garnishment, with time to respond to the court. The debtor can plead for a reduction in the amount taken off his or her wages and can stop the garnishment if it can be shown that steps are being taken to handle the debt problems. Sometimes, when more than one creditor has obtained a judgment against a debtor, the court may divide the funds collected by each garnishment order among the creditors, rather than handle the claims sequentially.

Garnishment is governed by a number of regulations, including some that exempt certain persons, some that exempt a portion of wages, and some that protect employees from being dismissed when their wages have been garnisheed. Income from social security programs—i.e., welfare, Employment Insurance, or Old Age Security—is exempt from garnishment. Provincial laws specify what proportion of wages may be garnisheed: 70 percent to 80 percent of gross wages may be exempt, and that proportion can be increased if the debtor can persuade the court of need. An employer that receives a garnishment order may be inclined to dismiss the employee on the assumption that he or she is not very reliable. Provincial laws attempt to prevent this, but sometimes the real reason for dismissal is difficult to find out. Home owners are occasionally surprised to receive garnishment orders for temporarily employed tradespeople who have outstanding judgment debts.

A **bank account garnishment** can be taken to obtain money from a debtor's account to satisfy a judgment debt. As with a wage garnishment, the process for doing this is initiated through the court. One difference is that a bank garnishment order may take 100 percent of an account to satisfy a debt. Bank account garnishments are sometimes used to collect debts from persons receiving welfare.

DEMAND ON A THIRD PARTY   A demand on a third party may be issued by the federal government for debts incurred against the federal government (such as income tax arrears and Employment Insurance benefit overpayments). The demand on a third party is like a garnishment in many ways, but it does not require a court judgment and it allows attachment (seizure) of a larger share of income. In the case of a self-employed individual, a demand on a third party may be issued against the person's bank account.

FAMILY COURT GARNISHMENT   Whenever payments on a maintenance order are not kept up-to-date, the family court can issue an attachment on wages, or **family court garnishment,** that has a continuing effect, similar to a demand on a third party. Again, these are circumstances under which the percentage of the person's wages that can be attached may exceed the limits set under provincial wage legislation. In Ontario, the Director of Support Custody Enforcement can issue a garnishment for 50 percent of gross wages minus CPP, E.I., union dues, and taxes. To apply for relief, the person must file a dispute with the courts and await a hearing. At the hearing, the judge decides whether or not to reduce the percentage garnisheed.

EXECUTION ORDER   A creditor who has obtained a favourable judgment has the right to seize and sell some of the debtor's property to satisfy the debt. In legal terms, this process is called **executing against the debtor's property.** The goods seized must be completely owned by the debtor, without liens or mortgages attached to them. Each province's *Execution Act* exempts certain possessions, such as essential household furnishings, from seizure.

Consumer Issues

Two issues of great concern to consumer credit users relate to (i) protecting the privacy of personal data and (ii) handling the credit records of married women.

Privacy of Personal Data

Technology now enables commercial enterprises and financial institutions to know a great deal about a consumer's personal habits. The use of credit cards, debit cards, and the Internet has made many people's lives an open book. Federal privacy legislation dating from 1983 controls the use of information collected by the federal government. On April 13, 2000, royal assent was given to *Bill C-6, The Personal Information Protection and Electronic Documents Act*. The act came into force on January 1, 2001. Passed by the federal government, it gives individuals legal rights concerning how their personal information is collected and used by the private sector. At the time of writing, Quebec was still the only province with legislation that governs how the private sector uses such information.

Credit Records of Married Women

In the past, when a woman married, the credit bureau combined her credit file with her husband's. Now that does not happen; if it does, a woman can ask to have a separate file set up. The credit bureau normally maintains a separate file for each individual. When a couple co-signs a loan or mortgage, this information is entered into both their credit files. Anyone who has any doubts about how his or her record is stored can make an appointment at the credit bureau to discuss the file. Some women make a special effort to develop an independent credit history by using credit in their own names, without a co-signer. A credit report cannot be drawn for the spouse of a person who is applying for credit unless the spouse also signs the application.

Overindebtedness: Why Does It Happen?

Overindebtedness

Overindebtedness is the condition of having more debts than one can or is willing to repay. An overindebted person is often found to have several accounts in arrears, with creditors and collectors actively pressing for payment. As we saw earlier in this chapter (under "Debt Collection"), reneging on a promise to a lender may prompt gentle reminders that lead to

Taking the Pressure Off

Larson is a 21-year-old university student. While in high school, he worked part-time at a supermarket and applied for and received several credit cards. He had a good summer job, earning $12 000 each year, and he earned $100 a week in the library during the semester. With credit, Larson learned to like many of the good things in life and now has a DVD, cell phone, and a new laptop. For the past two winters, Larson has gone on a trip to Venezuela with his two closest friends. As a result of his lifestyle, even with his summer wages, he is often short of cash, what with tuition, textbooks, rent, and entertainment. Now, at the start of his third year he owes $30 000 in student loans and credit card debt. For the past three years he has only managed to pay off the minimum monthly payment on his credit card. It has an outstanding balance of $6 000 on which he pays over $1 000 a year in interest. Realizing the enormity of his problems, Larson decided to take his mother's advice and go to a credit counselling service that caters to students. After several sessions, Larson was given the following advice:

Stop buying DVDs. At the rate of one a week, you will save over $100 a month or $1 200 a year.
Get rid of your cell phone and save $35 per month or $420 a year.
Take no more expensive vacations and save $2 000 a year.
Purchase less expensive clothes and save $500 a year.
Eat out less often on weekends and save approximately $600 per year.
Make your own lunch and save approximately $600 per year.
Move back home and reduce your expenses by $3 600 per year.

If Larson agrees, he will reduce his spending by over $9 000 per year. The credit counsellor recommends that he sell his laptop for $2 000, use the money to pay off some of his credit card debt, and stop using his credit cards. In addition, the credit counsellor suggests that he create a spending plan for his income so that he spends his money wisely.

more urgent requests, possible enforcement of security, and eventual referral of the debt to a collection department or agency. If all these measures fail to obtain results, the lender may sue the debtor in court. A lender who wins a court case gains some additional ways of collecting a debt, such as garnisheeing wages or seizing property and possessions. Of course, at any stage of overindebtedness, the debtor can take the initiative by contacting the creditor and trying to negotiate a new arrangement, by consulting a credit counsellor for help in identifying possible solutions to debt problems (see Personal Finance in Action Box 14.1, "Taking the Pressure Off"), or by talking with a trustee in bankruptcy (or an administrator).

Why Debtors Default

There are different degrees of overindebtedness, just as there are many reasons for becoming overindebted. Some people are unable to repay their debts because of an unexpected loss of income, unforeseen large expenses, personal difficulties, poor financial management, or some similar reason. A few are unwilling to pay, either because of disputes with creditors or retailers or because of their own irresponsibility. Those with a small amount of overindebtedness and reasonable earning capacity have the potential to get their affairs under control, perhaps with some professional help. Others are too deeply in debt and have such limited capacity to repay that more drastic measures are necessary.

The causes of personal bankruptcy are many and often quite complex. Personal and lifestyle problems, sometimes compounded as a result of illiteracy, are frequently to blame. These problems may include one or more of the following:

(a) a poor education,

(b) the inability to socialize and form lasting, meaningful relationships,

(c) marrying or forming a relationship at a young age,

(d) addiction,

(e) serious medical problems or disabilities,

(f) large student loans,

(g) loss of job and income.

A POOR EDUCATION Children learn most of what they know about financial management from their parents. Unfortunately, many parents know very little about finance themselves and are therefore unable to properly prepare their children to face the economic world. This problem is often compounded by an incomplete education. Many young people thus enter the world functionally and financially illiterate. As a result, they may be unable to find a good job and may be forced to live at the margins of society. Many make poor use of consumer credit, and soon find themselves in financial difficulty (see Personal Finance in Action Box 14.2, "It's Never Too Young to Start.").

THE INABILITY TO SOCIALIZE AND FORM LASTING, MEANINGFUL RELATIONSHIPS Broken homes and dysfunctional families have become quite common in Canada. Children from such a background, following the example of their parents, may never learn to properly socialize and form stable relationships. When families break up, they must maintain two homes instead of one. The extra financial burden on single parents can become unbearable. Consumer debt is often a result.

MARRYING OR FORMING A RELATIONSHIP AT A YOUNG AGE People who marry or live together at a young age often lack the financial resources necessary to run a home. They may see credit as their only option for acquiring the furniture and appliances they need.

Personal Finance in Action 14.2

It's Never Too Young to Start

When Dominic finished college, he had a large student loan. It took him over six years to pay off this debt. He now has a good job and is determined that Frankie, his eight-year-old son, will never run into the same problems.

Frankie is given a weekly allowance of $10.00. If he wants more, Dominic lends him the money. Frankie also has a line of credit of $2.00 per week and is charged interest at a rate of 18 percent if he uses it. Frankie also has to keep an account book showing his income and where he spends his money. Even the smallest expenditure has to be recorded. Frankie has learned not to borrow because he hates having to pay the interest. If he wants something badly enough, he saves his money until he can afford it.

Since their incomes are often low, the burden of debt can soon become intolerable. Financial pressures can then lead to the end of the relationship and further financial hardship.

ADDICTION Gambling has become a popular form of entertainment in Canada, stimulated by government-run lotteries and casinos. For a minority of players, casinos, video lottery terminals, and lotteries have become an addiction. Such a dependency can be as hard to beat as that for alcohol or drugs; and, like those and other addictions, may lead to financial chaos.

Shopping is also an addiction for some people. Because buying provides pleasure it becomes an end in itself. Fuelled by the easy availability of credit, such shoppers can soon accumulate more debt than they can afford.

SERIOUS MEDICAL PROBLEMS OR DISABILITIES Sometimes very ill people find themselves inz debt because the cost of their medications, special treatments, or special equipment is so great. Those with disabilities may be unable to find jobs that pay well and may therefore end up in debt. Problems like these occur less often today than in the past as the barriers facing disabled people continue to come down.

LARGE STUDENT LOANS Many students require a loan in order to go to college or university. Paying off this debt is rarely difficult for those who ultimately graduate and find a full-time job. But for those who drop out or who fail to find appropriate employment after graduating (a common problem in the 1990s), such a debt can lead to bankruptcy.

LOSS OF JOB AND INCOME Unfortunately, expenses do not stop with the loss of employment. The recent and continuing waves of corporate and public downsizing in Canada have led to more debt and bankruptcy. Those who had debts before being laid off may find themselves in an impossible situation and see bankruptcy as the only solution.

SOME COMMON SYMPTOMS OF INSOLVENCY A number of symptoms are often found in cases of bankruptcy. These may include one or more of the following:

(a) the debtor does not understand what happened,

(b) the debtor does not know how to handle money,

(c) the debtor does not understand basic consumer credit concepts,

(d) the debtor has never saved money and does not understand the principle,

(e) the debtor does not make budgets and does not understand the concept.

Alternatives for the Overcommitted Debtor

A creditor has a number of options to try to force a debtor to repay a debt, some of which may be quite unpleasant. What rights does the debtor have, and what steps can he or she take? If debt commitments exceed the debtor's capacity to repay them, the debtor's options include the following:

(a) negotiating new terms with creditors,

(b) obtaining a consolidation loan,

(c) seeking help from a credit counselling service,

(d) declaring insolvency and filing a consumer proposal,

(e) making an assignment in bankruptcy.

Unfortunately, whether from fear or ignorance, some overextended debtors do nothing at all, letting the situation worsen rapidly.

Negotiating with Creditors

If you ever become overindebted, talk to your creditors as soon as you realize that things are getting out of hand. Tell them what has happened, and ask what adjustments can be arranged. Creditors vastly prefer to see their money returned, even if its return is slightly delayed, rather than being forced to take strong measures. A particular institution's policies will determine which alternatives may be available to debtors who encounter financial difficulties. The creditor may offer to freeze the loan—that is, to accept no payments at all for a time. Additional interest payments may or may not be charged for this period, but the completion date for the credit contract will of course be moved forward.

Consolidation Loan

Some lenders offer consolidation loans to overcommitted debtors. A **consolidation loan** is a new loan that is used to discharge a number of existing debts; such loans are usually requested by a debtor who is unable to maintain previous repayment commitments. Advertisements often exhort credit users to borrow enough money to pay off all their debts and thus owe just one company. Unfortunately, this is not a perfect solution. Borrowing sufficient funds to cover all outstanding obligations and yet make smaller monthly payments than before has two predictable consequences: the new loan must be for a longer term, and the total interest charges may be increased. (See Personal Finance in Action Box 14.3, "Karen Considers a Consolidation Loan.")

Personal Finance in Action 14.3

Karen Considers a Consolidation Loan

When Rafi loses his job, he and Karen quickly realize that their monthly loan payments of $733.16 have become more than they can handle. Karen visits the credit union to inquire about a consolidation loan to tide them over until Rafi finds work. She takes along the following list of their current debts:

CREDITOR	BALANCE OUTSTANDING	INTEREST RATE (%)	MONTHLY PAYMENT	TERM REMAINING	TOTAL INTEREST
Sears	$1 000	28.8	$ 54.89	24 mo.	$ 317.00
Canadian Tire	1 000	28.8	55.30	24	327.00
MasterCard	2 000	18.9	100.24	24	405.00
Visa	1 100	18.99	54.12	24	198.00
Associates*	1 500	29.95	146.19	12	254.00
Avco*	7 600	29.95	322.42	36	4 007.00
TOTALS	$14 200		$733.16		5 508.00

*Finance company charges vary with the individual and his or her creditworthiness.

The credit union tells Karen that they can get a consolidation loan of $14 200, at 9 percent interest, with a choice of a two-, three-, or four-year term.

continued

Consolidation Loan Possibilities

	OPTION 1	OPTION 2	OPTION 3
Terms			
Term (years)	2	3	4
Monthly payment	$ 648.72	$ 451.56	$ 353.37
Total interest	$1 369.00	$2 056.00	$2 761.00
Costs and benefits compared to present loans:			
Change in monthly payment	–$ 84.44	–$ 281.60	–$ 379.79
Change in total interest cost	–$4 139.00	–$3 452.00	–$2 747.00

Karen notices an inverse relation between the term of the loan and the monthly payment: a longer term means lower payments. At first they are attracted by the low payments of $353.37 offered by Option 3. Then, they realize that it will take four years to repay, and the total interest cost will be $2 761.00. Recognizing that while the first option would not reduce their monthly payment enough, the third one would be too costly, they finally decide on Option 2.

A consolidation loan may be a reasonable solution in some cases, but for many people it can be the beginning of a vicious cycle from which it is difficult to escape. Unfortunately, the smaller monthly payments tempt many debtors to take on even more debt; thus the problem worsens.

Before deciding on a consolidation loan, examine the interest rate that will be charged, comparing it with the rates on your existing obligations. It is unwise to transfer to a consolidation loan any debts that currently carry a lower interest rate or that are not interest-bearing. (Consolidation loans may carry quite high rates of interest, because they are extended to people who are not very good credit risks.) Also, for any loan contract that is close to completion, the final payments consist mostly of principal and very little interest. If you prepay such a contract with funds from a consolidation loan and transfer the amount owing to the original creditor to the new creditor (i.e., the one who is extending the consolidation loan), you will significantly increase the amount of interest you pay.

During the recession of the early 1990s, banks became less eager to offer consolidation loans because of the high number of defaults on such loans. Some people were getting consolidation loans to lower their monthly debt payments, but then running up more debt on their credit cards.

Credit Counselling

Another option for the overcommitted debtor involves approaching one of the government- or community-sponsored credit or debt counselling services that are found in many larger centres. Although their organizational structure varies from province to province, all such agencies have the same objective; many offer services without charge. They help clients find an appropriate solution to their financial problems; in some instances, this involves mediating between overindebted families and their creditors to alleviate the crisis and facilitate the eventual repayment of the debt. Credit counselling usually begins with an assessment interview, followed by a review of possible solutions.

ASSESSMENT INTERVIEW The credit counsellor begins by interviewing the debtor, along with his or her partner; obtaining detailed information about the family's financial situation allows the counsellor to consider what type of solution might be appropriate. This financial analysis includes a complete listing of income, living expenses, and debts. If the family's monthly income is sufficient to cover living expenses and debt obligations, the counsellor may discuss ways of improving their financial management so that the family can make their income stretch from one payday to the next. If there is a prospect of allocating a reasonable amount toward debt repayment, although less than the family's present commitment, a debt repayment plan may be developed. But if there is insufficient income to cover living expenses and partial debt payments, another solution may be needed, such as applying for insolvency protection under the *Bankruptcy and Insolvency Act*.

DEBT REPAYMENT PROGRAM The counsellor will work out with the family the amount that can be used to repay debts, and allocate this amount among the family's creditors in proportion to each creditor's share of the total outstanding debt (pro rata). This process is a debt repayment program, also known as debt management or a prorate or a debt pooling plan. The creditor who is owed the largest part of the family's total debt will receive the largest share of any repayment. Once a debt repayment plan that is acceptable to both the debtors and the creditors is set up, the debtor signs a contract specifying the amount to be forwarded to the counselling agency on a regular basis. The agency, acting as a trustee, handles the distribution of the funds to the creditors.

  The success of a debt repayment program depends on the family's ability to live within the budget drawn up in consultation with the counsellor, the stability of the family's circumstances, and the creditor's willingness to participate in the plan. Often creditors will cooperate because they prefer to accept reduced but regular payments instead of trying more collection procedures or writing the account off as a bad debt. If the family fails to maintain the agreed-upon payments, the agency will cancel the plan. Personal Finance in Action Box 14.4, "A Debt Repayment Plan," illustrates how a debt repayment program may be set up.

Personal Finance in Action 14.4

A Debt Repayment Plan

Constant strife about bills has made life so unpleasant that Michael and Susan have decided to seek the help of a credit counselling service. With the counsellor's assistance, they begin for the first time to get a clear picture of their financial situation. When the counsellor asks them to list all their expenses and all their income, they are surprised at the result. They discover that their monthly living costs currently exceed their income before they make any consumer debt payments. The chart below shows that they are short nearly $1 250 a month.

MONTHLY CASH FLOW

Total family take-home pay	$2 750
Living expenses	$2 865
Debt commitment	$1 135
Total monthly expenses	$4 000
Difference between income and expenses	–$1 250

  Michael and Susan are also surprised to learn how much their total debt is; they know that their loan balance at the credit union is low, but since they have never before added up the rest of what they owe, they hadn't realized how quickly their credit card debts

continued

were mounting up. When the counsellor goes over the monthly statements from their various credit cards with them, they get another surprise: the balances are increasing, despite their sporadic payments and recent purchasing restraints.

After carefully reviewing their financial affairs, the counsellor discusses several possible solutions with them, helping them analyze each one. Michael and Susan decide that they will go on an agency-administered debt repayment program. The counsellor explains that this approach will require them to reduce their living expenses, increase their income, or do both. They think that the potential for augmenting their income is low, but feel that they can cut back on some of their expenses.

For a start, they decide to reduce their gift-giving and forgo vacations until their situation improves. The effect of these changes on their deficit will be approximately $100 per month. They propose cutting their expenses a further $90 a month by dropping the premium channels from their TV cable package and reducing the number of restaurant and take-out meals they consume. Before encouraging them to make any more sacrifices, the counsellor suggests that they take some time to consider the implications of these modifications and to decide what other actions they might take.

When Susan and Michael return to the counselling agency a week later, they offer several new ideas: to reduce the phone bill by making fewer long-distance calls, and to lower child-care costs by having their eldest child take more responsibility. They estimate that these new approaches will save about $125 a month. But they now realize that they were a little overzealous last week; they have since decided even if they do not go away for vacations, they will spend some extra money while they are off work—probably $200 a year. The counsellor, who also recognizes that such changes are easier to plan than to carry out, suggests that they allocate $650 per month toward repaying their consumer debt.

The counsellor confirms the outstanding balances with each creditor and is not surprised to find that the couple's debt is about $747 more than they have estimated—a total of $19 186. The counsellor's debt profile for this family shows the following list of creditors and amounts of debt, and the proportions of the total to be paid each month to each creditor.

CREDITOR	REASON FOR DEBT	MONTHLY PAYMENT	CONFIRMED BALANCE	PERCENT OF TOTAL LOAN	PRORATE* PAYMENT
Credit union	Car	$295	$4 917	25.6	$166.40
The Bay	Stove, refrigerator, dishwasher, stereo	49	4 023	21.0	136.50
Zellers	Clothing, household goods, Christmas gifts	227	3 813	19.9	129.35
Sears	Washer, dryer, clothes, gifts, VCR	228	3 967	20.7	134.55
Visa	Car repairs, vacuum, cash advances, misc.	136	2 304	12.0	78.00
Esso	Gas		162	0.8	5.20
Total		$935	$19 186	100.0	$650.00

* To prorate is to distribute proportionally.

Susan and Michael will require between 3.5 and 4 years to repay these debts; during that time, they must also refrain from assuming any new ones. If they successfully make the necessary lifestyle adjustments, they will probably eliminate their debt and become more effective financial managers. Unfortunately, some families cannot accept such a regimen, or their circumstances change and they do not complete the debt management program.

Consumer Proposals and Bankruptcy

Another solution to overindebtedness is to apply for insolvency protection under the federal *Bankruptcy and Insolvency Act*, either by filing a consumer proposal or by making an assignment in bankruptcy. These procedures are discussed in some detail in the following sections.

Bankruptcy and Insolvency

This discussion covers procedures that relate to consumers under 1992's federal *Bankruptcy and Insolvency Act*, which was amended in 1997. The law allows for a formal process of declaring insolvency by filing either a consumer proposal or an assignment in bankruptcy; eventually, the debtor obtains a certificate indicating that the conditions of the consumer proposal have been met or declaring the debtor to have been **discharged from bankruptcy.** Declaring insolvency, the last resort of the overindebted, is much dreaded because of the social stigma attached to this drastic measure and because of its detrimental effect on the bankrupt's credit rating. But it may be the only alternative for families that do not have enough income to cover their regular living expenses and also repay their debts in full. A **consumer proposal** is a plan for paying creditors a portion of the total debt. **Bankruptcy** allows an insolvent debtor to obtain relief from a financial crisis, with any assets distributed in an orderly fashion among creditors. After the conditions of the proposal or bankruptcy are met, the insolvent debtor is free to start over. The bankruptcy process can be painful. The steps involved are explained in Personal Finance in Action Box 14.5.

Bankruptcy in Canada

In 1999, 83 023 people declared bankruptcy in Canada . While this was a drop of 4 percent from 1998, the numbers jumped sharply in 2000. Overall in Canada, bankruptcies were up by 12 percent in August. The biggest increases came in Newfoundland, New Brunswick, and Saskatchewan with Newfoundland topping the list with 47 percent.

The federal *Bankruptcy and Insolvency Act*, passed in 1992 and amended in 1997, currently offers more options for seriously indebted consumers than were previously available. Earlier legislation was designed for bankrupt businesses and was very out-of-date. Today, approximately 90 percent of all bankruptcies are consumer bankruptcies, not commercial bankruptcies.

The 1992 legislation was designed to respond to some of the needs of overindebted consumers with a more streamlined process and an emphasis on rehabilitation. It is based on the premise that the best that the insolvency system can do for society is to return bankrupts to the marketplace as better-informed and more responsible citizens, with an enhanced ability to contribute to the economy. Recovery of funds is actually less important. In most consumer bankruptcies, there are few assets (other than income tax refunds) to distribute, and there is little potential for repaying debts from income. A bankrupt's family tends to have an income that is only 40 percent of the Canadian average.

In all provinces, both corporate and personal bankruptcies are regulated by the federal *Bankruptcy and Insolvency Act*. In the past, bankruptcy was managed by the federal Office of the Superintendent of Bankruptcy without provincial involvement. Trustees in bankruptcy are still federally appointed, but certain tasks are now delegated to provinces that wish to accept them. Those provinces already offering Orderly Payment of Debts programs have agreed to handle consumer proposals as well. The Ontario government no longer offers an Orderly Payment of Debts program (funding was stopped in 1991). But the Ontario Association of Credit Counselling Services offers a debt repayment program with the assistance of the Canadian Bankers Association but without government funding.

ORDERLY PAYMENT OF DEBTS   The federal *Bankruptcy and Insolvency Act* provides for an Orderly Payment of Debts (OPD) program (that is, a debt repayment plan) to be administered by the provinces if they so choose. Six provinces—British Columbia, Alberta, Saskatchewan, Manitoba, Nova Scotia, and Prince Edward Island—have implemented the OPD program, but there is no particular uniformity in procedures among these provinces. Essentially, this section of the Act permits a debt administration program to be established under provincial government sponsorship.

Personal Finance in Action 14.5

Bankruptcy or Asset Liquidation?

When a credit counsellor encounters a family whose debts far exceed their ability to repay, a consumer proposal or an agency-administered debt management plan may not be possible options. Shanti is such a case. Until her separation from her alcoholic husband, Shanti managed to keep all the bills paid; the family lived well on a combined income of over $100 000. After the separation, she hoped that with her salary as an executive secretary and substantial support payments for the two young children, she would still be able to keep on top of her expenses. But her ex-husband lost his middle-management job a few months after the separation, and the sporadic support payments have now ceased.

Shanti is currently behind on the mortgage and owes the gas company for fuel; the bank is threatening to take her car; her credit cards and charge accounts are at their limit. She still owes money to the lawyer who handled her separation. The pressures from these financial problems sometimes make Shanti wonder if she and the children are really better off living apart from her abusive husband. It seems to her that things are always going wrong.

The situation that Shanti finds herself in is not uncommon in today's climate of frequent marriage and relationship breakdowns and employment instability. Expenses that are manageable on two incomes are not always manageable on one. Shanti is so angry at what she feels to be the injustice of her circumstances that it is hard for her to take any kind of objective look at her financial affairs. The counsellor tries to help Shanti focus on one problem at a time.

It soon becomes evident to both Shanti and the counsellor that keeping the house is not going to be possible; nor, on her income alone, will she be able to meet her other monthly debt commitments. The counsellor suggests two alternatives. Since Shanti is insolvent, bankruptcy is one possibility. Another option is to use the equity in her home, along with some valuable antiques, by selling them and offering her creditors a cash settlement from the proceeds. Neither solution is ideal. The credit counsellor also recommends that Shanti seek legal advice, particularly concerning her right to sell the house and the antiques.

Shanti is also encouraged to seek psychological counselling for herself and for the children concerning their feelings about the separation.

Basics of the Insolvency Process

A hopelessly indebted person who applies for insolvency protection under the *Bankruptcy and Insolvency Act* now has a new option that was not available in the past—filing a consumer proposal.

ELIGIBILITY An applicant for a consumer proposal must be insolvent and must have less than $75 000 in debts (excluding a mortgage on the applicant's principal residence). To file for bankruptcy, a debtor must owe at least $1 000.

INITIATING THE PROCESS Insolvency proceedings are usually started when a debtor applies either to an administrator of consumer proposals or to a trustee in bankruptcy.

INSOLVENCY ACTORS There are five main actors in the insolvency or bankruptcy drama:

(a) the **insolvent,** who is unable to meet his or her debt obligations,

(b) the **creditors,** who are all those who can prove a claim against the insolvent,

(c) the **official receiver,** the federal civil servant who oversees the insolvency process,

(d) the **trustee in bankruptcy,** a federally licensed official (usually a chartered accountant) who carries out the insolvency process,

(e) the **administrator of consumer proposals,** who has more limited powers than a trustee (trustees may handle both bankruptcies and consumer proposals, while administrators are limited to handling only consumer proposals and the related counselling).

RESPONSIBILITIES OF THE DEBTOR The insolvent person must reveal complete information about his or her assets, debts, and income and may be asked to meet the official receiver and answer questions under oath. If there is a meeting of creditors, the debtor is expected to be there to provide information. Several counselling sessions must be attended, and regular statements about income and expenses must be submitted. The debtor is expected to cooperate with the insolvency officials.

RESPONSIBILITIES OF THE CREDITORS In bankruptcy cases, all creditors are invited to a meeting to consider the debtor's affairs and to confirm the trustee's appointment; creditors may also appoint inspectors to act as their agents in the bankruptcy process. But in a streamlined consumer bankruptcy process, some of these steps may be unnecessary. Finally, the creditors' agreement is necessary to discharge the insolvent person from bankruptcy. In the case of a consumer proposal, the creditors must accept the plan before it can be put into effect.

DUTIES OF THE OFFICIAL RECEIVER The official receiver generally oversees the whole insolvency process, performing tasks that include receiving petitions or proposals from the trustee or the administrator, making decisions about holding creditors' meetings, and submitting applications to court.

DUTIES OF THE TRUSTEE IN BANKRUPTCY When a person inquires about insolvency protection, the trustee investigates that person's financial situation by conducting an assessment interview and possibly by checking with creditors. The debtor decides whether to submit a consumer proposal (which is the option the trustee will normally advise taking wherever possible under the circumstances) or file for bankruptcy. If the debtor decides on a consumer proposal, the trustee changes hats, becoming an administrator of consumer proposals. Either a trustee or an administrator can handle the legally required counselling sessions and can prepare a consumer proposal, but only a trustee may look after the bankruptcy process.

DUTIES OF THE ADMINISTRATOR OF CONSUMER PROPOSALS An administrator of consumer proposals may be a trustee in bankruptcy or another person appointed to this task. The administrator can provide counselling, conduct an assessment interview, help the debtor file a consumer proposal, and disburse funds to creditors. If, at the assessment interview, the debtor decides to file for bankruptcy, the client must be transferred to a trustee.

COSTS OF INSOLVENCY The fees and costs of a bankruptcy depend upon the size of the estate in question and are set by the *Bankruptcy and Insolvency Act*. There are two classifications of bankruptcies. Estates of less than $10 000 are known as summary bankruptcies. The fees for such a bankruptcy are as follows:

$50 filing fee.	35% of the next $1 025.
$100 administration fee.	50% over $2 000 to a maximum of $4 000.
100% of the first $975.	

For estates over $10 000, the rate is not fixed. It will depend on the size and complexity of the estate but must be considered reasonable. In addition to paying any fees charged by the Trustee in Bankruptcy, the bankrupt must attend two couselling sessions at a cost of $85 per session. There is also a $50 filing fee.

Counselling Sessions

The legislation, with its focus on rehabilitation, offers the possibility of three counselling sessions. The first occurs when the overindebted person contacts a trustee or an administrator to discuss possible solutions to the insolvency problem. The administrator or trustee examines the debtor's whole financial situation and reviews possible alternatives. The second counselling session takes place a month or two after filing either a consumer proposal or an assignment in bankruptcy. At this session, the emphasis is on identifying the root causes of the financial difficulties and on finding ways to change the situation. Failure to attend the second counselling session results in a penalty: the debtor will not be eligible for an automatic discharge from bankruptcy. The third counselling session, which is optional, takes place within six months of filing a proposal or making an assignment. It is intended to provide the debtor and his or her family with further guidance in financial management or assistance with such personal problems as substance abuse, gambling, relationship difficulties, or compulsive shopping. The first counselling session must be done on an individual basis, but subsequent counselling may be done in groups.

The legislation requires that an administrator or trustee who agrees to assist an insolvent debtor must provide for at least two counselling sessions. The trustee or administrator can either do the counselling or delegate it to another qualified person. The counselling fees are paid out of the debtor's estate (i.e., his or her assets) before any distribution to creditors.

Consumer Proposals

As we have seen, a consumer proposal is a plan for reorganizing a debtor's personal financial affairs for presentation to his or her creditors. The debtor, with help from an administrator, prepares a plan for repaying all or part of the debt within five years. If the proposal is accepted by the court and the creditors, it becomes binding on the debtor and the creditors. Generally, a consumer proposal does not release a debtor from certain kinds of obligations, such as fines, penalties, alimony, maintenance agreements, or co-signer responsibilities. It does, however, protect the debtor from any claims for accelerated payments or discontinued service by public utilities; it nullifies the effect of any existing wage assignments; and it prohibits an employer from taking any disciplinary action because the employee has made a consumer proposal. If a person's creditors accept a consumer proposal, bankruptcy can be avoided; if they reject the proposal, an assignment in bankruptcy may follow.

CERTIFICATE OF PERFORMANCE When all the conditions of a consumer proposal have been met, the debtor receives a certificate to that effect.

Bankruptcy

The first step in bankruptcy is the assignment of all the debtor's assets to a licensed trustee. From this time until he or she is released from debts by the court, the debtor is an undischarged bankrupt. Next, the trustee will call a meeting of creditors. At this meeting, the appointment of the trustee is affirmed and instructions are given concerning the administration of the estate. The trustee then proceeds to liquidate the estate. All the debtor's property is available for payment of debts, except that which is exempt from execution or seizure under the laws of the debtor's province (see Personal Finance in Action Box 14.6, "The Bankruptcy Process"). All creditors must prove their claims against the estate; secured creditors will be paid first, because they have a claim on specific assets. Any remaining assets are then distributed in a specified order, with payment for the cost of administering the bankruptcy taking precedence over other claims.

Assets Exempt from Seizure

Provincial laws exempt some assets from seizure by the trustee in bankruptcy.

The exemptions in Ontario are as follows:

(a) Necessary clothing of the debtor and family, not exceeding $1 000.

(b) Household furniture, utensils, food, equipment, and fuel, not exceeding $2 000.

(c) Items used in the practice of the debtor's trade, not exceeding $2 000.

(d) Livestock, tools, and implements used by a farmer, not exceeding $5 000.

(e) Enough seed to allow a farmer to sow 100 acres.

The exemptions in British Columbia are as follows:

(a) Equity in a home in Vancouver or Victoria of $12 000 and $9 000 in the rest of the province.

(b) Household items equal to $4 000.

(c) Equity in a vehicle of $5 000.

(d) Equity in tools of $10 000.

Personal Finance in Action 14.6

The Bankruptcy Process

Brenda is in a financial mess. Since the break-up of her marriage, she has been unable to make ends meet. Her income, even though she is a full-time teacher, never seems to be enough. She has cut her expenses to the bone, but still owes over $8 000. Her creditors are becoming nastier with each passing month. At her friend Gail's suggestion, Brenda makes an appointment to talk with a Trustee in Bankruptcy. The Trustee explains that bankruptcy would immediately stop the legal

continued

actions of her creditors and also help to eliminate most of her debts. Since she owes more than $1 000, she does qualify for bankruptcy. The Trustee explains the process, if she decides to file.

1. She might be examined by an official receiver to determine the cause of her bankruptcy.
2. She will have to attend a meeting of her creditors to tell them about the bankruptcy and confirm the appointment of the Trustee.

3. She will have to attend two counselling sessions to assess her finances and discuss her problems.
4. Since this is Brenda's first bankruptcy, after she receives counselling, she will be eligible for an automatic discharge in nine months.
5. If the creditors make an objection, Brenda may have to attend a bankruptcy court. However, the Trustee said the court will grant her an absolute discharge.

DISCHARGE FROM BANKRUPTCY   Once the debtor's existing assets have been distributed, the court may grant the bankrupt a discharge. This document releases the debtor from all claims of creditors except fines imposed by a court, money owed as a result of theft, items obtained by misrepresentation, liability for support or maintenance of spouse or child under an agreement or cout order, damages awarded by a court for assault, and student loans. If there is no opposition from creditors, and if the counselling sessions have been attended, a first-time bankrupt is eligible for an automatic discharge nine months after declaring bankruptcy.

Complexities of Overindebtedness

Personal Finance in Action Box 14.7, "Debt Problems of a Blended Family," illustrates how interconnected family relations and financial matters can become. None of the alternatives identified appears to be a perfect solution, a situation that will force the family to look for the least costly option.

Personal Finance in Action 14.7

Debt Problems of a Blended Family

When the letter carrier brings Robert a summons to appear in family court regarding arrears in his support payments, it is the last straw. He persuades Denise that they had better get some help.

Robert and Denise are obviously feeling very overburdened and stressed by their financial situation when they approach the credit counselling agency. They are seriously considering separating. In addition to their debt difficulties, Denise's recurring medical problem has flared up again, and the school principal has called about some serious problems Denise's son, Tim, was having at school. Denise has been missing a fair

amount of work recently, and Robert's boss has told him to do something about his personal problems. It is apparent to the counsellor that the family needs relief from its financial problems soon.

The counsellor asks the couple to outline their family situation as necessary background for any new plans. Denise and Robert explain that they have been living common-law for several years and are caring for Denise's 12-year-old son from a previous marriage. Robert, who has also been married before, is required by a court order to pay $1 200 per month to his ex-wife for the support of their three

continued

teenaged children. These children spend every other weekend, as well as much of the summer, with Denise and Robert. Both Robert and Denise resent having to make such large support payments; Denise feels as if she works for Robert's ex-wife. To make matters worse, Denise's ex-husband is $2 400 behind in support payments to her, since he rarely sends his court-ordered $300-a-month payments.

When Robert and his wife separated two and a half years ago, he had to assume their debts of approximately $12 000 ($7 000 for the car and $5 000 on charge accounts) because she went on long-term social assistance.

Anxious to establish her own credit rating after her separation, Denise borrowed $5 000 to buy a car; her elderly parents served as co-signers. Denise still owes about $3 500 on that loan, and she also has another $2 500 in credit card debt. Cash advances on Robert's credit cards and loans from her family have

allowed them to keep up their commitments, but have added a further $6 500 to their debts.

Their resources for financial aid have been exhausted for months now; creditors have begun to call both Robert and Denise at work about their delinquent payments. Robert has received a summons to appear in family court regarding $1 050 that he owes in support payments. The arrears accumulated when Denise was laid off earlier in the year. The only payments that are up-to-date are those related to the bank loan for which Denise's parents co-signed. Denise says that she would starve before she would let her parents use their pension to pay that debt.

Before the counsellor can help this couple look at possible solutions to their problems, everyone needs to have a clearer picture of their financial position. The counsellor's assessment reveals the following.

BALANCE SHEET

Assets

Small bank account, two cars, household furnishings	$9 500	
Support arrears owed to Denise	2 400	
Total Assets		$11 900

Liabilities

Robert's old debts	$12 000	
Robert's support payments in arrears	1 050	
Denise's loan	3 500	
Robert's current debts	6 500	
Total Liabilities		$23 050

Net Worth | | –$11 150

MONTHLY CASH FLOW

Income | | $3 022

Expenses

Net living expenses	2 286	
Robert's support payments	1 200	
Consumer debt payments		
Charge accounts, credit cards	675	
Bank loans	502	

Total Expenses | | **$4 663**

Deficit | | –$1 641   *continued*

The counsellor helps the couple to look objectively at their situation, and together they draw up the following possible solutions.

1. **Both seek legal recourse regarding support payments that are in arrears.** Denise might be successful in obtaining a form of garnishment for current and future support payments as well as for those in arrears. This could increase the family's income by at least $300 a month. Robert could apply to the family court for a reduction in support payments, but it seems unlikely that a judge would be sympathetic to his situation.

2. **Find cheaper living accommodation.** Robert and Denise are renting a four-bedroom townhouse so that there will be space for Robert's children when they come to visit. They could reduce their housing expenses by at least $300 a month if they moved into a two-bedroom apartment. But they would then be very cramped when Robert's children came to stay.

3. **Consolidate their debts.** Charge account and credit card interest rates are usually higher than consumer loans. A consolidation loan might reduce their monthly debt load and the total amount owed. Unfortunately, since the couple currently has a negative net worth, it is doubtful that they could find a lender willing to give them a loan for the total owed.

4. **Arrange a debt repayment program.** This may be done through a governmental or social agency and would allow the couple to repay their debts with more manageable monthly payments, over a longer period of time. There are risks involved in this choice. If the pro rata share on Denise's bank loan were less than the contractual amount, the bank might ask Denise's parents to make up the deficit. Unless interest concessions are negotiated, though, the total debt could increase substantially through accrued interest charges. It is possible that a creditor might decide to exercise his or her rights to security, and thus take possession of household chattels or of a car. And last, but not necessarily least, the family would have to make lifestyle changes in order to reduce living expenses, and would need to exert considerable self-discipline for approximately four years in order for the program to be a success.

5. **Declare bankruptcy.** This action would relieve the family of their monthly debt burden, with the exception of support arrears. But they would undoubtedly lose some of their possessions. There is also a stigma attached to bankruptcy; as well, having been bankrupt may limit the ability of an individual or family to get credit in the future. Denise's elderly parents would, no doubt, be forced to take over her bank loan if she were to file for bankruptcy.

What do you think they should do?

Summary

Using credit is an economic fact of life for most consumers, as the popularity of credit cards proves. In order to help lenders assess each would-be borrower's risk potential, credit bureaus collect information about consumers and sell it to their members. Provincial legislation specifies what kind of information may be included in a person's credit file and how long negative facts may remain part of the record. Your credit rating is determined by the lender after reviewing the information in your credit file.

Debts in arrears may be collected by the creditor or turned over to a collection agency. There are several possible avenues for collecting bad debts, starting with polite requests and culminating in legal action.

Serious debt problems may be caused by a foolish use of credit or by circumstances beyond a person's control. People with insurmountable debt problems may choose from several options, which include negotiating for reduced or delayed payment terms, talking with a credit counsellor, and applying for insolvency protection. The latter approach, depending on the debtor's circumstances, will take the form of either a consumer proposal or a declaration of bankruptcy.

Key Terms

administrator of consumer proposals (p. 443)

bank account garnishment (p. 432)

bankruptcy (p. 441)

collection agency (p. 429)

consolidation loan (p. 437)

consumer information (p. 428)

consumer proposal (p. 441)

credit bureau (p. 422)

credit scoring (p. 427)

creditor (p. 443)

discharge from bankruptcy (p. 441)

execution against debtor's property (p. 433)

family court garnishment (p. 432)

information exchanges (p. 429)

insolvent (p. 443)

investigative agency (p. 429)

judgment debt (p. 432)

official receiver (p. 443)

overindebtedness (p. 433)

personal information (p. 428)

trustee in bankruptcy (p. 443)

wage garnishment (p. 432)

Problems

1. Answer true or false:

   (a) All provinces have passed laws governing how the private sector handles personal information.

   (b) The federal government now has legislation governing the collection and use of personal information by the private sector.

   (c) Citizens of BC are allowed to keep their homes, no matter how expensive, if they declare bankruptcy.

   (d) Alimony payments are usually discharged as a result of a bankruptcy.

   (e) Student loans are not forgiven as a result of bankruptcy.

2. Refer to Personal Finance in Action box 14.2, "It's Never Too Young to Start". Why do you suppose that more parents don't teach their children how to handle money?

3. Since the abuse of credit is considered a major cause of personal insolvency and bankruptcy, should the granting of credit be conditional upon the passing of a financial literacy test?

4. A course in the use and abuse of credit should be included in school curricula at a very early age and be stressed as much as literacy and numeracy. Discuss.

5. Explain the similarities and differences between the following pairs of terms:

(a)   a credit file and a credit report,

(b)   a collection agency and a collection department,

(c)   consumer information and personal information,

(d)   a credit bureau and a collection agency,

(e)   a garnishment and an execution order,

(f)   a demand on a third party and a family court garnishment,

(g)   a wage assignment and a wage garnishment.

6.   Do you AGREE or DISAGREE with each of the following statements? Explain.

(a)   Most debts can be collected without aggressive action.

(b)   Collection agencies and collection departments are essentially the same.

(c)   The amount a creditor can obtain through garnishment is limited by provincial legislation or by a court decision.

7.   Do you think there is enough information about the use of credit available to the general public?

8.   Refer to Personal Finance in Action Box 14.1, "Taking the Pressure Off." Larson's story is all too common today. How can this kind of financial mess be explained?

9.   Refer to Personal Finance in Action Box 14.4, "A Debt Repayment Plan," and to Personal Finance in Action Box 14.5, "Bankruptcy or Asset Liquidation?"

(a)   Which aspects of these cases are similar and which are different?

(b)   Do you think Shanti should file for bankruptcy or try for a negotiated settlement? What are the advantages and disadvantages of each alternative?

(c)   How does a credit counsellor arrive at an expenditure plan for an overcommitted debtor?

(d)   Should Michael and Susan continue to make their debt payments to the agency for four years, or should they assume responsibility for their financial affairs before that time?

(e)   What would be the consequences for Susan and Michael if they failed to maintain the repayment schedule established by the agency?

10.   Should a debtor arrange a prorate (a debt pooling plan) directly with creditors—that is, without enlisting the help of a counselling agency? Under what circumstances would such an approach work? Would it cause any problems?

11.   (a)   Why was the counsellor so unsuccessful?

(b)   Could a more experienced counsellor have helped this family? What would you have done?

(c)   What changes would be necessary to improve this family's success in managing their finances?

12.   Refer to Personal Finance in Action Box 14.7, "Debt Problems of a Blended Family."

(a)   Do you think this family should declare bankruptcy? What would be the advantages if they did?

The Novice Counsellor

My first assignment in a student counselling practicum involved Glen and Maria. An administrator for the local housing authority wanted me to visit them because they had fallen behind in their rent payments. I made my first call at their house, confident that with a bit of help from me, this family would soon find itself able to cope with its financial problems.

When I arrived at their home at the appointed time, Maria was out shopping, but she returned within the hour. This friendly woman, in her mid-thirties, seemed most cooperative, telling me that her husband is employed at a local factory, that she works part-time at a nursing home, and that they have three children between the ages of 5 and 13. During this interview, I tried to determine the actual amount of their debts, but Maria remained very vague about the amounts.

My second visit was equally pleasant. Maria seemed to be making every attempt to answer my questions. Unfortunately, it appeared that she really did not know much about their financial situation. For example, she wasn't sure what her husband's usual take-home pay is. Still, we managed to estimate their main debts, which totalled about $14 000.

I was astonished to find two large TV sets in the middle of a rather poorly furnished living room. According to Maria, both units are quite new and in splendid working condition; they bought the first one about a year ago and the second one last month. "The man who sold them to us," Maria confided, "is a very good friend of ours. Whenever he gets a really good deal, he calls us and we go down and look at it. He is awfully nice about letting us pay for the televisions when we can."

When I looked at the contracts for their television sets, I realized that they were paying a substantial amount in credit charges. I mentioned this to Maria, who was very surprised: evidently she hadn't realized that her friend was charging them anything extra. She says that they are paying off the TVs fairly quickly, because every so often they use Glen's whole paycheque for some of the television debt. I asked what they do about their other debts on these occasions, and Maria said that they often let hydro, rent, and telephone bills accumulate for a few months. As we talked about their debts, it became obvious to me that Maria had virtually no understanding of credit contracts or credit costs.

During the period of my visits to this household, Glen absolutely refused to meet me, although I was willing to stop by when he would be at home. I discovered that they have two cars—although Maria doesn't drive. The whole family enjoys going out to eat once or twice a week, and Glen usually meets a friend to have a few drinks at their club every week.

My visits ended without my ever meeting Maria's husband. Maria herself had stated repeatedly that unless Glen agrees to make some changes, there is very little that she can do. I later learned that they will probably be evicted from their low-rental townhouse. This experience has helped me to realize that solving financial problems is more complicated than I had thought: simply providing this family with information clearly will not change much about their situation. This particular couple does not seem eager to change, and until they become motivated to review their goals and values in the light of their actual resources, a counsellor cannot help them. This experience was obviously more beneficial for me than it was for the family I was "counselling."

(b) Can the family afford the cost of bankruptcy?

(c) Will the creditors get anything if the family goes bankrupt?

(d) Will the family lose their household furnishings?

(e) How will bankruptcy affect the family's credit rating if another loan is needed?

(f) What could the family have done to avoid this predicament?

(g) Are there any other solutions to this family's financial problems that might have been discussed in another interview? Discuss.

13. Why might a debtor decide to file a consumer proposal instead of making an assignment in bankruptcy?

14. Can someone be too poor to go bankrupt? Discuss.

15. Review the case studies in this chapter (that is, Personal Finance in Action Boxes 14.1 through 14.7). For each situation described, try to determine the reasons for the overindebtedness.

16. Try to determine from the research available whether there is a connection between gambling and insolvency.

17. Contact the Ministry of Education in your province to find out whether any courses in personal finance are offered in the province's elementary or secondary schools. If there are such courses, find out what topics they cover.

18. Apply for a Visa, a MasterCard, an American Express card, or a major retail store credit card. Describe your experience. Did you find it difficult or easy to get a card?

19. Displays of credit card applications are a common sight at colleges and universities every fall. Should students, who typically have either no income or only a very limited income, be given credit when they lack the financial resources to pay off their bills and will therefore incur high interest charges? Discuss.

20. Find out what services are available at your college or university to help students who get into financial difficulty. What percentage of the students at your institution make use of these services?

21. Find out the rate of interest currently charged by the major credit cards. Why is it so high? Should the cards' interest rates be lowered, as members of Parliament frequently suggest?

22. The Canadian media are filled with stories of family violence, severe antisocial behaviour at schools, and teen suicides. Try to determine whether such antisocial behaviour has anything to do with financial distress.

23. Prepare arguments for and against the introduction of a casino into your community. How would you feel if your city or town council voted in favour of developing a casino?

24. Contact the National Council of Welfare, 2nd Floor, 1010 Somerset Street West, Ottawa, ON K1A 0J9 (Phone 613-957-2961, Fax 613-957-0680), to find out whether there are any social patterns to gambling in Canada. What kinds of people buy lottery tickets and go to casinos? Is there a larger proportion of lower-income people, or do people from all socioeconomic classes participate?

25. Go to Industry Canada's Web site, www.strategis.gc.ca. Click on Strategies for Consumers. Then click on Credit Card Calculator. Proceed with the Calculator Service. Say no to the first question. When asked to identify your average monthly balance, choose a large amount. The results are then more dramatic. Also indicate that you have a large advance and that you use it frequently at both your bank's ABM as well as the ABM of another bank. Then compare the total annual charge at the following institutions:

   (a) Bank of Montreal with a standard card

   (b) National Bank

   (c) Bank of Nova Scotia with a standard card

   (d) TD Bank

   (e) American Express with a standard card

   Is there much difference in the charges at the various institutions?

References

BOOKS AND OTHER PRINT REFERENCES

BAKER, MURRAY. *The Debt Free Graduate: How to Survive College or University Without Going Broke.* Toronto: HarperPerennial, 1996. A book every student should read.

BAUM, DANIEL JAY.

Saving and Spending. Toronto, IPI Publishing, 1990. Contains a lot of commonsense information that too many people ignore.

BENNER, DAVID G. *Money Madness and Financial Freedom.* Calgary, Alberta: Detselig, 1996.

BENNETT, FRANK. *Bankruptcy and Insolvency Act with Draft Regulation 1992.* Toronto: CCH CANADIAN LIMITED, 1992. Like the next entry, this is a standard text on bankruptcy.

_____. *Bennett on Going Broke: A Practical Guide to Bankruptcy for Individuals and Small Businesses.* North York, ON: CCH Canadian, 1994.

BERGER, ESTHER M., and CONNIE CHURCH HASBUN. *Money Smart: Secrets Women Always Wanted to Know About Money.* New York: Simon and Shuster, 1993. Contains much useful advice.

CANADIAN BANKERS ASSOCIATION. *Credit Wise: A Guide to Consumer Credit.* Toronto: Canadian Bankers Association, 1994. A very useful guide.

_____. *Managing Money: A Guide To Budgeting, Credit Use, and Avoiding Money Mishaps.* Toronto: Canadian Bankers Association, 1997. Just as useful as *Credit Wise*, the guide cited in the previous entry.

_____. *Safeguarding Your Interests: A Guide to Protecting Money and Resolving Bank Problems.* Toronto: Canadian Bankers Association, 1998. Provides information on credit card security and fraud.

CIBC. *A Guide to Student Credit.* Burlington, ON: CIBC National Student Centre. A useful pamphlet that should be available at all student financial aid offices.

_____. *We've Changed the Student Loan Experience: Convenience and Advice.* Burlington, ON: CIBC National Student Centre. Contains some excellent questions and answers on bankruptcy. Also available at www.cibc.com/needs/student and 1-800-563-2422.

COVIENSKY, JUDITH. *My Money My Self: Create a Positive Relationship with Money*. Toronto: Chimes, 1997. A source of good advice.

DEPARTMENT OF FINANCE. *The Canadian Opportunities Strategy: Helping Manage Student Debt*. Ottawa: Department of Finance, 1998. Students who struggle with the high cost of student debt should find this pamphlet helpful.

DYMOND, MARY JOY. *The Canadian Woman's Legal Guide*. Toronto: Doubleday, 1989. A valuable reference.

FINLAY, REBECCA. *U-Choose: A Student's Guide to Financial Freedom*. Don Mills, ON: Moving Publications Ltd., 1997. Another valuable reference.

HATCH, JAMES, E., and LARRY WYNANT. *Canadian Commercial Lending: A Guide To Credit Decision Making*. Toronto: Carswell, 1995. Useful for anyone who wants more information on how credit is granted.

HORNUNG, SANDRA. *Consumer Power: A Guide to the Basics of Consumer Law in Saskatchewan*. Public Legal Education, 1996.

INDUSTRY CANADA. *All About Bankruptcy Mediation*. Ottawa: Industry Canada, 1998.This pamphlet stresses the role of mediation in the settling of disputes related to bankruptcy.

KPMG PEAT MARWICK. *Personal Bankruptcy and Consumer Proposals: The Most Often Asked Questions and Answers*. 1998. An excellent guide.

LIPTRAP, PATRICIA R., and AMY E.G. COUSINEAU. *Manual for Credit Counsellors*. Grimsby, ON: Ontario Association of Credit Counselling Services, 1983. The association's address is Box 189, Grimsby, Ontario, L3M 4E3.

LONG, CHARLES. *How to Survive Without a Salary: Learning to Live*. Toronto: Warwick, 1996. Should prove invaluable in view of the considerable public and private downsizing that has taken place in Canada.

ONTARIO ASSOCIATION OF CREDIT COUNSELLING SERVICES (OACCS). *Standards Manual*, Third Edition. Grimsby, ON: OACCS 1997. This volume replaces the previous publication, *Guidelines and Standards for Credit Counsellors*. For ordering information, contact the association at Box 189, Grimsby, ON L3M 4E3. Will interest anyone considering a career in credit counselling.

PARKER, ALLAN A. *Credit, Debt, and Bankruptcy*. Eighth Edition. Vancouver: International Self-Counsel Press, 1990. A standard book on these controversial topics.

STEINBERG, EVELYN, and MARILYN WILLIAMS, editors. *The Little Book of Money*. Vancouver: Arsenal Publishers, 1994. Interesting and useful.

WALLACE, MARY, and LARRY PITZ. *Mathematics for the Informed Consumer*. Toronto: ITP Nelson, 1985. A valuable book that should be available in any library.

YOUNG, JENNIFER. *Small Claims Court Guide for Ontario*. Seventh Edition. Vancouver: International Self-Counsel Press, 1992. A standard reference on the subject in Ontario.

ZINKHOFER, FRED. *Small Claims Court Guide for Alberta*. Fourth Edition. Vancouver: International Self-Counsel Press, 1985. The standard book of its kind in Alberta.

PERIODICALS

Canadian Commercial Law Guide. Don Mills, ON: CCH Canadian, Topical Law Reports. Subscription service in two volumes on federal and provincial law regarding the sale of personal property and consumer protection.

Personal Finance on the Web

Asset Find Canada
www.AssetFindCanada.com/ Provides asset information on people and companies.

Bank of Montreal Student Services
www.bmo.com/BrainMoney/ Provides information on student loans and lines of credit.

Bankruptcy & Insolvency Canada
www.insolvency.com/law/canada.htm The home page of the Canadian Justice Department.

Bankruptcy Canada
www.bankruptcycanada.com/ Provides information on insolvency and how to choose a trustee.

CIBC Students and Parents
www.cibc.com./english/personal_services/students Provides useful information on student loans.

Credit Bureau of Sudbury
www.porcupinecomputers.com/sudbury/ Provides credit reporting and collection services in northern Ontario.

Credit Counselling Service of Toronto
www.creditcanada.com Canada's largest non-profit credit counselling service.

Credit Institute of Canada
www.creditedu.org/ Provides education for credit and financial professionals.

Credit Union Central of Canada
www.cucentral.ca/ The umbrella organization for all provincial credit unions.

Debt 911 Network
www.bankruptcy-ont.com On-line bankruptcy assessment.

Dun & Bradstreet Credit Information
www.dbsina.com This firm only deals with commercial credit.

Equifax Canada
www.equifax.ca/ Canada's largest credit rating service, Equifax also provides access to commercial credit information on-line.

Industry Canada
www.strategis.gc.ca Includes a credit card calculator that allows you to enter the amount of the balance owing and see a cost comparison of 28 credit cards.

Insolvency Institute of Canada
www.insolvency.ca Provides useful background information.

Institute of Chartered Accountants
www.cica.ca/

Office of the Superintendent of Bankruptcy
Strategis.ic.gc.ca/sc_mrk.sv/bankrupt/engdoc/superint.ca

Privacy Commissioner of Canada
   www.privcom.gc.ca

COLLECTION AGENCIES: A sampling of the available sites.

Mr.Bailiff Inc.
   www.mbailiff.com/

Credit Management Solutions
   http://creditmansolutions.com/

Eastern Recovery Services Limited
   www.easternrecovery.com

Sterling Bailiffs Inc.
   www.sterbail.com/

Vanguard Collection Agencies
   www.vanguardcollection.com/

S. Wilson and Co.
   www.swilsonbailiffs.com

TRUSTEES IN BANKRUPTCY

CA-Xchange
   www.cax.org Provides a list of chartered accountants.

Deloitte and Touche
   deloitte.ca

Ernst & Young
   www.ey.com/

KPMG Peat Marwick
   www.personalbankruptcy.com

Mendlowitz and Associates
   www.oak.net/ma/

E. Sands and Associates Inc.
   www.sands-trustee.com Contains the complete text of the Bankruptcy and Insolvency
   Act. Telephone: 1-800-661-3030 (toll-free in British Columbia).

Soberman, Isenbaum and Colomby
   www.soberman.com/home

Index